WOMAN'S WORK

IN THE CIVIL WAR:

A RECORD OF

HEROISM, PATRIOTISM. AND PATIENCE.

BY

L. P. BROCKETT, M.D.,

AND

MRS. MARY C. VAUGHAN.

1867

COPYRIGHT 2015 BIG BYTE BOOKS

Discover more lost history from BIG BYTE BOOKS

Contents

PREFACE ... 2
INTRODUCTION ... 6
INTRODUCTORY CHAPTER ... 18
DOROTHEA L. DIX ... 44
CLARA HARLOWE BARTON ... 55
IN CAMP, FIELD, AND GENERAL HOSPITALS ... 75
AID SOCIETIES AND SUPPLIES ... 401
AMONG THE FREEDMEN AND REFUGEES ... 530
SOLDIERS' HOMES, REFRESHMENT SALOONS, HOSPITAL TRANSPORTS ... 557
LADIES DISTINGUISHED FOR OTHER SERVICES ... 577
OTHER DEFENDERS OF THE FLAG ... 590
MILITARY HEROINES ... 593
THE FAITHFUL BUT LESS CONSPICUOUS LABORERS ... 606

THE LOYAL WOMEN OF AMERICA

WHOSE PATRIOTIC CONTRIBUTIONS, TOILS AND SACRIFICES, ENABLED THEIRSISTERS, WHOSE HISTORY IS HERE RECORDED, TO MINISTERRELIEF AND CONSOLATION TO OUR WOUNDEDAND SUFFERING HEROES;

AND WHO BY THEIR DEVOTION, THEIR LABORS, AND THEIR PATIENT ENDURANCE OF PRIVATION AND DISTRESS OF BODY AND SPIRIT, WHEN CALLED TO GIVE UP THEIR BELOVED ONES FOR THE

NATION'S DEFENSE,

HAVE WON FOR THEMSELVES ETERNAL HONOR, AND THE UNDYING REMEMBRANCE OF THE PATRIOTS OF ALL TIME,

WE DEDICATE THIS VOLUME.

PREFACE

THE preparation of this work, or rather the collection of material for it, was commenced in the autumn of 1863. While engaged in the compilation of a little book on "The Philanthropic Results of the War" for circulation abroad, in the summer of that year, the writer became so deeply impressed with the extraordinary sacrifices and devotion of loyal women, in the national cause, that he determined to make a record of them for the honor of his country. A voluminous correspondence then commenced and continued to the present time, soon demonstrated how general were the acts of patriotic devotion, and an extensive tour, undertaken the following summer, to obtain by personal observation and intercourse with these heroic women, a more clear and comprehensive idea of what they had done and were doing, only served to increase his admiration for their zeal, patience, and self-denying effort.

Meantime the war still continued, and the collisions between Grant and Lee, in the East, and Sherman and Johnston, in the South, the fierce campaign between Thomas and Hood in Tennessee, Sheridan's annihilating defeats of Early in the valley of the Shenandoah, and Wilson's magnificent expedition in Mississippi, Alabama, and Georgia, as well as the mixed naval and military victories at Mobile and Wilmington, were fruitful in wounds, sickness, and death. Never had the gentle and patient ministrations of woman been so needful as in the last year of the war; and never had they been so abundantly bestowed, and with such zeal and self-forgetfulness.

From Andersonville, and Millen, from Charleston, and Florence, from Salisbury, and Wilmington, from Belle Isle, and Libby Prison, came also, in these later months of the war, thousands of our bravest and noblest heroes, captured by the rebels, the feeble remnant of the tens of thousands imprisoned there, a majority of whom had perished of cold, nakedness, starvation, and disease, in those charnel houses, victims of the fiendish malignity of the rebel leaders. These poor fellows, starved to the last degree of emaciation, crippled and dying from frost and gangrene, many of them idiotic from their sufferings, or with the fierce fever of typhus, more deadly than sword or minie bullet, raging in their veins, were brought to Annapolis and to Wilmington, and unmindful of the deadly infection, gentle and tender women ministered to them as faithfully and lovingly, as if they were their own brothers. Ever and anon, in these works of mercy, one of these fair ministrants died a martyr to her faithfulness, asking, often only, to be buried beside her "boys," but the work never ceased while there was a soldier to be nursed. Nor were these the only fields in which noble service was rendered to humanity by the women of our time. In the larger associations of our cities, day after day, and year after year, women served in summer's heat and winter's cold, at their desks, corresponding with auxiliary aid societies, taking account of goods received for sanitary supplies, re-packing and shipping them to the points where they were needed, inditing and sending out circulars appealing for aid, in work more prosaic but equally needful and patriotic with that performed in the hospitals; and throughout every village and hamlet in the country, women were toiling, contriving, submitting to privation, performing unusual and severe labors, all for the soldiers. In the general hospitals of the cities and larger towns, the labors of the special diet kitchen, and of the hospital nurse were performed steadily, faithfully, and uncomplainingly, though there also, ever and anon, some fair toiler laid down her life in the service. There were many too in still other fields of labor, who showed their love for their country; the faithful women who, in the Philadelphia Refreshment Saloons, fed the hungry soldier on his way to or from the battle-field, till in the aggregate, they had dispensed nearly eight hundred thousand meals, and had cared for thousands of sick and wounded; the matrons of the Soldiers' Homes, Lodges, and Rests; the heroic souls who devoted themselves to the noble work of raising a nation of bondmen to intelligence and freedom; those who attempted the still more hopeless task of rousing the blunted intellect and cultivating the moral nature of the degraded and abject poor whites; and those who in circumstances of the greatest peril, manifested their fearless and undying attachment to their country and its flag; all these were entitled to a place in such a record. What wonder, then, that, pursuing his self-appointed task assiduously, the writer found it growing upon him; till the question came, not, who should be inscribed in this roll, but who could be omitted, since it was evident no single volume could do justice to all.

In the autumn of 1865, Mrs. Mary C. Vaughan, a skilful and practiced writer, whose tastes and sympathies led her to take an interest in the work, became associated with the writer in its preparation, and to her zeal in collecting, and skill in arranging the materials obtained, many of the interesting sketches of the volume are due. We have in the prosecution of our work been constantly embarrassed, by the reluctance of some who deserved a prominent place, to suffer anything to be communicated concerning their labors; by the promises, often repeated but never fulfilled, of others to furnish facts and incidents which they alone could supply, and by the forwardness of a few, whose services were of the least moment, in presenting their claims.

We have endeavored to exercise a wise and careful discrimination both in avoiding the introduction of any name unworthy of a place in such a record, and in giving the due meed of honor to those who have wrought most earnestly and acceptably. We cannot hope that we have been completely successful; the letters even now, daily received, render it probable that there are some, as faithful and self-sacrificing as any of those whose services we have recorded, of whom we have failed to obtain information; and that some of those who entered upon their work of mercy in the closing campaigns of the war, by their zeal and earnestness, have won the right to a place. We have not, knowingly, however, omitted the name of any faithful worker, of whom we could obtain information, and we feel assured that our record is far more full and complete, than any other which has been, or is likely to be prepared, and that the number of prominent and active laborers in the national cause who have escaped our notice is comparatively small.

We take pleasure in acknowledging our obligations to Rev. Dr. Bellows, President of the United States Sanitary Commission, for many services and much valuable information; to Honorable James E. Yeatman, the President of the Western Sanitary Commission, to Rev. J. G. Forman, late Secretary of that Commission, and now

Secretary of the Unitarian Association, and his accomplished wife, both of whom were indefatigable in their efforts to obtain facts relative to western ladies; to Rev. N. M. Mann, now of Kenosha, Wisconsin, but formerly Chaplain and Agent of the Western Sanitary Commission, at Vicksburg; to Professor J. S. Newberry, now of Columbia College, but through the war the able Secretary of the Western Department of the United States Sanitary Commission; to Mrs. M. A. Livermore, of Chicago, one of the managers of the Northwestern Sanitary Commission; to Rev. G. S. F. Savage, Secretary of the Western Department of the American Tract Society, Boston, Rev. William De Loss Love, of Milwaukee, author of a work on "Wisconsin in the War." Samuel B. Fales, Esq., of Philadelphia, so long and nobly identified with the Volunteer Refreshment Saloon, Dr. A. N. Read, of Norwalk, Ohio, late one o the Medical Inspectors of the Sanitary Commission, Di. Joseph Parrish, of Philadelphia, also a Medical Inspector of the Commission, Mrs. M. M. Husband, of Philadelphia, one of the most faithful workers in field hospitals during the war, Miss Katherine P. Wormeley, of Newport, Rhode Island, the accomplished historian of the Sanitary Commission, Mrs. W. H. Holstein, of Bridgeport, Montgomery County, Pennsylvania, Miss Maria M. C. Hall, of Washington, District of Columbia, and Miss Louise Titcomb, of Portland, Maine. From many of these we have received information indispensable to the completeness and success of our work; information too, often afforded at great inconvenience and labor. We commit our book, then, to the loyal women of our country, as an earnest and conscientious effort to portray some phases of a heroism which will make American women famous in all the future ages of history; and with the full conviction that thousands more only lacked the opportunity, not the will or endurance, to do, in the same spirit of self-sacrifice, what these have done.

L. P. B.

BROOKLYN, N. Y., February, 1867.

INTRODUCTION

A RECORD of the personal services of our American women in the late Civil War, however painful to the modesty of those whom it brings conspicuously before the world, is due to the honor of the country, to the proper understanding of our social life, and to the general interests of a sex whose rights, duties and capacities are now under serious discussion. Most of the women commemorated in this work inevitably lost the benefits of privacy, by the largeness and length of their public services, and their names and history are to a certain extent the property of the country. At any rate they must suffer the penalty which conspicuous merit entails upon its possessors, especially when won in fields of universal interest. • Notwithstanding the pains taken to collect from all parts of the country, the names and history of the women who in any way distinguished themselves in the War, and in spite of the utmost impartiality of purpose, there is no pretence that all who served the country best, are named in this record. Doubtless thousands of women, obscure in their homes, and humble in their fortunes, without official position even in their local society, and all human trace of whose labors is forever lost, contributed as generously of their substance, and as freely of their time and strength, and gave as unreservedly their hearts and their prayers to the cause, as the most conspicuous on the shining list here unrolled. For if

"The world knows nothing of its greatest men,"

it is still more true of its noblest women. Unrewarded by praise, unsullied by self-complacency, there is a character "of no reputation," which formed in strictest retirement, and in the patient exercise of unobserved sacrifices, is dearer and holier in the eye of Heaven, than the most illustrious name won by the most splendid services. Women there were in this war who without a single relative in the army, denied themselves for the whole four years, the comforts to which they had been always accustomed; went thinly clad, took the extra blanket from their bed, never tasted tea, or sugar, or flesh, that they might wind another bandage round some unknown soldier's wound, or give some parched lips in the hospital another sip of wine. Others never let one leisure moment, saved from lives of pledged labor which barely earned their bread, go unemployed in the service of the soldiers. God Himself keeps this record! It is too sacred to be trusted to men.

But it is not such humble, yet exalted souls that will complain of the praise which to their neglect, is allotted to any of their sisters. The ranks always contain some heroes braver and better than the most fortunate and conspicuous officers of staff or line—but they feel themselves best praised when their regiment, their corps, or their general is gazetted. And the true-hearted workers for the soldiers among the women of this country will gladly accept the recognition given to the noble band of their sisters whom peculiar circumstances lifted into distinct view, as a tribute offered to the whole company. Indeed, if the lives set forth in this work, were regarded as exceptional in their temper and spirit, as they certainly were in their incidents and largeness of sphere, the whole lesson of the Record would be misread. These women in their sacrifices, their patriotism, and their persistency, are only fair representatives of the spirit of their whole sex. As a rule, American women exhibited not only an intense feeling for the soldiers in their exposures and their sufferings, but an intelligent sympathy with the national cause, equal to that which furnished among the men, two million and three hundred thousand volunteers.

It is not unusual for women of all countries to weep and to work for those who encounter the perils of war. But the American women, after giving up, with a principled alacrity, to the ranks of the gathering and advancing army, their husbands and sons, their brothers and lovers, proceeded to organize relief for them; and they did it, not in the spasmodic and sentimental way, which has been common elsewhere, but with a self-controlled and rational consideration of the wisest and best means of accomplishing their purpose, which showed them to be in some degree the products and representatives of a new social era, and a new political development.

The distinctive features in woman's work in this war, were magnitude, system, thorough co-operativeness with the other sex, distinctness of purpose, business-like thoroughness in details, sturdy persistency to the close. There was no more general rising among the men, than among the women. Men did not take to the musket, more commonly than women took to the needle; and for every assembly where men met for mutual excitation in the service of the country, there was some corresponding gathering of women, to stir each other's hearts and fingers in the same sacred cause. All the caucuses and political assemblies of every kind, in which speech and song quickened the blood of the men, did not exceed in number the meetings, in the form of Soldiers' Aid Societies, and Sewing Circles, which the women held, where they talked over the national cause, and fed the fires of sacrifice in each other's hearts. Probably never in any war in any country, was there so universal and so specific an acquaintance on the part of both men and women, with the principles at issue, and the interests at stake. And of the two, the women were clearer and more united than the men, because their moral feelings and political instincts were not so much affected by selfishness and business, or party considerations. The work which our system of popular education does for girls and boys alike, and which in the middle and upper classes practically goes further with girls than with boys, told magnificently at this crisis. Everywhere, well educated women were found fully able to understand and explain to their sisters, the public questions involved in the war. Everywhere the newspapers, crowded with interest and with discussions, found eager and appreciative readers among the gentler sex. Everywhere started up women acquainted with the order of public business; able to call, and preside over public meetings of their own sex; act as secretaries and committees, draft constitutions and bye-laws, open books, and keep accounts with adequate precision, appreciate system, and postpone private inclinations or preferences to general principles; enter into extensive correspondence with their own sex: co-operate in the largest and most rational plans proposed by men who had studied carefully the subject of soldiers' relief, and adhere through good report and through evil report, to organizations which commended themselves to their judgment, in spite of local, sectarian, or personal jealousies and detractions.

It is impossible to over-estimate the amount of consecrated work done by the loyal women of the North for the Army. Hundreds of thousands of women probably gave all the leisure they could command, and all the money they could save and spare, to the soldiers for the whole four years and more, of the War. Amid discouragements and fearful delays they never flagged, but to the last increased in zeal and devotion. And their work was as systematic as it was universal. A generous emulation among the Branches of the United States Sanitary Commission, managed generally by women, usually, however, with some aid from men, brought their business habits and methods to ah almost perfect finish. Nothing that men commonly think peculiar to their own methods was wanting in the plans of the women.

They acknowledged and answered, endorsed and filed their letters; they sorted their stores, and kept an accurate account of stock; they had their books and reports kept in the most approved forms; they balanced their cash accounts with the most pains-taking precision; they exacted of each other regularity of attendance and punctiliousness of official etiquette. They showed in short, a perfect aptitude for business, and proved by their own experience that men can devise nothing too precise, too systematic or too complicated for women to understand, apply and improve upon, where there is any sufficient motive for it.

It was another feature of the case that there was no jealousy between women and men in the work, and no disposition to discourage, underrate, or dissociate from each other. It seemed to be conceded that men had more invention, comprehensiveness and power of generalization, and that their business habits, the fruits of ages of experience, were at least worth studying and copying by women. On the other hand, men, usually jealous of woman's extending the sphere of her life and labors, welcomed in this case her assistance in a public work, and felt how vain men's toil and sacrifices would be without woman's steady sympathy and patient ministry of mercy, her more delicate and persistent pity, her willingness to endure monotonous details of labor for the sake of charity, her power to open the heart of her husband, and to keep alive and flowing the fountains of compassion and love.

No words are adequate to describe the systematic, persistent faithfulness of the women who organized and led the Branches of the United States Sanitary Commission. Their volunteer labor had all the regularity of paid service, and a heartiness and earnestness which no paid services can ever have. Hundreds of women evinced talents there, which, in other spheres and in the other sex, would have made them merchant-princes, or great administrators of public affairs. Storms nor heats could keep them from their posts, and they wore on their faces, and finally evinced in their breaking constitutions, the marks of the cruel strain put upon their minds and hearts. They engaged in a correspondence of the most trying kind, requiring the utmost address to meet the searching questions asked by intelligent jealousy, and to answer the rigorous objections raised by impatience or ignorance in the rural districts. They became instructors of whole townships in the methods of government business, the constitution of the Commissary and Quartermaster's Departments, and the forms of the Medical Bureau. They had steadily to contend with the natural desire of the Aid Societies for local independence, and to reconcile neighborhoods to the idea of being merged and lost in large generalizations. They kept up the spirit of the people distant from the war and the camps by a steady fire of letters full of touching incidents; and they were repaid not only by the most generous returns of stores, but by letters from humble homes and lonely hearts, so full of truth and tenderness, of wisdom and pity, of self-sacrifice and patriotic consecration, that the most gifted and educated women in America, many of them at the head of the Branches or among their Directors, felt constantly reproved by the nobleness, the sweetness, the depth of sentiment that welled from the hidden and obscure springs in the hearts of farmers' wives and factory-girls.

Nor were the talents and the sacrifices of those at the larger Depots or Centres, more worthy of notice than the skill and pains evinced in arousing, maintaining and managing the zeal and work of county or town societies. Indeed, sometimes larger works are more readily controlled than smaller ones; and jealousies and individual caprices obstruct the co-operation of villages more than of towns and cities.

In the ten thousand Soldiers' Aid Societies which at one time or another probably existed in the country, there was in each some master-spirit, whose consecrated purpose was the staple in the wall, from which the chain of service hung and on whose strength and firmness it steadily drew. I never visited a single town however obscure, that I did not hear some woman's name which stood in that community for "Army Service;" a name round which the rest of the women gladly rallied; the name of some woman whose heart was felt to beat louder and more firmly than any of the rest for the boys in blue.

Of the practical talent, the personal worth, the aptitude for public service, the love of self-sacrificing duty thus developed and nursed into power, and brought to the knowledge of its possessors and their communities, it is difficult to speak too warmly. Thousands of women learned in this work to despise frivolity, gossip, fashion and idleness; learned to think soberly and without prejudice of the capacities of their own sex; and thus, did more to advance the rights of woman by proving her gifts and her fitness for public duties, than a whole library of arguments and protests.

The prodigious exertions put forth by the women who founded and conducted the great Fairs for the soldiers in a dozen principal cities, and in many large towns, were only surpassed by the planning skill and administrative ability which accompanied their progress, and the marvellous success in which they terminated. Months of anxious preparation, where hundreds of committees vied with each other in long-headed schemes for securing the co-operation of the several trades or industries allotted to each, and during which laborious days and anxious nights were unintermittingly given to the wearing work, were followed by weeks of personal service in the fairs themselves, where the strongest women found their vigor inadequate to the task, and hundreds laid the foundations of long illness and some of sudden death. These sacrifices and far-seeing provisions were justly repaid by almost fabulous returns of money, which to the extent of nearly three millions of dollars, flowed into the treasury of the United States Sanitary Commission. The chief women who inaugurated the several great Fairs at New York, Philadelphia, Brooklyn, Boston, Chicago, Cincinnati, St. Louis, and administered these vast movements, were not behind the ablest men in the land in their grasp and comprehension of the business in hand, and often in comparison with the men associated with them, exhibited a finer scope, a better spirit and a more victorious faith. But for the women of America, the great Fairs would never have been born, or would have died ignominiously in their gilded cradles. Their vastness of conception and their splendid results are to be set as an everlasting crown on woman's capacity for large and money-yielding enterprises. The women who led them can never sink back into obscurity.

But I must pass from this inviting theme, where indeed I feel more at home than in what is to follow, to the consideration of what naturally occupies a larger space in this work—however much smaller it was in reality, i.e., to the labors of the women who actually went to the war, and worked in the hospitals and camps.

Of the labors of women in the hospitals and in the field, this book gives a far fuller history than is likely to be got from any other source, as this sort of service cannot be recorded in the histories of organized work. For, far the largest part of this work was done by persons of exceptional energy and some fine natural aptitude for the service, which was independent of organizations, and hardly submitted itself to any rules except the impulses of devoted love for the work—supplying tact, patience and resources. The women who did hospital service continuously, or who kept themselves near the base of armies in the field, or who moved among the camps, and travelled with the corps, were an exceptional class—as rare as heroines always are—a class, representing no social grade, but coming from all—belonging to no rank or age of life in particular; sometimes young and sometimes old, sometimes refined and sometimes rude; now of fragile physical aspect and then of extraordinary robustness—but in all cases, women with a mighty love and earnestness in their hearts—a love and pity, and an ability to show it forth and to labor in behalf of it, equal to that which in other departments of life, distinguishes poets,' philosophers, sages and saints, from ordinary or average men.

Moved by an indomitable desire to serve in person the victims of wounds and sickness, a few hundred women, impelled by instincts which assured them of their ability to endure the hardship, overcome the obstacles, and adjust themselves to the unusual and unfeminine circumstances in which they would be placed—made their way through all obstructions at home, and at the seat of war, or in the hospitals, to the bed-sides of the sick and wounded men. Many of these women scandalized their friends at home by what seemed their Quixotic resolution; or, they left their families under circumstances which involved a romantic oblivion of the recognized and usual duties of domestic life; they forsook their own children, to make children of a whole army corps; they risked their lives in fevered hospitals; they lived in tents or slept in ambulance wagons, for months together; they fell sick of fevers themselves, and after long illness, returned to the old business of hospital and field service. They carried into their work their womanly tenderness, their copious sympathies, their great-hearted devotion—and had to face and contend with the cold routine, the semi-savage professional indifference, which by the necessities of the case, makes ordinary medical supervision, in time of actual war, impersonal, official, unsympathetic and abrupt. The honest, natural jealousy felt by surgeons-in-charge, and their ward masters, of all outside assistance, made it necessary for every woman, who was to succeed in her purpose of holding her place, and really serving the men, to study and practice an address, an adaptation and a patience, of which not one candidate in ten was capable. Doubtless nine-tenths of all who wished to offer and thought themselves capable of this service, failed in their practical efforts. As many women fancied themselves capable of enduring hospital life, as there are always in every college, youth who believe they can become distinguished authors, poets and statesmen. But only the few who had a genius for the work, continued in it, and succeeded in elbowing room for themselves through the never-ending obstacles, jealousies and chagrins that beset the service. Every woman who keeps her place in a general hospital, or a corps hospital, has to prove her title to be trusted; her tact, discretion, endurance and strength of nerve and fibre. No one woman succeeded in rendering years of hospital service, who was not an exceptional person—a woman of larger heart, clearer head, finer enthusiasm, and more mingled tact, courage, firmness and holy will—' than one in a thousand of her sex. A grander collection of women— whether considered in their intellectual or their moral qualities, their heads or their hearts, I have not had the happiness of knowing, than the women I saw in the hospitals; they were the flower of their sex. Great as were the labors of those who superintended the operations at home—of collecting and preparing supplies for the hospitals and the field, I cannot but think that the women who lived in the hospitals, or among the soldiers, required a force of character and a glow of devotion and self-sacrifice, of a rarer kind. They were really heroines. They conquered their feminine sensibility at the sight of blood and wounds; their native antipathy to disorder, confusion and violence; subdued the rebellious delicacy of their more exquisite senses; lived coarsely, and dressed and slept rudely; they studied the caprices of men to whom their ties were simply human—men often ignorant, feeble-minded—out of their senses—raving with pain and fever; they had a still harder service to bear with the pride, the official arrogance, the hardness or the folly—perhaps the impertinence and presumption of half trained medical men, whom the urgencies of the case had fastened on the service. Their position was always critical, equivocal, suspected, and to be justified only by their undeniable and conspicuous merits;—their wisdom, patience and proven efficiency; justified by the love and reverence they exacted from the soldiers themselves!

True, the rewards of these women were equal to their sacrifices. They drew their pay from a richer treasury than that of the United States Government. I never knew one of them who had had a long service, whose memory of the grateful looks of the dying, of the few awkward words that fell from the lips of thankful convalescents, or the speechless eye-following of the dependent soldier, or the pressure of a rough hand, softened to womanly gentleness by long illness,—was not the sweetest treasure of all their lives. Nothing in the power of the Nation to give or to say, can ever compare for a moment with the proud satisfaction which every brave soldier who risked his life for his country, always carries in his heart of hearts. And no public recognition, no thanks from a saved Nation, can ever add anything of much importance to the rewards of those who tasted the actual joy of ministering with their own hands and hearts to the wants of one sick and dying man.

It remains only to say a word about the influence of the work of the women in the War upon the strength and unanimity of the public sentiment, and on the courage and fortitude of the army itself.

The participation by actual work and service in the labors of the War, not only took out of women's hearts the soreness which unemployed energies or incongruous pursuits would have left there, but it took out of their mouths the murmurs and moans which their deserted, husbandless, childless condition would so naturally have provoked. The women by their call to work, and the opportunity of pouring their energies, sympathies and affections into an ever open and practical channel, were quieted, reconciled, upheld. The weak were borne upon the bosoms of the strong. Banded together, and working together, their solicitude and uneasiness were alleviated. Following in imagination the work of their own hands, they seemed to be present on the field and in the ranks; they studied the course of the armies; they watched the policy of the Government; they learned the character of the Generals; they threw themselves into the war! And so they helped wonderfully to keep up the enthusiasm, or to rebuke the lukewarmness, or to check the despondency and apathy which at times settled over the people. Men were ashamed to doubt where women trusted, or to murmur where they submitted, or to do little where they did so much. If during the war, home life had gone on as usual; women engrossed in their domestic or social cares; shrinking from public questions; deferring to what their husbands or brothers told them, or seeking to amuse themselves with social pleasures and striving to forget the painful strife in frivolous caprices, it would have had a fearful effect on public sentiment, deepening the gloom of every reverse, adding to the discouragements which an embarrassed commerce and trade brought to men's hearts, by domestic echoes of weariness of the strife, and favoring the growth of a disaffected, compromising, unpatriotic feeling, which always stood ready to break out with any offered encouragement. A sense of nearness of the people to the Government which the organization of the women effected, enlarged their sympathies with its movements and disposed them to patience. Their own direct experience of the difficulties of all co-operative undertakings, broadened their views and rendered intelligible the delays and reverses which our national cause suffered. In short the women of the country were through the whole conflict, not only not softening the fibres of war, but they were actually strengthening its sinews by keeping up their own courage and that of their households, under the inspiration of the larger and more public life, the broader work and greater field for enterprise and self-sacrifice afforded them by their direct labors for the benefit of the soldiers. They drew thousands of lukewarm, or calculating, or self-saving men into the support of the national cause by their practical enthusiasm and devotion. They proved what has again and again been demonstrated, that what the women of a country resolve shall be done, will and must be done. They shamed recruits into the ranks, and made it almost impossible for deserters, or cowards, or malingerers to come borne; they emptied the pockets of social idlers, or wealthy drones, into the treasuries of the Aid Societies; and they compelled the shops and domestic trade of all cities to be favorable to the war. The American women were nearer right and more thoroughly united by this means, and their own healthier instincts, than the American men. The Army, whose bayonets were glittering needles, advanced with more unbroken ranks, and exerted almost a greater moral force than the army that carried loaded muskets.

The Aid Societies and the direct oversight the women sought to give the men in the field, very much increased the reason for correspondence between the homes and the tents.

The women were proud to write what those at the hearth-stone were doing for those who tended the camp-fires, and the men were happy and cheery to acknowledge the support they received from this home sympathy. The immense correspondence between the army and the homes, prodigious beyond belief as it was, some regiments sending home a thousand letters a week, and receiving as many more back; the constant transmission to the men of newspapers, full of the records of home work and army news, produced a homogeneousness of feeling between the soldiers and the citizens, which kept the men in the field, civilians, and made the people at home, of both sexes,' half-soldiers.

Thus there never grew up in the army any purely military and anti-social or anti-civil sentiments. The soldiers studied and appreciated all the time the moral causes of the War, and were acquainted with the political as well as military complications. They felt all the impulses of home strengthening their arms and encouraging their hearts. And their letters home, as a rule, were designed to put the best face upon things, and to encourage their wives and sweethearts, their sisters and parents, to bear their absence with fortitude, and even with cheerfulness.

The influence on the tone of their correspondence, exerted by the fact that the women were always working for the Army, and that the soldiers always knew they were working, and were always receiving evidence of their care, may be better imagined than described. It largely ministered to that sympathetic unity between the soldiers and the country, which made our army always a corrective and an inspiration to our Governmental policy, and kept up that fine reciprocal influence between civil and military life, which gave an heroic fibre to all souls at home, and finally restored us our soldiers with their citizen hearts beating regularly under their uniforms, as they dropped them off at the last drum-tap.

H. W. B.

INTRODUCTORY CHAPTER

AN intense and passionate love of country, holding, for the time, all other ties in abeyance, has been a not uncommon trait of character among women of all countries and climes, throughout the ages of human history. In the nomadic races it assumed the form of attachment to the patriarchal rules and chiefs of the tribe; in the more savage of the localized nations, it was reverence for the ruler, coupled with a filial regard for the resting-places and graves of their ancestors.

But in the more highly organized and civilized countries, it was the institutions of the nation, its religion, its sacred traditions, its history, as well as its kings, its military leaders, and its priests, that were the objects of the deep and intense patriotic devotion of its noblest and most gifted women.

The manifestations of this patriotic zeal were diverse in different countries, and at different periods in the same country. At one time it contented itself with triumphal pæans and dances over victories won by the nation's armies, as in the case of Miriam and the maidens of Israel at the destruction of the Egyptians at the Red Sea, or the victories of the armies led by David against the Philistines; or in the most heart-rending lamentations over the fall of the nation's heroes on the field of battle, as in the mourning of the Trojan maidens over the death of Hector; at other times, some brave and heroic spirit, goaded with the sense of her country's wrongs, girds upon her own fair and tender form, the armor of proof, and goes forth, the self-constituted but eagerly welcomed leader of its mailed hosts, to overthrow the nation's foes. We need only recall Deborah, the avenger of the Israelites against the oppressions of the King of Canaan; Boadicea, the daring Queen of the Britons, and in later times, the heroic but hapless maid of Orleans, Jeanne d'Arc; and in the Hungarian war of 1848, the brave but unfortunate Countess Teleki, as examples of these female patriots.

In rare instances, this sense of the nation's sufferings from a tyrant's oppression, have so wrought upon the sensitive spirit, as to stimulate it to the determination to achieve the country's freedom by the assassination of the oppressor. It was thus that Jael brought deliverance to her country by the murder of Sisera; Judith, by the assassination of Holofernes; and in modern times, Charlotte Corday sought the rescue of France from the grasp of the murderous despot, Marat, by plunging the poniard to his heart.

A far nobler, though less demonstrative manifestation of patriotic devotion than either of these, is that which has prompted women in all ages to become ministering angels to the sick, the suffering, and the wounded among their countrymen who have periled life and health in the nation's cause.

Occasionally, even in the earliest recorded wars of antiquity, we find high-born maidens administering solace to the wounded heroes on the field of battle, and attempting to heal their wounds by the appliances of their rude and simple surgery; but it was only the favorite leaders, never the common soldier, or the subordinate officer, who received these gentle attentions. The influence of Christianity, in its earlier development, tended to expand the sympathies and open the heart of woman to all gentle and holy influences, and it is recorded that the wounded Christian soldiers were, where it was possible, nursed and cared for by those of the same faith, both men and women.

In the fifth century, the Empress Helena established hospitals for the sick and wounded soldiers of the empire, on the routes between Rome and Constantinople, and caused them to be carefully nursed. In the dark ages that followed, and amid the downfall of the Roman Empire, and the uprearing of the Gothic kingdoms that succeeded, there was little room or thought of mercy; but the fair-haired women of the North encouraged their heroes to deeds of valor, and at times, ministered in their rude way to their wounds. The monks, at their monasteries, rendered some care and aid to the wounded in return for their exemption from plunder and rapine, and in the ninth century, an order of women consecrated to the work, the Beguines, predecessors of the modern Sisters of Charity, was established "to minister to the sick and wounded of the armies which then, and for centuries afterward, scarred the face of continental Europe with battle-fields." With the Beguines, however, and their successors, patriotism was not so much the controlling motive of action, as the attainment of merit by those deeds of charity and self-sacrifice.

In the wars of the seventeenth, eighteenth, and the early part of the nineteenth century, while the hospitals had a moderate share of fair ministrants, chiefly of the religious orders, the only female service on the battle-field or in the camp, often the scene of fatal epidemics, was that of the cantiniéres, vivandiéres, filles du regiment, and other camp followers, who, at some risk of reputation, accompanied the armies in their march, and brought to the wounded and often dying soldier, on the field of battle, the draught of water which quenched his raging thirst, or the cordial, which sustained his fast ebbing strength till relief could come. Humble of origin, and little circumspect in morals as many of these women were, they are yet deserving of credit for the courage and patriotism which led them to brave all the horrors of death, to relieve the suffering of the wounded of the regiments to which they were attached. Up to the period of the Crimean war in 1854, though there had been much that was praiseworthy in the manifestations of female patriotism in connection with the movements of great armies, there had never been any systematic ministration, prompted by patriotic devotion, to the relief of the suffering sick and wounded of those armies.

There were yet other modes, however, in which the women of ancient and modern times manifested their love of then' country. The Spartan mother, who, without a tear, presented her sons with them shields, with the stern injunction to return with them, or upon them, that is, with honor untarnished, or dead,—the fair dames and maidens of Carthage, who divested themselves of their beautiful tresses, to furnish bowstrings for their soldiers,—the Jewish women who preferred a death of torture, to the acknowledgment of the power of the tyrant over their country's rulers, and their faith—the women of the Pays-de Vaud, whose mountain fastnesses and churches were dearer to them than life—the thousands of wives and mothers, who in our revolutionary struggle, and in our recent war, gave up freely at their country's call, their best beloved, regretting only that they had no more to give; knowing full well, that in giving them up they condemned themselves to penury and want, to hard, grinding toil, and privations such as they had never before experienced, and not improbably to the rending, by the rude vicissitudes of war, of those ties, dearer than life itself—those who in the presence of ruffians, capable of any atrocity dared, and in many cases suffered, a violent death, and indignities worse than death, by their fearless defense of the cause and flag of their country—and yet again, those who, in peril of their lives, for the love they bore to them country, guided hundreds of escaped prisoners, through the regions haunted by foes, to safety and freedom—all these and many others, whose deeds of heroism we have not space so much as to name, have shown them love of country as fully and worthily, as those who in hospital, in camp or on battle-field have ministered to the battle-scarred hero, or those who, in all the panoply of war, have led their hosts to the deadly charge, or the fierce affray of contending armies.

Florence Nightingale, an English gentlewoman, of high social position and remarkable executive powers, was the first of her sex, at least among English-speaking nations, to systematize the patriotic ardor of her countrywomen, and institute such measures of reform in the care of sick and wounded soldiers in military hospitals, as should conduce to the comfort and speedy recovery of their inmates. She had voluntarily passed through the course of training, required of the hospital nurses and assistants, in Pastor Fliedner's Deaconess' Institution, at Kaiserswerth on the Rhine, before she entered upon her great mission in the hospitals at Scutari. She was ably seconded in her labors by other ladies of rank from England, who, actuated only by patriotic zeal, gave themselves to the work of bringing order out of chaos, cheerfulness out of gloom, cleanliness out of the most revolting filth, and the sunshine of health out of the lazar house of corruption and death. In this heroic undertaking they periled their lives, more certainly, than those who took part in the fierce charge of Balaclava. Some fell victims to their untiring zeal; others, and Miss Nightingale among the number, were rendered hopeless invalids for life, by their exertions.

Fifty years of peace had rendered our nation more entirely unacquainted with the arts of war, than was Great Britain, when, at the close of forty years of quiet, she again marshalled her troops in battle array. But though the transition was sudden from the arts of peace to the din and tumult of war, and the blunders, both from inexperience and dogged adherence to routine, were innumerable, the hearts of the people, and especially the hearts of the gentler sex, were resolutely set upon one thing; that the citizen soldiers of the nation should be cared for, in sickness or in health, as the soldiers of no nation had ever been before. Soldiers' Aid Societies, Sewing Circles for the soldiers, and Societies for Relief, sprang up simultaneously with the organization of regiments, in every village, town, and city throughout the North. Individual benevolence kept pace with organized charity, and the managers of the freight trains and expresses, running toward Washington, were in despair at the fearful accumulation of freight for the soldiers, demanding instant transportation. It was inevitable that there should be waste and loss in this lavish outpouring; but it was a manifestation of the patriotic feeling which throbbed in the hearts of the people, and which, through four years of war, never ceased or diminished aught of its zeal, or its abundant liberality. It was felt instinctively, that there would soon be a demand for nurses for the sick and wounded, and fired by the noble example of Florence Nightingale, though too often without her practical training, thousands of young, fair, and highly educated women offered themselves for the work, and strove for opportunities for their gentle ministry, as in other days they might have striven for the prizes of fortune.

Soon order emerged from the chaos of benevolent impulse; the Sanitary Commission and its affiliated Societies organized and wisely directed much of the philanthropic effort, which would otherwise have failed of accomplishing its intended work through misdirection; while other Commissions, Associations, and skilfully managed personal labors, supplemented what was lacking in its earlier movements, and ere long the Christian Commission added intellectual and religious aliment to its supplies for the wants of the physical man.

Of the thousands of applicants for the position of Hospital Nurses, the greater part were rejected promptly by the stern, but experienced lady, to whom the Government had confided the delicate and responsible duty of making the selection. The ground of rejection was usually the youthfulness of the applicants; a sufficient reason, doubtless, in most cases, since the enthusiasm, mingled in some instances, perhaps, with romance, which had prompted the offer, would often falter before the extremely unpoetic realities of a nurse's duties, and the youth and often frail health of the applicants would soon cause them to give way under labors which required a mature strength, a firm will, and skill in all household duties. Yet "to err is human," 'and it need not surprise us, as it probably did not Miss Dix, to learn, that in a few instances, those whom she had refused to commission on account of their youthfulness, proved in other fields, their possession of the very highest qualifications for the care of the sick and wounded. Miss Gilson was one of the most remarkable of these instances; and it reflects no discredit on Miss Dix's powers of discrimination, that she should not have discovered, in that girlish face, the indications of those high abilities, of which their possessor was as yet probably unconscious. The rejection of so many of these volunteer nurses necessitated the appointment of many from another class,—young women of culture and education, but generally from the humbler walks of life, in whose hearts the fire of patriotism was not less ardent and glowing than in those of their wealthier sisters. Many of these, though they would have preferred to perform their labors without fee or reward, were compelled, from the necessities of those at home, to accept the wholly inadequate pittance (twelve dollars a month and their food) which was offered them by the Government, but they served in their several stations with a fidelity, intelligence, and patient devotion which no money could purchase. The testimony received from all quarters to the faithfulness and great moral worth of these nurses, is greatly to them honor. Not one of them, so far as we can learn, ever disgraced her calling, or gave cause for reproach. "We fear that so general an encomium could not truthfully be bestowed on all the volunteer nurses.

But nursing in the hospitals, was only a small part of the work to which patriotism called American women. There was the collection and forwarding to the field, there to be distributed by the chaplains, or some specially appointed agent, of those supplies which the families and friends of the soldiers so earnestly desired to send to them; socks, shirts, handkerchiefs, havelocks, and delicacies in the way of food. The various states had their agents, generally ladies, in Washington, who performed these duties, during the first two years of the war, while as yet the Sanitary Commission had not fully organized its system of Field Relief. In the West, every considerable town furnished its quota of supplies, and, after every battle, voluntary agents undertook their distribution.

During McClellan's peninsular campaign, a Hospital Transport service was organized in connection with the Sanitary Commission, which numbered among its members several gentlemen and ladies of high social position, whose labors in improvising, often from the scantiest possible supplies, the means of comfort and healing for the fever-stricken and wounded, resulted in the preservation of hundreds of valuable lives.

Mrs. John Harris, the devoted and heroic Secretary of the Ladies' Aid Society of Philadelphia, had already, in the Peninsular campaign, encountered all the discomforts and annoyances of a life in the camp, to render what assistance she could to the sick and wounded, while they were yet in the field or camp hospital. At Cedar Mountain, and in the subsequent battles of

August, in Pope's Campaign, Miss Barton, Mrs. T. J. Fales, and some others also brought supplies to the field, and ministered to the wounded, while the shot and shell were crashing around them, and Antietam had its representatives of the fair sex, angels of mercy, but for whose tender and judicious ministrations, hundreds and perhaps thousands would not have seen another morning's light. In the race for Richmond which followed, Miss Barton's train was hospital and diet kitchen to the Ninth Corps, and much of the time for the other Corps also. At Fredericksburg, Mrs. Harris, Mrs. Lee, Mrs. Plummer, Mrs. Fales, and Miss Barton, and we believe also, Miss

Gilson, were all actively engaged. A part of the same noble company, though not all, were at Chancellorsville.

At Gettysburg, Mrs. Harris was present and actively engaged, and as soon as the battle ceased, a delegation of ladies connected with the Sanitary Commission toiled most faithfully to alleviate the horrors of war. In the subsequent battles of the Army of the Potomac, the Field Relief Corps of the Sanitary Commission with its numerous male and female collaborators, after, or at the time of all the great battles, the ladies connected with the Christian Commission and a number of efficient independent workers, did all in their power to relieve the constantly swelling tide of human suffering, especially during that period of less than ninety days, when more than ninety thousand men, wounded, dying, or dead, covered the battle-fields with their gore.

In the West, after the battle of Shiloh, and the subsequent engagements of Buell's campaign, women of the highest social position visited the battle-field, and encountered its horrors, to minister to those who were suffering, and bring them relief. Among these, the names of Mrs. Martha A. Wallace, the widow of General W. H. L. Wallace, who fell in the battle of Shiloh; of Mrs. Harvey, the widow of Governor Louis Harvey of Wisconsin, who was drowned while on a mission of philanthropy to the Wisconsin soldiers wounded at Shiloh; and the sainted Mario garet E. Breckinridge of St. Louis, will be readily recalled. During Grant's Vicksburg campaign, as well as after Rosecrans' battles of Stone River and Chickamauga, there were many of these heroic women who braved all discomforts and difficulties to bring healing and comfort to the gallant soldiers who had fallen on the field. Mrs. Hoge and Mrs. Livermore, of Chicago, visited Grant's camp in front of Vicksburg, more than once, and by their exertions, saved his army from scurvy; Mrs. Porter, Mrs. Bickerdyke, and several others are deserving of mention for their untiring zeal both in these and Sherman's Georgian campaigns. Mrs. Bickerdyke has won undying renown throughout the Western armies as pre-eminently the friend of the private soldier.

As our armies, especially in the West and Southwest, won more and more of the enemy's territory, the important towns of which were immediately occupied as garrisons, hospital posts, and secondary bases of the armies, the work of nursing and providing special diet and comfort in the general hospitals at these posts, which were often of great extent, involved a vast amount of labor and frequently serious privation, and personal discomfort on the part of the nurses. Some of these who volunteered for the work were remarkable for their earnest and faithful labors in behalf of the soldiers, under circumstances which would have disheartened any but the most resolute spirits. We may name without invidiousness among these, Mrs. Colfax, Miss Maertz, Miss Melcenia Elliott, Miss Parsons, Miss Adams, and Miss Brayton, who, with many others, perhaps equally faithful, by their constant assiduity in their duties, have given proof of their ardent love of their country.

To provide for the great numbers of men discharged from the hospitals while yet feeble and ill, and without the means of going to their often distant homes, and the hundreds of enfeebled and mutilated soldiers, whose days of service were over, and who, often in great bodily weakness, sought to obtain the pay due them from the Government, and not unseldom died in the effort; the United States Sanitary Commission and the Western Sanitary Commission established Soldiers' Homes at Washington, Cincinnati, Chicago, Louisville, Nashville, St. Louis, Memphis, Vicksburg, and other places. In these, these disabled men found food and shelter, medical attendance when needed, assistance in collecting their dues, and aid in their transportation homeward. To each of these institutions, a Matron was assigned, often with female assistants. The duties of these Matrons were extremely arduous, but they were performed most nobly. To some of these homes were attached a department for the mothers, wives and daughters of the wounded soldiers, who had come on to care for them, and who often found themselves, when ready to return, penniless, and without a shelter. To these, a helping hand, and a kind welcome, was ever extended.

To these should be added the Soldiers' Lodges, established at some temporary stopping-places on the routes to and from the great battle-fields; places where the soldier, fainting from his wearisome march, found refreshment, and if sick, shelter and care; and the wounded, on their distressing journey from the battle-field to the distant hospitals, received the gentle ministrations of women, to allay their thirst, relieve their painful positions, and strengthen their wearied bodies for further journeyings. There were also, in New York, Boston, and many other of the Northern cities, Soldiers' Homes or Depots, not generally connected with the Sanitary Commission, in which invalid soldiers were cared for and their interests protected. In all these there were efficient and capable Matrons. In the West, there were also Homes for Refugees, families of poor whites generally though not always sufferers for their Union sentiments, sent north by the military commanders from all the States involved in the rebellion. Reduced to the lowest depths of poverty, often suffering absolute starvation, usually dirty and of uncleanly habits, in many cases ignorant in the extreme, and intensely indolent, these poor creatures had often little to recommend them to the sympathy of their northern friends, save their common humanity, and their childlike attachment to the Union cause. Yet on these, women of high culture and refinement, women who, but for the fire of patriotism which burned in their hearts, would have turned away, sickened at the mental and moral degradation which seemed proof against all instruction or tenderness, bestowed their constant and unwearying care, endeavoring to rouse in them the instinct of neatness and the love of household duties; instructing their children, and instilling into the darkened minds of the adults some ideas of religious duty, and some gleams of intelligence. No mission to the heathen of India, of Tartary, or of the African coasts, could possibly have been more hopeless and discouraging; but they triumphed over every obstacle, and in many instances had the happiness of seeing these poor people restored to their southern homes, with higher aims, hopes, and aspirations, and with better habits, and more intelligence, than they had ever before possessed.

The camps and settlements of the freedmen were also the objects of philanthropic care. To these, many highly educated women volunteered to go, and establishing schools, endeavored to raise these former slaves to the comprehension of their privileges and duties as free men. The work was arduous, for though there was a stronger desire for learning, and a quicker apprehension of religious and moral instruction, among the freedmen than among the refugees, their slave life had made them fickle, untruthful, and to some extent, dishonest and unchaste. Yet the faithful and indefatigable teachers found their labors wonderfully successful, and accomplished a great amount of good.

Another and somewhat unique manifestation of the patriotism of our American women, was the service of the Refreshment Saloons at Philadelphia. For four years, the women of that portion of Philadelphia lying in the vicinity of the Navy Yard, responded, by night or by day, to the signal gun, fired whenever one or more regiments of soldiers were passing through the city, and hastening to the Volunteer or the Cooper Shop Refreshment Saloons, spread before the soldiers an ample repast, and served them with a cordiality and heartiness deserving all praise. Four hundred thousand soldiers were fed by these willing hands and generous hearts, and in hospitals connected with both Refreshment Saloons the sick were tenderly cared for.

In the large general hospitals of Washington, Philadelphia, New York, Cincinnati, and St. Louis, in addition to the volunteer and paid nurses, there were committees of ladies, who, on alternate days, or on single days of each week, were accustomed to visit the hospitals, bringing delicacies and luxuries, preparing special dishes for the invalid soldiers, writing to their friends for them, etc. To this sacred duty, many women of high social position devoted themselves steadily for nearly three years, alike amid the summer's heat and the winter's cold, never failing of visiting the patients, to whom their coming was the most joyous event of the otherwise gloomy day.

But these varied forms of manifestation of patriotic zeal would have been of but little material service to the soldiers, had there not been behind them, throughout the loyal North, a vast network of organizations extending to every village and hamlet, for raising money and preparing and forwarding supplies of whatever was needful for the welfare of the sick and wounded. We have already alluded to the spontaneity and universality of these organizations at the beginning of the war. They were an outgrowth alike of the patriotism and the systematizing tendencies of the people of the North. It might have been expected that the zeal which led to their formation would soon have cooled, and, perhaps, this would have been the case, but for two causes, viz.: that they very early became parts of more comprehensive organizations officered by women of untiring energy, and the most exalted patriotic devotion; and that the events of the war constantly kept alive the zeal of a few in each society, who spurred on the laggards, and encouraged the faint-hearted. These Soldiers' Aid Societies, Ladies' Aid Associations, Alert Clubs, Soldiers' Relief Societies, or by whatever other name they were called, were usually auxiliary to some Society in the larger cities, to which their several contributions of money and supplies were sent, by which their activity and labors were directed, and which generally forwarded to some central source of supply, their donations and its own. The United States Sanitary Commission had its branches, known under various names, as Branch Commissions, General Soldiers' Aid Societies, Associates, Local Sanitary Commissions, etc., at Boston, Albany, Philadelphia, Pittsburg, Buffalo, Cleveland, Cincinnati, and Chicago, and three central organizations, the Women's Central Association of Relief, in New York, the Sanitary Commission, at Washington, and the Western Depot of Supplies, at Louisville, Kentucky. Affiliated to these were over twelve thousand local Soldiers' Aid Societies. The Western Sanitary Commission had but one central organization, besides its own depot, viz.: The Ladies' Union Aid Society, of St. Louis, which had a very considerable number of auxiliaries in Missouri and Iowa. The Christian Commission had its branches in Boston, New York, Brooklyn, Baltimore, Buffalo, Cincinnati, Chicago, and St. Louis, and several thousand local organizations reported to these. Aside from these larger bodies, there were the Ladies' Aid Association of Philadelphia, with numerous auxiliaries in Pennsylvania, the Baltimore Ladies' Relief Association, the New England Soldiers' Relief Association of New York; and during the first two years of the war, Sanitary Commissions in Iowa, Indiana, and Illinois, and State Relief Societies in Wisconsin, Ohio, Michigan, New York, and some of the other States with their representative organizations in Washington. Several Central Aid Societies having large numbers of auxiliaries, acted independently for the first two years, but were eventually merged in the Sanitary Commission. Prominent among these were the Hartford Ladies' Aid Society, having numerous auxiliaries throughout Connecticut, the Pittsburg Relief Committee, drawing its supplies from the circumjacent country, and we believe, also, the Penn Relief Society, an organization among the Friends of Philadelphia and vicinity. The supplies for the Volunteer and Cooper Shop Refreshment Saloons of Philadelphia, were contributed by the citizens of that city and vicinity.

When it is remembered, that by these various organizations, a sum exceeding fifty millions of dollars was raised, during a little more than four years, for the comfort and welfare of the soldiers, their families, their widows, and their orphans, we may be certain that there was a vast amount of work done by them. Of this aggregate of labor, it is difficult to form any adequate idea. The ladies who were at the head of the Branch or Central organizations, worked day after day, during the long and hot days of summer, and the brief but cold ones of winter, as assiduously and steadily, as any merchant in his counting-house, or the banker at his desk, and exhibited business abilities, order, foresight, judgment, and tact, such as are possessed by very few of the most eminent men of business in the country. The extent of their operations, too, was in several instances commensurate with that of some of our merchant princes. Miss Louisa Lee Schuyler and Miss Ellen Collins, of the Women's Central Association of Relief at New York, received and disbursed in supplies and money, several millions of dollars in value; Mrs. Rouse, Miss Mary Clark Brayton, and Miss Ellen F. Terry, of the Cleveland Soldiers' Aid Society, somewhat more than a million; Miss Abby May, of Boston, not far from the same amount; Mrs. Hoge, and Mrs. Livermore, of the N. W. Sanitary Commission, over a million; while Mrs. Seymour, of Buffalo, Miss Valeria Campbell, of Detroit, Mrs. Colt, of Milwaukie, Miss Rachel W. McFadden, of Pittsburg, Mrs. Hoadley, and Mrs. Mendenhall, of Cincinnati, Mrs. Clapp, and Miss H. A. Adams, of the St. Louis Ladies' Aid Society, Mrs. Joel Jones, and Mrs. John Harris, of the Philadelphia Ladies' Aid Society, Mrs.

Stranahan, and Mrs. Archer, of Brooklyn, if they did not do quite so large a business, at least rivaled the merchants of the smaller cities, in the extent of their disbursements; and when it is considered, that these ladies were not only the managers and financiers of their transactions, but in most cases the bookkeepers also, we think their right to be regarded as possessing superior business qualifications will not be questioned.

But some of these lady managers possessed still other claims to our respect, for their laborious and self-sacrificing patriotism. It occurred to several ladies in different sections of the country, as they ascertained the suffering condition of some of the families of the soldiers, (the early volunteers, it will be remembered, received no bounties, or very trifling ones), that if they could secure for them, at remunerative prices, the making of the soldiers' uniforms, or of the hospital bedding and clothing, they might thus render them independent of charity, and capable of self-support.

Three ladies (and perhaps more), Mrs. Springer, of St. Louis, in behalf of the Ladies' Aid Society of that city, Miss Katherine P. Wormeley, of Newport, R. I., and Miss Helen L. Gilson, of Chelsea, Mass., applied to the Governmental purveyors of clothing, for the purpose of obtaining this work. There was necessarily considerable difficulty in accomplishing their purpose. The army of contractors opposed them strongly, and in the end, these ladies were each obliged to take a contract of large amount themselves, in order to be able to furnish the work to the wives and daughters of the soldiers. In St. Louis, the terms of the contract were somewhat more favorable than at the East, and on the expiration of one, another was taken up, and about four hundred women were supplied with remunerative work throughout the whole period of the war. The terms of the contract necessitated the careful inspection of the clothing, and the certainty of its being well made, by the lady contractors; but in point of fact, it was all cut and prepared for the sewing-women by Mrs. Springer and her associates, who, giving their services to this work, divided among their employes the entire sum received for each contract, paying them weekly for their work. The strong competition at the East, rendered the price paid for the work, for which contracts were taken by Miss Wormeley and Miss Gilson, less than at the west, but Miss Gilson, and, we believe, Miss Wormeley also, raised an additional sum, and paid to the sewing-women more than the contract price for the work. It required a spirit thoroughly imbued with patriotism and philanthropy to carry on this work, for the drudgery connected with it was a severe tax upon the strength of those who undertook it. In the St. Louis contracts, the officers and managers of the Ladies' Aid Society, rendered assistance to Airs. Springer, who had the matter in charge, so far as they could, but not satisfied with this, one of their number, the late Mrs. Palmer, spent a portion of every day in visiting the soldiers' families who were thus employed, and whenever additional aid was needed, it was cheerfully and promptly bestowed. In this noble work of Christian charity, Mrs. Palmer overtasked her physical powers, and after a long illness, she passed from earth, to be reckoned among that list of noble martyrs, who sacrificed life for the cause of their country.

But it was not the managers and leaders of these central associations alone whose untiring exertions, and patient fidelity to their patriotic work should excite our admiration and reverence. Though moving in a smaller circle, and dealing with details rather than aggregates, there were, in almost every village and town, those whose zeal, energy, and devotion to their patriotic work, was as worthy of record, and as heroic in character, as the labors of their sisters in the cities. We cannot record the names of those thousands of noble women, but their record is on high, and in the grand assize, their zealous toil to relieve their suffering brothers, who were fighting or had fought the nation's battles, will be recognized by Him, who regards every such act of love and philanthropy as done to Himself.

Nor are these, alone, among those whose deeds of love and patriotism are inscribed in the heavenly record. The whole history of the contributions for relief, is glorified by its abundant instances of self-sacrifice. The rich gave, often, largely and nobly from their wealth; but a full moiety of the fifty millions of voluntary gifts, came from the hard earnings, or patient labors of the poor, often bestowed at the cost of painful privation. Incidents like the following were of every-day occurrence, during the later years of the war: "In one of the mountainous countries at the North, in a scattered farming district, lived a mother and daughters, too poor to obtain by purchase, the material for making hospital clothing, yet resolved to do something for the soldier. Twelve miles distant, over the mountain, and accessible only by a road almost impassable, was the county-town, in which there was a Relief Association. Borrowing a neighbor's horse, either the mother or daughters came regularly every fortnight, to procure from this society, garments to make up for the hospital. They had no money; but though the care of their few acres of sterile land devolved upon themselves alone, they could and would find time to work for the sufferers in the hospitals. At length, curious to know the secret of such fervor in the cause, one of the managers of the association addressed them: "You have some relative, a son, or brother, or father, in the war, I suppose?" "No!" was the reply, "not now; our only brother fell at Ball's Bluff." "Why then," asked the manager, "do you feel so deep an interest in this work?" "Our country's cause is the cause of God, and we would do what we can, for His sake," was the sublime reply.

Take another example. "In that little hamlet on the bleak and barren hills of New England, far away from the great city or even the populous village, you will find a mother and daughter living in a humble dwelling. The husband and father has lain for many years'neath the sod in the graveyard on the hill slope; the only son, the hope and joy of both mother and sister, at the call of duty, gave himself to the service of his country, and left those whom he loved as his own life, to toil at home alone. By and bye, at Williamsburg, or Fair Oaks, or in that terrible retreat to James River, or at Cedar Mountain, it matters not which, the swift speeding bullet laid him low, and after days, or it may be weeks of terrible suffering, he gave up his young life on the altar of his country. The shock was a terrible one to those lone dwellers on the snowy hills. He was their all, but it was for the cause of Freedom, of Right, of God; and hushing the wild beating of their hearts they bestir themselves, in their deep poverty, to do something for the cause for which their young hero had given his life. It is but little, for they are sorely straitened; but the mother, though her heart is wrapped in the darkness of sorrow, saves the expense of mourning apparel, and the daughter turns her faded dress; the little earnings of both are carefully hoarded, the pretty chintz curtains which had made their humble room cheerful, are replaced by paper, and by dint of constant saving, enough money is raised to purchase the other materials for a hospital quilt, a pair of socks, and a shirt, to be sent to the Relief Association, to give comfort to some poor wounded soldier, tossing in agony in some distant hospital. And this, with but slight variation is the history of hundreds, and perhaps thousands of the articles sent to the soldiers' aid societies.

This fire of patriotic zeal, while it glowed alike in the hearts of the rich and poor, inflamed the young as well as the old. Little girls, who had not attained their tenth year, or who had just passed it, denied themselves the luxuries and toys they had long desired, and toiled with a patience and perseverance wholly foreign to childish nature, to procure or make something of value for their country's defenders. On a pair of socks sent to the Central Association of Relief, was pinned a paper with this legend: "These stockings were knit by a little girl five years old, and she is going to knit some more, for mother said it will help some poor soldier." The official reports of the Women's Soldiers' Aid Society of Northern Ohio, the Cleveland branch of the Sanitary Commission, furnish the following incident: "Every Saturday morning finds Emma Andrews, ten years of age, at the rooms of the Aid Society with an application for work. Her little basket is soon filled with pieces of half-worn linen, which, during the week, she cuts into towels or handkerchiefs; hems, and returns, neatly washed and ironed, at her next visit. Her busy fingers have already made two hundred and twenty-nine towels, and the patriotic little girl is still earnestly engaged in her work." Holidays and half holidays in the country were devoted by the little ones with great zeal, to the gathering of blackberries and grapes, for the preparations of cordials and native -wines for the hospitals, and the picking, paring and drying peaches and apples, which, in their abundance, proved a valuable safeguard against scurvy, which threatened the destruction or serious weakening of our armies, more than once. In the cities and large villages the children, with generous self-denial, gave the money usually expended for fireworks to purchase onions and pickles for the soldiers, to prevent scurvy. A hundred thousand dollars, it is said, was thus consecrated, by these little ones, to this benevolent work.

In the days of the Sanitary Fairs, hundreds of groups of little girls held their miniature fairs, stocked for the most part with articles of their own production, upon the door step, or the walk in front of their parents' dwellings, or in the wood-shed, or in some vacant room, and the sums realized from their sales, varying from five to one hundred dollars, were paid over, without any deduction for expenses, since labor and attendance were voluntary and the materials a gift, to the treasuries of the great fairs then in progress.

Nor were the aged women lacking in patriotic devotion. Such inscriptions as these were not uncommon. "The fortunate owner of these socks is secretly informed, that they are the one hundred and ninety-first pair knit for our brave boys by Mrs. Abner Bartlett, of Medford, Mass., now aged eighty-five years."

A barrel of hospital clothing sent from Conway, Mass., contained a pair of socks knit by a lady ninety-seven years old, who declared herself ready and anxious to do all she could. A homespun blanket bore the inscription, "This blanket was carried by Milly Aldrich, who is ninety-three years old, down hill and up hill, one and a-half miles, to be given to some soldier."

A box of lint bore this touching record, "Made in a sick-room where the sunlight has not entered for nine years, but where God has entered, and where two sons have bade their mother goodbye, as they have gone out to the war."

Every one knows the preciousness of the household linen which has been for generations an heirloom in a family. Yet in numerous instances, linen sheets, table-cloths, and napkins, from one hundred and twenty to two hundred years old, which no money could have purchased, were dedicated, often by those who had nought else to give, to the service of the hospital.

An instance of generous and self-denying patriotism related by Mrs. D. P. Livermore, of the Northwestern Sanitary Commission, deserves a record in this connection, as it was one which has had more than one counterpart elsewhere. "Some two or three months ago, a poor girl, a seamstress, came to our rooms. 'I do not feel right she said, that I am doing nothing for our soldiers in the hospitals, and have resolved to do something immediately. Which do you prefer—that I should give money, or buy material and manufacture it into garments?'"

"You must be guided by your circumstances," was the answer made her; "we need both money and supplies, and you must do that which is most convenient for you."

"I prefer to give you money, if it will do as much good." "Very well; then give money, which we need badly, and without which we cannot do what is most necessary for our brave sick men."

"Then I will give you the entire earnings of the next two weeks. I'd give more, but I have to help support my mother who is an invalid. Generally I make but one vest a day, but I will work earlier and later these two weeks." In two weeks she came again, the poor sewing girl, her face radiant with the consciousness of philanthropic intent. Opening her porte-monnaie, she counted out nineteen dollars and thirty-seven cents. Every penny was earned by the slow needle, and she had stitched away into the hours of midnight on every one of the working days of the week. The patriotism which leads to such sacrifices as these, is not less deserving of honor than that which finds scope for its energies in ministering to the wounded on the battle-field or in the crowded wards of a hospital.

Two other offerings inspired by the true spirit of earnest and active philanthropy, related by the same lady, deserve a place here.

"Some farmers' wives in the north of Wisconsin, eighteen miles from a railroad, had given to the Commission of their bed and table linen, their husbands' shirts and drawers, their scanty supply of dried and canned fruits, till they had exhausted their ability to do more in this direction. Still they were not satisfied. So they cast about to see what could be done in another way. They were all the wives of small farmers, lately moved to the West, all living in log cabins, where one room sufficed for kitchen, parlor, laundry, nursery and bed-room, doing their own house-work, sewing, baby-tending, dairy-work, and all. What could they do?

"They were not long in devising a way to gratify the longings of their motherly and patriotic hearts, and instantly set about carrying it into action. They resolved to beg wheat of the neighboring farmers, and convert it into money. Sometimes on foot, and sometimes with a team, amid the snows and mud of early spring, they canvassed the country for twenty and twenty-five miles around, everywhere eloquently pleading the needs of the blue-coated soldier boys in the hospitals, the eloquence everywhere acting as an open sesame to the granaries. Now they obtained a little from a rich man, and then a great deal from a poor man—deeds of benevolence are half the time in an inverse ratio to the ability of the benefactors—till they had accumulated nearly five hundred bushels of wheat. This they sent to market, obtained the highest market price for it, and forwarded the proceeds to the Commission. As we held this hard-earned money in our hands, we felt that it was consecrated, that the holy purpose and resolution of these noble women had imparted a sacredness to it.'

Very beautiful is the following incident, narrated by the same lady, of a little girl, one of thousands of the little ones, who have, during the war, given up precious and valued keepsakes to aid in ministering to the sick and wounded soldiers. "A little girl not nine years old, with sweet and timid grace, came into the rooms of the Commission, and laying a five dollar gold-piece on our desk, half frightened, told us its history. 'My uncle gave me that before the war, and I was going to keep it always; but he's got killed in the army, and mother says now I may give it to the soldiers if I want to—and I'd like to do so. I don't suppose it will buy much for them, will it?'" We led the child to the store-room, and proceeded to show her how valuable her gift was, by pointing out what it would buy—so many cans of condensed milk, or so many bottles of ale, or pounds of tea, or codfish, etc. Her face brightened with pleasure. But when we explained to her that her five dollar gold-piece was equal to seven dollars and a half in greenbacks, and told her how much comfort we had been enabled to carry into a hospital, with as small an amount of stores as that sum would purchase, she fairly danced with joy.

"Oh, it will do lots of good, won't it?" And folding her hands before her, she begged, in her charmingly modest way, "Please tell me something that you've seen in the hospitals?" A narrative of a few touching events, not such as would too severely shock the little creature, but which plainly showed the necessity of continued benevolence to the hospitals, filled her sweet eyes with tears, and drew from her the resolution, "to save all her money, and to get all the girls to do so, to buy things for the wounded soldiers."

Innumerable have been the methods by which the loyalty and patriotism of our countrywomen have manifested themselves; no memorial can ever record the thousandth part of their labors, their toils, or their sacrifices; sacrifices which, in so many instances, comprehended the life of the earnest and faithful worker. A grateful nation and a still more grateful army will ever hold in remembrance, such martyrs as Margaret Breckinridge, Anna M. Boss, Arabella Griffith Barlow, Mrs. Howland, Mrs. Plummer, Mrs. Mary E. Palmer, Mrs. S. C. Pomeroy, Mrs. C. M. Kirkland, Mrs. David Dudley Field, and Sweet Jenny Wade, of Gettysburg, as well as many others, who, though less widely known, laid down their lives as truly for the cause of their country; and their names should be inscribed upon the ever during granite, for they were indeed the most heroic spirits of the war, and to them, belong its unfading laurels and its golden crowns.

And yet, we are sometimes inclined to hesitate in our estimate of the comparative magnitude of the sacrifices laid upon the Nation's altar; not in regard to these, for she who gave her life, as well as her services, to the Nation's cause, gave all she had to give; but in reference to the others, who, though serving the cause faithfully in their various ways, yet returned unscathed to their homes. Great and noble as were the sacrifices made by these women, and fitted as they were to call forth our admiration, were they after all, equal to those of the mothers, sisters, and daughters, who, though not without tears, yet calmly, and with hearts burning with the fire of patriotism, willingly, gave up their best beloved to fight for the cause of their country and their God? A sister might give up an only brother, the playmate of her childhood, her pride, and her hope; a daughter might bid adieu to a father dearly beloved, whose care and guidance she still needs and will continue to need. A mother might, perchance, relinquish her only son, he on whom she had hoped to lean, as the strong staff and the beautiful rod of her old age; all this might be, with sorrow indeed, and a deep and abiding sense of loneliness, not to be relieved, except by the return of that father, brother, or son. But the wife, who, fully worthy of that holy name, gave the parting hand to a husband who was dearer, infinitely dearer to her than father, son, or brother, and saw him go forth to the battle-field, where severe wounds or sudden and terrible death, were almost certainly to be his portion, sacrificed in that one act all but life, for she relinquished all that made life blissful. Yet even in this holocaust there were degrees, gradations of sacrifice. The wife of the officer might, perchance, have occasion to see how her husband was honored and advanced for his bravery and good conduct, and while he was spared, she was not likely to suffer the pangs of poverty. In these particulars, how much more sad was the condition of the wife of the private soldier, especially in the earlier years of the war. To her, except the letters often long delayed or captured on their route, there were no tidings of her husband, except in the lists of the wounded or the slain; and her home, often one of refinement and taste, was not only saddened by the absence of him who was its chief joy, but often stripped of its best belongings, to help out the scanty pittance which rewarded her own severe toil, in furnishing food and clothing for herself and her little ones. Cruel, grinding poverty, was too often the portion of these poor women. At the West, women tenderly and carefully reared, were compelled to undertake the rude labors of the field, to provide bread for their families. And when, to so many of these poor women who had thus struggled with poverty, and the depressing influences of loneliness and weariness, there came the sad intelligence, that the husband so dearly loved, was among the slain, or that he had been captured and consigned to death by starvation and slow torture at Andersonville, where even now he might be filling an unknown grave, what wonder is it that in numerous cases the burden was too heavy for the wearied spirit, and insanity supervened, or the broken heart found rest and reunion with the loved and lost in the grave.

Yet in many instances, the heart that seemed nigh to breaking, found solace in its sorrow, in ministering directly or indirectly to the wounded soldier, and forgetting its own misery, brought to other hearts and homes consolation and peace. This seems to us the loftiest and most divine of all the manifestations of the heroic spirit; it is nearest akin in its character to the conduct of Him, who while "he was a man of sorrows and acquainted with grief," yet found the opportunity, with his infinite tenderness and compassion, to assuage every sorrow and soothe every grief but his own.

The effect of this patriotic zeal and fervor on the part of the wives, mothers, sisters, and daughters of the loyal North, in stimulating and encouraging the soldiers to heroic deeds, was remarkable. Napoleon sought to awaken the enthusiasm and love of fame of his troops in Egypt, by that spirit-stirring word, "Soldiers, from the height of yonder pyramids forty centuries look down upon you." But to the soldier fighting the battles of freedom, the thought that in every hamlet and village of the loyal North, patriotic women were toiling and watching for his welfare, and that they were ready to cheer and encourage him in the darkest hour, to medicine his wounds, and minister to his sickness and sorrows in the camp, on the battle-field, or in the hospital wards, was a far more grateful and inspiring sentiment, than the mythical watch and ward of the spectral hosts of a hundred centuries of the dead past.

The loyal soldier felt that he was fighting, so to speak, under the very eyes of his countrywomen, and he was prompted to higher deeds of daring and valor by the thought. In the smoke and flame of battle, he bore, or followed the flag, made and consecrated by female hands to his country's service; many of the articles which contributed to his comfort, and strengthened his good right arm, and inspired his heart for the day of battle were the products of the toil and the gifts of his countrywomen; and he knew right well, that if he should fall in the fierce conflict, the gentle ministrations of woman would be called in requisition, to bind up his wounds, to cool his fevered brow, to minister to his fickle or failing appetite, to soothe his sorrows, to communicate with his friends, and if death came to close his eyes, and comfort, so far as might be those who had loved him. This knowledge strengthened him in the conflict, and enabled him to strike more boldly and vigorously for freedom, until the time came when the foe, dispirited and exhausted, yielded up his last vantage ground, and the war was over.

The Rebel soldiers were not thus sustained by home influences. At first, indeed, Aid Societies were formed all over the South, and supplies forwarded to their armies; but in the course of a year, the zeal of the Southern ladies cooled, and they contented themselves with waving their handkerchiefs to the soldiers, instead of providing for their wants; and thenceforward, to the end of the war, though there were no rebels so bitter and hearty in their expressions of hostility to the North, as the great mass of Southern women, it was a matter of constant complaint in the Rebel armies, that their women did nothing for their comfort. The complaint was doubtless exaggerated, for in their hospitals there were some women of high station who did minister to the wounded, but after the first year, the gifts and sacrifices of Southern women to their army and hospitals, were not the hundredth, hardly the thousandth part of those of the women of the North to their countrymen.

A still more remarkable result of this wide-spread movement among the women of the North, was its effect upon the sex themselves. Fifty years of peace had made us, if not "a nation of shop-keepers," at least a people given to value too highly, the pomp and show of material wealth, and our women were as a class, the younger women especially, devoting to frivolous pursuits, society, gaiety and display, the gifts wherewith God had endowed them most bountifully. The war, and the benevolence and patriotism which it evoked, changed all this. The gay and thoughtless belle, the accomplished and beautiful leader of society, awoke at once to a new life. The soul of whose existence she had been almost as unconscious as Fouqud's Undine, began to assert its powers, and the gay and fashionable woman, no longer ennuyd by the emptiness and frivolity of life, found her thoughts and hands alike fully occupied, and rose into a sphere of life and action, of which, a month before, she would have considered herself incapable.

Saratoga and Newport, and the other haunts of fashion were not indeed deserted, but the visitors there were mostly new faces, the wives and daughters of those who had grown rich through the contracts and vicissitudes of the war, while their old habituds were toiling amid the summer's heat to provide supplies for the hospitals, superintending sanitary fairs, or watching and aiding the sick and wounded soldiers in the hospitals, or at the front of the army. In these labors of love, many a fair face grew pale, many a light dancing step became slow and feeble, and ever and anon the light went out of eyes, that but a little while before had flashed and glowed in conscious beauty and pride. But though the cheeks might grow pale, the step feeble, and the eyes dim, there was a holier and more transcendent beauty about them than in their gayest hours. "We looked daily," says one who was herself a participant in this blessed work, in speaking of one who, after years of self-sacrificing devotion, at last laid down her young life in patriotic toil, "we looked daily to see the halo surround her head, for it seemed as if God would not suffer so pure and saintly a soul to walk the earth without a visible manifestation of his love for her." Work so ennobling, not only elevated and etherealized the mind and soul, but it glorified the body, and many times it shed a glory and beauty over the plainest faces, somewhat akin to that which transfigured the Jewish lawgiver, when he came down from the Mount. But it has done more than this. The soul once ennobled by participation in a great and glorious work, can never again be satisfied to come down to the heartlessness, the frivolities, the petty jealousies, and littlenesses of a life of fashion. Its aspirations and sympathies lie otherwheres, and it must seek in some sphere of humanitarian activity or Christian usefulness, for work that will gratify its longings.

How pitiful and mean must the brightest of earth's gay assemblages appear, to her who, day after day, has held converse with the souls of the departing, as they plumed their wings for the flight heavenward, and accompanying them in their upward journey so far as mortals may, has been privileged with some glimpse through the opening gates of pearl, into the golden streets of the city of our God!

With such experiences, and a discipline so purifying and ennobling, we can but anticipate a still higher and holier future, for the women of our time. To them, we must look for the advancement of all noble and philanthropic enterprises; the lifting vagrant and wayward childhood from the paths of ruin; the universal diffusion of education and culture; the succor and elevation of the poor, the weak, and the down-trodden; the rescue and reformation of the fallen sisterhood; the improvement of hospitals and the care of the sick; the reclamation of prisoners, especially in female prisons; and in general, the genial ministrations of refined and cultured womanhood, wherever these ministrations can bring calmness, peace and comfort. Wherever there is sorrow, suffering, or sin, in our own or in other lands, these heaven-appointed Sisters of Charity will find their mission and their work.

Glorious indeed will be the results of such labors of love and Christian charity. Society will be purified and elevated; giant evils which have so long thwarted human progress, overthrown; the strongholds of sin, captured and destroyed by the might of truth, and the "new earth wherein dwelleth righteousness," so long foretold by patriarch, prophet, and apostle, become a welcome and enduring reality.

And they who have wrought this good work, as, one after another, they lay down the garments of their earthly toil to assume the glistening robes of the angels, shall find, as did Enoch of old, that those who walk with God, shall be spared the agonies of death and translated peacefully and joyfully to the mansions of their heavenly home, while waiting choirs of the blessed ones shall hail their advent to the transcendent glories of the world above.

DOROTHEA L. DIX.

AMONG all the women who devoted themselves with untiring energy, and gave talents of the highest order to the work of caring for our soldiers during the war, the name of Dorothea L. Dix will always take the first rank, and history will undoubtedly preserve it long after all others have sunk into oblivion. This her extraordinary and exceptional official position will secure. Others have doubtless done as excellent a work, and earned a praise equal to her own, but her relations to the government will insure her historical mention and remembrance, while none will doubt the sincerity of her patriotism, or the faithfulness of her devotion.

Dorothea L. Dix is a native of Worcester, Mass. Her father was a physician, who died while she was as yet young, leaving her almost without pecuniary resources.

Soon after this event, she proceeded to Boston, where she opened a select school for young ladies, from the income of which she was enabled to draw a comfortable support.

One day during her residence in Boston, while passing along a street, she accidentally overheard two gentlemen, who were walking before her, conversing about the state prison at Charlestown, and expressing their sorrow at the neglected condition of the convicts. They were undoubtedly of that class of philanthropists who believe that no man, however vile, is all bad, but, though sunk into the lowest depths of vice, has yet in his soul some white spot which 1397 the taint has not reached, but which some kind hand may reach, and some kind heart may touch.

Be that as it may, their remarks found an answering chord in the heart of Miss Dix. She was powerfully affected and impressed, so much so, that she obtained no rest until she had herself visited the prison, and learned that in what she had heard there was no exaggeration. She found great suffering, and great need of reform.

Energetic of character, and kindly of heart, she at once lent herself to the work of elevating and instructing the degraded and suffering classes she found there, and becoming deeply interested in the welfare of these unfortunates, she continued to employ herself in labors pertaining to this field of reform, until the year 1834.

At that time her health becoming greatly impaired, she gave up her school and embarked for Europe. Shortly before this period, she had inherited from a relative sufficient property to render her independent of daily exertion for support, and to enable her to carry out any plans of charitable work which she should form. Like all persons firmly fixed in an idea which commends itself alike to the judgment and the impulses, she was very tenacious of her opinions relating to it, and impatient of opposition. It is said that from this cause she did not always meet the respect and attention which the important objects to which she was devoting her life would seem to merit. That she found friends and helpers however at home and abroad, is undoubtedly true she remained abroad until the year 1837, when returning to her native country she devoted herself to the investigation of the condition of paupers, lunatics and prisoners. In this work she was warmly aided and encouraged by her friend and pastor the Rev. Dr. Channing, of whose children she had been governess, as well as by many other persons whose hearts beat a chord responsive to that long since awakened in her own.

Since 1841 until the breaking out of the late war, Miss Dix devoted herself to the great work which she accepted as the special mission of her life. In pursuance of it, she, during that time, is said to have visited every State of the Union east of the Rocky Mountains, examining prisons, poor-houses, lunatic asylums, and endeavoring to persuade legislatures and influential individuals to take measures for the relief of the poor and wretched.

Her exertions contributed greatly to the foundation of State lunatic asylums in Rhode Island, Pennsylvania, New York, Indiana, Illinois, Louisiana and North Carolina. She presented a memorial to Congress during the Session of 1848-9, asking an appropriation of five hundred thousand acres of the public lands to endow hospitals for the indigent insane.

This measure failed, but, not discouraged, she renewed the appeal in 1850 asking for ten millions of acres. The Committee of the House to whom the memorial was referred, made a favorable report, and a bill such as she asked for passed the House, but failed in the Senate for want of time. In April, 1854, however, her unwearied exertions were rewarded by the passage of a bill by both houses, appropriating ten millions of acres to the several States for the relief of the indigent insane. Bui this bill was vetoed by President Pierce, chiefly on the ground that the General Government had no constitutional power to make such appropriations.

Miss Dix was thus unexpectedly checked and deeply disappointed in the immediate accomplishment of this branch of the great work of benevolence to which she had more particularly devoted herself.

From that time she seems to have given herself, with added zeal, to her labors for the insane. This class so helpless, and so innocently suffering, seem to have always been, and more particularly during the later years of her work, peculiarly the object of her sympathies and labors. In the prosecution of these labors she made another voyage to Europe in 1858 or '59, and continued to pursue them with indefatigable zeal and devotion.

The labors of Miss Dix for the insane were continued without intermission until the occurrence of those startling events which at once turned into other and new channels nearly all the industries and philanthropies of our nation. With many a premonition, and many a muttering of the coming storm, unheeded, our people, inured to peace, continued unappalled in their quiet pursuits. But while the actual commencement of active hostilities called thousands of men to arms, from the monotony of mechanical, agricultural and commercial pursuits and the professions, it changed as well the thoughts and avocations of those who were not to enter the ranks of the military.

And not to men alone did these changes come. Not they alone were filled with a new fire of patriotism, and a quickened devotion to the interests of our nation. Scarcely had the ear ceased thrilling with the tidings that our country was indeed the theatre of civil war, when women as well as men began to inquire if there were not for them some part to be played in this great drama.

Almost, if not quite the first among these was Miss Dix. Self-reliant, accustomed to rapid and independent action, conscious of her ability for usefulness, with her to resolve was to act. Scarcely had the first regiments gone forward to the defense of our menaced capital, when she followed, full of a patriotic desire to offer to her country whatever service a woman could perform in this hour of its need, and determined that it should be given.

She passed through Baltimore shortly after that fair city had covered itself with the indelible disgrace of the 16th of April, 1861, and on her arrival at Washington, the first labor she offered on her country's altar, was the nursing of some wounded soldiers, victims of the Baltimore mob. Thus was she earliest in the field.

Washington became a great camp. Every one was willing, nay anxious, to be useful and employed. Military hospitals were hastily organized. There were many sick, but few skilful nurses. The opening of the rebellion had not found the government, nor the loyal people prepared for it. All was confusion, want of discipline, and disorder. Organizing minds, persons of executive ability, leaders, were wanted.

The services of women could be made available in the hospitals. They were needed as nurses, but it was equally necessary that some one should decide upon their qualifications for the task, and direct their efforts.

Miss Dix was present in Washington. Her ability, long experience in public institutions and high character were well known. Scores of persons of influence, from all parts of the country, could vouch for her, and she had already offered her services to the authorities for any work in which they could be made available.

Her selection for the important post of Superintendent of Female Nurses, by Secretary Cameron, then at the head of the War Department, on the 10th of June, 1861, commanded universal approbation.

This at once opened for her a wide and most important field of duty and labor. Except hospital matrons, all women regularly employed in the hospitals, and entitled to pay from the Government, were appointed by her. An examination of the qualifications of each applicant was made. A woman must be mature in years, plain almost to homeliness in dress, and by no means liberally endowed with personal attractions, if she hoped to meet the approval of Miss Dix. Good health and an unexceptionable moral character were always insisted on. As the war progressed, the applications were numerous, and the need of this kind of service great, but the rigid scrutiny first adopted by Miss Dix continued, and many were rejected who did not in all respects possess the qualifications which she had fixed as her standard. Some of these women, who in other branches of the service, and under other auspices, became eminently useful, were rejected on account of their youth; while some, alas! were received, who afterwards proved themselves quite unfit for the position, and a disgrace to their sex.

But in these matters no blame can attach to Miss Dix. In the first instance she acted no doubt from the dictates of a sound and mature judgment; and in the last was often deceived by false testimonials, by a specious appearance, or by applicants who, innocent at the time, were not proof against the temptations and allurements of a position which all must admit to be peculiarly exposed and unsafe.

Besides the appointment of nurses the position £f Miss Dix imposed upon her numerous and onerous duties. She visited hospitals, far and near, inquiring into the wants of their occupants, in all cases where possible, supplementing the Government stores by those with which she was always supplied by private benevolence, or from public sources; she adjusted disputes, and settled difficulties in which her nurses were concerned; and in every way showed her true and untiring devotion to her country, and its suffering defenders. She undertook long journeys by land and by water, and seemed ubiquitous, for she was seldom missed from her office in Washington, yet was often seen elsewhere, and always bent upon the same fixed and earnest purpose. We cannot, perhaps, better describe the personal appearance of Miss Dix, and give an idea of her varied duties and many sacrifices, than by transcribing the following extract from the printed correspondence of a lady, herself an active and most efficient laborer in the same general field of effort, and holding an important position in the Northwestern Sanitary Commission.

"It was Sunday morning when we arrived in Washington, and as the Sanitary Commission held no meeting that day, we decided after breakfast to pay a visit to Miss Dix.

"We fortunately found the good lady at home, but just ready to start for the hospitals. She is slight and delicate looking, and seems physically inadequate to the work she is engaged in. In her youth she must have possessed considerable beauty, and she is still very comely, with a soft and musical voice, graceful figure, and very winning manners. Secretary Cameron vested her with sole power to appoint female nurses in the hospitals. Secretary Stanton, on succeeding him ratified the appointment, and she has installed several hundreds of nurses in this noble work—all of them Protestants, and middle-aged. Miss Dix's whole soul is in this work. She rents two large houses, which are depots for sanitary supplies sent to her care, and houses of rest and refreshment for nurses and convalescent soldiers, employs two secretaries, owns ambulances and keeps them busily employed, prints and distributes circulars, goes hither and thither from one remote point to another in her visitations of hospitals,—and pays all the expenses incurred from her private purse. Her fortune, time and strength are laid on the altar of the country in this hour of trial.

"Unfortunately, many of the surgeons in the hospitals do not work harmoniously with Miss Dix. They are jealous of her power, impatient of her authority, find fault with her nurses, and accuse her of being arbitrary, opinionated, severe and capricious. Many to rid themselves of her entirely, have obtained permission of Surgeon-General Hammond to employ Sisters of Charity in their hospitals, a proceeding not to Miss Dix's liking. Knowing by observation that many of the surgeons are wholly unfit for their office, that too often they fail to bring skill, morality, or humanity to their work, we could easily understand how this single-hearted, devoted, tireless friend of the sick and wounded soldier would come in collision with these laggards, and we liked her none the less for it."

Though Miss Dix received no salary, devoting to the work her time and labors without remuneration, a large amount of supplies were placed in her hands, both by the Government and from private sources, which she was always ready to dispense with judgment and caution, it is true, but with a pleasant earnestness alike grateful to the recipient of the kindness, or to the agent who acted in her stead in this work of mercy.

It was perhaps unfortunate for Miss Dix that at the time when she received her appointment it was so unprecedented, and the entire service was still in such a chaotic state, that it was simply impossible to define her duties or her authority. As, therefore, no plan of action or rules were adopted, she was forced to abide exclusively by her own ideas of need and authority. In a letter to the writer, from an official source, her position and the changes that became necessary are thus explained:

"The appointment of nurses was regulated by her ideas of their prospective usefulness, good moral character being an absolute prerequisite. This absence of system, and independence of action, worked so very unsatisfactorily, that in October, 1863, a General Order was issued placing the assignment, or employment of female nurses, exclusively under control of Medical Officers, and limiting the superintendency to a 'certificate of approval without which no woman nurse could be employed, except by order of the Surgeon-General. This materially reduced the number of appointments, secured the muster and pay of those in service, and established discipline and order."

The following is the General Order above alluded to.

GENERAL ORDERS, No. 351.

WAR DEPARTMENT, ADJUTANT-GENERAL'S OFFICE, WASHINGTON, October 29, 1863.

The employment of women nurses in the United States General Hospitals will in future be strictly governed by the following rules:

Persons approved by Miss Dix, or her authorized agents, will receive from her, or them, "certificates of approval," which must be countersigned by Medical Directors upon their assignment to duty as nurses within their Departments.

Assignments of "women nurses" to duty in General Hospitals will only be made upon application by the Surgeons in charge, through Medical Directors, to Miss Dix or her agents, for the number they require, not exceeding one to every thirty beds.

No females, except Hospital Matrons, will be employed in General Hospitals, or, after December 31, 1863, born upon the Muster and Pay Polls, without such certificates of approval and regular assignment, unless specially appointed by the Surgeon-General.

Women nurses, while on duty in General Hospitals, are under the exclusive control of the senior medical officer, who will direct their several duties, and may be discharged by him when considered supernumerary, or for incompetency, insubordination, or violation of his orders. Such discharge, with the reasons therefor, being endorsed upon the certificate, will be at once returned to Miss Dix.

BY ORDER OF THE SECRETARY OF WAR:

E. D. TOWNSEND, Assistant Adjutant-General.

OFFICIAL:

By this Order the authority of Miss Dix was better defined, but she continued to labor under the same difficulty which had from the first clogged her efforts. Authority had been bestowed upon her, but not the power to enforce obedience. There was no penalty for disobedience, and persons disaffected, forgetful, or idle, might refuse or neglect to obey with impunity. It will at once be seen that this fact must have resulted disastrously upon her efforts. She doubtless had enemies (as who has not)? and some were jealous of the power and prominence of her position, while many might even feel unwilling, under any circumstances, to acknowledge, and yield to the authority of a woman. Added to this she had, in some cases, and probably without any fault on her part, failed to secure the confidence and respect of the surgeons in charge of hospitals. In these facts lay the sources of trials, discouragements, and difficulties, all to be met, struggled with, and, if possible, triumphed over by a woman, standing quite alone in a most responsible, laborious, and exceptional position. It indeed seems most wonderful—almost miraculous— that under such circumstances, such a vast amount of good was accomplished. Had she not accomplished half so much, she still would richly have deserved that highest of plaudits—Well done good and faithful servant!

Miss Dix has one remarkable peculiarity—undoubtedly remarkable in one of her sex which is said, and with truth—to possess great approbativeness. She does not apparently desire fame, she does not enjoy being talked about, even in praise. The approval of her own conscience, the consciousness of performing an unique and useful work, seems quite to suffice her. Few women are so self-reliant, self-sustained, self-centered. And in saying this we but echo the sentiments, if not the words, of an eminent divine who, like herself, was during the whole war devoted to a work similar in its purpose, and alike responsible and arduous.

"She (Miss Dix) is a lady who likes to do things and not have them talked about. She is freer from the love of public reputation than any woman I know. Then her plans are so strictly her own, and always so wholly controlled by her own individual genius and power, that they cannot well be participated in by others, and not much understood.

"Miss Dix, I suspect, was as early in, as long employed, and as self-sacrificing as any woman who offered her services to the country. She gave herself—body, soul and substance—to the good work. I wish we had any record of her work, but we have not.

"I should not dare to speak for her—about her work—except to say that it was extended, patient and persistent beyond anything I know of, dependent on a single-handed effort."

All the testimony goes to show that Miss Dix is a woman endowed with warm feelings and great kindness of heart. It is only those who do not know her, or who have only met her in the conflict of opposing wills, who pronounce her, as some have done, a cold and heartless egotist. Opinionated she may be, because convinced of the general soundness of her ideas, and infallibility of her judgment. If the success of great designs, undertaken and carried through single-handed, furnish warrant for such conviction, she has an undoubted right to hold it.

Her nature is large and generous, yet with no room for narrow grudges, or mean reservations. As a proof of this, her stores were as readily dispensed for the use of a hospital in which the surgeon refused and rejected her nurses, as for those who employed' them.

She had the kindest care and oversight over the women she had commissioned. She wished them to embrace every opportunity for the rest and refreshment rendered necessary by their arduous labors. A home for them was established by her in Washington, which at all times opened its doors for their reception, and where she wished them to enjoy that perfect quiet and freedom from care, during their occasional sojourns, which were the best remedies for their weariness and exhaustion of body and soul.

In her more youthful days Miss Dix devoted herself considerably to literary pursuits. She has published several works anonymously—the first of which—"The Garland of Flora," was published in Boston in 1829. This was succeeded by a number of books for children, among which were "Conversations about Common Things," "Alice and Ruth," and "Evening Hours." She has also published a variety of tracts for prisoners, and has written many memorials to legislative bodies on the subject of the foundation and conducting of Lunatic Asylums.

Miss Dix is gifted with a singularly gentle and persuasive voice, and her manners are said to exert a remarkably controlling influence over the fiercest maniacs.

She is exceedingly quiet and retiring in her deportment, delicate and refined in manner, with great sweetness of expression. She is far from realizing the popular idea of the strong-minded woman—loud, boisterous and uncouth, claiming as a right, what might, perhaps, be more readily obtained as a courteous concession. On the contrary, her successes with legislatures and individuals, are obtained by the mildest efforts, which yet lack nothing of persistence; and few persons beholding this delicate and retiring woman would imagine they saw in her the champion of the oppressed and suffering classes.

Miss Dix regards her army work but as an episode in her career. She did what she could, and with her devotion of self and high patriotism she would have done no less. She pursued her labors to the end, and her position was not resigned until many months after the close of the war. In fact, she tarried in Washington to finish many an uncompleted task, for some time after her office had been abolished.

When all was done she returned at once to that which she considers her life's work, the amelioration of the condition of the insane.

A large portion of the winter of 1865-6 was devoted to an attempt to induce the Legislature of New York to make better provision for the insane of that State, and to procure, or erect for them, several asylums of small size where a limited number under the care of experienced physicians, might enjoy greater facilities for a cure, and a better prospect of a return to the pursuits and pleasures of life.

Miss Dix now resides at Trenton, New Jersey, where she has since the war fixed her abode, travelling thence to the various scenes of her labors. Wherever she may be, and however engaged, we may be assured that her object is the good of some portion of the race, and is worthy of the prayers and blessings of all who love humanity and seek the promotion of its best interests. And to the close of her long and useful life, the thanks, the heartfelt gratitude of every citizen of our common country so deeply indebted to her, and to the many devoted and self-sacrificing women whose efforts she directed, must as assuredly follow her. She belongs now to History, and America may proudly claim her daughter.

CLARA HARLOWE BARTON

IF those whom the first blast of the war trump roused and called to lives of patriotic devotion and philanthropic endeavor, some were led instinctively to associated labor, and found their zeal inflamed, their patriotic efforts cheered and encouraged by communion with those who were like-minded. To these the organizations of the Soldiers Aid Societies and of the Sanitary and Christian Commissions were a necessity; they provided a place and way for the exercise and development of those capacities for noble and heroic endeavor, and generous self-sacrifice, so gloriously manifested by many of our American women, and which it has given us so much pleasure to record in these pages.

But there were others endowed by their Creator with greater independence of character and higher executive powers, who while not less modest and retiring in disposition than their sisters, yet preferred to mark out their own career, and pursue a comparatively independent course. They worked harmoniously with the various sanitary and other organizations when brought into contact with them, but their work was essentially distinct from them, and was pursued without interfering in any way with that of others.

In the preparation of this sketch of Miss Barton, we have availed ourselves, as far as practicable, of a paper prepared for us by a clerical friend of the lady, who had known her from childhood. The passages from this paper are indicated by quotation marks.

To this latter class pre-eminently belongs Miss Clara Harlowe Barton.

Quiet, modest, and unassuming in manner and appearance, there is beneath this quiet exterior au intense energy, a comprehensive intellect, a resolute will, and an executive force, which is found in few of the stronger sex, and which mingled with the tenderness and grace of refined womanhood eminently qualifies her to become an independent power.

Miss Barton was born in North Oxford, Worcester County, Massachusetts. Her father, Stephen Barton, Sr., was a man highly esteemed in the community in which he dwelt, and by which his worth was most thoroughly known. In early youth he had served as a soldier in the West under General Wayne, the "Mad Anthony" of the early days of the Republic, and his boyish eyes had witnessed the evacuation of Detroit by the British in 1796. "His military training may have contributed to the sterling uprightness, the inflexible will, and the devotion to law and order and rightful authority for which he was distinguished." The little Clara was the youngest by several years in a family of two brothers and three sisters. She was early taught that primeval benediction, miscalled a curse, which requires mankind to earn their bread. Besides domestic duties and a very thorough public school training she learned the general rules of business by acting as clerk and book-keeper for her eldest brother. Next she betook herself to the district school, the usual stepping-stone for all aspiring men and women in New England. She taught for several years, commencing when very young, in various places in Massachusetts and New Jersey. The large circle of friends thus formed was not without its influence in determining her military career. So many of her pupils volunteered in the first years of the war that at the second battle of Bull Run she found seven of them, each of whom had lost an arm or a leg.

"One example will show her character as a teacher. She went to Bordentown, N. J., in 1853, where there was not, and never had been, a public school. Three or four unsuccessful attempts had been made, and the idea had been abandoned as not adapted to that latitude. The brightest boys in the town ran untaught in the streets. She offered to teach a free school for three months at her own expense, to convince the citizens that it could be done; and she was laughed at as a visionary. Six weeks of waiting and debating induced the authorities to fit up an unoccupied building at a little distance from the town. She commenced with six outcast boys, and in five weeks the house would not hold the number that came. The commissioners, at her instance, erected the present school-building of Bordentown, a three-story brick building, costing four thousand dollars; and there, in the winter of 1853-4, she organized the city free-school with a roll of six hundred pupils. But the severe labor, and the great amount of loud speaking required, in the newly plastered rooms, injured her health, and for a time deprived her of her voice—the prime agent of instruction. Being unable to teach, she left New Jersey about the 1st of March, 1854, seeking rest and a milder climate, and went as far south as Washington. While there, a friend and distant relative, then in Congress, voluntarily obtained for her an appointment in the Patent Office, where she continued until the fall of 1857. She was employed at first as a copyist, and afterwards in the more responsible work of abridging original papers, and preparing records for publication. As she was an excellent chirographer, with a clear head for business, and was paid by the piece and not by the month, she made money fast, as matters were then reckoned, and she was very liberal with it. I met her often during those years, as I have since and rarely saw her without some pet scheme of benevolence on her hands which she pursued with an enthusiasm that was quite heroic, and sometimes amusing. The roll of those she has helped, or tried to help, with her purse, her personal influence or her counsels, would be a long one; orphan children, deserted wives, destitute women, sick or unsuccessful relatives, men who had failed in business, and boys who never had any business—all who were in want, or in trouble, and could claim the slightest acquaintance, came to her for aid and were never repulsed. Strange it was to see this generous girl, whose own hands ministered to all her wants, always giving to those around her, instead of receiving, strengthening the hands and directing the steps of so many who would have seemed better calculated to help her. She must have had a native genius for nursing; for in her twelfth year she was selected as the special attendant of a sick brother, and remained in his chamber by day and by night for two years, with only a respite of one half-day in all that time. Think, O reader! of a little girl in short dresses and pantalettes, neither going to school nor to play, but imprisoned for years in the deadly air of a sick room, and made to feel, every moment, that a brother's life depended on her vigilance. Then followed a still longer period of sickness and feebleness ou her own part; and from that time to the present, sickness, danger and death have been always near her, till they have grown familiar as playmates, and she has come to understand all the wants and ways and waywardness of the sick; has learned to anticipate their wishes and cheat them of their fears. Those who have been under her immediate care, will understand me when I say there is healing in the touch of her hand, and anodyne in the low melody of her voice. In the first year of Mr. Buchanan's administration she was hustled out of the Patent Office on a suspicion of anti-slavery sentiments. She returned to New England, and devoted her time to study and works of benevolence. In the winter following the election of Mr. Lincoln, she returned to Washington at the solicitation of her friends there, and would doubtless have been reinstated if peace had been maintained. I happened to see her a day or two after the news came that Fort Sumter had been fired on. She was confident, even enthusiastic. She had feared that the Southern aristocracy, by their close combination and superior political training, might succeed in gradually subjugating the whole country; but of that there was no longer any danger.

The war might be long and bloody, but the rebels had voluntarily abandoned a policy in which the chances were in favor of their ultimate success, for one in which they had no chance at all. For herself, she had saved a little in time of peace, and she intended to devote it and herself to the service of her country and of humanity. If war must be, she neither expected nor desired to come out of it with a dollar. If she survived, she could no doubt earn a living; and if she did not, it was no matter. This is actually the substance of what she said, and pretty nearly the words—without appearing to suspect that it was remarkable." Three days after Major Anderson had lowered his flag in Charleston Harbor, the Sixth Massachusetts Militia started for Washington. Their passage through Baltimore, on the 19th of April, 1861, is a remarkable point in our national history. The next day about thirty of the sick and wounded were placed in the Washington Infirmary, where the Judiciary Square Hospital now stands. Miss Barton proceeded promptly to the spot to ascertain their condition and afford such voluntary relief as might be in her power. Hence, if she was not the first person in the country in this noble work, no one could have been more than a few hours before her. The regiment was quartered at the Capitol, and as those early volunteers will remember, troops on their first arrival were often very poorly provided for. The 21st of April happened to be Sunday. No omnibuses ran that day, and street cars as yet were not; so she hired five colored persons, loaded them with baskets of ready prepared food, and proceeded to the Capitol. The freight they bore served as countersign and pass; she entered the Senate Chamber, and distributed her welcome store. Many of the soldiers were from her own neighborhood, and as they thronged around her, she stood upon the steps to the Vice President's chair and read to them from a paper she had brought, the first written history of their departure and their journey. These two days were the first small beginnings of her military experience,—steps which naturally led to much else. Men wrote home their own impressions of what they saw; and her acts found ready reporters. Young soldiers whom she had taught or known as boys a few years before, called to see her on their way to the front. Troops were gathering rapidly, and hospitals—the inevitable shadows of armies—were springing up and getting filled. Daily she visited them, bringing to the sick news, and delicacies and comforts of her own procuring, and writing letters for those who could not write themselves. Mothers and sisters heard of her, and begged her to visit this one and that, committing to her care letters, socks, jellies and the like. Her work and its fame grew week by week, and soon her room, for she generally had but one, became sadly encumbered with boxes, and barrels and baskets, of the most varied contents. Through the summer of 1862, the constant stock she had on hand averaged about five tons. The goods were mainly the contributions of liberal individuals, churches and sewing-circles to whom she was personally known. But, although articles of clothing, lint, bandages, cordials, preserved fruits, liquors, and the like might be sent, there was always much which she had to buy herself.

During this period as in her subsequent labors, she neither sought or received recognition by any department of the Government, by which I mean only that she had no acknowledged position, rank, rights or duties, was not employed, paid, or compensated in any way, had authority over no one, and was subject to no one's orders. She was simply an American lady, mistress of herself and of no one else; free to stay at home, if she had a home, and equally free to go where she pleased, if she could procure passports and transportation, which was not always an easy matter. From many individual officers, she received most valuable encouragement and assistance; from none more than from General Rucker, the excellent Chief Quartermaster at Washington. He furnished her storage for her supplies when necessary, transportation for herself and them, and added to her stores valuable contributions at times when they were most wanted. She herself declares, with generous exaggeration, that if she has ever done any good, it has been due to the watchful care and kindness of General Rucker.

About the close of 1861, Miss Barton returned to Massachusetts to watch over the declining health of her father, now in his eighty-eighth year, and failing fast. In the following March she placed his remains in the little cemetery at Oxford, and then returned to Washington and to her former labors. But, as the spring and summer campaigns progressed, Washington ceased to be the best field for the philanthropist. In the hospitals of the Capitol the sick and wounded found shelter, food and attendance. Private generosity now centered there; and the United States Sanitary Commission had its office and officers there to minister to the thousand exceptional wants not provided for by the Army Regulations. There were other fields where the harvest was plenteous and the laborers few. Yet could she as a young and not unattractive lady, go with safety and propriety among a hundred thousand armed men, and tell them that no one had sent her? She would eucounter rough soldiers, and camp-followers of every nation, and officers of all grades of character; and could she bear herself so wisely and loftily in all trials as to awe the impertinent, and command the respect of the supercilious, so that she might be free to come and go at her will, and do what should seem good to her? Or, if she failed to maintain a character proof against even innuendoes, would she not break the bridge over which any successor would have to pass? These questions she pondered, and prayed and wept over for months, and has spoken of the mental conflict as the most trying one of her life. She had foreseen and told all these fears to her father; and the old man, on his death-bed, advised her to go wherever she felt it a duty to go. He reminded her that he himself had been a soldier, and said that all true soldiers would respect her. He was naturally a man of great benevolence, a member of the

Masonic fraternity, of the Degree of Royal Arch Mason; and in his last days he spoke much of the purposes and noble charities of the Order. She had herself received the initiation accorded to daughters of Royal Arch Masons, and wore on her bosom a Masonic emblem, by which she was easily recognized by the brotherhood, and which subsequently proved a valuable talisman. At last she reached the conclusion that it was right for her to go amid the actual tumult of battle and shock of armies. And the fact that she has moved and labored with the principal armies in the North and in the South for two years and a half, and that now no one who knows her would speak of her without the most profound respect, proves two things—that there may be heroism of the highest order in American women—and that American armies are not to be judged of, by the recorded statements concerning European ones.

Her first tentative efforts at going to the field were cautious and beset with difficulties. Through the long Peninsula campaign as each transport brought its load of suffering men, with the mud of the Chickahominy and the gore of battle baked hard upon them like the shells of turtles, she went down each day to the wharves with an ambulance laden with dressings and restoratives, and there amid the turmoil and dirt, and under the torrid sun of Washington, toiled day by day, alleviating such suffering as she could. And when the steamers turned their prows down the river, she looked wistfully after them, longing to go to those dread shores whence all this misery came. But she was alone and unknown, and how could she get the means and the permission to go? The military authorities were overworked in those days and plagued with unreasonable applications, and as a class are not very indulgent to unusual requests. The first officer of rank who gave her a kind answer was a man who never gave an unkind reply without great provocation—Dr. R. H. Coolidge, Medical Inspector. Through him a pass was obtained from Surgeon-general Hammond, and she was referred to Major Rucker, Quartermaster, for transportation. The Major listened to her story so patiently and kindly that she was overcome, and sat down and wept. It was then too late in the season to go to McClellan's army, so she loaded a railroad car with supplies and started for Culpepper Court-House, then crowded with the wounded from the battle of Cedar Mountain. With a similar car-load she was the first of the volunteer aid that reached Fairfax Station at the close of the disastrous days that culminated in the second Bull Run, and the battle of Chantilly. On these two expeditions, and one to Fredericksburg, Miss Barton was accompanied by friends, at least one gentleman and a lady in each case, but at last a time came, when through the absence or engagements of these, she must go alone or not at all.

On Sunday, the 14th of September, 1862, she loaded an army wagon with supplies and started to follow the march of General McClellan. Her only companions were Mr. Cornelius M. Welles, the teacher of the first contraband school in the District of Columbia—a young man of rare talent and devotion—and one teamster She travelled three days along the dusty roads of Maryland, buying bread as she went to the extent of her means of conveyance, and sleeping in the wagon by night. After dark, on the night of the sixteenth, she reached Burnside's Corps, and found the two armies lying face to face along the opposing ridges of hills that bound the valley of the Antietam. There had already been heavy skirmishing far away on the right where Hooker had forded the creek and taken position on the opposite hills; and the air was dark and thick with fog and exhalations, with the smoke of camp-fires and premonitory death. There was little sleep that night, and as the morning sun rose bright and beautiful over the Blue Ridge and dipped down into the Valley, the firing on the right was resumed. Reinforcements soon began to move along the rear to Hooker's support. Thinking the place of danger was the place of duty, Miss Barton ordered her mules to be harnessed and took her place in the Swift train of artillery that was passing. On reaching the scene of action, they turned into a field of tall corn, and drove through it to fi large barn. They were dose upon the line of battle; the rebel shot and shell flew thickly around and over them; and in the barn-yard and among the corn lay torn and bleeding men—the worst cases—just brought from the places where they had fallen. The army medical supplies had not yet arrived, the small stock of dressings was exhausted, and the surgeons were trying to make bandages of corn-husks. Miss Barton opened to them her stock of dressings, and proceeded with her companions to distribute bread steeped in wine to the wounded and fainting. In the course of the day she picked up twenty-five men who had come to the rear with the wounded, and set them to work administering restoratives, bringing and applying water, lifting men to easier' positions, stopping hemorrhages, etc., etc. At length her bread was all spent; but luckily a part of the liquors she had brought were found to have been packed in meal, which suggested the idea of making gruel. A farm-house was found connected with the barn, and on searching the cellar, she discovered three barrels of flour, and a bag of salt, which the rebels had hidden the day before. Kettles were found about the house, and she prepared to make gruel on a large scale, which was carried in buckets and distributed along the line for miles. On the ample piazza of the house were ranged the operating tables, where the surgeons performed their operations; and on that piazza she kept her place from the forenoon till nightfall, mixing gruel and directing her assistants, under the fire of one of the greatest and fiercest battles of modern times. Before night her face was as black as a negro's, and her lips and throat parched with the sulphurous smoke of battle. But night came at last, and the wearied armies lay down on the ground to rest; and the dead and wounded lay everywhere. Darkness too had its terrors, and as the night closed in, the surgeon in charge at the old farm-house, looked despairingly at a bit of candle and said it was the only one on the place; and no one could stir till morning. A thousand men dangerously wounded and suffering terribly from thirst lay around, and many must die before the light of another day. It was a fearful thing to die alone and in the dark, and no one could move among the wounded, for fear of stumbling over them. Miss Barton replied, that, profiting by her experience at Chantilly, she had brought with her thirty lanterns, and an abundance of candles. It was worth a journey to Antietam, to light the gloom of that night. On the morrow, the fighting had ceased, but the work of caring for the wounded was resumed and continued all day. On the third day the regular supplies arrived, and Miss Barton having exhausted her small stores, and finding that continued fatigue and watching were bringing on a fever, turned her course towards Washington. It was with difficulty that she was able to reach home, where she was confined to her bed for some time. When she recovered sufficiently to call on Colonel Rucker, and told him that with five wagons she could have taken supplies sufficient for the immediate wants of all the wounded in the battle, that officer shed tears, and charged her to ask for enough next time.

It was about the 23d of October, when another great battle was expected, that she next set out with a well appointed and heavily laden train of six wagons and an ambulance, with seven teamsters, and thirty-eight mules. The men were rough fellows, little used or disposed to be commanded by a woman; and they mutinied when they had gone but a few miles. A plain statement of the course she should pursue in case of insubordination, induced them to proceed and confine themselves, for the time being, to imprecations and grumbling. When she overtook the army, it was crossing the Potomac, below Harper's Ferry. Her men refused to cross. She offered them the alternative to go forward peaceably, or to be dismissed and replaced by soldiers. They chose the former, and from that day forward were all obedience, fidelity and usefulness. The expected battle was not fought, but gave place to a race for Richmond. The Army of the Potomac had the advantage in regard to distance, keeping for a time along the base of the Blue Ridge, while the enemy followed the course of the Shenandoah. There was naturally a skirmish at every gap. The rebels were generally the first to gain possession of the pass, from which they would attempt to surprise some part of the army that was passing, and capture a portion of our supply trains. Thus every day brought a battle or a skirmish, and its accession to the list of sick and wounded; and for a period of about three weeks, until Warrenton Junction was reached, the national army had no base of operations, nor any reinforcements or supplies. The sick had to be carried all that time over the rough roads in wagons or ambulances. Miss Barton with her wagon train accompanied the Ninth Army Corps, as a general purveyor for the sick. Her original supply of comforts was very considerable, and her men contrived to add to it every day such fresh provisions as could be gathered from the country. At each night's encampment, they lighted their fires and prepared fresh food and necessaries for the moving hospital. Through all that long and painful march from Harper's Ferry to Fredericksburg, those wagons constituted the hospital larder and kitchen for all the sick within reach.

It will be remembered that after Burnside assumed command of the Army of the Potomac, the route by Fredericksburg was selected, and the march was conducted down the left bank of the Rappahannock to a position opposite that city. From Warrenton Junction Miss Barton made a visit to Washington, while her wagons kept on with the army, which she rejoined with fresh supplies at Falmouth. She remained in camp until after the unsuccessful attack on the works behind Fredericksburg. She was on the bank of the river in front of the Lacy House, within easy rifle shot range of the enemy, at the time of the attack of the 11th December—witnessed the unavailing attempts to lay pontoon bridges directly into the city, and the heroic crossing of the 19th and 20th Massachusetts Regiments and the 7th Michigan. During the brief occupation of the city she remained in it, organizing the hospital kitchens; and after the withdrawal of the troops, she established a private kitchen for supplying delicacies to the wounded. Although it was now winter and the weather inclement, she occupied an old tent while her train was encamped around; and the cooking was performed in the open air. When the wounded from the attack on the rebel batteries were recovered by flag of truce, fifty of them were brought to her camp at night. They had lain several days in the cold, and were wounded, famished and frozen. She had the snow cleaned away, large fires built and the men wrapped in blankets. An old chimney was torn down, the bricks heated in the fire, and placed around them. As she believed that wounded men, exhausted and depressed by the loss of blood, required stimulants, and as Surgeon-General Hammond, with characteristic liberality had given her one hundred and thirty gallons of confiscated liquor, she gave them with warm food, enough strong hot toddy to make them all measurably drunk. The result was that they slept comfortably until morning, when the medical officers took them in charge. It was her practice to administer a similar draught to each patient on his leaving for Acquia Creek, en route to the Washington hospitals.

A circumstance which occurred during the battle of Fredericksburg, will illustrate very strikingly the courage of Miss Barton, a courage which has never faltered in the presence of danger, when what she believed to be duty called. In the skirmishing of the 12th of December, the day preceding the great and disastrous battle, a part of the Union troops had crossed over to Fredericksburg, and after a brief fight had driven back a body of rebels, wounding and capturing a number of them whom they sent as prisoners across the river to Falmouth, where Miss Barton as yet had her camp. The wounded rebels were brought to her for care and treatment. Among them was a young officer, mortally wounded by a shot in the thigh. Though she could not save his life, she ministered to him as well as she could, partially staunching his wound, quenching his raging thirst, and endeavoring to make his condition as comfortable as possible. Just at this time, an orderly arrived with a message from the Medical Director of the Ninth Army Corps requesting her to come over to Fredericksburg, and organize the hospitals and diet kitchens for the corps. The wounded rebel officer heard the request, and beckoning to her, for he was too weak to speak aloud, he whispered a request that she would not go. She replied that she must do so; that her duty to the corps to which she was attached required it. "Lady," replied the wounded rebel, "you have been very kind to me. You could not save my life, but you have endeavored to render death easy. I owe it to you to tell you what a few hours ago I would have died sooner than have revealed. The whole arrangement of the Confederate troops and artillery is intended as a trap for your people. Every street and lane of the city is covered by our cannon. They are now concealed, and do not reply to the bombardment of your army, because they wish to entice you across. When your entire army has reached the other side of the Rappahannock and attempts to move along the streets, they will find Fredericksburg only a slaughter pen, and not a regiment of them will be allowed to escape. Do not go over, for you will go to certain death!" While her tender sensibilities prevented her from adding to the suffering of the dying man, by not apparently heeding his warning, Miss Barton did not on account of it forego for an instant her intention of sharing the fortunes of the Ninth Corps on the other side of the river. The poor fellow was almost gone, and waiting only to close his eyes on all earthly objects, she crossed on the frail bridge, and was welcomed with cheers by the Ninth Corps, who looked upon her as their guardian angel. She remained with them until the evening of their masterly retreat, and until the wounded men of the corps in the hospitals were all safely across. While she wits in Fredericksburg, after the battle of the 13th, some soldiers of the corps who had been roving about the city, came to her quarters bringing with great difficulty a large and very costly and elegant carpet. "What is this for?" asked Miss Barton. "It is for you, ma'am," said one of the soldiers; "you have been so good to us, that we wanted to bring you something." "Where did you get it?" she asked. "Oh! ma'am, we confiscated it," said the soldiers. "No! no!" said the lady; "that will never do. Governments confiscate. Soldiers when they take such things, steal. I am afraid, my men, you will have to take it back to the house from which you took it.' I can't receive a stolen carpet." The men looked sheepish enough, but they shouldered the carpet and carried it back. In the wearisome weeks that followed the Fredericksburg disaster, when there was not the excitement of a coming battle, and the wounded whether detained in the hospitals around Falmouth or forwarded through the deep mud to the hospital transports on the Potomac, still with saddened countenances and depressed spirits looked forward to a dreary future, Miss Barton toiled on, infusing hope and cheerfulness into sad hearts, and bringing the consolations of religion to her aid, pointed them to the only true source of hope and comfort.

In the early days of April, 1863, Miss Barton went to the South with the expectation of being present at the combined land and naval attack on Charleston. She reached the wharf at Hilton Head on the afternoon of the 7th, in time to hear the crack of Sumter's guns as they opened in broadside on Dupont's fleet. That memorable assault accomplished nothing unless it might be to ascertain that Charleston could not be taken by water. The expedition returned to Hilton Head, and a period of inactivity followed, enlivened only by unimportant raids, newspaper correspondence, and the small quarrels that naturally arise in an unemployed army.

Later in the season Miss Barton accompanied the Gilmore and Dahlgren expedition, and was present at nearly all the military operations on James, Folly, and Morris Islands. The ground occupied on the latter by the army, during the long siege of Fort Wagner, was the low sand-hills forming the sea-board of the Island. No tree, shrub, or weed grew there; and the only shelter was light tents without floors. The light sand that yielded to the tread, the walker sinking to the ankles at almost every step, glistened in the sun, and burned the feet like particles of fire, and as the ocean winds swept it, it darkened the air and filled the eyes and nostrils. There was no defense against it, and every wound speedily became covered with a concrete of gore and sand. Tent pins would not hold in the treacherous sand, every vigorous blast from the sea, overturned the tents, leaving the occupants exposed to the storm or the torrid sun. It was here, under the fire of the heaviest of the rebel batteries, that Miss Barton spent the most trying part of the summer. Her employment was, with three or four men detailed to assist her, to boil water in the lee of a sand-hill, to wash the wounds of the men who were daily struck by rebel shot, to prepare tea and coffee, and various dishes made from dried fruits, farina, and desiccated milk and eggs. On the 19th of July, when the great night assault was made on Wagner, and everybody expected to find rest and refreshments within the rebel fortress, she alone, so far as I can learn, kept up her fires and preparations. She alone had anything suitable to offer the wounded and exhausted men who streamed back from the repulse, and covered the sand-hills like a flight of locusts.

Through all the long bombardment that followed, until Sumter was reduced, and Wagner and Gregg was ours, amid the scorching sun and the prevalence of prostrating diseases, though herself more than once struck down with illness, she remained at her post, a most fearless and efficient co-worker with the indefatigable agent of the Sanitary Commission, Dr. M. M. Marsh, in saving the lives and promoting the health of the soldiers of the Union army. "How could you," said a friend to her subsequently, "how could you expose your life and health to that deadly heat?" ""Why," she answered, evidently without a thought of the heroism of the answer, "the other ladies thought they could not endure the climate, and as I knew somebody must take care of the soldiers, I went."

In January, 1864, Miss Barton returned to the North, and after spending four or five weeks in visiting her friends and recruiting her wasted strength, again took up her position at "Washington, and commenced making preparations for the coming campaign which from observation, she was convinced would be the fiercest and most destructive of human life of any of the war. The first week of the campaign found her at the secondary base of the army at Belle Plain, and thence with the great army of the wounded she moved to Fredericksburg. Extensive as had been her preparations, and wide as were the circle of friends who had entrusted to her the means of solace and healing, the slaughter had been so terrific that she found her supplies nearly exhausted, and for the first time during the war was compelled to appeal for further supplies to her friends at the North, expending in the meantime freely, as she had done all along, of her own private means for the succor of the poor wounded soldiers. Moving on to Port Royal, and thence to the James River, she presently became attached to the Army of the James, where General Butler, at the instance of his Chief Medical Director, Surgeon McCormick, acknowledging her past services, and appreciating her abilities, gave her a recognized position, which greatly enhanced her usefulness, and enabled her, with her energetic nature, to contribute as much to the welfare and comfort of the army in that year, as she had been able to do in all her previous connection with it. In January, 1865, she returned to Washington, where she was detained from the front for nearly two months by the illness and death of a brother and nephew, and did not again join the army in the field.

By this time, of course, she was very generally known, and the circle of her correspondence was wide. Her influence in high official quarters was supposed to be considerable, and she was in the daily receipt of inquiries and applications of various kinds, in particular in regard to the fate of men believed to have been confined in Southern prisons. The great number of letters received of this class, led her to decide to spend some months at Annapolis, among the camps and records of paroled and exchanged prisoners, for the purpose of answering the inquiries of friends. Her plan of operation was approved by President Lincoln, March 11, 1865, and notice of her appointment as "General Correspondent for the friends of Paroled Prisoners," was published in the newspapers extensively, bringing in a torrent of inquiries and letters from wives, parents, State officials, agencies, the Sanitary Commission and the Christian Commission. On reaching Annapolis, she encountered obstacles that were vexatious, time-wasting, and in fact, insupportable. Without rank, rights or authority credited by law, the officials there were at a loss how to receive her. The town was so crowded that she could find no private lodgings, and had to force herself as a scarce welcome guest upon some one for a few days, while her baggage stood out in the snow. Nearly two months were consumed in negotiations before an order was obtained from the War Department to the effect that the military authorities at Annapolis might allow her the use of a tent, and its furniture, and a moderate supply of postage stamps. This was not mandatory, but permissive; and negotiations could now be opened with the gentlemen at Annapolis. In the meantime the President had been assassinated, Richmond taken, and Lee's army surrendered. The rebellion was breaking away. All prisoners were to be released from parole, and sent home, and nothing would remain at Annapolis but the records. Unfortunately these proved to be of very little service—but a small per centage of those inquired for, were found on the rolls, and obviously these, for the most part, were not men who had been lost, but who had returned. She was also informed, on good authority, that a large number of prisoners had been exchanged without roll or record, and that some rolls were so fraudulent and incorrect, as to be worthless. Poor wretches in the rebel pens seemed even to forget the names their mother called them. The Annapolis scheme was therefore abandoned, with mortification that thousands of letters had lain so long unanswered, that thousands of anxious friends were daily waiting for tidings of their loved and lost. The pathos and simplicity of these letters was often touching. An old man writes that he has two sons and three grandsons in the army, and of two of the five he could get no tidings. Another says she knew her son was brave, and if he died, he died honorably. He was all she had and she gave him freely to the country. If he be really lost she will not repine; but she feels she has a right to be told what became of him. Many of the writers seemed to have a very primitive idea of the way information was to be picked up. They imagined that Miss Barton was to walk through all hospitals, camps, armies and prisons, and narrowly scrutinizing every face, would be able to identify the lost boy by the descriptions given her. Hence the fond mother minutely described her boy as he remained graven on her memory on the day of his departure. The result of these delays was the organization, by Miss Barton, at her own cost, of a Bureau of Records of Missing Men of the Armies of the United States, at Washington. Here she collected all rolls of prisoners, hospital records, and records of burials in the rebel prisons and elsewhere, and at short intervals published Rolls of Missing Men, which, by the franks of some of her friends among the Members of Congress, were sent to all parts of the United States, and posted in prominent places, and in many instances copied into local papers. The method adopted for the discovery of information concerning these missing men, and the communication of that information to their friends who had made inquiries concerning them may be thus illustrated.

A Mrs. James of Kennebunk, Maine, has seen a notice in the paper that Miss Clara Barton of Washington will receive inquiries from friends of "missing men of the Army," and will endeavor to obtain information for them without fee or reward. She forthwith writes to Miss Barton that she is anxious to obtain tidings of her husband, Eli James, Sergeant Company F. Fourth Maine Infantry, who has not been heard of since the battle of—. This letter, when received, is immediately acknowledged, registered in a book, endorsed and filed away for convenient reference. The answer satisfied Mrs. James for the time, that her letter was not lost and that some attention is given to her inquiry. If the fate of Sergeant James is known or can be learned from the official rolls the information is sent at once. Otherwise the case lies over until there are enough to form a roll, which will probably be within a few weeks. A roll of Missing Men is then made up—with an appeal for information respecting them, of which from twenty thousand to thirty thousand copies are printed to be posted all over the United States, in all places where soldiers are most likely to congregate. It is not impossible, that in say two weeks' time, one James Miller, of Keokuk, Iowa, writes that he has seen the name of his friend James posted for information; that he found him lying on the ground, at the battle of mortally wounded with a fragment of shell; that he, James, gave the writer a few articles from about his person, and a brief message to his wife and children, whom he is now unable to find; that the national troops fell back from that portion of the field leaving the dead within the enemy's lines, who consequently were never reported. When this letter is received it is also registered in a book, endorsed and filed, and a summary of its contents is sent to Mrs. James, with the intimation that further particulars of interest to her can be learned by addressing James Miller, of Keokuk, Iowa.

Soon after entering fully upon this work in Washington, and having obtained the rolls of the prison hospitals of Wilmington, Salisbury, Florence, Charleston, and other Rebel prisons of the South, Miss Barton ascertained that Dorrance Atwater, a young Connecticut soldier, who had been a prisoner at Andersonville, Georgia, had succeeded in obtaining a copy of all the records of interments in that field of death, during his employment in the hospital there, and that he could identify the graves of most of the thirteen thousand who had died there the victims of Rebel cruelty.

Atwater was induced to permit Government officers to copy his roll, and on the representation of Miss Barton that no time should be lost in putting up head-boards to the graves of the Union Soldiers, Captain James M. Moore, Assistant Quartermaster, was ordered to proceed to Andersonville with young Atwater and a suitable force, to lay out the grounds as a cemetery and place head-boards to the graves; and Miss Barton was requested by the Secretary of War to accompany him. She did so, and the grounds were laid out and fenced, and all the graves except about four hundred which could not be identified were marked with suitable head-boards. On their return, Miss Barton resumed her duties, and Captain Moore caused Atwater's arrest on the charge of having stolen from the Government the list he had loaned them for copying, and after a hasty trial by Court-martial, he was sentenced to be imprisoned in the Auburn State Prison for two years and six months. The sentence was immediately carried into effect.

Miss Barton felt that this whole charge, trial and sentence, was grossly unjust; that Atwater had committed no crime, not even a technical one, and that he ought to be relieved from imprisonment. She accordingly exerted herself to have the case brought before the President. This was done; and in part through the influence of General Benjamin F. Butler, an order was sent on to the Warden of the Auburn Prison to set the prisoner at liberty. Atwater subsequently published his roll of the Andersonville dead, to which Miss Barton prefixed a narrative of the expedition to Andersonville. Her Bureau had by this time become an institution of great and indispensable importance not only to the friends of missing men but to the Sanitary Commission, and to the Government itself, which could not without daily and almost hourly reference to her records settle the accounts for bounties, back pay, and pensions. Thus far, however, it had been sustained wholly at her own cost, and in this and other labors for the soldiers she had expended her entire private fortune of eight or ten thousand dollars. Soon after the assembling of Congress, Hon. Henry Wilson, of Massachusetts, who had always been her firm friend, moved an appropriation of fifteen thousand dollars to remunerate her for past expenditure, and enable her to maintain the Bureau of Records of Missing Men, which had proved of such service. To the honor of Congress it should be said, that the appropriation passed both houses by a unanimous vote. Miss Barton still continues her good work, and has been instrumental in sending certainty if not solace to thousands of families, who mourned their loved ones as lying in unknown graves.

In person Miss Barton is about of medium height, her form and figure indicating great powers of endurance. Though not technically beautiful, her dark expressive eye is attractive, and she possesses, evidently unconsciously to herself, great powers of fascination. Her voice is soft, low, and of extraordinary sweetness of tone. As we have said she is modest, quiet and retiring in manner, and is extremely reticent in speaking of anything she has done, while she is ever ready to bestow the full meed of praise on the labors of others. Her devotion to her work has been remarkable, and her organizing abilities are unsurpassed among her own sex and equalled by very few among the other. She is still young, and with her power and disposition for usefulness is destined we hope to prove greatly serviceable to the country she so ardently loves.

IN CAMP, FIELD, AND GENERAL HOSPITALS

HELEN LOUISE GILSON

MISS HELEN LOUISE GILSON is a native of Boston, but removed in childhood to Chelsea, Massachusetts, where she now resides. She is a niece of Hon. Frank B. Fay, former Mayor of Chelsea, and was his ward. Mr. Fay, from the commencement of the war took the most active interest in the National cause, devoting his time, his wealth and his personal efforts to the welfare of the soldiers. In the autumn of 1861 he went in person to the seat of war, and from that time forward, in every battle in which the Army of the Potomac was engaged, he was promptly upon the field with his stores and appliances of healing, and moved gently though rapidly among the dead and wounded, soothing helpless, suffering and bleeding men parched with fever, crazed with thirst, or lying neglected in the last agonies of death. After two years of this independent work performed when as yet the Sanitary Commission had no field agencies, and did not attempt to minister to the suffering and wounded until they had come under the hands of the surgeons, Mr. Fay laid before the Sanitary Commission, in the winter of 1863-4, his plans for an Auxiliary Relief Corps, to afford personal relief in the field, to the wounded soldier, and render him such assistance, as should enable him to bear with less injury the delay which must ensue before he could come under the surgeon's care or be transferred to a hospital, and in cases of the slighter wounds furnish the necessary dressings and attention.

The Sanitary Commission at once adopted these plans and made Mr. Fay chief of the Auxiliary Relief Corps. In this capacity he performed an amount of labor of which few men were capable, till December, 1864, when he retired from it but continued his independent work till the close of the war. During his visits at home he was active in organizing and directing measures for raising supplies and money for the Sanitary Commission and the independent measures of relief.

Influenced by such an example of lofty and self-sacrificing patriotism, and with her own young heart on fire with love for her country, Miss Gilson from the very commencement of the war, gave herself to the work of caring for the soldiers, first at home, and afterward in the field. In that glorious uprising of American women, all over the North, in the spring of 1861, to organize Soldiers' Aid Societies she was active and among the foremost in her own city. She had helped to prepare and collect supplies, and to arrange them for transportation. She had also obtained a contract for the manufacture of army clothing, from the Government, by means of which she provided employment for soldiers' wives and daughters, raising among the benevolent and patriotic people of Chelsea and vicinity, a fund which enabled her to pay a far more liberal sum than the contractors' prices, for this labor.

When Mr. Fay commenced his personal services with the Army of the Potomac, Miss Gilson, wishing to accompany him, applied to Miss D. L. Dix, Government Superintendent of Female Nurses, for a diploma, but as she had not reached the required age she was rejected. This, however, did not prevent her from fulfilling her ardent desire of ministering to the sick and wounded, but served in a measure to limit her to services upon the field, where she could act in concert with Mr. Fay, or otherwise under the direction of the Sanitary Commission.

During nearly the whole term of Miss Gilson's service she was in company with Mr. Fay and his assistants. The party had their own tent, forming a household, and carrying with them something of home-life.

In this manner she, with her associates, followed the Army of the Potomac, through its various vicissitudes, and was present at, or near, almost every one of its great battles except the first battle of Bull Run.

In the summer of 1862 Miss Gilson was for some time attached to the Hospital Transport service, and was on board the *Knickerbocker* when up the Pamunky River at White House, and afterward at Harrison's Landing during the severe battles which marked McClellan's movement from the Chickahominy to the James River. Amidst the terrible scenes of those eventful days, the quiet energy, the wonderful comforting and soothing power, and the perfect adaptability of Miss Gilson to her work were conspicuous.

Whatever she did was done well, and so noiselessly that only the results were seen. When not more actively employed she would sit by the bed-sides of the suffering men, and charm away their pain by the magnetism of her low, calm voice, and soothing words. She sang for them, and, kneeling beside them, where they lay amidst all the agonizing sights and sounds of the hospital wards, and even upon the field of carnage, her voice would ascend in petition, for peace, for relief, for sustaining grace in the brief journey to the other world, carrying with it their souls into the realms of an exalted faith.

As may be supposed, Miss Gilson exerted a remarkable personal influence over the wounded soldiers as well as all those with whom she was brought in contact. She always shrank from notoriety, and strongly deprecated any publicity in regard to her work; but the thousands who witnessed her extraordinary activity, her remarkable executive power, her ability in evoking order out of chaos, and providing for thousands of sick and wounded men where most persons would have been completely overwhelmed in the care of scores or hundreds, could not always be prevented from speaking of her in the public prints. The uniform cheerfulness and buoyancy of spirit with which all her work was performed, added greatly to its efficiency in removing the depressing influences, so common in the hospitals and among the wounded.

From some of the reports of agents of the Sanitary Commission we select the following passages referring to her, as expressing in more moderate language than some others, the sentiments in regard to her work entertained by all who were brought into contact with her.

"Upon Miss Gilson's services, we scarcely dare trust ourselves to comment. Upon her experience we relied for counsel, and it was chiefly due to her advice and efforts, that the work in our hospital went on so successfully. Always quiet, self-possessed, and prompt in the discharge of duty, she accomplished more than any one else could for the relief of the wounded, besides being a constant example and embodiment of earnestness for all. Her ministrations were always grateful to the wounded men, who devotedly loved her for her self-sacrificing spirit. Said one of the Fifth New Jersey in our hearing, 'There isn't a man in our regiment who wouldn't lay down his life for Miss Gilson.'

"We have seen the dying man lean his head upon her shoulder, while she breathed into his ear the soothing prayer that calmed, cheered and prepared him for his journey through the dark valley.

"Under the direction of Miss Gilson, the special diet was prepared, and we cannot strongly enough express our sense of the invaluable service she rendered in this department. The food was always eagerly expected and relished by the men, with many expressions of praise."

After the battle of Gettysburg Mr. Fay and his party went thither on their mission of help and mercy. And never was such a mission more needed. Crowded within the limits, and in the immediate vicinity, of that small country-town, were twenty-five thousand wounded men, thirteen thousand seven hundred and thirteen of our own, and nearly twelve thousand wounded rebel prisoners. The Government in anticipation of the battle had provided medical and surgical supplies and attendance for about ten thousand. Had not the Sanitary Commission supplemented this supply, and sent efficient agents to the field, the loss of life, and the amount of suffering, terrible as they were with the best appliances, must have been almost incredibly great.

Here as elsewhere Miss Gilson soon made a favorable impression on the wounded men. They looked up to her, reverenced and almost worshipped her. She had their entire confidence and respect. Even the roughest of them yielded to her influence and obeyed her wishes, which were always made known in a gentle manner and in a voice peculiarly low and sweet.

It has been recorded by one who knew her well, that she once stepped out of her tent, before which a group of brutal men were fiercely quarrelling, having refused, with oaths and vile language, to carry a sick comrade to the hospital at the request of one of the male agents of the Commission, and quietly advancing to their midst, renewed the request as her own. Immediately every angry tone was stilled. Their voices were lowered, and modulated respectfully. Their oaths ceased, and quietly and cheerfully, without a word of objection, they lifted their helpless burden, and tenderly carried him away.

At the same time she was as efficient in action as in influence. Without bustle, and with unmoved calmness, she would superintend the preparation of food for a thousand men, and assist in feeding them herself. Just so she moved amidst the flying bullets upon the field, bringing succor to the wounded; or through the hospitals amidst the pestilent air of the fever-stricken wards. Self-controlled, she could control others, and order and symmetry sprung up before her as a natural result of the operation of a well-balanced mind.

In all her journeys Miss Gilson made use of the opportunities afforded her wherever she stopped to plead the cause of the soldier to the people, who readily assembled at her suggestion. She thus stimulated energies that might otherwise have flagged, and helped to swell the supplies continually pouring in to the depots of the Sanitary Commission. But Miss Gilson's crowning work was performed during that last protracted campaign of General Grant from the Rapidan to Petersburg and the Appomattox, a campaign which by almost a year of constant fighting finished the most terrible and destructive war of modern times. She had taken the field with Mr. Fay at the very commencement of the campaign, and had been indefatigable in her efforts to relieve what she could of the fearful suffering of those destructive battles of May, 1864, in which the dead and wounded were numbered by scores of thousands. To how many poor sufferers she brought relief from the raging thirst and the racking agony of their wounds, to how many aching hearts her words of cheer and her sweet songs bore comfort and hope, to how many of those on whose countenances the Angel of death had already set his seal, she whispered of a dying and risen Saviour, and of the mansions prepared for them that love him, will never be known till the judgment of the great day; but this we know, that thousands now living speak with an almost rapturous enthusiasm, of "the little lady who in their hours of agony, ministered to them with such sweetness, and never seemed to weary of serving them." a young physician in the service of the Sanitary Commission, Dr. William Howell Reed, who was afterwards for many months associated with her and Mr. Fay in their labors of auxiliary relief, thus describes his first opportunity of observing her work. It was at Fredericksburg in May, 1864, when that town was for a time the base of the Army of the Potomac, and the place to which the wounded were brought for treatment before being sent to the hospitals at Washington and Baltimore. The building used as a hospital, and which she visited was the mansion of John L. Marie, a large building, but much of it in ruins from the previous bombardment of the city. It was crowded with wounded in every part. Dr. Reed says:—

"One afternoon, just before the evacuation, when the atmosphere of our rooms was close and foul, and all were longing for a breath of our cooler northern air, while the men were moaning in pain, or were restless with fever, and our hearts were sick with pity for the sufferers, I heard a light step upon the stairs; and looking up I saw a young lady enter, who brought with her such an atmosphere of calm and cheerful courage, so much freshness, such an expression of gentle, womanly sympathy, that her mere presence seemed to revive the drooping spirits of the men, and to give a new power of endurance through the long and painful hours of suffering. First with one, then at the side of another, a friendly word here, a gentle nod and smile there, a tender sympathy with each prostrate sufferer, a sympathy which could read in his eyes his longing for home love, and for the presence of some absent one—in those few minutes hers was indeed an angel ministry. Before she left the room she sang to them, first some stirring national melody, then some sweet or plaintive hymn to strengthen the fainting heart; and I remember how the notes penetrated to every part of the building. Soldiers with less severe wounds, from the rooms above, began to crawl out into the entries, and men from below crept up on their hands and knees, to catch every note, and to receive of the benediction of her presence—for such it was to them. Then she went away. I did not know who she was, but I was as much moved and melted as any soldier of them all. This is my first reminiscence of Helen L. Gilson."

Thus far Miss Gilson's cares and labors had been bestowed almost exclusively on the white soldiers; but the time approached when she was to devote herself to the work of creating a model hospital for the colored soldiers who now formed a considerable body of troops in the Army of the Potomac. She was deeply interested in the struggle of the African race upward into the new life which seemed opening for them, and her efforts for the mental and moral elevation of the freedmen and their families were eminently deserving of record.

Dr. Reed relates how, as they were passing down the Rappahannock and up the York and Pamunky rivers to the new temporary base of the army at Port Royal, they found a government barge which had been appropriated to the use of the "contrabands," of whom about a thousand were stowed away upon it, of all ages and both sexes, all escaped from their former masters in that part of Virginia. The hospital party heard them singing the negroes' evening hymn, and taking a boat from the steamer rowed to the barge, and after a little conversation persuaded them to renew their song, which was delivered with all the fervor, emotion and abandon of the negro character.

When their song had ceased, Miss Gilson addressed them. She pictured the reality of freedom, told them what it meant and what they would have to do, no longer would there be a master to deal out the peck of corn, no longer a mistress to care for the old people or the children. They were to work for themselves, provide for their own sick, and support their own infirm; but all this was to be done under new conditions. No overseer was to stand over them with the whip, for their new master was the necessity of earning their daily bread. Very soon new and higher motives would come; fresh encouragements, a nobler ambition, would grow into their new condition. Then in the simplest language she explained the difference between their former relations with the then master and their new relations with the northern people, showing that labor here was voluntary, and that they could only expect to secure kind employers by faithfully doing all they had to do. Then, enforcing truthfulness, neatness, and economy, she said,—

"You know that the Lord Jesus died and rose again for you. You love to sing his praise and to draw near to him in prayer.

But remember that this is not all of religion. You must do right as well as pray right. Your lives must be full of kind deeds towards each other, full of gentle and loving affections, full of unselfishness and truth: this is true piety. You must make Monday and Tuesday just as good and pure as Sunday is, remembering that God looks not only at your prayers and your emotions, but at the way you live, and speak, and act, every hour of your lives."

Then she sang Whittier's exquisite hymn:—

"O, praise an' tanks,—the Lord he come
To set de people free; an' massa tink it day ob doom,
An' we ob jubilee.
De Lord dat heap de Eed Sea wabes,
He just as'trong as den;
He say de word, we last night slabes,
To-day de Lord's free men."

Here were a thousand people breathing their first free air. They were new born with this delicious sense of freedom. They listened with moistened eyes to every word which concerned their future, and felt that its utterance came from a heart which could embrace them all in its sympathies. Life was to them a jubilee only so far as they could make it so by a consciousness of duty faithfully done. They had hard work before them, much privation, many struggles. They had everything to learn—the new industries of the North, their changed social condition, and how to accept their new responsibilities.

As she spoke the circle grew larger, and they pressed round her more eagerly. It was all a part of their new life. They welcomed it; and, by every possible expression of gratitude to her, they showed how desirous they were to learn. Those who were present can never forget the scene—a thousand dusky faces, expressive of such fervency and enthusiasm, their large eyes filled with tears, answering to the throbbing heart below, all dimly outlined by the flickering rays of a single lamp. And when it was over, we felt that we could understand our relations to them, and the new duties which this great hour had brought upon us.

It was not till the sanguinary battles of the 15th, 16th, 17th, and 18th of June, 1864, that there had been any considerable number of the colored troops of the Army of the Potomac wounded. In those engagements however, as well as in the subsequent ones of the explosion of the mine, and the actions immediately around Petersburg, they suffered terribly. The wounded were brought rapidly to City Point, where a temporary hospital had been provided. We give a description of this hospital in the words of Dr. Reed, who was associated subsequently with Miss Gilson in its management.

"It was, in no other sense a hospital, than that it was a depot for wounded men. There were defective management and chaotic confusion. The men were neglected, the hospital organization was imperfect, and the mortality was in consequence frightfully large. Their condition was horrible. The severity of the campaign in a malarious country had prostrated many with fevers, and typhoid, in its most malignant forms, was raging with increasing fatality.

"These stories of suffering reached Miss Gilson at a moment when the previous labors of the campaign had nearly exhausted her strength; but her duty seemed plain. There were no volunteers for the emergency, and she prepared to go. Her friends declared that she could not survive it; but replying that she could not die in a cause more sacred, she started out alone. A hospital was to be created, and this required all the tact, finesse and diplomacy of which a woman is capable. Official prejudice and professional pride was to be met and overcome. A new policy was to be introduced, and it was to be done without seeming to interfere. Her doctrine and practice always were instant, silent, and cheerful obedience to medical and disciplinary orders, without any qualification whatever; and by this she overcame the natural sensitiveness of the medical authorities.

"A hospital kitchen was to be organized upon her method of special diet; nurses were to learn her way, and be educated to their duties; while cleanliness, order, system, were to be enforced in the daily routine. Moving quietly on with her work of renovation, she took the responsibility of all changes that became necessary; and such harmony prevailed in the camp that her policy was vindicated as time rolled on. The rate of mortality was lessened, and the hospital was soon considered the best in the department. This was accomplished by a tact and energy which sought no praise, but modestly veiled themselves behind the orders of officials. The management of her kitchen was like the ticking of a clock—regular discipline, gentle firmness, and sweet temper always. The diet for the men was changed three times a day; and it was her aim to cater as far as possible to the appetites of individual men. Her daily rounds in the wards brought her into personal intercourse with every patient, and she knew his special need. At one time, nine hundred men were supplied from her kitchen (with seven hundred rations daily).

The following passage from the pen of Harriet Martineau, in regard to the management of the kitchen at Scutari, by Florence Nightingale, is true also of those organized by Miss Gilson in Virginia. The parallel is so close, and the illustration of the daily administration of this department of her work so vivid, that, if the circumstances under which it was written were not known, I should have said it was a faithful picture of our kitchen in the Colored Hospital at City Point:—

"The very idea of that kitchen was savory in the wards; for out of it came, at the right moment, arrowroot, hot and of the pleasantest consistence; rice puddings, neither hard on the one hand or clammy on the other; cool lemonade for the feverish; cans full of hot tea for the weary, and good coffee for the faint. When the sinking sufferer was lying with closed eyes, too feeble to make moan or sigh, the hospital spoon was put between his lips, with the mouthful of strong broth or hot wine, which rallied him till the watchful nurse came round again. The meat from that kitchen was tenderer than any other, the beef tea was more savory. One thing that came out of it was the lesson on the saving of good cookery. The mere circumstance of the boiling water being really boiling there, made a difference of two ounces of rice in every four puddings, and of more than half the arrowroot used. The same quantity of arrowroot which made a pint thin and poor in the general kitchen, made two pints thick and good in Miss Nightingale's.

"Again, in contrasting the general kitchen with the light or special diet prepared for the sicker men, there was all the difference between having placed before them the cold mutton chop with its opaque fat, the beef with its caked gravy, the arrowroot stiff and glazed, all untouched, as might be seen by the bed-sides in the afternoons, while the patients were lying back, sinking for want of support and seeing 'the quick and quiet nurses enter as the clock struck, with their hot water tins, hot morsels ready cut, bright knife, and fork, and spoon,—and all ready for instant eating!'

"The nurses looked for Miss Gilson's word of praise, and labored for it; and she had only to suggest a variety in the decoration of the tents to stimulate a most honorable rivalry among them, which soon opened a wide field for displaying ingenuity and taste, so that not only was its standard the highest, but it was the most cheerfully picturesque hospital at City Point.

"This colored hospital service was one of those extraordinary tasks, out of the ordinary course of army hospital discipline, that none but a woman could execute. It required more than a man's power of endurance, for men fainted and fell under the burden. It required a woman's discernment, a woman's tenderness, a woman's delicacy and tact; it required such nerve and moral force, and such executive power, as are rarely united in any woman's character. The simple grace with which she moved about the hospital camps, the gentle dignity with which she ministered to the suffering about her, won all hearts. As she passed through the wards, the men would follow her with their eyes, attracted by the grave sweetness of her manner; and when she stopped by some bed-side, and laid her hand upon the forehead and smoothed the hair of a soldier, speaking some cheering, pleasant word, I have seen the tears gather in his eyes, and his lips quiver, as he tried to speak or to touch the fold of her dress, as if appealing to her to listen, while he opened his heart about the mother, wife, or sister far away. I have seen her in her sober gray flannel gown, sitting motionless by the dim candle-light,—which was all our camp could afford,—with her eyes open and watchful, and her hands ever ready for all those endless wants of sickness at night, especially sickness that may be tended unto death, or unto the awful struggle between life and death, which it was the lot of nearly all of us at some time to keep watch over until the danger had gone by. And in sadder trials, when the life of a soldier whom she had watched and ministered to was trembling in the balance between earth and heaven, waiting for Him to make all things new, she has seemed, by some special grace of the Spirit, to reach the living Christ, and draw a blessing down as the shining way was opened to the tomb. And I have seen such looks of gratitude from weary eyes, now brightened by visions of heavenly glory, the last of many recognitions of her ministry. Absorbed in her work, unconscious of the spiritual beauty which invested her daily life,—whether in her kitchen, in the heat and overcrowding incident to the issues of a large special diet list, or sitting at the cot of some poor lonely soldier, whispering of the higher realities of another world,—she was always the same presence of grace and love, of peace and benediction. I have been with her in the wards when the men have craved some simple religious services,—the reading of Scripture, the repetition of a psalm, the singing of a hymn, or the offering of a prayer,—and invariably the men were melted to tears by the touching simplicity of her eloquence.

"These were the tokens of her ministry among the sickest men; but it was not here alone that her influence was felt in the hospital. Was there jealousy in the kitchen, her quick penetration detected the cause, and in her gentle way harmony was restored; was there profanity among the convalescents, her daily presence and kindly admonition or reproof, with an occasional glance which spoke her sorrow for such sin, were enough to check the evil; or was there hardship or discontent, the knowledge that she was sharing the discomfort too, was enough to compel patient endurance until a remedy could be provided. And so, through all the war, from the seven days' conflict upon the Peninsula, in those early July days of 1862, through the campaigns of Antietam and Fredericksburg, of Chancellorsville and Gettysburg, and after the conflicts of the Wilderness, and the fierce and undecided battles which were fought for the possession of Richmond and Petersburg, in 1864 and 1865, she labored steadfastly on until the end. Through scorching heat and pinching cold, in the tent or upon the open field, in the ambulance or on the saddle, through rain and snow, amid unseen perils of the enemy, under fire upon the field, or in the more insidious dangers of contagion, she worked quietly on, doing her simple part with all womanly tact and skill, until now the hospital dress is laid aside, and she rests, with the sense of a noble work done, and with the blessings and prayers of the thousands whose sufferings she has relieved, or whose lives she has saved."

Amid all these labors, Miss Gilson found time and opportunity to care for the poor negro washerwomen and their families, who doing the washing of the hospital were allowed rations and a rude shelter by the government in a camp near the hospital grounds. Finding that they were suffering from overcrowding, privation, neglect, and sickness, she procured the erection of comfortable huts for them, obtained clothing from the North for the more destitute, and by example and precept encouraged them in habits of neatness and order, while she also inculcated practical godliness in all their life. In a short time from one of the most miserable this became the best of the Freedmen's camps.

As was the case with nearly every woman who entered the service at the seat of war, Miss Gilson suffered from malarious fever. As often as possible she returned to her home for a brief space, to recruit her wasted energies, and it was those brief intervals of rest which enabled her to remain at her post until several months after the surrender of Lee virtually ended the war.

She left Richmond in July, 1865, and spent the remainder of the summer in a quiet retreat upon Long Island, where she partially recovered her impaired health, and in the autumn returned to her home in Chelsea.

In person Miss Gilson is small and delicately proportioned. Without being technically beautiful, her features are lovely both in form and expression, and though now nearly thirty years of age she looks much younger than she actually is. Her voice is low and soft, and her speech gentle and deliberate. Her movements correspond in exact harmony with voice and speech. But, under the softness and gentleness of her external demeanor, one soon detects a firmness of determination, and a fixedness of will. No doubt, once determined upon the duty and propriety of any course, she will pursue it calmly and persistently to the end. It is to these qualifications, and physical and moral traits, that she owes the undoubted power and influence exercised in her late mission.

MRS. JOHN HARRIS

HE would have been a man of uncommon sagacity and penetration, who in the beginning of 1861, should have chosen Mrs. Harris as capable of the great services and the extraordinary power of endurance with which her name has since been identified. A pale, quiet, delicate woman, often an invalid for months, and almost always a sufferer; the wife of a somewhat eminent physician, in Philadelphia, and in circumstances which did not require constant activity for her livelihood, refined, educated, and shrinking from all rough or brutal sights or sounds, she seemed one of those who were least fitted to endure the hardships, and encounter the roughnesses of a life in the camp or field hospitals.

But beneath that quiet and frail exterior, there dwelt a firm and dauntless spirit. She had been known by her neighbors, and especially in the church of which she was an honored member, as a woman of remarkable piety and devotion, and as an excellent and skilful attendant upon the sick. When the war commenced, she was one of the ladies who assembled to form the Ladies' Aid Society of Philadelphia, and was chosen, we believe unanimously, Corresponding Secretary. She seems to have entered upon the work from the feeling that it was a part of her duty, a sacrifice she was called to make, a burden which she ought to bear. And through the war, mainly from her temperament, which inclined her to look on the dark side, she never seemed stimulated or strengthened in her work by that abiding conviction of the final success of our arms, which was to so many of the patient workers, the day-star of hope. Like Bunyan's Master Fearing, she was always apprehensive of defeat and disaster, of the triumph of the adversary • and when victories came, her eyes were so dim with tears for the bereaved and sorrow-stricken, and her heart so heavy with their griefs that she could not join in the songs of triumph, or smile in unison with the nation's rejoicings. We speak of this not to depreciate her work or zeal, but rather to do the more honor to both. The despondent temperament and the intense sympathy with sorrow were constitutional, or the result of years of ill-health, and that under their depressing influence, with no step of her way lighted with the sunshine of joy, she should have not only continued faithful to her work, but have undergone more hardships and accomplished more, for the soldiers than most others, reflects the highest credit upon her patience, perseverance and devotion to the cause.

We have elsewhere in this volume given an account of the origin and progress of the Ladies' Aid Society, of Philadelphia. Mrs. Harris, though continued as its Corresponding Secretary through the war, was, during the greater part of the time, its correspondent in the field, and left to the other officers, the work of raising and forwarding the money and supplies, while she attended in person to their distribution. This division of labor seems to have satisfied her associates, who forwarded to her order their hospital stores and money with the most perfect confidence in her judicious disposition of both. Other Societies, such as the Penn Belief, the Patriotic Daughters of Lancaster, and Aid Societies from the interior of Pennsylvania, as well as the Christian and Sanitary Commissions, made her their almoners, and she distributed a larger amount of stores, perhaps, than any other lady in the field.

The history of her work during the war, is given very fully, in her correspondence with the Ladies' Aid Society, published in their semi-annual reports. From these we gather that she had visited in 1861, and the winter of 1862, before the movement of the army to the peninsula, more than one hundred hospitals of the army of the Potomac, in and around Washington, and had not only ministered to the physical wants of the sick and wounded men, but had imparted religious instruction and consolation to many of them. Everywhere her coming had been welcomed; in many instances, eyes dimmed by the shadow of the wings of the death-angel, saw in her the wife or mother, for whose coming they had longed and died, with the hallowed word "mother" on their lips.

When in the spring of 1862, the army of the Potomac moved to the Peninsula, Mrs. Harris went thither, first distributing as far as practicable, her stores among the men. Soon after her arrival on the Peninsula, she found ample employment for her time. The Chesapeake and Hygeia hospitals at Fortress Monroe, filled at first mostly with the sick, and the few wounded in the siege of Yorktown, were, after the battles of Williamsburg and West Point crowded with such of the wounded, both Union and Confederate soldiers as could be brought so far from the battle-fields. She spent two or three weeks here, aiding the noble women who were acting as Matrons of these hospitals. From thence she went on board the Vanderbilt, then just taken as a Government Transport for the wounded from the bloody field of Fair Oaks.

She thus describes the scene and her work:

"There were eight hundred on board. Passage-ways, state-rooms, floors from the dark and foetid hold to the hurricane deck, were all more than filled; some on mattresses, some on blankets, others on straw; some in the death-struggle, others nearing it, some already beyond human sympathy and help; some in their blood as they had been brought from the battle-field of the Sabbath previous, and all hungry and thirsty, not having had anything to eat or drink, except hard crackers, for twenty-four hours.

"The gentlemen who came on with us hurried on to the White House, and would have had us go with them, but something held us back; thank God it was so. Meeting Dr. Cuyler, Medical Director, he exclaimed, 'Here is work for you 1' He, poor man, was completely overwhelmed with the general care of all the hospitals at Old Point, and added to these, these mammoth floating hospitals, which are coming in from day to day with their precious cargoes. Without any previous notice, they anchor, and send to him for supplies, which it would be extremely difficult to improvise, even in our large cities, and quite impossible at Old Point. 'No bakeries, no stores, except small sutlers.' The bread had all to be baked; the boat rationed for two days; eight hundred on board.

"When we went aboard, the first cry we met was for tea and bread. 'For God's sake, give us bread,' came from many of our wounded soldiers. Others shot in the face or neck, begged for liquid food. With feelings of a mixed character, shame, indignation, and sorrow blending, we turned away to see what resources we could muster to meet the demand. A box of tea, a barrel of cornmeal, sundry parcels of dried fruit, a few crackers, ginger cakes, dried rusk, sundry jars of jelly and of pickles, were seized upon, soldiers and contrabands impressed into service, all the cooking arrangements of three families appropriated, by permission, and soon three pounds of tea were boiling, and many gallons of gruel blubbering. In the meantime, all the bread we could buy, twenty-five loaves, were cut into slices and jellied, pickles were got in readiness, and in an incredibly short time, we were back to our poor sufferers.

"When we carried in bread, hands from every quarter were outstretched, and the cry, 'Give me a piece, O please! I have had nothing since Monday;' another, 'Nothing but hard crackers since the fight,' etc. When we had dealt out nearly all the bread, a surgeon came in, and cried, 'Do please keep some for the poor fellows in the hold; they are so badly off for everything.' So with the remnant we threaded our way through the suffering crowd, amid such exclamations as 'Oh! please don't touch my foot,' or, 'For mercy's sake, don't touch my arm;' another, 'Please don't move the blanket; I am so terribly cut up,' down to the hold, in which were not less than one hundred and fifty, nearly all sick, some very sick. It was like plunging into a vapor bath, so hot, close, and full of moisture, and then in this dismal place, we distributed our bread, oranges, and pickles, which were seized upon with avidity. And here let me say, at least twenty of them told us next day that the pickles had done them more good than all the medicine they had taken. The tea was carried all around in buckets, sweetened, but no milk in it. How much we wished for some concentrated milk. The gruel, into which we had put a goodly quantity of wine, was relished, you cannot know how much. One poor wounded boy, exhausted with the loss of blood and long fasting, looked up after taking the first nourishment be could swallow since the battle of Saturday, then four days, and exclaimed, with face radiant with gratitude and pleasure, 'Oh! that is life to me; I feel as if twenty years were given me to live.' He was shockingly wounded about the neck and face, and could only take liquid food from a feeding-cup, of which they had none on board. We left them four, together with a number of tin dishes, spoons, etc. After hours spent in this va;, we returned to the Hygeia Hospital, stopping on our way to stew a quantity of dried fruit, which served for supper, reaching the Hygeia wet through and through, every garment saturated. Disrobed, and bathing with bay rum, was glad to lie down, every bone aching, and head and heart throbbing, unwilling to cease work where so much was to be done, and yet wholly unable to do more. There I lay, with the sick, wounded, and dying all around, and slept from sheer exhaustion, the last sounds falling upon my ear being groans from the operating room."

Her ministrations to the wounded on the Vanderbilt were unexpectedly prolonged by the inability of the officers to get the necessary supplies on board, but two days after she was on the Knickerbocker, a Sanitary Commission Transport, and on her way to White House Landing where in company with Miss Charlotte Bradford, she spent the whole night on the Transport Louisiana, dressing and caring for the wounded. When she left the boat at eleven o'clock the next night she was obliged to wash all her skirts which were saturated with the mingled blood of the Union and Confederate soldiers which covered the floor, as she kneeled between them to wash their faces. She had torn up all her spare clothing which could be of use to them for bandages and compresses. From White House she proceeded to the battleground of Fair Oaks, and presently pitched her tent on the Dudley Farm, near Savage Station, to be near the group of field hospitals, to which the wounded in the almost daily skirmishes and the sick smitten with that terrible Chickahominy fever were sent.

The provision made by the Medical Bureau of the Government at this time for the care and comfort of the wounded and fever-stricken was small and often inappropriate. Where tents were provided, they were either of the wedge pattern or the bivouacking tent of black cloth, and in the hot sun of a Virginia summer absorbed the sun's rays till they were like ovens; many of the sick were put into the cabins and miserable shanties of the vicinity, and not unfrequently in the attics of these, where amid 20 the intense heat they were left without food or drink except when the Sanitary Commission's agents or some of the ladies connected with other organizations, like Mrs. Harris, ministered to their necessities. One case of this kind, not by any means the worst, but told with a simple pathos deserves to be quoted:

"Passing a forlorn-looking house, we were told by a sentinel that a young Captain of a Maine regiment laid in it very sick; we went in, no door obstructing, and there upon a stretcher in a corner of the room opening directly upon the road lay an elegant-looking youth struggling with the last great enemy. His mind wandered; and as we approached him he exclaimed: 'Is it not cruel to keep me here when my mother and sister, whom I have not seen for a year, are in the next room; they might let me go in?' His mind continued to wander; only for an instant did he seem to have a glimpse of the reality, when he drew two rings from his finger, placed there by a loving mother and sister, handed them to an attendant, saying: 'Carry them home,' and then he was amid battle scenes, calling out, 'Deploy to the left;' 'Keep out of that ambuscade;' 'Now go, my braves, double quick, and strike for your flag! On, on,' and he threw up his arms as if cheering them, 'you'll win the day;' and so he continued to talk, whilst death was doing its terrible work. As we looked upon the beautiful face and manly form, and thought of the mother and sister in their distant home, surrounded by every luxury wealth could purchase, worlds seemed all too cheap to give to have him with them. But this could not be. The soldier of three battles, he was not willing to admit that he was sick until his strength failed, and he was actually dying. He was carried to this cheerless room, a rude table the only furniture; no door, no window-shutters; the western sun threw its hot rays in upon him,—no cooling shade for his fevered brow: and so he lay unconscious of the monster's grasp, which would not relax until he had done his work. His last expressions told of interest in his men. He was a graduate of Waterville College. Twenty of his company graduated at the same institution. He was greatly beloved; his death, even in this Golgotha, was painfully impressive. There was no time to talk to him of that spirit-land upon which he was so soon to enter. Whispered a few verses of Scripture into his ear; he looked with a sweet smile and thanked me, but his manner betokened no appreciation of the sacred words. He was an only son. His mother and sister doted on him. He had everything to bind him to life, but the mandate had gone forth."

Of the scenes of the retreat from the Chickahominy to Harrison's Landing, Mrs. Harris was an active and deeply interested witness; she remained at Savage Station caring for the wounded, for some time, and then proceeded to Seven Pines, where a day was passed in preparing the wounded for the operations deemed necessary, obtaining, at great personal peril, candles to light the darkness of the field hospital, and was sitting down, completely exhausted with her trying and wearisome labors, when an army chaplain, an exception it is to be hoped to most of his profession, in his unwillingness to serve the wounded, came to her and said, "They have just brought in a soldier with a leg blown off; he is in a horrible condition; could you wash him?" Wearied as she was, she performed the duty tenderly, but it was scarcely finished when death claimed him. Her escape to White House, and thence to Harrison's Landing, was made not a minute too soon; she was obliged to abandon her stores, and to come off on the steamer in a borrowed bonnet.

At this trying time, her constitutional tendency to despondency took full possession of her. "The heavens are filled with blackness," she writes; "I find myself on board the Nelly Baker, on my way to City Point, with supplies for our poor army, if we still have one; I am not always hopeful, you see. Alarming accounts come to us. Prepare for the worst, but hope for the best. We do not doubt we are in a very critical condition, out of which only the Most High can bring us." This is not the language of fear or cowardice. There was no disposition on her part to seek her own personal safety, but while she despaired of success, she was ready to brave any danger for the sake of the wounded soldiers. This courage in the midst of despair, is really greater than that of the battle-field.

The months of July and August, 1862, except a brief visit home, were spent at Harrison's Landing, amid the scenes of distress, disease, wounds and suffering, which abounded there. The malaria of the Chickahominy swamps had done much to demoralize the finest army ever put into the field; tens of thousands were ill with it, and these, with the hosts of wounded accumulated more rapidly than the transports, numerous as they were, could carry them away. Their condition at Harrison's Landing was pitiable; the medical bureau seemed to have shared in the general demoralization. The proper diet, the necessai-y hospital arrangements, everything required for the soldiers' restoration to health, was wanting; the pasty, adhesive mud was everywhere, and the hospital tents, old, mildewed, and leaky, were pitched in it, and no floors provided; hard tack, salt junk, fat salt pork, and cold, greasy bean soup, was the diet provided for men suffering from typhoid fever, and from wounds which rendered liquid food indispensable. Soft bread was promised, but was not obtained till just before the breaking up of the encampment. Nor was the destitution of hospital clothing less complete. In that disastrous retreat across the peninsula, many of the men had lost their knapsacks; the government did not provide shirts, drawers, undershirts, as well as mattresses, sheets, blankets, etc., in anything like the quantity needed, and men had often lain for weeks without a change of clothing, in the mud and filth. So far as a few zealous workers could do it, Mrs. Harris, and her willing and active coadjutors sought to remedy these evils; the clothing, and the more palatable and appropriate food they could and did provide for most of those who remained. Having accomplished all for these which she could, and the army having left the James River, after spending a few days at the hospitals near Fortress Monroe, Mrs. Harris came up the Potomac in one of the Government transports, reaching Alexandria on the 31st of August. Here she found ample employment in bestowing her tender care upon the thousands of wounded from Pope's campaigns.

On the 8th of September, she followed, with her supplies, the army on its march toward South Mountain and Antietam. She reached Antietam the day after the battle, and from that time till the 3rd of November, aided by a corps of most devoted and earnest laborers in the work of mercy, among whom were Mrs. M. M. Husband, Miss M. M, C. Hall, Mrs. Mary W. Lee, Miss Tyson, and others. Mrs. Harris gave herself to the work of caring for the wounded. Sad were the sights she was often called to witness. She bore ample testimony to the patience and the uncomplaining spirit of our soldiers; to their filial devotion, to the deep love of home, and the dear ones left behind, which would be manifested in the dying hour, by brave, noble-hearted men, and to the patriotism which even in the death agony, made them rejoice to lay down their lives for their country.

Early in November, 1862, Mrs. Harris left Smoketown General Hospital, near Antietam, and came to Washington. In the hospitals in and around that city thirty thousand sick and wounded men were lying, some of them well and tenderly cared for, some like those in the Parole and Convalescent Camps near Alexandria, (the "Camp Misery" of those days), suffering from all possible privations. She did all that she could to supply the more pressing needs of these poor men. After a few weeks spent in the vicinity of the Capitol, news of the disastrous battle of Fredericksburg came to Washington. Though deeply depressed by the intelligence, she hastened to the front to do what she could for the thousands of sufferers. From this time till about the middle of June, 1863, Mrs. Harris had her quarters in the Lacy House, Falmouth, and aided by Mrs. Beck and Mrs. Lee, worked faithfully for the soldiers, taking measures to re eve and cure the ailing, and to prevent illness from the long and severe exposures to which the troops were subject on picket duty, or special marches, through that stormy and inclement winter. This work was in addition to that in the camp and field hospitals of the Sixth Corps. Another part of her work and one of special interest and usefulness, was the daily and Sabbath worship at her rooms, in which such of the soldiers as were disposed, participated. The contrabands were also the objects of her sympathy and care, and she assembled them for religious worship and instruction on the Sabbath.

But the invasion of Pennsylvania was approaching, and she went forward to Harrisburg, which was at first thought to be threatened, on the 25th of June. After two or three days, finding that there was no probability of an immediate battle there, she returned to Philadelphia, and thence to Washington, which she reached on the 30th of June. The next three days were spent in the effort to forward hospital stores, and obtain transportation to Gettysburg. The War Department then, as in most of the great battles previously, refused to grant this privilege, and though she sought with tears and her utmost powers of persuasion, the permission to forward a single car-load of stores, she was denied, even on the 3rd of July. She could not be restrained, however, from going where she felt that her services would be imperatively needed, and at five P. M., of the 3rd of July, she left Washington carrying only some chloroform and a few stimulants, reached Westminster at four A. M., of the 4th, and was carried to the battle-field of Gettysburg, in the ambulance which had brought the wounded General Hancock to Westminster. The next week was spent day and night amid the horrors of that field of blood, horrors which no pen can describe. That she and her indefatigable aid, (this time a young lady from Philadelphia), were able to alleviate a vast amount of suffering, to give nourishment to many who were famishing; to dress hundreds of wounds, and to point the dying sinner to the Saviour, or whisper words of consolation to the agonized heart, was certain. On the night of the 10th of July, Mrs. Harris and her friend Miss B. left for Frederick, Maryland, where a battle was expected; but as only skirmishing took place, they kept on to Warrenton and Warrenton Junction, where their labors were incessant in earing for the great numbers of wounded and sick in the hospitals. Constant labor had so far impaired her health, that on the 18th of August she attempted to get away from her work for a few days rest; but falling in with the sick men of the Sixth Michigan Cavalry, she went to work with her usual zeal to prepare food and comforts for them, and when they were supplied returned to her work; going to Culpepper Court House, where there were four hospitals, and remaining there till the last of September.

The severe battle of Chickamauga, occurring on the 19th and 20th of September, roused her to the consciousness of the great field for labor, offered by the Western armies, and about the 1st of October, she went to Nashville, Tennessee, taking her friends Miss Tyson and Mrs. Beck with her. It was her intention to go on to Chattanooga, but she found it impossible at that time to procure transportation, and she and her friends at once commenced work among the refugees, the "poor white trash," who were then crowding into Nashville. For a month and more they labored zealously, and with good results, among these poor, ignorant, but loyal people, and then Mrs. Harris, after a visit to Louisville to provide for the inmates of the numerous hospitals in Nashville, a Thanksgiving dinner, pushed forward to the front, reaching Bridgeport, on the 28th of November, and Chattanooga the next day. Here she found abundant work, but her protracted labors had overtasked her strength, and she was for several weeks so ill that her life was despaired of. She was unable to resume her labors until the latter part of January, 1864, and then she worked with a will for the half-starved soldiers in the hospitals, among whom scurvy and hospital gangrene were prevailing. After two months of faithful labor among these poor fellows, she went back to Nashville, and spent four or five months more among the refugees. She returned home early in May, 1864, hoping to take a brief period of rest, of which she was in great need; but two weeks later, she was in Fredericksburg, attending to the vast numbers of wounded brought from the battles of the Wilderness and Spottsylvania, and followed on with that sad procession of the wounded, the dead, and the dying, to Port Royal, White House, and City Point. Never had been there so much need for her labors, and she toiled on, though suffering from constant prostration of strength, until the close of June, when she was obliged to relinquish labor for a time, and restore the almost exhausted vital forces. In September, she was again in the field, this time with the Army of the Shenandoah, at Winchester, where she ministered to the wounded for some weeks. She was called home to attend her mother in her last illness, and for three or four months devoted herself to this sacred duty. Early in the spring of 1865, she visited North Carolina, and all the sympathy of her nature was called out in behalf of the poor released prisoners from Andersonville and Salisbury, to whom she ministered with her usual faithfulness. At the close of the war, she returned to her home, more an invalid than ever from the effects of a sun-stroke received while in attendance on a field hospital in Virginia.

MRS. ELIZA C. PORTER

MRS. ELIZA C. PORTER, the subject of the following sketch, is the wife of the Rev. Jeremiah Porter, a Presbyterian clergyman of Chicago, Illinois.

Of all the noble band of Western women who during the late war devoted time, thought, and untiring exertions to the care of our country's defenders, very few, if any are more worthy of honorable mention, and the praise of a grateful nation, than Mrs. Porter. Freely she gave all, withholding not even the most precious of her possessions and efforts—her husband, her sons, her time and strength, the labor of hands and brain, and, above all, her prayers. Few indeed at a time when sacrifices were general, and among the women of our country the rule rather than the exception, made greater sacrifices than she. Her home was broken up, and the beloved circle scattered, each member in his or her own appropriate sphere, actively engaged in the great work which the war unfolded.

A correspondent thus describes Mrs. Porter; "Mrs. Porter is from forty-five to fifty years of age, a quiet, modest, lady-like woman, very gentle in her manners, and admirably qualified to soothe, comfort and care for the sick and wounded." But this description, by no means includes, or does justice to the admirable fitness for the work which her labors have developed, her quiet energy, her great executive and organizing ability, and her tact ever displayed in doing and saying the right thing at precisely the right time. Of the value of this latter qualification few can form an estimate who have not seen excellent and praiseworthy exertions so often wither unfruitfully for the lack alone of an adjunct so nearly indispensable.

Mrs. Porter was early stimulated to exertion and sacrifice. In the spring of 1861, immediately after the breaking out of the war, while sitting one morning at her breakfast table, her husband, eldest son and two nephews being present, she exclaimed fervently; "If I had a hundred sons, I would gladly send them all forth to this work of putting down the rebellion."

The three young men then present all entered the army. One of them after three years' service was disabled by wounds and constant labor. The other two gave themselves anew to their country, all they could give.

During the summer of 1861 Mrs. Porter visited Cairo where hospitals had been established, and in her labors and experiences there carried what things were most needed by the sick and wounded soldiers. In October of that year, Illinois was first roused to co-operation in the work of the Sanitary Commission. The Northwestern Sanitary Commission was established, and at the request of Mr. E. W. Blatchford and others, Mrs. Porter was induced to take charge of the Commission Rooms which were opened in Chicago. Her zeal and abilities, as well as the hospital experiences of the summer, had fitted her for the arduous task, and as opening to her a field of great usefulness, she accepted the appointment. How she devoted herself to that work, at what sacrifice of family comfort, and with what success, is well known to the Commission, and to thousands of its early contributors.

In April, 1862, she became satisfied that she could be more useful in the field, by taking good nurses to the army hospitals, and herself laboring with them. Pier husband, who the previous winter had been commissioned as Chaplain of the First Illinois Light Artillery, was then at Cairo, where he had been ordered to labor in hospitals; and Mrs. Porter, visiting Cairo and Paducah, entered earnestly into the work of placing the nurses she had brought with her from Chicago. Some of these devoted themselves constantly to the service, and proved equally successful and valuable.

At Cairo, Mrs. Porter made the acquaintance of Miss Mary J. Safford, since known as the "Cairo Angel," and co-operating with her there, and with Mr. Porter and various surgeons and philanthropists, aided in receiving, and temporarily caring for seven hundred men from the field of Pittsburgh Landing, and in transferring them to the hospitals of Mound City, Illinois.

From four o'clock in the morning until ten at night, Mrs. Porter and her friends labored, and then, their work accomplished and their suffering charges made as comfortable as circumstances would permit, they were forced, by the absence of hotel accommodations, to spend the night upon the steamer where the staterooms being occupied, they slept upon chairs.

Soon afterward she went, accompanied by Miss Safford, to Pittsburgh Landing. There she obtained from the Medical Director, Dr. Charles McDougal, an order for several female nurses for his department. She hastened to Chicago, secured them, and accompanying them to Tennessee placed them at Savannah with Mrs. Mary Bickerdyke, who had been with the wounded since the battle of Shiloh. From thence she went to Corinth, then just taken by General Grant. She was accompanied by several benevolent ladies from Chicago, like herself bent on doing good to the sick and wounded. At Corinth she joined her husband, and he being ordered to join his regiment at Memphis, she went thither in his company.

Here, principally in the hospital of the First Light' Artillery at Fort Pickering, she labored through the summer of 1862, and afterwards returned to visit some of the southern towns of Illinois in search of stores from the farmers, which she added to the supplies forwarded by the Commission.

While at Memphis, Airs. Porter became deeply interested in the welfare of the escaped slaves and their families congregated there.

Receiving aid from friends at the North, she organized a school for them, and spent all her leisure hours in giving them instruction. One of the nurses she had brought thither desired to aid in the work, and obtaining needful books and charts she organized a school for Miss Humphrey at Shiloh.

Mrs. Porter was very successful in this work. In her youth she had gathered an infant school among the half-breed children at Mackinac and Point St. Ignace, and understood well how to deal with these minds scarce awakened from the dense slumber of ignorance.

The school flourished, and others entered into the work, and other schools were established. Ministering to their temporal wants as well, clothing, feeding, medicating these unfortunate people, visiting their hospitals as well as those of the army, Mrs. Porter remained at Memphis and in its vicinity until June, 1863.

Her schools having by that time become well-established, and general interest in the scheme awakened, Mrs. Porter felt herself constrained to once more devote herself exclusively to the soldiers, a large number of whom were languishing in Southern hospitals in an unhealthy climate. Failing in her attempts to get them rapidly removed to the North, through correspondence with the Governors of Ohio and Illinois, she went North for the purpose of obtaining interviews with these gentlemen. At Green Bay, Wisconsin, she joined Mrs. Governor Harvey, who was striving to obtain a State Hospital for Wisconsin. Here she proposed to Senator T. O. Howe to draft a petition to the President, praying for the establishment of such hospitals. Judge Howe was greatly pleased to comply, and accordingly drew up the petition to which Mrs. Howe and others obtained over eight thousand names. Mrs. Harvey desired Mrs. Porter to accompany her to Washington with the petition, but she declined, and

Mrs. Harvey went alone, and as the result of her efforts, succeeded in the establishment of the Harvey Hospital at Madison, Wisconsin.

Other parties took up the matter in Illinois, and Mrs. Porter returned to her beloved work at the South, visiting Natchez and Vicksburg. At the latter place she joined Mrs. Harvey and Mrs. Bickerdyke, all three ministering by Sanitary stores and personal aid to the sick and wounded in hospitals and regiments.

While on her way, at Memphis, she learned that the battery, in which were her eldest son and a nephew, had gone 'with Sherman's army toward Corinth, and started by rail to overtake them. At Corinth, standing in the room of the Sanitary Commission, she saw the battery pass in which were her boys. It was raining, and mud-bespattered and drenched, her son rode by in an ague chill, and could only give her a look of recognition as he passed on to the camp two miles beyond. The next morning she went out to his camp, but missed him, and returning found him at the Sanitary Rooms in another chill. The next day she nursed him through a third chill, and then parting she sent her sick boy on his way toward Knoxville and Chattanooga.

After a short stay at Vicksburg she once more returned to Illinois to plead with Governor Yates to bring home his disabled soldiers, then went back, by way of Louisville and Nashville, to Huntsville,

Alabama, where she met and labored indefatigably with Mrs. Lincoln Clark and her daughter, of Chicago, and Mrs. Bickerdyke.

After a few weeks spent there in comforting the sick, pointing the dying to the Saviour, and ministering to surgeons, officers, and soldiers, she followed our conquering arms to Chattanooga, Resaca, Kingston, Allatoona Pass, Marietta and Atlanta.

As a memorial of her earlier movements in this campaign, we extract the following letter from the Report for January and February, 1864, of the Northwestern Sanitary Commission.

"From a mass of deeply interesting correspondence on hand, we select the following letter from Rev. Mrs. Jeremiah Porter, who, with Mrs. Bickerdyke, the widely known and very efficient Hospital Matron, has been laboring in the hospitals of the 15th Army Corps, most of the time since the battle of Chickamauga mrs. Bickerdyke was assigned to hospital duty in this corps, at the request of General Sherman, and is still actively engaged there. This letter affords glimpses of the hardships and privations of our brave men, whose sufferings in Southern and Eastern ' Tennessee during the months of December and January, have been unparalleled."

"IN CAMP, NOVEMBER 4TH, FIELD HOSPITAL,

"CHATTANOOGA, January 24, 1864.

"I reached this place on New Year's Eve, making the trip of the few miles from Bridgeport to Chattanooga, in twenty-four hours. New Year's morning was very cold. I went immediately to the Field Hospital about two miles out of town, where I found Mrs. Bickerdyke hard at work, as usual, endeavoring to comfort the cold and suffering, sick and wounded. The work done on that day told most happily on the comfort of the poor wounded men.

"The wind came sweeping around Lookout Mountain, and uniting with currents from the valleys of Mission Ridge, pressed in upon the hospital tents, overturning some, and making the inmates of all tremble with cold and anxious fear. The cold had been preceded by a great rain, which added to the general discomfort. Mrs. Bickerdyke went from tent to tent in the gale, carrying hot bricks and hot drinks to warm and to cheer the poor fellows. 'She is a power of good,' said one soldier. 'We fared mighty poor till she came here said another. 'God bless the Sanitary Commission,' said a third, 'for sending women among us!' The soldiers fully appreciate 'Mother Bickerdyke as they call her, and her work.

"Mrs. Bickerdyke left Vicksburg at the request of General Sherman, and other officers of his corps, as they wished to secure her services for the then approaching battle. The Field Hospital of the 15th (Sherman's) Army Corps, was situated on the north bank of the Genesee river, on a slope at the base of Mission Ridge, where, after the struggle was over, seventeen hundred of our wounded and exhausted soldiers were brought. Mrs. Bickerdyke reached there before the din and smoke of battle were well over, and before all were brought from the field of blood and carnage. There she remained the only female attendant for four weeks. Never has she rendered more valuable service. Dr. Newberry arrived in Chattanooga with Sanitary goods which Mrs. Bickerdyke had the pleasure of using, as she says, 'just when and where needed and never were Sanitary goods more deeply felt to be good goods. 'What could we do without them?' is a question I often hear raised, and answered with a hearty 'God bless the Sanitary Commission!' which is now, everywhere, acknowledged as a great power for good.

"The Field Hospital was in a forest, about five miles from Chattanooga, wood was abundant, and the camp was warmed by immense burning 'log heaps which were the only fire-places or cooking-stoves of the camp or hospitals. Men were detailed to fell the trees and pile the logs to heat the air, which was very wintry. And beside them Mrs. Bickerdyke made soup and toast, tea and coffee, and broiled mutton, without a gridiron, often blistering her fingers in the process. A house in due time was demolished to make bunks for the worst cases, and the brick from the chimney was converted into an oven, when Mrs. Bickerdyke made bread, yeast having been found in the Chicago boxes, and flour at a neighboring mill, which had furnished flour to secessionists through the war until now. Great multitudes were fed from these rude kitchens. Companies of hungry soldiers were refreshed before those open fire-places, and from those ovens. On one occasion, a citizen came and told the men to follow him, he would show them a reserve of beef and sheep which had been provided for General Bragg's army, and about thirty head of cattle and twenty sheep was the prize. Large potash kettles were found, which were used over the huge log fires, and various kitchen utensils for cooking were brought into camp from time to time, almost every day adding to our conveniences. After four weeks of toil and labor, all the soldiers who were able to leave were furloughed home, and the rest brought to the large hospital where I am now located. About nine hundred men are here, most of them convalescents, and waiting anxiously to have the men and mules supplied with food, so that they may have the benefit of the cars, which have been promised to take them home.

"There was great joy in the encampment last week, at the announcement of the arrival of a train of cars from Bridgeport. You at home can have little appreciation of the feelings of the men as that sound greeted their ears. Our poor soldiers had been reduced to half and quarter rations for weeks, and those of the poorest quality. The mules had fallen by the wayside from very starvation. You cannot go a mile in any direction without seeing these animals lying dead from starvation—and this state of things had to continue until the railroad was finished to Chattanooga, and the cars could bring in sustenance for man and beast. You will not wonder then at the huzzas of the men in the hospitals and camps, as the whistle of the long looked for train was heard.

"The most harrowing scenes are daily witnessed here. A wife came on yesterday only to learn that her dear husband had died the morning previous. Her lamentations were heart-breaking. 'Why could he not have lived until I came? Why?' In the evening came a sister, whose aged parents had sent her to search for their only son. She also came too late. The brother had gone to the soldier's grave two days previous. One continued wail of sorrow goes up from all parts of this stricken land.

"I have protracted this letter, I fear, until you are weary. I write in great haste, not knowing how to take the time from pressing duties which call me everywhere. Yours, etc.,

"ELIZA C. PORTER."

In illustration of her services at this time, and of the undercurrent of terror and sadness of this triumphal march, we can do no better than to give some extracts from her journal, kept during this period, and published without her knowledge in the Sanitary Commission Bulletin. It was commenced on the 15th of May, 1864, as she was following Mrs. Bickerdyke to Binggold, Georgia. Together they arrived at Sugar Creek, where but two miles distant the battle was raging, and spent the night at General Logan's headquarters, within hearing of its terrific sounds. All night, and all day Sunday, they passed thus, not being permitted to go upon the field, but caring for the wounded as rapidly as possible, as they were brought to the rear. She says:

"The wounded were brought into hospitals, quickly and roughly prepared in the forest, as near the field as safety would permit. What a scene was presented! Precious sons of northern mothers, beloved husbands of northern wives were already here to undergo amputation, to have wounds probed and dressed, or broken limbs set and bandaged. Some were writhing under the surgeon's knife, but bore their sufferings bravely and uncomplainingly. There were many whose wounds were considered slight, such as a shot through the hand, arm, or leg, which but for the contrast with severer cases, would seem dreadful. Never was the presence of women more joyfully welcomed. It was touching to see those precious boys looking up into our faces with such hope and gladness. It brought to their minds mother and home, as each testified, while his wounds were being dressed; 'This seems a little like having mother about,' was the reiterated expression of the wounded, as one after another was washed and had his wounds dressed. Mrs. Bickerdyke and myself assisted in the operation. Poor boys! how my heart ached that I could do so little.

"After doing what we could in Hospital No. 1, to render the condition of the poor fellows tolerable, we proceeded to No. 2, and did what we could there, distributing our sanitary comforts in the most economical manner, so as to make them go as far as possible. We found that what we brought in the ambulance was giving untold comfort to our poor exhausted wounded men, whose rough hospital couches were made by pine boughs with the stems cut out, spread upon the ground over which their blankets were thrown. This forms the bed, and the poor fellows blouses, saturated with their own blood, is their only pillow, their knapsacks being left behind when they went into battle. More sanitary goods are on the way, and will be brought to relieve the men as soon as possible."

Amidst all this care for others, there was little thought for her own comfort. She says in another place:

"Our bed was composed of dry leaves, spread with a rubber and soldier's blanket—our own blankets, with pillows and all, having been given out to sufferers long before night."

In this diary we find another illustration of her extreme modesty. Though intended but for the eyes of her own family, she says much of Mrs. Bickerdyke's work, and but little of her own. Two, three, or four hundred men, weary and exhausted, would be sent to them, and they must exert every nerve to feed them, while they snatched a little rest. Pickles, sauer-kraut, coffee and hard bread they gave to these—for the sick and wounded they reserved their precious luxuries. With a fire made out of doors, beneath a burning sun, and in kettles such as they could find, and of no great capacity, they made coffee, mush, and cooked dried fruit and vegetables, toiling unweariedly through the long hot days and far into the nights. Many of the men knew Mrs. Bickerdyke, for many of them she had nursed through 22 wounds and sickness during the two years she had been with this army, and she was saluted as "Mother" on all sides. Not less grateful were they to Mrs. Porter. Again she says:

"The failing and faint-hearted are constantly coming in. They report themselves sick, and a few days of rest and nourishing food will restore most of them, but some have made their last march, and will soon be laid in a soldier's grave! Mrs. Bickerdyke has sent gruel and other food, which I have been distributing according to the wants of the prostrate multitude, all on the floor. Some are very sick men. It is a pleasure to do something for them. They are all dear to some circle, and are a noble company."

Again she gives a sort of summary of her work in a letter, dated Kingston, Georgia, June 1st: "We have received, fed, and comforted at this hospital, during the past week, between four and five thousand wounded men, and still they come. All the food and clothing have passed under our supervision, and, indeed, almost every garment has been given out by our hands. Almost every article of special diet has been cooked by Mrs. Bickerdyke personally, and all has been superintended by her. I speak of this particularly, as it is a wonderful fulfillment of the promise, 'As thy day is, so shall thy strength be.'"

Again, muting from Alatoona, Georgia, June 14th: "I have just visited a tent filled with I amputated cases.' They are noble young men, the pride and hope of loving families at the North, but most of them are so low that they will never again return to them. Each had a special request for something that he could relish.' I made my way quickly down from the heights, where the hospital tents are pitched, and sought for the food they craved. I found it among the goods of the Sanitary Commission—and now the dried currants, cherries, and other fruit are stewing; we have unsoddered cans containing condensed milk and preserved fruit—and the poor fellows will not be disappointed in their expectations."

In the foregoing sketch we have given but a very brief statement of the labors and sacrifices of Mrs. Porter which were not intermitted until the close of the war. We have said that her sons were in the army. Her eldest son re-enlisted at the close of his first term, and the youngest, after a hundred days' service, returned to college to fit himself for future usefulness in his regenerated country. Mr. Porter's services, as well as those of his wife were of great value, and her son, James B. Porter, though serving as a private only, in Battery A, First Illinois Light Artillery, has had frequent and honorable mention.'

At the close of Sherman's campaign Mrs. Porte; finished her army service by caring for the travel-worn and wearied braves as they came into camp at Washington where, with Mrs. Stephen Barker and others, she devoted herself to the distribution of sanitary stores, attending the sick and in various ways comforting and relieving all who needed her aid after the toils of the Grand March.

MRS. MARY A. BICKERDYKE

AMONG the hundreds who with untiring devotion have consecrated their services to the ministrations of mercy in the Armies of the Union, there is but one "Mother" Bickerdyke. Others may in various ways have made as great sacrifices, or displayed equal heroism, but her measures and methods have been peculiarly her own, and "none but herself can be her parallel."

She is a widow, somewhat above forty years of age, of humble origin, and of but moderate education, with a robust frame and great powers of endurance, and possessing a rough stirring eloquence, a stern, determined will and extraordinary executive ability. No woman connected with the philanthropic work of the army has encountered more obstacles in the accomplishment of her purposes, and none ever carried them through more triumphantly. She has two little sons, noble boys, to whom she is devotedly attached, but her patriotic zeal was even stronger than her love for her children, and she gave herself up to the cause of her country most unhesitatingly.

At the commencement of the war, she was, it is said, housekeeper in the family of a gentleman in Cleveland, but she commenced her labors among the sick and wounded men of the army very early, and never relinquished her work until the close of the conflict. It has been one of her peculiarities that she devoted her attention almost exclusively to the care of the private soldiers; the officers, she said, had enough to look after them; but it was the men, poor fellows, with but a private's pay, a private's fare, and a private's dangers, to whom she was particularly called. They were dear to somebody, and she would be a mother to them. And it should be said, to the honor of the private soldiers of the Western Armies, that they returned her kindness with very decided gratitude and affection. If they were her "boys" as she always insisted, she was "Mother Bickerdyke" to the whole army. Nothing could exceed the zeal and earnestness with which she has always defended their interests. For her "boys," she would brave everything; if the surgeons or attendants at the hospitals were unfaithful, she denounced them with a terrible vehemence, and always managed to secure their dismission; if the Government officers were slow or delinquent in forwarding needed supplies, they were sure to be reported at headquarters by her, and in such a way that their conduct would be thoroughly investigated. Yet while thus stern and vindictive toward those who through negligence or malice wronged the soldiers of the army, no one could be more tender in dealing with the sick and wounded. On the battlefield, in the field, camp, post or general hospitals, her vigorous arm was ever ready to lift the wounded soldier as tenderly as his own mother could have done, and her ready skill was exerted with equal facility in dressing his wounds, or in preparing such nourishment for him as should call back his fleeting strength or tempt his fickle and failing appetite. She was a capital forager, and for the sake of a sick soldier she would undergo any peril or danger, and violate military rules without the least hesitation. For herself she craved nothing—would accept nothing—if "the boys in the hospital" could be provided for, she was supremely happy. The soldiers were ready to do anything in their power for her, while the contrabands regarded her almost as a divinity, and would fly with unwonted alacrity to obey her commands.

We are not certain whether she was an assistant in one of the hospitals, or succored the wounded in any of the battles in Kentucky or Missouri, in the autumn of 1861; we believe she was actively engaged in ministering to the "wounded after the fall of Fort Donelson, and at Shiloh after the battle she rendered great and important services. It was here, or rather at Savannah, Tennessee, where one of the largest hospitals was established, soon after the battle, and placed in her charge, that she first met Mrs. Eliza C. Porter, who was afterward during Sherman's Grand March her associate and companion. Mrs. Porter brought from Chicago a number of nurses, whom she placed under Mrs. Bickerdyke's charge.

The care of this hospital occupied Mrs. Bickerdyke for some months, and we lose sight of her till the battle of Perrysville where amid difficulties which would have appalled any ordinary spirit, she succeeded in dressing the wounds of the soldiers and supplying them with nourishment. But with her untiring energy, she was not satisfied with this. Collecting a large number of negro women who had escaped from the plantations along the route of the Union Army, she set them to work gathering the blankets and clothing left on the field, and such of the clothing of the slain and desperately wounded as could be spared, and having superintended the washing and repairing of these articles, distributed them to the wounded who were in great need of additional clothing. She also caused her corps of contrabands to pick up all the arms and accoutrements left on the field, and turn them over to the Union Quartermaster. Having returned after a time to Louisville, she was appointed Matron of the Gayoso Hospital, at Memphis. This hospital occupied the Gayoso House, formerly the largest hotel in Memphis. It was Mrs. Bickerdyke's ambition to make this the best hospital of the six or eight in the city, some of them buildings erected for hospital purposes. A large hotel is not the best structure for a model hospital, but before her energy and industry all obstacles disappeared. By an Army regulation or custom, convalescent soldiers were employed as nurses, attendants and ward-masters in the hospitals; an arrangement which though on some accounts desirable, yet was on others objectionable. The soldiers not yet fully recovered, were often weak, and incapable of the proper performance of their duties; they were often, also, peevish and fretful, and from sheer weakness slept at their posts, to the detriment of the patients. It was hardly possible with such assistance to maintain that perfect cleanliness so indispensable for a hospital. Mrs. Bickerdyke determined from the first that she would not have these convalescents as nurses and attendants in her hospital. Selecting carefully the more intelligent of the negro women who flocked into Memphis in great numbers, she assigned to them the severer work of the hospital, the washing, cleaning, waiting upon the patients, and with the aid of some excellent women nurses, paid by Government, she soon made her hospital by far the best regulated one in the city. The cleanliness and ventilation were perfect. The patients were carefully and tenderly nursed, their medicine administered at the required intervals, and the preparation of the special diet being wholly under Mrs. Bickerdyke's supervision, herself a cook of remarkable skill, was admirably done. Nothing escaped her vigilance, and under her watchful care, the affairs of the hospital were admirably managed. She would not tolerate any neglect of the men, either on the part of attendants, assistant surgeons or surgeons.

On one occasion, visiting one of the wards containing the badly wounded men, at nearly eleven o'clock, A. M., she found that the assistant surgeon, in charge of that ward, who had been out on a drunken spree the night before, and had slept very late, had not yet made out the special diet list for the ward, and the men, faint and hungry, had had no breakfast. She denounced him at once in the strongest terms, and as he came in, and with an attempt at jollity inquired, "Hoity-toity, what's the matter?" she turned upon him with "Matter enough, you miserable scoundrel! Here these men, any one of them worth a thousand of you, are suffered to starve and die, because you want to be off upon a drunk! Pull off your shoulder-straps," she continued, as he tried feebly to laugh off her reproaches, "pull off your shoulder-straps, for you shall not stay in the army a week longer." The surgeon still laughed, but he turned pale, for he knew her power. She was as good as her word. Within three days she had caused his discharge. He went to headquarters and asked to be reinstated. Major-General Sherman, who was then in command, listened patiently, and then inquired who had procured his discharge. "I was discharged in consequence of misrepresentation," answered the surgeon, evasively. "But who caused your discharge?" persisted the general. Why," said the surgeon, hesitatingly, "I suppose it was that woman, that Mrs. Bickerdyke." "Oh!" said Sherman, "well, if it was her, I can do nothing for you. She ranks me."

We may say in this connection, that the commanding generals of the armies in which Mrs. Bickerdyke performed her labors, Generals Sherman, Hurlburt, Grant, and Sherman again, in his great march, having become fully satisfied how invaluable she was in her care of the private soldiers, were always ready to listen to her appeals and to grant her requests. She was, in particular, a great favorite with both Grant and Sherman, and had only to ask for anything she needed to get it, if it was within the power of the commander to obtain it. It should be said in justice to her, that she never asked anything for herself, and that her requests were always for something that would promote the welfare of the men.

Some months after the discharge of the assistant surgeon, the surgeon in charge of the hospital, who was a martinet in discipline, and somewhat irritated for some cause, resolved, in order to annoy her, to compel the discharge of the negro nurses and attendants, and require her to employ convalescent soldiers, as the other hospitals were doing. For this purpose he procured from the medical director an order that none but convalescent soldiers should be employed as nurses in the Memphis hospitals. The order was issued, probably, without any knowledge of the annoyance it was intended to cause Mrs. Bickerdyke. It was to take effect at nine o'clock the following morning. Mrs. Bickerdyke heard of it just at night. The Gayoso Hospital was nearly three-fourths of a mile from headquarters. It was raining heavily, and the mud was deep; but she was not the woman to be thwarted in her plans by a hospital surgeon, without a struggle; so, nothing daunted, she sallied out, having first had the form of an order drawn up, permitting the employment of contrabands as nurses, at the Gayoso Hospital. Arrived at headquarters, she was told that the commanding general, Sherman's successor, was ill and could not be seen. Suspecting that his alleged illness was only another name for over-indulgence in strong drink, she insisted that she must and would see him, and in spite of the objections of his staff-officers, forced her way to his room, and finding him in bed, roused him partially, propped him up, put a pen in his hand, and made him sign the order she had brought. This done, she returned to her hospital, and the next morning, when the surgeon and medical director came around to enforce the order of the latter, she quietly handed them the order of the commanding general, permitting her to retain her contrabands.

While in charge of this hospital, she made several journeys to Chicago and other cities of the Northwest, to procure aid for the suffering soldiers. The first of these were characteristic of her energy and resolution. She had found great difficulty in procuring, in the vicinity of Memphis, the milk, butter, and eggs needed for her hospital. She had foraged from the secessionists, had traded with them her own clothing and whatever else she could spare, for these necessaries for her "boys," until there was nothing more left to trade. The other hospitals were in about the same condition. She resolved, therefore, to have a dairy for the hospitals. Going among the farmers of Central Illinois, she begged two hundred cows and a thousand hens, and returned in with her flock of hens and her drove of cows. On reaching Memphis, her cattle and fowls made such a lowing and cackling, that the secessionists of the city entered their complaints to the commanding general, who assigned her an island in the Mississippi, opposite the city, where her dairy and hennery were comfortably accommodated. It was we believe, while on this expedition that, at the request of Mrs. Hoge and Mrs. Livermore, the Associate Managers of the Northwestern Sanitary Commission, she visited Milwaukie, Wisconsin. The Ladies' Aid Society of that city had memorialized their Chamber of Commerce to make an appropriation to aid them in procuring supplies for the wounded soldiers, and were that day to receive the reply of the chamber.

Mrs. Bickerdyke went with the ladies, and the President of the Chamber, in his blandest tones, informed them that the Chamber of Commerce had considered their request, but that they had expended so much recently in fitting out a regiment, that they thought they must be excused from making any contributions to the Ladies' Aid Society. Mrs. Bickerdyke asked the privilege of saying a few words in the way of answer. For half an hour she held them enchained while she described, in simple but eloquent language, the life of the private soldier, his privations and sufferings, the patriotism which animated him, and led him to endure, without murmuring, hardships, sickness, and even death itself, for his country. She contrasted this with the sordid love of gain which not only shrank from these sacrifices in person, but grudged the pittance necessary to alleviate them, while it made the trifling amount it had already contributed, an excuse for making no further donations, and closed with this forcible denunciation: "And you, merchants and rich men of Milwaukie, living at your ease, dressed in your broad-cloth, knowing little and caring less for the sufferings of these soldiers from hunger and thirst, from cold and nakedness, from sickness and wounds, from pain and death, all incurred that you may roll in wealth, and your homes and little ones be safe; you will refuse to give aid to these poor soldiers, because, forsooth, you gave a few dollars some time ago to fit out a regiment! Shame on you— you are not men—you are cowards—go over to Canada—this country has no place for such creatures!" The Chamber of Commerce was not prepared for such a rebuke, and they reconsidered their action, and made an appropriation at once to the Ladies' Aid Society.

Immediately after the surrender of Vicksburg, Mrs. Bickerdyke surrendered her hospital at Memphis into other hands, and went thither to care for the wounded. She accompanied Sherman's corps in their expedition to Jackson, and amid all the hardships and exposures of the field, ministered to the sick and wounded. Cooking for them in the open air, under the burning sun and the heavy dews, she was much exposed to the malarious fevers of that sickly climate, but her admirable constitution enabled her to endure fatigue and exposure, better even than most of the soldiers. Though always neat and cleanly in person, she was indifferent to the attractions of dress, and amid the flying sparks from her fires in the open air, her calico dresses would often take fire, and as she expressed it, "the soldiers would put her out," i e. extinguish the sparks which were burning her dresses. In this way it happened that she had not a single dress which had not been more or less riddled by these sparks. With her clothing in this plight she visited Chicago again late in • the summer of 1863, and the ladies of the Sanitary Commission replenished her wardrobe, and soon after sent her a box of excellent clothing for her own use. Some of the articles in this box, the gift of those who admired her earnest devotion to the interests of the soldiers, were richly wrought and trimmed. Among these were two elegant night dresses, trimmed with ruffles and lace. On receiving the box, Mrs. Bickerdyke, who was again for the time in charge of a hospital, reserving for herself only a few of the plainest and cheapest articles, traded off the remainder, except the two night dresses, with the rebel women of the vicinity, for butter, eggs, and other delicacies for her sick soldiers, and as she purposed going to Cairo soon, and thought that the night dresses would bring more for the same purpose in Tennessee or Kentucky, she reserved them to be traded on her journey. On her way, however, at one of the towns on the Mobile and Ohio railroad, she found two poor fellows who had been discharged from some of the hospitals with their wounds not yet fully healed, and their exertions in traveling had caused them to break out afresh. Here they were, in a miserable shanty, sick, bleeding, hungry, penniless, and with only their soiled clothing. Mrs. Bickerdyke at once took them in hand. Washing their wounds and staunching the blood, she tore off the lower portions of the night dresses for bandages, and as the men had no shirts, she arrayed them in the remainder of these dresses, ruffles, lace, and all. The soldiers modestly demurred a little at the ruffles and lace, but Mrs. Bickerdyke suggested to them that if any inquiries were made, they could say that they had been plundering the secessionists.

Visiting Chicago at this time, she was again invited to Milwaukie, and went with the ladies to the Chamber of Commerce. Here she was very politely received, and the President informed her that the Chamber feeling deeply impressed with the good work, she and the other ladies v ere doing in behalf of the soldiers, had voted a contribution of twelve hundred dollars a month to the Ladies' Aid Society. Mrs. Bickerdyke was not, however, disposed to tender them the congratulations, to which perhaps they believed themselves entitled for their liberality. "You believe yourselves very generous, no doubt, gentlemen," she said, "and think that because you have voted this pretty sum, you are doing all that is required of you. But I have in my hospital a hundred poor soldiers who have done more than any of you. Who of you would contribute a leg, an arm, or an eye, instead of what you have done? How many hundred or thousand dollars would you consider an equivalent for either? Don't deceive yourselves, gentlemen. The poor soldier who has given an arm, a leg, or an eye to his country (and many of them have given more than one) has given more than you have or can. How much more, then, he who has given his life? No! gentlemen, you must set your standard higher yet or you will not come up to the full measure of liberality in giving."

On her return to the South Mrs. Bickerdyke spent a few weeks at Huntsville, Alabama, in charge of a hospital, and then joined Sherman's Fifteenth Corps in their rapid march toward Chattanooga. It will be remembered that Sherman's Corps, or rather the Army of the Tennessee which he now commanded were hurried into action immediately on their arrival at Chattanooga. To them was assigned the duty of making the attack against that portion of the enemy who were posted on the northern termination of Mission Ridge, and the persistent assaults on Fort Buckner were attended with severe slaughter, though they made the victory elsewhere possible. The Field Hospital of the Fifteenth Army Corps was situated on the north bank of the Genesee River, on a slope at the base of Mission Ridge, where after the struggle was over seventeen hundred of our wounded and exhausted soldiers were brought. Mrs. Bickerdyke reached there before the din and smoke of battle were well over, and before all were brought from the field of blood and carnage. There she remained the only female attendant for four weeks. The supplies she had been able to bring with her soon gave out, but Dr. Newberry, the Western Secretary of the Sanitary Commission, presently arrived with an ample supply which she used freely.

The Field Hospital was in a forest, about five miles from Chattanooga; wood was abundant, and the camp was warmed by immense burning log heaps, which were the only fire-places or cooking-stoves of the camp or hospitals. Men were detailed to fell the trees and pile the logs to heat the air, which was very wintry. Beside these fires Mrs. Bickerdyke made soup and toast, tea and coffee, and broiled mutton without a gridiron, often blistering her fingers in the process. A house in due time was demolished to make bunks for the worst cases, and the bricks from the chimney were converted into an oven, where Mrs. Bickerdyke made bread, yeast having been found in the Chicago boxes, and flour at a neighboring mill which had furnished flour to secessionists through the war until that time. Great multitudes were fed from these rude kitchens, and from time to time other conveniences were added and the labor made somewhat less exhausting. After four weeks of severe toil all the soldiers who were able to leave were furloughed home, and the remainder, about nine hundred, brought to a more comfortable Field Hospital, two miles from Chattanooga. In this hospital Mrs. Bickerdyke continued her work, being joined, New Year's eve, by Mrs. Eliza C. Porter, who thenceforward was her constant associate, both being employed by the Northwestern Sanitary Commission to attend to this work of special field relief in that army. Mrs. Porter says that when she arrived there it was very cold, and the wind which had followed a heavy rain was very piercing, overturning some of the hospital tents and causing the inmates of all to tremble with cold and anxious fear. Mrs. Bickerdyke was going from tent to tent in the gale carrying hot bricks and hot drinks to warm and cheer the poor fellows. It was touching to see the strong attachment the soldiers felt for her. "She is a power of good," said one soldier. "We fared mighty poor till she came here," said another. "God bless the Sanitary Commission," said a third, "for sending women among us." True to her attachment to the private soldiers, Mrs. Bickerdyke early sought an interview with General Grant, and told him in her plain way, that the surgeons in some of the hospitals were great rascals, and neglected the men shamefully; and that unless they were removed and faithful men put in their places, he would lose hundreds and perhaps thousands of his veteran soldiers whom he could ill afford to spare. "You must not," she said, "trust anybody's report in this matter, but see to it yourself. Disguise yourself so that the surgeons or meu won't know you, and go around to the hospitals and see for yourself how the men are neglected."

"But, Mrs. Bickerdyke," said the general, "that is the business of my medical director, he must attend to that. I can't see to everything in person."

"Well," was her reply, "leave it to him if you think best; but if you do you will lose your men."

The general made no promises, but a night or two later the hospitals were visited by a stranger who made very particular inquiries, and within a week about half a dozen surgeons were dismissed and more efficient men put in their places. At the opening of spring, Mrs. Bickerdyke and Mrs. Porter returned to Huntsville and superintended the distribution of Sanitary Supplies in the hospitals there, and at Pulaski and other points.

No sooner was General Sherman prepared to move on his Atlanta Campaign than he sent word to Mrs. Bickerdyke to come up and accompany the army in its march. She accordingly left Huntsville on the 10th of May for Chattanooga, and from thence went immediately to Ringgold, near which town the army was then stationed. As the army moved forward to Dalton and Resaca, she sent forward teams laden with supplies, and followed them in an ambulance the next day. On the 16th of May she and her associate Mrs. Porter proceeded at once to the Field Hospitals which were as near as safety would permit to the hardfought battle-ground of the previous day, washed the wounded, dressed their wounds, and administered to them such nourishment as could be prepared. There was at first seme little delay in the receipt of sanitary stores, but with wonderful tact and ingenuity Mrs. Bickerdyke succeeded in making palatable dishes for the sick from the hard tack, coffee and other items of the soldier's ration. Soon however the sanitary goods came up, and thenceforward, with her rare executive ability the department of special relief for that portion of the army to which she was assigned was maintained in its highest condition of efficiency, in spite of disabilities which would have completely discouraged any woman of less resolution. The diary of her associate, Mrs. Porter, is full of allusions to the extraordinary exertions of Mrs. Bickerdyke during this campaign. We quote two or three as examples.

"To-day every kettle which could be raised has been used in making coffee. Mrs. Bickerdyke has made barrel after barrel, and it is a comfort to know that multitudes are reached, and cheered, and saved. Two hundred and sixty slightly wounded men just came to this point on the cars on their way North, all hungry and weary, saying, 'We are so thirsty 'Do give us something to eat Mrs. Bickerdyke was engaged in giving out supper to the three hundred in wards here, and told them she could not feed them then. They turned away in sorrow and were leaving, when learning who they were—wounded men of the Twentieth Army Corps, and their necessity—she told them to wait a few moments, she would attend to them. She gave them coffee, krout, and potato pickles, which are never eaten but by famished men, and for once they were a luxury. I stood in the room where our supplies were deposited, giving to some crackers, to some pickles, and to each hungry man something. One of the green cards that come on all the stores of the Northwestern Commission Mrs. Bickerdyke had tacked upon the wall, and this told the inquirers from what branch of the Commission the supplies were obtained. The men were mostly from New York, Pennsylvania and New Jersey, and most grateful recipients were they of the generosity of the Northwest. You can imagine the effort made to supply two barrels of coffee with only three camp kettles, two iron boilers holding two pailfuls, one small iron teakettle and one saucepan, to make it in. These all placed over a dry rail-fire were boiled in double-quick time, and were filled and refilled till all had a portion. Chicago canned milk never gave more comfort than on this occasion, I assure you. Our cooking conveniences are muck the same as at Mission Ridge, but there is to be a change soon. The Medical Director informs me that this is to be a recovering hospital, and cooking apparatus will soon be provided."

"Mrs. Bickerdyke was greeted on the street by a soldier on horseback; I Mother said he, 'is that you? Don't you remember me? I was in the hospital, my arm amputated, and I was saved by your kindness. I am so glad to see you,' giving her a beautiful bouquet of roses, the only token of grateful remembrance he could command. Mrs. Bickerdyke daily receives such greetings from men, who say they have been saved from death by her efforts."

"To-day three hundred and twelve men have been fed and comforted here. This morning Mrs. Bickerdyke made mush for two hundred, having gathered up in various places kettles, so that by great effort out of doors she can cook something. Potatoes, received from Iowa, and dried fruit and canned, have been distributed among the men. Many of them are from Iowa. 'What could we do without these stores?' is the constant inquiry."

"Almost every article of special diet has been cooked by Mrs. Bickerdyke personally, and all has been superintended by her."

After the close of the Atlanta Campaign and the convalescence of the greater part of the wounded, Mrs. Bickerdyke returned to Chicago for a brief period of rest, but was soon called to Nashville and Franklin to attend the wounded of General Thomas's Army after the campaign which ended in Hood's utter discomfiture. When Savannah was surrendered she hastened thither, and after organizing the supply department of its hospitals, she and Mrs. Porter, who still accompanied her, established their system of Field Relief in Sherman's Campaign through the Carolinas. When at last in June, 1865, Sherman's veterans reached the National Capitol and were to be mustered out, the Sanitary Commission commenced its work of furnishing the supplies of clothing and other needful articles to these grim soldiers, to make their homeward journey more comfortable and their appearance to their families more agreeable. The work of distribution in the Fifteenth and Seventeenth Army Corps was assigned to Mrs. Bickerdyke and Mrs. Porter, and was performed, says Mrs. Barker, who had the general superintendence of the distribution, admirably. With this labor Mrs. Bickerdyke's connection with the sanitary work of the army ceased. She had, however, been too long engaged in philanthropic labor, to be content to sit down quietly, and lead a life of inaction; and after a brief period of rest, she began to gather the more helpless of the freedmen, in Chicago, and has since devoted her time and efforts to a "Freedmen's Home and Refuge" in that city, in which she is accomplishing great good. Out of the host of zealous workers in the hospitals and in the field, none have borne to their homes in greater measure the hearty and earnest love of the soldiers, as none had been more zealously and persistently devoted to their interests.

MARGARET E. BRECKINRIDGE

A TRUE heroine of the war was Margaret Elizabeth Breckinridge. Patient, courageous, self-forgetting, steady of purpose and cheerful in spirit, she belonged by nature to the heroic order, while all the circumstances of her early life tended to mature and prepare her for her destined work. Had her lot been cast in the dark days of religious intolerance and 'persecution, her steadfast enthusiasm and holy zeal would have earned for her a martyr's cross and crown; but, born in this glorious nineteenth century, and reared in an atmosphere of liberal thought and active humanity, the first spark of patriotism that flashed across the startled North at the outbreak of the rebellion, set all her soul aglow, and made it henceforth an altar of living sacrifice, a burning and a shining light, to the end of her days. Dearer to her gentle spirit than any martyr's crown, must have been the consciousness that this God-given light had proved a guiding beacon to many a faltering soul feeling its way into the dim beyond, out of the drear loneliness of camp or hospital. With her slight form, her bright face, and her musical voice, she seemed a ministering angel to the sick and suffering soldiers, while her sweet womanly purity and her tender devotion to their wants made her almost an object of worship among them. "Ain't she an angel?" said a gray-headed soldier as he watched her one morning as she was busy getting breakfast for the boys on the steamer "City of Alton." "She never seems to tire, she is always smiling, and don't seem to walk—she flies, all but—God bless her!" Another, a soldier boy of seventeen said to her, as she was smoothing his hair and saying cheering words about mother and home to him, "Ma'am, where do you come from? How could such a lady as you are come down here, to take care of us poor, sick, dirty boys?" She answered—"I consider it an honor to wait on you, and wash off the mud you've waded through for me."

Another asked this favor of her, "Lady, please write down your name, and let me look at it, and take it home, to show my wife who wrote my letters, and combed my hair and fed me. I don't believe you're like other people." In one of her letters she says, "I am often touched with their anxiety not to give trouble, not to bother, as they say. That same evening I found a poor, exhausted fellow, lying on a stretcher, on which he had just been brought in. There was no bed for him just then, and he was to remain there for the present, and looked uncomfortable enough, with his knapsack for a pillow. 'I know some hot tea will do you good,' I said. 'Yes, ma'am,' he answered, 'but I am too weak to sit up with nothing to lean against;

it's no matter,— don't bother about me,' but his eyes were fixed longingly on the smoking tea. Everybody was busy, not even a nurse in sight, but the poor man must have his tea. I pushed away the knapsack, raised his head, and seated myself on the end of the stretcher; and, as I drew his poor tired head back upon my shoulder and half held him, he seemed, with all his pleasure and eager enjoyment of the tea, to be troubled at my being so bothered with him. He forgot I had come so many hundred miles on purpose to be bothered."

One can hardly read this simple unaffected statement of hers, without instinctively recalling the touching story told of a soldier in one of the hospitals of the Crimea who, when Florence Nightingale had passed, turned and kissed the place upon his pillow where her shadow fell. The sweet name of the fair English nurse might well be claimed by many of our American heroines, but, when we think of Margaret's pure voice, singing hymns with the soldiers on the hospital-boat, filling the desolate woods along the Mississippi shores with solemn music in the still night, we feel that it belongs especially to her and that we may call her, Without offense to the others, our Florence Nightingale.

Her great power of adaptation served her well in her chosen vocation. Unmindful of herself, and always considerate of others, she could suit herself to the need of the moment and was equally at home in making tea and toast for the hungry, dressing ghastly wounds for the sufferers, and in singing hymns and talking of spiritual things with the sick and dying.

She found indeed her true vocation. She saw her way and walked fearlessly in it she knew her work and did it with all her heart and soul. When she first began to visit the hospitals in and around St. Louis, she wrote "I shall never be satisfied till I get right into a hospital, to live till the war is over. If you are constantly with the men, you have hundreds of opportunities and moments of influence in which you can gain their attention and their hearts, and do more good than in any missionary field." Once, on board a steamer near Vicksburg, during the fearful winter siege of that city, some one said to her, "You must hold back, you are going beyond your strength, you will die if you are not more prudent!" "Well," said she, with thrilling earnestness, "what if I do? Shall men come here by tens of thousands and fight, and suffer, and die, and shall not some women be willing to die to sustain and succor them?" No wonder that such sincerity won all hearts and carried all before it! Alas! the brave spirit was stronger than the frail casket that encased it, and that yielded inevitably to the heavy demands that were made upon it.

A rare and consistent life was hers, a worthy and heroic death. Let us stop a moment to admire the truth and beauty of the one, and to do reverence to the deep devotion of the other. The following sketch is gathered from the pages of a "Memorial" published by her friends shortly after her death, which occurred at Niagara Falls, July 27th, 1864.

"Margaret Elizabeth Breckinridge was born in Philadelphia, March 24th, 1832. Her paternal grandfather was John Breckinridge, of Kentucky, once Attorney-General of the United States. Her father, the Rev. John Breckinridge, D. D., was his second son, a man of talent and influence, from whom Margaret inherited good gifts of mind and heart, and an honored name. Her mother, who was the daughter of Rev. Samuel Miller, of Princeton, N. J., died when Margaret was only six years old, at which time she and her sister Mary went to live with their grandparents at Princeton. Their father dying three years afterwards, the home of the grandparents became their permanent abode. They had one brother, now Judge Breckinridge of St. Louis. Margaret's school-days were pleasantly passed, for she had a genuine love of study, an active intellect, and a very retentive memory. When her school education was over, she still continued her studies, and never gave up her prescribed course until the great work came upon her which absorbed all her time and powers. In the year 1852 her sister married Mr. Peter A. Porter of Niagara Falls, a gentleman of culture and accomplishments, a noble man, a true patriot. At his house the resort of literary and scientific men, the shelter of the poor and friendless, the centre of sweet social life and domestic peace, Margaret found for a time a happy home.

"Between her and her sister, Mrs. Porter, there was genuine sisterly love, a fine intellectual sympathy, and a deep and tender affection. The first great trial of Miss Breckinridge's life was the death of this beloved sister which occurred in 1854, only two years after her marriage. She died of cholera, after an illness of only a few hours. Margaret had left her but a few days before, in perfect health. The shock was so terrible that for many years she could not speak her sister's name without deep emotion; but she was too brave and too truly religious to allow this blow, dreadful as it was, to impair her usefulness or unfit her for her destined work. Her religion was eminently practical and energetic. She was a constant and faithful Sunday-school teacher, and devoted her attention especially to the colored people in whom she had a deep interest. She had become by inheritance the owner of several slaves in Kentucky, who were a source of great anxiety to her, and the will of her father, though carefully designed to secure their freedom, had become so entangled with state laws, subsequently made, as to prevent her, during her life, from carrying out what was his wish as well as her own. By her will she directed that they should be freed as soon as possible, and something given them to provide against the first uncertainties of self-support.

So the beginning of the war found Margaret ripe and ready for her noble womanly work; trained to self-reliance, accustomed to using her powers in the service of others, tender, brave, and enthusiastic, chastened by a life-long sorrow, she longed to devote herself to her country, and to do all in her power to help on its noble defenders. During the first year of the struggle duty constrained her to remain at home, but heart and hands worked bravely all the time, and even her ready pen was pressed into the service.

But Margaret could not be satisfied to remain with the Home Guards. She must be close to the scene of action and in the foremost ranks. She determined to become a hospital-nurse. Her anxious friends combated her resolution in vain; they felt that her slender frame and excitable temperament could not bear the stress and strain of hospital work, but she had set her mark and must press onward let life or death be the issue. In April, 1862, Miss Breckinridge set out for the West, stopping a few weeks at Baltimore on her way. Then she commenced her hospital service; then, too, she contracted measles, and, by the time she reached Lexington, Kentucky, her destination, she was quite ill; but the delay was only temporary, and soon she was again absorbed in her work. A guerrilla raid, under John Morgan, brought her face to face with the realities of war, and soon after, early in September she found herself in a beleaguered city, actually in the grasp of the Rebels, Kirby Smith holding possession of Lexington and its neighborhood for about six weeks. It is quite evident that Miss Breckinridge improved this occasion to air her loyal sentiments and give such help and courage to Unionists as lay in her power. In a letter written just after this invasion she says, "At that very time, a train of ambulances, bringing our sick and wounded from Richmond, was leaving town on its way to Cincinnati. It was a sight to stir every loyal heart; and so the Union people thronged round them to cheer them up with pleasant, hopeful words, to bid them God speed, and last, but not least, to fill their haversacks and canteens. We went, thinking it possible we might be ordered off by the guard, but they only stood off, scowling and wondering.

"Good-by said the poor fellows from the ambulances, we're coming back as soon as ever we get well.'

"'Yes, yes,' we whispered, for there were spies all around us, 'and every one of you bring a regiment with you.'"

As soon as these alarms were over, and Kentucky freed from rebel invaders, Miss Breckinridge went on to St. Louis, to spend the winter with her brother. As soon as she arrived, she began to visit the hospitals of the city and its neighborhood, but her chief work, and that from the effects of which she never recovered, was the service she undertook upon the hospital boats, which were sent down the Mississippi to bring up the sick and wounded from the posts below. She made two excursions of this kind, full of intense experiences, both of pleasure and pain. These boats went down the river empty unless they chanced to carry companies of soldiers to rejoin their regiments, but they returned crowded with the sick and dying, emaciated, fever-stricken men, sadly in need of tender nursing but with scarcely a single comfort at command. Several of the nurses broke down under this arduous and difficult service, but

Margaret congratulated herself that she had held out to the end. These expeditions were not without danger as well as privation. One of her letters records a narrow escape. "To give you an idea of the audacity of these guerrillas; while we lay at Memphis that afternoon, in broad daylight, a party of six, dressed in our uniform, went on board a government boat, lying just across the river, and asked to be taken as passengers six miles up the river, which was granted; but they had no sooner left the shore than they drew their pistols, overpowered the crew, and made them go up eighteen miles to meet another government boat coming down loaded with stores, tied the boats together and burned them, setting the crew of each adrift in their own yawl, and nobody knew it till they reached Memphis, two hours later. Being able to hear nothing of the wounded, we pushed on to Helena, ninety miles below, and here dangers thickened. We saw the guerrillas burning cotton, with our own eyes, along the shore, we saw their little skiffs hid away among the bushes on the shore; and just before we got to Helena, had a most narrow escape from their clutches. A signal to land on the river was in ordinary times never disregarded, as the way business of freight and passengers was the chief profit often of the trip, and it seems hard for pilots and captains always to be on their guard against a decoy. At this landing the signal was given, all as it should be, and we were just rounding to, when, with a sudden jerk, the boat swung round into the stream again. The mistake was discovered in time, by a government officer on board, and we escaped an ambush. Just think! we might have been prisoners in Mississippi now, but God meant better things for us than that."

Her tender heart was moved by the sufferings of the wretched colored people at Helena. She says, "But oh! the contrabands! my heart did ache for them. Such wretched, uncared-for, sad-looking creatures I never saw. They come in such swarms that it is impossible to do anything for them, unless benevolent people take the thing into their hands. They have a little settlement in one end of the town, and the government furnishes them rations, but they cannot all get work, even if they were all able and willing to do it; then they get sick from exposure, and now the small pox is making terrible havoc among them. They have a hospital of their own, and one of our Union Aid ladies has gone down to superintend it, and get it into some order, but it seems as if there was nothing before them but suffering for many a long day to come, and that sad, sad truth came back to me so often as I went about among them, that no people ever gained their freedom without a baptism of fire."

Miss Breckinridge returned to St. Louis on a small hospital boat on which there were one hundred and sixty patients in care of herself and one other lady. A few extracts from one of her letters will show what brave work it gave her to do.

"It was on Sunday morning, 25th of January, that Mrs. C. and I went on board the hospital boat which had received its sad freight the day before, and was to leave at once for St. Louis, and it would be impossible to describe the scene which presented itself to me as I stood in the door of the cabin. Lying on the floor, with nothing under them but a tarpaulin and their blankets, were crowded fifty men, many of them with death written on their faces; and looking through the half-open doors of the staterooms, we saw that they contained as many more. Young, boyish faces, old and thin from suffering, great restless eyes that were fixed on nothing, incoherent ravings of those who were wild with fever, and hollow coughs on every side—this, and much more that I do not want to recall, was our welcome to our new work; but, as we passed between the two long rows, back to our own cabin, pleasant smiles came to the lips of some, others looked after us wonderingly, and one poor boy whispered, 'Oh, but it is good to see the ladies come in!' I took one long look into Mrs. C.'s eyes to see how much strength and courage was hidden in them. We asked each other, not in words, but in those fine electric thrills by which one soul questions another, 'Can we bring strength, and hope, and comfort to these poor suffering men?' and the answer was, 'Yes, by God's help we will!' The first thing was to give them something like a comfortable bed, and, Sunday though it was, we went to work to run up our sheets into bed-sacks. Every man that had strength enough to stagger was pressed into the service, and by night most of them had something softer than a tarpaulin to sleep on. 'Oh, I am so comfortable now!' some of them said; 'I think I can sleep to-night,' exclaimed one little fellow, half-laughing with pleasure. The next thing was to provide something that sick people could eat, for coffee and bread was poor food for most of them. We had two little stoves, one in the cabin and one in the chambermaid's room, and here, the whole time we were on board, we had to do the cooking for a hundred men. Twenty times that day I fully made up my mind to cry with vexation, and twenty times that day I laughed instead; and surely, a kettle of tea was never made under so many difficulties as the one I made that morning. The kettle lid was not to be found, the water simmered and sang at its leisure, and when I asked for the poker I could get nothing but an old bayonet, and, all the time, through the half-open door behind me, I heard the poor hungry fellows asking the nurses, 'Where is that tea the lady promised me?' or 'When will my toast come?' But there must be an end to all things, and when I carried them their tea and toast, and heard them pronounce it 'plaguey good,' and 'awful nice,' it was more than a recompense for all the worry.

"One great trouble was the intense cold. We could not keep life in some of the poor emaciated frames. 'Oh dear! I shall freeze to death!' one poor little fellow groaned, as I passed him. Blankets seemed to have no effect upon them, and at last we had to keep canteens filled with boiling water at their feet.

"There was one poor boy about whom from the first I had been very anxious. He drooped and faded from day to day before my eyes. Nothing but constant stimulants seemed to keep him alive, and, at last I summoned courage to tell him—oh, how hard it was!—that he could not live many hours. 'Are you willing to die?' I asked him. He closed his eyes, and was silent a moment; then came that passionate exclamation which I have heard so often, 'My mother, oh! my mother!' and, to the last, though I believe God gave him strength to trust in Christ, and willingness to die, he longed for his mother. I had to leave him, and, not long after, he sent for me to come, that he was dying, and wanted me to sing to him. He prayed for himself in the most touching words; he confessed that he had been a wicked boy, and then with one last message for that dear mother, turned his face to the pillow and died; and so, one by one, we saw them pass away, and all the little keepsakes and treasures they had loved and kept about them, laid away to be sent home to those they should never see again. Oh, it was heart-breaking to see that!"

After the "sad freight" had reached its destination, and the care and responsibility are over, true woman that she is, she breaks down and cries over it all, but brightens up, and looking back upon it declares: "I certainly never had so much comfort and satisfaction in anything in all my life, and the tearful thanks of those who thought in their gratitude that they owed a great deal more to us than they did, the blessings breathed from dying lips, and the comfort it has been to friends at home to hear all about the last sad hours of those they love, and know their dying messages of love to them; all this is a rich, and full, and overflowing reward for any labor and for any sacrifice." Again she says: "There is a soldier's song of which they are very fond, one verse of which often comes back to me:

'So I've had a sight of drilling,

And I've roughed it many days;

Yes, and death has nearly had me,

Yet, I think, the service pays.'

Indeed it does,—richly, abundantly, blessedly, and I thank God that he has honored me by letting me do a little and suffer a little for this grand old Union, and the dear, brave fellows who are fighting for it."

Early in March she returned to St. Louis, expecting to make another trip down the river, but her work was nearly over, and the seeds of disease sown in her winter's campaign were already overmastering her delicate constitution. She determined to go eastward for rest and recovery, intending to return in the autumn and fix herself in one of the Western hospitals, where she could devote herself to her beloved work while the war lasted. At this time she writes to her Eastern friends: "I shall soon turn my face eastward, and I have more and more to do as my time here grows shorter. I have been at the hospital every day this week, and at the Government rooms, where we prepare the Government work for the poor women, four hundred of whom we supply with work every week. I have also a family of refugees to look after, so I do not lack employment."

Early in June, Miss Breckinridge reached Niagara on her way to the East, where she remained for a month. For a year she struggled against disease and weakness, longing all the time to be at work again, making vain plans for the time when she should be "well and strong, and able to go back to the hospitals." With this cherished scheme in view she went in the early part of May, 1864, into the Episcopal Hospital in Philadelphia, that she might acquire experience in nursing, especially in surgical cases, so that in the autumn, she could begin her labor of love among the soldiers more efficiently and confidently than before. She went to work with her usual energy and promptness, following the surgical nurse every day through the wards, learning the best methods of bandaging and treating the various wounds. She was not satisfied with merely seeing this done, but often washed and dressed the wounds with her own hands, saying, "I shall be able to do this for the soldiers when I get back to the army." The patients could not understand this, and would often expostulate, saying, "Oil no, Miss, that is not for the like of you to do!" but she would playfully insist and have her way. Nor was she satisfied to gain so much without giving something in return. She went from bed to bed, encouraging the despondent, cheering the weak and miserable, reading to them from her little Testament, and singing sweet hymns at twilight,—a ministering angel here as well as on the hospital-boats on the Mississippi.

On the 2d of June she had an attack of erysipelas, which however was not considered alarming, and under which she was patient and cheerful.

Then came news of the fighting before Richmond and of the probability that her brother-in-law, Colonel Porter, had fallen.

Her friends concealed it from her until the probability became a sad certainty, and then they were obliged to reveal it to her. The blow fell upon her with overwhelming force. One wild cry of agony, one hour of unmitigated sorrow, and then she sweetly and submissively bowed herself to the will of her Heavenly Father, and was still; but the shock was too great for the wearied body and the bereaved heart. Gathering up her small remnant of strength and courage she went to Baltimore to join the afflicted family of Colonel Porter, saying characteristically, "I can do more good with them than anywhere else just now." After a week's rest in Baltimore she proceeded with them to Niagara, bearing the journey apparently well, but the night after her arrival she became alarmingly ill, and it was soon evident that she could not recover from her extreme exhaustion and prostration. For five weeks her life hung trembling in the balance, and then the silver cord was loosed and she went to join her dear ones gone before.

"Underneath are the everlasting arms," she said to a friend who bent anxiously over her during her sickness. Yes, "the everlasting arms" upheld her in all her courageous heroic earthly work they cradle her spirit now in eternal rest.

MRS. STEPHEN BARKER

MRS. BARKER is a lady of great refinement and high culture, the sister of the Hon. William Whiting, late Attorney-General of Massachusetts, and the wife of the Rev. Stephen Barker, during the war, Chaplain of the First Massachusetts Heavy Artillery.

This regiment was organized in July, 1861, as the Fourteenth Massachusetts Infantry (but afterwards changed as above) under the command of Colonel William B. Green, of Boston, and was immediately ordered to Fort Albany, which was then an outpost of defense guarding the Long Bridge over the Potomac, near Washington.

Having resolved to share the fortunes of this regiment in the service of its hospitals, Mrs. Barker followed it to Washington in August, and remained in that city six months before suitable quarters were arranged for her at the fort.

During her stay in Washington, she spent much of her time in visiting hospitals, and in ministering to their suffering inmates. Especially was this the case with the E. Street Infirmary, which was destroyed by fire in the autumn of that year. After the fire the inmates were distributed to other hospitals, except a few whose wounds would not admit of a removal. These were collected together in a small brick school-house, which stands on the corner of the lot now occupied by the Judiciary Square Hospital, and there was had the first Thanksgiving Dinner which was given in an army hospital.

After dinner, which was made as nice and home-like as possible, they played games of checkers, chess, and backgammon on some new boards presented from the supplies of the Sanitary Commission, and Mrs. Barker read aloud "The Cricket on the Hearth." This occupied all the afternoon and made the day seem so short to these poor convalescents that they all confessed afterwards that they had no idea, nor expectation that they could so enjoy a day which they had hoped to spend at home; and they always remembered and spoke of it with pleasure.

This was a new and entirely exceptional experience to Mrs. Barker. Like all the ladies who have gone out as volunteer nurses or helps in the hospitals, she had her whole duty to learn. In this she was aided by a sound judgment, and an evident natural capacity and executive ability. Without rules or instructions in hospital visiting, she had to learn by experience the best methods of aiding sick soldiers without coming into conflict with the regulations peculiar to military hospitals. Of course, no useful work could be accomplished without the sanction and confidence of the surgeons, and these could only be won by strict and honorable obedience to orders.

The first duty was to learn what Government supplies could properly be expected in the hospitals; next to be sure that where wanting they were not withheld by the ignorance or carelessness of the sub-officials; and lastly that the soldier was sincere and reliable in the statement of his wants. By degrees these questions received their natural solution; and the large discretionary power granted by the surgeons, and the generous confidence and aid extended by the Sanitary Commission, in furnishing whatever supplies she asked for, soon gave Airs. Barker all the facilities she desired for her useful and engrossing work.

In March, 1862, Mrs. Barker removed to Fort Albany, and systematically commenced the work which had first induced her to leave her home. This work was substantially the same that she had done in Washington, but was confined to the Regimental Hospitals. But it was for many reasons pleasanter and more interesting. As the wife of the Chaplain of the Regiment, the men all recognized the fitness of her position, and she shared with him all the duties, not strictly clerical, of his office, finding great happiness in their mutual usefulness and sustaining power. She also saw the same men oftener, and became better acquainted, and more deeply interested in their individual conditions, and she had here facilities at her command for the preparation of all the little luxuries and delicacies demanded by special cases.

While the regiment held Fort Albany, and others of the forts forming the defenses of Washington, the officers' quarters were always such as to furnish a comfortable home, and Mrs. Barker had, consequently, none of the exposures and hardships of those who followed the army and labored in the field. As she, herself, has written in a private letter—"It was no sacrifice to go to the army, because my husband was in it, and it would have been much harder to stay at home than to go with him. I cannot even claim the merit of acting from a sense of duty—for I wanted to work for the soldiers, and should have been desperately disappointed had I been prevented from doing it."

And so, with a high heart, and an unselfish spirit, which disclaimed all merit in sacrifice, and even the existence of the sacrifice, she entered upon and fulfilled to the end the arduous and painful duties which devolved upon her.

For nearly two years she continued in unremitting attendance upon the regimental hospitals, except when briefly called home to the sick and dying bed of her father.

All this time her dependence for hospital comforts was upon the Sanitary Commission, for though the regiment was performing the duties of a garrison it was not so considered by the War Department, and the hospital received none of the furnishings it would have been entitled to as a Post Hospital. Most of the hospital bedding and clothing, as well as delicacies of diet came from the Sanitary Commission, and a little money contributed from private sources helped to procure the needed furniture. Mrs. Barker found this "camp life" absorbing and interesting. She became identified -with the regiment and was accustomed to speak of it as a part of herself. And even more closely and intimately did sha identify herself with her suffering patients in the hospital.

On Sundays, while the chaplain was about his regular duties, she was accustomed to have a little service of her own for the patients, which mostly consisted in reading aloud a printed sermon of the Rev. Henry Ward Beecher, which appeared in the Weekly Traveller, and which was always listened to with eager interest.

The chaplain's quarters were close by the hospital, and at any hour of the day and till a late hour of the night Mr and Mrs. Barker could assure themselves of the condition and wants of any of the patients, and be instantly ready to minister to them. Mrs. Barker, especially, bore them continually in her thoughts, and though not with them, her heart and time were given to the work of consolation, either by adding to the comforts of the body or the mind.

In January, 1864, it became evident to Mrs. Barker that she could serve in the hospitals more effectually by living in Washington, than by remaining at Fort Albany. She therefore offered her services to the Sanitary Commission without other compensation than the expenses of her board, and making no stipulation as to the nature of her duties, but only that she might remain within reach of the regimental hospital, to which she had so long been devoted.

Just at this time the Commission had determined to secure a more sure and thorough personal distribution of the articles intended for soldiers, and she was requested to become a visitor in certain hospitals in Washington. It was desirable to visit bedsides, as before, but henceforth as a representative of the Sanitary Commission, with a wider range of duties, and a proportionate increase of facilities. Soldiers were complaining that they saw nothing of the Sanitary Commission, when the shirts they wore, the fruits they ate, the stationery they used, and numerous other comforts from the Commission abounded in the hospitals. Mrs. Barker found that she had only to refuse the thanks which she constantly received, and refer them to the proper object, to see a marked change in the feeling of the sick toward the Sanitary Commission. And she was so fully convinced of the beneficial results of this remarkable organization, that she found the greatest pleasure in doing this.

In all other respects her work was unchanged. There was the same need of cheering influences—the writing of letters and procuring of books, and obtaining of information. There were the thousand varied calls for sympathy and care which kept one constantly on the keenest strain of active life, so that she came to feel that no gift, grace, or accomplishment could be spared without leaving something wanting of a perfect woman's work in the hospitals.

Nine hospitals, in addition to the regimental hospital, which she still thought of as her "own," were assigned her. Of these Harewood contained nearly as many patients as all the others. During the summer of 1864, its wards and tents held twenty-eight hundred patients. It was Mrs. Barker's custom to commence here every Monday morning at the First Ward, doing all she saw needful as she went along, and to go on as far as she could before two o'clock, when she went to dinner. In the afternoon she would visit one of the smaller hospitals, all of whose inmates she could see in the course of one visit, and devote the whole afternoon entirely to that hospital.

The next morning she would begin again at Harewood, where she stopped the day before, doing all she could there, previous to two o'clock, and devoting the afternoon to a smaller hospital. When Harewood was finished, two hospitals might be visited in a day, and in this manner she would complete the entire round weekly.

It was not necessary to speak to every man, for on being recognized as a Sanitary Visitor the men would tell her their wants, and her eye was sufficiently practiced to discern where undue shyness prevented any from speaking of them. An assistant always went with her, who drove the horses, and who, by his knowledge of German, was a great help in understanding the foreign soldiers. They carried a variety of common articles with them, so that the larger proportion of the wants could be supplied on the spot. In this way a constant distribution was going on, in all the hospitals of

Washington, whereby the soldiers received what was sent for them with certainty and promptness.

In the meantime the First Heavy Artillery had been ordered to join the army before Petersburg. On the fourth day after it left the forts round Washington, it lost two hundred men killed, wounded and taken prisoners. As soon as the sick or wounded men began to be sent back to Washington, Mrs. Barker was notified of it by her husband, and sought them out to make them the objects of her special care.

At the same time the soldiers of this regiment, in the field, were constantly confiding money and mementoes to Mr. Barker, to be sent to Mrs. Barker by returning Sanitary Agents, and forwarded by her to their families in New England. Often she gave up the entire day to the preparation of these little packages for the express, and to the writing of letters to each person who was to receive a package, containing messages, and a request for a reply when the money was received. Large as this business was, she never entrusted it to any hands but her own, and though she sent over two thousand dollars in small sums, and numerous mementoes, she never lost an article of all that were transmitted by express.

But whatever she had on hand, it was, at this time, an especial duty to attend to any person who desired a more thorough understanding of the work of hospitals; and many days were thus spent with strangers who had no other means of access to the information they desired, except through one whose time could be given to such purposes.

These somewhat minute details of Mrs. Barker's labors are given as being peculiar to the department of service in which she worked, and to which she so conscientiously devoted herself for such a length of time.

In this way she toiled on until December, 1864, when a request was made by the Women's Central Association that a hospital visitor might be sent to the Soldiers' Aid Societies in the State of New York. Few of these had ever seen a person actually engaged in hospital work, and it was thought advisable to assure them that their labors were not only needed, but that their results really reached and benefited the sick soldiers.

Mrs. Barker was chosen as this representative, and the programme included the services of Mr. Barker, whose regiment was now mustered out of service, as a lecturer before general audiences, while Mrs. Barker met the Aid Societies in the same places. During the month of December, 1864, Mr and Mrs. Barker, in pursuance of this plan, visited Harlem, Brooklyn, Astoria, Hastings, Irvington, Rhinebeck, Albany, Troy, Rome, Syracuse, Auburn, and Buffalo, presenting the needs of the soldier, and the benefits of the work of the Sanitary Commission to the people generally, and to the societies in particular, with great acceptance, and to the ultimate benefit of the cause. This tour accomplished, Mrs. Barker returned to her hospital work in Washington.

After the surrender of Lee's army, Mrs. Barker visited Richmond and Petersburg, and as she walked the deserted streets of those fallen cities, she felt that her work was nearly done. Almost four years, in storm and in sunshine, in heat and in cold, in hope and in discouragement she had ceaselessly toiled on, and all along her path were strewed the blessings of thousands of grateful hearts.

The increasing heats of summer warned her that she could not withstand the influences of another season of hard work in a warm climate, and on the day of the assassination of President Lincoln, she left Washington for Boston.

Mrs. Barker had been at home about six weeks when a new call for effort came, on the return of the Army of the Potomac encamped around Washington previous to its final march for home. To it was presently added the Veterans of Sherman's grand march, and all were in a state of destitution. The following extract from the Report of the Field Relief Service of the United States Sanitary Commission with the Armies of the Potomac, Georgia, and Tennessee, in the Department of Washington, May and June, 1865, gives a much better idea of the work required than could otherwise be presented.

"Armies, the aggregate strength of which must have exceeded two hundred thousand men, were rapidly assembling around this city, previous to the grand review and their disbandment. These men were the travel-worn veterans of Sherman, and the battle stained heroes of the glorious old Army of the Potomac, men of whom the nation is already proud, and whom history will teach our children to venerate. Alas! that veterans require more than 'field rations;' that heroes will wear out or throw away their clothes, or become diseased with scurvy or chronic diarrhoea.

"The Army of the West had marched almost two thousand miles, subsisting from Atlanta to the ocean almost wholly upon the country through which it passed. When it entered the destitute regions of North Carolina and Virginia it became affected with scorbutic diseases. A return to the ordinary marching rations gave the men plenty to cat, but no vegetables. Nor had foraging put them in a condition to bear renewed privation.

"The Commissary Department issued vegetables in such small quantities that they did not affect the condition of the troops in any appreciable degree. Surgeons immediately sought the Sanitary Commission. The demand soon became greater than the supply. At first they wanted nothing but vegetables, for having these, they said, all other discomforts would become as nothing.

"After we had secured an organization through the return of agents and the arrival of transportation, a division of labor was made, resulting ultimately in three departments, more or less distinct. These were:

"First, the supply of vegetables;

"Second, the depots for hospital and miscellaneous supplies; and,

"Third, the visitation of troops for the purpose of direct distribution of small articles of necessity or comfort."

These men, war-worn—and many of them sick—veterans, were without money, often in rags, or destitute of needful clothing, and they were not to be paid until they were mustered out of the service in their respective States. Generous, thorough and rapid distribution was desirable, and all the regular hospital visitors, as well as others temporarily employed in the work, entered upon the duties of field distribution. In twenty days, such was the system and expedition used, every regiment, and all men on detached duty, had been visited and supplied with necessaries on their camping grounds; and frequent expressions of gratitude from officers and men, attested that a great work had been successfully accomplished.

This was the conclusion of Mrs. Barker's army work, and what it was, how thorough, kind, and every way excellent we cannot better tell than by appending to this sketch her own report to the Chief of Field Belief Corps.

"WASHINGTON, D. C., June 29, 1865.

"A. M. SPERRY—Sir: It was my privilege to witness the advance of the army in the spring of 1862, and the care of soldiers in camp and hospital having occupied all my time since then, it was therefore gratifying to close my labors by welcoming the returning army to the same camping grounds it left four years ago. The circumstances under which it went forth and returned were so unlike, the contrast between our tremulous farewell and our exultant welcome so extreme, that it has been difficult to find an expression suited to the hour. The Sanitary Commission adopted the one method by which alone it could give for itself this expression. It sent out its agents to visit every regiment and all soldiers on detached duty, to ascertain and relieve their wants, and by words and acts of kindness to assure them of the deep and heartfelt gratitude of the nation for their heroic sufferings and achievements.

"The Second, Fifth, Sixth, Ninth, Fourteenth, Fifteenth, Seventeenth, and Twentieth army corps have been encamped about the capital. They numbered over two hundred thousand men.

"Our first work was to establish stations for sanitary stores in the camps, wherever it was practicable, to which soldiers might come for the supply of their wants without the trouble of getting passes into Washington. Our Field Relief Agents, who have followed the army from point to point, called on the officers to inform them of our storehouse for supplies of vegetables and pickles. The report of the Superintendent of Field Relief will show how great a work has been done for the army in these respects. How great has been the need of a full and generous distribution of the articles of food and clothing may be realized by the fact, that here were men unpaid for the last six months, and yet to remain so till mustered out of the service in their respective States; whose government accounts were closed, with no sutlers in their regiments, and no credit anywhere. Every market-day, numbers of these war-worn veterans have been seen asking for some green vegetable from the tempting piles, which were forbidden fruits to them.

"In order to make our work in the army as thorough, rapid, and effective as possible, it was decided to accept the services of the 'Hospital Visitors.' They have been at home in the hospitals ever since the war began, but never in the camp. But we believed that even here they would be safe, and the gifts they brought would be more valued because brought by them.

"Six ladies have been employed by the Sanitary Commission as Hospital Visitors. These were temporarily transferred from their hospitals to the field.

"The Second and Fifth Corps were visited by Mrs. Steel and Miss Abby Francis.

"The Sixth Corps by Mrs. Johnson, Miss Armstrong, and Mrs. Barker; on in each division.

"The Ninth Corps by Miss Wallace, whose illness afterward obliged her to yield her place to Mrs. Barker.

"The Fourteenth Corps by Miss Armstrong.

"The Fifteenth and Seventeenth Corps by ladies belonging to those corps— Mrs. Porter and Mrs. Bickerdyke—whose admirable services rendered other presence superfluous.

"The Twentieth Corps was visited by Mrs. Johnson.

"The articles selected for their distribution were the same for all the corps; while heavy articles of food and clothing were issued by orders from the field agents, smaller articles—like towels, handkerchiefs, stationery, sewing materials, combs, reading matter, etc.—were left to the ladies.

"This division of labor has been followed, except in cases where no field agent accompanied the lady, and there was no sanitary station in the corps. Then the lady agent performed double duty. She was provided with a vehicle, and followed by an army wagon loaded with supplies sufficient for her day's distribution, which had been drawn from the Commission storehouse upon a requisition approved by the chief clerk. On arriving at the camp, her first call was at headquarters, to obtain permission to distribute her little articles, to learn how sick the men were, in quarters or in hospital, and to find out the numbers in each company. The ladies adopted two modes of issuing supplies: some called for the entire company, giving into each man's hand the thing he needed; others gave to the orderly sergeant of each company the same proportion of each article, which he distributed to the men. The willing help and heartfelt pleasure of the officers in distributing our gifts among their men have added much to the respect and affection already felt for them by the soldiers and their friends.

"In Mrs. Johnson's report of her work in the Twentieth Army Corps, she says: 'In several instances officers have tendered the thanks of their regiments, when they were so choked by tears as to render their voices unheard.'

"I remember no scenes in camp more picturesque than some of our visits have presented. The great open army wagon stands under some shade-tree, with the officer who has volunteered to help, or the regular Field Agent, standing in the midst of boxes, bales, and bundles. Wheels, sides, and every projecting point are crowded with eager soldiers, to see what the Sanitary has brought for them. By the side of the great wagon stands the light wagon of the lady, with its curtains all rolled up, while she arranges before and around her the supplies she is to distribute. Another eager crowd surrounds her, patient, kind, and respectful as the first, except that a shade more of softness in their look and tone attest to the ever-living power of woman over the rough elements of manhood. In these hours of personal communication with the soldier, she finds the true meaning of her work. This is her golden opportunity, when by look, and tone, and movement she may call up, as if by magic, the pure influences of home, which may have been long banished by the hard necessities of war. Quietly and rapidly the supplies are handed out for Companies A. B, C., etc., first from one wagon, then the other, and as soon as a regiment is completed the men hurry back to their tents to receive their share, and write letters on the newly received paper, or apply the long needed comb, or mend the gaping seams in their now 'historic garments.' When at last the supplies are exhausted, and sunset reminds us that we are yet many miles from home, we gather up the remnants, bid good by to the friendly faces which already seem like old acquaintances, promising to come again to visit new regiments to-morrow, and hurry home to prepare for the next day's work.

"Every day, from the first to the twentieth day of June, our little band of missionaries has repeated a day's work such as I have now described. Every regiment, except some which were sent home before we were able to reach them, has shared alike in what we had to give. And I think I speak for all in Baying that among the many pleasant memories connected with our sanitary work, the last but not the least will be our share in the Field Relief.

"Yours respectfully,

"MRS. STEPHEN BARKER."

AMY M. BRADLEY

VERY few individuals in our country are entirely ignorant of the beneficent work performed by the Sanitary Commission during the late war; and these, perhaps, are the only ones to whom the name of Amy M. Bradley is unfamiliar. Very early in the war she commenced her work for the soldiers, and did not discontinue it until some months after the last battle was fought, completing fully her four years of service, and making her name a synonym for active, judicious, earnest work from the beginning to the end.

Amy M. Bradley is a native of East Vassalboro', Kennebec County, Maine, where she was born September 12th, 1823, the youngest child of a large family. At six years of age she met with the saddest of earthly losses, in the death of her mother. From early life it would appear to have been her lot to make her way in life by her own active exertions. Her father ceased to keep house on the marriage of his older daughters, and from that time until she was fifteen she lived alternately with them. Then she made her first essay in teaching a small private school.

At sixteen she commenced life as a teacher of public schools, and continued the same for more than ten years, or until 1850.

To illustrate her determined and persistent spirit during the first four years of her life as a teacher she taught country schools during the summer and winter, and during the spring and fall attended the academy in her native town, working for her board in private families.

At the age of twenty-one, through the influence of Noah Woods, Esq., she obtained an appointment as principal of one of the Grammar Schools in Gardiner, Maine, where she remained until the fall of 1847. At the end of that time she resigned and accepted an appointment as assistant in the Winthrop Grammar School, Charlestown, Massachusetts, obtained for her by her cousin, Stacy Baxter, Esq., the principal of the Harvard Grammar School in the same city. There she remained until the winter of 1849-50, when she applied for a similar situation in the Putnam Grammar School, East Cambridge (where higher salaries were paid) and was successful. She remained, however, only until May, when a severe attack of acute bronchitis so prostrated her strength as to quite unfit her for her duties during the whole summer. She had previously suffered repeatedly from pneumonia. Her situation was held for her until the autumn, when finding her health not materially improved, she resigned and prepared to spend the winter at the South in the family of a brother residing at Charleston, South Carolina.

Miss Bradley returned from Charleston the following spring. Her winter in the South had not benefited her as she had hoped and expected, and she found herself unable to resume her occupation as a teacher.

During the next two years her active spirit chafed in forced idleness, and life became almost a burden. In the autumn of 1853, going to Charlestown and Cambridge to visit friends, she met the physician who had attended her during the severe illness that terminated her teacher-life. He examined her lungs, and gave it as his opinion that only a removal to a warmer climate could preserve her life through another winter, and that the following months of frost and cold spent in the North must undoubtedly in her case develop pulmonary consumption.

To her these were words of doom. Not possessed of the means for travelling, and unable, as she supposed, to obtain a livelihood in a far off country, she returned to Maine, and resigned herself with what calmness she might, to the fate in store for her.

But Providence had not yet developed the great work to which she was appointed, and though sorely tried, and buffeted, she was not to be permitted to leave this mortal scene until the objects of her life were fulfilled. Through resignation to death she was, perhaps, best prepared to live, and even in that season when earth seemed receding from her view, the wise purposes of the Ruler of all in her behalf were being worked out in what seemed to be an accidental manner.

In the family of her cousin, Mr. Baxter, at Charlestown, Massachusetts, there had been living, for two years, three Spanish boys from Costa Rica, Central America. Mr. Baxter was an instructor of youth and they were his pupils. About this period their father arrived to fetch home a daughter who was at school in New York, and to inquire what progress these boys were making in their studies. He applied to Mr. Baxter to recommend some lady who would be willing to go to Costa Rica for two or three years to instruct his daughters in the English language. Mr. Baxter at once recommended Miss Bradley as a suitable person and as willing and desirous to undertake the journey. The situation was offered and accepted, and in November, 1853, she set sail for Costa Rica.

After remaining a short time with the Spanish family, she accepted a proposition from the American Consul, and accompanied his family to San Jose, the Capital, among the mountains, some seventy miles from Punta Arenas, where she opened a school receiving as pupils, English, Spanish, German, and American children. This was the first English school established in Central America. For three months she taught from a blackboard, and at the end of that time received from New York, books, maps, and all the needful apparatus for a permanent school.

This school she taught with success for three years. At the end of that time learning that the health of her father, then eighty-three years of age, was rapidly declining, and that he was unwilling to die without seeing her, she disposed of the property and "good-will" of her school, and as soon as possible bade adieu to Costa Rica. She reached home on the 1st of June, 1857, after an absence of nearly four years. Her father, however, survived for several months.

Her health which had greatly improved during her stay in the salubrious climate of San Jose, where the temperature ranges at about 70° Fahrenheit the entire year, again yielded before the frosty rigors of a winter in the Pine Tree State, and for a long time she was forced to lead a very secluded life. She devoted herself to reading, to the study of the French and German languages, and to teaching the Spanish, of which she had become mistress during her residence in Costa Rica.

In the spring of 1861, she went to East Cambridge, where she obtained the situation of translator for the New England Glass Company, translating commercial letters from English to Spanish, or from Spanish to English as occasion required.

This she would undoubtedly have found a pleasant and profitable occupation, but the boom of the first gun fired at Sumter upon the old flag stirred to a strange restlessness the spirit of the granddaughter of one who starved to death on board the British Prison Ship Jersey, during the revolution. She felt the earnest desire, but saw not the way to personal action, until the first disastrous battle of Bull Run prompted her to immediate effort.

She wrote to Dr. G. S. Palmer, Surgeon of the Fifth Regiment Maine Volunteers, an old and valued friend, to offer her services in caring for the sick and wounded. His reply was quaint and characteristic. "There is no law at this end of the route, to prevent your coming j but the law of humanity requires your immediate presence."

As soon as possible she started for the seat of war, and on the 1st of September, 1861, commenced her services as nurse in the hospital of the Fifth Maine Regiment.

The regiment had been enlisted to a great extent from the vicinity of Gardiner, Maine, where, as we have said, she had taught for several years, and among the soldiers both sick and well were a number of her old pupils.

The morning after her arrival, Dr. Palmer called at her tent, and invited her to accompany him through the hospital tents. There were four of these, filled with fever cases, the result of exposure and hardship at and after the battle of Bull Run.

In the second tent, were a number of patients delirious from the fever, whom the surgeon proposed to send to Alexandria, to the General Hospital. To one of these she spoke kindly, asking if he would like to have anything; with a wild look, and evidently impressed with the idea that he was about to be ordered on a long journey, he replied, "I would like to see my mother and sisters before I go home." Miss Bradley was much affected by his earnestness, and seeing that his recovery was improbable, begged Dr. Palmer to let her care for him for his mother and sisters' sake, until he went to his last home. He consented, and she soon installed herself as nurse of most of the fever cases, several of them her old pupils. From morning till night she was constantly employed in ministering to these poor fellows, and her skill in nursing was often of more service to them than medicine.

Colonel Oliver O. Howard, the present Major-General and Commissioner of the Freedmen's Bureau, had been up to the end of September, 1861, in command of the Fifth Maine Regiment, but at that time was promoted to the command of a brigade, and Dr. Palmer was advanced to the post of brigade surgeon, while Dr. Brickett succeeded to the surgeoncy of the Fifth Regiment.

By dint of energy, tact and management, Miss Bradley had brought the hospital into fine condition, having received cots from friends in Maine, and supplies of delicacies and hospital clothing from the Sanitary Commission. General Slocum, the new brigade commander, early in October made his first round of inspection of the regimental hospitals of the brigade. He found Dr. Brickett's far better arranged and supplied than any of the others, and inquired why it was so. Dr. Brickett answered that they had a Maine woman who understood the care of the sick, to take charge of the hospital, and that she had drawn supplies from the Sanitary Commission. General Slocum declared that he could have no partiality in his brigade, and proposed to take two large buildings, the Powell House and the Octagon House, as hospitals, and Miss Bradley as lady superintendent of the Brigade Hospital. This was done forthwith, and with further aid from the Sanitary Commission, as the Medical Bureau had not yet made any arrangement for brigade hospitals, Miss Bradley assisted by the zealous detailed nurses from the brigade soon gave these two houses a decided "home" appearance. The two buildings would accommodate about seventy-five patients, and were soon filled. Miss Bradley took a personal interest in each case, as if they -were her own brothers, and by dint of skilful nursing raised many of them from the grasp of death.

A journal which she kept of her most serious cases, illustrates very forcibly her deep interest and regard for all "her dear boys" as she called them. She would not give them up, even when the surgeon pronounced their cases hopeless, and though she could not always save them from death, she undoubtedly prolonged life in many instances by her assiduous nursing.

On the 10th of March, 1862, Centreville, Virginia, having been evacuated by the rebels, the brigade to which Miss Bradley was attached were ordered to occupy it, and five days later the Brigade Hospital was broken up and the patients distributed, part to Alexandria, and part to Fairfax Seminary General Hospital. In the early part of April Miss Bradley moved with the division to "Warrenton Junction, and after a week's stay in and about Manassas the order came to return to Alexandria and embark for 23

Yorktown. Returning to Washington, she now offered her services to the Sanitary Commission, and on the 4th of May was summoned by a telegraphic despatch from Mr. F. L. Olmstead, the energetic and efficient Secretary of the Commission, to come at once to Yorktown. On the 6th of May she reached Fortress Monroe, and on the 7th was assigned to the Ocean Queen as lady superintendent. We shall give some account of her labors here when we come to speak of the Hospital Transport service. Suffice it to say, in this place that her services which were very arduous, were continued either on the hospital ships or on the shore until the Army of the Potomac left the Peninsula for Acquia Creek and Alexandria, and that in several instances her kindness to wounded rebel officers and soldiers, led them to abandon the rebel service and become hearty, loyal Union men. She accompanied the flag of truce boat three times, when the Union wounded were exchanged, and witnessed some painful scenes, though the rebel authorities had not then begun to treat our prisoners with such cruelty as they did later in the war. Early in August she accompanied the sick and wounded men on the steamers from Harrison's Landing to Philadelphia, where they were distributed among the hospitals. During all this period of hospital transport service, she had had the assistance of that noble, faithful, worker Miss Annie Etheridge, the "Gentle Annie" of the Third Michigan regiment, of whom we shall have more to say in another place. For a few days, after the transfer of the troops to the vicinity of Washington, Miss Bradley remained unoccupied, and endeavored by rest and quiet to recover her health, which had been much impaired by her severe labors.

A place was, however, in preparation for her, which, while it would bring her less constantly in contact with the fearful wounds and terrible sufferings of the soldiers in the field, would require more administrative ability and higher business qualities than she had yet been called to exercise.

The Sanitary Commission in their desire to do what they could for the soldier, had planned the establishment of a Home at Washington, where the private soldier could go and remain for a few days while awaiting orders, without being the prey of the unprincipled villains who neglected no opportunity of fleecing every man connected with the army, whom they could entice into their dens; where those who were recovering from serious illness or wounds could receive the care and attention they needed; where their clothing often travel-stained and burdened with the "Sacred Soil of Virginia," could be exchanged for new, and the old washed, cleansed and repaired. It was desirable that this Home should be invested with a "home" aspect; that books, newspapers and music should be provided, as well as wholesome and attractive food, and that the presence of woman and her kindly and gentle ministrations, should exert what influence they might to recall vividly to the soldier the home he had left in a distant state, and to quicken its power of influencing him to higher and purer conduct, and more earnest valor, to preserve the institutions which had made that home what it was.

Kev. F. N. Knapp, the Assistant Secretary of the Commission, on whom devolved the duty of establishing this Home, had had opportunity of observing Miss Bradley's executive ability in the Hospital Transport Service, as well as in the management of a brigade hospital, and he selected her at once, to take charge of the Home, arrange all its details, and act as its Matron. She accepted the post, and performed its duties admirably, accommodating at times a hundred and twenty at once, and by her neatness, good order and cheerful tact, dispensing happiness among those who, poor fellows, had hitherto found little to cheer them.

But her active and energetic nature was not satisfied with her work at the Soldiers Home. Her leisure hours, (and with her prompt business habits, she secured some of these every day), were consecrated to visiting the numerous hospitals in and around Washington, and if she found the surgeons or assistant surgeons negligent and inattentive, they were promptly reported to the medical director. The condition of the hospitals in the city was, however, much better than that of the hospitals and convalescent camps over the river, in Virginia. A visit which she made to one of these, significantly named by the soldiers, "Camp Misery," in September, 1862, revealed to her, wretchedness, suffering and neglect, such as she had not before witnessed; and-she promptly secured from the Sanitary Commission such supplies as were needed, and in her frequent visits there for the next three months, distributed them with her own hands, while she encouraged and promoted such changes in the management and arrangements of the camp as greatly improved its condition.

This "Camp Misery" was the original Camp of Distribution, to which were sent, 1st, men discharged from all the hospitals about Washington, as well as the regimental, brigade, division and post hospitals, as convalescent, or as unfit for duty, preparatory to their final discharge from the army; 2d, stragglers and deserters, recaptured and collected here preparatory to being forwarded to their regiments; 3d, new recruits awaiting orders to join regiments in the field. Numerous attempts had been made to improve the condition of this camp, but owing to the small number and inefficiency of the officers detailed to the command, it had constantly grown "worse. The convalescents, numbering nine or ten thousand, were lodged, in the depth of a very severe winter, in wedge and Sibley tents, without floors, with no fires, or means of making any, amid deep mud or frozen clods, and were vciy poorly supplied with clothing, and many of them without blankets. Under such circumstances, it was not to be expected that their health could improve. The stragglers and deserters, and the new recruits were even worse off than the convalescents. The assistant surgeon and his acting assistants, up to the last of October, 1862, were too inexperienced to be competent for their duties.

In December, 1862, orders were issued by the Government for the construction of a new Rendezvous of Distribution, at a point near Fort Barnard, Virginia, on the Loudon and Hampshire Railroad, the erection of new and more comfortable barracks, and the removal of the men from the old camp to it. The barracks for the convalescents were fifty in number and intended for the accommodation of one hundred men each, and they were completed in February, 1863, and the new regulations and the appointment of new and efficient officers, greatly improved the condition of the Rendezvous.

In December, 1862, while the men were yet in Camp Misery, Miss Bradley was sent there as the Special Relief Agent of the Sanitary Commission, and took up her quarters there. As we have said the condition of the men was deplorable. She arrived on the 17th of December, and after setting up her tents, and arranging her little hospital, cook-room, store-room, washroom, bath-room, and office, so as to be able to serve the men most effectually, she passed round with the officers, as the men were drawn up in line for inspection, and supplied seventy-five men with woollen shirts, giving only to the very needy. In her hospital tents she soon had forty patients, all of them men who had been discharged from the hospitals as well; these were washed, supplied with clean clothing, warmed, fed and nursed. Others had discharge papers awaiting them, but were too feeble to stand in the cold and wet till their turn came. She obtained them for them, and sent the poor invalids to the Soldiers' Home in Washington, en route for their own homes. From May 1st to December 31st, 1863, she conveyed more than two thousand discharged soldiers from the Rendezvous of Distribution to the Commission's Lodges at Washington; most of them men suffering from incurable disease, and who but for her kind ministrations must most of them have perished in the attempt to reach their homes. In four months after she commenced her work she had had in her little hospital one hundred and thirty patients, of whom fifteen died. For these patients as well as for other invalids who were unable to write she wrote letters to their friends, and to the friends of the dead she sent full accounts of the last hours of their lost ones. The discharged men, and many of those who were on record unjustly as deserters, through some informality in their papers, often found great difficulty in obtaining their pay, and sometimes could not ascertain satisfactorily how much was due them, in consequence of errors on the part of the regimental or company officers. Miss Bradley was indefatigable in her efforts to secure the correction of these papers, and the prompt payment of the amounts due to these poor men, many of whom, but for her exertion, would have suffered on their arrival at their distant homes. Between May 1st and December 31st, 1863, she procured the reinstatement of one hundred and fifty soldiers who had been dropped from their muster rolls unjustly as deserters, and secured their arrears of pay to them, amounting in all to nearly eight thousand dollars.

On the 8th of February, 1864, the convalescents were, by general orders from the War Department, removed to the general hospitals in and about Washington, and the name changed from Camp Distribution to Rendezvous of Distribution, and only stragglers and deserters, and the recruits awaiting orders, or other men fit for duty were to be allowed there. For nearly two months Miss Bradley was confined to her quarters by severe illness. On her recovery she pushed forward an enterprise on which she had set her heart, of establishing a weekly paper at the Rendezvous, to be called "The Soldiers' Journal," which should be a medium of contributions from all the more intelligent soldiers in the camp, and the profits from which (if any accrued), should be devoted to the relief of the children of deceased soldiers. On the 17th of February the first number of "The Soldiers' Journal" appeared, a quarto sheet of eight pages; it was conducted with considerable ability and was continued till the breaking up of the Rendezvous and hospital, August 22, 1865, just a year and a half. The profits of the paper were twenty-one hundred and fifty-five dollars and seventy-five cents, beside the value of the printing-press and materials, which amount was held for the benefit of orphans of soldiers who had been connected with the camp, and was increased by contributions from other sources. Miss Bradley, though the proprietor, was not for any considerable period the avowed editor of the paper, Mr. R. A. Cassidy, and subsequently Mr. Thomas V. Cooper, acting in that capacity, but she was a large contributor to its columns, and her poetical contributions which appeared in almost every number, indicated deep emotional sensibilities, and considerable poetic talent. Aside from its interesting reading matter, the Journal gave instructions to the soldiers in relation to the procurement of the pay and clothing to which they were entitled; the requisites demanded by the government for the granting of furloughs; and the method of procuring prompt settlement of their accounts with the government without the interference of claim agents. During the greater part of 1864, and in 1865, until the hospital was closed, Miss Bradley, in addition to her other duties, was Superintendent of Special Diet to the Augur General Hospital, and received and forwarded from the soldiers to their friends, about forty-nine hundred and twenty-five dollars.

The officers and soldiers of the Rendezvous of Distribution were not forgetful of the unwearied labors of Miss Bradley for their benefit. On the 22d of February, 1864, she was presented with an elegant gold watch and chain, the gift of the officers and private soldiers of Camp Convalescent, then just broken up. The gift was accompanied with a very appropriate address from the chaplain of the camp, Rev. William J. Potter. She succeeded in winning the regard and esteem of all with whom she was associated. When, in August, 1865, she retired from the service of The Sanitary Commission, its secretary, John S. Blatchford, Esq., addressed her in a letter expressive of the high sense the Commission entertained of her labors, and the great good she had accomplished, and the Treasurer of the Commission forwarded her a check as for salary for so much of the year 1865 as was passed, to enable her to take the rest and relaxation from continuous labor which she so greatly needed. In person Miss Bradley is small, erect, and possesses an interesting and attractive face, thoughtful, and giving evidence in the lines of the mouth and chin, of executive ability, energy and perseverance. Her manners are easy, graceful and winning, and she evinces in a marked degree the possession of that not easily described talent, of which our record furnishes numerous examples, which the Autocrat of the Breakfast Table calls "faculty."

MRS. ARABELLA G. BARLOW

A ROMANTIC interest encircles the career of this brilliant and estimable lady, which is saddened by her early doom, and the grief of her young husband bereaved before Peace had brought him that quiet domestic felicity for which he doubtless longed.

Arabella Griffith was born in Somerville, New Jersey, but was brought up and educated under the care of Miss Eliza Wallace of Burlington, New Jersey, who was a relative upon her father's side. As she grew up she developed remarkable powers. Those who knew her well, both as relatives and in the social circle, speak of her warm heart, her untiring energy, her brilliant conversational powers, and the beauty and delicacy of thought which marked her contributions to the press. By all who knew her she was regarded as a remarkable woman.

That she was an ardent patriot, in more than words, who can doubt? She sealed her devotion to her country's cause by the sublimest sacrifices of which woman is capable—sacrifices in which she never faltered even in the presence of death itself.

Arabella Griffith was a young and lovely woman, the brilliant centre of a large and admiring fcircle. Francis C. Barlow was a rising young lawyer with a noble future opening before him. These two were about to unite their destinies in the marriage relation.

Into the midst of their joyful anticipations, came the echoes of the first shot fired by rebellion. The country sprang to arms.

These ardent souls were not behind their fellow-countrymen and countrywomen in their willingness to act and to suffer for the land and the Government they loved.

On the 19th of April, 1861, Mr. "Barlow enlisted as a private in the Twelfth Regiment New York Militia. On the 20th of April they were married, and on the 21st Mr. Barlow left with his regiment for Washington.

In the course of a week Mrs. Barlow followed her husband, and remained with him at Washington, and at Harper's Ferry, where the Twelfth was presently ordered to join General Patterson's command, until its return home, August 1st, 1861.

In November, 1861, Mr. Barlow re-entered the service, as Lieutenant-Colonel of the Sixty-first New York Volunteers, and Mrs. Barlow spent the winter with him in camp near Alexandria, Virginia. She shrank from no hardship which it was his lot to encounter, and was with him, to help, to sustain, and to cheer him, whenever it was practicable for her to be so, and neglected no opportunity of doing good to others which presented itself. •

Colonel Barlow made the Peninsular Campaign in the spring and summer of 1862 under McClellan. After the disastrous retreat from before Richmond, Mrs. Barlow joined the Sanitary Commission, and reached Harrison's Landing on the 2d of July, 1862.

Exhausted, wounded, sick and dying men were arriving there by scores of thousands—the remnants of a great army, broken by a series of terrible battles, disheartened and well-nigh demoralized. Many of the best and noblest of our American women were there in attendance, ready to do their utmost amidst all the hideous sights, and fearful sufferings of the hospitals, for these sick, and maimed, and wounded men. Mrs. Barlow remained, doing an untold amount of work, and good proportionate, until the army left in the latter part of August.

Soon after, with Short space for rest, she rejoined her husband in the field during the campaign in Maryland, but was obliged to go north upon business, and was detained and unable to return until the day following the battle of Antietam.

She found her husband badly wounded, and of course her first efforts were for him. She nursed him tenderly and unremittingly, giving such assistance as was possible in her rare leisure to the other wounded. We cannot doubt that even then she was very useful, and with her accustomed energy and activity, made these spare moments of great avail.

General Barlow was unfit for further service until the following spring. His wife remained in attendance upon him through the winter of 1862-3, and in the spring accompanied him to the field, and made the campaign with him from Falmouth to Gettysburg.

At this battle her husband was again severely wounded. He was within the enemy's lines, and it was only by great effort and exposure that she was able to have him removed within our own. She remained here, taking care of him, and of the other wounded, during the dreadful days that followed, during which the sufferings of the wounded from the intense heat, and the scarcity of medical and other supplies were almost incredible, and altogether indescribable. It was after this battle that the efficient aid, and the generous supplies afforded by the Sanitary Commission and its agents, were so conspicuous, and the results of this beneficent organization in the saving of life and suffering perhaps more distinctly seen than on any other occasion. Mrs. Barlow, aside from her own special and absorbing interest in her husband's case, found time to demonstrate that she had imbibed its true spirit.

Again, through a long slow period of convalescence she watched beside her husband, but the spring of 1864 found her in the field prepared for the exigencies of Grant's successful campaign of that year.

At times she was with General Barlow in the trenches before Petersburg, but on the eve of the fearful battles of the Wilderness, and the others which followed in such awfully bewildering succession, she was to be found at the place these foreshadowed events told that she was most needed. At Belle Plain, at Fredericksburg, and at White House, she was to be found as ever actively working for the sick and wounded. A friend and fellow-laborer describes her work as peculiar, and fitting admirably into the more exclusive hospital work of the majority of the women who had devoted themselves to the care of the soldiers. Her great activity and inexhaustible energy showed themselves in a sort of roving work, in seizing upon and gathering up such things as her quick eye saw were needed. "We called her the Raider" says this friend, who was also a warm admirer. "At Fredericksburg she had in some way gained possession of a wretched-looking pony, and a small cart or farmer's wagon, with which she was continually on the move, driving about town or country in search of such provisions or other articles as were needed for the sick and wounded. The surgeon in charge had on one occasion assigned her the task of preparing a building, which had been taken for a hospital, for a large number of wounded who were expected almost immediately. I went with my daughter to the building. It was empty, containing not the slightest furniture or preparation for the sufferers, save a large number of bed-sacks, without straw or other material to fill them.

"On requisition a quantity of straw was obtained, but not nearly enough for the expected need, and we were standing in a kind of mute despair, considering if it were indeed possible to secure any comfort for the poor fellows expected, when Mrs. Barlow came in. 'I'll find some more straw was her cheerful reply, and in another moment she was urging her tired beast toward another part of the town where she remembered having seen a bale of the desired article earlier in the day. Half an hour afterward the straw had been confiscated, loaded upon the little wagon by willing hands, and brought to the hospital. She then helped to fill and arrange the sacks, and afterwards drove about the town in search of articles, which, by the time the ambulances brought in their freight of misery and pain, had served to furnish the place with some means of alleviation.

Through all these awful days she labored on unceasingly. Her health became somewhat impaired, but she paid no heed to the warning. Her thoughts were not for herself, her cares not for her own sufferings. Earlier attention to her own condition might perhaps, have arrested the threatening symptoms, but she was destined to wear the crown of martyrdom, and lay down the beautiful life upon which so many hopes clung, her last sacrifice upon the altar of her country. The extracts which we append describe better the closing scenes of her life than we can. The first is taken from the Sanitary Commission Bulletin, of August 15, 1864, and we copy also the beautiful tribute to the memory of the departed contributed by Dr. Francis Lieber, of Columbia College, to the New York Evening Post. The briefer extract is from a letter which appeared in the columns of the New York Herald of July 31st, 1864.

"Died at "Washington, July 27, 1864, Mrs. Arabella Griffith Barlow, wife of Brigadier-General Francis C. Barlow, of fever contracted while in attendance upon the hospitals of the Army of the Potomac at the front.

"With the commencement of the present campaign she became attached to the Sanitary Commission, and entered upon her sphere of active work during the pressing necessity for willing hands and earnest hearts, at Fredericksburg. The zeal, the activity, the ardent loyalty and the scornful indignation for everything disloyal she then displayed, can never be forgotten by those whose fortune it was to be with her on that occasion. Ever watchful of the necessities of that trying time, her mind, fruitful in resources, was always busy in devising means to alleviate the discomforts of the wounded, attendant upon so vast a campaign within the enemy's country, and her hand was always ready to carry out the devices of her mind.

"Many a fractured limb rested upon a mattress improvised from materials sought out and brought together from no one knew where but the earnest sympathizing woman who is now no more.

"At Fredericksburg she labored with all her heart and mind. The sound of battle in which her husband was engaged, floating back from Chancellorsville, stimulated her to constant exertions. She faltered not an instant. Remaining till all the wounded had been removed from Fredericksburg, she left with the last hospital transport for Port Royal, where she again aided in the care of the wounded, as they were brought in at that point. From thence she went to White House, on one of the steamers then in the service of the Commission, and immediately going to the front, labored there in the hospitals, after the battle of Cold Harbor. From White House she passed to City Point, and arrived before the battles in front of Petersburg. Going directly to the front, she labored there with the same energy and devotion she had shown at Fredericksburg and White House.

"Of strong constitution, she felt capable of enduring all things for the cause she loved; but long-continued toil, anxiety and privation prepared her system for the approach of fever, which eventually seized upon her.

"Yielding to the solicitation of friends she immediately returned to Washington, where, after a serious illness of several weeks, she, when apparently convalescing, relapsed, and fell another martyr to a love of country."

Dr. Lieber says: "Mi's. Barlow, (Arabella Griffith before she married), was a highly cultivated lady, full of life, spirit, activity and charity.

"General Barlow entered as private one of our Hew York volunteer regiments at the beginning of the war. The evening before he left

New York for Washington with his regiment, they were married in the Episcopal Church in Lafayette Place. Barlow rose, and as Lieutenant-Colonel, made the Peninsular campaign under General McClellan. He was twice severely wounded, the last time at Antietam. Since then we have always read his name most honorably mentioned, whenever Major General Hancock's Corps was spoken of. Mrs. Barlow in the meantime entered the Sanitary service. In the Peninsular campaign she was one of those ladies who worked hard and nobly, close to the battle-field, as close indeed as they were permitted to do. "When her husband was wounded she attended, of course, upon him. In the present campaign of General Grant she has been at Belle Plain, White House, and everywhere where our good Sanitary Commission has comforted the dying and rescued the many wounded from the grave, which they would otherwise have found. The last time I heard of her she was at White House, and now I am informed that she died of typhus fever in Washington. No doubt she contracted the malignant disease in performing her hallowed and self-imposed duty in the field.

"Her friends will mourn at the removal from this life of so noble a being. All of us are the poorer for her loss; but our history has been enriched by her death. Let it always be remembered as one of those details which, like single pearls, make up the precious string of history, and which a patriot rejoices to contemplate and to transmit like inherited jewels to the rising generations. Let us remember as American men and women, that here we behold a young advocate, highly honored for his talents by all who knew him. He joins the citizen army of his country as a private, rises to command, is wounded again and again, and found again and again at the head of his regiment or division, in the fight where decision centres. And here is his bride—accomplished, of the fairest features, beloved and sought for in society —who divests herself of the garments of fashion, and becomes the assiduous nurse in the hospital and on the field, shrinking from no sickening sight, and fearing no typhus—that dreadful enemy, which in war follows the wings of the angel of death, like the fever-bearing currents of air—until she, too, is laid on the couch of the camp, and bidden to rest from her weary work, and to let herself be led by the angel of death to the angel of life. God bless her memory to our women, our men, our country.

"There are many glories of a righteous war. It is glorious to fight or fall, to bleed or to conquer, for so great and good a cause as ours; it is glorious to go to the field in order to help and to heal, to fan the fevered soldier and to comfort the bleeding brother, and thus helping, may be to die with him the death for our country. Both these glories have been vouchsafed to the bridal pair."

The Herald correspondent, writing from Petersburg, July 31, says:

"General Miles is temporarily in command of the First Division during the absence of General Barlow, who has gone home for a few days for the purpose of burying his wife. The serious loss which the gallant young general and an extensive circle of friends in social life have sustained by the death of Mrs. Barlow, is largely Shared by the soldiers of this army. She smoothed the dying pillow of many patriotic soldiers before she received the summons to follow them herself; and many a surviving hero who has languished in army hospitals will tenderly cherish the memory of her saintly ministrations when they were writhing with the pain of wounds received in battle or lost in the delirium of consuming fevers."

To these we add also the cordial testimony of Dr. W. H. Reed, one of her associates, at City Point, in his recently published "Hospital Life in the Army of the Potomac:"

"Of our own more immediate party, Mrs. General Barlow was the only one who died. Her exhausting work at Fredericksburg, where the largest powers of administration were displayed, left but a small measure of vitality with which to encounter the severe exposures of the poisoned swamps of the Pamunky, and the malarious districts of City Point. Here, in the open field, she toiled with Mr. Marshall and Miss Gilson, under the scorching sun, with no shelter from the pouring rains, with no thought but for those who were suffering and dying all around her. On the battle-field of Petersburg, hardly out of range of the enemy, and at night witnessing the blazing lines of fire from right to left, among the wounded, with her sympathies and powers of both mind and body strained to the last degree, neither conscious that she was working beyond her strength, nor realizing the extreme exhaustion of her system, she fainted at her work, and found, only when it was too late, that the raging fever was wasting her life away. It was strength of will which sustained her in this intense activity, when her poor, tired body was trying to assert its own right to repose. Yet to the last, her sparkling wit, her brilliant intellect, her unfailing good humor, lighted up our moments of rest and recreation. So many memories of her beautiful constancy and self-sacrifice, of her bright and genial companionship, of her rich and glowing sympathies, of her warm and loving nature, come back to me, that I feel how inadequate would be any tribute I could-pay to her worth."

MRS. NELLIE MARIA TAYLOR

THE Southwest bore rank weeds of secession and treason, spreading poison and devastation over that portion of our fair national heritage. But from the same soil, amidst the ruin and desolation which followed the breaking out of the rebellion, there sprang up growths of loyalty and patriotism, which by flowering and fruitage, redeemed the land from the curse that had fallen upon it among the women of the Southwest have occurred instances of the most devoted loyalty, the most self-sacrificing patriotism. They have suffered deeply and worked nobly, and their efforts alone have been sufficient to show that no part of our fair land was irrecoverably doomed to fall beneath the ban of a government opposed to freedom, truth, and progress.

Prominent among these noble women, is Mrs. Nellie Maria Taylor, of New Orleans, whose sufferings claim our wannest sympathy, and whose work our highest admiration and gratitude.

Mrs. Taylor, whose maiden name was Dewey, was born in Watertown, Jefferson county, New York, in the year 1821, of New England parentage. At an early age she removed -with her parents to the West, where, as she says of herself, she "grew up among the Indians," and perhaps, by her free life, gained something of the firmness of health and strength of character and purpose, which have brought her triumphantly through the trials and labors of the past four years.

She married early, and about the year 1847 removed with her husband, Dr. Taylor, and her two children, to New Orleans, where she has since resided. Consequently she was there through the entire secession movement, during which, by her firm and unswerving loyalty, she contrived to render herself somewhat obnoxious to those surrounding her, of opposite sentiments.

Mrs. Taylor watched anxiously the progress of the movements which preceded the outbreak, and fearlessly, though not obtrusively, expressed her own adverse opinions. At this time her eldest son was nineteen years of age, a noble and promising youth. He was importuned by his friends and associates to join some one of the many companies then forming, but as he was about to graduate in the high school, he and his family made that an objection. As soon as he graduated a lieutenancy was offered him in one of the companies, but deferring an answer, he left immediately for a college in the interior. Two months after the college closed its doors, and the students, urged by the faculty, almost en-masse entered the army. Mrs. Taylor, to remove her son, sent him at once to the north, and rejoiced in the belief that he was safe.

Immediately after this her persecutions commenced. Her husband had been ill for more than two years, while she supported her family by teaching, being principal of one of the city public schools. One day she was called from his bed-side to an interview with one of the Board of Directors of the schools.

By him she was accused (?) of being a Unionist, and informed that it was believed that she had sent her son away "to keep him from fighting for his country." Knowing the gentleman to be a northern man, she answered freely, saying that the country of herself and son was the whole country, and for it she was -willing he should shed his last drop of blood, but not to divide and mutilate it, would she consent that he should ever endanger himself.

The consequence of this freedom of speech was her dismissal from her situation on the following day. With her husband ill unto death, her house mortgaged, her means of livelihood taken away, she could only look upon the future with dark forebodings which nothing but her faith in God and the justice of her cause could subdue.

A short time after a mob assembled to tear down her house. She stepped out to remonstrate with them against pulling down the house over the head of a dying man. The answer was, "Madam, we give you five minutes to decide whether you are for the South or the North. If at the end of that time you declare yourself for the South, your house shall remain; if for the North, it must come down."

Her answer was memorable.

"Sir, I will say to you and your crowd, and to the world if you choose to summon it—I am, always have been, and ever shall be, for the Union. Tear my house down if you choose!"

Awed perhaps by her firmness, and unshrinking devotion, the spokesman of the mob looked at her steadily for a moment, then turning to the crowd muttered something, and they followed him away, leaving her unmolested. This man was a renegade Boston Yankee.

Such was her love for the national flag that during all this period of persecution, previous to General Butler's taking possession of the city she never slept without the banner of the free above her head, although her house was searched no less than seven times by a mob of chivalrous gentlemen, varying in number from two or three score to three hundred, led by a judge who deemed it not beneath his dignity to preside over a court of justice by day, and to search the premises of a defenseless woman by night, in the hope of finding the Union flag, in order to have an excuse for ejecting her from the city, because she was well known to entertain sentiments inimical to the interests of secession.

Before the South ran mad with treason, Mrs. Taylor and the wife of this judge were intimate friends, and their intimacy had not entirely ceased so late as the early months of 1862. It was late in February of that year that Mrs. Taylor was visiting at the judge's house, and during her visit the judge's son, a young man of twenty, taunted her with various epithets, such as a "Lincoln Emissary," "a traitor to her country," "a friend of Lincoln's hirelings," etc. She listened quietly, and then as quietly remarked that "he evidently belonged to that very numerous class of young men in the South who evinced their courage by applying abusive epithets to women and defenseless persons, but showed a due regard to their own safety, by running away—as at Donelson—whenever they were likely to come into contact with "Lincoln's hirelings."

The same evening, at a late hour, while Mrs. Taylor was standing by the bed-side of her invalid husband, preparing some medicine for him, she heard the report of a rifle and felt the wind of a minie bullet as it passed close to her head and lodged in the wall. In the morning she dug the ball out of the wall and took it over to the judge's house which was opposite to her own. When the young man came in Mrs. Taylor handed it to him, and asked if he knew what it was. He turned pale, but soon recovered his composure sufficiently to reply that "it looked like a rifle-ball." "Oh, no," said Mrs. Taylor, "you mistake! It is a piece of Southern chivalry fired at a defenseless woman, in the middle of the night, by the son of a judge, whose courage should entitle him to a commission in the Confederate army."

Still, brave as she was, she could not avoid some feeling, if not of trepidation, at least of anxiety, at being thus exposed to midnight assassination, while her life was so necessary to her helpless family.

These are but a few instances out of many, of the trials she had to endure. Her son hearing of them, through the indiscretion of a school-friend, hastened home, determined to enlist in the Confederate army to save his parents from further molestation. He enlisted for ninety days, hoping thus to shield his family from persecution, but the Conscription Act, which shortly after went into effect, kept him in the position for which his opinions so unfitted him. From the spring of 1862, he remained in the Confederate army, gaining rapid promotion, and distinguished for his bravery, until the close of the war, when he returned home unchanged in sentiment, and unharmed by shot or shell—in this last particular more fortunate than thousands of others forced by conscription into the ranks, and sacrificing their lives for a cause with which they had no sympathy.

From the time of her son's enlistment Mrs. Taylor was nearly free from molestation, and devoted herself to the care of her family, until the occupation of New Orleans by the Union forces. She was then reinstated in her position as teacher, and after the establishment of Union hospitals, she spent all her leisure moments in ministering to the wants of the sick and wounded.

In 1863, we hear of her as employing all her summer vacation, as well as her entire leisure-time when in school, in visiting the hospitals, attending the sick and wounded soldiers, and preparing for them such delicacies and changes of food and other comforts as she could procure from her own purse, and by the aid of others. From that time forward until the close of the war, or until the hospitals were closed by order of the Government, she continued this work, expending her whole salary upon these suffering men, and never omitting anything by which she might minister to their comfort.

Thousands of soldiers can bear testimony to her unwearied labors; it is not wanting, and will be her best reward. One of these writers says, "I do assure you it affords me the greatest pleasure to be able to add my testimony for that good, that noble, that blessed woman, Mrs. Taylor. I was wounded at Port Hudson in May, 1863, and lay in the Barracks General Hospital at New Orleans for over three months, when I had an excellent opportunity to see and know her work. She worked every day in the hospital—all her school salary she spent for the soldiers—night after night she toiled, and long after others were at rest she was busy for the suffering." And another makes it a matter of personal thankfulness that he should have been applied to for information in regard to this "blessed woman," and repeats his thanks "for himself and hundreds of others," that her services are to be recorded in this book.

Having great facility in the use of her pen, Mrs. Taylor made herself especially useful in writing letters for the soldiers. During the year from January 1864 to January 1865, she wrote no less than eleven hundred and seventy-four letters for these men, and even now, since the close of the war, her labors in that direction do not end. She is in constant communication with friends of soldiers in all parts of the country, collecting for them every item of personal information in her power, after spending hours in searching hospital records, and all other available sources for obtaining the desired knowledge.

During the summer of 1864, her duties were more arduous than at any other time. She distributed several thousands of dollars worth of goods, for the Cincinnati Branch of the United States Sanitary Commission, and on the 1st of June, when her vacation commenced, she undertook the management of the Dietetic Department in the University Hospital, the largest in New Orleans. From that time till October 1st, she, with her daughter and four other ladies, devoted like herself to the work, with their own hands, with the assistance of one servant only, cooked, prepared, and administered all the extra diet to the patients, numbering frequently five or six hundred on diet, at one time.

Two of these ladies were constantly at the hospital, Mrs. Taylor frequently four days in the week, and when not there, in other hospitals, not allowing herself one day at home during the whole vacation. When obliged to return to her school, her daughter, Miss Alice Taylor, took her place, and with the other ladies continued, Mrs. Taylor giving her assistance on Saturday and Sun day, till January 1st, 1865, when the hospital was finally closed.

Mrs. Taylor has been greatly aided by her children; her daughter, as nobly patriotic as herself, in the beginning of the war refusing to present a Confederate flag to a company unless beneath an arch ornamented, and with music the same as on occasion of presenting a banner to a political club the preceding year —viz: the arch decorated with United States flags, and the national airs played.. Her son "Johnnie" is as well known and as beloved by the soldiers as his mother, and well nigh sacrificed his noble little life to his unwearied efforts in their behalf.

It is out of the fiery furnace of trial that such nobly devoted persons as Mrs. Taylor and her family come forth to their mission of beneficence. Persecuted, compelled to make the most terrible and trying sacrifices, in dread and danger continually, the work of the loyal women of the South stands pre-eminent, among the labors of the noble daughters of America. And of these, Mrs. Taylor and her associates, and of Union women throughout the South, it may well and truly be said, in the words of Holy Writ: Many daughters have done virtuously, but thou excellest them all.

MRS. ADALINE TYLER

MRS. TYLER, the subject of the following sketch, is a native of Massachusetts, and for many years was a resident of Boston, in which city from her social position and her piety and benevolence she was widely known. She is a devout member of the Protestant Episcopal Church, greatly trusted and respected both by clergy and laity.

In 1856, she removed from Boston to Baltimore, Maryland. It was the desire of Bishop Whittingham of that Diocese to institute there a Protestant Sisterhood, or Order of Deaconesses, similar to those already existing in Germany, England, and perhaps other parts of Europe. Mrs. Tyler, then a widow, was invited to assume the superintendence of this order—a band of noble and devout women who turning resolutely from the world and its allurements and pleasures, desired to devote their lives and talents to works of charity and mercy.

To care for the sick, to relieve all want and suffering so far as lay in their power, to administer spiritual comfort, to give of their own substance, and to be the almoners of those pious souls whose duties lay in other directions, and whose time necessarily absorbed in other cares, did not allow the same self-devotion—this was the mission which they undertook, and for years prosecuted with untiring energy, and undoubted success.

In addition to her general superintendence of the order, Mrs. Tyler administered the affairs of the Church Home, a charitable Institution conducted by the Sisterhood, and occupied herself in a variety of pious and benevolent duties, among which were visiting the sick, and comforting the afflicted and prisoners. Among other things she devoted one day in each week to visiting the jail of Baltimore, at that time a crowded and ill-conducted prison, and the abode of a great amount of crime and suffering.

Mrs., then known as Sister Tyler, had been five years in Baltimore, filling up the time with her varied duties and occupations, when the storm that had so long threatened the land, burst in all the thunderbolts of its fury. Secession had torn from the Union some of the fairest portions of its domain, and already stood in hostile attitude all along the borders of the free North. The President, on the 15th of April, 1861, issued his first proclamation, announcing the presence of rebellion, commanding the insurgents to lay down their arms and return to their allegiance within twenty days, and calling on the militia of the several loyal States to the number of seventy-five thousand, to assemble for the defense of their country.

This proclamation, not unexpected at the North, yet sent a thrill of mingled feeling all through its bounds. The order was promptly obeyed, and without delay the masses prepared for the struggle which lay before them, but of which, as yet, no prophetic visions foretold the progress or result. Immediately regiment after regiment was hurried forward for the protection of the Capitol, supposed to be the point most menaced. Among these, and of the very earliest, was the Sixth Regiment Massachusetts Volunteers, of which the nucleus was the Lowell City Guards.

On the memorable and now historical 19th of April, this regiment while hurrying to the defense of Washington was assailed by a fierce and angry mob in the streets of Baltimore, and several of its men were murdered; and this for marching to the defense of their country, to which the citizens of Baltimore, their assailants, were equally pledged.

This occurred on a Friday, the day as before stated, set apart by Mrs. Tyler for her weekly visit to the jail. The news of the riot reached her as she was about setting out upon this errand of mercy, and caused her to postpone her visit for several hours, as her way lay through some portion of the disturbed district.

When, at last, she did go, a degree of quiet prevailed, though she saw wounded men being conveyed to their homes, or to places where they might be cared for, and it was evident that the public excitement had not subsided with hostilities. Much troubled concerning the fate of the Northern men—men, it must be remembered, of her own State—who had been stricken down, she hastened to conclude as soon as possible her duties at the jail, and returning homeward despatched a note to a friend asking him to ascertain and inform her what had become of the wounded soldiers. The reply soon came, with the tidings that they had been conveyed to one of the Station Houses by the Police, and were said to have been cared for, though the writer had not been allowed to enter and satisfy himself that such was the case.

This roused the spirit of Mrs. Tyler. Here was truly a work of "charity and mercy," and it was clearly her duty, in pursuance of the objects to which she had devoted her life, to ensure the necessary care of these wounded and suffering men who had fallen into the hands of those so inimical to them.

It was now late in the afternoon. Mrs. Tyler sent for a carriage which she was in the habit of using whenever need required, and the driver of which was honest and personally friendly, though probably a secessionist, and proceeded to the Station House. By this time it was quite dark, and she was alone. Alighting she asked the driver to give her whatever aid she might need, and to come to her should he even see her beckon from a window, and he promised compliance.

She knocked at the door, but on telling her errand was denied admittance, with the assurance that the worst cases had been sent to the Infirmary, while those who were in the upper room of the Station House had been properly cared for, and were in bed for the night. She again asked to be allowed to see them, adding that the care of the suffering was her life work, and she would like to assure herself that they needed nothing. She was again denied more peremptorily than before.

"Very well," she replied, "I am myself a Massachusetts woman, seeking to do good to the citizens of my own state. If not allowed to do so, I shall immediately send a telegram to Governor Andrew, informing him that my request is denied."

This spirited reply produced the desired result, and after a little consultation among the officials, who probably found the Governor of a State a much more formidable antagonist than a woman, coming alone on an errand of mercy, the doors were opened and she was conducted to that upper room where the fallen patriots lay.

Two were already dead. Two or three were in bed, the rest lay in their misery upon stretchers, helpless objects of the tongue abuse of the profane wretches who, "dressed in a little brief authority," walked up and down, thus pouring out their wrath. All the wounded had been drugged, and were either partially or entirely insensible to their miseries. Some eight or ten hours had elapsed since the wounds were received, but no attention had been paid to them, further than to staunch the blood by thrusting into them large pieces of cotton cloth. Even their clothes had not been removed. One of them (Coburn) had been shot in the hip, another (Sergeant Ames) was wounded in the back of the neck, just at the base of the brain, apparently by a heavy glass bottle, for pieces of the glass yet remained in the wound, and lay in bed, still in his soldier's overcoat, the rough collar of which irritated the ghastly wound. These two were the most dangerously hurt.

Airs. Tyler with some difficulty obtained these men, and procuring, by the aid of her driver, a furniture van, had them laid upon it and conveyed to her house, the Deaconesses' Home. Here a surgeon was called, their wounds dressed, and she extended to them the care and kindness of a mother, until they were so nearly well as to be able to proceed to their own homes. She during this time refused protection from the police, and declared that she felt no fears for her own safety while thus strictly in the line of the duties to which her life was pledged.

This was by no means the last work of this kind performed by Sister Tyler. Other wounded men were received and cared for by her—one a German, member of a Pennsylvania Regiment, (who was accidentally shot by one of his own comrades) whom she nursed to health in her own house.

For her efforts in behalf of the Massachusetts men she received the personal acknowledgments of the Governor, President of the Senate, and Speaker of the House of Representatives of that State, and afterwards resolutions of thanks were passed by the Legislature, or General Court, which, beautifully engrossed upon parchment, and sealed with the seal of the Commonwealth, were presented to her.

In all that she did, Mrs. Tyler had the full approval of her Bishop, as well as of her own conscience, while soon after at the suggestion of Bishop Whittingham, the Surgeon-General offered, and indeed urged upon her, the superintendency of the Camden Street Hospital, in the city of Baltimore. Her experience in the management of the large institution she had so long superintended, her familiarity with all forms of suffering, as well as her natural tact and genius, and her high character, eminently fitted her for this position.

Her duties were of course fulfilled in the most admirable manner, and save that she sometimes came in contact with the members of some of the volunteer associations of ladies who, in their commendable anxiety to minister to the suffering soldiers, occasionally allowed their zeal to get the better of-their discretion, gave satisfaction to all concerned. She did not live in the Hospital, but spent the greater part of the time there during the year of her connection with it. Circumstances at last decided her to leave. Her charge she turned over to Miss Williams, of Boston, whom she had herself brought thither, and then went northward to visit her friends.

She had not long been in the city of New York before she was urgently desired by the Surgeon-General to take charge of a large hospital at Chester, Pennsylvania, just established and greatly needing the ministering aid of women. She accepted the appointment, and proceeding to Boston selected from among her friends, and those who had previously offered their services, a corps of excellent nurses, who accompanied her to Chester.

In this hospital there was often from five hundred to one thousand sick and wounded men, and Mrs. Tyler had use enough for the ample stores of comforts which, by the kindness of her friends in the east, were continually arriving. Indeed there was never a time when she was not amply supplied with these, and with money for the use of her patients.

She remained at Chester a year, and was then transferred to Annapolis, where she was placed in charge of the Naval School Hospital, remaining there until the latter part of May, 1864.

This was a part of her service which perhaps drew more heavily than any other upon the sympathies and heart of Mrs. Tyler. Here, during the period of her superintendency, the poor wrecks of humanity from the prison pens of Andersonville and Belle Isle were brought, an assemblage of such utter misery, such dreadful suffering, that words fail in the description of it. Here indeed was a "work of charity and mercy," such as had never before been presented to this devoted woman; such, indeed, as the world had never seen.

Most careful, tender, and kindly were the ministrations of Mrs. Tyler and her associates—a noble band of women—to these wretched men. 'Filth, disease, and starvation had done their work upon them. Emaciated, till only the parchment-like skin covered the protruding bones, many of them too feeble for the least exertion, and their minds scarcely stronger than their bodies, they were indeed a spectacle to inspire, as they did, the keenest sympathy, and to call for every effort of kindness.

Mrs. Tyler procured a number of photographs of these wretched men, representing them in all their squalor and emaciation. These were the first which were taken, though the Government afterwards caused some to be made which were widely distributed. With these Mrs. Tyler did much good. She had a large number of copies printed in Boston, after her return there, and both in this country and in Europe, which she afterwards visited, often had occasion to bring them forward as unimpeachable witnesses of the truth of her own statements. Sun pictures cannot lie, and the sun's testimony in these brought many a heart shudderingly to a belief which it had before scouted. In Europe, particularly, both in England and upon the Continent, these pictures compelled credence of those tales of the horrors and atrocities of rebel prison pens, which it had long been the fashion to hold as mere sensation stories, and libels upon the chivalrous South.

Whenever referring to her work at Annapolis for the returned prisoners, Mrs. Tyler takes great pleasure in expressing her appreciation of the valuable and indefatigable services of the late Dr. Vanderkieft, Surgeon in charge of the Naval School Hospital. In his efforts to resuscitate the poor victims of starvation and cruelty, he was indefatigable, never sparing himself, but bestowing upon them his unwearied personal attention and sympathy. In this he was aided by his wife, herself a true Sister of Charity.

Mrs. Tyler also gives the highest testimony to the services and personal worth of her co-workers, Miss Titcomb, Miss Hall, and others, who gave themselves with earnest zeal to the cause, and feels how inadequate would have been her utmost efforts amid the multitude of demands, but for their aid. It is to them chiefly due that so many healthy recreations, seasons of amusement and religious instruction were given to the men.

During and subsequent to the superintendency of Mrs. Tyler fit Annapolis a little paper was published weekly at the hospital, under the title of "The Crutch." This was well supplied with articles, many of them of real merit, both by officials and patients. "Whenever an important movement took place, or a battle, it was the custom to issue a small extra giving the telegraphic account; when, if it were a victory, the feeble sufferers who had sacrificed so much for their country, would spend the last remnants of their strength, and make the very welkin ring, with their shouts of gladness.

Exhausted by her labors, and the various calls upon her efforts, Mrs. Tyler, in the spring of 1864, was at length obliged to send in her resignation. Her health seemed utterly broken down, and her physicians and friends saw in an entire change of air and scene the best hope of her recovery. She had for some time been often indisposed, and her illness at last terminated in fever and chills. Though well accustomed during her long residence to the climate of Maryland, she no longer possessed her youthful powers of restoration and reinvigoration. Accordingly it was determined that a sea voyage, and a tom in Europe were therefore advised as essential to her recovery.

She left the Naval School Hospital on the 27th of May, 1864, and set sail from New York on the 15th of June.

The disease did not succumb at once, as was hoped. She endured extreme illness and lassitude during her voyage, and was completely prostrated on her arrival in Paris where she lay three weeks ill, before being able to proceed by railroad to Lucerne, Switzerland, and rejoin her sister who had been some months in Europe, and who, with her family, were to be the traveling companions of Mrs. Tyler. Arrived at Lucerne, she was again prostrated by chills and fever, and only recovered after removal to the dryer climate of Berlin. The next year she was again ill with the same disease after a sojourn among the dykes and canals of Holland.

Mrs. Tyler spent about eighteen months in Europe, traveling over various parts of the Continent, and England, where she remained four or five months, returning to her native land in November, 1865, to find the desolating war which had raged here at the time of her departure at an end. Her health had been by this time entirely re-established, and she is happy in the belief that long years of usefulness yet remain to her.

Ardent and fearless in her loyalty to her Government, Mrs. Tyler had ample opportunities, never neglected, to impress the truth in regard to our country and its great struggle for true liberty, upon the minds of persons of all classes in Europe. Her letters of introduction from her friends, from Bishop Whittingham and others, brought her iuto frequent contact with people of cultivation and refinement who, like the masses, yet held the popular belief in regard to the oppression and abuse of the South by the North, a belief which Mrs. Tyler even at the risk of offending numerous Southern friends by her championship, was sure to combat. Like other intelligent loyal Americans she was thus the means of spreading right views, and accomplishing great good, even while in feeble health and far from her own country. For her services in this regard she might well have been named a Missionary of Truth and Liberty.

One instance of her experience in contact with Southern sympathizers with the Rebellion, we take the liberty to present to the readers of this sketch. Mrs. Tyler was in London when the terrible tidings of that last and blackest crime of the Rebellion— the assassination of Abraham Lincoln was received. She was paying a morning visit to an American friend, a Southerner and a Christian, when the door was suddenly thrust open and a fiendish-looking man rushed in, vociferating, "Have you heard the news? Old Abe is assassinated! Seward too! Johnson escaped. Now if God will send an earthquake and swallow up the whole North—men, women, and children, I will say His name be praised!"

All this was uttered as in one breath, and then the restless form, and fierce inflamed visage as suddenly disappeared, leaving 32 horrid imprecations upon the ears of the listeners, who never supposed the fearful tale could be true. Mrs. Tyler's friend offered the only extenuation possible—the man had "been on board the Alabama and was very bitter." But in Mrs. Tyler's memory that fearful deed is ever mingled with that fiendish face and speech.

The next day the Rebel Commissioner Mason, replying to some remarks of the American Minister, Mr. Adams, in the Times, took occasion most emphatically to deprecate the insinuation that the South had any knowledge of, or complicity in this crime.

MRS. WILLIAM H. HOLSTEIN

AT the opening of the war Mrs. Holstein was residing in a most pleasant and delightful country home at Upper Merion, Montgomery County, Pennsylvania. In the words of one who knows and appreciates her well—"Mr and Mrs. Holstein are people of considerable wealth, and unexceptionable social position, beloved and honored by all who know them, who voluntarily abandoned their beautiful home to live for years in camps and hospitals. Their own delicacy and modesty would forbid them to speak of the work they accomplished, and no one can ever know the greatness of its results."

As Mrs. Holstein was always accompanied by her husband, and this devoted pair were united in this great patriotic and kindly work, as in all the other cases, duties and pleasures of life, it would be almost impossible, even if it were necessary, to give any separate account of her services for the army. This is shown in the following extracts from a letter, probably not intended for publication, but which, in a spirit far removed from that of self-praise, gives an account of the motives and feelings which actuated her, and of the opening scenes of her public services.

"The story of my work, blended as it is, (and should be) so intimately with that of my husband, in his earnest wish to carry out what we felt to be simply a matter of duty, is like an 'oft told tale' not worth repeating. Like all other loyal women in our land, at the first sound and threatening of war, there sprang up in my heart an uncontrollable impulse to do, to act; for anything but idleness when our country was in peril and her sons marching to battle.

"It seemed that the only help woman could give was in providing comforts for the sick and wounded, and to this, for a time, I gave my undivided attention. I felt sure there was work for me to do in this war; and when my mother would say 'I hope, my child, it will not be in the hospitals,'—my response was ever the same—'Wherever or whatever it may be, it shall be done with all my heart.'

"At length came the battle of Antietam, and from among us six ladies went to spend ten days in caring for the wounded. But craven-like I shrank instinctively from such scenes, and declined to join the party. But when my husband returned from there, one week after the battle, relating such unheard of stories of suffering, and of the help that was needed, I hesitated no longer. In a few days we collected a car load of boxes, containing comforts and delicacies for the wounded, and had the satisfaction of taking them promptly to their destination.

"The first wounded and the first hospitals I saw I shall never forget, for then flashed across my mind, 'This is the work God has given you to do,' and the vow was made, I While the war lasts we stand pledged to aid, as far as is in our power, the sick and suffering. We have no right to the comforts of our home, while so many of the noblest of our land so willingly renounce theirs.' The scenes of Antietam are graven as with an 'iron pen' upon my mind. The place ever recalls throngs of horribly wounded men strewn in every direction. So fearful it all looked to me then, that I thought the choking sobs and blinding tears would never admit of my being of any use. To suppress them, and to learn to be calm under all circumstances, was one of the hardest lessons the war taught.

"We gave up our sweet country home, and from that date were dwellers in tents occupied usually in field hospitals, choosing that work because there was the greatest need, and knowing that while many were willing to work at home, but few could go to the front."

From that time, the early autumn of 1862, until July, 1865, Mrs. Holstein was constantly devoted to the work, not only in camps and hospitals, but in traveling from place to place and enlisting the more energetic aid of the people by lecturing and special appeals.

At Antietam Mrs. Holstein found the men she had come to care for, those brave, suffering men, lying scattered all over the field, in barns and sheds, under the shelter of trees and fences, in need of every comfort, but bearing their discomforts and pain without complaint or murmuring, and full of gratitude to those who had it in their power to do anything, ever so little, for their relief.

Here she encountered the most trying scenes—a boy of seventeen crying always for his mother to come to him, or to be permitted to go to her, till the great stillness of death fell upon him; agonized wives seeking the remains of the lost, sorrowing relatives, of all degrees, some confirmed in their worst fears, some reassured and grateful—a constant succession of bewildering emotions, of hope, fear, sadness and joy.

The six ladies from her own town, were still for a long time busy in their work of mercy distributing freely, as they had been given, the supplies with which they had been provided. This was eminently a work of faith. Often the stores, of one, or of many kinds, would be exhausted, but in no instance did Providence fail to immediately replenish those most needed.

During the stay of Mr and Mrs. Holstein in Sharpsburg, an ambulance was daily placed at their disposal, and they were continually going about with it and finding additional cases in need of every comfort. Supplies were continually sent from friends at home, and they remained until the wounded had all left save a few who were retained at Smoketown and Locust Spring Hospitals.

While the army rested in the vicinity of Sharpsburg, scores of fever patients came pouring in, making a fearful addition to the hospital patients, and greatly adding to the mortality.

The party, consisting of Mr and Mrs. Holstein and a friend of theirs, a lady, remained until their services were no longer required, and then, about the 1st of December, returned home. Busied in arrangement for the collection and forwarding of stores, and in making trips to Antietam, Harper's Ferry, and Frederick City, on similar business, the days wore away until the battle of Fredericksburg. Soon after this they went to Virginia, and entered the Second Corps Hospital near Falmouth. There in a Sibley tent whose only floor was of the branches of the pines—in that little Hospital on the bleak hill-side, the winter wore slowly away. The needful army movements had rendered the muddy roads impassable. Ho chaplain came to the camp until these roads were again in good order. Men sickened and died with no other religious services performed in their hearing than the simple reading of Scripture and prayers which Mrs. Holstein was in the habit of using for them, and which were always gladly listened to.

Just previous to the battle of Chancellorsville, Mrs. Holstein returned home for a few days, and was detained on coming back to her post by the difficulty of getting within the lines. She found the hospital moved some two miles from its former location, and that many of her former patients had died, or suffered much in the change. After the battle there was of course a great accession of wounded men. Some had lain long upon the field—one group for eleven days, with wounds undressed, and almost without food. The rebels, finding they did not die, reluctantly fed them with some of their miserable corn bread, and afterwards sent them within the Union lines.

The site of the hospital where Mrs. Holstein was now stationed, was very beautiful. The surgeon in charge had covered the sloping hill-side with a flourishing garden. The convalescents had slowly and painfully planted flower seeds, and built rustic arbors. All things had begun to assume the aspect of a beautiful home.

But suddenly, on the 13th of June, 1863, while at dinner, the order was received to break up the hospital. In two hours the wounded men, so great was their excitement at the thought of going toward home, were on their way to Washington.

All was excitement, in fact. The army was all in motion as soon as possible. Through the afternoon the work of destruction went on. As little as possible was left for the enemy, and when Mrs. Holstein awoke the following morning, the plain below was covered by a living mass, and the bayonets were gleaming in the brilliant sunlight, as the long lines were put in motion, and the Army of the Potomac began its northern march.

Mr and Mrs. Holstein accompanied it, bearing all its dangers and discomforts in company with the men with whom they had for the time cast their lot. The heat, dust, and fatigue were dreadful, and danger from the enemy was often imminent. At Sangster's Station, the breaking down of a bridge delayed the crossing of the infantry, and the order was given to reduce the officers' baggage to twenty pounds then came many of the officers to beg leave to entrust to the care of Mr and Mrs. Holstein, money and valuables. They received both in large amounts, and had the satisfaction of carrying all safely, and having them delivered at last to their rightful owners.

At Union Mills a battle was considered imminent, and Mrs. Holstein's tent in the rear of the Union army, was within bugle call of the rebel lines. In the morning it was deemed best for them to proceed by railroad to Alexandria and Washington, whence they could readily return whenever needed.

. At Washington, Mr. Holstein was threatened by an attack of malarious fever, and they returned at once to their home. While there, and he still unable to move, the battle of Gettysburg was fought. In less than a week he left his bed, and the devoted pair proceeded thither to renew their services, where they were then so greatly needed.

Mrs. Holstein's first night in this town was passed upon the parlor floor of a hotel, with only a satchel for a pillow, where fatigue made her sleep soundly. The morning saw them at the Field Hospital of the Second Corps, where they were enthusiastically welcomed by their old friends. Here, side by side, just as they had been brought in from the field, lay friends and enemies.

Experience had taught Mr and Mrs. Holstein how and what to do. Very soon their tent was completed, their "Diet Kitchen" arranged, the valuable supplies they had brought with them ready for distribution, and their work moving on smoothly and beneficially amid all the horrors of this terrible field.

"There," reports Mrs. Holstein, "as in all places where I have known our brave Union soldiers, they bore their sufferings bravely, I might almost say exultingly, because they were for 'The Flag' and our country."

The scenes of horror and of sadness enacted there, have left their impress upon the mind of Mrs. Holstein in unfading characters. And yet, amidst these there were some almost ludicrous, as for instance, that of the soldier, White, of the Twentieth Massachusetts, who, supposed to be dead, was borne, with two of his comrades, to the grave side, but revived under the rude shock with which the stretcher was set down, and looking down into the open grave in which lay a brave lieutenant of his own regiment, declared, with grim fun, that he would not be "buried by that raw recruit," and ordered the men to "carry him back." This man, though fearfully wounded in the throat, actually lived and recovered.

The government was now well equipped with stores and supplies, but Mrs. Holstein writes her testimony, with that of all others, to the most valuable supplementary aid of the Sanitary and Christian Commissions, in caring for the vast army of wounded and suffering upon this dreadful field.

By the 7th of August all had been removed who were able to bear transportation, to other hospitals. Three thousand remained, who were placed in the United States General Hospital on York Turnpike. The Second Corps Hospital was merged in this, and Mrs. Holstein remained as its matron until its close, and was fully occupied until the removal of the hospital and the dedication of the National Cemetery.

She then returned home, but after rest she was requested by the Sanitary Commission to commence a tour among the Aid Societies of the State, for the purpose of telling the ladies all that her experience had taught her of the soldier's needs, and the best way of preparing and forwarding clothing, delicacies and supplies of all kinds. She felt it impossible to be idle, and however disagreeable this task, she would not shrink from it. The earnestness with which she was listened to, and the consciousness of the good to result from her labors, sustained her all through the arduous winter's work, during which she often met two or three audiences for an "hour and a half talk," in the course of the day. Her husband as usual accompanied her, and in the spring, with the commencement of Grant's campaign over the Rapidan, they both went forward as agents of the Sanitary Commission.

Through all this dread campaign they worked devotedly. They could not rest to be appalled by its horrors. They could not think of the grandeur of its conceptions or the greatness of its victories—they could only work and wait for leisure to grasp the wonder of the passing events. As Mrs. Holstein herself says: While living amidst so much excitement—in the times which form history—we were unconscious of it all—it was our daily life!"

Of that long period, Mrs. Holstein records two grand experiences as conspicuous—the salute which followed the news of the completion of Sherman's "March to the Sea," and the explosion of the mine at City Point.

With the first, one battery followed another with continuous reverberation, till all the air was filled with the roar of artillery. The other was more awful. The explosion was fearful. The smoke rose in form like a gigantic umbrella, and from its midst radiated every kind of murderous missile—shells were thrown and burst in all directions, muskets and every kind of arms fell like a shower around. Comparatively few were killed—many of the men were providentially out of the way. Until the revelations upon the trial of Wirz, it was supposed to have been caused by an accident, but then men learned that it was part of a fiendish plot to destroy lives and Government property.

The summer of 1864 was noted for its intense heat and dust, but Mr and Mrs. Holstein remained with the army, absorbed in their work, till November, when Mr. Holstein's health again failed and they went home for rest. It was not thought prudent for them to return, and Mrs. Holstein, still accompanied by him, resumed her travels and spent some time in "talking" to the women and children of the State. She had the satisfaction of establishing several societies which worked vigorously during the remainder of the war.

In January, 1865, they went to Annapolis to do what they could for the returned Andersonville prisoners, and to learn their actual condition and sufferings that Mrs. Holstein might have a better hold upon the minds of the people, to whom she talked. Let us give these brief allusions to her experiences here, in her own words.

"All of horror I had seen, or known, throughout the war, faded into insignificance when contrasted with the results of this heinous sin— a systematic course of starvation of brave men, made captive by the chances of v ar. My note-book is filled with fearful records of suffering, and hardships unparalleled, written just as I took the statements from the fleshless lips of these living skeletons. In appearance they reminded me more of the bodies I had seen washed out upon Antietam, and other battle-fields, than of anything else— only they had ceased to suffer and were at rest,—these were still living, breathing, helpless skeletons.

'In treason's prison-hold

Their martyred spirits grew

To stature like the saints of old,

While, amid agonies untold,

They starved for me—and you.'

"We remained at Annapolis from January to July, when, the war being closed, the men were mustered out of service. The few remaining were sent to Baltimore, and the hospitals were vacated and restored to their former uses.

"Much of the summer was occupied in unfinished hospital work, and in looking after some special cases of great interest. The final close of the war brought with it, for the first time in all these long years, perfect rest to overtasked mind and wearied body."

MRS. CORDELIA A. P. HARVEY

THE State of Wisconsin is justly proud of a name, which, while standing for what is noble and true in man, has received an added lustre in being made to express also, the sympathy, the goodness, and the power of woman. The death of the honored husband, and the public labors of the heroic wife, in the same cause—the great cause that has absorbed the attention and the resources of the country for four years—have given each to the other a peculiar and thrilling interest to every loyal American heart.

It will be remembered that shortly after the battle of Shiloh, Governor Harvey proceeded to the front with supplies and medical aid to assist in caring for the wounded among the soldiers from his State, after rendering great service in alleviating their sufferings by the aid and comfort he brought with him, and reviving their spirits by his presence. As he was about to embark at Savannah for home, in passing from one boat to another, he fell into the river and was drowned. This was on the 19th of April, 1862, a day made memorable by some of the most important events in our country's history. Two days before he wrote to Mrs. Harvey the last sacred letter as follows:

"PITTSBURG LANDING, April 17, 1862.

"DEAR WIFE:—Yesterday was the day of my life. Thank God for the impulse that brought me here. I am well and have done more good by coming than I can well tell you. In haste,

Louis."

With these words ringing in her ears as from beyond the tomb, the conviction forced itself upon her mind that the path of duty for her lay in the direction he had so faithfully pointed out. But for a while womanly feeling overcame all else, and she gave way beneath the shock of her affliction, coming so suddenly and taking away at once the pride, the hope, and the joy of life. For many weeks it seemed that the tie that bound her to the departed was stronger than that which held her to the earth, and her friends almost despaired of seeing her again herself.

Hers was indeed a severe affliction. A husband, beloved and honored by all, without a stain upon his fair fame, with a bright future and hope of long life before him, had fallen—suddenly as by a bullet—at the front, where his great heart had led him to look after the wants of his own brave troops—fallen to be remembered with the long list of heroes who have died that their country might live, and in making themselves immortal, have made a people great. Nor was this sacrifice without its fruit. It was this that put it into her heart to work for the soldiers, and from the grave of HARVEY have sprung those flowers of Love and Mercy whose fragrance has filled the land.

Looking back now, it is easy to see how much this bereavement had to do in fitting Mrs. Harvey for her work. It is the experience of sorrow that prepares us to minister to others in distress. At home none could say they had given more for their country than she, few could feel a sorrow she had not known or with which she could not sympathize, out of something in her own experience. In the army, in camps and hospitals, who so fit to speak in the place of wife or mother to the sick and dying soldier, as she, in whom the tenderest feelings of the heart had been touched by the hand of Death?

With the intention of devoting herself to this work, she asked of the Governor permission to visit hospitals in the Western Department, as agent for the State, which was cordially granted, and early in the autumn of 1862, set out for St. Louis to commence her new work.

To a lady who had seen nothing of military life, of course, all was strange. The experiment she was making was one in which very many kind-hearted women have utterly failed—rushing to hospitals from the impulse of a tender sympathy, only to make themselves obnoxious to the surgeons by their impertinent zeal, and, by their inexperience and indiscretion, useless, and sometimes detrimental, to the patients. With the wisdom that has marked her course throughout, she at once comprehended the delicacy of the situation, and was not long in perceiving what she could best do, and wherein she could accomplish the most good. The facility with which she brought, not only her own best powers, but the influence universally accorded to her position, to bear for the benefit of the suffering soldiers, is subject of remark and wonder among all who have witnessed her labors.

At that time St. Louis was the theater of active military operations, and the hospitals were crowded with sick and wounded from the camps and battle-fields of Missouri and Tennessee. The army was not then composed of the hardy veterans whose prowess has since carried victory into every rebellious State, but of boys and young men unused to hardship, who, in the flush of enthusiasm, had entered the army. Time had not then brought to its present perfection the work of the Medical Department, and but for the spontaneous generosity of the people in sending forward assistance and supplies for the sick and wounded, the army could scarcely have existed. Such was the condition of things when Airs. Harvey commenced her work of mercy in visiting the hospitals of that city, filled with the victims of battle and disease. How from morning till night for many a weary week she waited by the cots of these poor fellows, attending to their little wants, and speaking words of cheer and comfort, those who knew her then all well remember. The work at once became delightful and profitable to her, calling her mind away from its own sorrows to the physical suffering of those around her. In her eagerness to soothe their woes, she half forgot her own, and came to them always with a joyous smile and words of cheerful consolation. During her stay in St. Louis her home was at the hospitable mansion of George Partridge, Esq., an esteemed member of the Western Sanitary Commission, whose household seem to have vied with each other in attention and kindness to their guest.

Hearing of great suffering at Cape Girardeau, she went there about the 1st of August, just as the First Wisconsin Cavalry were returning from their terrible expedition through the swamps of Arkansas. She had last seen them in all their pride and manly beauty, reviewed by her husband, the Governor, before they left their State. Now how changed! The strongest, they that could stand, just tottering about, the very shadows of their former selves. The building taken as a temporary hospital, was filled to overflowing, and the surgeons were without hospital supplies, the men subsisting on the common army ration alone. The heat was oppressive, and the diseases of the most fearfully contagious character. The surgeons themselves were appalled, and the attendants shrank from the care of the sick and the removal of the dead. In one room she found a corpse which had evidently lain for many hours, the nurses fearing to go near and see if the man was dead. With her own hands she bound up the face, and emboldened by her coolness, the burial party were induced to coffin the body and remove it from the house. Here was a field for self-forgetfulness and heroic devotion to a holy cause; and here the light of woman's sympathy shone brightly when all else was fear and gloom. Patients dying with the noxious camp fever breathed into her ear their last messages to loved ones at home, as she passed from cot to cot, undaunted by the bolts of death which fell around her thick as on the battle-field. She set herself to work procuring furloughs for such as were able to travel, and discharges for the permanently disabled, to get them away from a place of death. To this end she brought all the art of woman to work. Once convinced that the object she sought was just and right, she left no honorable means untried to secure it. Surgeons were flattered and coaxed, whenever coaxing and flattering availed; or, failing in this, she knew when to administer a gentle threat, or an intimation that a report might go up to a higher official. One resource failing she always had another, and never attempted anything without carrying it out.

Mrs. Harvey relates many touching incidents of her experience at this place which want of space forbids us to repeat. One of her first acts was to telegraph Mr. Yeatman, President of the 'Western Sanitary Commission, at St. Louis, for hospital stores, and in two days, by his promptness and liberality, she received an abundant supply.

After several weeks' stay at Cape Girardeau, during which time the condition of the hospital greatly improved, Mrs. Harvey continued her tour of visitation which was to embrace all the general hospitals on the Mississippi river, as well as the regimental hospitals of the troops of her own State. Her face, cheerful with all the heart's burden of grief, gladdened every ward where lay a Union soldier, from Keokuk as far down as the sturdy legions of GRANT had regained possession of the Father of Waters.

At Memphis she was able to do great service in procuring furloughs for men who would else have died. Often has the writer heard brave men declare, with tearful eyes, their gratitude to her for favors of this kind. Many came to have a strange and almost superstitious reverence for a person exercising so powerful an influence, and using it altogether for the good of the common soldier. The estimate formed of her authority by-some of the more ignorant class, often exhibited itself in an extremely ludicrous manner. She would sometimes receive letters from homesick men begging her to give them a furlough to visit their families! and often, from deserters and others confined in military prisons, asking to be set at liberty, and promising faithful service thereafter!

The spring of 1863 found General Grant making his approaches upon the last formidable position held by the rebels on the Mississippi. Young's Point, across the river from Vicksburg, the limit of uninterrupted navigation at that time, will be remembered by many as a place of great suffering to our brave boys. The high water covering the low lands on which they were encamped during the famous canal experiment, induced much sickness. Intent to be where her kind offices were most needed, Mrs. Harvey proceeded thither about the first of April. After a few weeks' labor, she, herself, overcome by the terrible miasma, was taken seriously ill, and was obliged to return homeward. Months of rest, and a visit to the seaside, were required to bring back a measure of her wonted strength, and so for the summer her services were lost to the army.

But though for a while withheld from her chosen work, Mrs. Harvey never forgot the sick soldier. Her observation while with the army, convinced her of the necessity of establishing general hospitals in the Northern States, where soldiers suffering from diseases incurable in the South, might be sent with prospect of recovery. Her own personal experience deepened her conviction, and, although the plan found little favor then among high officials, she a once gave her heart to its accomplishment. Although repeated efforts had been made in vain to lead the Government into this policy, Mrs. Harvey determined to go to Washington and make her plea in person to the president.

As the result of her interview with Mr. Lincoln, which was of the most cordial character, a General Hospital was granted to the State of Wisconsin; and none who visit the city of Madison can fail to observe, with patriotic pride, the noble structure known as Harvey Hospital. As proof of the service it has done, and as fully verifying the arguments urged by Mrs. Harvey to secure 34 its establishment, the reader is referred to the reports of the surgeon in charge of the hospital.

Her mission at Washington accomplished, Mrs. Harvey returned immediately home, where she soon received official intelligence that the hospital would be located at Madison and be prepared for the reception of patients at the earliest possible moment. Upon this, she went immediately to Memphis, Tennessee, where she was informed by the medical director of the Sixteenth Army Corps, that there were over one hundred men in Fort Pickering (used as a Convalescent Camp) who had been vacillating between camp and hospital for a year, and who would surely die unless removed North. At his suggestion, she accompanied these sick men up the river, to get them, if possible, north of St. Louis. She landed at Cairo, and proceeded to St. Louis by rail, and, on the arrival of the transport, had transportation to Madison ready for the men. As they were needy, and had not been paid, she procured of the Western Sanitary Commission a change of clothing for every one. Out of the whole number, only seven died, and only five were discharged. The remainder returned, strong and healthy, to the service.

Returning South, she visited all points on the river down to New Orleans, coming back to make her home for the time at Vicksburg, as the place nearest the centre of her field of labor. The Superintendent and Matrons of the Soldiers' Home extended to her a hearty welcome, happy to have their institution honored by her presence, and receive her sympathizing and kindly aid. So substantial was the reputation she had won among the army, that her presence alone, at a military post in the West, was a power for good. Officers and attendants in charge of hospitals knew how quick she was to apprehend and bring to light any delinquency in the performance of their duties, and profited by this knowledge to the mutual advantage of themselves and those thrown upon their care.

During the summer of 1864, the garrison of Vicksburg suffered much from diseases incident to the season in that latitude. Perhaps in no regiment was the mortality greater than in the Second Wisconsin Cavalry. Strong men sickened and died within a few days, and others lingered on for weeks, wasting by degrees, till only skin and bone were left. The survivors, in evidence of their appreciation of her sympathy and exertions for them in their need, presented her an elegant enameled gold watch, beautifully set with diamonds. The presentation was an occasion on which she could not well avoid a public appearance, and those who were present, must have wondered that one of such power in private conversation should have so little control, even of her own feelings, before an assembly. Mrs. Harvey has never distinguished herself as a public speaker. Resolute, impetuous, confident to a degree bordering on the imperious, with power of denunciation to equip an orator, she yet shrinks from the gaze of a multitude with a woman's modesty, and the humility of a child. She does not underestimate the worth of true womanhood by attempting to act a distinctively manly part.

Although known as the agent of the State of Wisconsin, All's. Harvey has paid little regard to state lines, and has done a truly national work. Throughout the time of her stay with the army, applications for her aid came as often from the soldiers of other states as from those of her own, and no one was ever refused relief if to obtain it was in her power. Acting in the character of a friend to every Union soldier, from whatever state, she has had the entire confidence of the great Sanitary Commissions, and rendered to their agents invaluable aid in the distribution of goods. The success that has everywhere attended Mrs. Harvey's efforts, directly or indirectly, to benefit the soldier, has given to her life an unusual charm, and established for her a national reputation.

In years to come, the war-scarred veteran will recount to listening children around the domestic hearth, along with many a thrilling deed of valor performed by his own right arm, the angel visits of this lady to his cot, when languishing with disease, or how, when ready to die, her intercessions secured him a furlough, and sent him home to feel the curative power of his native air and receive the care of loving hands and hearts. Not a few unfortunates will remember, if they do not tell, how her care reached them, not only in hospital but in prison as well, bringing clothing and comfort to them when shivering in their rags; while others, again, will not be ashamed to relate, as we have heard them, with tears, their gratitude for release from unjust imprisonment, secured by her faithful exertions.

The close of the war has brought Mrs. Harvey back to her home, and closed her work for the soldiers. Her attention now is turned in the direction of soothing the sorrows the war has caused among the households of her State. Many a soldier who has died for his country, has left his little ones to the charity of the world. Through her exertions the State of Wisconsin now has a Soldiers' Orphan Asylum, where all these children of our dead heroes shall be gathered in. By a visit to Washington she has recently obtained from the United States Government, the donation of its interest in Harvey Hospital, and has turned it into an institution of this kind, and has set her hand and heart to the work of securing from the people a liberal endowment for it.

Happy indeed has she been in her truly Christian work, begun in sadness and opening into the joy that crowns every good work. The benedictions of thousands of the brave and victorious rest upon her, and the purest spirits of the martyred ones have her in their gentle care! May America be blest with many more like her to teach us by example the nature and practice of a true Christian heroism.

MRS. SARAH R. JOHNSTON.

OUR. northern women have won the highest meed of praise for their devotion and self-sacrifice in the cause of their country, but great as their labors and sacrifices have been, they are certainly inferior to those of some of the loyal women of the South, who for the love they bore to their country and its flag, braved all the contempt, obloquy and scorn which Southern women could heap upon them—who lived for years in utter isolation from the society of relatives, friends, and neighbors, because they would render such aid and succor as was in their power to the defenders of the national cause, in prison, in sorrow and in suffering. Often were the lives of those brave women in danger, and the calmness with which they met those who thirsted for their blood gave evidence of their position of a spirit as undaunted and lofty as any which ever faced the cannon's mouth or sought death in the high places of the field. Among these heroines none deserves a higher place in the records of womanly patriotism and courage than Mrs. Sarah R. Johnston.

At the breaking out of the war Mrs. Johnston was teaching a school at Salisbury, North Carolina, where she was born and always resided. When the first prisoners were brought into that place, the Southern women turned out in their carriages and with a band escorted them through the town, and when they filed past saluted them with contemptuous epithets. From that time Mrs. Johnston determined to devote herself to the amelioration of the condition of the prisoners; and the testimony of thousands of the Union soldiers confined there proved how nobly she performed the duties she undertook. It was no easy task, for she was entirely alone, being the only woman who openly advocated Union sentiments and attempted to administer to the wants of the prisoners. For fifteen months none of the women of Salisbury spoke to her or called upon her, and every possible indignity was heaped on her as a "Yankee sympathizer." Her scholars were withdrawn from her school, and it was broken up, and her means were very limited; nevertheless, she accomplished more by systematic arrangements than many would have done with a large outlay of money.

When the first exchange of prisoners was made, she went to the depot to arrange some pallets for some of the sick who were leaving, when she stumbled in the crowd, and looking down she found a young Federal soldier who had fainted and fallen, and was in danger of being trodden to death. She raised him up and called for water, but none of the people would get a drop to save a "Yankee's" life. Some of the soldiers who were in the cars threw their canteens to her, and she succeeded in reviving him; during this time the crowd heaped upon her every insulting epithet they could think of, and her life even was ill danger. But she braved all, and succeeded in obtaining permission from Colonel Godwin, then in command of the post, who was a kindhearted man, to let her remove him to her own house, promising to take care of him as if he were her own son, and if he died to give him Christian burial. He was in the last stages of consumption, and she felt sure he would die if taken to the prison hospital. None of the citizens of the place would even assist in carrying him, and after a time two gentlemen from Richmond stepped forward and helped convey him to her house. There she watched over him for hours, as he was in a terrible state from neglect, having had blisters applied to his chest which had never been dressed and were full of vermin.

The poor boy, whose name was Hugh Berry, from Ohio, only lived a few days, and she had a grave dug for him in her garden in the night, for burial had been refused in the public graveyard, and she had been threatened that if she had him interred decently his body should be dug up and buried in the street. They even attempted to take his body from the house for that purpose, but she stood at her door, pistol in hand, and said to them that the first man who dared to cross her threshold for such a purpose should be shot like a dog. They did not attempt it, and she performed her promise to the letter.

During the first two years she was enabled to do a great many acts of kindness for the prisoners, but after that time she was watched very closely as a Yankee sympathizer, and the rules of the prison were stricter, and what she could do was dene by strategy.

Her means were now much reduced, but she still continued in her good work, cutting up her carpets and spare blankets to make into moccasins, and when new squads of prisoners arrived, supplied them with bread and water as they halted in front of her house, which they were compelled to do for hours, waiting the routine of being mustered into the prison. They were not allowed to leave their ranks, and she would turn an old-fashioned windlass herself for hours, raising water from her well; for the prisoners were often twenty-four to forty-eight hours on the railroad without rations or water.

Generally the officer in command would grant her request, but once a sergeant told her, in reply, if she gave any of them a drop of water or a piece of bread, or dared to come outside her gate for that purpose, he would pin her to the earth with his bayonet. She defied him, and taking her pail of water in one hand, and a basket of bread in the other, she walked directly past him on her errand of mercy; he followed her, placing his bayonet between her shoulders, just so that she could feel the cold steel. She turned and coolly asked him why he did not pin her to the earth, as he had threatened to do, but got no reply. Then some of the rebels said, "Sergeant, you can't make anything on that woman, you had better let her alone," and she performed her work unmolested.

Not content with these labors, she visited the burial-place where the deceased Union prisoners of that loathsome prison-pen at Salisbury were buried, and transcribed with a loving fidelity every inscription which could be found there, to let the sorrowing friends of those martyrs to their country know where their beloved ones are laid. The number of these marked graves is small, only thirty-one in all, for the greater part of the four or five thousand dead starved and tortured there till they relinquished their feeble hold on life, were buried in trenches four or five deep, and no record of their place of burial was permitted. Mrs. Johnston also copied from the rebel registers at Salisbury after the place was captured the statistics of the Union prisoners, admitted, died, and remaining on hand in each month from October, 1864, to April, 1865. The aggregates in these six months were four thousand and fifty-four admitted, of whom two thousand three hundred and ninety-seven died, and one thousand six hundred and fifty-seven remained.

Mrs. Johnston came North in the summer of 1865, to visit her daughter, who had been placed at a school in Connecticut by the kindness of some of the officers she had befriended in prison; transportation having been given her by Generals Schofield and Carter, who testified to the services she had rendered our prisoners, and that she was entitled to the gratitude of the Government and all loyal citizens.

EMILY E. PARSONS

[See the letters of this extraordinary woman in Fearless Purpose.]

AMONG the honorable and heroic women of New England whose hearts were immediately enlisted in the cause of their country, in its recent struggle against the rebellion of the slave States, and who prepared themselves to do useful service in the hospitals as nurses, was Miss Emily E. Parsons, of Cambridge, Massachusetts, a daughter of Professor Theophilus Parsons, of the Cambridge Law School, and granddaughter of the late Chief Justice Parsons, of Massachusetts.

Miss Parsons was born in Taunton, Massachusetts, was educated in Boston, and resided at Cambridge at the beginning of the war. She at once foresaw that there would be need of the same heroic work on the part of the women of the country as that performed by Florence Nightingale and her army of women nurses in the Crimea, and with her father's approval she consulted with Dr. Wyman, of Cambridge, how she could acquire the necessary instruction and training to perform the duties of a skilful nurse in the hospitals. Through his influence with Dr. Shaw, the superintendent of the Massachusetts General Hospital, she was received into that institution as a pupil in the work of caring for the sick, in the dressing of wounds, in the preparation of diet for invalids, and in all that pertains to a well regulated hospital. She was thoroughly and carefully instructed by the surgeons of the hospital, all of whom took great interest in fitting her for the important duties she proposed to undertake, and gave her every opportunity to practice, with her own hands, the labors of a good hospital nurse. Dr. Warren and Dr.

Townshend, two distinguished surgeons, took special pains to give her all necessary information and the most thorough instruction. At the end of one year and a half of combined teaching and practice, she was recommended by Dr. Townshend to Fort Schuyler Hospital, on Long Island Sound, where she went in October, 1862, and for two months performed the duties of hospital nurse, in the most faithful and satisfactory manner, when she left by her father's wishes, on account of the too great exposure to the sea, and went to New York.

While in New York Miss Parsons wrote to Miss Dix, the agent of the Government for the employment of women nurses, offering her services wherever they might be needed, and received an answer full of encouragement and sympathy with her wishes. At the same time she also made the acquaintance of Mrs. John C. Fremont, who wrote to the Western Sanitary Commission at St. Louis, of her qualifications and desire of usefulness in the hospital service, and she was immediately telegraphed to come on at once to St. Louis.

At this time, January, 1863, every available building in St. Louis was converted into a hospital, and the sick and wounded were brought from Vicksburg, and Arkansas Post, and Helena up the river to be cared for at St. Louis and other military posts. At Memphis and Mound City, (near Cairo) at Quincy, Illinois, and the cities on the Ohio River, the hospitals were in equally crowded condition. Miss Parsons went immediately to St. Louis and -was assigned by Mr. James E. Yeatman, (the President of the Western Sanitary Commission, and agent for Miss Dix), to the Lawson Hospital. In a few weeks, however, she was needed for a still more important service, and was placed as head nurse on the hospital steamer "City of Alton," Surgeon Turner in charge. A large supply of sanitary stores were entrusted to her care by the Western Sanitary Commission, and the steamer proceeded to Vicksburg, where she was loaded v'th about four hundred invalid soldiers, many of them sick past recovery, and returned as far as Memphis. On this trip the strength and endurance of Miss Parsons were tried to the utmost, and the ministrations of herself and her associates to the poor, helpless and suffering men, several of whom died on the passage up the river, were constant and unremitting. At Memphis, after transferring the sick to the hospitals, an order was received from General Grant to load the boat with troops and return immediately to Vicksburg, an order prompted by some military exigency, and Miss Parsons and the other female nurses were obliged to return to St. Louis.

For a few weeks after her return she suffered from an attack of malarious fever, and on her recovery was assigned to duty as superintendent of female nurses at the Benton Barracks Hospital, the largest of all the hospitals in St. Louis, built out of the amphitheatre and other buildings in the fair grounds of the St. Louis Agricultural Society, and placed in charge of Surgeon Ira Russell, an excellent physician from Natick, Mass. In this large hospital there were often two thousand patients, and besides the male nurses detailed from the army, the corps of female nurses consisted of one to each of the fifteen or twenty wards, whose duty it was to attend to the special diet of the feebler patients, to see that the wards were kept in order, the beds properly made, the dressing of wounds properly done, to minister to the wants of the patients, and to give them words of good cheer, both by reading and conversation— softening the rougher treatment and manners of the male nurses, by their presence, and performing the more delicate offices of kindness that are natural to woman.

In this important and useful service these women nurses, many of them having but little experience, needed one of their own number of superior knowledge, judgment and experience, to supervise their work, counsel and advise with them, instruct them in their duties, secure obedience to every necessary regulation, and good order in the general administration of this important branch of hospital service. For this position Miss Parsons was most admirably fitted, and discharged its duties with great fidelity and success for many months, as long as Dr. Russell continued in charge of the hospital. The whole work of female nursing was reduced to a perfect system, and the nurses under Miss Parsons' influence became a sisterhood of noble women, performing a great and loving service to the maimed and suffering defenders of their country. In the organization of this system and the framing of wise rules for carrying it into effect Dr. Russell and Mr. Yeatman lent their counsel and assistance, and Dr. Russell, as the chief surgeon, entertained those enlightened and liberal views which gave the system a full chance to accomplish the best results. Under his administration, and Miss Parsons' superintendence of the nursing, the Benton Barracks Hospital became famous for its excellence, and for the rapid recovery of the patients.

It was not often that the army surgeons could be induced to give so fair a trial to female nursing in the hospitals. Too often they allowed their prejudices to interfere, and used their authority to thwart instead of aid the best plans for making the services of women all that was needed in the hospitals. But in the ease of Dr. Russell, enlightened judgment and humane sympathies combined to make him friendly to the highest exertions of woman, in this holy service of humanity. And the result entirely justified the most sanguine expectations.

Having served six months in this capacity, Miss Parsons went to her home at Cambridge, on a furlough from the Sanitary Commission, to recruit her health. After a short period of rest she returned to St. Louis and resumed her position at Benton Barracks, in which she continued till August, 1864, when in consequence of illness, caused by malaria, she returned to her home in Cambridge a second time. On her recovery she concluded to enter upon the same work in the eastern department, but the return of peace, and the disbanding of a large portion of the army rendered her services in the hospitals no longer necessary.

From this time she devoted herself at home to working foi the freedmen and refugees, collecting clothing and garden seeds for them, many boxes of which she shipped to the Western Sanitary Commission, at St. Louis, to be distributed in the Mississippi Valley, where they were greatly needed, and were received as a blessing from the Lord by the poor refugees and freedmen, who in many instances were without the mens to help themselves, or to buy seed for the next year's planting.

In the spring of 1865, she took a great interest in the Sanitary Fair held at Chicago, collected many valuable gifts for it, and was sent for by the Committee of Arrangements to go out as one of the managers of the department furnished by the New Jerusalem Church—the different churches having separate departments in the Fair. This duty she fulfilled, with great pleasure and success, and the general results of the Fair were all that could be desired.

Returning home from the Chicago Fair, and the war being ended, Miss Parsons conceived a plan of establishing in hei own city of Cambridge, a Charity Hospital for poor women and children. For this most praiseworthy object she has already collected a portion of the necessary funds, which she has placed in the hand of a gentleman who consents to act as Treasurer, and is entirely confident of the ultimate success of her enterprise. There is no doubt but that she possesses the character, good judgment, Christian motive and perseverance to carry it through, and she has the encouragement, sympathies and prayers of many friends to sustain her in the noble endeavor.

In concluding this sketch of the labors of Miss Parsons in the care and nursing of our sick and wounded soldiers, and in the Sanitary and other benevolent enterprises called forth bv the war, it is but just to say that in every position she occupied she performed her part with judgment and fidelity, and always brought to her work a spirit animated by the highest motives, and strengthened by communion with the Infinite Spirit, from whom all love and wisdom come to aid and bless the children of men. Everywhere she went among the sick and suffering she brought the sunshine of a cheerful and loving heart, beaming from a countenance expressive of kindness, and good will and sympathy to all. Her presence in the hospital was always a blessing, and cheered and comforted many a despondent heart, and compensated in some degree, for the absence of the loved ones at home. Her gentle ministrations so faithful and cheering, might well have received the reverent worship bestowed on the shadow of Florence Nightingale, so admirably described by Longfellow in his Saint Filomena:

"And slow, as in a dream of bliss

The speechless sufferer turned to kiss

Her shadow as it falls Upon the darkening walls."

MRS. ALMIRA FALES

MRS. FALES, it is believed, was the first woman in America who performed any work directly tending to the aid and comfort of the soldiers of the nation in the late war. In truth, her labors commenced before any overt acts of hostility had taken place, even so long before as December, 1860. Hostility enough there undoubtedly was in feeling, but the fires of secession as yet only smouldered, not bursting into the lurid flames of war until the following spring.

Yet Mrs. Fales, from her home in Washington, was a keen observer of the "signs of the times," and read aright the portents of rebellion. In her position, unobserved herself, she saw and heard much, which probably would have remained unseen and unheard by loyal eyes and ears, had the haughty conspirators against the nation's life dreamed of any danger arising from the knowledge of their projects, obtained by this humble woman.

So keen was the prescience founded on these things that, as has been said, she, as early as December, 1860, scarcely a month after the election of Abraham Lincoln, gave a pretext for secession which its leaders were eager to avail themselves of, "began to prepare lint and hospital stores for the soldiers of the Union, not one of whom had then been called to take up arms."

Of course, she was derided for this act. Inured to peace, seemingly more eager for the opening of new territory, the spread of commerce, the gain of wealth and power than even for the highest national honor, the North would not believe in the possibility of war until the boom of the guns of Sumter, reverberating from the waves of the broad Atlantic, and waking the echoes all along its shores, burst upon their ears to tell in awful tones that it had indeed commenced.

But there was one—a woman in humble life, yet of wonderful benevolence, of indomitable energy, unflagging perseverance, and unwavering purpose, who foresaw its inevitable coming and was prepared for it.

Almira Fales was no longer young. She had spent a life in doing good, and was ready to commence another. Her husband had employment under the government in some department of the civil service, her sons entered the army, and she, too,—a soldier, in one sense, as truly as they—since she helped and cheered on the fight.

From that December day that commenced the work, until long after the war closed, she gave herself to it, heart and soul—mind and body. No one, perhaps, can tell her story of work and hardship in detail, not even herself, for she acts rather than talks or writes. "Such women, always doing, never think of pausing to tell their own stories, which, indeed, can never be told; yet the hint of them can be given, to stir in the hearts of other women a purer emulation, and to prove to them that the surest way to happiness is to serve others and forget yourself."

In detail we have only this brief record of what she has done, yet what volumes it contains, what a history of labor and of self-sacrifice!

"After a life spent in benevolence, it was in December, 1860, that Almira Fales began to prepare lint and hospital stores for the soldiers of the Union, not one of whom had then been called to take up arms. People laughed, of course; thought it a 'freak;' said that none of these things would ever be needed. Just as the venerable Dr. Mott said, at the women's meeting in Cooper Institute, after Sumter had been fired: 'Go on, ladies! Get your lint ready, if it will do your dear hearts any good, though I don't believe myself that it will ever be needed. Since that December Mrs. Fales has emptied over seven thousand boxes of hospital stores, and distributed with her own hands over one hundred and fifty thousand dollars worth of comforts to sick and wounded soldiers. Besides, she supplied personally between sixty and seventy forts with reading matter. She was months at sea—the only woman on hospital ships nursing the wounded and dying men. She was at Corinth, and at Pittsburg Landing, serving our men in storm and darkness. She was at Pair Oaks. She was under fire through the seven days fight on the

Peninsula, with almost breaking heart ministering on those bloody fields to the saddest creatures that she ever saw.

"Through all those years, every day, she gave her life, her strength, her nursing, her mother-love to our soldiers. For her to be a soldier's nurse meant something very different from wearing a white apron, a white cap, sitting by a moaning soldier's bed, looking pretty. It meant days and nights of untiring toil; it meant the lowliest office, the most menial service; it meant the renouncing of all personal comfort, the sharing of her last possession with the soldier of her country; it meant patience, and watching, and unalterable love. A mother, every boy who fought for his country was her boy; and if she had nursed him in infancy, she could not have cared for him with a tenderer care. Journey after journey this woman has performed to every part of the land, carrying with her some wounded, convalescing soldier, bearing him to some strange cottage that she never saw before, to the pale, weeping woman within, saying to her with smiling face, 'I have brought back your boy. Wipe your eyes, and take care of him. Then, with a fantastic motion, tripping away as if she were not tired at all, and had done nothing more than run across the street. Thousands of heroes on earth and in heaven gratefully remember this woman's loving care to them in the extremity of anguish. The war ended, her work does not cease. Every day you may find her, with her heavily-laden basket, in hovels of white and 36 black, which dainty and delicate ladies would not dare to enter. No wounds are so loathsome, no disease so contagious, no human being so abject, that she shrinks from contact, if she can minister to their necessity."

During the Peninsular campaign Mrs. Fales was engaged on board the Hospital Transports, during most of the trying season of 1862. She was at Harrison's Landing in care of the wounded and wearied men worn down by the incessant battles and hard marches which attended the "change of base" from the Chickahominy to the James. She spent a considerable time in the hospitals at Fortress Monroe; and was active in her ministrations upon the fields in the battles of Centreville, Chantilly, and the second battle of Bull Run, indeed most of those of Pope's campaign in Virginia in the autumn of 1862.

At the battle of Chancellorsville, or rather at the assault upon Marye's Heights, in that fierce assault of Sedgwick's gallant Sixth Corps on the works which had on the preceding December defied the repeated charges of Burnside's best troops, Mrs. Fales lost a son. About one-third of the attacking force were killed or badly wounded in the assault, and among the rest the son of this devoted mother, who at that very hour might have been ministering to the wounded and dying son of some other mother. This loss was to her but a stimulus to further efforts and sacrifices. She mourned as deeply as any mother, but not as selfishly, as some might have done. In this, as in all her ways of life, she but carried out its ruling principle which was self-devotion, and deeds not words.

Mrs. Fales may not, perhaps, be held up as an example of harmonious development, but she has surely shown herself great in self-forgetfulness and heroic devotion to the cause of her country. In person she is tall, plain in dress, and with few of the fashionable and stereotyped graces of manner. No longer young, her face still bears ample traces of former beauty, and her large blue eyes still beam with the clear brightness of youth. But her hands tell the story of hardship and sacrifice.

"Poor hands! darkened and hardened by work, they never shirked any task, never turned from any drudgery, that could lighten the load of another. Dear hands! how many bloodstained faces they have washed, how many wounds they have bound up, how many eyes they have closed in dying, how many bodies they have sadly yielded to the darkness of death!"

She is full of a quaint humor, and in all her visits to hospitals her aim seemed to be to awake smiles, and arouse the cheerfulness of the patients; and she was generally successful in this, being everywhere a great favorite. One more quotation from the written testimony of a lady who knew her well and we have done.

"An electric temperament, a nervous organization, with a brain crowded with a variety of memories and incidents that could only come to one in a million—all combine to give her a pleasant abruptness of motion and of speech, which I have heard some very fine ladies term insanity. 'Now don't you think she is crazy, to spend all her time in such ways?' said one. When we remember how rare a thing utter unselfishness and self-forgetfulness is, we must conclude that she is crazy. If the listless and idle lives which we live ourselves are perfectly sane, then Almira Fales must be the maddest of mortals. But would it not be better for the world, and for us all, if we were each of us a little crazier in the same direction?"

MISS CORNELIA HANCOCK

AMONG the most zealous and untiring of the women who ministered to the wounded men "at the front," in the long and terrible campaign of the Army of the Potomac in 1864-5, was Miss Cornelia Hancock, of Philadelphia. Of this lady's early history or her previous labors in the war, we have been unable to obtain any very satisfactory information. She had, we are told, been active in the United States General Hospitals in Philadelphia, and had there learned what wounded men need in the way of food and attention. She had also rendered efficient services at Gettysburg. Of her work among the wounded men at Belle Plain and Fredericksburg, Mr. John Yassar, one of the most efficient agents of the Christian Commission, writes as follows:

"Miss Cornelia Hancock was the first lady who arrived at Fredericksburg to aid in the care of the wounded. As one of the many interesting episodes of the war, it has seemed that her good deeds should not be unheralded. She was also among the very first to arrive at Gettysburg after the fearful struggle, and for days and weeks ministered unceasingly to the suffering. During the past winter she remained constantly with the army in winter quarters, connecting herself with the Second Division of the Second Corps. So attached were the soldiers, and so grateful for her ministration in sickness, that they built a house for her, in which she remained until the general order for all to leave was given.

"When the news of Grant's battles reached the North, Miss Hancock left Philadelphia at once for Washington. Several applications were made by Members of Congress at the War Department for a permit for her to go to the wounded. It was each time declined, as being unfeasible and improper. With a woman's tact, she made application to go with one of the surgeons then arriving, as assistant, as each surgeon was entitled to one. The plan succeeded, and I well remember the mental ejaculation made when I saw her at such a time on the boat. I lost sight of her at Belle Plain, and had almost forgotten the circumstance, when, shortly before our arrival at Fredericksburg, she passed in an ambulance. On being assigned to a hospital of the Second Corps, I found she had preceded me, and was earnestly at work. It was no fictitious effort, but she had already prepared soup and farina, and was dispensing it to the crowds of poor fellows lying thickly about.

"All day she worked, paying little attention to others, only assiduous in her sphere. When, the next morning, I opened a new hospital at the Methodist Church, I invited her to accompany me; she did so; and if success and amelioration of suffering attended the effort, it was in no small degree owing to her indefatigable labors. Within an hour from the time one hundred and twenty had been placed in the building, she had seen that good beef soup and coffee was administered to each, and during the period I was there, no delicacy or nutriment attainable was wanting to the men.

"Were any dying, she sat by to soothe their last moments, to receive the dying message to friends at home, and when it was over to convey by letter the sad intelligence. Let me rise ever so early, she had already preceded me at work, and during the many long hours of the day, she never seemed to weary or flag; in the evening, when all in her own hospital had been fully cared for, she would go about the town with delicacies to administer to officers who were so situated they could not procure them. At night she sought a garret (and it was literally one) for her rest.

"One can but feebly portray the ministrations of such a person. She belonged to no association—had no compensation. She commanded respect, for she was lady-like and well educated; so quiet and undemonstrative, that her presence was hardly noticed, except by the smiling faces of the wounded as she passed. While she supervised the cooking of the meats and soups and coffee, all nice things were made and distributed by herself. How the men watched for the dessert of farina and condensed milk, and those more severely wounded for the draughts of milk punch!

"Often would she make visits to the offices of the Sanitary and Christian Commissions, and when delicacies arrived, her men were among the first to taste them. Oranges, lemons, pickles, soft bread and butter, and even apple-sauce, were one or the other daily distributed. Such unwearied attention is the more appreciated, when one remembers the number of females who subsequently arrived, and the desultory and fitful labor performed. Passing from one hospital to another, and bestowing general sympathy, with small works, is not what wounded men want. It was very soon perceptible how the men in that hospital appreciated the solid worth of the one and the tinsel of the other.

"This imperfect recognition is but a slight testimonial to the lady-like deportment and the untiring labors in behalf of sick and wounded soldiers of Miss Hancock."

MRS MARY MORRIS HUSBAND

THERE are some noble souls whose devotion to duty, to the welfare of the suffering and sorrowing, and to the work which God has set before them, is so complete that it leaves them no time to think of themselves, and no consciousness that what they have done or are doing, is in any way remarkable. To them it seems the most natural thing in the world to undergo severe hardships and privations, to suffer the want of all things, to peril health and even life itself, to endure the most intense fatigue and loss of rest, if by so doing they may relieve another's pain or soothe the burdened and aching heart; and with the utmost ingenuousness, they will avow that they have done nothing worthy of mention; that it is the poor soldier who has been the sufferer, and has made the only sacrifices worthy of the name.

The worthy and excellent lady who is the subject of this sketch, is one of the representative women of this class. Few, if any, have passed through more positive hardships to serve the soldiers than she; but few have as little consciousness of them.

Mrs. Mary Morris Husband, is a granddaughter of Robert Morris, the great financier of our Revolutionary War, to whose abilities and patriotism it was owing that we had a republic at all. She is, in her earnest patriotism, well worthy of her ancestry. Her husband, a well-known and highly respectable member of the Philadelphia bar, her two sons and herself constituted her household at the commencement of the war, and her quiet home in the Quaker City, was one of the pleasantest of the many delightful homes in that city. The patriotic instincts were strong in the family; the two sons enlisted in the army at the very beginning of the conflict, one of them leaving his medical studies to do so; and the mother, as soon as there was any hospital work to do was fully prepared to take her part in it. She had been in poor health for some years, but in her anxiety to render aid to the suffering, her own ailings were forgotten. She was an admirable nurse and a skilful housewife and cook, and her first efforts for the sick and wounded soldiers in Philadelphia, were directed to the preparation of suitable and palatable food for them, and the rendering of those attentions which should relieve the irksomeness and discomforts of sickness in a hospital. The hospital on Twenty-second and Wood streets, Philadelphia, was the principal scene of these labors.

But the time had come for other and more engrossing labors for the sick and wounded, and she was to be inducted into them by the avenue of personal anxiety for one of her sons. In that fearful "change of base" which resulted in the seven days' battle on the peninsula, when from the combined influence of marsh malaria, want of food, overmarching, the heat and fatigue of constant fighting, and the depression of spirits incident to the unexpected retreat, more of our men fell down with mortal sickness than were slain or wounded in the battles, one of Mrs. Husband's sons was among the sufferers from disease, and word was sent to her that he was at the point of death. She hastened to nurse him, and after a great struggle and frequent relapses, he rallied, and began to recover. Meantime she had not been so wholly engrossed with her care for him as to be neglectful of the hundreds and thousands around, who, like him, were suffering from the deadly influences of that pestilential climate and soil, or of the wounded who were wearing out their lives in agony, with but scant attention or care; and every moment that could be spared from her sick boy, was given to the other sufferers around her.

It was in this period of her work that she rendered the service to a young soldier, now a physician of Brooklyn, New York, so graphically described in the following extract from a letter addressed to the writer of this sketch:

"I was prostrated by a severe attack of camp dysentery, stagnant water and unctuous bean soup not being exactly the diet for a sick person to thrive on. I got "no better" very rapidly, till at length, one afternoon, I lay in a kind of stupor, conscious that I was somewhere, though where, for the life of me I could not say. As I lay in this state, I imagined I heard my name spoken, and opening my eyes with considerable effort, I saw bending over me a female form. I think the astonishment restored me to perfect consciousness (though some liquor poured into my mouth at the same time, may have been a useful adjunct). As soon as I could collect myself sufficiently, I discovered the lady to be a Mrs. Husband, who, with a few other ladies, had just arrived on one of the hospital boats. Having lost my own mother when a mere child, you may imagine the effect her tender nursing had upon me, and when she laid her hand upon my forehead, all pain seemed to depart. I sank into a sweet sleep, and awoke the next morning refreshed and strengthened in mind and in body. From that moment my recovery was rapid, and in ten days I returned to my duty."

As her son began to recover, she resolved, in her thankfulness for this mercy, to devote herself to the care of the sick and wounded of the army. She was on one of the hospital transports off Harrison's Landing, when the rebels bombarded it, and though it was her first experience "under fire," she stood her ground like a veteran, manifesting no trepidation, but pursuing her work of caring for the sick as calmly as if in perfect safety. Finding that she was desirous of rendering assistance in the care of the disabled soldiers, she was assigned, we believe, by the Sanitary Commission, to the position of Lady Superintendent of one of the hospital transports which bore the wounded and sick to New York. She made 37 four trips on these vessels, and her faithful attention to the sick, her skilful nursing, and her entire forgetfulness of self, won for her the hearty esteem and regard of all on board. The troops being all transferred to Acquia Creek and Alexandria, Mrs. Husband went to Washington, and endeavored to obtain a pass and transportation for supplies to Pope's army, then falling back, foot by foot, in stern but unavailing resistance to Lee's strong and triumphant force. These she was denied, but Miss Dix requested her to take charge temporarily of the Camden Street Hospital, at Baltimore, the matron of which had been stricken down with illness. After a few weeks' stay here, she relinquished her position, and repaired to Antietam, where the smoke of the great battle was just rolling off over the heights of South Mountain. Here, at the Smoketown Hospital, where the wounded from French's and some other divisions were gathered, she found abundant employment, and at the request of that able surgeon and excellent man, Dr. Yanderkieft, she remained in charge two months. Mrs. Harris was with her here for a short time, and Miss Maria M. C. Hall, during her entire stay. Her presence at this hospital brought perpetual sunshine. Arduous as were her labors, for there were very many desperately wounded, and quite as many dangerously sick, she never manifested weariness or impatience, and even the sick and wounded men, usually exacting, because forgetful of the great amount of labor which their condition imposes upon the nurses, wondered that she never manifested fatigue, and that she was able to accomplish so much as she did. Often did they express their anxiety lest she should be compelled from weariness and illness to leave them, but her smiling, cheerful face reassured them. She and Miss Hall occupied for themselves and their stores, a double hospital tent, and let the weather be what it might, she was always at her post in the hospitals promptly at her hours, and dispensed with a liberal hand to those who needed, the delicacies, the stimulants, and medicines they required. She had made a flag for her tent by sewing upon a breadth of calico a figure of a bottle cut out of red flannel, and the battleflag flew to the wind at all times, indicative of the medicines which were dispensed from the tent below. We have endeavored to give a view of this tent, from which came daily such quantities of delicacies, such excellent milk-punch to nourish and support the patients whose condition was most critical, such finely flavored flaxseed tea for the army of patients suffering from pulmonic diseases ("her flaxseed tea," says one of her boys, "was never insipid"), lemonades for the feverish, and something for every needy patient. See her as she comes out of her tent for her round of hospital duties, a substantial comely figure, with a most benevolent and motherly face, her hands filled with the good things she is bearing to some of the sufferers in the hospital; she has discarded hoops, believing with Florence Nightingale, that they are utterly incompatible with the duties of the hospital; she has a stout serviceable apron nearly covering her dress, and that apron is a miracle of pockets; pockets before, behind, and on each side; deep, wide pockets, all stored full of something which will benefit or amuse her "boys" an apple, an orange, an interesting book, a set of chess-men, checkers, dominoes, or puzzles, newspapers, magazines, everything desired, comes out of those capacious pockets. As she enters a ward, the whisper passes from one cot to another, that "mother" is coming, and faces, weary with pain, brighten at her approach, and sad hearts grow glad as she gives a cheerful smile to one, says a kind word to another, administers a glass of her punch or lemonade to a third, hands out an apple or an orange to a fourth, or a book or game to a fifth, and relieves the hospital of the gloom which seemed brooding over it. But not in these ways alone does she bring comfort and happiness to these poor wounded and fever-stricken men. She encourages them to confide to her their sorrows and troubles, and the heart that, like the caged bird, has been bruising itself against the bars of its cage, from grief for the suffering; or sorrow of the loved ones at home or oftener still, the soul that finds itself on the confines of an unknown hereafter, and is filled with distress at the thought of the world to come, pours into her attentive ear, the story of its sorrows, and finds in her a wise and kind counsellor and friend, and learns from her gentle teachings to trust and hope.

Hers was a truly heroic spirit. Darkness, storm, or contagion, had no terrors for her, when there was suffering to be alleviated, or anguish to be soothed. Amid the raging storms of the severe winter of 1862-3, she often left her tent two or three times in the night and went round to the beds of those who were apparently near death, from the fear that the nurses might neglect something which needed to be done for them. When diphtheria raged in the hospital, and the nurses fearing its contagious character, fled from the bed-sides of those suffering from it, Mrs. Husband devoted herself to them night and day, fearless of the exposure, and where they died of the terrible disease received and forwarded to their friends the messages of the dying.

It is no matter of surprise that when the time came for her to leave this hospital, where she had manifested such faithful and self-sacrificing care and tenderness for those whom she knew only as the defenders of her country, those whom she left, albeit unused to the melting mood, should have wept at losing such a friend. "There were no dry eyes in that hospital," says one who was himself one of its inmates; "all, from the strong man ready again to enter the ranks to the poor wreck of humanity lying on his death-bed gave evidence of their love for her, and sorrow at her departure in copious tears. On her way home she stopped for an hour or two at camps A and B in Frederick, Maryland, where a considerable number of the convalescents from Antietam had been sent, and these on discovering her, surrounded her ambulance and greeted her most heartily, seeming almost wild with joy at seeing their kind friend once more. After a brief stay at Philadelphia, during which she visited the hospitals almost constantly, she hastened again to the front, and at Falmouth early in 1863, after that fearful and disastrous battle of Fredericksburg she found ample employment for her active and energetic nature. As matron of Humphreys' Division Hospital (Fifth Corps) she was constantly engaged in ministering to the comfort of the wounded, and her solicitude for the welfare and prosperity of the men did not end with their discharge from the hospital. The informalities or blunders by which they too often lost their pay and were sometimes set down as deserters attracted her attention, and so far as possible she always procured the correction of those errors. Early in April, 1863, she made a flying visit to Philadelphia, and thus details in a letter to a friend, at the time the kind and amount of labor which almost always filled up every hour of those journeys. "Left Monday evening for home, took two discharged soldiers with me; heard that I could not get a pass to return; so instead of going directly through, stayed in Washington twenty-four hours, and fought a battle for a pass. I came off conqueror of course, but not until wearied almost to death—my boys in the meantime had gotten their pay—so I took them from the Commission Lodge (where I had taken them on arriving) to the cars, and off for Baltimore. There I placed them in the care of one of the gentlemen of the Relief Associations, and arrived home at 1.30 A. M. I carried money home for some of the boys, and had business of my own to attend to, keeping me constantly going on Wednesday and Thursday; left at midnight (Thursday night) for Washington, took the morning boat and arrived here this afternoon." This record of five days of severe labor such as few men could have gone through without utter prostration, is narrated in her letter to her friend evidently without a thought that there was anything extraordinary in it; yet it was in a constant succession of labors as wearing as this that she lived for full three years of her army life.

Immediately after the battles of Chancellorsville she went to United States Ford, but was not allowed to cross, and joined two Maine ladies at the hospital on the north side of the Rappahannock, where they dressed wounds until dark, slept in an ambulance, and early in the morning went to work again, but were soon warned to leave, as it was supposed that the house used as a hospital would be shelled. They left, and about half a mile farther on found the hospital of the Third and Eleventh Corps. Here the surgeon in charge urged Mrs. Husband to remain and assist him, promising her transportation. She accordingly left her ambulance and dressed wounds until midnight. By this time the army was in full retreat and passing the hospital. The surgeon forgot his promise, and taking care of himself, left her to get away as best she could. It was pitch dark and the rain pouring in torrents. She was finally offered a part of the front seat of an army (medicine) wagon, and after riding two or three miles on the horrible roads the tongue of the wagon broke, and she was compelled to sit in the drenching rain for two or three hours till the guide could bring up an ambulance, in which she reached Falmouth the next day.

The hospital of which she was lady matron was broken up at the time of this battle, but she was immediately installed in the same position in the hospital of the Third Division of the Third Corps, then filled to overflowing with the Chancellorsville wounded. Here she remained until compelled to move North with the army by Lee's raid into Pennsylvania in June and July, 1863.

On the 3d of July, the day of the last and fiercest of the Gettysburg battles, Mrs. Husband, who had been, from inability to get permission to go to the front, passing a few anxious days at Philadelphia, started for Gettysburg, determined to go to the aid and relief of the soldier boys, who, she well knew, needed her services. She reached the battle-field on the morning of the 4th by way of Westminster, in General Meade's mail-wagon. She made her way at first to the hospital of the Third Corps, and labored there till that as well as the other field hospitals were broken up, when she devoted herself to the wounded in Camp Letterman. Here she was attacked with miasmatic fever, but struggled against it with all the energy of her nature, remaining for three weeks ill in her tent. She was at length carried home, but as soon as she was convalescent, went to Camp Parole at Annapolis, as agent of the Sanitary Commission, to fill the place of Miss Clara Davis, (now Mrs. Edward Abbott), who was prostrated by severe illness induced by her severe and continued labors.

In December, 1863, she accepted the position of matron to her old hospital, (Third Division of the Third Corps), then located at Brandy Station, where she remained till General Grant's order issued on the 15th of April caused the removal of all civilians from the army.

A month had not elapsed, before the terrible slaughter of the "Wilderness" and "Spottsylvania," had made that part of Virginia a field of blood, and Mrs. Husband hastened to Fredericksburg where no official now barred her progress with his "red tape" prohibitions; here she remained till the first of June, toiling incessantly, and then moving on to Port Royal and White House, where the same sad scenes were repeated, and where, amid so much suffering and horror, it was difficult to banish the feeling of depression. At White House, she took charge of the low diet kitchen for the whole Sixth

Corps, to which her division had been transferred. The number of wounded was very large, this corps having suffered severely in the battle of Cold Harbor, and her duties were arduous, but she made no complaint, her heart being at rest, if she could only do something for her brave soldier boys.

When the base was transferred to City Point, she made her way to the Third Division, Sixth Corps' Hospital at the front, where she remained until the Sixth Corps were ordered to the Shenandoah Valley, when she took charge of the low diet kitchen of the Second Corps' Hospital at City Point, and remained there until the end. Her labors among the men in this hospital were constant and severe, but she won all hearts by her tenderness, cheerfulness, and thoughtful consideration of the needs of every particular case. Each one of those under her care felt that she was specially his friend, and interesting and sometimes amusing were the confidences imparted to her, by the poor fellows. The one bright event of the day to all was the visit of "Mother" Husband to their ward. The apron, with its huge pockets, always bore some welcome gift for each, and however trifling it might be in itself, it was precious as coming from her hands. Her friends in Philadelphia, by their constant supplies, enabled her to dispense many articles of comfort and luxury to the sick and wounded, which could not otherwise have been furnished.

On the 6th of May, 1865, Mrs. Husband was gratified by the sight of our gallant army marching through Richmond. As they passed, in long array, they recognized her, and from hundreds of the soldiers of the Second, Third, and Sixth Corps, rang out the loud and hearty "Hurrah for Mother Husband!" while their looks expressed their gratitude to one who had been their firm and faithful friend in the hour of suffering and danger.

Mrs. Husband felt that she must do something more for her "boys" before they separated and returned to their distant homes; she therefore left Richmond immediately, and traveling with her accustomed celerity, soon reached Philadelphia, and gathering up from her liberal friends and her own moderate means, a sufficient sum to procure the necessary stores, she returned with an ample supply, met the soldiers of the corps to which she had been attached at Bailey's Cross Roads, and there spent six or seven days in distributing to them the clothing and comforts which they needed. Her last opportunity of seeing them was a few days later at the grand review in Washington.

There was one class of services which Mrs. Husband rendered to the soldiers, which we have not mentioned, and in which we believe she had no competitor. In the autumn of 1863, her attention was called to the injustice of the finding and sentence of a court martial, which had tried a private soldier for some alleged offence and sentenced him to be shot. She investigated the case and, with some difficulty, succeeded in procuring his pardon from the President.

She began from this time to take an interest in these cases of trial by summary court martial, and having a turn for legal investigation, to which her early training and her husband's profession had inclined her, and a clear judicial mind, she made each one her study, and though she found that there were some cases in which summary punishment was merited, yet the majority were deserving of the interposition of executive clemency, and she became their advocate with the patient and kind-hearted Lincoln. In scores of instances she secured, not without much difficulty, and some abuse from officials "dressed in a little brief authority," who disliked her keen and thorough investigation of their proceedings, the pardon or the commutation of punishment of those sentenced to death. Rarely, if ever, did the President turn a deaf ear to her pleadings; for he knew that they were prompted by no sinister motive, or simple humane impulse. Every case which she presented had been thoroughly and carefully examined, and her knowledge of it was so complete, that he felt he might safely trust her.

Through all these multifarious labors and toils, Mrs. Husband has received no compensation from the Government or the Sanitary Commission. She entered the service as a volunteer, and her necessities have been met from her own means, and she has also given freely to the soldiers and to their families from her not over-full purse. Her reward is in the sublime consciousness of having been able to accomplish an amount of good which few could equal. All over the land, in hundreds of homes, in thousands of hearts, her name is a household word, and as the mother looks upon her son, the wife upon her husband, the child upon its father, blessings are breathed forth upon her through whose skilful care and watchful nursing these loved ones are spared to 38 be a joy and support. The contributions and mementoes presented by her soldier boys form a large and very interesting museum in her home. There are rings almost numberless, carved from animal bones, shells, stone, vulcanite, etc., miniature tablets, books, harps, etc., inlaid from trees or houses of historic memory, minie bullets, which have traversed bone and flesh of patient sufferers, and shot and shell which have done their part in destroying the fortresses of the rebellion. Each memento has its history, and all are precious in the eyes of the recipient, as a token of the love of those whom she has watched and nursed.

Her home is the Mecca of the soldiers of the Army of the Potomac, and if any of them are sick or in distress in Philadelphia, Mother Husband hastens at once to their relief. Late may she return to the skies; and when at last in the glory of a ripe and beautiful old age, she lies down to rest, a grateful people shall inscribe on her monument, "Here lies all that was mortal of one whom all delighted to honor."

HOSPITAL TRANSPORT SERVICE

AMONG the deeds which entitle the United States Sanitary Commission to the lasting gratitude of the American people, was the organization and maintenance of the "Hospital Transport Service" in the Spring and Summer of 1862. When the Army of the Potomac removed from the high lands about Washington, to the low marshy and miasmatic region of the Peninsula, it required but little discernment to predict that extensive sickness would prevail among the troops; this, and the certainty of sanguinary battles soon to ensue, which would multiply the wounded beyond all previous precedents, were felt, by the officers of the Sanitary Commission, as affording sufficient justification, if any were needed for making an effort to supplement the provision of the Medical Bureau, which could not fail to be inadequate for the coming emergency.

Accordingly early in April, 1862, Mr. F. L. Olmstead, the Secretary of the Commission, having previously secured the sanction of the Medical Bureau, made application to the Quartermaster-General to allow the Commission to take in hand some of the transport steamboats of his department, of which a large number were at that time lying idle, to fit them up and furnish them in all respects suitable for the reception and care of sick and wounded men, providing surgeons and other necessary attendance without cost to Government. After tedious delays and disappointments of various kinds—one fine largo boat having been assigned, partially furnished by the Commission, and then withdrawn—au order was at length received, authorizing the Commission to take possession of any of the Government transports, not in actual use, which might at that time be lying at Alexandria. Under this authorization the Daniel Webster was assigned to the Commission on the 25th of April, and having been fitted up, the stores shipped, and the hospital corps for it assembled, it reached York River on the 30th of April.

Other boats were subsequently, (several of them, very soon) assigned to the Commission, and were successively fitted up, and after receiving their freights of sick and wounded, sent to Washington, Philadelphia, New York and other points with their precious cargoes, which were to be transferred to the general hospitals. Among these vessels were the "Ocean Queen," the "S. R. Spaulding," the "Elm City," the "Daniel Webster," No. 2, the "Knickerbocker," the clipper ships Euterpe and St. Mark, and the Commission chartered the "Wilson Small," and the "Elizabeth," two small steamers, as tender and supply boats. The Government were vacillating in their management in regard to these vessels, often taking them from the Commission just when partially or wholly fitted up, on the plea of requiring them for some purpose and assigning another vessel, often poorly adapted to their service, on board of which the labor of fitting and supplying must be again undergone, when that too would be withdrawn.

To each of these hospital transports several ladies were assigned by the Commission to take charge of the diet of the patients, assist in dressing their wounds, and generally to care for their comfort and welfare. Mr. Olmstead, and Mr. Knapp, the Assistant Secretary, had also in their company, or as they pleasantly called them, members of their staff, four ladies, who remained in the service, not leaving the vicinity of the Peninsula, until the transfer of the troops to Acquia Creek and Alexandria late in August. These ladies remained for the most part on board the Daniel Webster, or the Wilson Small, or wherever the headquarters of the Commission in the field might be. Their duties consisted in nursing, preparing food for the sick and wounded, dressing wounds, in connexion with the surgeons and medical students, and in general, making themselves useful to the great numbers of wounded and sick who were placed temporarily under their charge. Often they provided them with clean beds and hospital clothing, and suitable food in preparation for their voyage to Washington, Philadelphia, or New York. These four ladies were Miss Katherine P. Wormeley, of Newport, R. I., Mrs. William P. Griffin, of New York, one of the executive board of the Woman's Central Association of Relief, Mrs. Eliza W. Howland, wife of Colonel (afterward General) Joseph Howland, and her sister, Miss Georgiana Woolsey, both of New York.

Among those who were in charge of the Hospital Transports for one or more of their trips to the cities we have named, and by their tenderness and gentleness comforted and cheered the poor sufferers, and often by their skilful nursing rescued them from the jaws of death, were Mrs. George T. Strong, the wife of the Treasurer of the Commission, who made four or five trips; Miss Harriet Douglas Whetten, who served throughout the Peninsular Campaign as head of the Women's Department on the S. R. Spaulding; Mrs. Laura Trotter, (now Mrs. Charles Parker) of Boston, who occupied, a similar position on the Daniel Webster; Mrs. Bailey, at the head of the Women's Department on the Elm City; Mrs. Charlotte Bradford, a Massachusetts lady who made several trips on the Elm City and Knickerbocker; Miss Amy M. Bradley, whose faithful services are elsewhere recorded; Mrs. Annie Etheridge, of the Fifth Michigan, Miss Bradley's faithful and zealous co-worker; Miss Helen L. Gilson, who here as well as everywhere else proved herself one of the most eminently useful women in the service; Miss M. Gardiner, who was on several of the steamers; Mrs. Balustier, of New York, one of the most faithful and self-sacrificing of the ladies of the Hospital Transport service-; Mrs. Mary Morris Husband, of Philadelphia, who made four voyages, and whose valuable services are elsewhere recited; Mrs. Bellows, the wife of the President of the Commission, who made one voyage; Mrs. Merritt, and several other ladies.

But let us return to the ladies who remained permanently at the Commission's headquarters in the Peninsula. Their position and duties were in many respects more trying and arduous than those who accompanied the sick and wounded to the hospitals of the cities. The Daniel Webster, which, as we have said, reached York River April 30, discharged her stores except what would be needed for her trip to New York, and having placed them in a store-house on shore, began to supply the sick in camp and hospital, and to receive such patients on board as it was deemed expedient to send to New York. These were washed, their clothing changed, they were fed and put in good clean beds, and presently sent off to their destination. The staff then commenced putting the Ocean Queen, which had just been sent to them, into a similar condition of fitness for receiving the sick and wounded. She had not, on her arrival, a single bunk or any stores on board; and before any preparation could be made, the regimental and brigade surgeons on shore (who never would wait) began to send their sick and wounded on board; remonstrance was useless, and the whole party worked with all their might to make what provision was possible. One of the party went on shore, found a rebel cow at pasture, shot her, skinned her with his pocket-knife, and brought off the beef. A barrel of Indian meal, forgotten in discharging the freight of the vessel, was discovered in the hold and made into gruel almost by magic, and cups of it were ladled out to the poor fellows as they tottered in, with their faces flushed with typhoid fever; by dint of constant hard work, bunks were got up, stores brought on board, two draught oxen left behind by Franklin's Division found and slaughtered, and nine hundred patients having been taken on board, the vessel's anchors were weighed and she went out to sea. This was very much the experience of the party during their stay in the Peninsula. Hard, constant, and hurrying work were the rule, a day of comparative rest was the exception. Dividing themselves into small parties of two or three, they boarded and supplied with the stores of the Commission, the boats which the Medical officers of the army had pressed into the service filled with wounded and sent without comfort, food or attendance, on their way to the hospitals in the vicinity of Fortress Monroe; superintended the shipping of patients on the steamers which returned from the North; took account of the stores needed by these boats and saw that they were sent on board; fitted up the new boats furnished to the Commission by the Quartermaster's orders; received, sorted and distributed the patients brought to the landing on freight-cars, according to orders; fed, cleansed, and gave medical aid and nursing to all of them, and selected nurses for those to be sent North; and when any great emergency came did their utmost to meet it the amount of work actually performed was very great; but it was performed in such a cheerful triumphant spirit, a spirit that rejoiced so heartily in doing something to aid the nation's defenders, in sacrificing everything that they might be saved, that it was robbed of half its irksomeness and gloom, and most of the zealous workers retained their health and vigor even in the miasmatic air of the bay and its estuaries. Miss Wormeley, one of the transport corps, has supplied, partly from her own pen, and partly from that of Miss Georgiana Woolsey, one of her coworkers, some vivid pictures of their daily life, which, with her permission, we here reproduce from her volume on the "United States Sanitary Commission," published in 1863.

"The last hundred patients were brought on board" (imagine any of the ships, it does not matter which) "late last night. Though these night-scenes are part of our daily living, a fresh eye would find them dramatic. We are awakened in the dead of night by a sharp steam-whistle, and soon after feel ourselves clawed by little tugs on either side of our big ship, bringing off the sick and wounded from the shore. And, at once, the process of taking on hundreds of men—many of them crazed with fever —begins. There is the bringing of the stretchers up the sideladder between the two boats; the stopping at the head of it, where the names and home addresses of all who can speak are written down, and their knapsacks and little treasures numbered and stacked; then the placing of the stretchers on the platform; the row of anxious faces above and below deck; the lantern held over the hold; the word given to 'Lower;' the slow-moving ropes and pulleys; the arrival at the bottom; the turning down of the anxious faces; the lifting out of the sick man, and the lifting him into his bed; and then the sudden change from cold, hunger and friendlessness, into positive comfort and satisfaction, winding up with his invariable verdict, if he can speak,—'This is just like home!'

"We have put 'The Elm City' in order, and she began to fill up last night. I wish you could hear the men after they are put into bed. Those who can speak, speak with a will; the others grunt, or murmur their satisfaction. 'Well, this bed is most too soft; I don't know as I shall sleep, for thinking of it.' 'What have you got there?' 'That is bread; wait till I put butter on it.' 'Butter, on soft bread!' he slowly ejaculates, as if not sure that he isn't Aladdin with a genie at work upon him. Instances of such high unselfishness happen daily, that, though I forget them daily, I feel myself strengthened in my trust in human nature, without making any reflections about it. Last night, a man comfortably put to bed in a middle berth (there were three tiers, and the middle one incomparably the best) seeing me point to the upper berth as the place to put the man on an approaching stretcher, cried out: 'Stop! put me up there. Guess I can stand h'isting better'n him' It was agony to both.

"I have a long history to tell you, one of these days, of the gratefulness of the men. I often wish,—as I give a comfort to some poor fellow, and see the sense of rest it gives him, and hear the favorite speech: 'O, that's good, it's just as if mother was here—that the man or woman who supplied that comfort were by to see how blessed it is. Believe me, you may all give and work in the earnest hope that yon alleviate suffering, but none of you realize what you do; perhaps you can't conceive of it, unless you could see your gifts in use.

"We are now on board 'The Knickerbocker,' unpacking and arranging stores, and getting pantries and closets in order. I am writing on the floor, interrupted constantly to join in a laugh.

Missis sorting socks, and pulling out the funny little balls of yam, and big darning-needles stuck in the toes, 'with which she is making a fringe across my back. Do spare us the darning needles! Reflect upon us, rushing in haste to the linen closet, and plunging our hands into the bale of stockings! I certainly will make a collection of sanitary clothing. I solemnly aver that yesterday I found a pair of drawers made for a case of amputation at the thigh. And the slippers! Only fit for pontoon bridges!"

This routine of fitting up the ships as they arrived, and of receiving the men on board as they came from the front, was accompanied by constant hard work in meeting requisitions from regiments, with ceaseless battlings for transportation to get supplies to the front for camps and hospitals; and was diversified by » short excursions, which we will call "special relief;" such, for instance, as the following:—

"At midnight two steamers came alongside 'The Elm City,' each with a hundred sick, bringing word that 'The Daniel Webster No. 2' (a side wheel vessel, not a Commission boat) was aground at a little distance, with two hundred more, having no one in charge of them, and nothing to eat. Of course they had to be attended to. So, amidst the wildest and most beautiful storm of thunder and lightning, four of us pulled off to her in a little boat, with tea, bread, brandy, and beef-essence. (No one can tell how it tries my nerves to go toppling round at night in little boats, and clambering up ships' sides on little ladders). We 39 fed them,—the usual process. Poor fellows! they were so crazy! —And then 'The Wissahickon' came alongside to transfer them to 'The Elm City.' Only a part of them could go in the first load. Dr. "Ware, with his constant thoughtfulness, made me go in her, to escape returning in the small boat. Just as we pushed off, the steam gave out, and we drifted end on to the shore. Then a boat had to put off from 'The Elm City,' with a line to tow us up. All this time the thunder was incessant, the rain falling in torrents, whilst every second the beautiful crimson lightning flashed the whole scene open to us. Add to this, that there were three men alarmingly ill, and (thinking to be but a minute in reaching the other ship) I had not even a drop of brandy for them. Do you wonder, therefore, that I forgot your letters?"

Or, again, the following:—

"Sixty men were heard of as lying upon the railroad without food, and no one to look after them. Some of us got at once into the stern-wheeler 'Wissahickon,' which is the Commission's carriage, and, with provisions, basins, towels, soap, blankets, etc., went up to the railroad bridge, cooking tea and spreading bread and butter as we went. A tremendous thunder-storm came up, in the midst of which the men were found, put on freight-cars, and pushed to the landing;—fed, washed, and taken on the tug to 'The Elm City.' Dr. Ware, in his hard working on shore, had found fifteen other sick men without food or shelter,—there being 'no room' in the tent-hospital. He had studied the neighborhood extensively for shanties; found one, and put his men in it for the night. In the morning we ran up on the tug, cooking breakfast for them as we ran, scrambling eggs in a wash-basin over a spirit-lamp:—and such eggs! nine in ten addled! It must be understood that wash-basins in the rear of an army are made of tin"

And here is one more such story: "We were called to go on board 'The Wissahickon, from thence to 'The Sea-shore' and run down in the latter to West Point, to bring off twenty-five men said to be lying there sick and destitute. Two doctors went with us. After hunting an hour for 'The Sea-shore' in vain, and having got as low as Cumberland, we decided (ice being Mrs. Howland and I, for the doctors were new and docile, and glad to leave the responsibility upon us women) to push on in the tug, rather than leave the men another night on the ground, as a heavy storm of wind and rain had been going on all the day. The pilot remonstrated, but the captain approved; and, if the firemen had not suddenly let out the fires, and detained us two hours, we might have got our men on board, and returned, comfortably, soon after dark. But the delay lost us the precious daylight. It was night before the last man was got on board. There were fifty-six of them, ten very sick ones. The boat had a little shelter cabin. As we were laying mattresses on the floor, whilst the doctors were finding the men, the captain stopped us, refusing to let us put typhoid fever below the deck, on account of the crew, he said, and threatening to push off, at once, from the shore. Mrs. Howland and I looked at him! I did the terrible, and she the pathetic,—and he abandoned the contest. The return passage was rather an anxious one. The river is much obstructed with sunken ships and trees; the night was dark, and we had to feel our way, slackening speed every ten minutes. If we had been alone it wouldn't have mattered; but to have fifty men unable to move upon our hands, was too heavy a responsibility not to make us anxious. The captain and pilot said the boat was leaking, and remarked awfully that the water was six fathoms deep about there;' but we saw their motive and were not scared. we were safe alongside 'The Spaulding' by midnight; but Mr. Olmstead's tone of voice, as he said, 'You don't know how glad I am to see you,' showed how much he had been worried. And yet it was the best thing we could have done, for three, perhaps five, of the men would have been dead before morning. To-day (Sunday) they are living and likely to live. Is this Sunday? what days our Sundays have been! I think of you all at rest, and the sound of church bells in your ears, with a strange, distant feeling."

This was the general state of things at the time when the battle of Fair Oaks was fought, June 1, 1862. All the vessels of the Commission except "The Spaulding"—and she was hourly expected—were on the spot, and ready. "The Elm City" happened to be full of fever cases. A vague rumor of a battle prevailed, soon made certain by the sound of the cannonading; and she left at once (4 A. M.) to discharge her sick at Yorktown, and performed the great feat of getting back to White House, cleaned, and with her beds made, before sunset of the same day. By that time the wounded were arriving. The boats of the Commission filled up calmly. The young men had a system by which they shipped their men; and there was neither hurry nor confusion, as the vessels, one by one,—"The Elm City," "The Knickerbocker," "The Daniel Webster,"—filled up and left the landing. After them, other boats, detailed by the Government for hospital service, came up. These boats were not under the control of the Commission. There was no one specially appointed to take charge of them; no one to receive the wounded at the station; no one to see that the boats were supplied with proper stores. A frightful scene of confusion and misery ensued. The Commission came forward to do what it could; but it had no power, only the right of charity. It could not control, scarcely check, the fearful confusion that prevailed, as train after train came in, and the wounded were brought and thrust upon the various boats. But it did nobly what it could. Night and day its members worked: not, it must be remembered, in its own well-organized service, but in the hard duty of making the best of a bad case. Not the smallest preparation was found, on at least three of the boats, for the common food of the men; and, as for sick-food, stimulants, drinks, there was nothing of the kind on any one of the boats, and not a pail nor a cup to distribute food, had there been any.

No one, it is believed, can tell the story, as it occurred, of the next three days;—no one can tell distinctly what boats they were, on which they lived and worked through those days and nights. They remember scenes and sounds, but they remember nothing as a whole; and, to this day, if they are feverish and weary, comes back the sight of men in every condition of horror, borne, shattered and shrieking, by thoughtless hands, who banged the stretchers against pillars and posts, dumped them anywhere, and walked over the men without compassion. Imagine an immense river-steamboat filled on every deck: every berth, every square inch of room, covered with wounded men,—even the stairs and gangways and guards filled with those who were less badly wounded; and then imagine fifty well men, on every kind of errand, hurried and impatient, rushing to and fro, every touch bringing agony to the poor fellows, whilst stretcher after stretcher comes along, hoping to find an empty place; and then imagine what it was for these people of the Commission to keep calm themselves, and make sure that each man, on such a boat as that, was properly refreshed and fed. Sometimes two or even three such boats were lying side by side, full of suffering and horrors.

This was the condition of things with the subordinates. With the chiefs it was aggravated by a wild confusion of conflicting orders from headquarters, and conflicting authority upon the ground, until the wonder is that any method could have been obtained. But an earnest purpose can do almost everything, and out of the struggle came daylight at last. The first gleam of it was from a hospital tent and kitchen, which, by the goodness and thoughtfulness of Captain (now Colonel) Sawtelle, Assistant Quartermaster, was pitched for the Commission, just at the head of the wharf, and near the spot where the men arrived in the cars. This tent (Dr. Ware gave to its preparation the only hour when he might have rested through that long nightmare) became the strength and the comfort of the Commission people. As the men passed it, from cars to boat, they could be refreshed and stimulated, and from it meals were sent to all the boats at the landing. During that dreadful battle-week, three thousand men were fed from that tent. It was not the Vale of Cashmere, but many dear associations cluster round it.

After the pressure was over, the Commission went back to its old routine, but upon a new principle. A member of the Commission came down to White House for a day or two, and afterward wrote a few words about that work. As he saw it with a fresh eye, his letter will be given here. He says:—

"I wish you could have been with me at White House during my late visit, to see how much is being done by our agents there to alleviate the sufferings of the sick and wounded soldiers. I have seen a good deal of suffering among our volunteers, and observed the marvellous variety and energy of the beneficence bestowed by the patriotic and philanthropic in camp, in hospital, and on transports for the sick; but nothing has ever impressed me so deeply as this. Perhaps I can better illustrate my meaning by sketching a few of the daily labors of the agents of the Commission as I saw them. The sick and wounded were usually sent down from the front by rail, a distance of about twenty miles, over a rough road, and in the common freight-cars. A train generally arrived at White House at nine P. M., and another at two A. M. In order to prepare for the reception of the sick and wounded, Mr. Olmstead, with Drs. Jenkins and Ware, had pitched, by the side of the railway, at White House, a large number of tents, to shelter and feed the convalescent. These tents were their only shelter while waiting to be shipped. Among them was one used as a kitchen and work-room, or pantry, by the ladies in our service, who prepared beef-tea, milk-punch, and other food and comforts, in anticipation of the arrival of the trains. By the terminus of the railway the large Commission steamboat 'Knickerbocker' lay in the Pamunkey, in readiness for the reception of four hundred and fifty patients, provided with comfortable beds and a corps of devoted surgeons, dressers, nurses, and litter-bearers. Just outside of this vessel lay 'The Elizabeth a steam-barge, loaded with the hospital stores of the Commission, and in charge of a storekeeper, always ready to issue supplies. Outside of this again lay I The Wilson Small the headquarters of our Commission. As soon as a train arrived, the moderately sick were selected and placed in the tents near the railroad and fed; those more ill were carried to the upper saloon of 'The Knickerbocker while the seriously ill, or badly wounded, were placed in the lower saloon, and immediately served by the surgeons and dressers. During the three nights that I observed the working of the system, about seven hundred sick and wounded were provided with quarters and ministered to in all their wants with a tender solicitude, and skill that excited my deepest admiration. To see Drs. Ware and Jenkins, lantern in hand, passing through the trains, selecting the sick with reference to their necessities, and the ladies following to assuage the thirst, or arouse, by judiciously administered stimulants, the failing strength of the brave and uncomplaining sufferers, was a spectacle of the most touching character. If you had experienced the debilitating influence of the Pamunkey climate, you would be filled with wonder at the mere physical endurance of our corps, who certainly could not have been sustained in the performance of duties, involving labor by day and through sleepless nights, without a strong sense of their usefulness and success.

"At Savage's Station, too, the Commission had a valuable depot, where comfort and assistance was dispensed to the sick when changing from the ambulances to the cars. I wish I could do justice to the subject of my hasty narrative, or in any due measure convey to your mind the impressions left on mine in observing, even casually, the operations in the care of the sick at these two points.

"When we remember what was done by the same noble band of laborers after the battles of Williamsburg and Fair Oaks, in ministering to the wants of thousands of wounded, I am sure that we shall join with them in gratitude and thankfulness that they were enabled to be there."

But the end of it all was at hand; the "change of base of which the Commission had some private intelligence, came to pass. The sick and wounded were carefully gathered up from the tents and hospitals, and sent slowly away down the winding river—"The "Wilson Small lingering as long as possible, till the telegraph wires had been cut, and the enemy was announced, by mounted messengers, to be at "Tunstall's; in fact, till the roar of the battle came nearer, and we knew that Stoneman with his cavalry was falling back to Williamsburg, and that the enemy were about to march into our deserted places.

"All night we sat on the deck of 'The Small slowly moving away, watching the constantly increasing cloud and the fire-flashes over the trees towards the White House; watching the fading out of what had been to us, through these strange weeks, a sort of home, where all had worked together and been happy; a place which is sacred to some of us now for its intense living remembrances, and for the hallowing of them all by the memory of one who, through months of death and darkness, lived and worked in self-abnegation, lived in and for the suffering of others, and finally gave himself a sacrifice for them.

"We are coaling here to-night ('Wilson Small, off Norfolk, June 30th, 1862). We left White House Saturday night, and rendezvoused at West Point. Captain Sawtelle sent us off early, with despatches for Fortress Monroe; this gave us the special fun of being the first to come leisurely into the panic then raging at Yorktown. 'The Small was instantly surrounded by terror-stricken boats; the people of the big 'St. Mark leaned, pale, over their bulwarks, to question us. Nothing could be more delightful than to be as calm and monosyllabic as we were. We leave at daybreak for Harrison's Bar, James River, where our gunboats are said to be; we hope to get further up, but General Dix warns us that it is not safe. What are we about to learn? No one here can tell. (Harrison's Bar, July 2d). We arrived here yesterday to hear the thunder of the battle, and to find the army just approaching this landing; last night it was a verdant shore, to-day it is a dusty plain. The Spaulding' has passed and gone ahead of us; her ironsides can carry her safely past the rifle-pits which line the shore. No one can tell us as yet what work there is for us; the wounded have not come.

"Hospital Transport Spaulding,' July 3d.—Reached Harrison's Bar at 11 A. M., July 1st, and were ordered to go up the James River, as far as Carter's Landing. To do this we must pass the batteries at City Point. We were told there was no danger if we should carry a yellow flag; yellow flag we had none, so we trusted to the red Sanitary Commission, and prepared to run it. 'The Galena' hailed us to keep below, as we passed the battery. Shortly after, we came up with 'The Monitor,' and the little captain, with his East India hat, trumpet in hand, repeated the advice of The Galena,' and added, that if he heard firing, he would follow us. Our cannon pointed its black muzzle at the shore, and on we went. As we left 'The Monitor,' the captain came to me, with his grim smile, and said, I'll take those mattresses you spoke of.' We had joked, as people will, about our danger, and I had suggested mattresses round the wheel-house, never thinking that he would try it. But the captain was in earnest; when was he anything else? So the contrabands brought up the mattresses, and piled them against the wheel-house, and the pilot stood against the mast, with a mattress slung in the rigging to protect him. In an hour we had passed the danger and reached Carter's Landing, and there was the army, 'all that was left of it.'

Over all the bank, on the lawns of that lovely spot, under the shade of the large trees that fringed the outer park, lay hundreds of our poor boys, brought from the battle-fields of six days. It seemed a hopeless task even to feed them. We went first into the hospital, and gave them refreshment all round. One man, burnt up with fever, burst into tears when I spoke to him. I held his hand silently, and at last he sobbed out, 'You are so kind,—I—am so weak.' We were ordered by the surgeon in charge to station ourselves on the lawn, and wait the arrival of the ambulances, so as to give something (we had beef-tea, soup, brandy, etc., etc.) to the poor fellows as they arrived. Late that night came peremptory orders from the Quartermaster, for 'The Spaulding' to drop down to Harrison's Landing. We took some of the wounded with us; others went by land or ambulances, and some—it seems incredible—walked the distance.

Others were left behind and taken prisoners; for the enemy reached Carter's Landing as we left it."

The work of the Commission upon the hospital transports was about to close.

But before it was all over, the various vessels had made several trips in the service of the Commission, and one voyage of "The Spaulding" must not pass unrecorded.

"We were ordered up to City Point, under a flag of truce, to receive our wounded men who were prisoners in Richmond. At last the whistle sounded and the train came in sight. The poor fellows set up a weak cheer at the sight of the old flag, and those who had the strength hobbled and tumbled off the train almost before it stopped. We took four hundred and one on board. TWO other vessels which accompanied us took each two hundred more. The rebel soldiers had been kind to our men,— so they said,—but the citizens had taken pains to insult them. One man burst into tears as he was telling me of their misery: 'May God defend me from such again.' God took him to Himself, poor suffering soul! He died the next morning,—died because he would not let them take off his arm. I wasn't going to let them have it in Richmond; I said I would take it back to old Massachusetts.' Of course we had a hard voyage with our poor fellows in such a condition, but, at least, they were cleaned and well fed."

OTHER LABORS OF SOME OF THE MEMBERS OF THE HOSPITAL TRANSPORT CORPS.

MOST of the ladies connected with this Hospital Transport service, distinguished themselves in other departments of philanthropic labor for the soldiers, often net less arduous, and sometimes not cheered by so pleasant companionship. Miss BRADLEY, as we have seen accomplished a noble work in connection with the Soldiers' Home at Washington, and the Rendezvous of Distribution; Miss GILSON and Mrs. HUSBAND were active in every good word and work; Mrs CHARLOTTE BRADFORD succeeded Miss Bradley in the charge of the Soldiers' Home at Washington, where she accomplished a world of good.

Mrs. W. P. GRIFFIN, though compelled by illness contracted during her services on the Peninsula, returned with quickened zeal and more fervid patriotism to her work in connection with the "Woman's Central Association of Relief," in New York, of which she was up to the close of the war one of the most active and untiring managers. Miss HARRIET DOUGLAS WHETTEN, who after two or three voyages back and forth in different vessels, was finally placed in charge of the Woman's Department on board of the Spaulding, where she remained until that vessel was given up by the Commission, and indeed continued on board for two or three voyages after the vessel became a Government hospital transport. Her management on board the Spaulding was admirable, eliciting the praise of all who saw it. When the Portsmouth Grove General Hospital in Rhode Island was opened, under the charge of Miss Wormeley, as Lady Superintendent, that lady invited her to become her assistant; she accepted the invitation and remained there a year, when she was invited to become Lady Superintendent of the Carver General Hospital, at Washington, D. C., a position of great responsibility, which she filled with the greatest credit and success, retaining it to the close of the war.

An intimate friend, who was long associated with her, says of her, "Miss Whetten's absolute and untiring devotion to the sick men was beyond all praise. She is a born nurse. She was perhaps less energetic and rapid than others, but no one could quite come up to her in tender care, and in that close watching and sympathetic knowledge about a patient which belongs only to a true nurse. And when I say that she was less energetic than some, I am in fact saying something to her honor. Her nature was calmer and less energetic, but she worked as hard and for a longer time together than any of us, and this was directly in opposition to her habits and disposition, and was in fact a triumph over herself. She did more than any one personally for the men —the rest of us worked more generally— when a man's sufferings or necessities were relieved, we thought no more about him—but she took a warm personal interest in the individual. In the end this strain upon her feelings wore down her spirits, but it was a feature of her success, and there must be many a poor fellow, who if he heard her name "would rise up and call her blessed."

Three or four of the ladies especially connected with the headquarters of the Commission in the Hospital Transport Service, from their important services elsewhere, are entitled to a fuller notice. Among these we must include the accomplished historian of the earlier work of the Commission.

KATHERINE P. WORMELEY

AMONG the many of our countrywomen who have been active and ardent in the soldier's cause, some may have devoted themselves to the service for a longer period, but few with more earnestness and greater ability than the lady whose name stands at the head of this sketch, and few have entered into a greater variety of details in the prosecution of the work.

Katherine Prescott Wormeley was born in England. Her father though holding the rank of a Pear-Admiral in the British Navy, was a native of Virginia. Her mother is a native of Boston, Massachusetts. Miss Wormeley may therefore be said to be alien to her birth-place, and to be an American in fact as in feelings. She now resides with her mother at Newport, Rhode Island.

Miss Wormeley was among the earliest to engage in the work of procuring supplies and aid for the volunteer soldiery. The work began in Newport early in July, 1861. The first meeting of women was held informally at the house of Miss wormeley's mother. An organization was obtained, rooms secured (being lent for the purpose), and about two thousand dollars subscribed. The Society, which assumed the name of the "Woman's Union Aid Society" immediately commenced the work with vigor, and shortly forwarded to the Sanitary Commission at Washington their first cases of clothing and supplies. Miss Wormeley remained at the head of this society until April, 1862. It was kept in funds by private gifts, and by the united efforts of all the churches of Newport, and the United States Naval Academy which was removed thither from Annapolis, Maryland, in the spring of 1861.

During the summer of 1861 several ladies (summer residents of Newport), were in the habit of sending to Miss wormeley many poor women, with the request that she would furnish them with steady employment upon hospital clothing, the ladies paying for the work. After they left, the poor women whom they had thus benefited, felt the loss severely, and the thought occurred to Miss wormeley that the outfitting of a great army must furnish much suitable work for them could it be reached.

After revolving the subject in her own mind, she wrote to Quartermaster-General Meigs at Washington, making inquiries, and was by him referred to the Department Quartermaster General, Colonel D. H. Vinton, United States Army, office of army clothing and equipage, New York. Colonel Vinton replied in the kindest manner, stating the difficulties of the matter, but expressing his willingness to give Miss wormeley a contract if she thought she could surmount them.

Miss wormeley found her courage equal to the attempt, and succeeded far more easily than she had expected in carrying out her plans. She engaged rooms at a low rent, and found plenty of volunteer assistance on all sides. Ladies labored unweariedly in cutting and distributing the work to the applicants. Gentlemen packed the cases, and attended to the shipments. During the winter of 1861-2 about fifty thousand army shirts were thus made, not one of which was returned as imperfect, and she was thus enabled to circulate in about one hundred families, a sum equal to six thousand dollars, which helped them well through the winter.

Colonel Vinton, as was the case with other officers very generally throughout the war, showed great kindness and appreciation of these efforts of women. And though this contract must have given him far more trouble than contracts with regular clothing establishments, his goodness, which was purely benevolent, never flagged.

During all this time the work of the Women's Union Aid Society was also carried on at Miss Wormeley's rooms, and a large number of cases were packed and forwarded thence, either to New York or directly to Washington. Miss Wormeley, herself, still superintended this matter, and though an Associate Manager of the New England Women's Branch of the Sanitary Commission, preferred this direct transmission as a saving both of time and expense.

The Society was earnest and indefatigable in its exertions, acting always with great promptness and energy while under the direction of Miss Wormeley. On one occasion, as an instance, a telegraphic message from Washington brought at night an urgent call for a supply of bed-sacks. Early in the morning all the material in Newport was bought up, as many sewing-machines as possible obtained, and seventy-five bed-sacks finished and sent off that day, and as many more the following day.

Miss Wormeley was just closing up her contract when, in April, 1802, the "Hospital Transport Service" was organized, principally by the efforts of Mr. Frederick Law Olmstead, the General Secretary of the Sanitary Commission. The sudden transfer of the scene of active war from the high grounds bordering the Potomac to a low and swampy region intersected by a network of creeks and rivers, made necessary appliances for the care of the sick and wounded, which the Government was not at that time prepared to furnish. Hence arose the arrangement by which certain large steamers, chartered, but then unemployed by the Government, were transferred to the Sanitary Commission to be fitted up as Hospital Transports for the reception and conveyance of the sick and wounded. To the superintendence of this work, care of the sick, and other duties of this special service, a number of agents of the Commission, with volunteers of both sexes, were appointed, and after protracted and vexatious delays in procuring the first transports assembled at Alexandria, Virginia, on the 25th of April, and embarked on the Daniel Webster for York River, which they reached on the 30th of April bliss Wormeley was one of the first to become connected with this branch of the service, and proceeded at once to her field of duty. She remained in this employment until August of the same year, and passed through all the horrors of the Peninsula campaign. By this, of course, is not understood the battles of the campaign, nor the army movements, but the reception, washing, feeding, and ministering to the sick and the wounded—scenes which are too full of horror for tongue to tell, or pen to describe, but which must always remain indelibly impressed upon the minds and hearts of those who were actors in them.

The ladies, it may be observed, who were attached to the Hospital Transport Corps at the headquarters of the Commission, were all from the higher walks of society, women of the greatest culture and refinement, and unaccustomed to toil or exhausting care. Yet not one of them shrank from hardship, or revolted at any labor or exertion which could serve to bring comfort to the sufferers under their charge.

Active and endowed with extraordinary executive ability, Miss Wormeley was distinguished for her great usefulness during this time of fierce trial, when the malaria of the Chickahominy swamps was prostrating its thousands of brave men, and the battles of Williamsburg, White House, and Fair Oaks, and the disastrous retreat to Harrison's Landing were marked by an almost unexampled carnage.

While the necessity of exertion continued, Miss Wormeley and her associates bore up bravely, but no sooner was this ended than nearly all succumbed to fever, or the exhaustion of excessive and protracted fatigue. Nevertheless, within a few days after bliss Wormeley's return home, the Surgeon-General, passing through Newport, came to call upon her and personally solicit her to take charge of the "Woman's Department of the Lowell General Hospital, then being organized at Portsmouth Grove, R. I. After a brief hesitation, on account of her health, Miss Wormeley assented to the proposal, and on the 1st of September, 1862, went to the hospital. She was called, officially, the "Lady Superintendent," and her duties were general; they consisted less of actual nursing, than the organization and superintendence of her department. Under her charge were the Female Nurses, the Diet Kitchens, and Special diet, the Linen Department, and the Laundry, where she had a steam Washing Machine, which was capable of washing and mangling four thousand pieces a day.

The hospital had beds for two thousand five hundred patients. Four friends of Miss Wormeley joined her here, and were her

Assistant Superintendents—Misses G. M. and J. S. Woolsey, Miss Harriet D. Whetten, of New York, and Miss Sarah C. Woolsey, of New Haven. Each of these had charge of seven Wards, and was responsible to the surgeons for the nursing and diet of the sick men. To the exceedingly valuable co-operation of these ladies, Miss Wormeley has, on all occasions, attributed in a great measure the success which attended and rewarded her services in this department of labor, as also to the kindness of the Surgeon in charge, Dr. Lewis A. Edwards, and of his Assistants.

She remained at Portsmouth Grove a little more than a year, carrying on the arrangements of her department with great ability and perfect success. On holidays, through the influence of herself and her assistants, the inmates received ample donations for the feasts appropriate to the occasions, and at all times liberal gifts of books, games, &c., for their instruction and entertainment. But in September, 1863, partly from family reasons, and partly because her health gave way, she was forced to resign and return home.

From that time her labors in hospital ceased. But, in the following December, at the suggestion of Mr and Mrs. George Ticknor, of Boston, and of other friends, she prepared for the Boston Sanitary Fair, a charming volume entitled, "The United States Sanitary Commission; A Sketch of its Purposes and its Work."

This book, owing to unavoidable hindrances, was not commenced till so late that but eleven days were allowed for its completion. But, with her accustomed energy, having most of her materials at hand, Miss Wormeley commenced and finished the book within the specified time, without other assistance than that volunteered by friends in copying and arranging papers. Graceful in style, direct in detail, plain in statement and logical in argument, it shows, however, no traces of hasty writing. It met with great and deserved success, and netted some hundreds of dollars to the fair.

Miss Wormeley attributes much of the success of her work, in all departments, to the liberality of her friends. During the war she received from the community of Newport, alone, over seventeen thousand dollars, beside, large donations of brandy, wine, flannel, etc., for the Commission and hospital use. The Newport Aid Society, which she assisted in organizing, worked well and faithfully to the end, and rendered valuable services to the Sanitary Commission, and she was enabled at all times to add largely to its funds. Since the completion of her book, her health has not permitted her to engage in active service.

THE MISSES WOOLSEY

WE are not aware of any other instance among the women who have devoted themselves to works of philanthropy and patriotism during the recent war, in which four sisters have together consecrated their sendees to the cause of the nation. In social position, culture, refinement, and all that could make life pleasant, Misses Georgiana and Jane C. Woolsey, and their married sisters, Mrs. Joseph and Mrs. Robert Howland, were blessed above most women; and if there were any who might have deemed themselves excused from entering upon the drudgery, the almost menial service incident to the Hospital Transport service, to the position of Assistant Superintendent of a crowded hospital, of nurse in field hospitals after a great battle, or of instructors and superintendents of freedmen and freedwomen; these ladies might have pleaded an apology for some natural shrinking from the work, from its dissimilarity to all their previous pursuits. But to the call of duty and patriotism, they had no such objections to urge.

Airs. Joseph Howland was the wife of a Colonel in the Union army, and felt it a privilege to do something for the brave men with whom her husband's interests were identified, and accompanying him to the camp whenever this was permitted, she ministered to the sick or wounded men of his command with a tenderness and gentleness which won all hearts. When the invitation was given to her and her sister to unite with others in the Hospital Transport service, she rejoiced at the opportunity for wider usefulness in the cause she loved; how faithfully, earnestly, and persistently she toiled is partially revealed in the little work published by some of her associates, under the title of "Hospital Transports," but was fully known only by those who shared in her labors, and those who were the recipients of her kind attentions. One of these, a private in the

Sixteenth New York Regiment (her husband's regiment), and who had been under her care on one of the Commission's transports at White House, expressed his gratitude in the following graceful lines:

"From old St. Paul till now

Of honorable women, not a few

Have left their golden ease, in love to do

The saintly work which Christ-like hearts pursue.

"And such an one art thou? God's fair apostle,

Bearing his love in war's horrific train;

Thy blessed feet follow its ghastly pain, and misery and death without disdain.

"To one borne from the sullen battle's roar,

Dearer the greeting of thy gentle eyes

When he, a-weary, torn, and bleeding lies,

Than all the glory that the victors prize.

"When peace shall come and homes shall smile again,

A thousand soldier hearts, in northern climes,

Shall tell their little children in their rhymes

Of the sweet saints who blessed the old war times."

On the Chickahominy, June 12th, 1862.

Impaired health, the result of the excessive labors of that battle summer, prevented Mrs. Howland from further active service in the field; but whenever her health permitted, she visited and labored in the hospitals around Washington, and her thoughtful attention and words of encouragement to the women nurses appointed by Miss Dix, and receiving a paltry stipend from the Government, were most gratefully appreciated by those self-denying, hard-working, and often sorely-tried women—many of them the peers in culture, refinement and intellect of any lady in the land, but treated with harshness and discourtesy by boy surgeons, who lacked the breeding or instincts of the gentleman. Her genuine modesty and humility have led her, as well as her sisters, to deprecate any notoriety or public notice of their work, which they persist in regarding as unworthy of record; but so will it not be regarded by the soldiers who have been rescued from inevitable death by their persistent toil, nor by a nation grateful for the services rendered to its brave defenders.

Mrs. Robert S. Howland was the wife of a clergyman, and an earnest worker in the hospitals and in the Metropolitan Sanitary Fair, and her friends believed that her over-exertion in the preparation and attendance upon that fair, contributed to shorten a life as precious and beautiful as was ever offered upon the altar of patriotism. Mrs. Howland possessed rare poetic genius, and some of her effusions, suggested by incidents of army or hospital life, are worthy of preservation as among the choicest gems of poetry elicited by the war. "A Rainy Day in Camp," "A Message from the Army," etc., are poems which many of our readers will recall with interest and pleasure. A shorter one of equal merit and popularity, we copy not only for its brevity, but because it expresses so fully the perfect peace which filled her heart as completely as it did that of the subject of the poem.

Miss Georgiana M. Woolsey, was one of the most efficient ladies connected with the Hospital Transport service, where her constant cheerfulness, her ready wit, her never failing resources of contrivance and management in any emergency, made the severe labor seem light, and by keeping up the spirits of the entire party, prevented the scenes of suffering constantly presented from rendering them morbid or depressed. She took the position of assistant superintendent of the Portsmouth Grove General Hospital, in September, 1862, when her friend, Miss Wormeley, became superintendent, and remained there till the spring of 1863, was actively engaged in the care of the wounded at Falmouth after the battle of Chancellorsville, was on the field soon after the battle of Gettysburg, and wrote that charming and graphic account of the labors of herself and a friend at Gettysburg in the service of the Sanitary Commission which was so widely circulated, and several times reprinted in English reviews and journals. We cannot refrain from introducing it as one of those narratives of actual philanthropic work of which we have altogether too few.

THREE WEEKS AT GETTYSBURG

"July, 1863.

"DEAR: What we did at Gettysburg, for the three weeks we were there, you will want to know. 'We are Mrs.— and I, who, happening to be on hand at the right moment, gladly fell in with the proposition to do what we could at the Sanitary Commission Lodge after the battle. There were, of course, the agents of the Commission, already on the field, distributing supplies to the hospitals, and working night and day among the wounded. I cannot pretend to tell you what was done by all the big wheels of the concern, but only how two of the smallest ones went round, and what turned up in the going.

"Twenty-four hours we were in making the journey between Baltimore and Gettysburg, places only four hours apart in ordinary running time; and this will give you some idea of the difficulty there was in bringing up supplies when the fighting was over, and of the delays in transporting wounded. Coming toward the town at this crawling rate, we passed some fields where the fences were down and the ground slightly tossed up: I That's where Kilpatrick's Cavalry-men fought the rebels some one said; I and close by that barn a rebel soldier was found day before yesterday, sitting dead'— no one to help, poor soul,—'near the whole city full.' The railroad bridge broken up by the enemy, Government had not rebuilt as yet, and we stopped two miles from the town, to find that, as usual, just where the Government had left off the Commission came in. There stood their temporary lodge and kitchen, and here, hobbling out of their tents, came the wounded men who had made their way down from the corps-hospitals, expecting to leave at once in the return-cars.

"This is the way the thing was managed at first: The surgeons left in care of the wounded three or four miles out from the town, went up and down among the men in the morning, and said, 'Any of you boys who can make your way to the cars can go to Baltimore So off start all who think they feel well enough; anything better than the 'hospitals so called, for the first few days after a battle. Once the men have the surgeons' permission to go, they are off; and there may be an interval of a day, or two days, should any of them be too weak to reach the train in time, during which these poor fellows belong to no one,—the hospital at one end, the railroad at the other,—with far more than a chance of falling through between the two. The Sanitary Commission knew this would be so of necessity, and, coming in, made a connecting link between these two ends.

"For the first few days the worst cases only came down in ambulances torn the hospitals; hundreds of fellows hobbled along as best they could in heat and dust, for hours, slowly toiling; and many hired farmers' wagons, as hard as the farmers' fists themselves, md were jolted down to the railroad, at three or four dollars the man. Think of the disappointment of a soldier, sick, body and heat, to find, at the end of this miserable journey, that his effort to get away, into which he had put all his remaining stock of strength, was useless; that 'the cars had gone,' or 'the cars were full;' but while he was coming others had stepped down before him, and that he must turn all the weary way back again, or sleep on the road-side till the next train to-morrow!' Think what this would have been, and you are ready to appreciate the relief and comfort that was. No men were turned back. You fed and you sheltered them just when no one else could have done so; and out of the bores and barrels of good and nourishing things, which you people at home had supplied, we took all that was needed. Some of you sent a stove (that is, the money to get it), some of you the beef-stock, some of you the milk and fresh bread; and all of you would have been thankful that you had done so, could you have seen the refreshment and comfort received through these things.

"As soon as the men hobbled up to the tents, good hot soup was given all round; and that over, their wounds were dressed, —for the gentlemen of the Commission are cooks or surgeons, as occasion demands,—and, finally, with their blankets spread over the straw, the men stretched themselves out and were happy and contented till morning, and the next train.

"On the day that the railroad bridge was repaired, we moved up to the depot, close by the town, and had things ii perfect order; a first-rate camping-ground, in a large field directly by the track, with unlimited supply of delicious cool wafer. Here we set up two stoves, with four large boilers, always left full of soup and coffee, watched by four or five black men, who did the cooking, under our direction, and sang (not under »ur direction) at the top of their voices all day,—

'Oh darkies, hab you seen my Massa?'

'When this cruel war is over.'

Then we had three large hospital tents, holding about thirty-five each, a large camp-meeting supply tent, where barrels of goods were stored, and our own smaller tent, fitted up with tables, where jelly-pots, and bottles of all kinds of good syrups, blackberry and black currant, stood in rows. Barrels were ranged round the tent-walls; shirts, drawers, dressing-gowns, socks, and slippers (I wish we had had more of the latter), rags and bandages, each in its own place on one side; on the other, boxes of tea, coffee, soft crackers, tamarinds, cherry brandy, etc. Over the kitchen, and over this small supply-tent, we women rather reigned, and filled up our wants b requisition on tjie Commission's depot. By this time there lad arrived a 'delegation' of just the right kind from Canandagua, New York, with surgeons' dressers and attendants, bringing a first-rate supply of necessities and comforts for the wounded, which they handed over to the Commission.

"Twice a day the trains left for Baltimore or Harrisburg, and twice a day we fed all the wounded who arrived for them. Things were systematized now, and the men came down in long ambulance trains to the ears; baggage-ears they were, filled with straw for the wounded to lie on, and broken open at either end to let in the air. A Government surgeon was always present to attend to the careful lifting of the soldiers from ambulance to car. Many of the men could get along very nicely, holding one foot up, and taking great jumps on their crutches. The latter were a great comfort; we had a nice supply at the Lodge; and they traveled up and down from the tents to the ears daily. Only occasionally did we dare let a pair go on with some very lame soldier, who begged for them; we needed them to help the new arrivals each day, and trusted to the men being supplied at the hospitals at the journey's end. Pads and crutches are a standing want,—pads particularly. We manufactured them out of the rags we had, stuffed with sawdust from brandy-boxes; and with half a sheet and some soft straw, Mrs made a poor dying boy as easy as his sufferings would permit. Poor young fellow, he was so grateful to her for washing and feeding and comforting him. He was too ill to bear the journey, and went from our tent to the church hospital, and from the church to Lis grave, which would have been coffinless but for the care of; for the Quarter master's Department was overtaxed, and for many days our dead were simply wrapped in their blankets and put into the earth. It is a soldierly way, after all, of lying wrapped in the old warworn blanket,—the little dust returned to dust.

"When the surgeons had the wounded all placed, with as much comfort as seemed possible under the circumstances, on board the train, our detail of men -would go from car to car, with soup made of beef-stock or fresh meat, full of potatoes, turnips, cabbage, and rice, with fresh bread and coffee, and, when stimulants were needed, with ale, milk-punch, or brandy. Water-pails were in great demand for use in the cars on the journey, and also empty bottles to take the place of canteens. All our whisky and brandy bottles were washed and filled up at the spring, and the boys went off carefully hugging their extemporized canteens, from which they would wet their wounds, or refresh themselves till the journey ended. I do not think that a man of the sixteen thousand who were transported during our stay, went from Gettysburg without a good meal. Rebels and Unionists together, they all had it, and were pleased and satisfied. 'Have you friends in the army, madam? a rebel soldier, lying on the floor of the car, said to me, as I gave him some milk. 'Yes, my brother is on's staff.' 'I thought so-, ma'am. You can always tell; when people are good to soldiers they are sure to have friends in the army.' 'We are rebels, you know, ma'am,' another said. 'Do you treat rebels so?' It was strange to see the good brotherly feeling come over the soldiers, our own and the rebels, when side by side they lay in our tents. 'Hullo, boys! this is the pleasantest way to meet, isn't it? We are better friends when we are as close as this than a little farther off.' And then they would go over the battles together, 'We were here,' and 'you were there,' in the friendliest way.

"After each train of cars daily, for the three weeks we were in Gettysburg, trains of ambulances arrived too late—men who must spend the day with us until the five P. M. cars went, and men too late for the five P. M. train, who must spend the night till the ten A. M. cars went. All the men who came in this way, under our own immediate and particular attention, were given the best we had of care and food. The surgeon in charge of our camp, with his most faithful dresser and attendants, looked after all their wounds, which were often in a shocking state, particularly among the rebels. Every evening and morning they were dressed. Often the men would say, 'That feels good. I haven't had my wound so well dressed since I was hurt. Something cool to drink is the first thing asked for after the long, dusty drive; and pailfuls of tamarinds and water, 'a beautiful drink the men used to say, disappeared rapidly among them.

"After the men's wounds were attended to, we went round giving them clean clothes; had basins and soap and towels, and followed these with socks, slippers, shirts, drawers, and those coveted dressing-gowns. Such pride as they felt in them! comparing colors, and smiling all over as they lay in clean and comfortable rows, ready for supper,— 'on dress parade they used to say. And then the milk, particularly if it were boiled and had a little whisky and sugar, and the bread, with butter on it, and jelly on the butter: how good it all was, and how lucky we felt ourselves in having the immense satisfaction of distributing these things, which all of you, hard at work in villages and cities, were getting ready and sending off, in faith.

"Canandaigua sent cologne with its other supplies, which went right to the noses and hearts of the men. 'That is good, now—'I'll take some of that—' worth a penny a sniff that kinder gives one life— and so on, all round the tents, as we tipped the bottles up on the clean handkerchiefs some one had sent, and when they were gone, over squares of cotton, on which the perfume took the place of hem,—'just as good, ma'am.' We varied our dinners with custard and baked rice puddings, scrambled eggs, codfish hash, corn-starch, and always as much soft bread, tea, coffee, or milk as they wanted. Two Massachusetts boys I especially remember for the satisfaction with which they ate their pudding. I carried a second plateful up to the cars, after they had been put in, and fed one of them till he was sure he had had enough. Young fellows they were, lying side by side, one with a right and one with a left arm gone.

"The Gettysburg women were kind and faithful to the wounded and their friends, and the town was full to overflowing of both. The first day, when Mrs and I reached the place, we literally begged our bread from door to door; but the kind woman who at last gave us dinner would take no pay for it. 'No, ma'am, I shouldn't wish to have that sin on my soul when the war is over.' She, as well as others, had fed the strangers flocking into town daily, sometimes over fifty of them for each meal, and all for love and nothing for reward; and one night we forced a reluctant confession from our hostess that she was meaning to sleep on the floor that we might have a bed, her whole house being full. Of course we couldn't allow this self-sacrifice, and hunted up some other place to stay in. We did her no good, however, for we afterwards found that the bed was given up that night to some other stranger who arrived late and tired: 'An old lady, you know; and I couldn't let an old lady sleep on the floor.' Such acts of kindness and self-denial were almost entirely confined to the women.

"Few good things can be said of the Gettysburg farmers, and I only use Scripture language in calling them 'evil beasts.' One of this kind came creeping into our camp three weeks after the battle. He lived five miles only from the town, and had 'never seen a rebel.' He heard we had some of them, and had come down to see them. 'Boys,' we said,—marching him into the tent which happened to be full of rebels that day, waiting for the train,—'Boys, here's a man who never saw a rebel in his life, and wants to look at you;' and there he stood with his mouth wide open, and there they lay in rows, laughing at him, stupid old Dutchman. 'And why haven't you seen a rebel?' Mrs said; 'why didn't you take your gun and help to drive them out of your town?' 'A feller might'er got hit!'—which reply was quite too much for the rebels; they roared with laughter at him, up and down the tent.

"One woman we saw, who was by no means Dutch, and whose pluck helped to redeem the other sex. She lived in a little house close up by the field where the hardest fighting was done,—a redcheeked, strong, country girl. 'Were you frightened when the shells began flying?' 'Well, no. You see we was all a-baking bread around here for the soldiers, and had our dough a-rising. The neighbors they ran into their cellars, but I couldn't leave my bread. When the first shell came in at the window and crashed through the room, an officer came and said, 'You had better get out of this;' but I told him I could not leave my bread; and I stood working it till the third shell came through, and then I went down cellar; but' (triumphantly) 'I left my bread in the oven.' 'And why didn't you go before?' 'Oh, you see, if I had, the rebels would'a'come in and daubed the dough all over the place.' And here she had stood, at the risk of unwelcome plums in her loaves, while great holes (which we saw) were made by shot and shell through and through the room in which she was working.

"The streets of Gettysburg were filled with the battle. People thought and talked of nothing else; even the children showed their little spites by calling to each other, 'Here, you rebel;' and mere scraps of boys amused themselves with percussion-caps and hammers. Hundreds of old muskets were piled on the pavements, the men who shouldered them a week before, lying underground now, or helping to fill the long trains of ambulances on their way from the field. The private houses of the town were, many of them, hospitals; the little red flags hung from the upper windows. Beside our own men at the Lodge, we all had soldiers scattered about whom we could help from our supplies; and nice little puddings and jellies, or an occasional chicken, were a great treat to men condemned by their wounds to stay in Gettysburg, and obliged to live on what the empty town could provide. There was a colonel in a shoe-shop, a captain just up-the street, and a private round the corner whose young sister had possessed herself of him, overcoming the military rules in some way, and carrying him off to a little room, all by himself, where I found her doing her best with very little. She came afterward to our tent and got for him clean clothes, and good food, and all he wanted, and was perfectly happy in being his cook, washer woman, medical cadet, and nurse. Besides such as these, we occasionally carried from our supplies something to the churches, which were filled with sick and wounded, and where men were dying,—men whose strong patience it was very hard to bear,— dying with thoughts of the old home far away, saying, as last words, for the women watching there and waiting with a patience equal in its strength, 'Tell her I love her

"Late one afternoon, too late for the cars, a train of ambulances arrived at our Lodge with over one hundred wounded rebels, to be cared for through the night. Only one among them seemed too weak and faint to take anything. He was badly hurt, and failing. I went to him after his wound was dressed, and found him lying on his blanket stretched over the straw,—a fair-haired, blue-eyed young lieutenant, with a face innocent enough for one of our own New England boys. I could not think of him as a rebel; he was too near heaven for that. He wanted nothing,— had not been willing to eat for days, his comrades said; but I coaxed him to try a little milk gruel, made nicely with lemon and brandy; and one of the satisfactions of our three weeks is the remembrance of the empty cup I took away afterward, and his perfect enjoyment of that supper. 'It was so good, the best thing he had had since he was wounded—and he thanked me so much, and talked about his 'good supper' for hours. Poor fellow, he had had no care, and it was a surprise and pleasure to find himself thought of; so, in a pleased, childlike way, he talked about it till midnight, the attendant told me, as long as he spoke of anything; for at midnight the change came, and from that time he only thought of the old days before he was a soldier, when he sang hymns in his father's church. He sang them now again in a clear, sweet voice. 'Lord, have mercy upon me and then songs without words—a sort of low intoning. His father was a Lutheran clergyman in South Carolina, one of the rebels told us in the morning, when we went into the tent, to find him sliding out of our care. All day long we watched him,—sometimes fighting his battles over, often singing his

Lutheran chants, till, in at the tent-door, close to which he lay, looked a rebel soldier, just arrived with other prisoners. He started when he saw the lieutenant, and quickly kneeling down by him, called, 'Henry! Henry!' But Henry was looking at some one a great way off, and could not hear him. 'Do you know this soldier?' we said. 'Oh, yes, ma'am; and his brother is wounded and a prisoner, too, in the cars, now.' Two or three men started after him, found him, and half carried him from the cars to our tent. 'Henry' did not know him, though; and he threw himself down by his side on the straw, and for the rest of the day lay in a sort of apathy, without speaking, except to assure himself that he could stay with his brother, without the risk of being separated from his fellow-prisoners. And there the brothers lay, and there we strangers sat watching and listening to the strong, clear voice, singing, 'Lord, have mercy upon me.' The Lord had mercy; and at sunset I put my hand on the lieutenant's heart, to find it still. All night the brother lay close against the coffin, and in the morning went away with his comrades, leaving us to bury Henry, having 'confidence;' but first thanking us for what we had done, and giving us all that he had to show his gratitude,— the palmetto ornament from his brother's cap and a button from his coat. Dr. W. read the burial service that morning at the grave, and wrote his name on the little head-board:

'Lieutenant Rauch, Fourteenth Regiment South Carolina Volunteers.'

"In the field where we buried him, a number of colored freedmen, working for Government on the railroad, had their camp, and every night they took their recreation, after the heavy work of the day was over, in prayer-meetings. Such an 'inferior race,' you know! We went over one night and listened for an hour, while they sang, collected under the fly of a tent, a table in the middle where the leader sat, and benches all round the sides for the congregation—men only,—all very black and very earnest.

They prayed with all their souls, as only black men and slaves can; for themselves and for the dear, white people who had come over to the meeting; and' for 'Massa Lincoln,' for whom they seemed to have a reverential affection,—some of them a sort of worship, which confused Father Abraham and Massa Abraham in one general cry for blessings. Whatever else they asked for, they must have strength, and comfort, and blessing for 'Massa Lincoln Very little care was taken of these poor men. Those who were ill during our stay were looked after by one of the officers of the Commission. They were grateful for every little thing. Airs went into the town and hunted up several dozen bright handkerchiefs, hemmed them, and sent them over to be distributed the next night after meeting. They were put on the table in the tent, and one by one, the men came up to get them. Purple, and blue, and yellow the handkerchiefs were, and the desire of every man's heart fastened itself on a yellow one; they politely made way for each other, though,—one man standing back to let another pass up first, although he ran the risk of seeing the particular pumpkin-color that riveted his eyes taken from before them. When the distribution is over, each man tied his head up in his handkerchief, and they sang one more hymn, keeping time all round, with blue and purple and yellow nods, and thanking and blessing the white people in their basket and in their store,' as much as if the cotton handkerchiefs had all been gold leaf. One man came over to our tent next day, to say, 'Missus, was it you who sent me that present? I never had anything so beautiful in all my life before;' and he only had a blue one, too.

"Among our wounded soldiers one night, came an elderly man, sick, wounded, and crazy, singing and talking about home. We did what we could for him, and pleased him greatly with a present of a red flannel shirt, drawers, and red calico dressing-gown, all of which he needed, and in which he dressed himself up, and then wrote a letter to his wife, made it into a little book with gingham covers, and gave it to one of the gentlemen to mail for him. The next morning he was sent on with the company from the Lodge; and that evening two tired women came into our camp—his wife and sister, who hurried on from their home to meet him, arriving just too late. Fortunately we had the queer little gingham book to identify him by, and when some one said, "It is the man, you know, who screamed so,' the poor wife was certain about him. He had been crazy before the war, but not for two years, now, she said. He had been fretting for home since he was hurt; and when the doctor told him there was no chance of his being sent there, he lost heart, and wrote to his wife to come and carry him away. It seemed almost hopeless for two lone women, who had never been out of their own little town, to succeed in finding a soldier among so many, sent in so many different directions; but we helped them as we could, and started them on their journey the next morning, back on their track, to use their common sense and Yankee privilege of questioning.

"A week after, Mrs had a letter full of gratitude, and saying that the husband was found and secured for home. That same night we had had in our tents two fathers, with their wounded sons, and a nice old German mother with her boy. She had come in from Wisconsin, and brought with her a patchwork bed-quilt for her son, thinking he might have lost his blanket; and there he laid all covered up in his quilt, looking so homelike, and feeling so, too, no doubt, with his good old mother close at his side. She seemed bright and happy,—had three sons in the Army,—one had been killed,—this one wounded; yet she was so pleased with the tents, and the care she saw taken there of the soldiers, that, while taking her tea from a barrel-head as table, she said, 'Indeed, if she was a man, she'd be a soldier too, right off.'

"For this temporary sheltering and feeding of all these wounded men, Government could make no provision. There was nothing for them, if too late for the cars, except the open field and hunger, in preparation for their fatiguing journey. It is expected when the ears are ready that the men will be promptly sent to meet them, and Government cannot provide for mistakes and delays; so that, but for the Sanitary Commission's Lodge and comfortable supplies, for which the wounded are indebted to the hard workers at home, men badly hurt must have suffered night and day, while waiting for the 'next train.' We had on an average sixty of such men each night for three weeks under our care,—sometimes one hundred, sometimes only thirty; and with the 'delegation,' and the help of other gentlemen volunteers, who all worked devotedly for the men, the whole thing was a great success, and you and all of us can't help being thankful that we had a share, however small, in making it so. Sixteen thousand good meals were given; hundreds of men kept through the day, and twelve hundred sheltered at night, their wounds dressed, their supper and breakfast secured—rebels and all. You will not, I am sure, regret that these most wretched men, these 'enemies,"sick and in prison,' were helped and eared for through your supplies, though, certainly, they were not in your minds when you packed your barrels and boxes. The clothing we reserved for our own men, except now and then when a shivering rebel needed it; but in feeding them we could make no distinctions.

"Our three weeks were coming to an end; the work of transporting the wounded was nearly over; twice daily AA e had filled and emptied our tents, and twice fed the trains before the long journey. The men came in slowly at the last,—a lieutenant, all the way from Oregon, being among the very latest. He came down from the corps hospitals (now greatly improved), having lost one foot, poor fellow, dressed in a full suit of the Commission's cotton clothes, just as bright and as cheerful as the first man, and all the men that we received had been. We never heard a complaint. 'would he like a little I ice soup?' 'Well, no, thank you, ma'am hesitating and polite. 'You have a long ride before you, and had better take a little; I'll just bring it and you can try.' So the good, thick soup came. He took a very little in the spoon to please me, and afterwards the whole cupful to please himself. He 'did not think it was this kind of soup I meant. He had some in camp, and did not think he cared for any more; his "cook" was a very small boy, though, who just put some meat in a little water and stirred it round.' 'Would you like a handkerchief?' and I produced our last one, with a hem and cologne too. 'Oh, yes; that is what I need; I have lost mine, and was just borrowing this gentleman's.' So the lieutenant, the last man, was made comfortable, thanks to all of you, though he had but one foot to carry him on his long journey home.

"Four thousand soldiers, too badly hurt to be moved, were still left in Gettysburg, cared for kindly and well at the large, new Government hospital, with a Sanitary Commission attachment.

"Our work was over, our tents were struck, and we came away after a flourish of trumpets from two military bands who filed down to our door, and gave us a farewell 'Red, white, and blue.'"

One who knows Miss Woolsey well says of her, "Her sense, energy, lightness, and quickness of action; her thorough knowledge of the work, her amazing yet simple resources, her shy humility which made her regard her own work with impatience, almost with contempt—all this and much else make her memory a source of strength and tenderness which nothing can take away." Elsewhere, the same writer adds, "Strength and sweetness, sound practical sense, deep humility, merriment, playfulness, a most ready wit, an educated intelligence—were among her characteristics. Her work I consider to have been better than any which I saw in the service. It was thorough, but accomplished rapidly. She saw a need before others saw it, and she supplied it often by some ingenious contrivance which answered every purpose, though no one but Georgy would ever have dreamt of it. Her pity foi the sufferings of the men was something pathetic in itself, but it was never morbid, never unwise, never derived from her own shoek at the sight, always practical and healthy." Miss Woolsey remained in the service through the war, a part of the time in charge of hospitals, but during Grant's great campaign of the spring, summer, and autumn of 1864, she was most effectively engaged at the front, or rather at the great depots for the wounded, at Belle Plain, Port Royal, Fredericksburg, White House, and City Point. Miss Jane S. Woolsey, also served in general hospitals as lady superintendent until the close of the war, and afterward transferred her efforts to the work among the Freedmen at Richmond, Virginia.

A cousin of these ladies, Miss Sarah C. Woolsey, daughter of President Woolsey of Yale College, was also engaged during the greater part of the war in hospital and other philanthropic labors for the soldiers. She was for ten months assistant superintendent of the Portsmouth Grove General Hospital, and her winning manners, her tender and skilful care of the patients, and her unwearied efforts to do them good, made her a general favorite.

ANNA MARIA ROSS

ANNA MARIA ROSS, the subject of this sketch, was a native of Philadelphia, in which city the greater part of her life was spent, and in which, on the 22d of December, 1863, she passed to her eternal rest.

It was a very beautiful life of which we have now to speak— a life of earnest activity in every work of benevolence and Christian kindness. She had gathered about her, in her native city, scores of devoted friends, who loved her in life, and mourned her in death with the sentiments of a true bereavement.

Miss Ross was patriotic by inheritance, as well as through personal loyalty. Her maternal relatives were largely identified with the war of American Independence. Her mother's uncle, Jacob Root, held a captain's commission in the Continental army, and it is related of her great grandmother that she served voluntarily as a moulder in an establishment where bullets were manufactured to be used in the cause of freedom.

Her mother's name was Mary Root, a native of Chester County, Pennsylvania. Her father was William Ross, who emigrated early in life from the county of Derry, Ireland. There may have been nothing in her early manifestations of character to foreshow the noble womanhood into which she grew. There remains, at any rate, a small record of her earliest years. The wonderful powers which she developed in mature womanhood possess a greater interest for those who know her chiefly in connection with the labors which gave her so just a claim to the title of "The Soldier's Friend."

Endowed by nature with great vigor of mind and uncommon activity and energy, of striking and commanding personal appearance and pleasing address, she had been, before the war, remarkably successful in the prosecution of those works of charity and benevolence which made her life a blessing to mankind. Well-known to the public-spirited and humane of her native city, her claims to attention were fully recognized, and her appeals in behalf of the needy and suffering were never allowed to pass unheeded.

"I have little hope of success," she said once to her companion, in going upon an errand of mercy: "yet we may get one hundred dollars. The lady we are about to visit is not liberal, though wealthy. Let us pray that her heart may be opened to us. Many of my most earnest prayers have been made while hurrying along the street on such errands as this." The lady gave her three hundred dollars.

On one occasion she was at the house of a friend, when a family was incidentally mentioned as being in great poverty and affliction. The father had been attacked with what is known as "black small pox," and was quite destitute of the comforts and attentions which his situation required, some of the members of his own family having left the house from fear of the infection. The quick sympathies of Miss Ross readily responded to this tale of want and neglect. "While God gives me health and strength," she earnestly exclaimed, "no man shall thus suffer!" With no more delay than was required to place in a basket articles of necessity and comfort she hastened to the miserable dwelling; nor did she leave the poor sufferer until he was beyond the reach of human aid forever. And her thoughtful care ceased not even here. From her own friends she sought and obtained the means of giving him a respectable burial.

The lady to whom the writer is indebted for the above incident, relates to at on the day when all that was mortal of Anna Maria Ross was consigned to its kindred dust, as she was entering a street-car, the conductor remarked, "I suppose you have been to see the last of Miss Ross." Upon her replying in the affirmative, he added, while tears flowed down his cheeks, "I did not know her, but she watched over my wife for four weeks when she had a terrible sickness. She was almost an entire stranger to her when she came and offered her assistance."

Her work for the soldier was chiefly performed in connection with the institution known as the Cooper Shop Hospital, a branch of the famous Cooper Shop Refreshment Saloon, for Soldiers. Miss Ross was appointed Lady Principal of this Institution, and devoted herself to it with an energy that never wearied. Day and night she was at her post—watching while others slept, dressing with her own hands the most loathsome wounds; winning the love and admiration of all with whom she was associated. Her tasks were arduous, her sympathies were drawn upon to the utmost, her responsibilities were great.

One who knew her well, and often saw her within the walls of the "Cooper Shop," thus gives us some incidents of her work there. The benevolence expressed in her glowing countenance, and the words of hearty welcome with which she greeted a humble coadjutor in her loving labors, will never be forgotten. It was impossible not to be impressed at once by the tender earnestness with which she engaged in her self-imposed duties, and her active interest in everything which concerned the well-being of those committed to her charge. When they were about to leave her watchful care forever, a sister's thoughtfulness was exhibited in her preparations for their comfort and convenience. The wardrobe of the departing soldier was carefully inspected, and everything needful 'was supplied. It was her custom also to furnish to each one who left, a sum of money, "that he might have something of his own" to meet any unexpected necessity by the way. And if the donation-box at the entrance of the hospital chanced to be empty, her own purse made good the deficiency.

The writer well remembers the anxious countenance with which she was met one morning by Miss Ross, when about taking her place for the day's duty. "I am so sorry!" was her exclamation. "When Cleft for Virginia last night I forgot, in the confusion, to give him money; and I am afraid that he has nothing of his own, for he had not received his pay. I thought of it after I was in bed, and it disturbed my sleep."

The tenderness of Miss Ross's nature was never more touchingly exhibited than in the case of Lieutenant B, of Saratoga,

New York. He was brought to the hospital by his father for a few days' rest before proceeding to his home. Mortally wounded, he failed so rapidly that he could not be removed. During two days and nights of agonizing suffering Miss Ross scarcely left his side, and while she bathed his burning brow and moistened his parched lips she mingled with these tender offices words of Christian hope and consolation. "Call me Anna," she said, "and tell me all which your heart prompts you to say." And as life ebbed away he poured into her sympathizing ear the confidences which his mother, alas! could not receive. With tearful eyes and sorrowing heart this new-found friend watched by him to the last— then closed the heavy eyes, and smoothed the raven locks, and sent the quiet form, lovely even in death, to her who waited its arrival in bitter anguish.

To those who best knew the subject of this sketch, it seems a hopeless task to enumerate the instances of unselfish devotion to the good of others with which that noble life was filled. It was the same tale again and again repeated. Alike the pain, the anxiety, the care; alike the support, the encouragement, the consolation. No marvel was it that the sinking soldier, far from home and friends, mistook the gentle ministry for that which marks 'earth's strongest tie, and at her approach whispered "mother."

It would be impossible to enumerate a tithe of the special instances of her kindly ministrations, but there are some that so vividly illustrate prominent points in her character that we cannot refrain from the record. One of these marked traits was her perseverance in the accomplishment of any plan for the good of her charges, and may well be mentioned here.

For a long time an Eastern soldier, named D, was an inmate of her hospital, and as, though improving, his recovery was slow, and it seemed unlikely that he would soon be fit for service in the ranks, she got him the appointment of hospital steward, and he remained where he could still have care.

After the battle of Gettysburg he relapsed, and from over-work and over-wrought feeling, sank into almost hopeless depression. The death of a beloved child, and an intense passionate longing to revisit his home and family, aided this deep grief, and gave it a force and power that threatened to deprive him of life or reason. It was at this crisis that with her accustomed energy Miss Ross directed all her efforts toward restoring him to his family. After the preliminary steps had been taken she applied to the captain of a Boston steamer, but he refused to receive a sick passenger on account of the want of suitable accommodations. The case was urgent. He must go or die. "There is no room," repeated the captain.

"Give him a place upon the floor," was the rejoinder, "and I will furnish everything needful." "But a sick man cannot have proper attendance under such circumstances," persisted the captain. "I will go with him if necessary," she replied, "and will take the entire charge of his comfort." "Miss Ross, I am sorry to refuse you, but I cannot comply with your request. This answer must be final."

What was to be done? The unsuccessful pleader covered her face with her hands for a few moments; then raising her head said, slowly and sadly, "Captain, I have had many letters from the friends of New England soldiers, thanking me with overflowing hearts for restoring to them the dearly loved husband, son, or brother while yet alive. From D. s wife I shall receive no such message. This is his only chance of life. He cannot bear the journey by land. He must go by water or die. He will die here—far from friends and home." This appeal could not be resisted. "I will take him, Miss Ross," was the answer; "but it must be only upon the condition that you will promise not to ask such a favor of me again whatever the case may be." "Never!" was the quick reply, "never will I bind myself by such a promise while an Eastern soldier needs a friend or a passage to his home! You are the first man to whom I should apply." "Then let him come without a promise. You have conquered; I will do for him all that can be done."

Could such friendship fail to win the hearts of those to whom this inestimable woman gave the cheerful service of her life's best days? "Do you want to see Florence Nightingale?" said one, who had not yet left the nursing care which brought him back to life and hope, to a companion whom he met. "If you do, just come to our hospital and see Miss Ross."

This was the only reward she craved—a word of thoughtful gratitude from those she sought to serve; and in this was lost all remembrance of days of toil and nights of weariness. So from week to week and from month to month the self-consecration grew more complete—the self-forgetfulness more perfect. But the life spent in the service of others was drawing near its end. The busy hands were soon to be folded, the heavy eyelids forever closed, the weary feet were hastening to their rest.

The spring of 1863 found Miss Ross still occupied in the weary round of her labors at the hospital. She had most remarkable strength and vigor of constitution, and that, with every other gift and talent she possessed was unsparingly used for the promotion of any good cause to which she was devoted. During this spring, in addition to all her other and engrossing labors, she was very busy in promoting the interests of a large fair for the purpose of aiding in the establishment of a permanent Home for discharged soldiers, who were incapacitated for active labor. She canvassed the city of Philadelphia, and also traveled in different parts of Pennsylvania and New Jersey in order to obtain assistance in this important undertaking. "Is it not wrong," a friend once asked, "that you should do so much, while so many are doing nothing?" "Oh, there are hundreds who would gladly work as I do," was her reply, "but they have not my powers of endurance."

The fair in which she was so actively interested took place in June, and a large sum was added to the fund previously obtained for the benefit of the "Soldiers' Home." The work now progressed rapidly, and the personal aid and influence of Miss Ross were exerted to forward it in every possible way. Yet while deeply absorbed in the promotion of this object, which was very near to her heart, she found time to brighten, with characteristic tenderness and devotion, the last hours of the Rev. Dr. Clay, the aged and revered minister of the ancient church, in which the marriage of her parents had taken place so many years before. With his Own family she watched beside his bed, and with them received his parting blessing.

The waning year found the noble undertaking, the object of so many prayers and the goal of such ardent desire, near a prosperous completion. A suitable building had been obtained, and many busy days were occupied in the delightful task of furnishing it. At the close of a day spent in this manner, the friend who had been Miss Boss's companion proposed that the remaining purchases should be deferred to another time, urging, in addition to her extreme fatigue, that many of the stores were closed. "Come to South Street with me," she replied. "They keep open there until twelve o'clock, and may find exactly what we want." The long walk AA as taken, and A hen the desired articles were secured she yielded to her friend's entreaties, and at a late hour sought her home. As she pursued her solitary way came there no foreshadowing of what was to be? no whisper of the hastening summons? no token of the quick release? Wearily were the steps ascended, which echoed for the lad; time the familiar tread. Slowly the door closed through which she should pass on angelic mission nevermore. Was there no warning?

"I am tired," she said, "and so cold that I feel as if I never could be warm again." It was an unusual complaint for her to whom fatigue had seemed almost unknown before. But it was very natural that exhaustion should follow a day of such excessive labor, and she would soon be refreshed. So thought those who loved her, unconscious of the threatening danger. The heavy chill retained its grasp, the resistless torpor of paralysis crept slowly on, and then complete insensibility. In this utter helplessness, which baffled every effort of human skill, night wore away, and morning dawned. There was no change and days passed before the veil was lifted.

She could not believe that her work was all done on earth and death near, "but," she said, "God has willed it—His will be done." There was no apparent mental struggle. Well she knew that she had done her uttermost, and that God was capable of placing in the field other laborers, and perhaps better ones than she; and she uttered no meaningless words when, without a murmur, she resigned herself to His will.

A few words of fond farewell, she calmly spoke to the weeping friends about her. Then with fainter and fainter breathing, life fled so gently that they knew not when the shadowy vale was passed. So, silently and peacefully the Death-angel had visited her, and upon her features lay the calm loveliness of perfect rest.

On the 22d of December, 1863, the friends, and sharers of her labors were assembled at the dedication of the Soldiers' Home. It was the crowning work of her life, and it was completed; and thus, at the same hour, this earthly crown was laid upon her dying brow, and the freed soul put on the crown of a glorious immortality.

Her funeral was attended by a sorrowing multitude, all of whom had known, and many, yea, most of whom, had been blest by her labors. For even they are blest to whom it has happened to know and appreciate a character like hers.

They made her a tomb, in the beautiful Monument Cemetery, beneath the shadow of a stately cedar. Nature itself, in the desolation of advancing winter, seemed to join in the lament that such loveliness and worth was lost to earth.

But with returning summer, the branches of her overshadowing cedar are melodious with the song of birds, while roses and many flowering plants scatter fragrance to every passing breeze as their petals falling hide the dark soil beneath. The hands of friends have planted these—an odorous tribute to the memory of her they loved and mourn, and have raised beside, in the enduring marble, a more lasting testimony of her worth.

The tomb is of pure white marble, surmounted by a tablet of the same, which in alto relief, represents a female figure ministering to a soldier, who lies upon a couch. Beneath, is this inscription:

ERECTED BY HER FRIENDS

IN MEMORY OF

ANNA M. ROSS,

DIED, DECEMBER 22, 1863.

Her piety was fruitful of good works. The friendless child, the fugitive slave, and the victim of intemperance were ever objects of her tenderest solicitude.

When civil war disclosed its horrors, she dedicated her life to the sick and wounded soldiers of her country, and died a martyr to Humanity and Patriotism.

So closes the brief and imperfect record of a beautiful life; but the light of its lovely example yet remains.

MRS. G. T. M. DAVIS

AMONG the large number of the ladies of New York city who distinguished themselves for their devotion to the welfare of the soldiers of our army, of whom so many in all forms of suffering were brought there during the war, it seems almost invidious to select any individual. But it is perhaps less so in the case of the subject of this sketch, than of many others, since from the very beginning of the war till long after its close, she quietly sacrificed the ease and luxury of her life to devote herself untiringly, and almost without respite, to the duties thus voluntarily assumed and faithfully performed.

Mrs. Davis is the wife of Colonel G. T. M. Davis, who served with great distinction in the Mexican war, but who, having entered into commercial pursuits, is not at present connected with the army. Her maiden name was Pomeroy, and she is a native of Pittsfield, Massachusetts. Her brother, Robert Pomeroy, Esq., of that town, a wealthy manufacturer, was noted for his liberal benefactions during the war, and with all his family omitted no occasion of showing his devotion to his country and to its wounded and suffering defenders. His daughter, near the close of the war, became the wife of one of the most distinguished young officers in the service, General Bartlett.

General Bartlett, at twenty-two, and fresh from the classic precincts of Harvard, entered the service as a private. He rose rapidly through the genius and force of his commanding character. He lost a leg, we believe at the siege of Yorktown, left the service, until partially recovered, when he again re-entered it as the Colonel of the Forty-ninth Massachusetts Regiment, which was raised in Berkshire County. For months he rode at the head of his regiment with his crutch attached to the back of his saddle. It was after his return from the South-west, (where the gallant Forty-ninth distinguished itself at Port Hudson, Plain's Stone, and other hard-won fields), with a maimed arm, that he was rewarded with the hand of one of Berkshire's fairest daughters, a member of this patriotic family. Several other young men, members of the same family, have also greatly distinguished themselves in the service of their country

At the very outset of the war, or as soon as the sick among the volunteers who were pouring into New York, demanded relief, Mrs. Davis began to devote time and care to them. Daily leaving her elegant home, she sought out and ministered to her country's suffering defenders, at the various temporary barracks erected for their accommodation.

When the Park Barracks Ladies' Association was formed, she became its Secretary, and so continued for a long period, most faithful and energetic in her ministrations. This association included in its work the Hospital on Bedloe's Island, and Mrs. Davis was one of the first who commenced making regular visits there.

Most of the men brought to Bedloe's Island in the earlier part of the war, were sick with the various diseases consequent upon the unaccustomed climate and the unwonted exposure they had encountered. They needed a very careful and regular diet, one which the army rations, though perhaps suitable and sufficient for men in health, were unable to supply. It was but natural that these ladies, full of the warm sympathy which prompted them to the unusual tasks they had undertaken, should shrink from seeing A half-convalescent fever patient fed with hard-bread and salt pork, or the greasy soups of which pork was the basis. They brought delicacies, often prepared by their own hands or in their own kitchens, and were undoubtedly injudicious, sometimes, in their administration. Out of this arose the newspaper controversy between the public and the surgeons in charge, at Bedloe's Island, which is probably yet fresh in many minds. It was characterized by a good deal of acrimony.

Mrs. Davis avers that neither she nor her friends gave food to the patients without the consent of the physicians. The affair terminated, as is well-known, by the removal of the surgeon in charge.

The Ladies Park Barracks' Association was, as a body, opposed to extending its benefactions beyond New York and its immediate vicinity. Mrs. Davis was of a different opinion, and was, beside, not altogether pleased with the management of the association. She therefore, after a time, relinquished her official connection with it, though never for one instant relaxing her efforts for the same general object.

For a long series of months Mrs. Davis repaired almost daily to the large General Hospital at David's Island, where thousands of sick and wounded men were sometimes congregated. Here she and her chief associates, Mrs. Chapman, and Miss Morris, established the most amicable relations with the surgeon in charge, Dr. McDougall, and were welcomed by him, as valued coadjutors.

On the opening of the Soldiers' Best, in Howard Street, an association of ladies was formed to aid in administering to the comfort of the poor fellows who tarried there during their transit through the city, or were received in the well-conducted hospital connected with the institution. Of this association Mrs. Davis was the Secretary, during the whole term of its existence.

This association, as well as the institution itself, was admirably conducted, and perhaps performed as much real and beneficial work as any other in the vicinity of New York. It was continued in existence till several months after the close of the war.

Besides her visits at David's Island and Howard Street, which were most assiduous, Mrs. Davis as often as possible visited the Central Park, or Mount St. Vincent Hospital, the Ladies' Home Hospital, at the corner of Lexington avenue and Fifty-first Street, and the New England Rooms in Broadway. At all of these she was welcomed, and her efforts most gratefully received. Seldom indeed did a day pass, during the long four years of the war, and for months after the suspension of hostilities, that her kind face was not seen in one or more of the hospitals.

Her social position, as well as her genuine dignity of manners enforced the respect of all the officials, and won their regard. Her untiring devotion and kindness earned her the almost worshipping affection of the thousands of sufferers to whom she ministered.

Letters still reach her, at intervals, from the men who owe, perhaps life, certainly relief and comfort to her cherishing care. Ignorant men, they may be, little accustomed to the amenities of life, capable only of composing the strangely-worded, ill-spelled letters they send, but the gratitude they express is so abundant and so genuine, that one overlooks the uncouthness of manner, and the unattractive appearance of the epistles. And seldom does she travel but at the most unexpected points scarred and maimed veterans present themselves before her, and with the deepest respect beg the privilege of once more offering their thanks. She may have forgotten the faces, that in the great procession of suffering flitted briefly before her, but they will never forget the face that bent above their couch of pain.

The native county of Mrs. Davis, Berkshire, Massachusetts, was famous for the abundance and excellence of the supplies it continually sent forward to the sick and suffering soldiers. The appeals of Mrs. Davis to the women of Berkshire, were numerous and always effective. Her letters were exceedingly graphic and spirited, and were published frequently in the county papers, reaching not only the villages in the teeming valleys but the scattered farm-houses among the hills; and they continually gave impulse and direction to the noble charities of those women, who, in their quiet homes, had already sent forth their dearest and best to the service of the country.

Mrs. Davis for herself disclaims all merit, but has no word of praise too much for these. They made the real sacrifices, these women who from their small means gave so much, who rose before the sun, alike in the cold of winter and the heat of summer, who performed the most menial tasks and the hardest toil that they might save for the soldiers, that they might gain time to work for the soldiers. It was they who gave much, not the lady who laid aside only the soft pleasures of a luxurious life, whose well-trained servants left no task unfinished during: her absence, whose bath, and dress, and dinner were always ready on her return from the tour of visiting, who gave only what was not missed from her abundance, and made no sacrifice but that of her personal ease. So speaks Mrs. Davis, in noble self-depreciation of herself and her class. There is a variety of gifts. God and her country will decide whose work was most worthy.

MISS MARY J. SAFFORD

MISS MARY J. SAFFORD, is a native of New England, having been born in Vermont, though her parents, very worthy people, early emigrated to the West, and settled in Northern Illinois, in which State she has since resided, making her home most of the time in Crete, Joliet, Shawneetown and Cairo; the last named place is her present home.

Miss Safford, early in life, evinced an unusual thirst for knowledge, and gave evidence of an intellect of a superior order; and, with an energy and zeal seldom known, she devoted every moment to the attainment of an education, the cultivation of her mind—and the gaining of such information as the means at hand afforded. Her love of the beautiful and good was at once marked, and every opportunity made use of to satisfy her desires in these directions.

Her good deeds date from the days of her childhood, and the remarkably high sense of duty of which she is possessed, makes her continually in search of some object of charity upon which to exert her beneficence and kindly care.

The commencement of the late rebellion, found her a resident of Cairo, Illinois, and immediately upon the arrival of the Union soldiers there, she set about organizing and establishing temporary hospitals throughout the different regiments, in order that the sick might have immediate and proper care and attention until better and more permanent arrangements could be effected.

Every day found her a visitor and a laborer among these sick soldiers, scores of whom now bear fresh in their memories the petite form, and gentle and loving face of that good angel of mercy to whom they are indebted, through her kind and watchful care and nursing, for the lives they are now enjoying.

The morning after the battle of Belmont, found her,—the only lady—early on the field, fearlessly penetrating far into the enemies' lines, with her handkerchief tied upon a little stick, and waving above her head as a flag of truce,—ministering to the wounded, which our army had been compelled to leave behind, to some extent—and many a Union soldier owes his life to her almost superhuman efforts on that occasion. She continued her labors with the wounded after their removal to the hospitals, supplying every want in her power, and giving words of comfort and cheer to every heart.

As soon as the news of the terrible battle of Pittsburg Landing reached her, she gathered together a supply of lints and bandages, and provided herself with such stimulants and other supplies as might be required, not forgetting a good share of delicacies, and hastened to the scene of suffering and carnage, where she toiled incessantly day and night in her pilgrimage of love and mission of mercy for more than three weeks, and then only returned with a steamboat-load of the wounded on their way to the general hospitals. She continued her labors among the hospitals at Cairo and the neighborhood, constantly visiting from one to the other. Any day she could be seen on her errands of mercy passing along the streets with her little basket loaded with delicacies, or reading-matter, or accompanied with an attendant carrying ample supplies to those who had made known to her their desire for some favorite dish or relish. On Christmas day, 1861, there were some twenty-five regiments stationed at Cairo, and on that day she visited all the camps, and presented to every sick soldier some little useful present or token. The number of sad hearts that she made glad that day no one will ever know save He who knoweth all things. Her zeal and energy in this good work was so far in excess of her physical abilities, that she labored beyond her endurance, and her health finally became so much impaired that she was induced to leave the work and make a tour in Europe, where at this writing she still is, though an invalid. Her good deeds even followed her in her travels in a foreign land, and no sooner had the German States become involved in war, than she was called upon and consulted as to the establishment of hospital regulations and appointments there— and even urged to take charge of and establish and direct the whole system.

Mrs. Mary A. Livermore, of the Northwestern Sanitary Commission, who has known as much of Miss Salford's work, as any one connected with the service, writes thus of her:

"Miss Salford commenced her labors immediately, when Cairo was occupied. I think she was the very first woman who went into the camps and hospitals, in the country; I know she was in the West. There was no system, no organization, nothing to do with. She systematized everything in Cairo, furnished necessaries with her own means, or rather with her brother's, who is wealthy; went daily to the work, and though surgeons and authorities everywhere were opposed to her efforts, she disarmed all opposition by her sweetness and grace and beauty. She did just what she pleased. At Pittsburg Landing, where she was found in advance of other women, she was hailed by dying soldiers, who did not know her name, but had seen her at Cairo, as the 'Cairo Angel.' She came up with boat-load after boat-load of sick and wounded soldiers who were taken to hospitals at Cairo, Paducah, St. Louis, etc., cooking all the while for them, dressing wounds, singing to them, and praying with them. She did not undress on the way up from Pittsburg Landing, but worked incessantly.

"She was very frail, as petite as a girl of twelve summers, and utterly unaccustomed to hardships. Sleeping in hospital tents, working on pestilential boats, giving up everything to this life, carrying the sorrows of the country, and the burdens of the soldier on her heart like personal griefs, with none of the aids in the work that came afterwards, she broke down at the end of the first eighteen months, and will never again be well. Her brother sent her immediately to Paris, where she underwent the severest treatment for the cure of the injury to the spine, occasioned by hei life in the army and hospitals. The physicians subsequently prescribed travel, and she has been since that time in Europe. She is highly educated, speaks French and German as well as English, and some Italian. She is the most indomitable little creature living, heroic, uncomplaining, self-forgetful, and will yet 'die in harness.' When the war broke out in Italy, she was in Florence, and at Madame Mario's invitation, immediately went to work to assist the Italian ladies in preparing for the sick and wounded of their soldiers. In Norway, she was devising ways and means to assist poor girls to emigrate to America, where they had relatives—and so everywhere. She must be counted among those who have given up health, and ultimately life for the country."

We add also the following extracts from a letter from Cairo, published in one of the Chicago papers, early in the war.

AN ANGEL AT CAIRO

"I cannot close this letter from Cairo without a passing word of one whose name is mentioned by thousands of our soldiers with gratitude and blessing. Miss Mary Safford is a resident of this town, whose life since the beginning of the war, has been devoted to the amelioration of the soldier's lot, and his comfort in the hospitals. She is a young lady, petite in figure, unpretending, but highly cultivated, by no means officious, and so wholly unconscious of her excellencies, and the great work she is achieving, that I fear this public allusion to her may pain her modest nature. Her sweet, young face, full of benevolence, pleasant voice, and winning manner instate her in every one's heart directly; and the more one sees her, the more he admires her great soul and her noble nature. Not a day elapses but she is found in the hospitals, unless indeed she is absent on an errand of mercy up the Tennessee, or to the hospitals in Kentucky.

"Every sick and wounded soldier in Cairo knows and loves her; and as she enters the ward, every pale face brightens at her approach. As she passes along, she inquires of each one how he has passed the night, if he is well supplied with reading matter, and if there is anything she can do for him. All tell her their story frankly—the man old enough to be her father, and the boy of fifteen, who should be out of the army, and home with his mother. One thinks he would like a baked apple if the doctor will allow it—another a rice pudding, such as she can make—a third a tumbler of buttermilk—a fourth wishes nothing, is discouraged, thinks he shall die, and breaks down utterly, in tears, and him she soothes and encourages, till he resolves for her sake, to keep up a good heart, and hold on to life a little longer—a fifth wants her to write to his wife—a sixth is afraid to die, and with him, and for him, her devout spirit wrestles, till light shines through the dark valley—a seventh desires her to sit by him and read, and so on. Every request is attended to, be it ever so trivial, and when she goes again, if the doctor has sanctioned the gratification of the sick man's wish, the buttermilk, baked apple, rice pudding, etc., are carried along. Doctors, nurses, medical directors, and army officers, are all her true friends; and so judicious and trustworthy is she, that the Chicago Sanitary Commission have given her carte blanche to draw on their stores at Cairo for anything she may need in her errands of mercy. She is performing a noble work, and that too in the quietest and most unconscious manner. Said a sick soldier from the back woods, in the splendid hospital at Mound City, who was transferred thither from one of the miserable regimental hospitals at Cairo, 'I'm taken care of here a heap better than I was at Cairo; but I'd rather be there than here, for the sake of seeing that little gal that used to come in every day to see us. I tell you what, she's an angel, if there is any.' To this latter assertion we say amen! most heartily."

Miss Safford is the sister of A. B. Safford, Esq., a well-known and highly respected banker at Cairo, Illinois, and of Hon. A. P. K. Safford of Nevada.

MRS. LYDIA G. PARRISH

AT the outbreak of hostilities Mrs. Parrish was residing at Media, Pennsylvania, near Philadelphia. Her husband, Dr. Joseph Parrish, had charge of an institution established there for idiots, or those of feeble mental capacity, and it cannot be doubted that Mrs. Parrish, with her kindly and benevolent instincts, and desire for usefulness, found there an ample sphere for her efforts, and a welcome occupation.

But as in the case of thousands of others, all over the country, Mrs. Parrish found the current of her life and its occupations marvellously changed, by the war. There was a new call for the efforts of woman, such an one as in our country, or in the world, had never been made. English women had set the example of sacrifice and work for their countrymen in arms, but their efforts were on a limited scale, and bore but a very small proportion to the great uprising of loyal women in our country, and their varied, grand persistent labors during the late civil war in America. Not a class, or grade, or rank, of our countrywomen, but was represented in this work. The humble dweller in the fishing cabins on the bleak and desolate coast, the woman of the prairie, and of the cities, the wife and daughter of the mechanic, and the farmer, of the merchant, and the professional man, the lady from the mansion of wealth, proud perhaps of her old name, of her culture and refinement—all met and labored together, bound by one common bond of patriotism and of sympathy.

Mrs. Parrish was one of the first to lay her talents and her efforts upon the altar of her country. In 1861, and almost as soon as the need of woman's self-sacrificing labors became apparent, she volunteered her services in behalf of the sick and wounded soldiers of the Union.

She visited Washington while the army was yet at the capital and in its vicinity. Her husband, Dr. Parrish, had become connected with the newly organized Sanitary Commission, and in company with him and other gentlemen similarly connected, she examined the different forts, barracks, camps, and hospitals then occupied by our troops, for the purpose of ascertaining their condition, and selecting a suitable sphere for the work in which she intended to engage.

On the first day of 1862, she commenced her hospital labors, selecting for that purpose the Georgetown Seminary Hospital. She wrote letters for the patients, read to them, and gave to them all the aid and comfort in her power; and she was thus enabled to learn their real wants, and to seek the means of supplying them. Their needs were many, and awakened all her sympathies and incited her to ever-renewed effort. After one day's trial of these new scenes, she wrote thus in her journal, January 2, 1862: "My heart is so oppressed with the sight of suffering I see around me that I am almost unfitted for usefulness; such sights are new to me. I feel the need of some resource, where I may apply for delicacies and comforts, which are positively necessary. The Sanitary Commission is rapidly becoming the sinew of strength for the sick and wounded, and I will go to their store-rooms." Application was made to the Commission, and readily and promptly responded to. She was authorized to draw from their stores, and was promised aid and protection from the organization.

Both camps and hospitals were rapidly filling up; the weather was inclement and the roads bad, but at the solicitation of other earnest workers, she made occasional visits to camps in the country, and distributed clothing, books and comforts of various kinds. The "Berdan Sharp-shooters" were encamped a few miles from the city, and needed immediate assistance. She was requested by the Secretary of the Commission to "visit the camps, make observations, inquire into their needs, and report to the Commission." She reached the camp through almost impassable roads, and was received by the officers with respect and consideration, upon announcing the object of her visit. She made calls upon the men in hospitals and quarters, returned to Washington, reported "two hundred sick, tents and streets needing police, small pox breaking out, men discouraged, and officers unable to procure the necessary aid, that she had distributed a few jellies to the sick, checker boards to a few of the tents, and made a requisition for supplies to meet the pressing want." This little effort was the means of affording speedy relief to many suffering men. She did not however feel at liberty to abandon her hospital service, as we learn from a note in her diary, that "this outside work does not seem to be my mission. I have become thoroughly interested in my daily rounds at the city hospitals, particularly at Georgetown Seminary, where my heart and energies are fully enlisted." She passed several weeks in this service, going from bed to bed with her little stores, which she dispensed under instructions from the surgeon, without being known by name to the many recipients of her attention and care.

The stores of the Commission were not then as ample as they afterward became, when its noble aims had become more fully understood, and its grand mission of benevolence more widely known, and the sick and wounded were in need of many things not obtainable from either this source or the Government supplies. Mrs. Parrish determined, therefore, to return to her northern home and endeavor to interest the people of her neighborhood in the cause she had so much at heart. She found the people ready to respond liberally to her appeals, and soon returned to Washington well satisfied with the success of her efforts.

She felt now that her time, and if need be her life, must be consecrated to this work, and as her diary expresses it, she "could not remain at home," and that if she could be of service in her new sphere of labor she "must return."

After her brief absence, she re-entered the Georgetown Seminary Hospital. Death had removed some of her former patients, others had returned to duty, but others whom she left there welcomed her with enthusiasm as the "orange lady," a title she had unconsciously earned from the fact that she had been in the habit of distributing oranges freely to such of the patients as were allowed to have them.

The experience of life often shows us the importance of little acts which so frequently have an entirely disproportionate result. Mrs. Parrish found this true in her hospital ministrations. Little gifts and attentions often opened the way to the closed hearts of those to whom she ministered, and enabled her to reach the innermost concealed thought-life of her patients.

A soldier sat in his chair, wrapped in his blanket, forlorn, haggard from disease, sullen, selfish in expression, and shrinking from her notice as she passed him. To her morning salutation, he would return only a cold recognition. He seemed to be bristling with defenses against encroachment. And thus it remained till one day a small gift penetrated to the very citadel of his fortress.

"Shall I read to you?" she commenced, kindly, to which he replied,' surlily, "Don't want reading." "Shall I write to any of your friends?" she continued. "I hav'n't any friends," he said in the sourest tone. Repulsed, but not baffled, she presently, and in the same kind manner, took an orange from her basket, and gently asked him if he would accept it. There was a perceptible brightening of his face, but he only answered, in the same surly tone, as he heid forth his hand, "Don't care if I do."

And yet, in a little time, his sullen spirit yielded—he spread all his troubles before the friend he had so long repulsed, and opening his heart, showed that what had seemed so selfish and moody in liim, arose from a deep sense of loneliness and discouragement, which disappeared the moment the orange had unlocked his heart, and admitted her to his confidence and affection.

About six weeks she spent thus in alternate visits to the various hospitals in the vicinity of Washington, though her labors were principally confined to the Georgetown Hospital, where they commenced, and where her last visit was made.

As her home duties called her at that time, she returned thither, briefly. Soon after she reached home, she received a letter from one of her former patients to whom she had given her address, requesting her to call at the Broad and Cherry Street Hospital, in Philadelphia. She did so, and on entering the building found herself surrounded by familiar faces. Her old Washington friends had just arrived, and welcomed her with cordial greetings. The stronger ones approached her with outstretched hands—some, too feeble to rise, covered their faces and wept with joy—she was the only person known to them in all the great lonely city. The surgeon-in-charge, observing this scene, urged her to visit the hospital often, where her presence was sure to do the men great good.

During her stay at home she assisted in organizing a Ladies Aid Society at Chester. She was appointed Directress for the township where she resided, and as the hospital was about to be located near Chester, she, with others, directed her attention to preparing and furnishing it. Sewing-circles were formed, and as a result of the efforts made, by the time the soldiers arrived, a plentiful supply of nice clothing, delicacies, etc., etc., was ready for them.

Mrs. Parrish united with other women of the vicinity in organizing a corps of volunteer nurses, who continued to perform their duties with regularity and faithfulness until some time after, a new order dispensed with their services.

Her labors during the summer and autumn of 1862 visibly affected her health, and were the cause of a severe illness which continued for several weeks.

Her health being at length restored, she went to "Washington, spent a few days in visiting the hospitals there, and then, with a pass sent her by Major-General Sumner, from Falmouth, she joined Mrs.

Dr. Harris and started, January 17th, 1863, for Falmouth via Acquia Creek.

The army was in motion and much confusion existed, but they found comfortable quarters at the Lacy House, where they were under the protection of the General and his staff.

Here Mrs. Parrish found much to do, there being a great deal of sickness among the troops. The weather was stormy, and the movement of the army was impeded; and though she underwent much privation for want of suitable food, and on account of the inclement season she continued faithful at her post and accomplished much good.

In December of the same year she accompanied her husband, with the Medical Director of the Department of Virginia and North Carolina, on a tour of inspection to the hospitals of Yorktown, Fortress Monroe, Norfolk, Portsmouth, and Newbern, North Carolina. While at Old Point she learned that there was about to be an exchange of prisoners, and desiring to render some services in this direction obtained permission from General Butler to proceed, in company with a friend, Miss L. C. on the flag-of-truce boat to City Point, witness the exchange, and render such aid as was possible to our men on their return passage.

There were five hundred Confederate prisoners on board, who, as her journal records, "sang our National airs, and seemed to be a jolly and happy healthy company."

Our men were in a very different condition—"sick and weary," and needing the Sanitary Commission supplies, which had been brought for them, yet shouting with feeble voices their gladness at being once more under the old flag, and in freedom. Mrs. Parrish fed and comforted these poor men as best she could, till the steamer anchored off Old Point again.

It had been intended to continue the exchange much further, but a dispute arising concerning the treatment of negro prisoners, the operations of the cartel were arrested, and the exchange suspended. She found, therefore, no further need of her services in this direction, and so returned home.

For many months to come, as one of the managers of the women's branch of the United States Sanitary Commission, she found ample employment in preparation for the great Philadelphia Fair, in which arduous service she continued until its close, in July, 1864. The exhausting labors of these mouths, and the heat of the weather during the continuance of the Fair, made it necessary for her to have a respite for the remainder of the summer.

It was in the early winter of this year that she accompanied her husband on a tour of inspection to the hospitals of Annapolis, and became so interested in the condition of the returned prisoners, who needed so much done for them in the way of personal care, that she gladly consented, at the solicitation of the medical officers and agent of the Commission, to serve there for a season.

Of the usefulness of her work among the prisoners, testimony is abundant. What she saw, and what she did, is most touchingly set forth in the following letters from her pen, extracted from the Bulletin of the United States Sanitary Commission:

ANNAPOLIS, December 1, 1864.

"The steamer Constitution arrived this morning with seven hundred and six men, one hundred and twenty-five of whom were sent immediately to hospitals, being too ill to enjoy more than the sight of their promised land.' Many indeed, were in a dying condition. Some had died a short time before the arrival of the boat. Those who were able, proceeded to the high ground above the landing, and after being divided into battalions, each was conducted in turn to the Government store-house, under charge of Captain Davis, who furnished each man with a new suit of clothes recorded his name, regiment and company.

They then passed out to another building near by, where warm water, soap, towels, brushes and combs awaited them.

"After their ablutions they returned to the open space in front of the building, to look around and enjoy the realities of their new life. Here they were furnished with paper, envelopes, sharpened pencils, hymn-books and tracts from the Sanitary Commission, and sat down to communicate the glad news of their freedom to friends at home. In about two hours most of the men who were able, had sealed their letters and deposited them in a large mail bag which was furnished, and they were soon sent on their way to hundreds of anxious kindred an! friends.

"Captain Davis very kindly invited me to accompany him to another building, to witness the administration of the food. Several cauldrons containing nice coffee, piles of new white bread, and stands covered with meat, met the eye. Three dealers were in attendance. The first gave to each soldier a loaf of bread, the second a slice of boiled meat, the third, dipping the new tin-cup from the hand of each, into the coffee cauldron, dealt out hot coffee; and how it was all received I am unable to describe. The feeble ones reached out their emaciated hands to receive gladly, that which they were scarcely able to carry, and with brightening faces and grateful expressions went on their way. The stouter ones of the party, however, must have their jokes, and such expressions as the following passed freely among them: 'No stockade about this bread 'This is no confederate dodge etc. One fellow, whose skin was nearly black from exposure, said, 'That's more bread than I've seen for two months.' Another, 'That settles a man's plate.' A bright-eyed boy of eighteen, whose young spirit had not been completely crushed out in rebeldom, could not refrain from a hurrah, and cried out, Hurrah for Uncle Sam, hurrah! No Confederacy about this bread.' One poor feeble fellow, almost too faint to hold his loaded plate, muttered out, 'Why, this looks as if we were going to live, there's no grains of corn for a man to swallow whole in this loaf.' Thus the words of cheer and hope came from almost every tongue, as they received their rations and walked away, each with his 'thank you, thank you;' and sat down upon the ground, which forcibly reminded me of the Scripture account where the multitude sat down in companies, 'and did eat and were filled.'

"Ambulances came afterwards to take those who were unable to walk to Camp Parole, which is two miles distant. One poor man, who was making his way behind all the rest to reach the ambulance, thought it would leave him, and with a most anxious and pitiful expression, cried out, 'Oh, wait for me!' I think I shall never forget his look of distress. When he reached the wagon he was too feeble to step in, but Captain Davis, and Rev. J. A. Whitaker, Sanitary Commission agent, assisted him till he was placed by the side of his companions, who were not in much better condition than himself. When he was seated, lie was so thankful that he wept like a child, and those who stood by to aid him could do no less. Soldiers—brave soldiers, officers and all, were moved to tears. That must he a sad discipline which not only wastes the manly form till the sign of humanity is nearly obuterated, but breaks the manly spirit till it is as tender as a child's."

"December 6, 1864.

"The St. John's College Hospital, is under the management of Dr. Palmer, surgeon-in-charge, and his executive officer, Dr. Tremaine. These gentlemen are worthy of praise for the systematic arrangement of its cleanly apartments, and for the very kind attention they bestow on their seven hundred patients. I visited the hospital a day or two ago, and, from what I saw there, can assure the relatives at home, that the sufferers are well provided for. If they could only be seen, how comfortable they look in their neat white-spread beds, much pain would be spared them. One of the surgeons informed me that all the appliances are bestowed either by the Government or the Sanitary Commission.

"As I passed through the different wards, I noticed that each one was well supplied with rocking-chairs, and alluding to the great comfort they must be to the invalids, the surgeon replied: 'Yes, this is one of the rich gifts made to us by the Sanitary Commission.' An invalid took up the words and remarked: 'I think it's likely that all about me is from the Sanitary, for I see my flannel shirt, this wrapper, and pretty much all I've got on, has the stamp of the United States Sanitary Commission on it.'

"The diet kitchen is under the care of Miss Rich, who, with her assistants, was busy preparing delicacies of various kinds, for two hundred patients who were not able to go to the convalescent's table. The whole atmosphere was filled with the odor of savory viands. On the stove I counted mutton-chops, beef-steaks, oysters, chicken, milk, tea, and other very palatable articles cooking. A man stood by a table, buttering nicely toasted bread; before him were eight to ten rows of the staff of life, rising up like pillars of strength to support the inner man. The chief cook in this department, informed me that he buttered twelve hundred slices of bread, or toast daily, for the diet patients, and prepared eighty-six different dishes at each meal. While in conversation with this good-natured person, the butcher brought in a supply of meat, amounting, he informed me, to one hundred pounds per day for the so-called diet kitchen, though this did not sound much like it. Before we left this attractively clean place the oysterman was met emptying his cansUpon inquiring how many oysters he had, he replied, 'Six gallons is my every day deposit hereand oh! they were so inexpressibly fine-looking, I could not resist robbing some poor fellow of one large bivalve to ascertain their quality. Next we were shown the store-room, where there was a good supply of Sanitary stores, pads, pillows, shirts, drawers, arm-slings, stock of crutches, fans, and other comforts, which the doctor said, had been deposited by the United States Sanitary Commission Agent. These were useful articles that were not furnished by the Government.

"The executive officer having given us permission to find our way among the patients, we passed several hours most profitably and interestingly, conversing with those who had none to cheer them for many months, and writing letters for those who were too feeble to use the pen. When the day closed our labors we felt like the disciple of old, who said, 'Master, it is good to be here,' and wished that we might set up our tabernacle and glorify the Lord by doing good to the sick, the lame, and those who had been in prison."

"December 8, 1864.

"No human tongue or pen can ever describe the horrible suffering we have witnessed this day.

"I was early at the landing, eight and a-half o'clock in the morning, before the boat threw out her ropes for security. The first one brought two hundred bad cases, which the Naval surgeon told me should properly go to the hospital near by, were it not that others were coming, every one of whom was in the most wretched condition imaginable. They were, therefore, sent in ambulances to

Camp Parole hospital, distant two miles, after being washed and fed at the barracks.

"In a short time another boat-load drew near, and oh! such a scene of suffering humanity I desire never to behold again. The whole deck was a bed of straw for our exhausted, starved, emaciated, dying fellow-creatures. Of the five hundred and fifty that left Savannah, the surgeon informed me not over two hundred would survive; fifty had died on the passage; three died while the boat was coming to the land. I saw five men dying as they were carried on stretchers from the boat to the Naval Hospital. The stretcher-bearers were ordered by Surgeon D. Vanderkieft to pause a moment that the names of the dying men might be obtained. To the credit of the officers and their assistants it should be known that everything was done in the most systematic and careful manner. Each stretcher had four attendants, who stood in line and came up promptly, one after the other, to receive the sufferers as they were carried off the boat. There was no confusion, no noise; all acted with perfect military order. Ah! it was a solemn funeral service to many a brave soldier, that was thus being performed by kind hearts and hands.

"Some had become insane; their wild gaze, and clenched teeth convinced the observer that reason had fled; others were idiotic; a few lying in spasms; perhaps the realization of the hope long cherished, yet oft deferred, or the welcome sound of the music, sent forth by the military band, was more than their exhausted nature could bear. When blankets were thrown over them, no one would have supposed that a human form lay beneath, save for the small prominences which the bony head and feet indicated. Oh I God of justice, what retribution awaits the perpetrators of such slow and awful murder.

"The hair of some was matted together, like beasts of the stall which lie down in their own filth. Vermin are over them in abundance. Nearly every man was darkened by scurvy, or black with rough scales, and with scorbutic sores. One in particular was reduced to the merest skeleton; his face, neck, and feet covered with thick, green mould. A number who had Government clothes given them on the boat were too feeble to put them on, and were carried ashore partially dressed, hugging their clothing with a death-grasp that they could not be persuaded to yield. It was not unfrequent to hear a man feebly call, as he was laid on a stretcher, "Don't take my clothes;" "Oh, save my new shoes" "Don't let my socks go back to Andersonville." In their wild death-struggle, with bony arms and hands extended, they would hold up their new socks, that could not be put on because of their swollen limbs, saying 'Save'em till I get home.' In a little while, however, the souls of many were released from their worn-out frames, and borne to that higher home where all things are registered for a great day of account.

"Let our friends at home have open purses and willing hands to keep up the supplies for the great demand that must necessarily be made upon them. Much more must yet be done.

"Thousands now languish in Southern prisons, that may yet be brought thus far toward home. Let every Aid Society be more diligent, that the stores of the Sanitary Commission may not fail in this great work."

Her services at Annapolis were cut short, and prematurely discontinued; for returning to her home for a short stay, to make preparations for a longer sojourn at Annapolis, she was again attacked by illness, which rendered it impossible for her to go thither again.

On her recovery, knowing that an immense amount of ignorance existed among officers and men concerning the operations of the Sanitary Commission, she compiled a somewhat elaborate, yet carefully condensed statement of its plans and workings, together with a great amount of useful information in relation to the facilities embraced in its system of special relief, giving a list of all Homes and Lodges, and telling how to secure back pay for soldiers, on furlough or discharged, bounties, pensions, etc., etc. Bound up with this, is a choice collection of hymns, adapted to the soldier's use, the whole forming a neat little volume of convenient size for the pocket.

The manuscript was submitted to the committee, accepted, and one hundred thousand copies ordered to be printed for gratuitous distribution in all the hospitals and camps. The "Soldiers' Friend," as it was called, was soon distributed in the different departments and posts of the army, and was even found in the Southern hospitals and prisons, while it was the pocket companion of men in the trenches, as well as of those in quarters and hospital. Many thousands were instructed by this little directory, where to find the lodges, homes and pension offices of the Commission, and were guarded against imposture and loss. So urgent was the demand for it, and so useful was it, that the committee ordered a second edition.

Perhaps no work published by the Sanitary Commission has been of more real and practical use than this little volume, or has had so large a circulation. It was the last public work performed for the Commission by Mrs. Parrish. At the close of the war her labors did not end; but transferring her efforts to the amelioration of the condition of the freedmen, she still found herself actively engaged in a work growing directly out of the war.

MRS. ANNIE WITTENMEYER

(See Wittenmyer's own account in the field in Under the Guns.)

MRS. ANNIE WITTENMEYER [a friend of Julia Dent Grant], who, during the early part of the war was widely known as the State Sanitary Agent of Iowa, and afterward as the originator of the Diet Kitchens, which being attached to hospitals proved of the greatest benefit as an adjunct of the medical treatment, was at the outbreak of the rebellion, residing in quiet seclusion at Keokuk. With the menace of armed treason to the safety of her country's institutions, she felt all her patriotic instincts and sentiments arousing to activity. She laid aside her favorite intellectual pursuits, and prepared herself to do what a woman might in the emergency which called into existence a great army, and taxed the Government far beyond its immediate ability in the matter of Hospital Supplies and the proper provision for, and care of the sick and wounded.

Early in 1861 rumors of the sufferings of the volunteer soldiery, called so suddenly to the field, and from healthy northern climates to encounter the unwholesome and miasmatic exhalations of more southern regions, as well as the pain of badly-dressed wounds, began to thrill and grieve the hearts which had willingly though sadly sent them forth in their country's defense. Mrs. Wittenmeyer saw at once that a field of usefulness opened before her. Her first movement was to write letters to every town in her State urging patriotic women in every locality to organize themselves into Aid Societies, and commence systematically the work of supplying the imperative needs of the suffering 374 soldiers. These appeals, and the intense sympathy and patriotism that inspired the hearts of the women of the North, proved quite sufficient. In Iowa the earlier Reports were addressed to her, and societies throughout the State forwarded their goods to the Keokuk Aid Society with which she was connected. As the agent of this society Mrs. Wittenmeyer went to the field and distributed these supplies.

Thus her work had its inception—and being still the chosen agent of distribution, she gave herself no rest. In fact, from the summer of 1861 until the close of the war, she was continually and actively employed in some department of labor for the soldiers, and did not allow herself so much as one week for rest.

From June, 1861, to April 1st, 1862, she had received and distributed goods to the value of $6,000. From that to July 1st, $12,564, and from that until September 25th, 1862, $2,000, making a total of $20,564 received before her appointment of that date by the Legislature as State Agent. From that time until her resignation of the office, January 13th, 1864, she received $115,876,93. Thus, in about two years and a half, she received and distributed more than $136,000 worth of goods and sanitary stores contributed for the benefit of suffering soldiers.

But while laboring so constantly in the army, Mrs. Wittenmeyer did not overlook the needs of the destitute at home. In October, 1863, a number of benevolent individuals, of whom she was one, called a Convention of Aid Societies, which had for its foremost object to take some steps toward providing for the wants of the orphans of soldiers. That Convention led to the establishment of the Iowa Soldiers Orphans' Home, an Institution of which the State is now justly proud, and which is bestowing upon hundreds of children bountiful care and protection.

While laboring in the hospitals at Chattanooga in the winter of 1863-4, Mrs. Wittenmeyer matured her long-cherished plan for supplying food for the lowest class of hospital patients, and this led to the establishment of Diet Kitchens. Believing her idea could be better carried out by the Christian Commission, than under any other auspices,' she soon after resigned her position as State agent, and became connected with that organization.

From a little work entitled "Christ in the Army," composed of sketches by different individuals, and published by the Christian Commission, and from the Fourth Report of the Maryland Branch of the Christian Commission, we make the following extracts, relative to Mrs. Wittenmeyer's labors in this sphere of effort:

"The sick and wounded suffer greatly from the imperfect cooking of the soldier nurses. To remedy this evil, a number of ladies have offered themselves as delegates of the Christian Commission, and arrangements have been made with the medical authorities to establish Diet Kitchens, where suitable food may be prepared by ladies' hands for our sick soldiers,—the Government furnishing the staple articles, and the Christian Commission providing the ladies and the delicacies and cordials. One of these at Knoxville is thus described by a correspondent of The Lutheran:—

"There have been several large hospitals in this city, but recently they have been all consolidated into one. In connection with this hospital is a 'Special Diet Kitchen.' Many of our readers will doubtless wonder what these 'Special Diet Kitchens' are. They have been originated by Mrs. Annie Wittenmeyer, of Keokuk, formerly State Sanitary Agent of Iowa. In her arduous labors in the Army of the Cumberland, she met with a large number of patients who suffered for want of suitably prepared, delicate and nutritious food. None of the benevolent institutions in connection with the army have been able to reach this class of persons. She says, in her report to the General Assembly of the State: 'This matter has given me serious and anxious thought for the past year, but I have recently submitted to the Christian Commission a plan by which I believe this class of patients may be reached and relieved. The plan proposed, is the establishment of "Special Diet Kitchens," in connection with that Commission, to be superintended by earnest, prudent Christian women, who will secure the distribution of proper food to this class of patients—taking such delicate articles of food as our good people supply to the very bed-sides of the poor languishing soldiers, and administering, with words of encouragement and sympathy, to their pressing wants; such persons to co-operate with the surgeons in all their efforts for the sick This plan of operations has been sanctioned and adopted by the United States Christian Commission. There is one in successful operation at Nashville, under the direction, I believe, of a daughter of the Honorable J. K. Moorehead, of Pittsburg. The one here is under the direction of Mrs. R. E. Conrad, of Keokuk, Iowa, and her two sisters. They are doing a great and good work now in Knoxville. From three to five hundred patients are thus daily supplied with delicate food, who would otherwise have scarcely anything to eat. The success of their labors has demonstrated beyond a doubt the practicability of the plan of Mrs. Wittenmeyer. The good resulting from their arduous labor proves that much can be done by these special efforts to rescue those who are laid upon languishing beds of sickness and pain, and have passed almost beyond the reach of ordinary means. The great need we have in connection with these 'Diet Kitchens is the want of canned fruits, jellies, preserves, etc. If our good people, who have already done so much, will provide these necessary means, they will be distributed to the most needy, and in such a way as to accomplish the most good." The War Department is so well satisfied with the value of these Diet Kitchens, in saving the lives of thousands of invalids, that it has issued the following special Order:—

SPECIAL ORDERS, No. 362.

WAR DEPARTMENT, ADJUTANT-GENERAL'S OFFICE, WASHINGTON, D. C., October 24, 1864. [EXTRACT.]

56. Permission to visit the United States General Hospitals, within the lines of the several Military Departments of the United States, for 43 the purpose of superintending the preparation of food in the Special Diet Kitchens of the same, is hereby granted Mrs. Annie Wittenmeyer, Special Agent United States Christian Commission, and such ladies as she may deem proper to employ, by request of the

United States surgeons. The Quartermaster's Department will furnish the necessary transportation.

BY ORDER OF THE SECRETARY OP WAR:

E. D. TOWNSEND, Assistant Adjutant-General.

OFFICIAL:

DIET KITCHENS.

Mrs. Annie Wittenmeyer suggested and introduced the use of the Diet Kitchen into the hospitals. The Kitchen was used extensively among the Branch Offices of the West. The design of the Kitchen was, to have prepared for the men who were under treatment, such articles of food and delicacies as are grateful to the sick, and at the same time may be allowed with safety. The ladies who were engaged in this department performed their labors under the direction of the surgeons, who appointed their stations and approved their preparations. The process was very much like that of the house in which the surgeon directs, and the family provides, the nourishing food that is needed for the patient.

Mrs. Wittenmeyer had the Diet Kitchens under her supervision. She was the agent of the Commission for the purpose. She operated under regulations which were approved by the Commission and by the War Department. These regulations were printed and circulated among the managers of the Kitchens. So effective were the orders under which the department was conducted, that not the least difficulty or misunderstanding occurred, notwithstanding the responsible relations of the co-operators, part being officials of the army and part under the direction of a voluntary service. Each of the managers was furnished with a copy of the rules, which, with the endorsement of the branch office with which the service was connected, constituted the commission of the manager.

The Special Diet Kitchens, were first adopted in the Department of the Cumberland, and in that of the Mississippi, and with results so unexpectedly beneficial, that Mrs. Wittenmeyer was earnestly solicited to extend the work to the Army of the Potomac. This she did in the winter of 1864, and it continued until the close of the war with great success.

Much of this success was undoubtedly owing to the class of ladies engaged in the work. Many of them were from the highest circles of society, educated, refined and accomplished, and each was required to maintain the life and character of an earnest Christian. They thus commanded the respect of officers and men, and proved a powerful instrument of good. As we have seen, the Christian Commission has borne ample testimony to the value of the efforts of Mrs. Wittenmeyer, and her associates in this department of hospital service.

Mrs. Wittenmeyer continued actively engaged in the service of the Christian Commission, in the organizing of Diet Kitchens, and similar labors, until the close of the war, and the disbanding of that organization, when she returned to her home in Keokuk, to resume the quiet life she had abandoned, and to gain needed repose, after her four years' effort in behalf of our suffering defenders.

MISS MELCENIA ELLIOTT

AMONG the heroic and devoted women who have labored for the soldiers of the Union in the late war, and endured all the dangers and privations of hospital life, is Miss Melcenia Elliott, of Iowa. Born in Indiana, and reared in the Northern part of Iowa, she grew to womanhood amid the scenes and associations of country life, with an artless, impulsive and generous nature, superior physical health, and a heart warm with the love of country and humanity. Her father is a prosperous farmer, and gave three of his sons to the struggle for the Union, who served honorably to the end of their enlistment, and one of them re-enlisted as a veteran, performing oftentimes the perilous duties of a spy, that he might obtain valuable information to guide the movements of our forces. The daughter, at the breaking out of the war, was pursuing her studies at Washington College, in Iowa, an institution open to both sexes, and under the patronage of the United Presbyterian Church. But the sound of fife and drum, the organization of regiments composed of her friends and neighbors, and the enlistment of her brothers in the grand army of the Union fired her ardent soul with patriotism, and an intense desire to help on the cause in which the soldiers had taken up the implements of warfare.

For many months her thoughts were far more with the soldiers in the field than on the course of study in the college, and as soon as there began to be a demand for female nurses in the hospitals, she was prompt to offer her services and was accepted.

The summer and autumn of 1862, found her in the hospitals in Tennessee, ready on all occasions for the most difficult posts of service, ministering at the bed-side of the sick and desponding, cheering them with her warm words of encouragement and sympathy, and her pleasant smile and ready mirthfulness, the very best antidote to the depression of spirits and home-sickness of the worn and tired soldier. In all hospital work, in the offices of nursing and watching, and giving of medicines, in the preparation of special diet, in the care and attention necessary to have the hospital beds clean and comfortable, and the wards in proper order, she was untiring and never gave way to weariness or failed in strength. It was pleasant to see with what ease and satisfaction she could lift up a sick soldier's head, smooth and arrange his pillow, lift him into an easier position, dress his wounds, and make him feel that somebody cared for him.

During the winter of 1862-3, she was a nurse in one of the hospitals at Memphis, and rendered most useful and excellent service. An example of her heroism and fortitude occurred here, that is worthy of being mentioned. In one of the hospitals there was a sick soldier who came from her father's neighborhood in Iowa, whom she had known, and for whose family she felt a friendly interest. She often visited him in the sick ward where he was, and did what she could to alleviate his sufferings, and comfort him in his illness. But gradually he became worse, and at a time when he needed her sympathy and kind attention more than ever, the Surgeon in charge of the hospital, issued an order that excluded all visitors from the wards, during those portions of the day when she could leave the hospital where she was on duty, to make these visits to her sick neighbor and friend. The front entrance of the hospital being guarded, she could not gain admission; but she had too much resolution, energy and courage, and too much kindness of heart, to be thwarted in her good intent ions by red tape. Finding that by scaling a high fence in the rear of the hospital, she could enter without being obstructed by guards, and being aided in her purpose by the nurses on duty in the ward, she made her visits in the evening to the sick man's bed-side till he died. As it was his dying wish that his remains might be carried home to his family, none of whom were present, she herself undertook the difficult and responsible task. Getting leave of absence from her own duties, without the requisite funds for the purpose, she was able, by her frank and open address, her self-reliance, intelligence and courage to accomplish the task, and made the journey alone, with the body in charge; all the way from Memphis to Washington, Iowa, overcoming all difficulties of procuring transportation, and reaching her destination successfully. By this act of heroism, she won the gratitude of many hearts, and gave comfort and satisfaction to the friends and relatives of the departed soldier returning as far as St. Louis, she was transferred to the large military hospital at Benton Barracks and did not return to Memphis. Here for many months, during the spring, summer and autumn of 1863, she served most faithfully, and was considered one of the most efficient and capable nurses in the hospital. At this place she was associated with a band of noble young women, under the supervision of that excellent lady, Miss Emily Parsons, of Cambridge, Massachusetts, who came out from her pleasant New England 'home to be at the head of the nursing department of this hospital, (then in charge of Surgeon Ira Russell, United States Volunteers), and to do her part towards taking care of the sick and wounded men who had perilled their lives for their country. A warm friendship grew up between these noble women, and Miss Parsons never ceased to regard with deep interest, the tall, heroic, determined girl, who never allowed any obstacle to stand between her and any useful service she could render to the defenders of her country.

Another incident of her fearless and undaunted bravery will illustrate her character, and especially the self-sacrificing spirit by which she was animated. During the summer of 1863, it became necessary to establish a ward for cases of erysipelas, a disease generating an unhealthy atmosphere and propagating itself by that means. The surgeon in charge, instead of assigning a female nurse of his own selection to this ward, called for a volunteer, among the women nurses of the hospital. There was naturally some hesitancy about taking so trying and dangerous a position, and, seeing this reluctance on the part of others, Miss Elliott promptly offered herself for the place. For several months she performed her duties in the erysipelas ward with the same constancy and regard for the welfare of the patients that had characterized her in other positions. It was here the writer of this sketch first became acquainted with her, and noticed the cheerful and cordial manner in which she waited upon the sufferers under her care, going from one to another to perform some office of kindness, always with words of genuine sympathy, pleasantry and good will.

Late in the fall of 1863, Miss Elliott yielded to the wishes of the Western Sanitary Commission, and became matron of the Refugee Home of St. Louis—a charitable institution made necessary by the events of the war, and designed to give shelter and assistance to poor families of refugees, mostly -widows and children, who were constantly arriving from the exposed and desolated portions of Missouri, Arkansas, Tennessee, Louisiana, Mississippi and Texas, sent North often by military authority as deck passengers on Government boats to get them away from the military posts in our possession further South. For one year Miss Elliott managed the internal affairs of this institution with great efficiency and good judgment, under circumstances that were very trying to her patience and fortitude. Many of the refugees were of the class called "the poor white trash" of the South, filthy, ragged, proud, indolent, ill-mannered, given to the smoking and chewing of tobacco, often diseased, inefficient, and either unwilling or unable to conform to the necessary regulations of the Home, or to do their own proper share of the work of the household, and the keeping of their apartments in a state of cleanliness and order.

It was a great trial of her Christian patience to see families of children of all ages, dirty, ragged, and ill-mannered, lounging in the halls and at the front door, and their mothers doing little better themselves, getting into disputes with each other, or hovering round a stove, chewing or smoking tobacco, and leaving the necessary work allotted to them neglected and undone. But out of this material and this confusion Miss Elliott, by her efficiency and force of character, brought a good degree of cleanliness and order. Among other things she established a school in the Home, gathered the children into it in the evening, taught them to spell, read and sing, and inspired them with a desire for knowledge.

At the end of a year of this kind of work Miss Elliott was called to the position of matron of the Soldiers' Orphans' Home, at Farmington, Iowa, which she accepted and filled for several months, with her usual efficiency and success, when, after long and arduous service for the soldiers, for the refugees and for the orphans of our country's defenders, she returned to the home of her family, and to the society and occupations for which she was preparing herself before the war.

MARY DWIGHT PETTES

O one who was accustomed to visit the military hospitals of St. Louis, during the first years of the war, the meeting with Mary Dwight Pettes in her ministry to the sick and wounded soldiers must always return as a pleasant and sacred memory. And such an one will not fail to recall how she carried to the men pleasant reading, how she sat by their bed-sides speaking words of cheer and sympathy, and singing songs of country, home, and heaven, with a voice of angelic sweetness. Nor, how after having by her own exertions procured melodeons for the hospital chapels, she would play for the soldiers in their Sabbath worship, and bring her friends to make a choir to assist in their religious services.

Slender in form, her countenance radiant with intelligence, and her dark eyes beaming with sympathy and kindness, it was indeed a pleasant surprise to see one so young and delicate, going about from hospital to hospital to find opportunities of doing good to the wan and suffering, and crippled heroes, who had been brought from hard-fought battle-fields to be cared for at the North.

But no one of the true Sisters of Mercy, who gave themselves ' to this service during the war, felt more intense and genuine satisfaction in her labors than she, and not one is more worthy of our grateful remembrance, now that she has passed away from the scene of her joys and her labors forever.

Mary Dwight Pettes was born in Boston, Massachusetts, in the year 1841, and belonged to a family who were eminent for their intelligence, and religious and moral worth. The circumstances of her early life and education are unknown to the writer of this sketch, but must have been such as to develope that purity of mind and manners, that sweetness and amiability of temper, that ready sympathy and disinterestedness of purpose and conduct, which, together with rare conversational and musical powers, she possessed in so high a degree.

Having an uncle and his family resident in St. Louis, the first year of the war found her in that city, engaged in the work of ministering to the soldiers in the hospitals with her whole hear! and soul. During the first winter of the great rebellion-(1862) St. Louis was filled with troops, and there were thirteen hospitals thronged with the sick and wounded from the early battle-fields of the war. On the 30th of January of that year she thus wrote to the Boston Transcript, over her own initials, some account of her labors and observations at that time. Speaking of the hospitals she said, "It is here that the evils and horrors of the war become very apparent. Here stout hearts are broken. You see great numbers of the brave young men of the Western States, who have left their homes to fight for their country. They were willing to be wounded, shot, to die, if need be, but after months of inaction they find themselves conquered by dysentery or fever. Some fifty or sixty each week are borne to their long home. This may have been unavoidable, but it is hard to bear.

Last night I returned home in the evening. It was dark, rainy, cold and muddy. I passed an ambulance in the street. The two • horses had each a leader walking beside them, which indicated that a very sick soldier was within. It was a sad sight; and yet this poor man could not be moved, when he arrived at the hospital-door, until his papers were examined to see if they conformed to I Army Regulations.' I protest against the coldness with which the Regulations treat the sick and wounded soldiers."

No doubt her sympathetic heart protested against all delays and all seeming indifference to the welfare of the poor fellows on whose bravery and devotion the salvation of the country depended.

In her devotion to the sick and wounded in the hospitals, and her labors of love among them, she sacrificed many of her own comforts and pleasures. Notwithstanding the delicacy of her own health she would go about among them doing them good.

She took great interest in seeing the soldiers engaged in religious worship, and in assisting to conduct the exercises of praise and thanksgiving. When these services were ended she used to go from ward to ward, and passing to the bed-side of those who were too weak to join the worship in the chapel would read to them the blessed words of comfort contained in the Book of Life, and sing to them the sweet hymn, "Jesus, I love thy charming name."

In one of her papers she has left this record. "For a year I have visited the hospitals constantly, and during that time they have been crowded with sick and wounded soldiers. I never had any idea what suffering was until I had been in the wards after the battles of Fort Donelson, Pittsburg Landing, and Pea Ridge. The poor fellows are so patient too, and so grateful for any little service or attention."

In another letter, speaking of the great civil war in which we were then engaged, she wrote, "Still I have hope, trusting in the justice of God. Being a constant visitor to the hospitals in and about this city, I have taken great pleasure in relieving the physical as well as the spiritual wants of the sick and wounded, as far as it has been in my power, proving to them that they have sympathizing friends near them, although their home-friends may be far away. I have encouraged them to be cheerful, and bear their sufferings with heroic fortitude, trusting in God, and a happier and better future. It has seemed to me that I do them some good when I find them watching for my coming, and that every face brightens as I enter the ward, while many say to me, 'We are always glad to see you come. It cheers and comforts us mightily to have you come so bright and smiling, asking us how we do, and saying always some pleasant word, and giving ns something good to read. Then we love to hear you sing to us. Sometimes it makes the tears come in our eyes, but it kind o' lifts us up, and makes us feel better. We sometimes wonder you come here so much among us poor fellows, but we have come to the conclusion that your heart is in the cause for which we are fighting, and that you want to help and cheer us so that we may get well and go back to our regiments, and finish up the work of putting down this infernal rebellion.'"

"One day as I lifted up the head of a poor boy, who was languidly drooping, and smoothed and fixed his pillow, he said, 'Thank you; that's nice. You are so gentle and good to me that I almost fancy I am at home, and that sister Mary is waiting upon me.'"

"Such expressions of their interest and gratitude," she adds, "encourage me in this work, and I keep on, though often my strength almost fails me, and my heart is filled with sadness, as I see one after another of the poor fellows wasting away, and in a few days their cots are empty and they sleep the sleep that knows no waking this side of the grave."

Thus she labored on in her work of self-sacrificing love and devotion, with no compensation but the satisfaction that she was doing good, until late in the month of December, 1862, she was attacked with the typhoid fever, which she, no doubt, had contracted in the infected air of the hospitals, and died on the 14th of January, 1863. During her five weeks of illness her thoughts were constantly with the soldiers, and in her delirium she would imagine she was among them in their sick wards, and would often speak to them words of consolation and sympathy.

In a letter of Rev. Dr. Eliot, the Unitarian Pastor, of St. Louis, published in the Christian Register on the following May, he gives the impression she had left upon those with whom she had been sometimes associated in her labors. Miss Pettes was a Unitarian in her religious faith, and this fact was known to one of the excellent

Chaplains who regularly officiated in the hospitals at St. Louis, and who belonged to the Old School Presbyterian Church. He had, however, been very glad of her co-operation and assistance in his work, and in conducting religious worship in the hospitals, and thus spoke of her to Dr. Eliot, some months after her death. "Chaplain P. said to me to-day, 'Can you not send me some one to take the place of Mary Pettes, who died literally a martyr to the cause six months ago?' 'I don't think said he, that you can find another as good as she, for her whole heart was in it, and she was like sunshine to the hospital. But he added, 'all your people [the Unitarians] work as if they really cared for the soldiers and loved the cause, and I want more of them.'"

Such was the impression of her goodness and worth, and moral beauty left by this New England girl upon the minds of those who saw her going about in the hospitals of St. Louis, during the first year and a-half of the war, trying to do her part in the great work given us to do as a nation, and falling a martyr, quite as much as those who fell on the field of battle, to the cause of her country and liberty:—such the brief record of a true and spotless life given, in its virgin purity and loveliness, as a sacrifice well pleasing to God.

LOUISA MAERTZ

DURING the winter of 1863, while stationed at Helena, Arkansas, the writer was greatly impressed with the heroic devotion to the welfare of the sick soldier, of a lady whom he often met in the hospitals, where she was constantly engaged in services of kindness to the suffering inmates, attending to their wants, and alleviating their distress. He soon learned that her name was Louisa Maertz, of Quincy, Illinois, who had come from her home all the way to Helena—at a time when the navigation of the river was rendered dangerous by the firing of guerrillas from the shore upon the passing steamers—that she might devote herself to the work of a hospital nurse. At a later period, when he learned that she had left a pleasant home for this arduous service, and saw how bravely she endured the discomforts of hospital life in Helena, where there was not a single well-ordered and well-provided hospital; how she went from one building to another through the filthy and muddy town, to carry the delicacies she had obtained from the Sanitary Commission, and dispense them to the sick, with her own hands, he was still more impressed with these evidences of her "good, heroic womanhood," and her disinterested benevolence. Recently he has procured a few particulars of her history, which will serve for a brief sketch.

Miss Maertz was born in Quincy, Illinois, in 1838. Her parents were of German birth, and among the early settlers of the place. From infancy she was of a delicate constitution, and 390 suffered much from ill health; and at the age of eighteen years she was sent to Europe in the hope that she might derive benefit from the mineral springs of Germany and from travel and change of climate. Two years in Germany, Switzerland and Italy were spent in traveling and in the society of her relatives, some of whom were the personal friends of the Monods of Paris, Guizot, the Gurneys of England, Merle D'Aubigne, of Geneva, and other literary people of Europe, with several of whom she became acquainted. From this visit abroad she received much benefit, and her general health was greatly improved.

From an early period she had cherished two strong aspirations, the desire of knowledge, and the wish to devote herself to works of charity. Her heart was always ready to sympathize with the sufferings and sorrows of humanity; and the cause of the orphan, the slave, the poor and the helpless excited a deep interest in her mind, and a desire to devote herself in some way to their relief. After her return from Europe it became an absorbing aspiration and the subject of earnest prayer that God would show her some way in which she could be useful to humanity.

As she was thus becoming prepared for the work upon which she afterwards entered, the great rebellion, which involved the country in the late civil war, broke forth; the early battles in Missouri, and at Fort Donelson and Belmont led to the establishment of hospitals in St. Louis, at Mound City, and at Quincy, Illinois; and the opportunity came to Miss Maertz, which she had so long desired, to undertake some work of charity and benevolence. During the months of October and November, 1861, she commenced the daily visitation of the hospitals in Quincy, carried with her delicacies for the sick and distributed them, procured the redress of any grievances they suffered, read the Scriptures and conversed with them, wrote letters for them to their friends, dressed their wounds, and furnished them books, papers, and sources of amusement. Although her physical strength at this period was very moderate, she seemed, on entering the hospital, and witnessing the sufferings of brave men, who had dared everything for their country, to be infused with a new and strange vigor that sustained her through every exertion.

In particular cases of tedious convalescence, retarded by inferior hospital accommodations, she—with her parents' consent—obtained permission to take them home, and nurse them till they were restored to health. Thus she labored on through the fall and winter of 1861-2 till the battles of Shiloh and Pea Ridge filled the hospitals with wounded men, at St. Louis and Mound City, and at Louisville and Evansville and Paducah, and she began to feel that she must go where her services were more needed, and give herself wholly to this work of caring for and nursing the wounded patriots of the war.

After waiting some time for an opportunity to go she wrote to Mr. James E. Yeatman, at St. Louis, the agent of Miss Dorothea L. Dix for the appointment of women nurses in the hospitals of the Western Department, and was accepted. On reporting herself at St. Louis she was commissioned as a nurse, and in the fall of 1862 proceeded to Helena, where the army of the Southwest had encamped the previous July, under Major-General Curtis, and where every church and several private buildings had to be converted into hospitals to accommodate the sick of his army.

It was here, during the winter of 1863, that the writer of this sketch first met with Miss Maertz, engaged in the work of a hospital nurse, enduring with rare heroism sacrifices and discomforts, labors and watchings in the service of the sick soldiers that won the reverence and admiration of all who saw this gentle woman thus nobly employed. It was of her the following paragraph was written in the History of the Western Sanitary Commission.

"Another one we also know whose name is likewise in this simple record, who, at Helena, Arkansas, in the fall and winter of 1862-3, was almost the only female nurse in the hospitals there, going from one building to another, in which the sick were quartered, when the streets were almost impassable with mud, administering sanitary stores and making delicate preparations of food, spending her own money in procuring milk and other articles that were scarce and difficult to obtain, and doing an amount of work which few persons could sustain, living without the pleasant society to which she had been accustomed at home, never murmuring, always cheerful and kind, preserving in the midst of a military camp such gentleness, strength and purity of character that all rudeness of speech ceased in her presence, and as she went from room to room she was received with silent benedictions, or an audible 'God bless you, dear lady from some poor sufferer's heart.'"

The last time I saw Miss Maertz, while engaged in her hospital work, was at the grave of a soldier, who was buried at Helena in the spring of 1863. He was one of the persecuted Union men of Arkansas, who had enlisted in the Union army on the march of General Curtis through Arkansas, and had fallen sick at Helena. For several weeks Miss Maertz had nursed and cared for him with all a woman's tenderness and delicacy, and perceiving that he must die had succeeded in sending a message to his wife, who lived sixty miles in the interior of Arkansas, within the enemy's lines. On the afternoon of his death and but a few hours before it she arrived, having walked the whole distance on foot with great difficulty, because she was partially blind; but had the satisfaction of receiving the parting words of her husband and attending his burial. Miss Maertz sent word to me, asking me to perform the burial service, and the next day I met her leading the half-blind widow, in her poverty and sorrow, to the grave. Some months later this poor soldier's widow came to the Refugee Home, at St. Louis, and was cared for, and being recognized and the scene of the lonely burial referred to, she related with tears of gratitude the kindness she received from the good lady, who nursed her husband in his last illness at Helena.

At a later period in the service, Miss Maertz was transferred 50 to the hospitals at Vicksburg, where she continued her work of benevolence till she was obliged to return home to restore her own exhausted energies. At this time her parents urged her to go with them to Europe, wishing to take her away from scenes of suffering, and prostrating disease, but she declined to go, and, on regaining a measure of health, entered the service again and continued in it at New Orleans to the end of the war.

In real devotion to the welfare of the soldiers of the Union; in high religious and patriotic motives; in the self-sacrificing spirit with which she performed her labors; in the heroism with which she endured hardship for the sake of doing good; in the readiness with which she gave up her own interests and the offer of personal advantages and pleasure to serve the cause of patriotism and humanity, she had few equals.

MRS. HARRIET R. COLFAX

THIS lady whose services merit all the praise which has been bestowed upon them, is a resident of Michigan City, Indiana, the still youthful widow of a near relative of the Honorable Schuyler Colfax, the present Speaker of the House of Representatives.

Her father, during her youth, was long an invalid, and his enforced seclusion from all business pursuits was spent in bestowing instruction upon his children. His conversations with his children, and the lessons in history which he gave them were made the means of instilling great moral ideas, and amidst all others an ardent love of their native country and its institutions. At the same period of the life of Mrs. Colfax, she was blest with a mother whose large and active benevolence led her to spend much time in visiting and ministering to the sick. Her daughter often accompanied her, and as often was sent alone upon like errands. Thus she learned the practice of the sentiments which caused her, in the hour of her country's trial, to lend such energetic and cheerful aid to its wounded defenders.

Previous to the commencement of the war Mrs. Colfax had lost her husband and her father. Her mother remained to advise and guide the young widow and her fatherless children, and it was to her that she turned for counsel, when, on the announcement of the need of female nurses in the hospitals that were so soon filled with sick and wounded, Mrs. Colfax felt herself impelled to devote herself to this service and ministry.

Her mother and other friends disapproved of her going, and said all they could in opposition. She listened, and delayed, but finally felt that she must yield to the impulse. The opposition was withdrawn, and on the last of October, 1861, she started for St. Louis to enter the hospitals there.

Her heart was very desolate as she entered this strange city alone, at ten o'clock at night. Mr. Yeatman, with whom communication had been opened relative to her coming, had neglected to give her definite directions how to proceed. But she heard some surgeons talking of the hospitals, and learned that they belonged to them. From them she obtained the address of Mr. Yeatman. A gentleman, as she left the cars, stepped forward and kindly and respectfully placed her in the omnibus which was to take her across the river. She turned to thank him, but he was gone. Yet these occurrences, small as they were, had given her renewed courage—she no longer felt quite friendless, but went cheerfully upon her way.

She proceeded to the Fifth Street Hospital, where Mr. Yeatman had his quarters, and was admitted by the use of his name. The night nurse, Mrs. Gibson, took kind charge of her for that night, and in the morning she was introduced to the matron, Mrs. Plummer, and to Mr. Yeatman. She had her first sight of wounded men on the night of her arrival, and the thought of their sufferings, and of how much could be done to alleviate them, made her forget herself, an obliviousness from which she did not for weeks recover.

She was assigned to the first ward in which there had been till then no female nurse, and soon found full employment for hands, mind and heart. The reception room for patients was on the same floor with her ward, and the sufferers had to be taken through it to reach the others, so that she was forced to witness every imaginable phase of suffering and misery, and her sympathies never became blunted. Many of these men lived but a short time after being brought in, and one man standing with his knapsack on to have his name and regiment noted down, fell to the floor as it was supposed in a swoon, but was found to be dead.

For some time when men were dying all around with typhus fever and wounds, no clergyman of any denomination visited them. Mrs. Colfax and other ladies would often at their request offer up prayers, but they felt that regular religious ministrations were needed. After a time through the intercession of a lady, a resident of St. Louis, the Rev. Dr. Schuyler came often to supply this want, giving great comfort to the sufferers.

About this time, the ward surgeon was removed, and another substituted in his place, Dr. Paddock. This gentleman thus speaks of the services and character of Mrs. Colfax:

ST. LOUIS, March 2d, 1866.

"Among the many patriotic and benevolent Christian ladies who volunteered their services to aid, comfort, and alleviate the suffering of the sick and wounded soldiers of the Union Army in the late wicked and woful Rebellion, I know of none more deserving of honorable mention and memory, than Mrs. Harriet R. Colfax. I first met her in the Fifth Street General Hospital of this city, where I was employed in the spring of 1862; and subsequently in the General Hospital, at Jefferson Barracks, in 1863. In both these hospitals she was employed in the wards under my care, and subject to my immediate orders and observation In both, she was uniformly the same industrous, indefatigable, attentive, kind, and sympathizing nurse and friend of the sick and wounded soldier. She prepared delicacies and cordials, and often obtained them to prepare from her friends abroad, in addition to such as were furnished by the Sanitary Commission. She administered them with her own hands in such a manner as only a sympathizing and loving woman can; and thus won the heartfelt gratitude and affection of every soldier to whom it was her duty and her delight to administer. No female nurse in either of the hospitals above named, and there was a large number in each of them, was more universally beloved and respected, than was Mrs. Colfax. I had not the opportunity to witness her services and privations, and vexations on hospital steamers, or elsewhere than in the two places named above; but I know that they were considerable; and that everywhere and under all circumstances, she was alike active and honored."

In Dr. Paddock, Mrs. Colfax truly found a friend, and she was able to accomplish a greater amount of good under his kind directions. The "Ward was crowded. The wounded arrived from

Fort Donelson in a miserable condition. From exposure, many were dangerously ill with pneumonia, and died very soon; few recovered, but the wounded did much better than the sick, and were so patient and cheerful, that even those suffering from the worst wounds, or amputations, would hardly have been known not to be well, save by their pale faces and weak voices. Many would not give way till the last moment, but with strong courage, and brave cheerfulness, would close their eyes on things of earth, and pass silently into the unseen world.

In the spring, Miss. Colfax, finding herself much worn by severe work and frequent colds, gladly availed herself of the change offered by a trip on the Hospital-boat, Louisiana, then just fitted up by the Sanitary Commission.

At Cairo, they received orders to proceed to Island No. 10, and there unexpectedly found themselves in the well-known battle which took place at that point on the 16th, 17th, and 18th of March, 1862.

The Batteries of the enemy, on the banks and Island, were engaged with the Union gunboats. The firing was incessant and protracted, but not very disastrous. At last the firing from one of the gunboats resulted in the killing and wounding of a number of the enemy, which last were brought on board the Louisiana for care. After remaining there ten days, the Louisiana returned to Cairo, and receiving on board the wounded from Mound City Hospital, carried them to Cincinnati. Mrs. Colfax and her friends were very busy in the care of these poor men, many of them very low, giving unceasing attentions to them, and even then feeling that they had not done half enough.

Immediately after their return to Cairo, they left for Savannah and Pittsburg Landing, on the Tennessee River. They took from the latter place two hundred and fifty men, leaving again before the battle of Shiloh. This took place immediately after they left, and they ran up to St. Louis, landed their freight of wounded, and returned immediately for another load.

Two hundred and seventy-five desperately wounded men from the battle of Shiloh, formed this load. They quickly made their way Northward with their freight of misery and suffering. This was beyond the power of the imagination to conceive, and the nurses were too busy in their cares to sleep or eat. The sorrowful labor was at last performed, the wounded were transferred to the hospitals at St. Louis, and Mrs. Colfax returned to her duties there.

After remaining some time in the Fifth Street Hospital, and making occasional trips on the Hospital-boats, Mrs. Colfax was sent to the Hospital at Jefferson Barracks, where she remained a long time, and where her services, so eminently kind, efficient and womanly, met the success they so much deserved.

She remained in the service as a hospital nurse two years and a half. Except while on the hospital boats, and during brief stays at the various hospitals of the South-west, while attached to the Transport Service, she spent the entire time at Fifth Street Hospital, St. Louis, and at Jefferson Barracks. In each and every place her services were alike meritorious, and though she encountered many annoyances, and unpleasant incidents, she does not now regret the time and labor she bestowed in doing her share of the woman's work of the war.

Like all earnest, unselfish workers, in this eminently unselfish service, Mrs. Colfax delights to bear testimony to the efficient labors of others.

All who worked with her were her friends, and she has the fullest appreciation of their best qualities, and their earnest efforts. Among those she names thus feelingly, are Mrs. Plummer, the matron of the Fifth Street Hospital, St. Louis, Miss Addie E. Johnson, Mrs. Gibson, and others, her fellow-workers there.

Early in 1864, quite worn out with her protracted labors, Mrs. Colfax returned to her home in Michigan City, where she still resides, honored, beloved and respected, as her character and services demand.

MISS CLARA DAVIS

THIS lady, now the wife of the Rev. Edward Abbott, of Cambridgeport, Massachusetts, was one of the earliest, most indefatigable and useful of the laborers for Union soldiers during the war. Her labors commenced early in the winter of 1861-62, in the hospitals of Philadelphia, in which city she was then residing.

Her visits were at first confined to the Broad and Cherry Street Hospital, and her purpose at first was to minister entirely to the religious wants of the sick, wounded and dying soldiers. Her interest in the inmates of that institution was never permitted to die out.

It was not patriotism,—for Miss Davis was not a native of this country—but rather a profound sympathy with the cause in which they were engaged which led her, in company with the late Rev. Dr. Vaughan of Philadelphia (of whose family she was an inmate) to visit this place and aid him in his philanthropic and official duties. The necessity of the case led her to labor regularly and assiduously to supply the lack of many comforts which was felt here, and the need of woman's nursing and comforting ways. By the month of May, ensuing, she was giving up her whole time to these ministrations, and this at a considerable sacrifice, and extending her efforts so as to alleviate the temporal condition of the sufferers, as well as to minister to their spiritual ones.

In the early part of this summer, memorable as the season of the Peninsula Campaign, she, in company with Mrs. M. M. Husband, of Philadelphia, entered upon the transport service on the James and Potomac Olivers, principally on board the steamer "John Brooks"—passing to and fro with the sick and wounded between Harrison's Landing, Fortress Monroe and Philadelphia. This joint campaign ended with a sojourn of two months at Mile Creek Hospital, Fortress Monroe.

Her friend, Mrs. H. thus speaks of her. "A more lovely Christian character, a more unselfishly devoted person, than Miss Davis, I have never known. Her happy manner of approaching the soldiers, especially upon religious subjects, was unequalled; the greatest scoffer would listen to her with respect and attention, while the majority followed her with a glance of veneration as if she were a being of a superior order. I heard one say, 'there must be wings hidden beneath her cloak.'"

After leaving Fortress Monroe, Miss Davis returned to Philadelphia, and recruited her supplies for the use of the soldiers. She was anxious to be permitted to serve in the field hospitals, but owing to unusual strictness of regulation at that time, she was not permitted to do so. Later in the season she accompanied Mrs. Husband to Frederick City, Harper's Ferry and Antietam, at which latter place, by the invitation of Surgeon Vanderkieft, and Miss Hall, she remained several weeks doing very acceptable service.

During the winter of 1863 she renewed her efforts to gain permission to serve in the field hospitals of the army, then in winter quarters between Falmouth and Acquia Creek, but was again repulsed. In the spring she once more renewed her efforts, but without success. Again visiting Washington, she was requested to become the agent of the Sanitary Commission, at Camp Parole, Annapolis, Maryland.

She commenced her laborious duties at Camp Parole about the 1st of May, 1863. She made numerous friends here, among all classes with whom she came in contact, and did a most admirable

51 work among the returned prisoners. She remained here the whole summer, never allowing herself one day's absence, until October. She suffered from ague, and her labors were far too great for her strength. Camp, or typhoid fever, seized her, and after long striving against weakness and pain, she was obliged to return to her home to recruit. She made great efforts to again take up her work where she had been obliged to leave it, but her strength would not admit.

She did not recover from this illness until the following February, nor even then could she be said to have fully recovered. As soon as the state of her health permitted, indeed before her physician gave his consent, she resumed her labors at Camp Parole, but in a few weeks the fever set in again, and further service was rendered impossible. Thus closed the ministrations in field and hospital, of one, of whom a friend who knew her well, and appreciated her fully, simply says, "Her deeds were beyond praise."

Her health was so undermined by her labors, that it has never been fully recovered, and she still suffers, as she perhaps will to the end of her life, from the weakness and diseases induced, by her unwonted exertions, and the fevers which so greatly prostrated her.

Nearly two years, as we have seen, she gave to her labors in camp and hospital, labors which, as we have seen, were principally directed to the relief of physical sufferings, though she never forgot to mingle with them the spiritual ministrations which were the peculiar feature of her usefulness.

The interest of Miss Davis was not limited to soldiers in hospitals, any more than were her labors confined to efforts for their relief. From her numerous friends, and from societies, she was in constant receipt of money, delicacies, reading matter, and many other things, both valuable and useful to the soldiers, and not embraced in the government supplies, nor sold by sutlers. These she distributed among both sick and well, as their needs required.

"She corresponded largely with the friends of sick soldiers; she represented their needs to those who had the means to relieve them; she used her influence in obtaining furloughs for the convalescents, and discharges for the incurables; she importuned tape-bound officials for passes, that the remains of the poor unpaid soldier might be buried beside his parents; she erected headboards at every soldier's grave at that time in the cemetery at West Philadelphia, as a temporary memorial and record."

In the heat of Virginian summers, and the inclement winters, it was with her the same steady unchanged work, till sickness put an end to her labors. Till the last her intercourse with the soldiers was always both pleasant, and in the highest sense profitable.

MRS. R. H. SPENCER

OF all the band of noble women who during the war gave their time and best labors with devotedness and singleness of purpose to the care of the suffering defenders of their country, few, perhaps, have been as efficient and useful in their chosen sphere as Mrs. Spencer.

That she left a home of quiet ease and comfort, and gave herself, with her whole soul, to the cause she loved, is not more than very many others have done, but she incited her husband to offer himself to his country, and gladly accompanied him, sharing all his privations, and creating for him, amid the rudest surroundings, home with all its comforts and enjoyments.

At the commencement of the war, Mrs. Spencer was living at Oswego, New York, which had been her residence for many years. Her husband, Captain R. H. Spencer, had been formerly commander of several of the finest vessels which sail from that port in the trade upon the upper lakes. But for some years lie had remained on shore, and devoted himself to the occupation of teaching, in which he had a very fine reputation. Mrs. Spencer was also a teacher, and both were connected with the public schools for which that city is celebrated.

Mr. Spencer was a member of that wing of the Democratic party which opposed the war, and his age already exempted him from military duty.

When, therefore, immediately after the battle of Antietam he announced to Mrs. Spencer that he had resolved to enlist in the

Regiment then rapidly forming in that city, she knew well, as did all who knew him, that only an imperative sense of personal duty had led to the decision.

Oswego had to mourn the most irreparable losses in that battle. The flower of her young men had been cut down, and many homes made desolate. Mr. Spencer, like many others, felt impelled to add himself to the patriot ranks, and help to fill the gaps left by the fallen.

Mrs. Spencer, whose name and person had long been familiar to the sick and suffering at home, had often longed for the power of ministering to those who had taken their lives in their hands, and gone forth in the service of their country. And she now not only gave her husband to the work, but resolved to aid him in it. She might not stand by his side, in the armed ranks, but there was, for her, service as arduous and important, for which she was peculiarly fitted, not only by the extreme kindness and benevolence of her nature, but by experience in the eare of the sick.

When her husband had enlisted and was sworn into the service, she, too, took the oath to faithfully serve her country, and her place by his side.

The regiment (one hundred and forty-seventh New York) left Oswego the 27th of September, 1862, and arrived in Washington the 1st of October. Mrs. Spencer, fatigued and ill, overcome with the excitement of preparation, perhaps, and the grief of parting with her friends, found herself thus in a strange city and upon the threshold of a strange new life. She obtained a little sleep upon a bench outside the Soldiers' Rest, and though scarcely refreshed commenced her duties early on the following morning by feeding from her own stores six wounded men from the battle of Antietam, who had arrived during the night. After making tea for them, and doing all she could for their comfort, she was obliged to leave, as the regiment was en route for Arlington Heights.

Mrs. Spencer remained in the neighborhood of "Washington until the middle of the December following. The regiment had gone forward some time previously, leaving herself and husband in charge of the hospital stores. Her husband was ward-master of the hospital, and she was matron and nurse.

"When the hospital tents and stores were sent to Acquia Creek, to the regiment, Mr and Mrs. Spencer remained for a time to care for the sick and wounded in Washington, and volunteered to take care of the wounded from the first battle of Fredericksburg, who were brought to the Patent Office.

On the 12th of January Mr. Spencer went to join the regiment at Falmouth, while Mrs. Spencer proceeded to New York for supplies, and on the 17th returned and joined the regiment at Belle Plain, proceeding almost immediately to Wind Mill Point, in company with the sick and wounded removed thither. Here she remained six months, engaged in her arduous duties as matron in the hospital of the First Corps, to which her husband was also attached.

From this place they were transferred to Belle Plain, and after a short stay from thence to Acquia Creek, where they remained attached to the hospital until the 13th of June, when they were ordered to report to their regiment, then lying near Falmouth.

Mrs. Spencer had by this time, by much practice, become an expert horse-woman, often foraging on her own account for supplies for the sick and wounded under her care. By the order of Dr. Hurd, the Medical Director of the First Corps, she took with her the horse she had been accustomed to ride, and a few days afterwards commenced on horseback the march to Gettysburg— now become historical.

Nearly two weeks were consumed in this march, one of which was spent in an encampment on Broad Run.

Mrs. Spencer's horse carried, besides herself, her bedding, sundry utensils for cooking, and a scanty supply of clothing, about three hundred and fifty pounds of supplies for the sick. In addition to this she often took charge of huge piles of coats belonging to the weary men, which otherwise they would have thrown away as superfluous during the intense heat of midday, to miss them sorely afterward amid the twilight dews, or the drenching rains.

The battle had already commenced as the long slow-moving train, to which they were attached, approached Gettysburg, and the awful roar of cannon and the scattering rattle of musketry reached their ears.

The day previous an ammunition-wagon in their train had exploded, and Mrs. Spencer had torn up the thick comforter which usually formed her bed, that the driver of the wagon, who was fearfully burned, might be wrapped in the cotton and bandaged by the calico of which it was made. Mr. Spencer remained to care for the man, and at night—a dark and rainy night—she found herself for the first time separated from her husband, and unprotected by any friend. But the respectful and chivalric instincts of American soldiers proved sufficient for her defense against any evil that might have menaced her. They spread their rubber blankets upon the muddy ground, and made a sort of tent with others, into which she crept and slept guarded and secure through the long dark hours. At morning they vied with each other in preparing her breakfast, and waiting upon her with every possible respect and attention, and she went on her way, rested and refreshed.

In the course of the morning Mr. Spencer rejoined her. After the firing was heard, telling the tale of the awful conflict that was progressing, she felt that she could no longer remain with the halting train, but must press on to some point where her work of mercy might commence.

This was found in an unoccupied barn, not far from the field, where, by the assistance of her husband, she got a fire and soon had her camp-kettles filled with fragrant coffee, which she distributed to every weary and wounded man who applied for the refreshing beverage.

"Wounded in considerable numbers from the Eleventh Corps were placed in this barn to gain which they crossed the fields between two rows of artillery, stationed there. Mrs. Spencer had two knapsacks and two haversacks suspended from her saddle, and supplied with materials for making tea, coffee and beef-tea— with these and crackers, she contrived to provide refreshment. Meanwhile the balls and shells were falling fast around the barn, and orders came to move further back.

But this brave woman with her husband chose to move forward rather, in search of her own regiment, though the enemy were then gaining upon the Union troops. As they went on toward the battle, they found their regiment stationed on a hill above them, and halting they made a fire and prepared refreshments which they gave to all they could reach.

"While working here the Surgeon of the First Division came hurrying past, and peremptorily called on Mrs. Spencer to go and help form a hospital. When she and Mr. Spencer found that many men of their own regiment were in the train of ambulances which was going slowly past with the sufferers, they followed.

They crossed to the White Church, on the Baltimore turnpike, about four miles from Gettysburg, and reached there after dark. They had sixty wounded undergoing every variety of suffering and torture. The church was small, having but one aisle, and the narrow seats were fixtures. A small building adjoining provided boards which were laid on the tops of the seats, and covered with straw, and on these the wounded were laid.

The supply train had been sent back fourteen miles. A number of surgeons were there, but none had instruments, and could do very little for the wounded, and Mrs. Spencer found the stores contained in her knapsacks and haversacks most useful in refreshing these sufferers.

In the course J£ a few days the confusion subsided. The hospital was thoroughly organized. The Sanitary and Christian Commissions and the people came and aided them, and order came out of the chaos that followed this awful battle.

On the 5th of July, the buildings and tents which formed this hospital contained over six hundred Union troops, and more than one hundred wounded prisoners, and Mrs. Spencer found herself constantly and fully employed, nursing the wounded, and daily riding into town for supplies.

It was here that she gained, and very justly as it would seem, the credit of saving the life of a wounded soldier, a townsman of her own. The man was shot in the mouth and throat, a huge gaping orifice on the side of his neck showing where the ball found exit. The surgeons gave him but a few days to live, as he could swallow nothing, the liquids which were all he even could attempt to take, passing out by the wound. Tearfully he besought Mrs. Spencer's aid. Young and strong, and full of life, he could not contemplate a death of slow starvation. Mrs. Spencer went to the surgeons and besought their aid. None of them could give hope, for none conceived the strength of will in nurse or patient.

"Do as I tell you , and you shall not die," said Mrs.

Spencer. "Can you bear to go without food a week?"

Gratefully the man signed "yes," and with the tough unyielding patience of a hero, he bore the pains of wound and hunger. In the meantime the chief appliance was the basin of pure cold water from which he was directed to keep his wound continually wet, that horrid wound which it seemed no human skill could heal.

In a few days the inflammation began to subside, even the surgeons decided the symptoms good, and began to watch the case with interest. The ragged edges of the wound, when the swelling subsided, could be closed up. Then, by direction of his kind nurse, he plunged his face into a basin of broth, and supped 52 from it strength, since it did not all escape from the still unhealed wound. Every day witnessed an improvement. In a little time he took his food like a human being; each day witnessed new strength and healing, and then he was saved, and the nurse proved wiser, for once, than the doctor!

For thiee weeks Mrs. Spencer remained in the white Church Hospital. She then accompanied some wounded to New York City, and took a brief respite from her duties, and the awful scenes she had witnessed.

On her return to Gettysburg, she received as a mark of the esteem felt for her by those who had witnessed her labors and devotion to the work, and the confidence reposed in her, the appointment of Agent of the State of New York, in the care of its sick and wounded soldiers in the field. Large discretionary powers, both as to the purchase and the distribution of supplies, were granted her; and every effort was made to have this appointment distinguished as a mark of the high appreciation and esteem which she had won in the discharge of her duties.

As her husband was detailed as clerk in the Medical Purveyor's Office, at Gettysburg, she remained there in the active performance of her duties for a considerable time.

Beside the supplies furnished by the State of New York, a large amount were entrusted to her, by various Ladies' Aid Societies, and kindred associations.

After leaving Gettysburg, Airs. Spencer was variously but usefully employed at various places, and in various ways, but always making her duties as State agent for the New York troops prominent, and of the first importance. She was for some time at Brandy Station. While there her husband received his discharge from the Volunteer Service, but immediately entered the regular service, as Hospital Steward, and was attached to the Medical Purveyor's Department.

From Brandy Station, Mrs. Spencer went to Alexandria, and remained there until after the battle of the Wilderness, when she was ordered by the Surgeon-General to repair to Rappahannock Station, with needful supplies for the wounded. On arriving there, no wounded were found, and it was rumored that the ambulances containing them had been intercepted by the enemy, and turned another way.

The party therefore returned to Alexandria, and there received orders to repair with stores to Belle Plain. The Steamer on which Mrs. Spencer was, arrived at day-break at its destination, but she could not for some time get on shore. As soon as possible she landed, anxious to let her services be of some avail to the many wounded who stood in immediate need of assistance, and thinking she might at least make coffee or tea for some of them.

After distributing what supplies she had, she found in another part of the field several Theological Students, delegates of the Sanitary Commission, who were making coffee in camp kettles for the wounded. Her services were thankfully accepted by them. All the day, and far into the night they worked, standing inches deep in the tenacious Virginia mud, till thousands had been served.

All the afternoon the wounded were arriving. Thousands were laid upon the ground, upon the hill-side, perhaps under the shelter of a bush, perhaps with only the sky above them, from which the rain poured in torrents.

All with scarcely an exception were patient, cheerful, and thoughtful—when asked as to their own condition, seeming more troubled by the risk she ran in taking cold, than of their own sufferings.

Late in the night, she remembered that she was alone, and must rest somewhere. A wagon driver willingly gave her his place in the wagon, and thoroughly drenched with rain, and covered with mud, she there rested for the first time in many hours. Her sad and anxious thoughts with her physical discomforts prevented sleep, but with the dawn she had rested so much, as to be able to resume her labors.

Another, and another day passed. The wounded from those fearful battles continued to arrive, and to be cared for, as well as was possible under the circumstances. The workers were shortly afterward made as comfortable as was possible. For two weeks Mrs. Spencer remained, and labored at Belle Plain, remained till her clothing of which, not expecting to remain, she had brought no change, was nearly worn out. The need was so pressing, of care for the wounded, that she scarcely thought of herself.

In the latter part of May, she left Belle Plain, and went to Port Royal, where similar scenes were enacted, save that there a shelter was provided. She had joined forces with the Sanitary Commission, and the facilities were now good and the workers numerous, yet it was barely possible, with all these, and with Government and Commission supplies, and private contributions, to feed the applicants.

The Medical Purveyor's boat with her husband on board, having arrived, Mrs. Spencer proceeded on that boat to "White House, where she was placed in Superintendence of the Government Cooking Barge, continuing at the same time her supervision of the wants of the New York soldiery.

Here they fed the first wounded who arrived from the field, and here Mrs. Spencer continued many days directing the feeding of thousands more, ever remembering the regiments from her own State, as her special charge, and assisted by many volunteers and others in her arduous task.

On the 18th of June, 1864, Mrs. Spencer arrived at City Point. The wounded were still arriving, and there was enough for all to do. A Hospital was here established, a mile from the landing. The Government kitchen was kept up, till the hospitals and their kitchens were in full operation, when it was discontinued, and Mrs. Spencer relieved from her double task.

From that time, Mrs. Spencer confined herself mostly to the duties of her agency, and continued to make City Point her headquarters and base of operations until the close of the war closed the agency, and left her free once again to seek the welcome seclusion of her home.

She occasionally visited the General Hospitals to distribute supplies to her Hew York soldiers and others, but these being now well organized, did not, owing to the plenty of attendants greatly need her services, and they were mostly confined to visits to soldiers in the field, at the Front, Field Hospitals, and in the Rifle Pits.

Her equestrian skill now often came in use. Often a ride of from twenty to forty miles in the day would enable her to visit some outlying regiment or picket station, or even to reach the Rifle Pits that honeycombed plain and hill-side all about Petersburg and Richmond, and return the same day. On these occasions she was warmly and enthusiastically welcomed by the soldiers, not only for what she brought, but for the comfort and solace of her presence.

She was often in positions of great peril from whizzing shot and bursting shell, but was never harmed during these dangerous visits. On one occasion, she was probably by reason of her black hat and feather, mistaken for an officer, as she for a moment carelessly showed the upper part of her person, from a slight eminence near the rifle pits, and was fired at by one of the enemy's sharp-shooters. The ball lodged in a tree, close by her side, from which she deliberately dug it out with her penknife, retaining it as a memento of her escape.

Few of us whose days have been passed in the serene quietude of home, can imagine the comfort and joy her presence and cheering words brought to the "boys" undergoing the privations and discomforts of their station at the "Front," in those days of peril and siege. As she approached, her name would be heard passing from man to man, with electric swiftness, and often the shouts that accompanied it, would receive from the enemy a warlike response in the strange music of the whistling shot, or the bursting shell.

Through all this she seemed to bear a charmed life. "I never believed I should be harmed by shot or shell," she says, and her simple faith was justified.

She even escaped nearly unharmed the fearful peril of the great explosion at City Point, when, as it is now supposed, by rebel treachery, the ammunition barge was fired, and hundreds of human beings without an instant's warning, were hurried into eternity.

when this event occurred, she was on horseback near the landing, and in turning to flee was struck, probably by a piece of shell, in the side. Almost as by a miracle she escaped with only a terrible and extensive bruise, and a temporary paralysis of the lower limbs. The elastic steel wires of her crinoline, had resisted the deadly force of the blow, which otherwise would undoubtedly have killed her. A smaller missile, nearly cut away the string of her hat, which was found next day covered by the ghastly smear of human blood and flesh, which also sprinkled all her garments.

After the surrender of Richmond, Mrs. Spencer, with a party of friends, visited that city, and she records that she experienced a very human sense of satisfaction, as she saw some rebel prisoners marching into that terrible Libby Prison, to take the place of the Union prisoners who had there endured such fearful and nameless sufferings.

On the 8th of April the President came to visit the hospitals at City Point, shaking hands with the convalescents, who were drawn up to receive him, and speaking cheering words to all. A week later he had fallen the victim of that atrocious plot which led to his assassination.

Mrs. Spencer remained at City Point, engaged in her duties, till all the wounded had been removed, and the hospitals broken up. On the 31st of May, she went on the medical supply boat to Washington. She there offered her services to aid in any way in care of the wounded, while she remained, which she did for several days. About the middle of June she once more found herself an inmate of her own home, and, after the long season of busy and perilous days, gladly retired to the freedom and quiet of private life. She remained in the service about three years, and the entire time, with only the briefest intervals of rest, was well and profitably occupied in her duties, a strong will and an excellent constitution having enabled her to endure fatigues which would soon have broken down a person less fitted, in these respects, for the work.

Mrs. Spencer has received from soldiers, (who are all her grateful friends) from loyal people in various parts of the country, and from personal friends and neighbors, many tokens of appreciation, which she enumerates with just pride and gratitude. Not the least of these is her house and its furniture, a horse, a sewing machine, silver ware, and expensive books; beside smaller articles whose chief value arises from the feeling that caused the gifts. Her health has suffered in consequence of her labors, but she now hopes for permanent recovery.

MRS. HARRIET FOOTE HAWLEY

By Mrs. Harriett Beecher Stowe

AMONG the many heroic women who gave their services to their country in our recent warfare, few deserve more grateful mention than Mrs. Harriet Foote Hawley, wife of Brevet Major-General Hawley, the present Governor of Connecticut.

Mrs. Hawley is of a fragile and delicate constitution, and one always regarded by her friends as peculiarly unfitted to have part in labors or hardships of any kind. But from the beginning to the end of the war, she was an exemplification of how much may be done by one "strong of spirit," even with the most delicate physical frame.

She went alone to Beaufort, South Carolina, in November, 1862, to engage in teaching the colored people. While there she regularly visited the army hospitals, and interested herself in the practical details of nursing, to which she afterwards more particularly devoted herself, and that spring and summer did the same at Fernandina and St. Augustine.

In November, 1863, she rejoined her husband on St. Helena Island, to which he had returned with his regiment from the siege of Charleston. She visited the Beaufort and Hilton Head General Hospitals, as well as the post hospital at St. Helena frequently during the winter, especially after the severe battle of Olustee, in February, 1864. When the Tenth Corps went to Fortress Monroe, to join General Butler's army, Mrs. Hawley went with them, and failing to find work in the Chesapeake Hospital, went to Washington and was assigned the charge of a ward in the Armory Square Hospital, on the very morning when the wounded began to arrive from the battles of the Wilderness.

Her ward was one of the two in the armory itself, which for a considerable time contained more patients than any other in that hospital. "Armory Square" being near the Potomac, usually received the most desperate cases, which could with difficulty be moved far. There could be no operating room connected with this ward, and the operations, however painful or dreadful, were of necessity performed in the ward itself. The scenes presented were enough to appall the stoutest nerves. The men exhausted by marching and by a long journey after their wounds, died with great rapidity—in one day forty-eight were carried out dead— many reaching the hospital only in time to die.

Among scenes like these Mrs. Hawley took up her abode, and labored with an untiring zeal over four months in the hottest of the summer weather—never herself strong—-often suffering to a degree that would have confined others to the bed of an invalid. She was ever at her post, a guiding, directing, and comforting presence, until worn-out nature required a temporary rest. After two months of repose she again returned to the same ward, and continued her labors from November to the last of March, 1865.

About the first of March, directly after its capture, her husband had been assigned to the command of Wilmington, North Carolina.

She arrived at Wilmington, directly after nine thousand Union prisoners had been delivered there, of whom more than three thousand needed hospital treatment.

The army was entirely unprovided with any means of meeting this exigency. The horrible condition of the prisoners, and the crowds of half-fed whites and blacks collected in the town, bred a pestilence. Typhus or jail fever appeared in its most dreadful form, and the deaths were terribly frequent. The medical officers tried all their energies to get supplies.

The garrison, the loyal citizens, and all good people gave their spare clothing, and all delicacies of food within reach, to alleviate the suffering. At one time nearly four thousand sick soldiers, together with some wounded from the main army, were scattered through the dwellings and churches of the town, and a considerable time elapsed before one clean garment could be found for each sufferer. The principal surgeon, Dr. Buzzell, of New Hampshire, died of over exertion and typhoid fever. Of five northern ladies, professional nurses, three were taken sick and two died. Chaplain Eaton died of the fever, and other chaplains were severely sick. To the detailed soldiers the fever and climate proved a greater danger than a battle-field. Through all these scenes of trial and danger Mrs. Hawley exerted herself to the utmost, in the hospitals, and among the poor of the town, avoiding no danger of contagion, not even that of small-pox.

Gradually supplies arrived, better hospitals were provided, the town was cleansed, and by the latter part of June—though the city was still unhealthy—but few eases remained in the hospitals.

NIrs. Hawley accompanied her husband to Richmond about the 1st of July, where he had been appointed chief of staff to General Terry. In October, while returning from the battle-ground of Five Forks, where she had been with an uncle to find the grave of his son (Captain Parmerlee, First Connecticut Cavalry) she received an injury on the head by the upsetting of the ambulance, through which unfortunately she remains still an invalid.

Her name and memory must be dear to hundreds whose sufferings she has shared and relieved, and she will be followed in her retirement by the prayers of grateful hearts.

Although it does not perhaps belong to the purpose of this book, it seems not inappropriate to make mention of the labors of Mrs. Hawley in the education of the freedmen and their families. Both she and her sister, Miss Kate Foote, labored in this sphere long and assiduously.

Governor Hawley was one of the speakers at the Boston anniversaries, in May, 1866. Colonel Higginson, in alluding to his personal services, said he would tell of his better half. When Colonel Hawley went as commander of the Seventh Connecticut to Port Royal, to do his share of conquering and to conquer, he took with him a thousand bayonets on one side, and a Connecticut woman with her school-books on the other (applause). Where he planted the standard of the Union, she planted its institutions; and where he waved the sword, she waved the primer.

ELLEN E. MITCHELL

THIS lady, better known among those to whom she ministered as "Nellie Mitchell," was at the opening of the late war a resident of Montrose, Pennsylvania, where, surrounded by friends, the inmate of a pleasant home, amiable, highly educated and accomplished, her early youth had been spent. Her family was one of that standing often named as "our first families," and her position one every way desirable.

Perhaps her own words extracted from a letter to the writer of this sketch will give the best statement of her views and motives.

"I only did my duty, did what I could, and did it because it would have been a great act of self-denial not to have done it.

"I have ever felt that those who cheerfully gave their loved ones to their country's cause, made greater sacrifices, manifested more heroism, were worthy of more honor by far, than those of us who labored in the hospitals or on the fields. I had not these 'dear ones' to give, so gave heartily what I could, myself to the cause, with sincere gratitude, I trust, to God, for the privilege of thus doing."

Miss Mitchell left her home in Montrose early in May, 1861, and proceeded to New York city, where she went through a course of instruction in surgical nursing at Bellevue Hospital, preparatory to assuming the duties of an army nurse. The unwonted labors, the terrible sights, and close attendance so impaired her health that after six weeks she concluded to go to Woodbury, Connecticut, where she remained with friends while awaiting orders, and in consequence did not join the army as soon as she otherwise would. Being absent from New York, one or two opportunities were lost, and it was not until September that her labors in the military hospitals commenced.

She had intended to give her services to her country, but after witnessing the frequent destitution of comforts among those to whom she ministered, she decided to receive the regular pay of a nurse from the Government, and appropriated it entirely to the benefit of the suffering ones around her.

Luxuries sent by her friends for her own use she applied in the same manner. The four years of her service were filled with self-sacrifice and faithful devoted labor.

Miss Mitchell spent the first three months in Elmore Hotel Hospital, Georgetown, District of Columbia. Around this place cluster some of the pleasantest, as well as the saddest memories of her life. The want of a well-arranged, systematic plan of action in this hospital, made the tasks of the nurses peculiarly arduous and trying. Yet Miss Mitchell records that she never found more delight in her labors, and never received warmer expressions of gratitude from her "boys." On being brought for the first time to a place associated in their minds only with gloom and suffering the joyful surprise of these poor fellows at finding kind hearts and willing hands ready to minister to their wants with almost motherly, or sisterly affection, exceeded words and called forth such manifestations of gratitude as amply regarded those who thus watched over them for all their toils. Often as they saw these kindly women engaged in their busy tasks of mercy, their eyes would glisten as they followed them with the most intense earnestness, and their lips would unconsciously utter remarks like these, so homely and spontaneous as to leave no doubt of their sincerity. "How good! how home-like to see women moving around! "We did not expect anything like this!"

But much as she loved her work and had become attached to her charges, circumstances of a very painful nature soon compelled Miss Mitchell to resign her post in this hospital. Very unworthy hands sometimes assume a ministry of kindness. There were associations here so utterly repugnant to Miss Mitchell, that with a sorrowful heart she at last forced herself to turn her back upon the suffering, in order to be free from them.

But Providence soon opened the way to another engagement. In less than two weeks she entered St. Elizabeth's Hospital. This was situated in Washington across the Eastern branch of the Potomac in an unfinished wing of the Insane Retreat.

Her initiation here was a sad, lonely night-watch, by the bedside of a dying nurse, who about ten o'clock the following day, with none but strangers to witness her dying conflicts, passed from this scene of pain and struggle it was about the last of December that she entered here, and in February she was compelled to relinquish the care of her ward by a severe and dangerous illness which lasted seven weeks. Her greatest joy in returning health consisted in her restoration to the duties in which she had learned to delight.

During this illness Miss Mitchell was constantly attended and nursed by Miss Jessie Home, a young woman of Scottish birth, of whom mention is made in another place, a most excellent and self-sacrificing woman who afterwards lost her life in the cause of her adopted country.

This kindly care and the assiduous and skilful attentions of Dr. Stevens, who was the surgeon of the hospital were, as she gratefully believes, the means of preserving her life.

Miss Mitchell had scarcely recovered from this illness when she was unexpectedly summoned home to stand by the death-bed of a beloved mother. After a month's absence, sadly occupied in this watch of affection, she again returned to Washington, whence she was sent directly to Point Lookout, in Maryland, at the entrance of the Potomac into Chesapeake Bay, where a hospital had recently been established.

She remained about two months at Point Lookout, and was surrounded there with great suffering in all its phases, besides meeting with peculiar trials, which rendered her stay at this hospital the most unsatisfactory part of her "soldier life."

Her next station was at the Ware House Hospital, Georgetown, District of Columbia, where she was employed in the care of the wounded from the second battle of Bull Run. Most of these poor men were suffering from broken limbs, had lain several days uncared for upon the field, and were consequently greatly reduced in strength. They had besides suffered so much from their removal in the jolting ambulances, that many of them expressed a wish that they had been left to die on the field, rather than to have endured such torment. Miss Mitchell found here a sphere decidedly fitted to her peculiar powers, for she was always best pleased to labor in the surgical wards, and would dress and care for wounds with almost the skill, and more than the tenderness of a practiced surgeon.

After some time this hospital being very open, became untenantable, and in February was closed, and Miss Mitchell was transferred to Union Hotel Hospital, where five of the nurses being at that time laid up by illness, her duties became unusually arduous.

Since her former labors here the hospital had been closed, refitted, and reopened under every way improved auspices. The "boys" found themselves in every respect so kindly cared for, and so surrounded by home-like experience that it was with great regret they saw the hospital broken up, in March.

Miss Mitchell's inclination would then, as often before, have led her to the front, but she was forced to obey orders, "soldierlike," and found herself transferred to Knight Hospital, New Haven, as the next scene' of her labors. Here she remained three months acti rely and usefully employed, but at the end of that time she had become so worn out with her long continued and arduous services, as to feel compelled to resign her position as army nurse. She soon after accepted a desirable situation in the Treasury Department, upon the duties of which she entered in July, 1863.

Miss Mitchell has never quite reconciled her conscience to this act, which she fears was too much tinged with selfishness and induced by interested motives. Feeling thus, she again enlisted as army nurse after a few months, resolving never again to abandon the service, while the war continued and strength was given her to labor.

This was in the beginning of May, 1864, and she was immediately sent to Fredericksburg to assist in earing for the wounded from the battle of the Wilderness. The scenes and labors of that terrible period are beyond description. Miss Mitchell was amidst them all, and like an angel of mercy made herself everywhere useful to the crowds of ghastly sufferers from those fields of awful carnage, which marked the onward march of Grant to victory, and the suppression of the rebellion.

When our army left Fredericksburg, most of the wounded were transferred to Washington, Miss Mitchell would again have preferred to go to the front, but obeyed orders, and went instead to Judiciary Square Hospital, Washington, where she found many of her former patients. After she had spent one day there, she would not willingly have left those poor men whom she found so greatly needing a woman's care. For weeks the mortality was fearful, and she found herself surrounded by the dead and dying, but gradually this was lessened, and she became engaged in the more delightful duty of superintending the improvement of convalescents, and watching the return to health of many a brave hero who had perhaps sacrificed limbs, and well-nigh life, in the service of his country. Here she remained, with ever-increasing satisfaction in her labors, until the final closing of the Hospital in June, 1865.

Here also ended her army services, with the occasion for them. She had rendered them joyfully, and she resigned them with regret and sadness at parting with those who had so long been her charge, and whom she would probably see no more forever. But in all joy or sadness, in all her life, she will not cease to remember with delight and gratitude how she was enabled to minister to the suffering, and thus perform a woman's part in the great struggle which redeemed our country from slavery, and made us truly a free people.

Few have done better service, for few have been so peculiarly adapted to their work. In all she gratefully acknowledges the aid and sustaining sympathy of her friends in New Milford, Pa., and elsewhere, to which she was so greatly indebted for the ability to minister with comforts to the sufferers under her charge.

As these lines are written some letters from a soldier who was long under her kind care in Washington, lie upon the writer's table with their appreciative mention of this excellent woman; which coming from one who knew and experienced her goodness, may well be regarded as the highest testimony of it. Here is one brief extract therefrom.

"As for Miss Mitchell herself—she has a cheerful courage, faith and patience which take hold of the duties of this place with a will that grasps the few amenities and pleasures found here, and works them all up into sunshine; and looks over and beyond the fatiguing work, and unavoidable brutalities of the present. Do we not call this happiness? Happiness is not to be pitied—nor is she!"

In another place he speaks of her unswerving, calm devotion—her entire self-abnegation, as beyond all he has seen of the like traits elsewhere. And still there were many devoted women —perhaps many Ellen Mitchells! Again he compares the hospital work of Miss Mitchell and her fellow-laborers with that of the sisters of charity, in whose care he had previously been— the one human, alert, sympathizing—uot loving sin, nor sinful 54 men, but laboring for them, sacrificing for them, pardoning them as Christ does—the other working with machine-like accuracy, but with as little apparent emotion, showing none in fact beyond a prudish shrinking from these sufferers from the outer world, of which they know nothing but have only heard of its wickedness. The contrast is powerful, and shows Miss Mitchell and her friends in fairest colors.

MISS JESSIE HOME

JESSIE HOME was a native of Scotland. Ho ties bound her to this, her adopted land. No relative of hers, resided upon its soil. She was alone—far from kindred and the friends of her early youth. But the country of her adoption had become dear to her. She loved it with the ardor and earnestness which were a part of her nature, and she was willing, nay anxious, to devote herself to its service.

At the commencement of the war Miss Home was engaged in a pleasant and lucrative pursuit, which she abandoned that she might devote herself to the arduous and ill-paid duties of a hospital nurse.

She entered the service early in the war, and became one of the corps of Government nurses attached to the hospitals in the vicinity of Washington. Like others, regularly enlisted, and under orders from Miss Dix, the Government Superintendent of nurses, she was transferred from point to point and from hospital to hospital, as the exigencies of the service required. But she had only to be known to be appreciated, and her companions, her patients, and the surgeons under whom she worked, were equally attached to her, and loud in her praises. She entered into her work with her whole soul—untiring, faithful, of a buoyant temperament, she possessed a peculiar power of winning the love and confidence of all with whom she came in contact.

She was quite dependent upon her own resources, and in giving herself to the cause yielded up a profitable employment and with

it her means of livelihood. Yet she denied herself all luxuries, everything but the merest necessities, that out of the pittance of pay received from the Government, out of the forty cents per day with which her labors were rewarded, she might save something for the wants of the suffering ones under her care.

And be it remembered always, that in this work it was not alone the well-born and the wealthy who made sacrifices, and gave grand gifts. Not from the sacrifice of gauds and frippery did the humble charities of these hired nurses come, but from the yielding up of a thousand needed comforts for themselves, and the forgetfulness of their own wants, in supplying the mightier wants of the suffering. It is impossible to mention them with words of praise beyond their merit.

For about two years Miss Home labored thus untiringly and faithfully, always alert, cheerful, active. During this time she had drawn to herself hosts of attached friends.

At the end of that period she fell a martyr to her exertions in the cause to which she had so nobly devoted herself.

When attacked with illness, she must have felt all the horrors of desolation—for she was without means or home. But Providence did not desert her in this last dread hour of trial. Miss Rebecca Bergen of Brooklyn, N. Y., who had learned her worth by a few months' hospital association, deemed it a privilege to receive the sufferer at her own home, and to watch over the last hours of this noble life as it drew to a close, ministering to her sufferings with all the kindness and affection of a sister, and smoothing her passage to the grave.

Thus, those, who without thought for themselves, devote their lives and energies to the welfare of others, are often unexpectedly cared for in the hour of their own extremity, and find friends springing up to protect them, and to supply their wants in the day of their need. Far from kindred and her native land, this devoted woman thus found friends and kindly care, and the stranger hands that laid her in an alien grave were warm with the emotion of loving hearts.

M. VANCE AND M. A. BLACKMAR

MISS MARY VANCE is a Pennsylvanian. Before the War, she was teaching among the Indians of Kansas or Nebraska, but it becoming unsafe there, she was forced to leave. She came to Miss Dix, who sent her to a Baltimore Hospital, in which she rendered efficient service, as she afterward did in Washington and Alexandria. In September, 1863, she went to the General Hospital, Gettysburg, where she was placed in charge of six wards, and no more indefatigable, faithful and judicious nurse was to be found on those grounds. She labored on continuously, going from point to point, as our army progressed towards Richmond, at Fredericksburg, suffering much from want of strengthening and proper food, but never murmuring, doing a vast amount of work, in such a quiet and unpretending manner, as to attract the attention from the lookers-on. Few, but the recipients of her kindness, knew her worth. At City Point, she was stationed in the Second Corps Hospital, where she, as usual, won the respect and esteem of the Surgeons and all connected with her.

Miss Vance labored the whole term of the War, with but three weeks' furlough, in all that time. A record, that no other woman can give, and but few soldiers.

Miss Blackmar, one of Michigan's worthy daughters, was one of the youngest of the band of Hospital nurses. She, for ten months, labored unceasingly at City Point. More than usually skilful in wound dressing, she rendered efficient service to her

Surgeons, as well as in saving many poor boys much suffering from the rough handling of inexperienced soldier-nurses. A lad was brought to her Wards, with a wound in the temple, which, in the course of time, ate into the artery. This she had feared, and was always especially careful in watching and attending to him. But, in her absence, a hemorrhage took place, the nurse endeavored to staunch the blood, but at last, becoming frightened, sent for a Surgeon. When she came back to the Ward, there lay her boy pale and exhausted, life almost gone. But she persevered in her efforts, and at last had the satisfaction of witnessing his recovery.

At City Point, Miss Vance and Miss Blackmar were tent-mates, and intimate friends—both noted for their untiring devotion to their work, their prudent and Christian deportment. As an instance of the wearying effects of the labors of a Hospital nurse, Mrs. Husband, who was the firm friend, and at City Point, the associate of these two young ladies, relates the following; these two ladies, wearied as usual, retired one very cold night, Miss Blackmar taking a hot brick with her, for her feet. They slept the sound sleep of exhaustion for some time, when Miss Vance struggled into consciousness, with a sensation of smothering, and found that the tent was filled with smoke. After repeatedly calling her companion, she was forced to rise and shake her, telling her that she must be on fire. This at last aroused Bliss Blackmar, who found that the brick had burned through the cloth in which it was wrapped, the straw-bed and two army blankets. By the application of water, the fire was quenched, and after airing the tent, they were soon sleeping as soundly as ever. But, in the morning, Bliss Blackmar, to her consternation, found that her feet and ankles were badly burned, covered with blisters and very painful, though her sleep had been too sound to feel it before.

H. A. DADA AND S. E. HALL

MISS HATTIE A. DADA, and Miss Susan E. Hall, were among the most earnest and persistent workers in a field which presented so many opportunities for labor and sacrifice. Both offered themselves to the Women's Central Association of Relief, New York, immediately on the formation of that useful organization for any service, or in any capacity, where their aid could be made available. Both had formerly been employed by one of the Missionary Societies, in mission labors among the Indians of the Southwest, and were eminently fitted for any sphere of usefulness which the existing condition of our country could present to woman.

They were received by the Association, and requested to join the class of women who, with similar motives and intentions, were attending the series of lectures and surgical instructions which was to prepare them for the duties of nurses in the army hospitals.

On Sunday, July 21st, 1861, a memorable day, the first battle of Bull Run took place. On the following day, the 22d, the disastrous tidings of defeat and rout was received in New York, and the country was thrilled with pain and horror.

At noon, on Monday, the 22d, Miss Dada and Miss Hall received instructions to prepare for their journey to the scene of their future labors, and at six P. M. they took the train for Washington, with orders to report to Miss Dix. Tuesday morning found them amidst all the terrible excitement which reigned in that city. The only question Miss Dix asked, was, "Are you ready to work?" and added, "You are needed in Alexandria."

And toward Alexandria they were shortly proceeding. There were apprehensions that the enemy might pursue our retreating troops, of whom they met many as they crossed the Long Bridge, and passed the fortifications all filled with soldiers watching for the coming foe who might then so easily have invaded the Federal City.

In some cabins by the road-side they first saw some wounded men, to whom they paused to administer words of cheer, and a "cup of cold water." They were in great apprehension that the road might not be safe, and a trip to Richmond, in the capacity of prisoners was by no means to be desired.

At last they reached Alexandria, and in a dark stone building on Washington Street, formerly a seminary, found their hospital. They were denied admittance by the sentinel, but the surgeon in charge was called, and welcomed them to their new duties.

There they lay, the wounded, some on beds, many on mattresses spread upon the floor, covered with the blood from their wounds, and the dust of that burning summer battle-field, many of them still in their uniforms. The retreat was so unexpected, the wounded so numerous, and the helpers so few, that all were at once extremely busy in bringing order and comfort to that scene of suffering.

Their labors here were exceedingly arduous. No soldiers were detailed as attendants for the first few weeks, and even the most menial duties fell upon these ladies. Sometimes a contraband was assigned them as assistant, but he soon tired of steady employment and left. They had little sleep and food that was neither tempting nor sufficient. So busy were they that two weeks elapsed before Miss Lada, whose letters furnish most of the material for this sketch, found time to write home, and inform her anxious friends "where she was."

A busy month passed thus, and then the numbers in the hospital began to decrease, many of the convalescent being sent North, or having furloughs, till only the worst cases remained.

As the winter approached typhus fever began to prevail among the troops, and many distressing cases, some of which despite all their efforts proved mortal, came under the care of these ladies.

About the beginning of April, 1862, soon after the battle of Winchester, and the defeat of Stonewall Jackson by General Shields, Miss Dada and Miss Hall were ordered thither to care for the wounded. Here they were transferred from one hospital to another, without time to become more than vaguely interested in the individual welfare of their patients. At length at the third, the Court-House Hospital, they were permitted to remain for several weeks. Here many interesting cases were found, and they became much attached to some of the sufferers under their care, and found great pleasure in their duties.

On the 22d of May they were ordered to Strasburg, and proceeded thither to the care of several hundred sick, entirely unsuspicious of personal danger, not dreaming that it could be met with beside the headquarters of General Banks. But on the following day troops were observed leaving the town on the FrontRoyal road, and the same night the memorable retreat was ordered.

It was indeed a sad sight which met their eyes in the gray of early dawn. Ambulances and army wagons filled the streets. Soldiers from the hospitals, scarcely able to walk, crawled slowly and painfully along, while the sick were crowded into the overfilled ambulances.

Pressing forward they arrived at Winchester at noon, but the ambulances did not arrive till many hours later, with their dismal freight. The fright and suffering had overpowered many, and many died as they were carried into the hospitals. A little later the wounded began to come in, and the faithful, hard-worked surgeons and nurses had their hands full. The retreating Union forces came pouring through the town, the rebels in close pursuit.

The shouts of the combatants, and the continued firing, created great confusion. Fear was in every heart, pallor on every cheek, anxiety in every eye, for they knew not what would be their fate, but had heard that the wounded had been bayonetted at Front Royal the previous day. Many dying men, in their fright and delirium, leaped from their beds, and when laid down soon ceased to breathe.

Soon the rebels had possession of the town, and the ladies found themselves prisoners with a rebel guard placed about their hospital.

Their supplies were now quite reduced, and it was not until personal application had been made by the nurses to the rebel authorities, that suitable food was furnished.

When the army left Winchester, enough men were ordered to remain to guard the hospitals, and an order was read to all the inmates, that any of them seen in the streets would be shot.

Miss Dada and her friend remained at this place until the months of June and July were passed. In August they were assigned to Armory Square Hospital, Washington.

Previous to the second battle of Bull Run, all the convalescent men were sent further North, and empty beds were in readiness for the wounded, who on the evening after the battle were brought in, in great numbers, covered with the dust and gore of the field of conflict. Here the ministering care of these ladies was most needed. They hastened with basins and sponges, cold water and clean clothes, and soon the sufferers felt the benefits of cleanliness, and were laid, as comfortably as their wounds would admit, in those long rows of white beds that awaited them. All were cheerful, and few regretted the sacrifices they had made. But in a few days many of these heroes succumbed before the mighty Conqueror. Their earthly homes they were never to see, but, one by one, they passed silently to their last home of silence and peace, where the war of battle and the pain of wounds never disturb. One poor fellow, a Michigan soldier, wounded in the throat, could take no nourishment, nor scarcely breathe. His sufferings were intense, and his restlessness kept him constantly in motion as long as the strength for a movement remained. But at last, he silently turned his face to the wall, and so died. Another, a victim of lockjaw, only yielded to the influence of chloroform. Another, whom the surgeons could only reach the second day, had his arm amputated, but too late. Even while he believed himself on the road to recovery, bad symptoms had intervened; and while with grateful voice he was planning how he would assist Miss Dada as soon as he was well enough, in the care of other patients, the hand of death was laid upon him, and he soon passed away.

Such are a few of the heart-rending scenes and incidents through which these devoted ladies passed.

The month of November found Miss Dada at Harper's Ferry. Miss Hall had been at Antietam, but the friends had decided to be no longer separated.

They found that the Medical Director of the Twelfth Army Corps was just opening a hospital there, and the next day the sick and wounded from the regimental hospitals were brought in. They had suffered for lack of care, but though the new hospital was very scantily furnished, they found that cause of trouble removed. Many of them had long been ill, and want of cleanliness and vermin had helped to reduce them to extreme emaciation. Their filthy clothes were replaced by clean ones, and burned or thrown into the river, their heads shaven, and their revolting appearance removed. But many a youth whom sickness and suffering had given the appearance of old age, succumbed to disease and suffering, and joined the long procession to the tomb.

These were sad days, the men were dying rapidly. One day a middle-aged woman came in inquiring for her son. Miss Dada took from her pocket a slip of paper containing the name of one who had died a day or two previously—it was the name of the son of this mother. She sought the surgeon, and together they undertook the painful task of conveying to the mother the tidings that her visit was in vain. Poor mother! How many, like her, returned desolate to broken homes, from such a quest!

May and June, 1863, Miss Dada and Miss Hall spent at Acquia Creek, in care of the wounded from the battle of Chancellorsville, and the 8th of July found them at Gettysburg—Miss Dada at the hospital of the Twelfth Army Corps, at a little distance from the town, and Miss Hall at that of the First Army Corps, which was within the town. The hospital of the Twelfth Army Corps was at a farm-house. The house and barns were filled with wounded, and tents were all around, crowded with sufferers, among whom were many wounded rebel prisoners, who were almost overwhelmed with astonishment and gratitude to find that northern ladies would extend to them the same care as to the soldiers of their own army.

The story of Gettysburg, and the tragical days that followed, has been too often told to need repetition. The history of the devotion of Northern women to their country's defenders, and of their sacrifices and labors was illustrated in brightest characters there. Miss Hall and Miss Dada remained there as long as their services could be made available.

In December, 1863, they were ordered to Murfreesboro', Tennessee, once a flourishing town, but showing everywhere the devastations of war. Two Seminaries, and a College, large blocks of stores, and a hotel, had been taken for hospitals, and were now filled with sick and wounded men. A year had passed since the awful battle of Stone River,—the field of which, now a wide waste lay near the town—but the hospitals had never been empty.

When they arrived, they reported to the medical director, who "did not care whether they stayed or not," but, "if they remained wished them to attend exclusively to the preparation of the Special Diet." They received only discouraging words from all they met. They found shelter for the night at the house of a rebel woman, and were next day assigned—Miss Hall to No. I Hospital, Miss Dada to No. 3.

When they reported, the surgeon of No. I Hospital, for their encouragement, informed them that the chaplain thought they had better not remain. Miss Dada also was coldly received, and it was evident that the Surgeons and chaplains were very comfortable, and desired no outside interference. They believed, however, that there was a work for them to do, and decided to remain.

Miss Dada found in the wards more than one familiar face from the Twelfth Army Corps, and the glad enthusiasm of her welcome by the patients, contrasted with the chilling reception of the officers.

Most of these men had been wounded at Lookout Mountain, a few days before, but many others had been suffering ever since the bloody battle of Chickamauga.

Miss Hall was able to commence her work at once, but Miss Dada was often exhorted to patience, while waiting three long weeks for a stove, before she could do more than, by the favor of the head cook of the full diet kitchen, occasionally prepare at his stove, some small dishes for the worst cases.

Here the winter wore away. Many a sad tale of the desolations of war was poured into their ears, by the suffering Union women who had lost their husbands, fathers, sons, in the wild warfare of the country in which they lived. And many a scene of sorrow and suffering they witnessed.

In January, they had a pleasant call from Dr. M, one of the friends they had known at Gettysburg. This gentleman, in conversation with the medical director, told him he knew two of the ladies there. The reply illustrates the peculiar position in which they were placed. "Ladies!" he answered with a sneer, "We have no ladies here! A hospital is no place for a lady. We have some women here, who are cooks!"

But they remembered that one has said—"The lowest post of service is the highest place of honor' and that Christ had humiliated himself to wash the feet of his disciples.

In the latter part of the ensuing May, they went to Chattanooga. They were most kindly received by the surgeons, and found much to be done. Car-loads of wounded were daily coming from the front, all who could bear removal were sent further north, and only the worst cases retained at Chattanooga. They were all in good spirits, however, and rejoicing at Sherman's successful advance—even those upon whom death had set his dark seal.

Miss Dada often rejoiced, while here, in the kindness of her friends at home, which enabled her to procure for the sick those small, but at that place, costly luxuries which their condition demanded.

As the season advanced to glowing summer, the mortality became dreadful. In her hospital alone, not a large one, and containing but seven hundred beds, there were two hundred and sixty-one deaths in the month of June, and there were from five to twenty daily. These were costly sacrifices, often of the best, noblest, most promising,—for Miss Dada records—"Daily I see devoted Christian youths dying on the altar of our country."

With the beginning of November came busy times, as the cars daily came laden with their freight of suffering from Atlanta. On the 26th, Miss Dada records, "One year to-day since Hooker's men fought above the clouds on Lookout. To-day as I look upon the grand old mountain the sun shines brightly on the graves of those who fell there, and all is quiet."

Again, after the gloomy winter had passed, she writes, in March, 1865, "Many cases of measles are being brought in, mostly new soldiers, many conscripts, and so down-spirited if they get sick. It was a strange expression a poor fellow made the other day, 'You are the God-blessedest woman I ever saw.' He only lived a few days after being brought to the hospital."

Their work of mercy was now well-nigh over, as the necessity for it seemed nearly ended. Patients were in May being mustered out of the service, and the hospitals thinning. Miss Dada and Miss Hall thought they could be spared, and started eastward. But when in Illinois, word reached them that all the ladies but one had left, and help was needed, and Miss Dada returned to Chattanooga. Here she was soon busy, for, though the war was over, there were still many sick, and death often claimed a victim.

Miss Dada remained till the middle of September, engaged in her duties, when, having given more than four years to the service of her country, she at last took her leave of hospital-life, and returned to home and its peaceful pleasures.

Before leaving she visited the historical places of the vicinity —saw a storm rise over Mission Ridge, and heard the thunders of heaven's artillery where once a hundred guns belched forth their fires and swept our brave boys to destruction. She climbed Lookout, amidst its vail of clouds, and visited "Picket Rock," where is the spring at which our troops obtained water the night after the battle, and the "Point" where, in the early morn, the Stars and Stripes proclaimed to the watching hosts below, that they were victors.

MRS. SARAH P. EDSON

MRS. EDSON is a native of Fleming, Cayuga County, New York, where her earlier youth was passed. At ten years of age she removed with her parents to Ohio, but after a few years again returned to her native place. Her father died while she was yet young, and her childhood and youth were clouded by many sorrows.

Gifted with a warm imagination, and great sensitiveness of feeling, at an early age she learned to express her thoughts in written words. Her childhood was not a happy one, and she thus found relief for a thousand woes. At length some of her writings found their way into print.

She spent several years as a teacher, and was married and removed to Pontiac, Michigan, in 1845. During her married life she resided in several States, but principally in Maysville, Kentucky.

Here she became well known as a writer, but her productions, both in prose and poetry, were usually written under various nommes de plume, and met very general acceptance.

She at various times edited journals devoted to temperance and general literature in the Western States, and became known as possessing a keenly observing and philosophic mind. This experience, perhaps, prepared and eminently fitted her for the service into which she entered at the breaking out of the war, and enabled her to comprehend and provide for the necessities and emergencies of "the situation."

Mrs. Edson arrived in "Washington November 1st, 1861, and commenced service as nurse in Columbia College Hospital. She remained there serving with great acceptance until early in March when the army was about to move and a battle was in anticipation, when by arrangement with the Division Surgeon, Dr. Palmer, she joined Sumner's Division, at Camp California, Virginia, where she was to remain and follow to render her services in case the anticipation was verified. The enemy, however, had stolen away, and "Quaker" guns being the only armament encountered, her services were not needed.

She soon after received an appointment from Surgeon-General Finley to proceed to Winchester, Virginia, to assist in the care of the wounded from General Banks' army. She found the hospital there in a most deplorable condition. Gangrene was in all the wards, the filth and foulness of the atmosphere were fearful. Men were being swept off by scores, and all things were in such a state as must ever result from inexperience, and perhaps incompetence, on the part of those in charge. Appliances and stores were scanty, and many of the surgeons and persons in charge, though doing the least that was possible, were totally unfit for their posts through want of experience and training.

The Union Hotel Hospital was placed in charge of Mrs. Edson, and the nurses who accompanied her were assigned to duty there. It was to be thoroughly cleansed and rendered as wholesome as possible.

The gratitude of the men for their changed condition, in a few days amply attested the value of the services of herself and associates, and demonstrated the fact that women have an important place in a war like ours.

Mrs. Edson next proceeded to join the army before York town, about the 1st of May, 1862, and was attached to the Hospital of General Sumner's corps. She arrived the day following the battle of Williamsburg, and learning that her son was among the wounded left in a hospital several miles from Yorktown, she at once started on foot to find him. After a walk of twelve miles she discovered him apparently in a dying state, he and his comrades imperatively demanding care. Here she spent four sleepless days and nights of terrible anxiety, literally flying from but to but of the rebel-built hospitals, to care for other sick and wounded men, whenever she could leave her son.

She remained thus till imperative orders were received to break up this hospital and go to York town. The men were laid in army wagons and transported over the rough roads from nine in the morning till six in the evening. Arriving exhausted by their terrible sufferings, they found no provision made for their reception. That was a dreadful day, and to an inexperienced eye and a sympathetic heart the suffering seemed frightful!

The 21st of May, Mrs. Edson went to Fortress Monroe, to care for her son and others, remaining a week. From thence she proceeded to White House and the "front." Arriving here the enemy were expected, and it was forbidden to land. At daylight the "only woman on board" was anxiously inquiring if there was any suffering to relieve. Learning that some wounded had just been brought in, she left the boat notwithstanding the prohibition, and found over three hundred bleeding and starved heroes lying upon the ground. The Sanitary Commission boats had gone, and no supplies were left but coffee and a little rice. As she stepped ashore, a soldier with a shattered arm came up to her, almost timidly, and with white trembling lips asked her if she could give them something to eat—they had lost everything three days before, and had been without food since. What an appeal to the sympathy of a warm heart!

It was feared that no food could be obtained, but after great search a barrel of cans of beef was found.. Some camp kettles were gathered up, and a fire kindled. In the shortest possible time beef soup and coffee were passing round among these delighted men. Their gratitude was beyond words. At four o'clock, that afternoon, the last man was put on board the ship which was to convey them within reach of supplies and care.

Mrs. Edson was left alone. One steamer only of the quartermaster's department remained. The quartermaster had no authority to admit her on board. But in view of the momently expected arrival of the enemy he told her to go on board and remain, promising not to interfere with her until she reached Harrison's Landing. And this was all that could be gained by her who was so busily working for the soldier—this the alternative of being left to the tender mercy of the enemy.

She remained at Harrison's Landing until the 12th of August, and passed through all the terrible and trying scenes that attended the arrival of the defeated, demoralized, and depressed troops of McClellan's army. These baffle description. Enough, that hands and heart were full—full of work, and full of sympathy, with so much frightful suffering all around her! She was here greatly aided and sustained by the presence and help of that excellent nan, Chaplain Arthur B. Fuller, who passed away to his reward long ere the close of the struggle, into which he had entered with so true an appreciation and devotion. Again, here as everywhere, gratitude for kindness, and cheerfulness in suffering marked the conduct of the poor men under her care.

When the army left she repaired again to Fortress Monroe, and was on duty there at Hygeia Hospital during the transit of the army.

She returned to Alexandria the 30th of August, and almost immediately heard rumors of the fighting going on at the front. She applied for permission to proceed to the field, but was informed that the army was retreating. The next tidings was of the second battle of Bull Run, and the other disastrous conflicts of Pope's campaign. As she could not go to the front to give aid and comfort to that small but heroic army in its retreat she did what she could for the relief of any sufferers who came under her notice, until the news of the conflict at A ntietain was received, with rumors of its dreadful slaughter. Her heart was fired with anxiety to proceed thither, but permission was again denied her, the surgeon-general replying that she was evidently worn out and must rest for a time. He was right, for on the ensuing day she was seized with a severe illness which prevented any further exertion for many weeks.

During the slow hours of convalescence from this illness she revolved a plan for systematizing the female branch of the relief service. Her idea was to provide a home for volunteer nurses, where they could be patiently educated and instructed in the necessities of the work they were to assume, and where they could retire for rest when needed, or in the brief intervals of their labors.

Her first labor on recovery was to proceed to Warrenton with supplies, but she found the army moving and the sick already on board the cars. She did what was possible for them under the circumstances. The trains moved off and she was left to wait for one that was to convey her back to Alexandria. This, however, was cut off by the rebels, and she found herself with no resource but to proceed with the army to Acquia Creek. She records that she reached Acquia, after several days, and a new and interesting experience, which was kindness and courtesy from all with whom she came in contact.

Immediately after her return to Washington, Mrs. Edson attempted to systematize her plan for a home and training school for nurses. A society was formed, and Mrs. Caleb B. Smith at first (but soon after in consequence of her resignation) Mrs. B. F. Wade, was appointed President, and Mrs. Edson, Secretary.

Many meetings were held. The attention of commanding and medical officers was drawn to the plan. Almost unanimously they expressed approval of it.

Mrs. Edson was the soul of the work, hers was the guiding brain, the active hand, and as is usual in similar cases most of the labor fell upon her. She visited the army at Fredericksburg, and carefully examined the hospitals to ascertain their needs in this respect. This with other journeys of the same kind occupied a considerable portion of the winter.

State Relief Societies had been consulted and approved the plan. Mrs. Edson visited the Sanitary Commission and laid the plan before them, but while they admitted the necessity of a home and place of rest for nurses, which they soon after established, they regarded a training school for them unnecessary, believing that those who were adapted to their work would best acquire the needed skill in it in the hospital itself, and that their imperative need of attendants in the hospitals and in the departments of special and field relief, did not admit of the delay required to educate nurses for the service.

The surgeon-general, though at first favorably impressed with the idea, on more mature consideration discouraged it, and withheld his approval before the Senate Committee, who had a bill before them for the establishment of such an institution. Thus thwarted in the prosecution of the plan on which she had set her heart, Mrs. Edson did not give up in despair, nor did she suffer her sympathy and zeal in its prosecution to prevent her from engaging in what she rightly regarded as the paramount work of every loyal woman who could enter upon it, the care of the sick and wounded after the great battles. The fearfully disastrous battle of Fredericksburg in December, 1862, called her to the front, and she was for several weeks at Falmouth caring tenderly for the wounded heroes there. This good work accomplished she returned to Washington, and thence visited New York city, and made earnest endeavors to enlist the aid of the wealthy and patriotic in this movement. She was familiar with Masonic literature and with the spirit of Masonry. Her husband had been an advanced member of the Order, and she had herself taken all the "Adoptive Degrees." These reasons induced her to seek the aid of the Order, and she was pleased to find that she met with much encouragement. The "Army Nurses' Association" was formed in New York, and commenced work under the auspices of the Masons. In the spring of 1864, when Grant's campaign commenced with the terrible battles of the Wilderness, Mrs. Edson hastened to the "front." Almost immediately the surgeons requested her to send for ten of the nurses then receiving instruction as part of her class at Clinton Hall, New York.

She did so. They were received, transportation found, and rations and pay granted. And they were found to be valuable workers, Mrs. Edson receiving from the Surgeons in charge, the highest testimonials of their usefulness. She had at first mentioned it to the Surgeons as an experiment, and said that funds and nurses would not be wanting if it proved a success. The day on which the order for the evacuation of Fredericksburg was issued, she was told that her "experiment was more than a success—it was a triumph." And this by one of the highest officials of the Medical department.

Eighty more nurses were at once ordered.

The interest taken by the Masons in this movement, led to the formation of the "Masonic Mission," with a strong "Advisory Board," composed of leading and wealthy Masons.

Airs. Edson, with unquestioning confidence in the integrity of Masons, and in the honor of the gentlemen who had given the movement the great strength of their names, continued ardently carrying out her plan. More nurses were sent out, and all received the promise of support by the "Mission." Much good— how much none may say, was performed by these women. They suffered and labored, and sacrificed much. They gave their best efforts and cares. Many of them were poor women, unable to give their time and labor without remuneration. But, alas! the purposes and promises of the Masonic Mission, were never fulfilled. Many of the women received no remuneration, and great suffering and dissatisfaction was the result. The good to the suffering of the army was perhaps the same.

Amidst all her sorrows and disappointments, Mrs. Edson continued her labors till the end of the war. Nothing could keep her from the fulfilment of what she regarded as an imperative duty, and nobly she achieved her purpose, so far as her individual efforts were concerned.

A lady, herself ardently engaged in the work of relief, and supply for the soldiers, visited the Army of the Potomac in company with Mrs. Edson, in the winter of 1865, not long before the close of the war. She describes the reception of Mrs. Edson, among these brave men to whom she had ministered during the terrific campaign of the preceding summer, as a complete ovation. The enthusiasm was overwhelming to the quiet woman who had come among them, not looking nor hoping for more than the privilege of a pleasant greeting from those endeared to her by the very self-sacrificing efforts by which she had brought them relief, and perhaps been the means of saving their lives.

Irrepressible shouts, cheers, tears and thanks saluted her on every side, and she passed on humbled rather than elated by the excess of this enthusiastic gratitude.

MISS MARIA M. C. HALL

ALTHOUGH the Federal City, Washington, was at the outbreak of the war more intensely Southern in sentiment than many of the

Southern cities, at least so far as its native, or long resident inhabitants could make it so, yet there were even in that Sardis, a few choice spirits, reared under the shadow of the Capitol, whose patriotism was as lofty, earnest and enduring as that of any of the citizens of any Northern or Western state.

Among these, none have given better evidence of their intense love of their country and its institutions, than Miss Hall. Born and reared in the Capital, highly educated, and of pleasing manners and address, she was well fitted to grace any circle, and to shine amid the gayeties of that fashionable and frivolous city. But the religion of the compassionate and merciful Jesus had made a deep lodgment in her heart, and in imitation of his example, she was ready to forsake the halls of gayety and fashion, if she might but minister to the sick, the suffering and the sorrowing. Surrounded by Secessionists, her father too far advanced in years to bear arms for the country he loved, with no brother old enough to be enrolled among the nation's defenders, her patriotism was as fervid as that of any soldier of the Republic, and she resolved to consecrate herself to the service of the nation, by ministrations to the sick and wounded. Her first opportunity of entering upon this duty was by the reception into her father's house of one of the sick soldiers before the first battle of Bull Run, who by her kindly care was restored to health. 'When the Indiana Hospital was established in the Patent Office building on the 1st of August, 1861, Miss Hall sought a position there as nurse; but Miss Dix had already issued her circular announcing that no nurses under thirty-five years of age would be accepted; and in vain might she plead her willingness and ability to undergo hardships and the uncomfortable duties pertaining to the nurse's position. She therefore applied to the kind-hearted but eccentric Mrs. Almira Pales, whose hearty and positive ways had given her the entree of the Government hospitals from the first, but she too discouraged her from the effort, assuring her, in her blunt way, that there was no poetry in this sort of thing, that the men were very dirty, hungry and rough, and that they would not appreciate refinement of manner, or be grateful for the attention bestowed on them by a delicate and educated lady. Finding that these representations failed to divert Miss Hall, and her sister who accompanied her, from their purpose, Mrs. Fales threw open the door of one of the wards, saying as she did so, "Well, girls, here they are, with everything to be done for them. You will find work enough."

There was, indeed, work enough. The men were very dirty, the "sacred soil" of Virginia clinging to their clothing and persons in plenty. Their hair was matted and tangled, and often, not free from vermin, and they were as Mrs. Fales had said, a rough set. But those apparently fragile and delicate girls had great energy and resolution, and the subject of our sketch was not disposed to undertake an enterprise and then abandon it. She had trials of other kinds, to bear. The surgeons afforded her few or no facilities for her work; and evidently expected that her whim of nursing would soon be given over. Then came the general order for the removal of volunteer nurses from the hospitals; this she evaded by enrolling herself as nurse, and drawing army pay, which she distributed to the men. For nearly a year she remained in this position, without command, with much hard work to do, and no recognition of it from any official source; but though the situation was not in any respect agreeable, there was a consciousness of usefulness, of service of the Master in it to sustain her; and while under her gentle ministrations cleanliness took the place of filth, order of disorder, and profanity was banished, because "the lady did not like it," it was also her privilege occasionally to lead the wanderer from God back to the Saviour he had deserted, and to point the sinner to the "Lamb of God that taketh away the sins of the world." In the summer of 1862, Miss Hall joined the Hospital Transport service, first on the Daniel Webster, Iso. 2, a steamer which had been used for the transportation of troops from Washington. After the sick and wounded of this transport had been disposed of, Miss Hall was transferred to the Daniel Webster, the original hospital transport of the Sanitary Commission, where she labored faithfully for some weeks after the change of base to Harrison's Landing, when she was associated with Mrs. Almira Fales in caring for the suffering wounded on shore. They found the poor fellows in a terrible plight, in rotten and leaky tents, and lying on the damp soil, sodden with the heavy rains, and poisonous from the malarial exhalations, in need of clothing, food, medicine, and comfort; and though but scantily supplied with the needful stores, these ladies spared no labor or exertion to improve their condition, and they were successful to a greater extent than would have seemed possible. When the army returned to Alexandria, Miss Hall visited her home for a short interval of rest; but the great battle of Antietam called her again to her chosen work; she went to the battle-field, intending to join Mrs. Harris, of the Ladies' Aid Society of Philadelphia, who was already at work there, and had telegraphed for her; but being unable to find her at first, she entered a hospital of wounded Rebel prisoners, and ministered to them until Mrs. Harris having ascertained her situation, sent for her to come to Smoketown General Hospital, where at that time the wounded of French's Division were gathered, and which ultimately received the wounded of the different corps who were unable to endure the fatigue of transportation to Washington, Baltimore or Philadelphia. Dr. Vanderldeft, an accomplished physician and a man of rare tenderness, amiability and goodness, was at this time the surgeon of the Smoketown Hospital, and appreciating Miss Hall's skill and adaptation to her work, he welcomed her cordially, and did everything in his power to render her position pleasant. Mrs. Harris was soon called to other scenes, and after Fredericksburg, went to Falmouth and remained there several months, but Miss Hall, and Mrs. Husband who was now associated with her remained at Smoketown; and when Mrs. Husband left, Miss Hall still continued till May, 1863, when the hospital was broken up, and the remaining inmates sent to other points.

The following letter addressed to Miss Hall, by one of the wounded soldiers under her care at the Smoketown Hospital, a Frenchman who, while a great sufferer, kept the whole tent full of wounded men cheerful and bright with his own cheerfulness, singing the Marseillaise and other patriotic songs, is but one example of thousands, of the regard felt for her, by the soldiers whose sufferings she had relieved by her gentle and kindly ministrations.

"MANCHESTER, MASS. June 28th, 1866.

"Miss M. M. C. Hall:—There are kind deeds received which a man cannot ever forget, more especially when they are done by one who does not expect any rewards for them, but the satisfaction of having helped humanity.

"But as one who first unfortunate, and next fortunate enough to come under your kind cares, I come rather late perhaps to pay you a tribute of gratitude which should have been done ere this. I say pay,—I do not mean that with few lines in a broken English, I expect to reward you for your good care of me while I was lying at Smoketown—no, words or gold could not repay you for your sufferings, privations, the painful hard sights which the angels of the battle-field are willing to face,—no, God alone can reward yon. Yet, please accept, Miss, the assurance of my profound respect, and my everlasting gratitude. May the God of Justice, Freedom and love, ever protect you, and reward you for your conduct on this earth is the wish of

"Your obedient and respectful servant,

"Junius F. RABARDY."

The Frenchman who sometimes sang the Marseillaise—formerly of the 12th Massachusetts Volunteers.

One feature of this Hospital-life both at Smoketown, and the other Hospitals with which Miss Hall was connected, a feature to which many of those under her care revert with great pleasure, was the evening or family prayers. Those of the convalescent soldiers who cared to do so were accustomed to assemble every evening at her tent, and engage in social worship, the chaplain usually being present and taking the lead of the meeting, and in the event of his absence, one of the soldiers being the leader. This evening hour was looked for with eagerness, and to sonm, we might say, to many, it was the beginning of new hopes and a new life. Many, after rejoining their regiments, wrote back to their friends, "We think of you all at the sweet hour of prayer, and know that you will remember us when you gather in the little tent." The life in the Hospital, was by this and other means, rendered the vestibule of a new and holy life, a life of faith and Christian endeavor to many, and this young Christian woman was enabled to exercise an influence for good which shall endure through the untold ages of eternity.

After a short period of rest, Miss Hall again reported for duty at the Naval Academy Hospital, Annapolis, whither considerable numbers of the wounded from Gettysburg were brought, and where her old friend Dr. Vanderkieft was the Surgeon-in-charge. After a time, the exchanged prisoners from Belle Isle and Libby Prison, and subsequently those from Andersonville, Florence, Salisbury and Wilmington, began to come into this Hospital, and it was Miss Hall's painful privilege to be permitted to minister to these poor victims of Hebei cruelty and hate, who amid the horrors of the charnel houses, had not only lost their health, but almost their semblance to humanity, and reduced by starvation and suffering to a condition of fatuity, often could not remember their own names. In these scenes of horror, with the patience and tenderness born only of Christianity, she ministered to these poor helpless men, striving to bring them back to life, and health, and reason, comforting them in their sufferings, pointing the dying to a suffering Saviour, and corresponding with their friends as circumstances required.

It was at Dr. Vanderkieft's request, that she came to this Hospital, and at first she was placed in charge of Section Five, consisting of the Hospital tents outside of the main building. Mrs. Adaline Tyler, (Sister Tyler), was at this time lady Superintendent of the entire Hospital, and administered her duties with great skill and ability. When, in the spring of 1864, as we have elsewhere recorded, the impaired health of Mrs. Tyler rendered her further stay in the Hospital impossible. Miss Hall, though young, was deemed by Dr. Vanderkieft, most eminently qualified to succeed her in the general superiutendency of this great Hospital, and she remained in charge of it till it was closed in the summer of 1865. Here she had at times, more than four thousand of these poor sufferers under her care, and although she had from ten to twenty assistants, each in charge of a section, yet her own labors were extremely arduous, and her care and responsibility such as few could have sustained. The danger, as well as the care, was very much increased by the prevalence of typhus fever, in a very malignant form in the Hospital, brought there by some of the poor victims of rebel barbarity from Andersonville. Three of her most valued assistants contracted this fearful disease from the patients whom they had so carefully watched over and died, martyrs to their philanthropy and patriotism.

During her residence at this Hospital, Miss Hall often contributed to "THE CRUTCH," a soldier's weekly paper, edited by Miss Titcomb, one of the assistant superintendents, to which the other ladies, the officers and some of the patients were also contributors. This paper created much interest in the hospital.

Our record of the work of this active and devoted Christian woman is but brief, for though there were almost numberless instances of suffering, of heroism and triumph passing constantly under her eye, yet the work of one day was so much like that of every other, that it afforded little of incident in her own labors to require a longer narrative. Painful as many of her experiences were, yet she found as did many others who engaged in it that it was a blessed and delightful work, and in the retrospect, more than a year after its close, she littered these words in regard to it, words to which the hearts of many other patriotic women will respond, "I mark my Hospital days as my happiest ones, and thank God for the way in which He led me into the good work, and for the strength which kept me through it all."

THE HOSPITAL CORPS AT ANNAPOLIS

THOUGH the Naval Academy buildings at Annapolis had been used for hospital purposes, from almost the first months of the war, they did not acquire celebrity, or accommodate a very large number of patients until August, 1863, when Surgeon Vanderkieft took charge of it, and it received great numbers of the wounded men from Gettysburg. As the number of these was reduced by deaths, convalescence and discharge from the army, their places were more than supplied by the returning prisoners, paroled or discharged, from Libby, Belle Isle, Andersonville, Millen, Salisbury, Florence and Wilmington. These poor fellows under the horrible cruelties, systematically practiced by the rebel authorities, with the avowed intention of weakening the Union forces, had been starved, frozen, maimed and tortured until they had almost lost the semblance of humanity, and one of the noble women who cared for them so tenderly, states that she often found herself involuntarily placing her hand upon her cheek to ascertain whether their flesh was like hers, human and vitalized. The sunken hollow cheeks, the parchment skiu drawn so tightly over the bones, the great, cavernous, lackluster eyes, the half idiotic stare, the dreamy condition, the loss of memory even of their own names, and the wonder with which they regarded the most ordinary events, so strange to them after their long and fearful experience, all made them seem more like beings from souie other world, than inhabitants of this. Many of them never recovered fully their memory or reason; the iron had entered the soul. Others lingered long on the confines of two worlds, now rallying a little and then falling back, till finally the flickering life went out suddenly; a few of the hardiest and toughest survived, and recovered partial though seldom or never complete health. During a part of the first year of Dr. Vanderkieft's administration, Mrs. Adaline Tyler ("Sister Tyler") was Lady Superintendent of the hospital, and the sketch elsewhere given of her life shows how earnestly and ably she labored to promote the interest of its inmates. During most of this time Miss Maria M. C. Hall had charge of section five, consisting of the hospital tents which occupied a part of the academical campus. Miss Helen M. Noye, a young lady from Buffalo, a very faithful, enthusiastic and cheerful worker, was her assistant, and remained for nearly a year in the hospital.

When in the spring of 1864, Miss Hall was appointed Mrs. Tyler's successor as Lady Superintendent of the hospital, its numerous large wards required several assistant superintendents who should direct the preparation of the special diet, and the other delicacies so desirable for the sick, attend to the condition of the men, ascertain their circumstances and history, correspond with their friends, and endeavor so far as possible to cheer, comfort and encourage their patients.

When the number of patients was largest twenty of these assistants were required, and the illness of some, or their change to other fields, rendered the list a varying one, over thirty different ladies being connected with the hospital during the two years from July, 1863, to July, 1865.

A considerable number of these ladies had accompanied Mrs. Tyler to Annapolis, having previously been her assistants in the general hospital at Chester, Pennsylvania. Among these were nine from Maine, viz., Miss Louise Titcomb, Miss Susan Newhall, Miss Rebecca R. Usher, Miss Almira Quimby, Miss Emily W. Dana, Miss Adeline Walker, Miss Mary E. Dupee, Miss Mary Pierson, and Mrs. Eunice D. Merrill, all -women of excellent abilities and culture, and admirably adapted to their work. One of this band of sisters, Miss Adeline Walker, died on the 28th of April, 1865, of malignant typhus, contracted in the discharge of her duties in the hospital.

Of her Miss Hall wrote in the Crutch, "She slept at sunset, sinking into the stillness of death as peacefully as a melted day into the darkness of the night. For two years and a half—longer than almost any other here—she had pursued her labors in this hospital, and with her ready sympathy with the suffering or wronged, had ministered to many needy ones the balm of comfort and healing. Her quick wit and keen repartee has served to brighten up many an hour otherwise dull and unhomelike in our little circle of workers, gathered in our quarters off duty.

"So long an inmate of this hospital its every part was familiar to her; its trees and flowers she loved; in all its beauties she rejoiced. We could almost fancy a hush in nature's music, as we walked behind her coffin, under the beautiful trees in the bright May sunshine.

"It was a touching thing to see the soldier-boys carrying the coffin of her who had been to them in hours of pain a minister of good and comfort. Her loss is keenly felt among them, and tears are on the face of more than one strong man as he speaks of her. One more veteran soldier has fallen in the ranks, one more faithful patriot-heart is stilled. No less to her than to the soldier in the field shall be awarded the heroic honor.

'For God metes to each his measure; and the woman's patient prayer,

No less than ball or bayonet Brings the victory unaware.'

Patient prayer and work for the victory to our country was the life of our sister gone from us; and in the dawning of our brighter days, and the coming glory of our regenerated country, it is hard to lay her away in unconsciousness; hard to close her eyes against 58 the bright sunshine of God's smile upon a ransomed people; hard to send her lifeless form away from us, alone to the grave in her far off home; hard to realize that one so familiar in our little band shall go no more in and out among us. But we say farewell to her not without hope. Her earnest spirit, ever eager in its questioning of what is truth, was not at rest with simply earthly things. Her reason was unsatisfied, and she longed for more than was revealed to her of the Divine. To the land of full realities she is gone. We trust that in his light she shall see light; that waking in his likeness, she shall be satisfied, and evermore at rest. We cannot mourn that she fell at her post. Her warfare is accomplished, and the oft-expressed thought of her heart is in her death fulfilled. She has said, 'It is noble to die at one's post, with the armor on; to fall where the work has been done.'"

One of her associates from her own State thus speaks of her: "Miss Walker left many friends and a comfortable home in Portland, in the second year of the war. Her devotion and interest in the work so congenial to her feelings, increased with every year's experience, until she found herself bound to it heart and hand. Her large comprehension, too, of all the circumstances connected with the soldier's experience in and outside of hospital, quickened her sympathies and adapted her to the part she was to share, as counsellor and friend. Many a soldier lives, who can pay her a worthy tribute of gratitude for her care and sympathy in his hour of need; and in the beyond, of the thousands who died in the cause of liberty, there are many who may call her 'blessed.'"

Massachusetts was also largely represented among the faithful workers of the Naval Academy Hospital, at Annapolis. Among these Miss Abbie J. Howe, of Brookfield; Miss Kate P. Thompson, of

Worcester, whose excessive labors and the serious illness which followed, have probably rendered her an invalid for life; Miss Eudora Clark, of Boston, Miss Ruth L. Ellis, of Bridgewater, Miss Sarah Allen, of Wilbraham, Miss Agnes Gillis, of Lowell, and Miss Maria Josslyn, of Roxbury, were those who were most laborious and faithful. From New Jersey there came a faithful and zealous worker, Miss Charlotte Ford, of Morristown. From New York there were Miss Helen M. Nove, of Buffalo, already named, Mrs. Guest, also of Buffalo, Miss Emily Gove, of Peru, Miss Mary Cary, of Albany, Miss Ella Wolcott, of Elmira, and Miss M. A. B. Young, of Morristown, New York. This lady, one of the most devoted and faithful of the hospital nurses, was also a martyr to her fidelity and patriotism, dying of typhus fever contracted in her attendance upon her patients, on the 12th of January, 1865.

Miss Young left a pleasant home in St. Lawrence County, New York, soon after the commencement of the war, with her brother, Captain James Young, of the Sixtieth New York Volunteers, and was an active minister of good to the sick and wounded of that regiment. She took great pride in the regiment, wearing its badge and having full faith in its valor. When the Sixtieth went into active service, she entered a hospital at Baltimore, but her regiment was never forgotten. She heard from it almost daily through her soldier-brother, between whom and herself existed the most tender devotion and earnest sympathy. From Baltimore she was transferred to Annapolis early in Mrs. Tyler's administration. In 1864, she suffered from the smallpox, and ever after her recovery she cared for all who were affected with that disease in the hospital.

Her thorough identity with the soldier's life and entire sacrifice to the cause, was perhaps most fully and touchingly evidenced by her oft repeated expression of a desire to be buried among the soldiers. When in usual health, visiting the graves of those to whom she had ministered in the hospital, she said, "If I die in hospital, let me buried here among my boys." This request was sacredly regarded, and she was borne to her last resting-place by soldiers to whom she had ministered in her own days of health.

Another of the martyrs in this service of philanthropy, was Miss Rose M. Billing, of Washington, District of Columbia, a young lady of most winning manners, and spoken of by Miss Hall as one of the most devoted and conscientious workers, she ever knew—an earnest Christian, caring always for the spiritual as well as the physical wants of her men. She was of delicate, fragile constitution, and a deeply sympathizing nature. From the commencement of the war, she had been earnestly desirous of participating in the personal labors of the hospital, and finally persuaded her mother, (who, knowing her frail health, was reluctant to have her enter upon such duties), to give her consent. She commenced her first service with Miss Hall, in the Indiana Hospital, in the Patent Office building, in the autumn of 1861, and subsequently served in the Falls Church Hospital, and at Fredericksburg. Early in 1863 she came to Annapolis, and no one of the nurses was more faithful and devoted in labors for the soldiers. Twice she had been obliged to leave her chosen work for a short time in consequence of illness, but she had hastened back to it with the utmost alacrity, as soon as she could again undertake her work. She had been eminently successful, in bringing up some cases of the fever, deemed by the surgeons, hopeless, and though she herself felt that she was exceeding her strength, or as she expressed it, "wearing out," she could not and would not leave her soldier boys while they were so ill; and when the disease fastened upon her, she had not sufficient vital energy left to throw it off. She failed rapidly and died on the 14th of January, 1865, after two weeks' illness. Her mother, after her death, received numerous letters from soldiers for whom she had cared, lamenting her loss and declaring that but for her faithful attentions, they should not have been in the land of the living. Among those who have given their life to the cause of their country in the hospitals, no purer or saintlier soul has exchanged the sorrows, the troubles and the pains of earth for the bliss of heaven, than Rose M. Billing.

OTHER LABORS OF SOME OF THE MEMBERS OF THE ANNAPOLIS HOSPITAL CORPS.

SOME of the ladies named in the preceding sketch had passed through other experiences of hospital life, before becoming connected with the Naval Academy Hospital at Annapolis. Among these, remarkable for their fidelity to the cause they had undertaken to serve, were several of the ladies from Maine, the Maine-stay of the Annapolis Hospital, as Hr. Vanderkieft playfully called them. We propose to devote a little space to sketches of some of these faithful workers.

Miss Louise Titcomb, was from Portland, Maine, a young lady of high culture and refinement, and from the beginning of the War, had taken a deep interest in working for the soldiers, in connection with the other patriotic ladies of that city. When in the early autumn of 1862, Mrs. Adaline Tyler, as we have already said in our sketch of her, took charge as Lady Superintendent of the Hospital at Chester, Pennsylvania, which had previously been in the care of a Committee of ladies of the village, she sought for volunteer assistants in her work, who would give themselves wholly to it.

Miss Titcomb, Miss Susan Newhall, and Miss Rebecca R. Usher, all from Portland, were among the first to enter upon this work. They remained there eight months, until the remaining patients had become convalescent, and the war had made such progress Southward that the post was too far from the field to be maintained as a general hospital.

The duties of these ladies at Chester, were the dispensing of the extra and low diet to the patients; the charge of their clothing; watching with, and attending personally to the wants of those patients whose condition was most critical; writing for and reading to such of the sick or wounded as needed or desired these services, and attending to innumerable details for their cheer and comfort. Dr. Le Comte, the Surgeon-in-charge, and the assistant Surgeons of the wards, were very kind, considerate and courteous to these ladies, and showed by their conduct how highly they appreciated their services.

In August, 1863, when Mrs. Tyler was transferred to the Naval Academy Hospital, at Annapolis, these ladies went thither with her, where they were joined soon after by Miss Adeline Walker, Miss Almira F. Quimby, and Miss Mary Pierson, all of Portland, and Miss Mary E. Dupee, Miss Emily W. Dana, and Mrs. Eunice D. Merrill, all from Maine. Their duties here were more varied and fatiguing than at Chester. One of them describes them thus: "The Hospital was often crowded with patients enduring the worst forms of disease and suffering; and added to our former duties were new and untried ones incident to the terrible and helpless condition of these returned prisoners. Evening Schools were instituted for the benefit of the convalescents, in which we shared as teachers; at the Weekly Lyceum, through the winter, the ladies in turn edited and read a paper, containing interesting contributions from inmates of the Hospital; they devised and took part in various entertainments for the benefit of the convalescents; held singing and prayer-meetings frequently in the wards; watched over the dying, were present at all the funerals, and aided largely in forwarding the effects, and where it was possible the bodies of the deceased to their friends. Five of these faithful nurses were attacked by the typhus fever, contracted by their attention to the patients, exhausted as they were by overwork, from the great number of the very sick and helpless men brought to the hospital in the winter of 1864-5; and the illness of these threw a double duty upon those who were fortunate enough to escape the epidemic. To the honor of these ladies, it should be said that not one of them shrank from doing her full proportion of the work, and nearly all who survived, remained to the close of the war. For twenty months, Miss Titcomb was absent from duty but two days, and others had a record nearly as satisfactory. Nearly all would have done so but for illness.

Miss Rebecca Usher, of whom we have spoken as one of Miss Titcomb's associates, in the winter of 1864-5, accepted the invitation of the Maine Camp and Hospital Association, to go to City Point, and minister to the sick and wounded, especially of the Maine regiments there. She was accompanied by Miss Mary A. Dupee, who was one of the assistants at Annapolis, from Maine.

The Maine Camp and Hospital Association, was au organization founded by benevolent ladies of Portland, and subsequently having its auxiliaries in all parts of the state, having for its object the supplying of needful aid and comfort, and personal attention, primarily to the soldiers of Maine, and secondarily to those from other states. Mrs. James E. Fernakl, Mrs. J. S. Eaton, Mrs. Elbridge Bacon, Mrs. William Preble, Miss Harriet Fox, and others were the managers of the association. Of these Mrs. J. S. Eaton, the widow of a Baptist clergyman, formerly a pastor in Portland, went very early to the front, with Mrs. Isabella Fogg, the active agent of the association, of whom we have more to say elsewhere, and the two labored most earnestly for the welfare of the soldiers. Mrs. Fogg finally went to the Western armies, and Mrs. Eaton invited Miss Usher and Miss Dupee, with some of the other Maine ladies to join her at City Point, in the winter of 1864-5. Mrs. Ruth S. Mayhew had been a faithful assistant at City Point from the first, and after Mrs. Fogg went to the West, had acted as agent of the association there. Miss Usher joined Mrs. Eaton and Mrs. Mayhew, in December, 1864, but Miss Dupee did not leave Annapolis till April, 1865.

The work at City Point was essentially different from that at Annapolis, and less saddening in its character. The sick soldiers from Maine were visited in the hospital and supplied with delicacies, and those who though in health were in need of extra clothing, etc., were supplied as they presented themselves. The Maine Camp and Hospital Association were always ready to respond to a call for supplies from their agents, and there was never any lack for any length of time. In May, 1865, Mrs. Eaton and her assistants established an agency at Alexandria, and they carried them supplies to the regiments encamped around that city, and visited the comparatively few sick remaining in the hospitals. The last of June their work seemed to be completed and they returned home.

Miss Mary A. Dupee was devoted to the cause from the beginning of the war. She offered her services when the first regiment left Portland, and though they were not then needed, she held herself in constant readiness to go where they were, working meantime for the soldiers as opportunity presented. When Mrs. Tyler was transferred to Annapolis, she desired Miss Susan Newhall, a most faithful and indefatigable worker for the soldiers, who had been with her at Chester, to bring with her another who was like-minded. The invitation was given to Miss Dupee, who gladly accepted it. At Annapolis she had charge of thirteen wards and had a serving-room, where the food was sent ready cooked, for her to distribute according to the directions of the surgeons to "her boys." Before breakfast she went out to see that that meal was properly served, and to ascertain the condition of the sickest patients. Then forenoon and afternoon, she visited each one in turn, ministering to their comfort as far as possible. The work, though wearing, and at times accompanied with some danger of contagion, she found pleasant, notwithstanding its connection with so many sad scenes. The consciousness of doing good more than compensated for any toil or sacrifice, and in the review of her work, Miss Dupee expresses the belief that she derived as much benefit from this philanthropic toil as she bestowed. As we have already said, she was for three months at City Point and elsewhere ministering to the soldiers of her native State.

Miss. Abbie J. Howe, of Brookfield, Massachusetts, was another of the Annapolis Hospital Corps deserving of especial mention for her untiring devotion to the temporal and spiritual welfare of the sick and wounded who were under her charge. We regret our inability to obtain so full an account of her work and its incidents as we desired, but we cannot suffer her to pass unnoticed. Miss Howe had from the beginning of the war been earnestly desirous to enter upon the work of personal service to the soldiers in the hospitals, but considerations of duty, the opposition of her friends, etc., had detained her at home until the way was unexpectedly opened for her in September, 1863. She came directly to Annapolis, and during her whole stay there had charge of the same wards which she first entered, although a change was made in the class of patients under her care in the spring of 1864. At first these wards were filled with private soldiers, but in April, 1864, they were occupied by the wounded and sick officers of the Officers Hospital at that time established in the Naval Academy under charge of Surgeon Vandcrkieft.

Miss Howe brought to her work not only extraordinary skill and tact in the performance of her duties, but a deep % l interest in her patients, a care and thoughtfulness for what might be best adapted to each individual case, as if each had been her own brother, and beyond this, an intense desire to promote their spiritual good. An earnest and devoted Christian, whose high motive of action was the desire to do something for the honor and glory of the Master she loved, she entered upon her duties in such a spirit as we may imagine actuated the saints and martyrs of the early Christian centuries.

We cannot forbear introducing here a brief description of her work from one who knew her well:—"She came to Annapolis with a spirit ready and eager to do all things and suffer all things 69 for the privilege of being allowed to work for the good of the soldiers. Nothing was too trivial for her to be engaged in for their sakes,— nothing was too great to undertake for the least advantage to one of her smallest and humblest patients. This was true of her regard to their bodily comfort and health—but still more true of her concern for their spiritual good. I remember very well that when she had been at work only a day or two she spoke to me with real joy of one of her sick patients, telling me of a hope she had that he was a Christian and prepared for death. She loved the soldiers for the cause for which they suffered—but she loved them most, because she was actuated in all things by her love for her Saviour, and for them He had died. I used to feel that her presence and influence, even if she had not been strong enough to work at all, would have been invaluable—the soldiers so instinctively recognized her true interest in them,—her regard for the right and her abhorrence of anything like deceit or untruthful ness, that they could not help trying to be good for her sake."

Miss Howe took a special interest in the soldier-nurses—the men detailed for extra duty in the wards. She had a very high opinion of their tenderness and faithfulness in their most trying and wearying work, and of their devotion to their suffering comrades. This estimate was undoubtedly true of most of those in her wards, and perhaps of a majority of those in the Naval Academy Hospital; but it would have been difficult for them to have been other than faithful and tender under the influence of her example and the loyalty they could not help feeling to a woman "so nobly good and true." Like all the others engaged in these labors among the returned prisoners,

Miss Howe speaks of her work as one which brought its own abundant reward, in the inexpressible joy she experienced in being able to do something to relieve and comfort those poor suffering ones, wounded, bleeding, and tortured for their country's sake, and at times to have the privilege of telling the story of the cross to eager dying men, who listened in their agony longing to know a Saviour's love.

MRS. A. H. AND MISS S. H. GIBBONS

MRS. GIBBONS is very well known in the City of New York where she resides, as an active philanthropist, devoting a large portion of her time and strength to the various charitable and reformatory enterprises in which she is engaged. This tendency to labors undertaken for the good of others, is, in part, a portion of her inheritance. The daughter of that good man, some years ago deceased, whose memory is so heartily cherished, by all to whom the record of a thousand brave and kindly deeds is known, so warmly by a multitude of friends, and by the oppressed and suffering—Isaac T. Hopper—we are justified in saying that his mantle has fallen upon this his favorite child.

The daughter of the noble and steadfast old Friend, could hardly fail to be known as a friend of the slave. Like her father she was ready to labor, and sacrifice and suffer in his cause, and had already made this apparent, had borne persecution, the crucial test of principle, before the war which gave to the world the prominent idea of freedom for all, and thus wiped the darkest stain from our starry banner, was inaugurated.

The record of the army work of Mrs. Gibbons, does not commence until the autumn of 1861. Previous to that time, her labors for the soldier had been performed at home, where there was much to be done in organizing a class of effort hitherto unknown to the women of our country. But she had always felt a strong desire to aid the soldiers by personal sacrifices.

It was quite possible for her to leave home, which so many mothers of families, whatever their wishes, were unable to do.

Accordingly, accompanied by her eldest daughter, Miss Sarah H. Gibbons, now Mrs. Emerson, she proceeded to Washington, about the time indicated.

There, for some weeks, mother and daughter regularly visited the hospitals, of which there were already many in the Capitol City, ministering to the inmates, and distributing the stores with which they were liberally provided by the kindness of friends, from their own private resources, and from those of "The Woman's Central Association of Relief," already in active and beneficent operation in New York.

Their work was, however, principally done in the Patent Office Hospital, where they took a regular charge of a certain number of patients, and rendered excellent service, where service was, at that time, greatly needed.

While thus engaged they were one day invited by a friend from New York to take a drive in the outskirts of the city. Washington was at that time like a great camp, and was environed by fortifications, with the camps of different divisions, brigades, regiments, to each of which were attached the larger and smaller hospitals, where the sick and suffering languished, afar from the comforts and affectionate cares of home, and not yet inured to the privations and discomforts of army life. It can without doubt be said that they were patient, and when we remember that the most of them ware volunteers, fresh from home, and new to war, that perhaps was all that could reasonably be expected of them.

The drive of Mrs. Gibbons, and her friends extended further than was at first intended, and they found themselves at Fall's Church, fifteen miles from the city. Here was a small force of New York troops, and their hospital containing about forty men, most of them very sick with typhoid fever.

Mrs. Gibbons and her daughter entered the hospital. All around were the emaciated forms, and pale, suffering faces of the men—their very looks an appeal for kindness which it was hardly possible for these ladies to resist.

One of them, a young man from Penn Yan, New York, fixed his sad imploring gaze upon the face of Mrs. Gibbons. Pale as if the seal of death had already been set upon his features, dreadfully emaciated, and too feeble for the least movement, except those of the large, dark, restless eyes, which seemed by the very intensity of their expression to draw her toward him. She approached and compassionately asked if there was anything she could do for him. The reply seemed to throw upon her a responsibility too heavy to be borne.

"Come and take care of me, and I shall get well. If you do not come, I shall die."

It was very hard to say she could not come, and with the constantly recurring thought of his words, every moment made it harder. It was, however, impossible at that time.

After distributing some little offerings they had brought, the party was forced to leave, carrying with them a memory of such suffering and misery as they had not before encountered. Pall's Church was situated in a nest of secessionists, who would have been open rebels except for the presence of the troops. No woman had ever shown her face within the walls of its hospital. The routine of duty had probably been obeyed, but there had been little sympathy and only the blundering care of men, entirely ignorant of the needs of the sick. The men were dying rapidly, and the number in the hospital fast diminishing, not by convalescence, but by death.

After she had gone away, the scene constantly recurred to Mrs. Gibbons, and she felt that a field of duty opened before her, which she had no right to reject. In a few days an opportunity for another visit occurred, which was gladly embraced. The young volunteer was yet living, but too feeble to speak. Again his eyes mutely implored help, and seemed to say that only that could beat back the advances of death. This time both ladies had come with the intention of remaining.

The surgeon was ready to welcome them, but told them there was no place for them to live. But that difficulty was overcome, as difficulties almost always are by a determined will. The proprietor of a neighboring "saloon," or eating-house, was persuaded to give the ladies a loft floored with unplaned boards, and boasting for its sole furniture, a bedstead and a barrel to serve as table and toilet. Here for the sum of five dollars per week, each, they were allowed to sleep, and they took their meals below.

There were at the date of their arrival thirty-nine sick men in the hospital, and six lay unburied in the dead-house. Two or three others died, and when they left, five or six weeks afterward, all had recovered, sufficiently at least to bear removal, save three whom they left convalescing. The young volunteer who had fastened his hope of life on their coming, had been able to be removed to his home, at Penn Yan, and they afterwards learned that he had entirely recovered his health.

Under their reign, cleanliness, order, quiet, and comfortable food, had taken the place of the discomfort that previously existed. The sick were encouraged by sympathy, and stimulated by it, and though they had persisted in their effort through great hardship, and even danger, for they were very near the enemy's lines, they felt themselves fully rewarded for all their toils and sacrifices.

During the month of January, their patients having nearly all recovered, Mrs and Miss Gibbons, cheerfully obeyed a request to proceed to Winchester, and take their places in the Seminary Hospital there. This hospital was at that time devoted to the worst cases of wounded.

There were a large number of these in this place, most of them severely wounded, as has been said, and many of them dangerously so. The closest and most assiduous care was demanded, and the ladies found themselves at once in a position to tax all their strength and efforts. They were in this hospital over four months, and afterwards at Strasburg, where they were involved in the famous retreat from that place, when the enemy took possession, and held the hospital nurses, even, as prisoners, till the main body of their army was safely on the road that led to Dixie.

Many instances of that retreat are of historical interest, but space forbids their repetition here. It is enough to state that these ladies heroically bore the discomfort of their position, and their own losses in stores and clothing, regretting only that it was out of their power to secure the comforts of the wounded, who were hurried from their quarters, jolted in ambulances in torture, or compelled to drag their feeble limbs along the encumbered road.

After the retreat, and the subsequent abandonment of the Valley by the enemy, Mrs. Gibbons and her daughter returned for a short time to their home in New York.

Their rest, however, was not long, for on the 19th of July, they arrived at Point Lookout, Maryland, where Hammond United States General Hospital was about to be opened.

On the 20th, the day following, the first installment of patients arrived, two hundred and eighteen suffering and famished men from the rebel prison of Belle Isle.

A fearful scene was presented on the arrival of these men. The transport on which they came was full of miserable-looking wretches, lying about the decks, many of them too feeble to walk, and unable to move without help. Not one of the two hundred and eighty, possessed more than one garment. Before leaving Belle Isle, they had been permitted to bathe. The filthy, vermin-infected garments, which had been their sole covering for many months, were in most cases thrown into the water, and the men had clothed themselves as best they could, in the scanty supply given them. Many were wrapped in sheets. A pair of trowsers was a luxury to which few attained.

They were mostly so feeble as to be carried on stretchers to the hospital. Mrs. Gibbons' first duty was to go on board the transport with food, wine and stimulants, to enable them to endure the removal; and when once removed, and placed in their clean beds, or wards, there was sufficient employment in reducing all to order, and nursing them back to health. Many were hopelessly broken down by their past sufferings, but most eventually recovered their strength.

Mrs and Miss Gibbons remained at Point Lookout fifteen months. After a short time Mrs. Gibbons finding her usefulness greatly impaired by being obliged to act under the authority of Miss Dix, who was officially at the head of all nurses, applied for, and received from Surgeon-General Hammond an independent appointment in this hospital, which gave her sole charge of it, apart from the medical supervision. In this appointment the Surgeon-General was sustained by the War Department. In her application Mrs. Gibbons was influenced by no antagonism to Miss Dix, but simply by her desire for the utmost usefulness.

The military post of Point Lookout was at that time occupied by two Maryland Regiments, of whom Colonel Rogers had the command. If not in sympathy with rebellion, they undoubtedly were with slavery. Large numbers of contrabands had flocked thither, hoping to be protected in their longings for freedom. In this, however, they were disappointed. As soon as the Maryland masters demanded the return of their absconding property, the Maryland soldiers were not only willing to accede to the demand, but to aid in enforcing it.

Mrs. Gibbons found herself in a continual unpleasant conflict with the authorities. Sympathy, feeling, sense of justice, the principles of a life, were all on the side of the enslaved, and their attempt to escape. She worked for them, helped them to evade the demands of their former masters, and often sent them on their way toward the goal of their hopes and efforts, the mysterious North.

She endured persecution, received annoyances, anonymous threats, and had much to bear, which was borne cheerfully for the sake of these oppressed ones. General Lockwood, then commander of the post, was always the friend of herself and her proteges, a man of great kindness of heart, and a lover of justice.

As has been said, they remained at Point Lookout fifteen months. The summer following her introduction to the place, Mrs. Gibbons visited home, and after remaining but a short time returned to her duties. She had left all at home tranquil and serene, and did not dream of the hidden fires which were even then smouldering, and ready to burst into flame.

She had not long returned before rumors of the riots in New York, the riots of July, 1863, reached Point Lookout.

"If private houses are attacked, ours will be one of the first," said Miss Gibbons, on the reception of these tidings, and though her mother would not listen to the suggestion, she very well knew it was far from impossible.

That night they retired full of apprehension, and had not fallen asleep when some one knocked at their door with the intimation that bad news had arrived for them. They asked if any one was dead, and on being assured that there was not, listened with comparative composure when they learned that their house in New York had been sacked by the mob, and most of its contents destroyed.

The remainder of the night was spent in packing, and in the morning they started for home.

It was a sad scene that presented itself on their arrival. There was not an unbroken pane of glass in any of the windows. The panels of the doors were many of them beaten in as with an axe. The furniture was mostly destroyed, bureaus, desks, closets, receptacles of all kinds had been broken open, and their contents stolen or rendered worthless; the carpets, soaked with a trampled conglomerate of mud and water, oil and filth, the debris left by the feet of the maddened, howling crowd, were entirely ruined; beds and bedding, mirrors, and smaller articles had been carried away, the grand piano had had a fire kindled on the key-board, as had the sofas and chairs upon their velvet seats, fires that were, none knew how, extinguished.

Over all were scattered torn books and valuable papers, the correspondence with the great minds of the country for years, trampled into the grease and filth, half burned and defaced. The relics of the precious only son, who had died a few years before—the beautiful memorial room, filled with pictures he had loved, beautiful vases, where flowers always bloomed; and a thousand tokens of the loved and lost, had shared the universal ruin. So had the writings and the clothing of the lamented father, Isaac T. Hopper—of all these priceless mementoes, there remained only the marble, life-size, bust of the son, which Mr. Gibbons had providentially removed to a place of safety, and a few minor objects. And all this ruin, and irreparable loss, had been visited upon this charitable and patriotic family, by a furious, demoniac mob, because they loved Freedom, Justice, and their country.

After this disaster the family were united beneath a hired roof for some time, while their own house was repaired, and the fragments of its scattered plenishing, and abundant treasures, were gathered together and reclaimed.

Mrs. Gibbons returned for a brief space to Point Lookout, where her purpose was to instal the Misses woolsey, and then leave them in charge of the hospital.

Circumstances, however, prevented her from leaving the Point for a much longer period than she had intended to stay, and when she did leave, she was accompanied by the Misses woolsey, and the whole party returned to New York together.

We have no record of the further army work of Mrs and Miss Gibbons until the opening of the grand campaign of the Army of the Potomac, the following May.

Immediately after the battle of the wilderness, Mrs. Gibbons received a telegram desiring her to come to the aid of the wounded. She resolved at once to go, and urged her daughter to accompany her, as she had always done before. Miss Gibbons had, in the meantime, married, and in the course of a few weeks become a widow. She felt reluctant to return to the work she had so loved, but her mother's wish prevailed. The next day they started, and in a very short space of time found themselves amidst the horrible confusion and suffering which prevailed at Belle Plain their stay there was but brief, and in a short time they were themselves established at Fredericksburg. There Mrs. Gibbons was requested to take charge of a hospital, or rather a large unfurnished building, which was to be used as one. In great haste straw was found to fill the empty bed-sacks, which were placed upon the floor, and the means to feed the suffering mass who were expected. The men, in all the forms of suffering, were placed upon these beds, and cared for as well as they could be, as fast as they arrived, and Mrs. Emerson prepared food for them, standing unsheltered in rain or sultry heat.

For weeks they toiled thus. One day when the town was beautiful and fragrant with the early roses, some regiments of Northern soldiers landed and marched through the town, on their way to the front. The patriotic women gathered there, cheered them as they marched on, and gathered roses which they offered in a fragrant shower, with which the men decorated caps and button-holes. They passed on; but two days later the long train of ambulances crept down the hill, bringing back these heroes to their pitying countrywomen, the roses withering on their breasts, and dyed'with their sacred patriot blood.

Through all the horrors of this sad campaign, Mrs. Gibbons and Mrs. Emerson remained, doing whatever their hands could find to do. When Fredericksburg was evacuated, they accompanied the soldiers, riding in the open box-cars, and on the way administering to them as they could.

They were for a time at 'White House, where thousands of wounded required and received their aid, and afterwards at City Point, where they remained for several weeks in charge of the hospital of the Second Division, being from first to last, among the most useful of the many noble women who were engaged in this work.

After their return home, Mrs. Gibbons accepted an appointment at the hospital in Beverly, New Jersey, where she had charge under Dr. Wagner, the excellent surgeon she had known, and to whom she had become much attached, at Point Lookout. As usual, Mrs. Emerson accompanied her to this place, and lent her efforts to the great work to which both had devoted themselves'.

There were about nineteen hundred patients in this hospital, and the duties were arduous. They boarded with the family of Dr. Wagner, adjacent to the hospital, and after the labors of the day were mostly finished, they went there to dine, at seven o'clock. Often, despite pleasant conversation, and attractive viands, the sense of fatigue, before unfelt, would attack Mrs. Gibbons, and at the table she would fall asleep. But the morning would find her with strength restored, and ready for the toil of the coming day.

The winter of 1865 will long be remembered in New York for the ravages of small-pox in that city. The victims were not confined to any class, or locality, and there were perhaps as many in the homes of wealth, as in the squalid dwelling-])!aces of the poor.

Mrs. Gibbons was suddenly summoned home to nurse her youngest daughter, in an attack of varioloid [smallpox]. This was accomplished, and the young lady recovered. But this closed the army labors of the mother. She did not return, though Mrs. Emerson remained till the close of the hospital the following spring, when the end of the war rendered their further services in this work unnecessary, and they once more found themselves settled in the quiet of home.

MRS. E. J. RUSSELL

WE have spoken in previous sketches of the faithfulness and devotion of many of the government nurses, appointed by Miss Dix. No salary, certainly not the meagre pittance doled out by the government could compensate for such services, and the only satisfactory reason which can be offered for their willingness to render them, is that their hearts were inspired by a patriotism equally ardent with that which actuated their wealthier sisters, and that this pitiful salary, hardly that accorded to a green Irish girl just arrived in this country from the bogs of Erin, was accepted rather as affording them the opportunity to engage more readily in their work, than from any other cause. In many instances it was expended in procuring necessary food or luxuries for their soldier patients, and in others, served to prevent dependence upon friends, who had the disposition but perhaps hardly the ability to furnish these heroic and self-denying nurses with the clothing or pocket money they needed in their work.

It is of one of these nurses, a lady of mature age, a widow, that we have now to speak. Mrs. E. J. Russell, of Plattekill, Ulster County, New York, was at the commencement of the war engaged in teaching in New York city. In common with the other ladies of the Reformed Dutch Church, in Ninth Street, of which she was a member, she worked for the soldiers at every spare moment, but the cause seemed to her to need her personal services in the hospital, and in ministrations to the wounded and sick, and when the call came for nurses, she waited upon Miss Dix, was accepted, and sent first to the Regimental Hospital of the Twentieth New York Militia, National Guard, then stationed at Annapolis Junction. On arriving there she found that the regiment consisted of men from her own county, her former neighbors and acquaintances. The regiment was soon after ordered to Baltimore, and being in the three months' service, was mustered out soon after, and Mrs. Russell was assigned by Miss Dix to Columbia College Hospital, Washington. Here she remained in the quiet discharge of her duties, until June, 1864, not without many trials and discomforts, for the position of the hired nurse in these hospitals about Washington, was often rendered very uncomfortable by the discourtesy of the young assistant surgeons. Her devotion to her duties had been so intense that her health was seriously impaired, and she resigned, but after a short period of rest, her strength was sufficiently recruited for her to resume her labors, and she reported for duty at West Building Hospital, Baltimore, where she remained until after Lee's surrender. She was in the service altogether four years, lacking eighteen days. During this time nine hundred and eighty-five men were under her care, for varying periods from a few days to thirteen months; of these ninety died, and she closed the eyes of seventy-six of them. Her service in Baltimore was in part among our returned prisoners, from Belle Isle, Libby and other prisons, and in part among the wounded rebel prisoners.

Many of the incidents which Mrs. Russell relates of the wounded who passed under her care are very touching. Many of her earlier patients were in the delirium of typhoid fever, and her ears and heart were often pained in hearing their piteous calls for their loved ones to come to them,—to forgive them—or to help them. Often had she occasion to offer the consolations of religion to those who were evidently nearing the river of death, and sometimes she was made happy in finding that those who were suffering terribly from racking pain, or the agony of wounds, were comforted and cheered by her efforts to bring them to think of the Saviour. One of these, suffering from an intense fever, as she seated herself by the side of his cot, and asked him in her quiet gentle way, if he loved Jesus as his Saviour, clasped her hand in his and folding it to his heart, asked so earnestly, Do you love Jesus too? Oh, yes, I love him. I do not fear to die, for then I shall join my dear mother who taught me to love him." He then repeated with great distinctness a stanza of the hymn, "Jesus can make a dying bed," etc., and inquired if she could sing. She could not, but she read several hymns to him. His joy and peace made him apparently oblivious of his suffering from the fever, and he endeavored as well as his failing strength would permit, to tell her of his hopes of immortality, and to commend to her prayers his only and orphaned sister.

Another, a poor fellow from Maine, dying of diphtheria, asked her to pray for him and to read to him from the Bible. She commended him tenderly to the Good Shepherd, and soon had the happiness of seeing, even amid his sufferings, that his face was radiant with joy. He selected a chapter of the Bible which he wished her to read, and then sent messages by her to his mother and friends, uttering the words with great difficulty, but passing away evidently in perfect peace.

Since the war, Mrs. Russell has resumed her profession as a teacher at Newburgh, New York.

MRS. MARY W. LEE

IT is somewhat remarkable that a considerable number of the most faithful and active workers in the hospitals and in other labors for the soldier during the late war, should have been of foreign birth. Their patriotism and benevolence was fully equal to that of our women born under the banner of the stars, and their joy at the final triumph of our arms was as fervent and hearty. Our readers will recall among these noble women, Miss Wormeley, Miss Clara Davis, Miss Jessie Home, Mrs. General Ricketts, Mrs. General Turchin, Bridget Divers, and others.

Among the natives of a foreign land, but thoroughly American in every fibre of her being, Mrs. Mary W. Lee stands among the foremost of the earnest persistent toilers of the great army of philanthropists. She was born in the north of Ireland, of Scotch parentage, but came with her parents to the United States when she was five years of age, and has ever since made Philadelphia her home. Here she married Mr. Lee, a gold refiner, and a man of great moral worth. An interesting family had grown up around them, all, like their parents thoroughly patriotic. One son enlisted early in the war, first, we believe, in the Pennsylvania Reserve Corps, and afterward in the Seventy-second Pennsylvania Volunteers, and served throughout the war, and though often in peril, escaped any severe wounds. A daughter, Miss Amanda Lee, imbued with her mother's spirit, accompanied her 480 in most of her labors, and emulated her example of active usefulness.

Mrs. Lee was one of the noble band of women whose hearts were moved with the desire to do something for our soldiers, when they were first hastening to the war in April, 1861, and in the organization of the Volunteer Refreshment Saloon at Philadelphia, an institution which fed, during the war, four hundred thousand of our soldiers as they passed to and from the battlefields, and brought comfort and solace to many thousands of the sick and wounded, she was one of the most active and faithful members of its committee. The regiments often arrived at midnight; but whatever the hour, whether night or day, at the firing of the signal gun, which announced that troops were on their way to Philadelphia, Mrs. Lee and her co-workers hastened to the Union Volunteer Refreshment Saloon, near the Navy Yard, and prepared an ample repast for the soldiers, caring at the same time for any sick or wounded among them. No previous fatigue or weariness, no inclemency of the weather, or darkness of the night was regarded by these heroic women as a valid excuse from these self-imposed duties or rather this glorious privilege, for so they deemed it, of ministering to the comfort of the defenders of the Union. And through the whole four and a-third years during which troops passed through Philadelphia, no regiment or company ever passed unfed. The supplies as well as the patience and perseverance of the women held out to the end, and scores of thousands who but for their voluntary labors and beneficence must have suffered severely from hunger, had occasion to bless God for the philanthropy and practical benevolence of the women of Philadelphia.

But this field of labor, broad as it was, did not fully satisfy the patriotic ardor of Mrs. Lee. She had heard of the sufferings and privations endured by our soldiers at the front, and in hospitals remote from the cities; and she longed to go and minister to their wants. Fortunately, she could be spared for a time at least from her home. Though of middle age, she possessed a vigorous constitution, capable of enduring all necessary hardships, and was in full health and strength. She was well known as a skilful cook, an admirable nurse, and an excellent manager of household affairs. The sickness of some members of her family delayed her for a time, but when this obstacle was removed, she felt that she could not longer be detained from her chosen work. It was July, 1862, the period when the Army of the Potomac exhausted by its wearisome march and fearful battles of the seven days, lay almost helpless at Harrison's Landing. The sick poisoned by the malaria of the Chickahominy Swamps, and the wounded, shattered and maimed wrecks of humanity from the great battles, were being sent off by thousands to the hospitals of Washington, Baltimore, Philadelphia, New York, and New England, and yet other thousands lay in the wretched field hospitals around the Landing, with but scant care, and in utter wretchedness and misery. The S. R. Spaulding, one of the steamers assigned to the United States Sanitary Commission for its Hospital Transport Service, had brought to Philadelphia a heavy cargo of the sick and wounded, and was about to return for another, when Mrs. Lee, supplied with stores by the Union Volunteer Refreshment Committee, and her personal friends, embarked upon it for Harrison's Landing, where she was to be associated with Mrs. John Harris in caring for the soldiers. The Spaulding arrived in due time in the James River, and lay off in the stream while the Ruffin house was burning. On landing, Mrs. Lee found Mrs. Harris, and the Rev. Isaac O. Sloan, one of the Agents of the Christian Commission ready to welcome her to the toilsome duties that were before her. Wretched indeed was the condition of the poor sick men, lying in mildewed, leaky tents without floors, and the pasty tenacious mud ankle deep around them, the raging thirst and burning fever of the marshes consuming them, with only the warm and impure river water to drink, and little even of this; with but a small supply of medicines, and no food or delicacies suitable for the sick, the bean soup, unctuous with rancid pork fat, forming the principal article of low diet; uncheered by kind words or tender sympathy, it is hardly matter of surprise that hundreds of as gallant men as ever entered the army died here daily.

The supplies of the Sanitary and Christian Commissions, and those sent to Mrs. Harris and Mrs. Lee, from the Ladies' Aid Society, and the Union Volunteer Refreshment Committee, administered by such skilful nurses as Mrs. Harris and Mrs. Lee, Mrs. Fales, Mrs. Husband, and Miss Hall, soon changed the aspect of affairs, and though the malarial fever still raged, there was a better chance of recovery from it, and the sick men were as rapidly as possible transferred to a better climate, and a healthier atmosphere. In the latter part of August, the Army of the Potomac having left the James River for Acquia Creek and Alexandria, Mrs. Lee returned home for a brief visit.

On the 5th of September, she started for Washington, to enter again upon her chosen work. Finding that the Army were just about moving into Maryland, she spent a few days in the Hospital of the Epiphany at Washington, nursing the sick and wounded there; but learning that the Army of the Potomac were in hot pursuit of the Rebel Army, and that a severe battle was impending, she could not rest; she determined to be near the troops, so that when the battle came, she might be able to render prompt assistance to the wounded. It was almost impossible to obtain transportation, the demand for the movement of sustenance and ammunition for the army filling every wagon, and still proving insufficient for their wants; but by the kind permission of Captain Gleason of the Seventy-first Pennsylvania Volunteers, she was permitted to follow with her stores in a forage wagon, and arrived at the rear of the army the night before the battle of Antietam. The battle commenced with the dawn on the 17th of September, and during its progress, she was stationed on the Sharpsburg road, 'where she had her supplies and two large tubs of water, one to bathe and bind up the wounds of those who had fallen in the fight, and the other to refresh them when suffering from the terrible thirst which gun-shot wounds always produce. As the hours drew on, the contents of one assumed a deeper and yet deeper crimson hue and the seemingly ample supply of the other grew less and less. Her supply of soft bread had given out, and she had bought of an enterprising sutler who had pushed his way to a place of danger in the hope of gain, at ten and twenty cents a loaf, till her money was nearly exhausted; but to the honor of this sutler, it should be said, that the noble example of Mrs. Lee, in seeking to alleviate the sufferings of the wounded so moved his feelings, that he exclaimed, "Great God! I can't stand this any longer; Take, this bread, and give it to that woman," (Mrs. Lee), and forgetting for the time the greed of gain which had brought him thither, he lent a helping hand most zealously to the care of the wounded. During the day, General McClellan's head-quarters were at Boonsboro', and his aids were constantly passing back and forth over the Sharpsburg road, near which Mrs. Lee had her station.

The battle closed with the night-fall, and Mrs. Lee immediately went into the Sedgwick Division Hospital, where were five hundred severely wounded men, and among the number, Major-General Sedgwick. Here she commenced preparing food for the wounded, but was greatly annoyed by a gang of villainous camp followers, who hung around her fires and stole everything from them if she was engaged for a moment. At last she entered the hospital, and inquired if there was any officer there who had the authority to order her a guard. General Sedgwick immediately responded to her request, by authorizing her to call upon the first soldier she could find for the purpose, and she had no further annoyance.

She remained for several days at this hospital, doing all she could with the means at her command, to make the condition of the wounded comfortable, but on the arrival of Mrs. Arabella Barlow, whose husband, then Colonel, afterward Major-General Barlow, was very severely wounded, she gave up the charge of this hospital to her, and went to the Hoffman Farm's Hospital, where there were over a thousand of the worst cases. Here she was the only lady for several weeks, until the hospital was removed to Smoketown, where she was joined by Miss M. M. C. Hall, Mrs. Husband, Mrs. Harris, and Miss Tyson, of Baltimore. She remained at Smoketown General Hospital, nearly three months. The worst cases, those which could not bear removal to Washington, Baltimore, or Philadelphia, were collected in this hospital, and there was much suffering and many deaths in it.

Mrs. Lee returned home on the 14th of December, 1862, and on the 29th of the same month, she again set out for the front, arriving safely at Falmouth on the 31st, where the wounded of Fredericksburg were gathered by thousands. After four weeks of earnest labor here, she again returned home, but early in March, she was again at the front, in the Hospital of the Second Corps, which had been removed from Falmouth to Potomac Creek. She continued in this Hospital until the battle of Chancellorsville, when she went up to the Lacy House, at Falmouth, to assist Mrs. Harris and Mrs. Beck. She accompanied Mrs. Harris, and several of the gentlemen of the Christian Commission in an Ambulance to take nourishment to the wounded of General Sedgwick's command, and witnessed the taking of Marye's Heights, the balls from the batteries passing over the heads of her company. Her anxiety in regard to this conflict was heightened by the fact that her son was in one of the regiments which made the charge upon the Heights, and great was her gratitude in finding that he was not among the wounded.

After the wounded were sent to Washington she returned to Potomac Creek, where she remained until Lee's second invasion of Maryland and Pennsylvania, when she moved with the army as far as Fairfax Court-House, enduring many hardships. From Fairfax Court-House she went to Alexandria to await the result of the movement, and after some delay returned home. The battle of Gettysburg called her again into the field. Arriving several days after the battle, she went directly to the Second Corps Hospital, and labored there until it was broken up. For her services in this hospital she received from the officers and men a gold medal—a trefoil, beautifully engraved, and with an appropriate inscription. She went next to Camp Letterman General Hospital, where she remained for some weeks, her stay at Gettysburg being in all about two months.

Her health was impaired by her excessive labors at Gettysburg and previously in Virginia, and she remained at home for a longer time than usual, giving her attention, however, meanwhile to the Volunteer Refreshment Saloon, but early in February, 1864, she established herself in a new hospital of the Second Division, Second Corps, at Brandy Station, Virginia. Here, soon after, her daughter joined her, and the old routine of the hospital at Potomac Creek was soon established. Mrs. Lee has the faculty of making the most of her conveniences and supplies. Her daughter writing home from this hospital thus describes the furniture of her "Special Diet Kitchen:"—"Mother has a small stove; until this morning it has smoked very much, but it is now doing very well. The top is about half a yard square. On this she is now boiling potatoes, stewing some chicken-broth, heating a kettle of water, and has a large bread-pudding inside. She has made milk-punch, lemonade, beef-tea, stewed cranberries, and I cannot think what else since breakfast." With all this intense activity the spiritual interests of her patients were not forgotten. Mrs. Lee is a woman of deep and unaffected piety, and her tact in speaking a word in season, and in bringing the men under religious influences was remarkable. This hospital soon became remarkable for its order, neatness and cheerfulness.

The order of General Grant on the 15th of April, 1864, for the removal of all civilians from the army, released Mrs. Lee and Miss—. Husband, who had been associated with her, from their duties at Brandy Station. But in less than a month both were recalled to the temporary base of the army at Belle Plain and Fredericksburg, to minister to the thousands of wounded from the destructive battles of the Wilderness and Spottsylvania. At Fredericksburg, where the whole town was one vast hospital, the surgeon in charge entrusted her with the care of the special diet of the Second Corps' hospitals. Unsupplied with kitchen furniture, and the surgeon being entirely at a loss how to procure any, her woman's wit enabled her to improvise the means of performing her duties. She remembered that Mrs. Harris had left at the Lacy House in Falmouth, opposite Fredericksburg, the year before, an old stove which might be there yet. Procuring an ambulance, she crossed the river, and found the old stove, much the worse for wear, and some kettles and other utensils, all of which were carefully transported to the other side, and after diligent scouring, the whole were soon in such a condition that boiling, baking, stewing and frying could proceed simultaneously, and during her stay in Fredericksburg, the old stove was kept constantly hot, and her skilful hands were employed from morning till night and often from night till morning again in the preparation of food and delicacies for the sick. Nothing but her iron constitution enabled her to endure this incessant labor.

From Fredericksburg she went over land to White House and there, aided by Miss Cornelia Hancock, her ministrations to the wounded were renewed. Thence soon after they removed to City Point. Here for months she labored amid such suffering and distress that the angels must have looked down in pity upon the accumulated human woe which 'met their sympathizing eyes Brave, noble-hearted men fell by hundreds and thousands, and died not knowing whether their sacrifices would be sufficient to save their country. At length wearied with her intense and protracted labors, Mrs. Lee found herself compelled to visit home and rest for a time. But her heart was in the work, and again she returned to it, and was in charge of a hospital near Petersburg at the time of Lee's surrender. She remained in the hospitals of Petersburg and Richmond, until the middle of May, and then returned to her quiet home, participating to the very last in the closing work of the Volunteer Refreshment Saloon, where she had commenced her labors for the soldiers. Other ladies may have engaged in more extended enterprises, may have had charge of larger hospitals, or undertaken more comprehensive and far-reaching plans for usefulness to the soldier—but in untiring devotion to his interests, in faithfully performed, though often irksome labor, carried forward patiently and perseveringly for more than four years, Mrs. Lee has a record not surpassed in the history of the deeds of American women.

MISS CORNELIA M. TOMPKINS

MISS CORNELIA M. TOMPKINS, of Niagara Falls, was one of the truly heroic spirits evoked by the war. Related to a distinguished family of the same name, educated, accustomed to the refinements and social enjoyments of a Christian home she left all to become a hospital nurse, and to aid in saving the lives of the heroes and defenders of her native land. Recommended by her friend, the late Margaret Breckinridge, of whom a biographical notice is given in this volume, she came to St. Louis in the summer of 1863, was commissioned as a nurse by Mr. Yeatman, and assigned to duty at the Benton Barracks Hospital, under the superintendence of Miss Emily E. Parsons, and the general direction of Surgeon Ira Russell. In this service she was one of the faithful band of nurses, who, with Miss Parsons, brought the system of nursing to such perfection at that hospital.

In the fall of that year she was transferred to the hospital service at Memphis, by Mr. Yeatman, to meet the great demand for nurses there, where she became favorably known as a most judicious and skilful nurse.

In the spring of 1864 she returned to St. Louis, and was again assigned to duty at Benton Barracks, where she remained till mid-summer, when having been from home a year, she obtained a furlough, and went home for a short period of rest, and to visit her family.

On her return to St. Louis she was assigned to duty at the large hospital at Jefferson Barracks, and continued there till the end of the war, doing faithful and excellent service, and receiving the cordial approbation of the surgeons in charge, and the Western Sanitary Commission, as well as the gratitude of the sick and wounded soldiers, to whom she was a devoted friend and a ministering angel in their sorrows and distress.

In her return to the quiet and enjoyment of her own home, within the sound of the great cataract, she has carried with her the consciousness of having rendered a most useful service to the patriotic and heroic defenders of her country, in their time of suffering and need, the approval of a good conscience and the smile of heaven upon her noble and heroic soul.

MRS. ANNA C. McMEENS

MRS. ANNA C. McMEENS, of Sandusky, Ohio, was born in Maryland, but removed to the northern part of Ohio, in company with her parents when quite young. She is therefore a western woman in her habits, associations and feelings, while her patriotism and philanthropy are not bounded by sectional lines. Her husband, Dr. McMeens, was appointed surgeon to an Ohio regiment, which was one of the first raised when Mr. Lincoln called for troops, after the firing upon Sumter. In the line of his duty he proceeded to Camp Dennison, where lie had for some time principal charge of the medical department. Mrs. McMeens resolved to accompany her husband, and share in the hardships of the campaign, for the purpose of doing good where she could find it to do. She was therefore one of the first,—if not the first woman in Ohio, to give her exclusive, undivided time in a military hospital, in administering to the necessities of the soldiers. "When the regiment left Camp Dennison, she accompanied it, until our forces occupied Nashville. Dr. McMeens then had a hospital placed under his charge, and his faithful wife assisted as nurse for several months, contributing greatly to the efficiency of the nursing department, and to the administration of consolation and comfort in many ways to our sick soldier boys, who were necessarily deprived of the comforts of home. Subsequently at the battle of Perryville, Mrs. McMeens' husband lost his life from excessive exertions while in attention to the sick and wounded.

Being deprived of her natural protector, she returned to her home in Sandusky, which was made desolate by an additional sacrifice to the demon of secession. While at home, not content to sit idle in her mourning for her husband, she was busily occupied in aiding the Sanitary Commission in obtaining supplies, of which she so well knew the value by her familiarity with the wants of the soldiers in field, camp and hospitals. She however very soon felt it her duty to participate more actively in immediate attentions upon the sick and wounded soldiers. A fine field offered itself in the hospitals at Washington, to which place she went; and remained nearly one year in attention, and rendering assistance daily among the various hospitals of the Nation's capital. It would be feeble praise to say that her duties were performed in the most energetic and judicious manner. Few women have made greater sacrifices in the war than the subject of our sketch • none have been made from a purer sense of duty, or a fuller knowledge of the magnitude of the cause in which we have been engaged.

At present the necessity for attention to soldiers has happily ceased, and we find her busily engaged in missionary work among the sailors, which she has an excellent opportunity of performing while at her beautiful summer home on the island of Gibraltar, Lake Erie.

MRS. JERUSHA R. SMALL

THIS young lady was one of the martyrs of the war. She resided in Cascade, Dubuque County, Iowa, and just previous to the commencement of the war had buried her only child, a sweet little girl of four years. When volunteers were called for from Iowa, her husband, Mr. J. E. Small, felt it his duty to take up arms for his country, and as his wife had no home ties she determined to go with him and make herself useful in caring for the sick and wounded of his regiment, or of other regiments in the same division. She proved a most excellent nurse, and for months labored with untiring energy in the regimental hospitals, and to hundreds of the wounded from Belmont, Donelson, and Shiloh, as well as to the numerous sick soldiers of General Grant's army she was an angel of mercy. Her constant care and devotion had considerably impaired her health before the battle of Shiloh.

At this battle her husband was badly wounded and taken prisoner, but was retaken by the Union troops. In the course of the battle, the tent which she occupied and where she was ministering to the wounded came within range of the enemy's shells, and she with her wounded husband and a large number of other wounded soldiers, were obliged to fly for their lives, leaving all their goods behind them. Previous to her flight, however, she had torn up all her spare clothing and dresses to make bandages and compresses and pillows for the wounded soldiers. She found her way with her wounded patients to one of the hospitals extemporized by the Cincinnati ladies. Her husband and many of his comrades of the Twelfth Iowa Regiment were among this company of wounded men. She craved admission for them and remained to nurse her husband and the others for several weeks, but when her husband became convalescent, she was compelled to take to her bed; her fatigue and exposure, acting upon a somewhat frail and delicate constitution had brought on galloping consumption. She soon learned from her physician that there was no hope of her recovery, and then the desire to return home and die in her mother's arms seemed to take entire possession of her soul. Permission was obtained for her to go, and for her husband to accompany her, and when she was removed from the boat to the cars, Mrs. Dr. Mendenhall of the Cincinnati Branch of the Sanitary Commission accompanied her to the cars, and having provided for her comfortable journey, gave her a parting kiss. Mrs. Small was deeply affected by this kindness of a stranger, and thanking her for her attention to herself and husband, expressed the hope that they should meet in a better world. A lady, who evidently had little sympathy with the war or with those who sought to alleviate the sufferings of the soldiers, stepped up and said to Mrs. Small; "You did very wrong to go and expose yourself as you have done when you were so young and frail." "No!" replied the dying woman, "I feel that I have done right, I think I have been the means of saving some lives, and that of my dear husband among the rest; and these I consider of far more value than mine, for now they can go and help our country in its hour of need."

Mrs. Small lived to reach home, but died a few days after her arrival. She requested that her dead body might be wrapped in the national flag, for next to her husband and her God, she loved the country which it represented, best. She was buried with military honors, a considerable number of the soldiers of the Twelfth Iowa who were home on furlough, taking part in the sad procession.

MRS. S. A. MARTHA CANFIELD

THIS lady was the wife of Colonel Herman Canfield, of the Seventy-first Ohio Regiment. She accompanied her husband to the field, and devoted herself to the care and succor of the sick and wounded soldiers, until the battle of Shiloh, where her husband was mortally wounded, and survived but a few hours. She returned home with his body and remained for a short time, but feeling that it was in her power to do something for the cause to which her husband had given his life, she returned to the Army of the Mississippi and became attached to the Sixteenth Army Corps, and spent most of her time in the hospitals of Memphis and its vicinity. But though she accomplished great good for the soldiers, she took a deep interest also in the orphans of the freedmen in that region, and by her extensive acquaintance and influence with the military authorities, she succeeded in establishing and putting upon a satisfactory basis, the Colored Orphan Asylum in Memphis. She devoted her whole time until the close of the war to these two objects; the welfare of the soldiers in the hospitals and the perfecting of the Orphan Asylum, and not only gave her time but very largely also of her property to the furthering of these objects. The army officers of that large and efficient army corps bear ample testimony to her great usefulness and devotion.

MRS. E. THOMAS, AND MISS MORRIS

THESE two ladies, sisters, volunteered as unpaid nurses for the War, from Cincinnati. They commenced their duties at the first opening of the Hospitals, and remained faithful to their calling, until the hospitals were closed, after the termination of the war. In cold or heat, under all circumstances of privation, and often when all the other nurses were stricken down with illness, they never faltered in their work, and, although not wealthy, gave freely of their own means to secure any needed comfort for the soldiers. Mrs. Mendenhall, of Cincinnati, who knew their abundant labors, speaks of them as unsurpassed in the extent and continuousness of their sacrifices.

MRS. SHEPARD WELLS

THIS lady, the wife of Rev. Shepard Wells, was, with her husband, driven from East Tennessee by the rebellion, because of their loyalty to the Union. They found their way to St. Louis at an early period of the War, where he entered into the work of the Christian Commission for the Union soldiers, and she became a member of the Ladies' Union Aid Society, of St. Louis, and gave herself wholly to sanitary labors for the sick and wounded in the Hospitals of that city, acting also as one of the Secretaries of the Society, and as its agent in many of its works of benevolence, superintending at one time the Special Diet Kitchen, established by the Society at Benton Barracks, and doing an amount of work which few women could endure, animated and sustained by a genuine love of doing good, by noble and Christian purposes, and by true patriotism and philanthropy.

The incidents of the persecutions endured by Mr and Mrs. Wells, in East Tennessee, and of her life and labors among the sick and wounded of the Union army, would add very much to the interest of this brief notice, but the particulars are not sufficiently familiar to the writer to be narrated by him, and he can only record the impressions he received of her remarkable faithfulness and efficiency, and her high Christian motives, in the labors she performed in connection with the Ladies' Union Aid Society, of St. Louis,—that noble Society of heroic women who, during the whole war, performed an amount of sanitary, hospital and philanthropic work for the soldiers, the refugees and the freedmen, second only to the Western Sanitary Commission itself, of which it was a most faithful ally and co-worker.

United with an earnest Christian faith, Mrs. Wells possessed a kind and generous sympathy with suffering, and a patriotic ardor for the welfare of the Union soldiers, so that she was never more in her element than when laboring for the poor refugees, for the families of those brave men who left their all to fight for their country, for the sick and wounded in the hospitals, and for the freedmen and their families. The labors she performed extended to all these objects of sympathy and charity, and, from the beginning to the end of her service, she never seemed weary in well-doing; and there can be no doubt that when her work on earth is finished, and she passes onward to the heavenly life, she will hear the approving voice of her Saviour, saying, "Well done, good and faithful servant, enter thou into the joy of thy Lord."

MRS. E. C. WITHERELL

IN the month of December, 1861, on a visit made by the writer to the Fourth Street Hospital, in St. Louis, he was particularly impressed with the great devotion of one of the female nurses to her sick patients. At the conclusion of a religious service held there, as he passed through the wards to call on those who had been too ill to attend worship, he found her seated by the bed-side of a sick soldier, suffering from pneumonia, on whose pale, thin face the marks of approaching dissolution were plainly visible. She held in her hand a copy of the New Testament, from which she had been reading to him, in a cheerful and hopeful manner, and a little book of prayers, hymns and songs from which she had been singing, "There is rest for the weary," and "The Shining Shore." The soldier's bed was neatly made; his special diet had been given; his head rested easily on his pillow; and his countenance beamed with a sweet and pleasant smile. It was evident the patient enjoyed the kind attentions, the conversation, the reading and singing of his faithful nurse. The lady who sat by his bedside was of middle age, having a countenance expressive of goodness, benevolence, purity of motive, intelligence and affection. It was plain that she regarded her patient with a tender care, and that her influence calmed and soothed his spirit. Her name was Mrs. E. C. Witherell, and the sick soldier was a mere boy, who had shouldered his musket to fight for the cause of the Union, and had contracted his fatal disease in the marches and the exposure of the army in Missouri, and was now about to die away from friends and home. The interest felt by Mrs. Witherell in this soldier boy, was motherly, full of affection and sympathy, and creditable to her noble and generous heart. As I drew near and introduced myself as a chaplain, she welcomed me, introduced me to the patient, and we sat down and conversed together; the young man was in a state of peaceful resignation; was willing to die for his country; and only regretted that he could not see his mother and sisters again; but he said that Mrs. Withered had been as a mother to him, and if he could have hold of her hand he should not be afraid to die. He even hoped that with her kind care and nursing he might get well. Mrs. Withered and myself then sang the "Shining Shore;" a brief prayer of hope and trust was offered; the other patients in the room seemed equally wed cared for, and interested in ad that was said and done; and I passed on to another ward, and never saw either the nurse or patient again. But I learned that the soldier died; and that Mrs. Withered continued in the service, until she also died, a martyr to her heroic devotion to the cause of the sick and wounded soldiers, for whom she laid down her life, that they might live to fight the battles of their country.

The only facts that I have been able to learn about this noble lady, were that at one time she resided in Louisville, and was greatly esteemed by her pastor, Rev. John H. Heywood, of the Unitarian Church; that she chose this work of the hospitals from the highest motives of religious patriotism and love of humanity; that after serving several months in the Fourth Street Hospital, at St. Louis, she was assigned to the hospital steamer, "Empress," in the spring of 1862, as matron, or head nurse; that she continued on this boat during the next few months, while so many sick and wounded were brought from Pittsburg Landing, after the battle of Shiloh, and from other battle-fields along the rivers, to the hospitals at Mound City and St. Louis; that she was always constant, faithful and never weary of doing good; and that at last, from her being so much in the infected atmosphere of the sick and wounded, she became the victim of a fever, and died on the 10th of July, 1862.

On the occurrence of the sad event, the Western Sanitary Commission, who had known and appreciated her services, and from whom she held her commission, passed a series of resolutions, as a tribute to her worth, and her blessed memory, in which she was described as one who was "gentle and unobtrusive, with a heart warm with sympathy, and unshrinking in the discharge of duty, energetic, untiring, ready to answer every call, and unwilling to spare herself where she could alleviate suffering, or minister to the comfort of others," as "not a whit behind the bravest hero on the battle-field and as worthy to be held "in everlasting remembrance."

MISS PHEBE ALLEN

THIS noble woman, who laid down her life in the cause of her country, was a teacher in Washington, Iowa, and left her school to enter the service as a hospital nurse. In the summer of 1863 she was commissioned by Mr. Yeatman, at St. Louis, and assigned to duty in the large hospital at Benton Barracks, where she belonged to the corps of women nurses, under the superintendence of Miss Emily E. Parsons, and under the general direction of Surgeon Ira Russell.

In the fulfilment of the duties of a hospital nurse she was very conscientious, faithful and devoted; won the respect and confidence of all who knew her, and is most pleasantly remembered by her associates and superior officers.

In the autumn of 1863 she went home on a furlough, was recalled by a letter from Miss Parsons; returned to duty, and continued in the service till the summer of 1864, when she was taken ill of malarious fever and died at Benton Barracks in the very scene of her patriotic and Christian labors, leaving a precious memory of her faithfulness and truly noble spirit to her friends and the world.

MRS. EDWIN GREBLE

AMONG the ardently loyal women of Philadelphia, by whom such great and untiring labors for the soldiers were performed, few did better service in a quiet and unostentatious manner than Mrs. Greble. Indeed so very quietly did she work that she almost fulfilled the Scripture injunction of secrecy as to good deeds.

The maiden name of Mrs. Greble was Susan Virginia Major. She was born in Chester County, Pennsylvania, being descended on the mother's side from a family of Quakers who were devoted to their country in the days of the Revolution with a zeal so active and outspoken as to cause them to lose their membership in the Society of Friends. Fighting Quakers there have been in both great American wars, men whose principles of peace, though not easily shaken, were less firm than their patriotism, and their traits have in many instances been emulated in the female members of their families. This seems to have been the case with Mrs. Greble.

Her eldest son, John, she devoted to the service of his country. He entered the Military Academy at West Point in 1850, at the age of sixteen, graduating honorably, and continuing in the service until June, 1861, when he fell at the disastrous battle of Great Bethel, one of the earliest martyrs of liberty in the rebellion. Another son, and the only one remaining after the death of the lamented Lieutenant Greble, when but eighteen years of age, enlisted, served faithfully, and nearly lost his life by typhoid fever. A son-in-law. Lieutenant-Colonel of the Ninetieth Pennsylvania Volunteers, and a brave soldier, was for many months a prisoner of war, and experienced the horrors of three different Southern prisons. Thus, by inheritance, patriotic, and by personal suffering and loss keenly aroused to sympathy with her country's brave defenders, Mrs. Greble from the first devoted herself earnestly and untiringly to every work of kindness and aid which suggested itself. Blessed with abundant means, she used them in the most liberal manner in procuring comforts for the sick and wounded in hospitals.

There was ample scope for such labors among the numerous hospitals of Philadelphia. Now it was blankets she sent to the hospital where they were most needed. Again a piece of sheeting already hemmed and washed. Almost daily in the season of fruit she drove to the hospitals with bushel baskets filled with the choicest the market afforded, to tempt the fever-parched lips, and refresh the languishing sufferers. Weekly she made garments for the soldiers. Leisure moments she employed in knitting scores of stockings. On holidays her contributions of poultry, fruit, and pies, went far toward making up the feasts offered by the like-minded, to the convalescents in the various institutions, or to soldiers on their way to or from the seat of war.

It was in this mode that Mrs. Greble served her country, amply and freely, but so quietly as to attract little notice. She withheld nothing that was in her power to bestow, giving even of her most precious treasures, her children, and continuing her labors unabated to the close of the war.

MRS. ISABELLA FOGG

AINE has given to the cause of the Union many noble heroes, brave spirits who have perilled life and health to put down the rebellion, and not a few equally brave and noble-hearted women, who in the ministrations of mercy have laid on the altar of patriotism their personal services, their ease and comfort, their health and some of them even life itself to bring healing and comfort to the defenders of their country. Among these, few, none perhaps save those who have laid down their lives in the service, are more worthy of honor than Mrs. Fogg.

The call for seventy-five thousand men to drive back the invaders and save the National Capital, met with no more hearty or patriotic responses than those that came from the extreme northeastern border of our Union, "away towards the sun-rising." Calais, in the extreme eastern part of Maine, raised its quota and more, upon the instant, and sent them forward promptly. The hearts of its women, too were stirred, and each was anxious to do something for the soldier. Mrs. Fogg felt that she was called to leave her home and minister in some way, she hardly knew, how, to the comfort of those who were to fight the nation's battles. At that time, however, home duties were so pressing that, most reluctantly, she was compelled to give up for the time the purpose. Three months later came the seeming disaster, the real blessing in disguise, of Bull Bun, and again was her heart moved, this time to more definite action, and a more determined purpose.

Her son, a mere boy, had left school and enlisted to hdp fill the ranks from his native State, and she was ready now to go also. Applying to the patriotic governor of Maine and to the surgeon-general of the State for permission to serve the State, without compensation, as its agent for distributing supplies to the sick and wounded soldiers of Maine, she was encouraged by them and immediately commenced the work of collecting hospital stores for her mission. In September, 1861, she in company with Mrs. Ruth S. Mayhew, went out with one of the State regiments, and caring for its sick, accompanied it to Annapolis. The regiment was ordered, late in the autumn, to join General T. AY. Sherman's expedition to Port Royal, and Airs. Fogg was desirous of accompanying it, but finding this impracticable, she turned her attention to the hospital at Annapolis, in which the spotted typhus fever had broken out and was raging with fearful malignity. The disease was exceedingly contagious, and there was great difficulty in finding nurses who were willing to risk the contagion with her high sense of duty, Mrs. Fogg felt that here was the place for her, and in company with Mrs. Alayhew, another noble daughter of Maine, she volunteered for service in this hospital. For more than three months did these heroic women remain at their post, on duty every day and often through the night for week after week, regardless of the infectious character of the disease, and only anxious to benefit the poor fever-stricken sufferers. The epidemic having subsided, Airs. Fogg placed herself under the direction of the Sanitary Commission, and took part in the spring of 1862, in that Hospital Transport Service which we have elsewhere so fully described. The month of June was passed by her at the front, at Savage's Station, with occasional visits to the brigade hospitals, and to the regimental hospitals of the most advanced posts. She remained at her post at Savage's Station, until the last moment, ministering to the wounded until the last load had been dispatched, and then retreating with the army, over land to Harrison's Landing. Here, under the orders of Mr. Letterman, the medical director, she took special charge of the diet of the amputation cases; and subsequently distributed the much needed supplies furnished by the Sanitary Commission to the soldiers in their lines.

When the camps at Harrison's Landing were broken up, and the army transferred to the Potomac, she accompanied a ship load of the wounded in the S. R. Spaulding, to Philadelphia, saw them safely removed to the general hospital, and then returned to Maine, for a brief period of rest, having been absent from home about a year. Her rest consisted mainly in appeals for further and larger supplies of hospital and sanitary stores for the wounded men of Maine, who in the battles of Pope's campaign, and Antietam had been wounded by hundreds. She was successful, and early in October returned to Washington and the hospitals of northern Maryland, where she proved an angel of mercy to the suffering. When McClellan's army crossed the Potomac, she followed, and early in December, 1862, was again at the front, where she was on the 13th, a sad spectator of the fatal disaster of Fredericksburg. The Maine Camp Hospital Association had been formed the preceding summer, and Mrs. J. S. Eaton, one of its managers, had accompanied Mrs. Fogg to the front. During the sad weeks that followed the battle of Fredericksburg, these devoted ladies labored with untiring assiduity in the hospitals, and dispensed their supplies of food and clothing, not only to the Maine boys, but to others who were in need.

When the battles of Chancellorsville were fought in the first days of May, 1863, Mrs. Fogg and Mrs. Eaton spent almost a week of incessant labor, much of the time day and night, in the temporary hospitals near United States Ford, their labors being shared for one or two days by Mrs. Husband, in dressing wounds, and attending to the poor fellows who had suffered amputation, and furnishing cordials and food to the wounded who were re-treating from the field, pursued by the enemy. One of these • Hospitals in which they had been thus laboring till they were completely exhausted, was shelled by the enemy while they were in it, and while it was filled with the wounded. The attack was of short duration, for the battery which had shelled them was soon silenced, but one of the wounded soldiers was killed by a shell.

In works like these, in the care of the wounded who were sent in by flag of truce, and the distribution to the needy of the stores received from Maine, the days passed quickly, till the invasion of Pennsylvania by General Lee, which culminated in the battle of Gettysburg. Mrs. Fogg pushed forward and reached the battle-field the day after the final battle, but she could not obtain transportation for her stores at that time, and was obliged to collect what she could from the farmers in the vicinity, and use what was put into her hands for distribution by others, until hers could be brought up. She labored with her usual assiduity and patience among this great mass of wounded and dying men, for nearly two weeks, and then, abundant helpers having arrived, she returned to the front, and was with the Army as a voluntary Special Relief agent, through all its changes of position on and about the Rapidan, at the affair of Mine Run, the retreat and pursuit to Bristow Station, and the other movements prior to General Grant's assumption of the chief command. In the winter of 1864, she made a short visit home, and the Legislature voted an appropriation of a considerable sum of money to be placed at her disposal, to be expended at her discretion for the comfort and succor of Maine soldiers.

At the opening of the great Campaign of May, 1864, she hastened to Belle Plain and Fredericksburg, and there, in company with scores of other faithful and earnest workers, toiled night and day to relieve so far as possible the indescribable suffering which filled that desolated city. After two or three weeks, she went forward to Port Royal, to White House, and finally to City Point, where, in connection with Mrs. Eaton of the Maine Camp Hospital Association, she succeeded in bringing one of the Hospitals up to the highest point of efficiency. This accomplished, she returned to Maine, and was engaged in stimulating the women of her State to more effective labors, when she received the intelligence that her son who had been in the Army of the Shenandoah, had been mortally wounded at the battle of Cedar-Run.

With all a mother's anxieties aroused, she abandoned her work in Maine, and hastened to Martinsburg, Virginia, to ascertain what was really her son's fate. Here she met a friend, one of the delegates of the Christian Commission, and learned from him, that her son had indeed been badly wounded, and had been obliged to undergo the amputation of one leg, but had borne the operation well, and after a few days had been transferred to a Baltimore Hospital. To that city she hastened, and greatly to her joy, found him doing well. Anxiety and over exertion soon prostrated her own health, and she was laid upon a sick bed for a month or more.

In November, her health being measurably restored, she returned to Washington, and asked to be assigned to duty by the Christian Commission. She was directed to report to Mrs. Annie Wittenmeyer, who was the Commission's Agent for the establishment of Special Diet Kitchens in the Hospitals. Mrs. Wittenmeyer assigned her a position in charge of the Special Diet Kitchen, on one of the large hospital-boats plying between Louisville and Nashville. While on duty on board this boat in January, 1865, she fell through one of the hatchways, and received injuries which will probably disable her for life, and her condition was for many months so critical as not to permit her removal to her native State. It would seem that here was cause for repining, had she been of a querulous disposition. Herself an invalid for life, among strangers, her only son permanently crippled from wounds received in battle, with none but stranger hands to minister to her necessities, who had done so much to soothe the anguish and mitigate the sorrows of others, there was but little to outward appearance, to compensate her for her four years of arduous toil for others, and her present condition of helplessness. Yet we are told, that amid all these depressing circumstances, this heroic woman was full of joy, that she had been permitted to labor so long, and accomplish so much for her country and its defenders, and that peace had at last dawned upon the nation. Even pain could bring no cloud over her brow, no gloom to her heart. To such a heroine, the nation owes higher honors than it has ever bestowed upon the victors of the battle-field.

MRS. E. E. GEORGE

OLD age is generally reckoned as sluggish, infirm, and not easily roused to deeds of active patriotism and earnest endeavor. The aged think and deliberate, but are slow to act. Yet in this glorious work of American Women during the late war, aged women were found ready to volunteer for posts of arduous labor, from which even those in the full vigor of adult womanhood shrank. We shall have occasion to notice this often in the work of the Volunteer Refreshment Saloons, the Soldiers' Homes, etc., where the heavy burdens of toil were borne oftenest by those who had passed the limits of three score years and ten.

Another and a noble example of heroism even to death in a lady advanced in years, is found in the case of Mrs. E. E. George. The Military Agency of Indiana, located at the capital of the State, became, under the influence and promptings of the patriotic and able Governor Morton, a power for good both in the State and in the National armies. Being in constant communication with every part of the field, it was readily and promptly informed of suffering, or want of supplies by the troops of the State at any point, and at once provided for the emergency. The supply of women-nurses for camp, field, or general hospital service, was also made a part of the work of this agency, and the efficient State Agent, Mr. Hannaman, sent into the service two hundred and fifty ladies, who were distributed in the hospitals and at the front, all over the region in insurrection.

One of these, Mrs. E. E. George, of Fort Wayne, Indiana, first applied to Mr. Hannaman for a commission in January, 1863. She brought with her strong recommendations, but her age was considered by the agent a serious objection. She admitted this, but her health was excellent, and she possessed more vigor than many ladies much younger. She was, besides, an accomplished and skilful nurse.

She was sent by Mr. Hannaman to Memphis where the wounded from the unsuccessful attack on Chickasaw Bluffs,—and the successful but bloody assault on Arkansas Post,—were gathered, and her thorough qualifications for her position, her dignity of manner and her high intelligence, soon gave her great influence. During the whole Vicksburg campaign, and into the autumn of 1863, she remained in the Memphis hospitals, working incessantly. After a short visit home, in September, she went to Corinth where Sherman's Fifteenth Corps were stationed, and remained there until their departure for Chattanooga. She then visited Pulaski and assisted in opening a hospital there, Mrs. Porter and Mrs. Bickerdyke co-operating with her, and several times she visited Indiana and procured supplies for her hospital. When Sherman commenced his forward movement toward Atlanta, in May, 1864,

Mrs. George and her friends, Mrs. Porter and Mrs. Bickerdyke, accompanied the army, and during the succession of severe battles of that campaign, she was always ready to minister to the wounded soldiers in the field. When Atlanta was invested in the latter part of July, 1864, she took charge of the Fifteenth Army Corps Hospital as Matron, and in the battles which terminated in the surrender of Atlanta, on the 1st of September, she was under fire. After the fall of Atlanta she returned home to rest and prepare for another campaign. She could not accompany Sherman's army to Savannah, but went to Nashville, where during and after Hood's siege of that city she found abundant employment.

Learning that Sherman's army was at Savannah, she set out for that city, via New York, intending to join the Fifteenth Corps, to which she had become strongly attached; but through some mistake, she was not provided with a pass, and visiting Washington to obtain one, Miss Dix persuaded her to change her plans and go to Wilmington, North Carolina, which had just passed into Union hands, and where great numbers of Union prisoners were accumulating. She had but just reached the dty when eleven thousand prisoners, just released from Salisbury, and in the worst condition of starvation, disease and wretchedness were brought in. Mrs. George, though supplied with but scant provision of hospital stores or conveniences, gave herself most heartily to the work of providing for those poor sufferers, and soon found an active coadjutor in Mrs. Harriet F. Hawley, the wife of the gallant general in command of the post. Heroically and incessantly these two ladies worked; Mrs. George gave herself no rest day or night. The sight of such intense suffering led her to such over exertion that her strength, impaired by her previous labors, gave way, and she sank under an attack of typhus, then prevailing among the prisoners. A skilful physician gave her the most careful attention, but it was of no avail. She died, another of those glorious martyrs, who more truly than the dying heroes of the battle-field have given their lives for their country. To such patient faithful souls there awaits in the "Better Land" that cordial recognition foreshadowed by the poet:

"While valor's haughty champions wait,

Till all their scars be shown,

Love walks unchallenged through the gate

To sit beside the Throne."

MRS. CHARLOTTE E. McKAY

THIS lady, a resident of Massachusetts, had early in the war been bereaved of her husband and only child, not by the vicissitudes of the battle-field but by sickness at home, and her heart worn with grief, sought relief, where it was most likely to find it, in ministering to the sufferings of others.

She accepted an appointment under Miss Dix as a hospital nurse, and commenced her hospital life in Frederick City, Maryland, in March, 1862, where she was entrusted with the care of a large number of wounded from the first battle of Winchester. Her life here passed without much of special interest, till September, 1862, when the little Maryland city was filled for two or three days with Stonewall Jackson's Corps on their way to South Mountain and Antietam. The rebels took possession of the hospital, and filled it for the time with their sick and wounded men. Resistance was useless, and Mrs. McKay treated the rebel officers and men courteously, and did what she could for the sick; her civility and kindness were recognized, and she was treated with respect by all. After the battle of Antietam, Frederick City and its hospitals were filled with the grounded, and Mrs. McKay's heart and hands were full—but as soon as the wounded became convalescent, she went to Washington and was assigned to duty for a time in the hospitals of the Capital. In January, she went to Falmouth and found employment as a nurse in the Third Corps Hospital. Here by her skill and tact she soon effected a revolution, greatly to the comfort of the poor fellows in the hospital. From being the worst it became the best of the corps hospitals at the front. General Birney and his excellent wife, seconded and encouraged all her efforts for its improvement.

The battles which though scattered over a wide extent of territory, and fought at different times and by different portions of the contending forces, have yet been known under the generic name of Chancellorsville, were full of horrors for Mrs. McKay. She witnessed the bloody but successful assault on Marye's Heights, and while ministering to the wounded who covered all the ground in front of the fortified position, received the saddening intelligence that her brother, who was with Hooker at Chancellorsville, had been instantly killed in the protracted fighting there. Other of her friends too had fallen, but crushing the agony of her own loss back into her heart, she went on ministering to the wounded. Six weeks later she was in Washington, awaiting the battle between Lee's forces and Hooker's, afterwards commanded by General Meade. When the intelligence of the three days' conflict at Gettysburg came, she went to Baltimore, and thence by such conveyance as she could find, to Gettysburg, reaching the hospital of her division, five miles from Gettysburg, on the 7th of July. Here she remained for nearly two months, laboring zealously for the welfare of a thousand or fifteen hundred wounded men. In the autumn she again sought the hospital of the Third Division, Third Corps, at the front, which for the time was at Warrenton, Virginia. After the battle of Mine Bun, she had ample employment in the care of the wounded; and later in the season she had charge of one of the hospitals at Brandy Station. Like the other ladies who were connected with hospitals at this place, she was compelled to retire by the order of April 15th; but like them she returned to her work early in May, at Belle Plain, Fredericksburg, White House, and City Point, where she labored with great assiduity and success. The changes in the army organization in June, 1864, removed most of her friends in the old third corps, and Mrs. McKay, on the invitation of the surgeon in charge of the cavalry corps hospital, took charge of the special diet of that hospital, where she remained for nearly a year, finally leaving the service in March, 1865, and remaining in Virginia in the care and instruction of the freedmen till late in the spring of 1866. The officers and men who had been under her care in the Cavalry Corps Hospital, presented her on Christmas day, 1864, with an elegant gold badge and chain, with a suitable inscription, as a testimonial of their gratitude for her services. She had previously received from the officers of the Seventeenth Maine Volunteers, whom she had cared for after the battle of Chancellorsville, a magnificent Kearny Cross, with its motto and an inscription indicating by whom it was presented.

MRS. FANNY L. RICKETTS

MRS. RICKETTS is the daughter of English parents, though born at Elizabeth, New Jersey. She is the wife of Major-General Ricketts, United States Volunteers, who at the time of their marriage was a Captain in the First Artillery, in the United States Army, and with whom she went immediately after their union, to his post on the Rio Grande. After a residence of more than three years on the frontier, the First Artillery was ordered in the spring of 1861, to Fortress Monroe, and her husband commenced a school of practice in artillery, for the benefit of the volunteer artillerymen, who, under his instruction, became expert in handling the guns.

In the first battle of Bull Run, Captain Ricketts commanded a battery of light artillery, and was severely, and it was supposed, mortally wounded and taken prisoner. The heroic wife at once applied for passes to go to him, and share his captivity, and if need be bring away his dead body. General Scott granted her such passes as he could give; but with the Rebels she found more difficulty, her parole being demanded, but on appeal to General J. E. Johnston, she was supplied with a pass and guide. She found her husband very low, and suffering from inattention, but his case was not quite hopeless. It required all her courage to endure the hardships, privations and cruelties to which the Union women were, even then, subject, but she schooled herself to endurance, and while caring for her husband during the long weeks when his life hung upon a slender thread, she became also a minister of mercy to the numerous Union prisoners, who had not a wife's tender care. When removed to Richmond, Captain Ricketts was still in great peril, and under the discomforts of his situation, grew rapidly worse. For many weeks he was unconscious, and his death seemed inevitable. At length four months after receiving his wound, he began very slowly to improve, when intelligence came that he was to be taken as one of the hostages for the thirteen privateersmen imprisoned in New York. Mrs. Ricketts went at once to Mrs. Cooper, the wife of the

Confederate Adjutant-General, and used such arguments, as led the Confederate authorities to rescind the order, so far as he was concerned. He was exchanged in the latter part of December, 1861, and having partially recovered from his wounds, was commissioned Brigadier-General, in March, 1862, and assigned to the command of a brigade in McDowell's Corps, at Fredericksburg. He passed unscathed through Pope's Campaign, but at Antietam was again wounded, though not so severely as before, and after two or three months' confinement, was in the winter of 1862-3, in Washington, as President of a Military Commission.

General Ricketts took part in the battles of Chancellorsville and Gettysburg, and escaped personal injury, but his wife in gratitude for his preservation, ministered to the wounded, and for months continued her labors of love among them.

In Grant's Campaign in 1864, General Ricketts distinguished himself for bravery in several battles, commanding a division; and at the battle of Monocacy, though he could not defeat the overwhelming force of the Rebels, successfully delayed their advance upon Baltimore. He then joined the Army of the Shenandoah, and in the battle of Middletown, October 19th, was again seriously, and it was thought mortally wounded. Again for four months did this devoted wife watch most patiently and tenderly over his couch of pain, and again was her tender nursing blessed to his recovery. In the closing scenes in the Army of the Potomac which culminated in Lee's surrender, General

Ricketts was once more in the field, and though suffering from his wounds, he did not leave his command till by the capitulation of the Rebel chief, the war was virtually concluded. The heroic wife remained at the Union headquarters, watchful lest he for whom she had periled life and health so often, should again be smitten down, but she was mercifully spared this added sorrow, and her husband was permitted to retire from the active ranks of the army, covered with scars honorably won.

MRS. JOHN S. PHELPS

AT the commencement of the War, Mrs. Phelps was residing in her pleasant home at Springfield, Missouri, her husband and herself, were both originally from New England, but years of residence in the Southwest, had caused them to feel a strong attachment for the region and its institutions. They were both, however, intensely loyal. Mr. Phelps was a member of Congress, elected as a Union man, and when it became evident that the South would resort to war, he offered his services to the General Government, raised a regiment and went into the field under the heroic Lyon. After the battle of Wilson's Creek, Mrs. Phelps succeeded in rescuing the body of General Lyon, and had it buried where it was within her control, and as soon as possible forwarded it to his friends in Connecticut. Her home was plundered subsequently by the Rebels, and nearly ruined. At the battle of Pea Ridge, Mrs. Phelps accompanied her husband to the field, and while the battle was yet raging, she assisted in the care of the wounded, tore up her own garments for bandages, dressed their wounds, cooked food, and made soup and broth for them, with her own hands, remaining with them as long as there was anything she could do, and giving not only words but deeds of substantial kindness and sympathy.

Col. Phelps was subsequently made Military Governor of Arkansas, and in the many bloody battles in that State, she was ready to help in every way in her power; and in her visits to the East, she plead the cause of the suffering loyalists of Missouri and Arkansas, among her friends with great earnestness and success.

MRS. JANE R. MUNSELL

MARYLAND, though strongly claimed by the Rebels as their territory almost throughout the War, had yet, many loyal men and women in its country villages as well as in its larger cities. The legend of Barbara Freitchie's defiance of Stonewall Jackson and his hosts, has been immortalized in Whittier's charming verse, and the equally brave defiance of the Rebels by Mrs. Effie Titlow, of Middletown, Maryland, who wound the flag about her, and stood in the balcony of her own house, looking calmly at the invading troops, who were filled with wrath at her fearlessness deserves a like immortality. Mrs. Titlow proved after the subsequent battle of Gettysburg, that she possessed the disposition to labor for the wounded faithfully and indefatigably, as well as the gallantly to defy their enemies.

Mrs. Jane R. Munsell, of Sandy Spring, Maryland, was another of these Maryland heroines, but her patriotism manifested itself in her incessant toils for the sick and wounded after Antietam and Gettysburg. For their sake, she gave up all; her home and its enjoyments, her little property, yea, and her own life also, for it was her excessive labor for the wounded soldiers which exhausted her strength and terminated her life. A correspondent of one of the daily papers of New York city, who knew her well, says of her: "A truer, kinder, or more lovely or loving woman never lived than she. Her name is a household word with the troops, and her goodnesses have passed into proverbs in the camps and sick-rooms and hospitals. She died a victim to her own kind-heartedness, for she went far beyond her strength in her blessed ministrations."

AID SOCIETIES AND SUPPLIES

WOMAN'S CENTRAL ASSOCIATION OF RELIEF

WHEN President Lincoln issued his proclamation, a quick thrill shot through the heart of every mother in New York. The Seventh Regiment left at once for the defense of Washington, and the women met at once in parlors and vestries. Perhaps nothing less than the maternal instinct could have forecast the terrible future so quickly. From the parlors of the Drs. Blackwell, and from Dr. Bellows' vestry, came the first call for a public meeting. On the 29th of April, 1861, between three and four thousand women met at the Cooper Union, David Dudley Field in the chair, and eminent men as speakers.

The object was to consecrate scattered efforts by a large and formal organization. Hence the "Woman's Central Association of Relief," the germ of the Sanitary Commission. Dr. Bellows, and Dr. E. Harris, left for Washington as delegates to establish those relations with the Government, so necessary for harmony and usefulness. The board of the Woman's Central, after many changes, consisted of,

VALENTINE MOTT, M. D., President,

HENRY W. BELLOWS, D. D., Vice President, GEORGE F. ALLEN, Esq., Secretary,

HOWARD POTTER, Esq., Treasurer.

EXECUTIVE COMMITTEE.

H. W. Bellows, D. D., Chairman. Valentine Mott, M. D.

Mrs. G. L. Schuyler. Mrs. T. d'Ordmieulx.

Miss Ellen Collins. W. H. Draper, M. D.

F. L. Olmstead, Esq. G. F. Allen, Esq.

REGISTRATION COMMITTEE.

E. Blackwell, M. D., Chairman. Mrs. W. P. Griffin, Secretary. Mrs. H. Baylis. Mrs. J. A. Swett.

Mrs. V. Botta. Mrs. C. Abernethy.

Wm. A. Muhlenburg, D. D. E. Harris, M. D.

FINANCE COMMITTEE.

Howard Potter, Esq. John D. Wolfe, Esq. "William Hague, D. D. J. H. Markoe, M. D.

Mrs. Hamilton Fish. Mrs. C. M. Kirkland. Mrs. C. W. Field. Asa D. Smith, D. D.

While in Washington, Dr. Bellows originated the "United States Sanitary Commission," and on the 24th of June, 1864, the Woman's Central voluntarily offered to become subordinate as one of its branches of supply. The following September this offer was accepted in a formal resolution, establishing also a semiweekly correspondence between the two boards, by which the wants of the army were made known to the Woman's Central.

Prominent and onerous were the duties of the Registration Committee. Its members met daily, to select from numberless applicants, women fitted to receive special training in our city hospitals for the position of nurses. So much of moral as well as mental excellence was indispensable, that the committee found its labors incessant. Then followed the supervision while in hospital, and while awaiting a summons, then the outfit and forwarding, often suddenly and in bands, and lastly, the acceptance by the War Department and Medical Bureau.

The chairman of the committee, Miss E. Blackwell, accompanied by its secretary, Mrs. Griffin, went to Washington in this service. Miss Blackwell's admirable report "on the selection and preparation of nurses for the army," will always be a source of pride to the Woman's Central.

In the meantime, the Finance and Executive Committees were struggling for a strong foothold. The chairman of the former, Mrs. Hamilton Fish, raised over five thousand dollars by personal effort. The latter committee had the liveliest contests, tor the Government declared itself through the Army Regulation, equal to any demands, and the people were disposed to cry amen. Rumors of "a ninety days' war," and "already more lint than would be needed for years," stirred the committee to open at once a correspondence with sewing-societies, churches, and communities in New York and elsewhere. Simultaneously, the Sanitary Commission issued an explanatory circular, urgent and minute, "To the loyal women of America."

Then began that slow yet sure stream of supplies which flow ed on to the close of the war, so slow, indeed, at first, and so impatiently hoped for, that the members of the committee could not wait, but must rush to the street to see the actual arrival of boxes and bales. Soon, however, that good old office, No. 10, Cooper Union, became rich in everything needed; rich, too, in young women to unpack, mark and repack, in old women to report forthcoming contributions from grocers, merchants and tradesmen, and richer than all, in those wondrous boxes of sacrifices from the country, the last blanket, the inherited quilt,' curtains torn from windows, and the coarse yet ancestral linen. In this personal self-denial the city had no part. What wonder that the whole corps of the Woman's Central felt their time and physical fatigue as nothing in comparison to these heart trials. Out of this responsive earnestness grew the carefully prepared reports and circulars, the filing of letters, thousands in number, contained in twenty-five volumes, their punctilious and grateful acknowledgement, and the thorough plan of books, three in number, by which the whole story of the Woman's Central may be learnt, and well would it repay the study.

First, The receiving book recorded the receipt and acknowledgement of box.

Second, in the day book, each page was divided into columns, in which was recorded, the letter painted on the cover of each box to designate it, and the kind and amount of supplies which each contained after repacking, only one description of supplies being placed in any one box. So many cases were received during the four years, that the alphabet was repeated seven hundred and twenty-seven times.

Third, The ledger with its headings of "shirts," "drawers," "socks," etc., so arranged, that on sudden demand, the exact number of any article on hand could be ascertained at a glance.

Thus early began through these minute details, the effectiveness of the Woman's Central. Every woman engaged in it learnt the value of precision.

A sub-committee for New York and Brooklyn was formed, consisting of Mrs. W. M. Fellows, and Mrs. Robert Colby, to solicit from citizens, donations of clothing, and supplies of all kinds. These ladies were active, successful and clerkly withal, giving receipts for every article received.

Those present at Dr. Bellows' Church in May, will never forget the first thrilling call for nurses on board the hospital transports. The duty was imperative, was untried and therefore startling. It was like a sudden plunge into unknown waters, yet many brave women enrolled their names. From the Woman's Central went forth Mrs. Griffin accompanied by Mrs david Lane. They left at once in the "Wilson Small," and went up the York and Pamunkey rivers, and to White House, thus tasting the first horrors of war. This experience would form a brilliant chapter in the history of the Woman's Central.

In June, 1861, the association met with a great loss in the departure of Mrs d'Ormieulx, for Europe. Of her Dr. Bellows said: "It would be ungrateful not to acknowledge the zeal, devotion and ability of one of the ladies of this committee, Mrs. d'Ordmieulx, now absent from the country, who labored incessantly in the earlier months of the organization, and gave a most vital start to the life of this committee." This lady resumed her duties after a year's absence, and continued her characteristic force and persistency up to the close.

At this time, Mr. S. W. Bridgham put his broad shoulders to the wheel. He had been a member of the board from the beginning, but not a "day-laborer" until now. And not this alone, for he was a night-laborer also. At midnight, and in the still "darker hours which precede the dawn," Mr. Bridgham and his faithful ally, Roberts, often left their beds to meet sudden emergencies, and to ship comforts to distant points. On Sundays too, he and his patriotic wife might be easily detected creeping under the half-opened door of Number 10, to gather up for a sudden requisition, and then to beg of the small city expresses, transportation to ship or railroad. This was often his Sunday worship. His heart and soul were given to the work.

In November, 1862, a council of representatives from the principal aid-societies, now numbering fourteen hundred and sixty-two, was held in Washington. The chief object was to obtain supplies more steadily. Immediately after a battle, but too late for the exigency, there was an influx, then a lull. The Woman's Central therefore urged its auxiliaries to send a monthly box. It also urged the Federal principle, that is, the bestowment of all supplies on United States troops, and not on individuals or regiments, and explained to the public that the Sanitary Commission acted in aid of, and not in opposition to the government.

In January, 1863, all supplies had been exhausted by the battles of Antietam and Fredericksburg. Everything was again needed. An able letter of inquiry to secretaries of the auxiliary societies with a preliminary statement of important facts, was drawn up by Miss Louisa L. Schuyler, and issued in pamphlet form. Two hundred and thirty-five replies were received, (all to be read)! which were for the most part favorable to the Sanitary Commission with its Federal principle as a medium, and all breathed the purest patriotism.

In February, the plan of "Associate Managers" borrowed from the Boston branch was adopted. Miss Schuyler assumed the whole labor. It was a division of the tributary states into sections, an associate manager to each, who should supervise, control and stimulate every aid-society in her section, going from village to village, and organizing, if need be, as she went. She should hold a friendly correspondence monthly, with the committee on correspondence (now separated from that on supplies) besides sending an official monthly report. To ascertain the right woman, one who should combine the talent, energy, tact and social influence for this severe field, was the difficult preliminary step. Then, to gain her consent, to instruct, and to place her in relations with the auxiliaries, involved an amount of correspondence truly frightful. It was done. Yet, in one sense, it was never done; for up to the close, innumerable little rills from "pastures new" were guided on to the great stream. The experience of every associate manager, endeared to the Woman's Central through the closest sympathy would be a rare record.

An elaborate and useful set of books was arranged by Miss Schuyler in furtherance of the work of the committee "on correspondence, and diffusion of information." Lecturers were also to be obtained by this committee, and this involved much forethought and preparation of the field. Three hundred and sixty-nine lectures were delivered upon the work of the Sanitary Commission, by nine gentlemen.

State agencies made great confusion in the hospitals. The Sanitary Commission was censured for employing paid agents, and its board of officers even, was accused of receiving salaries. Its agents were abused for wastefulness, as if the frugality so proper in health, were not improper in sickness. Reports were in circulation injurious to the honor of the Commission. Explanations had become necessary. The Woman's Central, therefore, published a pamphlet written by Mr. George T. Strong, entitled: "How can we best help our Camps and Hospitals'?" In this the absolute necessity of paid agents was conclusively vindicated; the false report of salaries to the board of officers was denied, and the true position of the Sanitary Commission with reference to the National Government and its medical bureau was again patiently explained. A series of letters from assistant-surgeons of the army and of volunteers, recommending the Commission to the confidence of the people, was also inserted.

About this time a Hospital Directory was opened at Number 10, Cooper Union.

In the spring of 1863, the Woman's Central continued to be harassed, not by want of money, for that was always promised by its undaunted treasurer, but by lack of clothing and edibles. The price of all materials had greatly advanced, the reserved treasures of every household were exhausted, the early days of havelocks and Sunday industry had gone forever, and the Sanitary Commission was frequently circumvented and calumniated by rival organizations. The members of the Woman's Central worked incessantly. Miss

Collins was always at her post. She had never left it. Her hand held the reins taut from the beginning to the end. She alone went to the office daily, remaining after office hours, which were from nine to six, and taking home to be perfected in the still hours of night those elaborate tables of supplies and their disbursement, which formed her monthly Report to the Board of the Woman's Central. These tables are a marvel of method and clearness.

To encourage its struggling Aid-Societies, who were without means, but earnest in their offers of time and labor, the Woman's Central offered to purchase for them materials at wholesale prices. This was eagerly accepted by many. A purchasing Committee was organized, consisting of Mrs. J. H. Swett, Mrs. H. Fish, Mrs. S. Weir Roosevelt.

Miss Schuyler's wise "Plan of organization for country Societies," and the founding of "Alert-clubs," as originated in Norwalk (Ohio), also infused new life into the tributaries. Her master-mind smoothed all difficulties, and her admirable Reports so full of power and pathos, probed the patriotism of all. Societies were urged to work as if the war had just begun. From these united efforts, supplies came in steadily, so that in the summer of 1863, the Woman's Central, was able to contribute largely to the Stations at Beaufort and Morris Island. The blessings thus poured in were dispensed by Hr and Mrs. Marsh, with their usual good judgment, and it is grateful to remember that the sufferers from that thrilling onslaught at Fort Wagner, were among the recipients.

In the summer of 1863, the Association lost its faithful Secretary, Mr. George F. Allen. Mr. S. W. Bridgham was elected in his place.

During this eventful summer, Miss Collins and Mrs. 'Griffin, had sole charge of the office, through the terrible New York riots. These ladies usually alternated in the summer months, never allowing the desk of the Supply Committee to be without a responsible bead. Mrs. Griffin also became Chairman of the Special Relief Committee organized in 1863, all of whom made personal visits to the sick, and relieved many cases of extreme suffering.

Early in January, 1864, a Council of women was summoned to Washington. Thirty-one delegates were present from the Eastern and Western branches. Miss Collins and Miss Schuyler were sent by the Woman's Central. This meeting gave a new impulse to the work. These toilers in the war met face to face, compared their various experiences, and suggested future expedients. Miss Schuyler took special pains to encourage personal intercourse between the different branches. Her telescopic eye swept the whole field. The only novelty proposed, was County Councils every three or six months, composed of delegates from the Aid-Societies. This would naturally quicken emulation, and prove a wholesome stimulus. "Westchester County led immediately in this movement.

About this time supplies were checked by the whirlwind of "Fairs." The Woman's Central, issued a Circular urging its Auxiliaries to continue their regular contributions, and to make their working for Fairs a pastime only. In no other way could it meet the increased demands upon its resources, for the sphere of the Sanitary Commission's usefulness had now extended to remotest States, and its vast machinery for distribution had become more and more expensive.

Letters poured in from the country, unflinching letters, but crying out, "we are poor." What was to be done? How encourage these devoted sewing-circles and aid-societies? Every article had advanced still more in price. A plan was devised to double the amount of any sum raised by the feeble Aid-Societies, not exceeding thirty dollars per month. Thus, any Society sending twenty dollars, received in return, goods to the value of forty. This scheme proved successful. It grew into a large business, increasing greatly the labors of the Purchasing Committee, involving a new set of account books and a salaried accountant. Duly the smaller Societies availed themselves of this offer. The Sanitary Commission, agreed to meet this additional expense of the Woman's Central, amounting to over five thousand dollars per month. Thus an accumulation was gathered for the coming campaign.

In November, 1864, The Woman's Central convened, and defrayed the expenses of a Soldiers' Aid Society Council, at which two hundred and fifteen delegates were present.

The Military Hospitals near the city had, from time to time, received assistance, though not often needed from the Association. The Navy too, received occasional aid.

In the spring of 1865, The Woman's Central lost its President, Dr. Mott, whose fame gave weight to its early organization. From respect to his memory, it was resolved that no other should fill his place.

At last, in April, 1865, came the glad tidings of great joy. Lee had surrendered. In May, Miss Collins wrote a congratulatory letter to the Aid-Societies, naming the 4th of July, as the closing day of the Woman's Central, and urging active work up to that time, as hospital and field supplies would still be needed. With tender forethought, she also begged them to keep alive their organizations, for "the privilege of cherishing the maimed and disabled veterans who are returning to us."

The receipts and disbursements of the Woman's Central are as astounding to itself as to the public. So much love and patriotism, so little money! As early as May, 1863, the Treasurer in his Report, remarks:

"That so small a sum should cover all the general amount of expenses of the Association in the transaction of a business w hich, during the year, has involved the receipt or purchase, assorting, cataloguing, marking, packing, storing and final distribution of nearly half a million of articles, will be no less satisfactory to the donors of the funds so largely economized for the direct benefit of the soldier, than to those friends of the Association from whose self-denying, patriotic and indefatigable personal labors, this economy has resulted."

In the Table of supplies received and distributed from May 1st, 1861, to July 7th, 1865, prepared by Miss Collins, the item of shirts alone amounts to two hundred and ninety-one thousand four hundred and seventy-five.

For four years' distribution, purchase of hospital delicacies, and all office expenses, except those of the committee which purchased material for the aid-societies amounting to seventy-nine thousand three hundred and ninety dollars and fifty-seven cents, the sum expended was only sixty-one thousand three hundred and eighty-six dollars and fifty-seven cents.

How was this accomplished by the Woman's Central except through its band of daily volunteers (the great unnamed) its devoted associate managers through whom came an increase of one hundred and thirty-eight new societies, the generosity of Express companies, the tender self-sacrifice of country-homes, and the indefatigable labors of the several committees, all of whom felt it a privilege to work in so sacred a cause. Neither land nor money, nothing less than sentiment and principle, could have produced these results.

To the Brooklyn Relief Association the Woman's Central always felt deeply indebted for supplies. Its admirable President, Mrs. Stranahan, was in close sympathy with the association, often pouring in nearly half of the woollen garments it received.

The careful dissemination of printed matter tended to sustain the interest of country societies. The voluminous reports of the Association arranged monthly by Miss Schuyler, who also contributed a series of twelve articles to the Sanitary Commission Bulletin, published semi-monthly by that board, the "Soldiers' Friend," "Nelly's Hospital," and other documents amounting in sixteen months to ninety-eight thousand nine hundred and eightyfour copies were issued by the committee "On Correspondence," etc. For the last two years that committee consisted of Miss L. L. Schuyler, chairman; Mrs. George Curtis, Mrs. David Lane, Miss A. Post, Miss C. Nash, H. W. Bellows, D.D.

For the last three years, to the first members of the committee on "Supplies," etc., were added Miss Gertrude Stevens, the Misses Shaw in succession, Miss Z. T. Detmold, Mr. Isaac Bronson. George Roberts remained the faithful porter through the whole four years.

The territory from which the Woman's Central received its supplies after the various branches of the Sanitary Commission were in full working condition, was eastern and central New York, Connecticut, Rhode Island, and partially from northern New Jersey, Massachusetts, Vermont and Canada. Generous contributions were also received from European auxiliaries.

On the 7th of July, 1865, the final meeting of the board of the Woman's Central took place. Its members, though scattered by midsummer-heat, did not fail to appear. It was a solemn and touching occasion. The following resolutions, deeply felt and still read with emotion by its members, were then unanimously adopted:

Resolved, That the Woman's Central Association of Relief cannot dissolve without expressing its sense of the value and satisfaction of its connection with the United States Sanitary Commission, whose confidence, guidance and support it has enjoyed for four years past. In now breaking the formal tie that has bound us together, we leave unbroken the bond of perfect sympathy, gratitude and affection, which has grown up between us.

Resolved, That we owe a deep debt of gratitude to our Associate Managers, who have so ably represented our interests, in the different sections of our field of duty, and, that to their earnest, unflagging and patriotic exertions, much of the success which has followed our labors is due.

Resolved, That to the Soldiers' Aid Societies, which form the working constituency of this Association, we offer the tribute of our profound respect and admiration for their zeal, constancy and patience to the end. Their boxes and their letters have been alike our support and our inspiration. They have kept our hearts hopeful, and our confidence in our cause always firm. Henceforth the women of America are banded in town and country, as the men are from city and field. We have wrought, and thought, and prayed together, as our soldiers have fought, and bled, and conquered, shoulder to shoulder, and from this hour the womanhood of our country is knit in a common bond, which the softening influences of Peace must not, and shall not weaken or dissolve. May God's blessing rest upon every Soldiers' Aid Society in the list of our contributors, and on every individual worker in their ranks.

Resolved, That to our band of Volunteer Aids, the ladies who, in turn, have so long and usefully labored in the details of our work at these rooms, we give our hearty and affectionate thanks, feeling that their unflagging devotion and cheerful presence have added largely to the efficiency and pleasure of oui labors. Their record, however hidden, is on high, and they have in their own hearts the joyful testimony, that in their country's peril and need they were not found wanting.

Resolved, That the thanks of this Association are due to the ladies who have, at different times, served upon the Board, but are no longer members of it; and that we recall in this hour of parting the memory of each and all who have lent us the light of their countenance, and the help of their hands. Especially do we recognize the valuable aid rendered by the members of our Registration Committee, who, in the early days of this Association, superintended the training of a band of one hundred women nurses for our army hospitals. The successful introduction of this system is chiefly due to the zeal and capacity of these ladies.

Resolved, That in dissolving this Association, we desire to express the gratitude we owe to Divine Providence for permitting the members of this Board to work together in so great and so glorious a cause, and upon so large and successful a scale, to maintain for so long a period, relations of such affection and respect, and now to part with such deep and grateful memories of our work and of each other.

Resolved, That, the close of the war having enabled this Association to finish the work for which it was organized, the Woman's Central Association of Relief for the Army and Navy of the United States, is hereby dissolved.

The meeting then adjourned sine die.

SAMUEL W. BRIDGHAM, Secretary.

For further and better knowledge of the Woman's Central, is it not written in the book of the Chronicles of the Board of the United States Sanitary Commission?

SOLDIERS' AID SOCIETY OF NORTHERN OHIO

AMONG the branches or centres of supply and distribution of the United States Sanitary Commission, though some with a wider field and a more wealthy population in that field have raised a larger amount of money or supplies, there was none which in so small and seemingly barren a district proved so efficient or accomplished so much as the "Soldiers' Aid Society of Northern Ohio."

This extraordinary efficiency was due almost wholly to the wonderful energy and business ability of its officers. The society which at first bore the name of The Soldiers' Aid Society of Cleveland, was composed wholly of ladies, and was organized on the 20th day of April, 1861, five days after the President's proclamation calling for troops. Its officers were (exclusive of vice-presidents who were changed once or twice and who were not specially active) Mrs. B. Rouse, President, Miss Mary Clark Brayton, Secretary, Miss Ellen F. Terry, Treasurer. These ladies continued their devotion to their work not only through the war, but with a slight change in their organization, to enable them to do more for the crippled and disabled soldier, and to collect without fee or reward the bounties, back pay and pensions coming to the defenders of the country, has remained in existence and actively employer! up to the present time.

No constitution or by-laws were ever adopted, and beyond a verbal pledge to work for the soldiers while the war should last, and a fee of twenty-five cents monthly, no form of membership was prescribed and no written word held the society together to its latest day. Its sole cohesive power was the bond of a common and undying patriotism.

In October, 1861, it was offered to the United States Sanitary Commission, as one of its receiving and disbursing branches, and the following month its name was changed to The Soldiers' Aid Society of Northern Ohio. Its territory was very small and not remarkable for wealth. It had auxiliaries in eighteen counties of Northeastern Ohio, (Toledo and its vicinity being connected with the Cincinnati Branch, and the counties farther west with Chicago), and a few tributaries in the counties of Michigan, New York, and Pennsylvania, which bordered on Ohio, of which that at Meadville, Pennsylvania, was the only considerable one.

In this region, Cleveland was the only considerable city, and the population of the territory though largely agricultural was not possessed of any considerable wealth, nor was the soil remarkably fertile.

In November, 1861, the society had one hundred and twenty auxiliaries. A year later the number of these had increased to four hundred and fifty, and subsequently an aggregate of five hundred and twenty was attained. None of these ever seceded or became disaffected, but throughout the war the utmost cordiality prevailed between them and the central office.

In the five years from its organization to April, 1866, this society had collected and disbursed one hundred and thirty thousand four hundred and five dollars and nine cents in cash, and one million and three thousand dollars in stores, making a grand total of one million one hundred and thirty-three thousand four hundred and five dollars and nine cents. This amount was received mainly from contributions, though the excess over one million dollars, was mostly received from the proceeds of exhibitions, concerts, and the Northern Ohio Sanitary Fair held in

February and March, 1864. The net proceeds of this fair were about seventy-nine thousand dollars.

The supplies thus contributed, as well as so much of the money as was not required for the other objects of the society, of which we shall say more presently, were forwarded to the Western Depôt of the Sanitary Commission at Louisville, except in a few instances where they were required for the Eastern armies. The reception, repacking and forwarding of this vast quantity of stores, as well as all the correspondence required with the auxiliaries and with the Western office of the Sanitary Commission, and the book-keeping which was necessary in consequence, involved a great amount of labor, but was performed with the utmost cheerfulness by the ladies whom we have named as the active officers of the society.

Among the additional institutions or operations of this society connected with, yet outside of its general work of receiving and disbursing supplies, the most important was the "Soldiers' Home," established first on the 17th of April, 1861, as a lodging room for disabled soldiers in transit, and having connected with it a system of meal tickets, which were given to deserving soldiers of this class, entitling the holder to a meal at the depot dining hall, the tickets being redeemed monthly by the society. In October, 1863, the "Soldiers' Home," a building two hundred and thirty-five feet long and twenty-five feet wide, erected and furnished by funds contributed by citizens of Cleveland at the personal solicitation of the ladies, was opened, and was maintained until June 1, 1866, affording special relief to fifty-six thousand five hundred and twenty registered inmates, to whom were given one hundred and eleven thousand seven hundred and seven meals, and twenty-nine thousand nine hundred and seventy-three lodgings, at an entire cost of twenty-seven thousand four hundred and eight dollars and three cents. No government support was received for this home, and no rations drawn from the commissary as in most institutions of this kind.

The officers of the society gave daily personal attention to the Home, directing its management minutely, and the superintendent, matron and other officials were employed by them.

The society also established a hospital directory for the soldiers of its territory, and recorded promptly the location and condition of the sick or wounded men from returns received from all the hospitals in which they were found; a measure which though involving great labor, was the means of relieving the anxiety of many thousands of the friends of these men.

In May, 1865, an Employment Agency was opened, and continued for six months. Two hundred and six discharged soldiers, mostly disabled, were put into business situations by the personal efforts of the officers of the society. The families of the disabled men were cared for again and again, many of them being regular pensioners of the society.

The surplus funds of the society, amounting June 1st, 1866, to about nine thousand dollars, were used in the settlement of all war claims of soldiers, bounties, back pay, pensions, etc., gratuitously to the claimant. For this purpose, an agent thoroughly familiar with the whole business of the Pension Office, and the bureaus before which claims could come, was employed, and Miss Brayton and Miss Terry were daily in attendance as clerks at the office. Up to August 1st, 1866, about four hundred claims had been adjusted.

The entire time of the officers of the society daily from eight o'clock in the morning to six and often later in the evening, was given to this work through the whole period of the war, and indeed until the close of the summer of 1866. The ladies being all in circumstances of wealth, or at least of independence, no salary was asked or received, and no traveling expenses were ever charged to the Society, though the president visited repeatedly every part of their territory, organizing and encouraging the auxiliary societies, and both secretary and treasurer went more than once to the front of the army, and to the large general hospitals at Louisville, Nashville, Chattanooga, etc., with a view to obtaining knowledge which might benefit their cause.

In August, 1864, a small printing office, with a hand-press, was attached to the rooms; the ladies learned how to set type and work the press, and issued weekly bulletins to their auxiliaries to encourage and stimulate their efforts. For two years from October, 1862, two columns were contributed to a weekly city paper by these indefatigable ladies for the benefit of their auxiliaries. These local auxiliary societies were active and loyal, but they needed constant encouragement, and incentives to action, to bring and keep them up to their highest condition of patriotic effort.

The Sanitary Fair at Cleveland was not, as in many other cases, originated and organized by outside effort, for the benefit of the Branch of the Sanitary Commission, but had its origin, its organization and its whole management directly from the Soldiers' Aid Society itself.

In November, 1865, the Ohio State Soldiers' Home was opened, and the Legislature having made no preparation for its immediate wants, the Soldiers' Aid Society made a donation of five thousand dollars for the support of its members.

With a brief sketch of each of these ladies, we close our history of the Soldiers' Aid Society of Northern Ohio.

Mrs. Rouse is a widow, somewhat advanced in life, small and delicately organized, and infirm in health, but of tireless energy and exhaustless sympathy for every form of human suffering. For forty years past she has been foremost in all benevolent movements among the ladies of Cleveland, spending most of her time and income in the relief of the unfortunate and suffering; yet it is the testimony of all who knew her, that she is entirely free from all personal ambition, and all love of power or notoriety. Though earnestly patriotic, and ready to do all in her power for her country, there is nothing masculine, or as the phrase goes, "strong-minded" in her demeanor. She is a descendant of Oliver Cromwell, and has much of his energy and power of endurance, but none of his coarseness, being remarkably unselfish, and ladylike in her manners. During the earlier years of the war, she spent much of her time in visiting the towns of the territory assigned to the society, and promoting the formation of local Soldiers' Aid Societies, and it was due to her efforts that there was not a town of any size in the region to which the society looked for its contributions which had not its aid society, or its Alert Club, or both. Though plain and petite in person, she possessed a rare power of influencing those whom she addressed, and never failed to inspire them with the resolution to do all in their power for the country. At a later period the laborious duties of the home office of the society required her constant attention.

Miss Mary Clark Brayton, the secretary of the society, is a young lady of wealth, high social position and accomplished education, but of gentle and modest disposition. Since the spring of 1861, she has isolated herself from society, and the pleasures of intellectual pursuits, and has given her whole time and thoughts to the one work of caring for the welfare of the soldiers. From early morning till evening, and sometimes far into the night, she has toiled in the rooms of the society, or elsewhere, superintending the receiving or despatch of supplies, conducting the immense correspondence of the society, preparing, setting up and printing its weekly bulletins, or writing the two columns weekly of matter for the Cleveland papers, on topics connected with the society's work, now in her turn superintending and purchasing supplies for the Soldiers' Home, looking out a place for some partially disabled soldier, or supplying the wants of his family; occasionally, though at rare intervals, varying her labors by a journey to the front, or a temporary distribution of supplies at some general hospital at Nashville, Huntsville, Bridgeport or Chattanooga, and then, having ascertained by personal inspection what was most necessary for the comfort and health of the army, returning to her work, and by eloquent and admirable 69 appeals to the auxiliaries, and to her personal friends in Cleveland, securing and forwarding the necessary supplies so promptly, that as the officers of the Commission at Louisville said, it seemed as if she could hardly have reached Cleveland, before the supplies began to flow in at the Commission's warehouses at Louisville. Miss Brayton possesses business ability sufficient to have conducted the enterprises of a large mercantile establishment, and the complete system and order displayed in her transaction of business would have done honor to any mercantile house in the world. Her untiring energy repeatedly impaired her health, but she has never laid down her work, and has no disposition to do so, while there is an opportunity of serving the defenders of her country.

Miss Ellen F. Terry, the treasurer of the society, is a daughter of Dr. Charles Terry, a professor in the Cleveland Medical College. Her social position, like that of Miss Brayton, is the highest in that city. She is highly educated, familiar, like her friend Miss Brayton, with most of the modern languages of Europe, but especially proficient in mathematics. During the whole period of the war, she devoted herself as assiduously to the work of the society as did Mrs. Bouse and Miss Brayton, She kept the books of the society (in itself a great labor), made all its disbursements of cash, and did her whole work with a neatness, accuracy and despatch which would have done honor to any business man in the country. No monthly statements of accounts from any of the branches of the Sanitary Commission reporting to its Western Office at Louisville were drawn up with such careful accuracy and completeness as those from the Cleveland branch, although in most of the others experienced and skilful male accountants were employed to make them up. Miss Terry also superintended the building of the Soldiers' Home, and took her turn with Miss Brayton in its management. She also assisted in the other labors of the society, and made occasional visits to the front and the hospitals. Since the close of the waj she and Miss Brayton have acted as clerks of the Free Claim Agency for recovering the dues of the soldiers, from the Government offices

We depart from our usual practice of excluding the writings of those who are the subjects of our narratives, to give the following sprightly description of one of the hospital trains of the Sanitary Commission, communicated by Miss Brayton to the Cleveland Herald, not so much to give our readers a specimen of her abilities as a writer, as to illustrate the thorough devotion to their patriotic work which has characterized her and her associates.

ON A HOSPITAL TRAIN

"Riding on a rail in the 'Sunny South' is not the most agreeable pastime in the world. Don't understand me to refer to that favorite argumentum ad hominem which a true Southerner applies to all who have the misfortune to differ from him, especially to Northern abolitionists; I simply mean that mode of traveling that Saxe in his funny little poem, calls so 'pleasant.' And no wonder! To be whirled along at the rate of forty miles an hour, over a smooth road, reposing on velvet-cushioned seats, with backs just at the proper angle to rest a tired head,—ice-water,— the last novel or periodical— all that can tempt your fastidious taste, or help to while away the time, offered at your elbow, is indeed pleasant; but wo to the fond imagination that pictures to itself such luxuries on a United States Military Railroad. Be thankful if in the crowd of tobacco-chewing soldiers you are able to get a seat, and grumble not if the pine boards are hard and narrow. Lay in a good stock of patience, for six miles an hour is probably the highest rate of speed you will attain, and even then you shudder to see on either hand strewn along the road, wrecks of cars and locomotives smashed in every conceivable manner, telling of some fearful accident or some guerrilla fight.

These are discomforts hard to bear even when one is well and strong; how much worse for a sick or wounded man. But thanks to the United States Sanitary Commission and to those gentlemen belonging to it, whose genius and benevolence originated, planned, and carried it out, a hospital-train is now running on almost all the roads over which it is necessary to transport sick or wounded men. These trains are now under the control of Government, but the Sanitary Commission continues to furnish a great part of the stores that are used in them. My first experience of them was a sad one. A week before, the army had moved forward and concentrated near Tunnel Hill. The dull, monotonous rumble of army wagons as they rolled in long trains through the dusty street; the measured tramp of thousands of bronzed and war-worn veterans; the rattle and roar of the guns and caissons as they thundered on their mission of death; the glittering sheen reflected from a thousand sabres, had all passed by and left us in the desolated town. We lived, as it were, with bated breath and eager ears, our nerves tensely strung with anxiety and suspense waiting to catch the first sound of that coming strife, where we knew so many of our bravest and best must fall. At last came the news of that terrible fight at Buzzard's Roost or Rocky Face Ridge, and the evening after, in came Dr. S. straight from the front, and said, 'The hospital-train is at the depot, wouldn't you like to see it?' 'Of course we would,' chorused Mrs. Dr. S and myself, and forthwith we rushed for our hats and cloaks, filled two large baskets with soft crackers and oranges, and started off. A walk of a mile brought us to the depot , and down in the further corner of the depot-yard we saw a train of seven or eight cars standing, apparently unoccupied.

'There it is,' said Dr. S. 'Why, it looks like any ordinary train,' I innocently remarked, but I was soon to find out the difference. We chanced to see Dr. Meyers, the Surgeon-in-charge, on the first car into which we went, and he made us welcome to do and to give whatever we had for the men, and so, armed with authority from the 'powers that be we went forward with confidence.

"Imagine a car a little wider than the ordinary one, placed on springs, and having on each side three tiers of berths or cots, suspended by rubber bands. These cots are so arranged as to yield to the motion of the car, thereby avoiding that jolting experienced even on the smoothest and best kept road. I didn't stop to investigate the plan of the car then, for I saw before me, on either hand, a long line of soldiers, shot in almost every conceivable manner, their wounds fresh from the battle-field, and all were patient and quiet; not a groan or complaint escaped them, though I saw some faces twisted into strange contortions with the agony of their wounds. I commenced distributing my oranges right and left, but soon realized the smallness of my basket and the largeness of the demand, and sadly passed by all but the worst cases. In the third car that we entered we found the Colonel, Lieutenant-Colonel, and Adjutant of the Twenty-ninth Ohio, all severely wounded. We stopped and talked awhile. Mindful of the motto of my Commission, to give 'aid and comfort,' I trickled a little sympathy on them. 'Poor fellows!' said I. 'No, indeed,' said they. 'We did suffer riding twenty miles' — it couldn't have been more than fourteen or fifteen, but a shattered limb or a ball in one's side lengthens the miles astonishingly—in those horrid ambulances to the cars. 'We cried last night like children, some of us,' said a Lieutenant, 'but we're all right now. This Hospital Train is a jolly thing. It goes like a cradle.' Seeing my sympathy wasted, I tried another tack. 'Did you know that Sherman was in Dalton?' 'No!' cried the Colonel and all the men who could, raised themselves up and stared at me with eager, questioning eyes. 'Is that so?' 'Yes,' I replied, 'It is true.' 'Then, I don't care for this little wound,' said one fellow, slapping his right leg, which was pierced and torn by a minie ball. Brave men! How I longed to take our whole North, and pour out its wealth and luxury at their feet.

"A little farther on in the car, I chanced to look down, and there at my feet lay a young man, not more than eighteen or nineteen years old; hair tossed back from his noble white brow; long brown lashes lying on his cheek; face as delicate and refined as a girl's. I spoke to him and he opened his eyes, but could not answer me. I held an orange before him, and he looked a Yes; so I cut a hole in it and squeezed some of the juice into his mouth. It seemed to revive him a little, and after sitting a short time I left him. Soon after, they carried him out on a stretcher—poor fellow! He was dying when I saw him, and I could but think of his mother and sisters who would have given worlds to stand beside him as I did. By this time it was growing dark, my oranges had given out, and we were sadly in the way; so we left, to be haunted for many a day by the terrible pictures we had seen on our first visit to a Hospital Train.

"My next experience was much pleasanter. I had the privilege of a ride on one from Chattanooga to Nashville, and an opportunity of seeing the plan of arrangement of the train. There were three hundred and fourteen sick and wounded men on board, occupying nine or ten cars, with the surgeon's car in the middle of the train. This car is divided into three compartments; at one end is the storeroom where are kept the eatables and bedding, at the other, the kitchen; and between the two the surgeon's room, containing his bed, secretary, and shelves and pigeon holes for instruments, medicines, etc. A narrow hall connects the store-room and kitchen, and great windows or openings in the opposite sides of the car give a pleasant draft of air. Sitting in a comfortable arm-chair, one would not wish a pleasanter mode of traveling, especially through the glorious mountains of East Tennessee, and further on, over the fragrant, fertile meadows, and the rolling hills and plains of Northern Alabama and middle Tennessee, clothed in their fresh green garments of new cotton and corn. This is all charming for a passenger, but a hospital train is a busy place for the surgeons and nurses.

"The men come on at evening, selected from the different hospitals, according to their ability to be moved, and after having had their tea, the wounds have to be freshly dressed. This takes till midnight, perhaps longer, and the surgeon must be on the watch continually, for on him falls the responsibility, not only of the welfare of the men, but of the safety of the train. There is a conductor and brakeman, and for them, too, there is no rest. Each finds enough to do as nurse or assistant. In the morning, after a breakfast of delicious coffee or tea, dried beef, dried peaches, soft bread, cheese, etc., the wounds have to be dressed a second time, and again in the afternoon, a third.

"In the intervals the surgeon finds time to examine individual cases, and prescribe especially for them, and perhaps to take a little rest. To fulfil the duties of surgeon in charge of such a train, or endure the terrible strain on brain and nerves and muscles, requires great skill, an iron will, and a mind undaunted by the shadow of any responsibility or danger. All this and more has Dr. J. P. Barnum, who has charge of the train formerly running between Louisville and Nashville, but now transferred to the road between Nashville and Chattanooga. With a touch gentle as a woman, yet with manly strength and firmness, and untiring watchfulness and thoughtful care, he seems wholly devoted to the work of benefiting our sick and wounded soldiers. All on board the train gave him the warmest thanks. As I walked through the car, I heard the men say, 'we haven't lived so well since we joined the army. We are better treated than we ever were before. This is the nicest place we were ever in etc Should the Doctor chance to see this, he will be shocked, for modesty, I notice, goes hand in hand with true nobility and generosity; but I risk his wrath for the selfish pleasure that one has in doing justice to a good man.

"After breakfast, in the morning, when the wounds were all dressed, I had the pleasure of carrying into one car a pitcher of delicious blackberry wine that came from the Soldiers Aid Society of Northern Ohio, and with the advice of Dr. Yates, the assistant surgeon, giving it to the men. The ear into which I went had only one tier of berths, supported like the others on rubber bands. Several times during the day I had an opportunity of giving some little assistance in taking care of wounded men, and it was very pleasant. My jonrney lasted a night and a day, and I think I can never again pass another twenty-four hours so fraught with sweet and sad memories as are connected with my second and last experience on a hospital train."

NEW ENGLAND WOMEN'S AUXILIARY ASSOCIATION

AMONG the branches of the United States Sanitary Commission, the Association which is named above, was one of the most efficient and untiring in its labors. It had gathered into its management, a large body of the most gifted and intellectual women of Boston, and its vicinity, women who knew how to work as well as to plan, direct and think. These were seconded in their efforts by a still larger number of intelligent and accomplished women in every part of New England, who, as managers and directors of the auxiliaries of the Association, roused and stimulated by their own example and their eloquent appeals, the hearts of their countrywomen to earnest and constant endeavour to benefit the soldiers of our National armies. The geographical peculiarities and connections of the New England States, were such that after the first year Connecticut and Rhode Island could send their supplies more readily to the field through New York than through Boston, and hence the Association from that time, had for its field of operations, only Maine, New Hampshire, Vermont, and Massachusetts. In these four States, however, it had one thousand and fifty auxiliaries, and during its existence, collected nearly three hundred and fifteen thousand dollars in money, and fully one million, two hundred thousand dollars in stores and supplies for the work of the Sanitary Commission. In December, 1863, it held a Sanitary Fair in Boston, the net proceeds of which were nearly one hundred and forty-six thousand dollars.

The first Chairman of the Executive Committee, was Mrs. D. Buck, and on her resignation early in 1864, Miss Abby W. May, an active and efficient member of the Executive Committee from the first was chosen Chairman. The rare executive ability displayed by Miss May in this position, and her extraordinary gifts and influence render a brief sketch of her desirable, though her own modest and retiring disposition would lead her to depreciate her own merits, and to declare that she had done no more than the other members of the Association. In that coterie of gifted women, it is not impossible that there may have been others who could have done as well, but none could have done better than Miss May; just as in our great armies, it is not impossible that there may have been Major-Generals, and perhaps even Brigadier-Generals, who, had they been placed in command of the armies, might have accomplished as much as those who did lead them to victory. The possibilities of success, in an untried leader, may or may not be great; but those who actually occupy a prominent position, must pay the penalty of their prominence, in the publicity which follows it.

Miss May is a native of Boston, born in 1829, and educated in the best schools of her natal city. She early gave indications of the possession of a vigorous intellect, which was thoroughly trained and cultivated. Her clear and quick understanding, her strong good sense, active benevolence, and fearlessness in avowing and advocating whatever she believed to be true and right, have given her a powerful influence in the wide circle of her acquaintance. She embarked heart and soul in the Anti-slavery movement while yet quite young, and has rendered valuable services to that cause.

At the very commencement of the war, she gave herself most heartily to the work of relieving the sufferings of the soldiers from sickness or wounds; laboring with great efficiency in the organization and extension of the New England Women's Auxiliary Association, and in the spring and summer of 1862, going into the Hospital Transport Service of the Sanitary Commission, where her labors were arduous, but accomplished great good. After her return, she was prevailed upon to take the Chairmanship of the Executive Committee of the Association, and represented it at Washington, at the meeting of the delegates from the Branches of the Sanitary Commission. Her executive ability was signally manifested in her management of the affairs of the Association, in her rapid and accurate dispatch of business, her prompt and unerring judgment on all difficult questions, her great practical talent, and her earnest and eloquent appeals to the auxiliaries. Yet fearless and daring as she has ever been in her denunciation of wrong, and her advocacy of right, and extraordinary as are the abilities she has displayed in the management of an enterprise for which few men would have been competent, the greatest charm of her character is her unaffected modesty, and disposition to esteem others better than herself. To her friends she declared that she had made no sacrifices in the work, none really worthy of the name—while there were abundance of women who had, but who were and must remain nameless and unknown. What she had done had been done from inclination and a desire to serve and be useful in her day, and in the great struggle, and had been a recreation and enjoyment.

To a lady friend who sought to win from her some incidents of her labors for publication, she wrote:

"The work in New England has been conducted with so much simplicity, and universal co-operation, that there have been no persons especially prominent in it. Rich and poor, -wise and simple, cultivated and ignorant, all—people of all descriptions, all orders of taste, every variety of habit, condition, and circumstances, joined hands heartily in the beginning, and have worked together as equals in every respect. There has been no chance for individual prominence. Each one had some power or quality desirable in the great work; and she gave what she could. In one instance, it was talent, in another, money,—in another, judgment,—in another, time,—and so on. Where all gifts were needed, it would be impossible to say what would make any person prominent, with this one exception. It was necessary that some one should be at the head of the work: and this place it was my blessed privilege to fill. But it was only an accidental prominence; and I should regret more than I can express to you, to have this accident of position single me out in any such manner as you propose; from the able, devoted, glorious women all about me, whose sacrifices, and faithfulness, and nobleness, I can hardly conceive of, much less speak of and never approach to.

"As far as I personally am concerned, I would rather your notice of our part of the work should be of New England women.' We shared the privileges of the work,—not always equally, that would be impossible. But we stood side by side— through it all, as New England women; and if we are to be remembered hereafter, it ought to be under that same good old title, and in one goodly company.

"When I begin to think of individual cases, I grow full of admiration, and wish I could tell you of many a special woman; but the number soon becomes appalling,—your book would be overrun, and all, or most of those who would have been omitted, might well have been there too."

In the same tone of generous appreciation of the labors of others, and desire that due honor should be bestowed upon all, Miss May, in her final Report of the New England Women's Auxiliary

Association, gives utterance to the thanks of the Executive Committee to its fellow-workers:

"We wish we could speak of all the elements that have conspired to our success in New England; but they are too numerous. From the representatives of the United States Government here, who remitted the duties upon soldiers' garments sent to us from Nova Scotia, down to the little child, diligently sewing with tiny fingers upon the soldier's comfort-bag, the co-operation has been almost universal. Churches, of all denominations, have exerted their influence for us; many schools have made special efforts in our behalf; the directors of railroads, express companies, telegraphs, and newspapers, and gentlemen of the business firms with whom we have dealt, have befriended us most liberally; and private individuals, of all ages, sexes, colors, and conditions, have aided us in ways that we cannot enumerate, that no one really knows but themselves. They do not seek our thanks, but we would like to offer them. Their service has been for the soldiers' sake; but the way in which they have rendered it has made us personally their debtors, beyond the power of words to express."

One of the most efficient auxiliaries of the New England Women's Auxiliary Association, from the thoroughly loyal spirit it manifested, and the persistent and patient labor which characterized its course was the Boston Sewing Circle, an organization started in November, 1862, and which numbered thenceforward to the end of the war from one hundred and fifty to two hundred workers. This Sewing Circle raised twenty-one thousand seven hundred and seventy-eight dollars in money, (about four thousand dollars of it for the Refugees in Western Tennessee), and made up twenty-one thousand five hundred and ninety-two articles of clothing, a large part of them of flannel, but including also shirts, drawers, etc., of cotton.

Its officers from first to last were Mrs. George Ticknor, President; Miss Ira E. Loring, Vice-President; Mrs. G. H. Shaw, Secretary; Mrs. Martin Brimmer, Treasurer. A part of these ladies, together with some others had for more than a year previous been engaged in similar labors, at first in behalf of the Second Regiment of Massachusetts Infantry, and afterward for other soldiers. This organization of which Mrs. George Ticknor was President, Miss Ticknor, Secretary, and Mrs. W. B. Rogers, Treasurer, raised three thousand five, hundred and forty-four dollars in money, and sent to the army four thousand nine hundred and sixty-nine articles of clothing of which one-third were of flannel.

Another "Boston notion' and a very excellent notion it was, was the organization of the Ladies' Industrial Aid Association, which we believe, but are not certain, was in some sort an auxiliary of the New England Women's Auxiliary Association. This society was formed in the beginning of the war and proposed first to furnish well made clothing to the soldiers, and second to give employment to their families, though it was not confined to these, but furnished work also to some extent to poor widows with young children, who had no near relatives in the army. In this enterprise were enlisted a large number of ladies of education, refinement, and high social position. During four successive winters, they carried on their philanthropic work, from fifteen to twenty of them being employed during most of the forenoons of each week, in preparing the garments for the sewing women, or in the thorough and careful inspection of those which were finished. From nine hundred to one thousand women were constantly supplied with work, and received in addition to the contract prices, (the ladies performing their labor without compensation) additional payment, derived from donations for increasing their remuneration. The number of garments (mostly shirts and drawers) made by the employes of this association in the four years, was three hundred and forty-six thousand seven hundred and fifteen, and the sum of twenty thousand thirty-three dollars and seventy-eight cents raised by donation, was paid as additional wages to the workwomen. The association of these poor women for so long a period with ladies of cultivation and refinement, under circumstances in which they could return a fair equivalent for the money received, and hence were not in the position of applicants for charity, could not fail to be elevating and improving, while the ladies themselves learned the lesson that as pure and holy a patriotism inspired the hearts of the humble and lowly, as was to be found among the gifted and cultivated. We regret that we cannot give the names of the ladies who initiated and sustained this movement.

Many of them were conspicuous in other works of patriotism and benevolence during the war, and some found scope for their earnest devotion to the cause in camp and hospital, and some gave vent to their patriotic emotion in battle hymns which will live through all coming time. Of these as of thousands of others 'in all the departments of philanthropy connected with the great struggle, it shall be said, "They have done what they could."

NORTHWESTERN SANITARY COMMISSION

WHEN the United States Sanitary Commission was first organized, though its members and officers had but little idea of the vast influence it was destined to exert on the labors which were before it, they wisely resolved to make it a National affair, and accordingly selected some of their corporate members from the large cities of the west. The Honorable Mark Skinner, and subsequently E. B. McCagg, Esq., and E. W. Blatchford, were chosen as the associate members of the Commission for Chicago. The Commission expected much from the Northwest, both from its earnest patriotism, and its large handed liberality. Its selection of associates was eminently judicious, and these very soon after their election, undertook the establishment of a branch Commission for collecting and forwarding supplies, and more effectively organizing the liberality of the Northwest, that its rills and streams of beneficence, concentrated in the great city of the Lakes, might flow thence in a mighty stream to the armies of the West. Public meetings were held, a branch of the United States Sanitary Commission with it rooms, its auxiliaries and its machinery of collection and distribution put in operation, and the office management at first entrusted to that devoted and faithful worker in the Sanitary cause, Mrs. Eliza Porter. The work grew in extent as active operations were undertaken in our armies, and early in 1862, the associates finding Mrs. Porter desirous of joining her husband in ministrations of 560 mercy at the front, entrusted the charge of the active labors of the Commission, its correspondence, the organization of auxiliary aid societies, the issuing of appeals for money and supplies, the forwarding of stores, the employment and location of women nurses, and the other multifarious duties of so extensive an institution, to two ladies of Chicago, ladies who had both given practical evidence of their patriotism and activity in the cause,—Mrs. A. H. Hoge and Mrs. M. A. Livermore. The selection was wisely made. No more earnest workers were found in any department of the Sanitary Commission's field, and their eloquence of pen and voice, the magnetism of their personal presence, their terse and vigorously written circulars appealing for general or special supplies, their projection and management of two great sanitary fairs, and their unwearied efforts to save the western armies from the fearful perils of scurvy, entitle them to especial prominence in our record of noble and patriotic women. The amount of money and supplies sent from this branch, collected from its thousand auxiliaries and its two great fairs, has not been up to this time, definitively estimated, but it is known to have exceeded one million of dollars.

This record of the labors of these ladies during the war would be incomplete without allusion to the fact that they were the prime movers in the establishment of a Soldiers' Home, in Chicago, and were, until after the war ended, actively identified with it. They early foresaw that this temporary resting-place, which became like "the shadow of a great rock in a weary land" to tens of thousands of soldiers, going to and returning from the camp, and hospital, and battle-field, would eventually crystallize into a permanent home for the disabled and indigent of Illinois' brave men—and in all their calculations for it, they took its grand future into account. That future which they foresaw, has become a verity, and nowhere in the United States is there a pleasanter, or more convenient, or more generously supported Soldiers' Home than in Chicago, standing on the shores of Lake Michigan.

MRS. A. H. HOGE

PERHAPS among all who have labored for the soldier, during the late war, among the women of our country, no name is better known that of Mrs. A. H. Hoge, the subject of this sketch. From the beginning until the successful close of the war, alike cheerful, ardent, and reliant, in its darkest, as in its brightest days, Mrs. Hoge dedicated to the service of her country and its defenders, all that she had to bestow, and became widely known all over the vast sphere of her operations, as one of the most faithful and tireless of workers; wise in council, strong in judgment, earnest in action.

Mrs. Hoge is a native of the city of Philadelphia, and was the daughter of George D. Blaikie, Esq., an East India shipping merchant—"a man of spotless character, and exalted reputation, whose name is held in reverence by many still living there."

Mrs. Hoge was educated at the celebrated seminary of John Brewer, A. M., (a graduate of Harvard University) who founded the first classical school for young ladies in Philadelphia, and which was distinguished from all others, by the name of the Young Ladies' College. She graduated with the first rank in her class, and afterward devoting much attention, with the advantage of the best instruction, to music, and other accomplishments, she soon excelled in the former. At an early age she became a member of the Old School Presbyterian Church, with which she still retains her connection, her husband being a ruling elder in the same church.

In her twentieth year she was married to Mr. A. H. Hoge, a merchant of Pittsburg, Pennsylvania, where she resided fourteen years. At the end of that period she removed to Chicago, Illinois, where she has since dwelt.

Mrs. Hoge has been the mother of thirteen children, five of whom have passed away before her. One of these, the Rev. Thomas Hoge, was a young man of rare endowments and promise.

As before stated; from the very beginning of the war, Mrs. Hoge identified herself with the interests of her country. Two of her sons immediately entered the army, and she at once commenced her unwearied personal services for the sick and wounded soldiers.

At first she entered only into that work of supply in which so large a portion of the loyal women of the North labored more or less continuously all through the war. But the first public act of her life as a Sanitary Agent, was to visit, at the request of the Chicago branch of the United States Sanitary Commission, the hospitals at Cairo, Mound City and St. Louis.

Of her visit to one of these hospitals she subsequently related the following incidents:

"The first great hospital I visited was Mound City, twelve miles from Cairo. It contained twelve hundred beds, furnished with dainty sheets, and pillows and shirts, from the Sanitary Commission, and ornamented with boughs of fresh apple blossoms, placed there by tender female nurses to refresh the languid frames of their mangled inmates. As I took my slow and solemn walk through this congregation of suffering humanity, I was arrested by the bright blue eyes, and pale but dimpled cheek, of a boy of nineteen summers. I perceived he was bandaged like a mummy, and could not move a limb; but still he smiled. The nurse who accompanied me said, 'We call this boy our miracle. Five weeks ago, lie was shot down at Donelson; both legs and arms shattered. To-day, with great care, he has been turned for the first time, and never a murmur has escaped his lips, but grateful words and pleasant looks have cheered us.' Said I to the smiling boy, some absent mother's pride, 'How long did you lie on the field after being shot?' 'From Saturday morning till Sunday evening,' he replied, 'and then I was chopped out, for I had frozen feet.' 'How did it happen that you were left so long?' 'Why, you see,' said he, 'they couldn't stop to bother with us, because they had to take the fort.' 'But,' said I, 'did you not feel'twas cruel to leave you to suffer so long?' 'Of course not! how could they help it? They had to take the fort, and when they did, we forgot our sufferings, and all over the battle-field went up cheers from the wounded, even from the dying. Men that had but one arm raised that, and voices so weak that they sounded like children's, helped to swell the sound.' 'Did you suffer much?' His brow contracted, as he said, 'I don't like to think of that; but never mind, the doctor tells me I won't lose an arm or a leg, and I'm going back to have another chance at them. There's one thing I can't forget though," said he, as his sunny brow grew dark, 'Jem and I (nodding at the boy in the adjoining cot) lived on our father's neighboring farms in Illinois; we stood beside each other and fell together. As he knows, we saw fearful sights that day. We saw poor wounded boys stripped of their clothing. They cut ours off, when every movement was torture. When some resisted, they were pinned to the earth with bayonets, and left writhing like worms, to die by inches. I can't forgive the devils for that.' 'I fear you've got more than you bargained for.' 'Not a bit of it; we went in for better or worse, and if we got worse, we must not complain.' Thus talked the beardless boy, nine months only from his mother's wing. As I spoke, a moan, a rare sound in a hospital, fell on my ear. I turned, and saw a French boy quivering with agony and crying for help. Alas! he had been wounded, driven several miles in an ambulance, with his feet projecting, had them frightfully frozen, and the surgeon had just decided the discolored, useless members must be amputated, and the poor boy was begging for the operation. Beside him, lay a stalwart man, with fine face, the fresh blood staining his bandages, his dark, damp hair clustering round his marble forehead. He extended his hand feebly and essayed to speak, as I bent over him, but speech had failed him. He was just brought in from a gunboat, where he had been struck with a piece of shell, and was slipping silently but surely into eternity. Two days afterward I visited Jefferson Barracks Hospital. In passing through the wards, I noticed a woman seated beside the cot of a youth, apparently dying. He was insensible to all around; she seemed no less so. Her face was bronzed and deeply lined with care and suffering. Her eyes were bent on the ground, her arms folded, her features rigid as marble. I stood beside her, but she did not notice me. I laid my hand upon her shoulder, but she heeded me not. I said 'Is this young man a relative of yours? No answer came. 'Can't I help you? With a sudden start that electrified me, her dry eyes almost starting from the sockets and her voice husky with agony, she said, pointing her attenuated finger at the senseless boy, 'He is the last of seven sons—six have died in the army, and the doctor says he must die to-night. The flash of life passed from her face as suddenly as it came, her arms folded over her breast, she sank in her chair, and became as before, the rigid impersonation of agony. As I passed through another hospital ward, I noticed a man whose dejected figure said plainly, 'he had turned his face to the wall to die. His limb had been amputated, and he had just been told his doom. Human nature rebelled. He cried out, 'I am willing to die, if I could but see my wife and children once more. In the silence that followed this burst of agony, the low voice of a noble woman, who gave her time and abundant means to the sick and wounded soldiers, was heard in prayer for him. The divine influence overcame his struggling heart, and as she concluded, he said, 'Thy will, O God, be done! 'Tis a privilege, even thus, to die for one's country.'

Before the midnight hour he was at rest. The vacant bed told the story next morning."

The object of these visits was to examine those hospitals which were under the immediate supervision of the Branch, and report their condition, also to investigate the excellent mode of working of the finely conducted, and at that time numerous hospitals in St. Louis. This report was made and acted upon, and was the means of introducing decided and much needed reforms into similar institutions.

The value of Mrs. Hoge's counsel, and the fruits of her great experience of life were generally acknowledged. In the several councils of women held in Washington, she took a prominent part, and was always listened to with the greatest respect and attention — not by any means lessened after her wide relations with the Sanitary Commission, and her special experience of its work, had become known in the following years.

Mrs. Hoge was accompanied to Washington, when attending the Women's Council in 1862, by her friend and fellow-laborer, Mrs. M. A. Livermore, of Chicago. After the return of these ladies they immediately commenced the organization of the Northwest for sanitary labor, being appointed agents of the Northwestern Sanitary Commission, and devoting their entire time to this work.

They opened a correspondence with leading women in all the cities and prominent towns of the Northwest. They prepared and circulated great numbers of circulars, relating to the mode and necessity of the concentrated efforts of the Aid Societies, and they visited in person very many towns and large villages, calling together audiences of women, and telling them of the hardships, sufferings and heroism of the soldiers, which they had themselves witnessed, and the pressing needs of these men, which were to be met by the supplies contributed by, and the work of loyal women of the North. They thus stimulated the enthusiasm of the women to the highest point, greatly increased the number of Aid Societies, and taught them how, by systematizing their efforts, they could render the largest amount of assistance, as well as the most important, to the objects of the Sanitary Commission.

The eloquence and pathos of these appeals has never been surpassed; and it is no matter of wonder that they should have opened the hearts and purses of so many thousands of the listeners. "But for these noble warriors," Mrs. Hoge would say, "who have stood a living wall between us and destruction, where would have been our schools, our colleges, our churches, our property, our government, our lives? Southern soil has been watered with their blood, the Mississippi fringed with their graves, measured by acres instead of numbers. The shadow of death has passed over almost, every household, and left desolate hearth-stones and vacant chairs. Thousands of mothers, wives and sisters at home have died and made no sign, while their loved ones have been hidden in Southern hospitals, prisons and graves—the separation, thank God, is short, the union eternal. I have only a simple story of these martyred heroes to tell you. I have been privileged to visit a hundred thousand of them in hospitals; meekly and cheerfully lying there, that you and I may be enabled to meet here, in peace and comfort to-day.

"Could I,' by the touch of a magician's wand, pass before you in solemn review, this army of sufferers, you would say a tithe cannot be told."

And then with simple and effective pathos she would proceed to tell of incidents which she had witnessed, so touching, that long ere she had concluded her entire audience would be in tears.

By two years of earnest and constant labor in this field, these ladies succeeded in adding to the packages sent to the Sanitary Commission, fifty thousand, mostly gifts directly from the Aid Societies, but in part purchased with money given. In addition to this, over four hundred thousand dollars came into the treasury through their efforts.

Early in 1863, Mrs. Hoge, in company with Mrs. Colt of Milwaukee, at the request of the Sanitary Commission, left Chicago for Vicksburg, with a large quantity of sanitary stores. The defeat of Sherman in his assault upon that city, had just taken place, and there was great want and suffering in the army. The boat upon which these ladies were traveling, was however seized as a military transport at Columbus, and pressed into the fleet of General Gorman, which was just starting for the forts at the mouth of the White River.

General Fisk, whose headquarters were upon the same boat, accorded to these ladies the best accommodations, and every facility for carrying out their work, which proved to be greatly needed. Their stores were found to be almost the only ones in the fleet, composed of thirty steamers filled with fresh troops, whose ranks were soon thinned by sickness, consequent upon the exposures and fatigues of the campaign.

Their boat became a refuge for the sick of General Fisk's brigade, to his honor be it said, and these ladies had the privilege of nursing hundreds of men during this expedition, and undoubtedly saved many valuable lives.

Early in the following spring, and only ten days after her return to Chicago, from the expedition mentioned above, Mrs. Hoge was again summoned to Vicksburg, opposite which, at Young's Point, the army under General Grant was lying and engaged, among other operations against this celebrated stronghold, in the attempt to turn the course of the river into a canal dug across the point. Scurvy was prevailing to a very considerable extent among the men, who were greatly in need of the supplies which accompanied her. Here she remained two weeks, and had the pleasure of distributing these supplies, and witnessing much benefit from their use. Her headquarters were upon the sanitary boat, Silver Wave, and she received constant support and aid from Generals Grant and Sherman, and from Admiral Porter, placed a tug boat at her disposal, in order that she might visit the camps and hospitals which were totally inaccessible in any other way, owing to the impassable character of the roads during the rainy season. Having made a tour of all the hospitals, and ascertained the condition of the sick, and of the army generally, she returned to the North, and reported to the Sanitary Commission the extent of that insidious army foe, the scurvy. They determined to act promptly and vigorously. Mrs. Hoge and Mrs. Livermore, as representatives of the Northwestern Sanitary Commission, by unremitting exertions, through the press and by circulars, and aided by members of the Commission, and by the noble Board of Trade of Chicago, succeeded in collecting, and in sending to the army, in the course of three weeks, over one thousand bushels of potatoes and onions, which reached them, were apportioned to them, and proved, as was anticipated, and has been universally acknowledged, the salvation of the troops.

Again, in the following June, on the invitation of General Fuller, Adjutant-General of the State of Illinois, Mrs. Hoge visited Vicksburg, on the Steamer City of Alton, which was despatched by Governor Yates, to bring home the sick and wounded Illinois soldiers. She remained till shortly before the surrender, which took place on the fourth of July, and during this time visited the entire circle of Hospitals, as well as the rifle-pits, where she witnessed scenes of thrilling interest, and instances, of endurance and heroism beyond the power of pen to describe.

She thus describes some of the incidents of this visit:

"The long and weary siege of Vicksburg, had continued many months previous to the terrific assaults of our brave army on the fortifications in the rear of that rebel stronghold. On the 19th and 22d of May, were made those furious attacks, up steep acclivities, in the teeth of bristling fortifications, long lines of riflepits, and sharp-shooters who fringed the hill-tops, and poured their murderous fire into our advancing ranks. It would seem impossible that men could stand, much less advance, under such a galling fire. They were mowed down as wheat before the sickle, 72 but they faltered not. The vacant places of the fallen were instantly filled, and inch by inch they gained the heights of Vicksburg. When the precipice was too steep for the horses to draw up the artillery, our brave boys did the work themselves, and then fought and conquered. When they had gained the topmost line of rifle-pits, they entered in and took possession; and when I made my last visit to the Army of the Mississippi, there they were ensconced as conies in the rock, enduring the heat of a vertical sun, and crouching, like beasts of prey, to escape the rebel bullets from the earthworks, almost within touching distance. The fierce and bloody struggle had filled long lines of field-hospitals with mangled victims, whose sufferings were soothed and relieved beyond what I could have conceived possible, and it rejoiced my heart to see there the comforts and luxuries of the Sanitary Commission. The main body of the army lay encamped in the valleys, at the foot of the rifle-pits, and spread its lines in a semicircle to a distance of fourteen miles. The health of the army was perfect, its spirit jubilant. They talked of the rebels as prisoners, as though they were guarding them, and answered questions implying doubt of success, with a scornful laugh, saying, 'Why, the boys in the rear could whip Johnston, and we not know it; and we could take Vicksburg if we chose, and not disturb them.' Each regiment, if not each man, felt competent for the work. One glorious day in June, accompanied by an officer of the 8th Missouri, I set out for the rifle-pits. When I reached them, I found the heat stifling; and as I bent to avoid the whizzing minies, and the falling branches of the trees, cut off by an occasional shell, I felt that war was a terrible reality. The intense excitement of the scene, the manly, cheerful bearing of the veterans, the booming of the cannon from the battlements, and the heavy mortars that were ever and anon throwing their huge iron balls into Vicksburg, and the picturesque panorama of the army encamped below, obuterated all sense of personal danger or fatigue. After a friendly talk with the men in the extreme front, and a peep again and again through the loop-holes, watched and fired upon continually, by the wary foe, I descended to the second ledge, where the sound of music reached us. "We followed it quickly, and in a few moments stood behind a rude litter of boughs, on which lay a gray-haired soldier, face downward, with a comrade on either side. They did not perceive us, but sang on the closing line of the verse:

'Come humble sinner in whose breast

A thousand thoughts revolve;

Come with thy sins and fears oppressed,

And make this last resolve.'

I joined in the second verse;

'I'll go to Jesus, though my sins

Have like a mountain rose,

I know His courts, I'll enter in,

Whatever may oppose.'

In an instant, each man turned and would have stopped, but I sang on with moistened eyes, and they continued. At the close, one burst out, 'Why, ma'am, where did you come from? Did you drop from heaven into these rifle-pits? You are the first lady we have seen here and then the voice was choked with tears. I said, 'I have come from your friends at home to see you, and bring messages of love and honor. I have come to bring you the comforts that we owe you, and love to give. I've come to see if you receive what they send you.' 'Do they think so much of us as that? Why, boys, we can fight another year on that, can't we?' 'Yes! yes!' they cried, and almost every hand was raised to brush away the tears. 'Why, boys,' said I, 'the women at home don't think of much else but the soldiers. If they meet to sew,'tis for you; if they have a good time,'tis to gather money for the Sanitary Commission; if they meet to pray,'tis for the soldiers; and even the little children, as they kneel at their mother's knees to lisp their good-night prayers, say,

God bless the soldiers A crowd of eager listeners had gathered from their hiding-places, as birds from the rocks. Instead of cheers as usual, I could only hear an occasional sob and feel solemn silence. The gray-haired veteran drew from his breast-pocket a daguerreotype, and said, 'Here are my wife and daughters. I think any man might be proud of them, and they all work for the soldiers and then each man drew forth the inevitable daguerreotype, and held it for me to look at, with pride and affection. There were aged mothers and sober matrons, bright-eyed maidens and laughing cherubs, all carried next these brave hearts, and cherished as life itself. Blessed art! It seems as though it were part of God's preparation work, for this long, cruel war. These mute memorials of home and its loved ones have proved the talisman of many a tempted heart, and the solace of thousands of suffering, weary veterans. I had much to do, and prepared to leave. I said, 'Brave men, farewell! When I go home, I'll tell them that men that never flinch before a foe, sing hymns of praise in the rifle-pits of Vicksburg. I'll tell them that eyes that never weep for their own suffering, overflow at the name of home and the sight of the pictures of their wives and children. They'll feel more than ever that such men cannot be conquered, and that enough cannot be done for them.' Three cheers for the women at home, and a grasp of multitudes of hard, honest hands, and I turned away to visit other regiments. The officer who was with me, grasped my hand; 'Madam,' said he, 'promise me you'll visit my regiment to-morrow—'twould be worth a victory to them. You don't know what good a lady's visit to the army does. These men whom you have seen to-day, will talk of your visit for six months to come. Around the camp fires, in the rifle-pits, in the dark nights or on the march, they will repeat your words, describe your looks, your voice, your size, your dress, and all agree in one respect, that yoi look like an angel, and exactly like each man's wife or mother. Such reverence have our soldiers for upright, tender-hearted women. In the valley beneath, just having exchanged the front line of rifle-pits, with the regiment now occupying it, encamped my son's regiment. Its ranks had been fearfully thinned by the terrible assaults of the 19th and 21st of May, as they had formed the right wing of the line of battle on that fearful day. I knew most of them personally, and as they gathered round me and inquired after home and friends, I could but look in sadness for many familiar faces, to be seen no more on earth. I said, 'Boys, I was present when your colors were presented to you by the Board of Trade. I heard your colonel pledge himself that you would bring those colors home or cover them with your blood, as well as glory. I want to see them, if you have them still, after your many battles.' With great alacrity, the man in charge of them ran into an adjoining tent, and brought them forth, carefully wrapped in an oil-silk covering. He drew it off and flung the folds to the breeze. 'What does this mean?' I said. 'How soiled and tattered, and rent and faded they look—1 should not know them.' The man who held them said, 'Why, ma'am,'twas the smoke and balls did that.' 'Ah! so it must have been,' I said. 'Well, you have covered them with glory, but how about the blood!' A silence of a minute followed, and then a low voice said, 'Four were shot down holding them—two are dead, and two in the hospital.' 'Verily, you have redeemed your pledge,' I said solemnly. 'How, boys, sing Rally round the Flag, Boys!'—and they did sing it. As it echoed through the valley, as we stood within sight of the green sward that had been reddened with the blood of those that had fought for and upheld it, methought the angels might pause to hear it, for it was a sacred song—the song of freedom to the captive, of hope to the oppressed of all nations. Since then, it seems almost profane to sing it with thoughtlessness or frivolity. After a touching farewell, I stepped into the ambulance, surrounded by a crowd of the brave fellows. The last sound that reached my ears was cheers for the Sanitary Commission, and the women at home. I soon reached the regimental hospital, where lay the wounded color-bearers. As I entered the tent, the surgeon met me and said, 'I'm so glad you've come, for It has been calling for you all day.' As I took his parched, feverish hand, he said, 'Oh! take me home to my wife and little ones to die.' There he lay, as noble a specimen of vigorous manhood as I had ever looked upon. His great,' broad chest heaved with emotion, his dark eyes were brilliant with fever, his cheeks flushed with almost the hue of health, his rich brown hair clustering in soft curls over his massive forehead, it was difficult to realize that he was entering the portals of eternity. I walked across the tent to the doctor, and asked if he could go with me. He shook his head, and said before midnight he would be at rest. I shrank from his eager gaze as I approached him. 'What does he say?' he asked quickly. 'You can't be moved.' The broad chest rose and fell, his whole frame quivered.' There was a pause of a few minutes. He spoke first, and said, 'Will you take my message to her?' 'I will,' I said, 'if I go five hundred miles to do it.' 'Take her picture from under my pillow, and my children's also. Let me see it once more.' As I held them for him, he looked earnestly, and then said, 'Tell her not to fret about me, for we shall meet in heaven. Tell her 'twas all right that I came. I don't regret it, and she must not. Tell her to train these two little boys, that we loved so well, to go to heaven to us, and tell her to bear my loss like a soldier's wife and a Christian.' He was exhausted by the effort. I sat beside him till his consciousness was gone, repeating God's precious promises. As the sun went to rest that night, he slept in his Father's bosom." Early in January, 1864, another Council of women connected with the Branch Commissions, Aid Societies, and general work of Supply, assembled in Washington, and was in session three days. Mrs. Hoge, was again a Delegate, and in relating the results of her now very large experience, helped greatly the beneficial results of the Council, and harmonized all the views and action of the various branches. As before, she was listened to with deference and attention, and we find her name mentioned in the most appreciative manner in the Reports of the meeting. Her remarks in regard to the value of free use of the Press, and of advertising, in the collection of supplies for the Army, stimulated the Commission to renewed effort in this direction, which they had partially abandoned under the censorious criticism of some portion of the public, who believed the money thus expended to be literally thrown away. The result was, instead, a very large increase of supplies.

In the two great Sanitary Fairs, which were held in Chicago, the efforts of Mrs. Hoge were unwearied from the inception of the idea until the close of the successful realization. Much of this success may be directly traced to her—her practical talent, great experience in influencing the minds and action of others, and sound judgment, as well as good taste, producing thus their natural results. The admirable conduct of these fairs, and the large amounts raised by them, are matters of history.

In an address delivered at a meeting of ladies in Brooklyn, New York, in March, 1865, Mrs. Hoge thus spoke of her work and that of the women, who like her, had given themselves to the duty of endeavoring to provide for the sick and suffering soldier:

"The women of the land, with swelling hearts and uplifted eyes asked 'Lord, what wilt thou have us to do?' The marvellous organization of the United States Sanitary Commission, with its various modes of heavenly activity, pointed out the way, saying 'The men must fight, the women must work, this is the way, follow me.' In accepting this call, there has been no reservation. Duty has been taken up, in whatever shape presented, nothing refused that would soothe a sorrow, staunch a wound, or heal the sickness of the humblest soldier in the ranks. Some have drifted into positions entirely new and heretofore avoided. They have gone forth from the bosom of their families, to visit hospitals, camps, and battle-fields; some even to appear as we do before you to-day, to plead for aid for our sick and wounded soldiers suffering and dying that we may live. The memory of their heroism is inspiring—the recollection of their patience and longsuffering is overwhelming. They form the most striking human exemplification of divine meekness and submission, the world has ever seen, and bring to mind continually the passage, 'He is brought as a lamb to the slaughter, and as a sheep before her shearers is dumb, so he opened not his mouth.'"

During the continuance of her labors, Mrs. Hoge was frequently the recipient of costly and elegant gifts, as testimonials of the respect and gratitude with which her exertions were viewed.

After a visit to the Ladies' Aid Society, of West Chester, Pennsylvania, she was presented by them with a testimonial, beautifully engrossed upon parchment, surmounted by an exquisitely painted Union flag the managers of the Philadelphia Fair, believing Mrs. Hoge to have had an important connection with that fair, presented to her a beautiful gift, in token of their appreciation of her services.

The Women's Relief Association, of Brooklyn, New York, presented her an elegant silver vase.

During the second Sanitary Fair in Chicago, a few friends presented her with a beautiful silver cup, bearing a suitable inscription in Latin, and during the same fair, she received as a gift a Roman bell of green bronze, or verd antique, of rare workmanship, and value , as an object of art.

Mrs. Hoge made three expeditions to the Army of the Southwest, and personally visited and ministered to more than one hundred thousand men in hospitals. Few among the many efficient workers, which the war called from the ease and retirement of home, can submit to the public a record of labors as efficient, varied, and long-continued, as hers.

MRS. MARY A. LIVERMORE

FEW of the busy and active laborers in the broad field of woman's effort during the war, have been more widely or favorably known than Mrs. Livermore. Her labors, with her pen, commenced with the commencement of the war; and in various spheres of effort, were faithfully and energetically given to the cause of the soldier and humanity, until a hard-won peace had once more "perched upon our banners," and the need of them, at least in that specific direction, no longer existed.

Mrs. Livermore is a native of Boston, where her childhood and girlhood were passed. At fourteen years of age she was a medal scholar of the "Hancock School," of that city, and three years later, she graduated from the "Charlestown (Mass)., Female Seminary," when she became connected with its Board of Instruction, as Teacher of Latin, French and Italian. With the exception of two years spent in the south of Virginia,—whence she returned an uncompromising anti-slavery woman—her home was in Boston until her marriage, to Rev. I). P. Livermore, after which she resided in its near vicinity, until twelve years ago, when with her husband and children she removed West. For the last ten years she has been a resident of Chicago. Her husband is now editor of the New Covenant, a paper published in Chicago, Illinois, in advocacy of Universalist sentiments, and, at the same time, of those measures of reform, which tend to elevate and purify erring and sinful human nature. Of this paper Mrs. Livermore is associate editor.

Mrs. Livermore is a woman of remarkable talent, and in certain directions even of genius, as the history of her labors in connection with the war amply evinces. Her energy is great, and her executive ability far beyond the average. She is an able writer, striking and picturesque in description, and strong and touching in appeal. She has a fine command of language, and in her conversation or her addresses to assemblies of ladies, one may at once detect the tone and ease of manner of a woman trained to pencraft. She is the author of several books, mostly poems, essays or stories, and is recognized as a member of the literary guild. The columns of her husband's paper furnished her the opportunity, she desired of addressing her patriotic appeals to the community, and her vigorous pen was ever at work both in its columns, and those of the other papers that were open to her. During the whole war, even in the busiest times, not a week was passed that she did not publish somewhere two or three columns at the least. Letters, incidents, appeals, editorial correspondence, —always something useful, interesting—head and hands were always busy, and the small implement, "mightier than the sword" was never allowed to rust unused in the ink-stand.

Before us, as we write, lies an article published in the New Covenant of May 18th, 1861, and as we see written scarcely a month after the downfall of Fort Sumter. It is entitled "Woman and the War," and shows how, even at that early day, the patriotism of American women was bearing fruit, and how keenly and sensitively the writer appreciated our peril.

"But no less have we been surprised and moved to admiration by the regeneration of the women of our land. A month ago, and we saw a large class, aspiring only to be I leaders of fashion,' and belles of the ball-room, their deepest anxiety clustering about the fear that the gored skirts, and bell-shaped hoops of the spring mode might not be becoming, and their highest happiness being found in shopping, polking, and the schottisch—pretty, petted, useless, expensive butterflies, whose future husbands and children were to be pitied and prayed for. But to-day, we find them lopping off superfluities, retrenching expenditures, deaf to the calls of pleasure, or the mandates of fashion, swept by the incoming patriotism of the time to the loftiest height of womanhood, willing to do, to bear, or to suffer for the beloved country. The riven fetters of caste and conventionality have dropped at their feet, and they sit together, patrician and plebeian, Catholic and Protestant, and make garments for the poorly-clad soldiery. An order came to Boston for five thousand shirts for the Massachusetts troops at the South. Every church in the city sent a delegation of needle-women to 'Union Hall a former aristocratic ball-room of Boston; the Catholic priest detailed five hundred sewing-girls to the pious work; suburban towns rang the bell to muster the seamstresses; the patrician Protestant of Beacon Street ran the sewing-machine, while the plebeian Irish Catholic of Broad Street basted—and the shirts were done at the rate of a thousand a day. On Thursday, bliss Dix sent an order for five hundred shirts for the hospital at Washington—on Friday they were ready. And this is but one instance, in one city, similar events transpiring in every other large city.

"But the patriotism of the Northern women has been developed in a nobler and more touching manner. We can easily understand how men, catching the contagion of war, fired with enthusiasm, led on by the inspiriting trains of martial music, and feeling their quarrel to be just, can march to the cannon's mouth, where the iron hail rains thickest, and the ranks are mowed down like grain in harvest. But for women to send forth their husbands, sons and brothers to the horrid chances of war, bidding them go with many a tearful 'good-by' and 'God bless you to see them, perhaps, no more—this calls for another sort of heroism. Only women can understand the fierce struggle, and exquisite suffering tliis sacrifice involves—and which has already been made by thousands."

The inception of that noble work, and noble monument of American patriotism, the United States Sanitary Commission, had its date in the early days of the war. We find in all the editorial writings of Mrs. Livermore, for the year 1861, constant warm allusions to this organization and its work, which show how strongly it commended itself to her judgment, how deeply she was interested in its workings, and how her heart was stirred by an almost uncontrollable impulse to become actively engaged with all her powers in the work.

In the New Covenant for December 18, 1861, we find over the signature of Mrs. Livermore, an earnest appeal to the women of the Northwest for aid, in furnishing Hospital supplies for the army. A "Sanitary Committee," had been formed in Chicago, to co-operate with the United States Sanitary Commission, which had opened an office, and was prepared to receive and forward supplies. These were designed to be sent, almost exclusively, to Western hospitals, and a Soldiers' Festival was at that time being held for the purpose of collecting aid, and raising funds for this Committee, to use in its charitable work.

This Committee did not long preserve a separate existence. About the beginning of the year 1862, the Northwestern branch of the United States Sanitary Commission was organized at Chicago, composed of some of the leading and most influential citizens of that city, and others in the Northwestern States. It at once became a power in the land, an instrument of almost incalculable good.

Soon afterward, Mrs. Livermore, and Mrs. A. H. Hoge, one of the most earnest, able and indefatigable of the women working in connection with the Sanitary Commission, and a resident of Chicago, were appointed agents of the Northwestern Commission, and immediately commenced their labors.

The writer is not aware that a complete and separate sketch of either the joint or individual labors of these ladies exists. For the outline of those of Mrs. Livermore, dependence is mostly made upon her communications to the New Covenant, and other Journals—upon articles not written with the design of furnishing information of personal effort, so much, as to give such statements of the soldier's need, and of the various efforts in that direction, as together with appeals, and exhortations to renewed benevolence and sacrifice, might best keep the public mind constantly stimulated and excited to fresh endeavor.

Running through these papers, we find everywhere evidences of the intense loyalty of this gifted woman, and also of the deep and equally outspoken scorn with which she regarded every evidence of treasonable opinion, or of sympathy with secession, on the part of army leaders, or the civil authorities. The reader will remember the repulse experienced in the winter of 1861-2, by the Hutchinsons, those sweet singers, whose "voices have ever been heard chanting the songs of Freedom—always lifted in harmonious accord in support of every good and noble cause." Mrs. Livermore's spirit was stirred by the story of their wrongs, and thus in keenest sarcasm, she gave utterance to her scorn of this weak and foolish deed of military tyrants encamping a winter through, before empty forts and Quaker guns, while they ventured only to make war upon girls: "While the whole country has been waiting in breathless suspense for six months, each one of which has seemed an eternity to the loyal people of the North, for the 'grand forward movement' of the army, which is to cut the Gordian knot of the rebellion, and perform unspeakable prodigies, not lawful for man to utter, a backward movement has been executed on the banks of tire Potomac, by the valiant commanders there stationed, for which none of us were prepared. No person, even though his imagination possessed a seven-leaguedboot-power of travel, could have anticipated the last great exploit of our generals, whose energies thus far, have been devoted to the achieving of a 'masterly inactivity.' The 'forward movement' has receded and receded, like the cup of Tantalus, but the backward movement came suddenly upon us, like a thief in the night."

"The Hutchinson family, than whom no sweeter songsters gladden this sorrow-darkened world, have been singing in Washington, to the President, and to immense audiences, everywhere giving unmixed delight. Week before last they obtained a pass to the camps the other side of the Potomac, with the laudable purpose of spending a month among them, cheering the hearts of the soldiers, and enlivening the monotonous and barren camp life with their sweet melody. But they ventured to sing a patriotic song—a beautiful song of Whittier's, which gave offense to a few semi-secessionists among the officers of the army, for which they were severely reprimanded by Generals Franklin and Kearny, their pass revoked by General McClellan, and they driven back to Washington. A backward movement was ordered instanter, and no sooner ordered, than executed. Brave Franklin! heroic Kearny! victorious McClellan! why did ye not order a Te Deum on the occasion of this great victory over a band of Vermont minstrels, half of whom were—girls! How must the hearts of the illustrious West-Pointers have pit-a-patted with joy, and dilated with triumph, as they saw the Hutchinson troupe—Asa B., and Lizzie C., little Dennett and Freddy, naive Viola, melodeon and all—scampering back through the mud, bowed beneath the weight of their military displeasure! Per contra to this expulsion, be it remembered that it occurred within sight of the residence of a family, in which there are some five or six young ladies, who, it is alleged, have been promised "passes" to go South whenever they are disposed to do so,—carrying, of course, all the information they can for the enemy. The bands of the regiments are also sent to serenade them, and on these occasions orders are given to suppress the national airs, as being offensive to these traitors in crinoline."

During the year 1862, Mrs. Livermore, besides the constant flow of communications from her pen, visited the army at various points, and in company with her friend, Mrs. Hoge, travelled over the Northwestern states, organizing numerous Aid Societies among the women of those states, who were found everywhere anxious for the privilege of working for the soldiers, and only desirous of knowing how best to accomplish this purpose, and through what channel they might best forward their benefactions.

In December of that year, the Sanitary Commission called a council, or convention of its members and branches at Washington, desiring that every Branch Commission in the North should be represented by at least two ladies thoroughly acquainted with its workings, who had been connected with it from the first. Mrs. Hoge and Mrs. Livermore were appointed by the Chicago Branch.

They accordingly proceeded to Washington—a long and arduous journey in mid winter, but these were not women to grudge toil or sacrifice, nor to shrink from duty.

Both these ladies had laid their talents upon the altar of the cause in which they were engaged, and both felt the pressing necessity at that time of a determined effort to relieve the frightful existing need. Sanitary supplies were decidedly on the decrease, while the demand for their increase was most piteously pressing. There was a strong call for the coming "council" of friends.

There were hindrances and delays. Delay at starting, in taking a regiment on board the cars, necessitating other delays, and waiting for trains on time through the whole distance.

The days spent in Washington were filled with good deeds, and a thousand incidents all connected in some way with the great work. Of the results of that council, the public was long since informed, and few who were interested in the work, did not learn to appreciate the more earnest labor, the greater sacrifice and self-devotion which soon spread from it through the country. Spirits, self-consecrated to so holy a work, could scarcely meet without the kindling of a flame that should spread all over the country, till every tender woman's heart, in all the land, had been touched by it, to the accomplishment of greater and brighter deeds.

While in Washington, Mrs. Livermore spent a day at the camp near Alexandria, set apart for convalescents from the hospitals, and known as "Camp Misery." The suffering there, as we have already stated in the sketch of Miss Amy M. Bradley's labors, was terrible from insufficient food, clothing and fuel, from want of drainage, and many other causes, any one of which might well have proved fatal to the feeble sufferers there crowded together. The pen of Mrs. Livermore carried the story of these wrongs all around the land. While she was in Washington, eighteen half sick soldiers died at the camp in one night, from cold and starvation. "The blood of the martyrs is the seed of the church," and the blood of these soaking into the soil where dwelt patriotic, warm-souled men and women, presently produced a noble growth and fruitage of charity, and sacrifice, and blessed deeds.

Mrs. Livermore has given her impressions of the President, gained from a visit made to the White House during this stay. She was one capable fully of appreciating the noble, simple, yet lofty nature of Abraham Lincoln.

Early in this year, Mrs. Livermore made a tour of the hospitals and military posts scattered along the Mississippi river. She was everywhere a messenger of good tidings. Sanitary supplies and cheering words seem to have been always about equally appreciated among the troops. Volunteers, fresh from home, and the quiet comfort of domestic life, willing to fight, and if need be die for the glorious idea of freedom, they yet had no thought of war as a profession. It was a sad, stern incident in their lives, but not the life they longed for, or meant to follow. Anything that was like home, the sight of a woman's face, or the sound of her voice, and all the sordid hardness of their present lives, all the martial pageantry faded away, and they remembered only that they were sons, brothers, husbands and fathers. Everywhere her reception was a kind, a respectful, and even a grateful one.•

There was much sickness among the troops, and the fearful ravages of scurvy and the deadly malaria of the swamps and bottom-lands along the great river were enemies far more to be dreaded than the thunder of artillery, or the hurtling shells.

During this trip she found in the hospitals, at St. Louis, and elsewhere, large numbers of female nurses, and ladies who had volunteered to perform these services temporarily. The surgeons were at that time, almost without exception, opposed to their being employed in the hospitals, though their services were afterwards, as the need increased, greatly desired and warmly welcomed. For these she soon succeeded in finding opportunities for rendering the service which they desired to the sick and wounded.

Were it possible in the space allowed for this sketch, to give a tithe of the incidents which came under the eyes of Mrs. Livermore, or even a small portion of her observations in steamer, train, or hospital, some idea of the magnitude and importance of her work might be gained. But this we cannot do, and must content ourselves with this partial allusion to her constant and indefatigable labors.

The premonitory symptoms of scurvy in the camps around Vicksburg, and its actual existence in many cases in the hospitals, so aroused the sympathies of Mrs. Livermore and Mrs. Hoge, on a second visit to these camps, that after warning General Grant of the danger which his medical directors had previously concealed from him, these two ladies hastened up the river, and by their earnest appeals and their stirring and eloquent circulars asking for onions, potatoes, and other vegetables, they soon awakened such an interest, that within three weeks, over a thousand bushels of potatoes and onions were forwarded to the army, and by their timely distribution saved it from imminent peril.

IN the autumn of 1863, the great Northwestern Sanitary Fair, the first of that series of similar fairs which united the North in a bond of large and wide-spread charity, occurred. It was Mrs. Livermore who suggested and planned the first fair, which netted almost one hundred thousand dollars to the Sanitary Commission. Mrs. Hoge, had at first, no confidence in the project, but she afterward joined it, and giving it her earnest aid, helped to carry it to a successful conclusion. It was indeed a giant plan, and it may be chiefly credited, from its inception to its fortunate close, to these indefatigable and skilful workers. The writer of this sketch was present at the convention of women of the Northwest called to meet at Chicago, and consider the feasibility of the project, and was forcibly impressed with the great and real power, the concentrated moral force, contained in that meeting, and left its doors without one doubt of the complete and ultimate success of the plan discussed. Mrs. Livermore held there a commanding position. A brilliant and earnest speaker, her words seemed to sway the attentive throng. Her commanding person, added to the power of her words. Gathered upon the platform of Bryan Hall, were Mrs. Hoge, Mrs. Colt, of Milwaukee, and many more, perhaps less widely known, but bearing upon their faces and in their attitudes, the impress of cultured minds, and an earnest active resolve to do, which seemed to insure success. Mrs. Livermore, seated below the platform, from time to time passed among the crowd, and her suggestions whether quietly made to individuals, or given in her clear ringing voice, and well selected language to the convention, were everywhere received with respect and deference. As all know, this fair which was about three months in course of preparation, was on a mammoth scale, and was a great success, and this result was no doubt greatly owing to the presence of that quality, which like every born leader, Mrs. Livermore evidently possesses—that of knowing how to select judiciously, the subordinates and instruments to be employed to carry out the plans which have originated in her mind.

"When this fair had been brought to a successful close, Mrs. Livermore returned to the particular work of her agency. When not traveling on the business connected with it, she spent many busy days at the rooms of the Commission in Chicago. The history of some of those days she has written—a history full of pathos and illuminated with scores of examples of noble and worthy deeds—of the sacrifices of hard-worked busy women for the soldiers—of tender self-sacrificing wives concealing poverty and sorrow, and swallowing bitter tears, and whispering no word of sorrows hard to bear, that the husband, far away fighting for his country, might never know of their sufferings; of the small but fervently offered alms of little children, of the anguish of parents waiting the arrival through this channel of tidings of their wounded or their dead; of heroic nurses going forth to their sad labors in the hospitals, with their lives in their hands, or returning in their coffins, or with broken health, the sole reward, beside the soldiers' thanks, for all their devotion.

Journey after journey Mrs. Livermore made, during the next two years, in pursuance of her mission, till her name and person were familiar not only in the camps and hospitals of the great West, but in the assemblies of patriotic women in the Eastern and Middle States. And all the time the tireless pen paused not in its blessed work.

In the spring of 1865, another fair was in contemplation. As before, Mrs. Livermore visited the Eastern cities, for the purpose of obtaining aid in her project, and as before was most successful.

In pursuance of this object, she made a flying visit to Washington, her chief purpose being to induce the President to attend the fair, and add the £clat of his presence and that of Mrs. Lincoln, to the brilliant occasion. An account of her interview with him whom she was never again to see in life, which, with her impressions of his character, we gain from her correspondence with the New Covenant, is appended.

"Our first effort was to obtain an interview with the President and Mrs. Lincoln—and this, by the way, is usually the first effort of all new comers. We were deputized to invite our Chief Magistrate to attend the great Northwestern Fair, to be held in May— and this was our errand. With the escort of a Senator, who takes precedence of all other visitors, it is very easy to obtain an interview with the President, and as we were favored in this respect, we were ushered into the audience chamber without much delay. The President received us kindly, as he does all who approach him. He was already apprised of the fair, and spoke of it with much interest, and with a desire to attend it. He gave us a most laughable account of his visit to the Philadelphia Fair, when, as he expressed it, "for two miles it was all people, where it wasn't houses,' and where 'he actually feared he should be pulled from the carriage windows.' We notified him that he must be prepared for a still greater crowd in Chicago, as the whole Northwest would come out to shake hands with him, and told him that a petition for his attendance at the fair, was in circulation, that would be signed by ten thousand women of Chicago. 'But,' said he, 'what do you suppose my wife will say, at ten thousand ladies coming after me in that style?' We assured him that the invitation included Mrs. Lincoln also, when he laughed heartily, and promised attendance, if State duties did not absolutely forbid. 'It would be wearisome,' he said, 'but it would gratify the people of the Northwest, and so he would try to come—and he thought by that time, circumstances would permit his undertaking a short tour West.' This was all that we could ask, or expect.

"We remained for some time, watching the crowds that surged through the spacious apartments, and the President's reception of them. Where they entered the room indifferently, and gazed at him as if he were a part of the furniture, or gave him simply a mechanical nod of the head, he allowed them to pass on, as they elected. But where he was met by a warm grasp of the hand, a look of genuine friendliness, of grateful recognition or of tearful tenderness, the President's look and manner answered the expression entirely. To the lowly and the humble he was especially kind; his worn face took on a look of exquisite tenderness, as he shook hands with soldiers who carried an empty coat sleeve, or swung themselves on crutches;

and not a child was allowed to pass him by without a kind word from him. A bright boy, about the size and age of the son he had buried, was going directly by, without appearing even to see the President. 'Stop, my little man,' said Mr. Lincoln, laying his hand on his shoulder, 'aren't you going to speak to me?' And stooping down, he took the child's hands in his own, and looked lovingly in his face, chatting with him for some moments."

The plans of Mrs. Livermore in regard to the fair were carried out—with one sad exception. It was a much greater success pecuniarily than the first. And the war was over, and it was the last time that wounded soldiers would call for aid. But alas! the great and good man whose presence she had coveted lay cold in death! She had promised him "days of rest" when he should come, and long ere then, he had entered his eternal rest, and all that remained of him had been carried through those streets, decked in mourning.

Like her friend, Mrs. Hoge, Mrs. Livermore was cheered during her labors by testimonials of appreciation from her co-laborers, and of gratitude from the brave men for whom she toiled. An exquisite silver vase was sent her by the Women's Relief Association, of Brooklyn, the counterpart of that sent Mrs. Hoge at the same time. From her co-workers in the last Sanitary Fair, she also received a gold-lined silver goblet, and a verd-antique Roman bell—the former bearing this complimentary inscription, "Poculum qui meruit fiat" But the gifts most prized by her are the comparatively inexpensive testimonials made by the soldiers to whom she ministered. At one time she rejoiced in the possession of fourteen photograph albums, in every style of binding, each one emblazoned with a frontispiece of the maimed or emaciated soldier who gave it.

GENERAL AID SOCIETY FOR THE ARMY, BUFFALO

THIS Society, a Branch of the Sanitary Commission, was organized in the summer of 1862, and became one of the Branches of the Commission in the autumn of 1862, had eventually for its field of operations, the Western Counties of New York, a few counties in Pennsylvania and Michigan, and received also occasional supplies from one or two of the border counties in Ohio, and from individuals in Canada West.

Its first President was Mrs. Joseph E. Follett, a lady of great tact and executive ability, who in 1862, resigned, in consequence of the removal of her husband to Minnesota. Mrs. Horatio Seymour, the wife of a prominent business man of Buffalo, was chosen to succeed Mrs. Follett, and developed in the performance of her duties, abilities as a manager, of the highest order. Through her efforts, ably seconded as they were by Miss Babcock and Miss Bird, the Secretaries of the Society, the whole field was thoroughly organized, and brought up to its highest condition of efficiency, and kept there through the whole period of the war.

A friendly rivalry was maintained between this branch and the Soldiers' Aid Society of Northern Ohio, and the perfect system and order with which both were conducted, the eloquent appeals and the stirring addresses by which both kept their auxiliaries up 590 to their work, and the grand and noble results accomplished by each, are worthy of all praise. In this, as in the Cleveland Society, the only paid officer was the porter. All the rest served, the President and Secretaries daily, the cutters, packers, and others, on alternate days, or at times semi-weekly, without fee or compensation. Arduous as their duties were, and far as they were from any romantic idea of heroism, or of notable personal service to the cause, these noble, patient, and really heroic women, rejoiced in the thought that by their labors they were indirectly accomplishing a good work in furnishing the means of comfort and healing to thousands of the soldiers, who, but for their labors would have perished from sickness or wounds, but through their care and the supplies they provided, were restored again to the ranks, and enabled to render excellent service in putting down the Rebellion in her closing report, Mrs. Seymour says:

We have sent nearly three thousand packages to Louisville, and six hundred and twenty-five to New York. We have cut and provided materials at our rooms, for over twenty thousand suits, and other articles for the army, amounting in all to more than two hundred thousand pieces. Little children, mostly girls under twelve years of age, have given us over twenty-five hundred dollars."

Like all the earnest workers of this class, Mrs. Seymour expresses the highest admiration for what was done by those nameless heroines, "the patriot workers in quiet country homes, who with self-sacrifice rarely equalled, gave their best spare-room linen and blankets, their choicest dried fruits, wines and pickles,—and in all seasons met to sew for the soldiers, or went about from house to house to collect the supplies to fill the box which came regularly once a month." Almost every woman who toiled thus, had a family whose sole care depended upon her, and many of them had dairies or other farm-work to occupy their attention, yet they rarely or never failed to have the monthly box filled and forwarded promptly. AYe agree with Mrs. Seymour in our estimate of the nobleness and self-sacrificing spirit manifested by these women; but the patriotic and self-denying heroines of the war were not in country villages, rural hamlets, and isolated farms alone; those ladies who for their love to the national cause, left their homes daily and toiled steadily and patiently through the long years of the war, in summer's heat and winter's cold, voluntarily secluding themselves from the society and social p , sition they were so well fitted to adorn, and in which they had been the bright particular stars, these too, for the great love they bore to their country should receive its honors and its heartfelt thanks.

MICHIGAN SOLDIERS' AID SOCIETY

FEW of the States of the Northwest, patriotic as they all were, present as noble a record as Michigan. Isolated by its position from any immediate peril from the rebel forces, (unless we reckon their threatened raids from Canada, in the last year of the War), its loyal and Union-loving citizens volunteered with a promptness, and fought with a courage surpassed by no troops in the Armies of the Republic. They were sustained in their patriotic sacrifices by an admirable home influence. The successive Governors of the State, during the war, its Senators and Representatives in Congress, and its prominent citizens at home, all contributed their full share toward keeping up the fervor of the brave soldiers in the field. Nor were the women of the State inferior to the other sex in zeal and self-sacrifice. The services of Mrs. Annie Etheridge, and of Bridget Divers, as nurses in the field-hospitals, and under fire are elsewhere recorded in this volume. Others were equally faithful and zealous, who will permit no account of their labors of love to be given to the public. There were from an early period of the war two organizations in the State, which together with the Northwestern Sanitary Commission, received and forwarded the supplies contributed throughout the State for the soldiers to the great depths of distribution at Louisville, St. Louis, and New York. These were "The Soldiers' Relief Committee," and the Soldiers" Aid Society of Detroit. There were also State agencies at Washington and New York, well managed, and which rendered early in the war great services to the Michigan troops. The Soldiers' Aid Society of Detroit, though acting informally previously, was formally organized in November, 1862, with Mrs. John Palmer, as President, and Miss Valeria Campbell, as Corresponding Secretary. In the summer of 1863, the Society changed its name to "The Michigan Soldiers' Aid Society," and the Soldiers' Relief Committee, having been merged in it, became the Michigan Branch of the Sanitary Commission, and addressed itself earnestly to the work of collecting and increasing the supplies gathered in all parts of the State, and sending them to the depots of the Commission at Louisville and New York, or directly to the front when necessary. At the time of this change, Hon. John Owen, one of the Associate members, of the Sanitary Commission, was chosen President, B. Vernor, Esq., Hon. James V. Campbell, and P. E. Demill, Esq., also Associates of the Commission, Miss S. A. Sibley, Mrs. H. L. Chipman, and Mrs. N. Adams, were elected Vice Presidents, and Miss Valeria Campbell, continued in the position of Recording Secretary, while the venerable Dr. Zina Pitcher, one of the constituent members of the Sanitary Commission was their counsellor and adviser.

Of this organization, Miss Campbell was the soul. Untiring in her efforts, systematic and methodical in her work, a writer of great power and eloquence, and as patriotic and devoted as any of those who served in the hospitals, or among the wounded men on the battle-field, she accomplished an amount of labor which few could have undertaken with success. The correspondence with all the auxiliaries, the formation of new Societies, and Alert clubs in the towns and villages of the State, the constant preparation and distribution of circulars and bulletins to stimulate the small societies to steady and persistent effort, the correspondence with the Western Office at Louisville, and the sending thither invoices of the goods shipped, and of the monthly accounts of the branch, these together, formed an amount of work which would have appalled any but the most energetic and systematic of women. In her labors, Miss Campbell received great and valuable assistance from Mrs. N. Adams, one of the Vice Presidents, Mrs. Brent, Mrs. Sabine, Mrs. Luther B. Willard, and Mrs. C. E. Russell. The two last named ladies, not satisfied with working for the soldiers at home, went to the army and distributed their supplies in person, and won the regard of the soldiers by their faithfulness and zeal.

In the year ending November 1st, 1864, one thousand two hundred and thirty-five boxes, barrels, etc., were sent from this branch to the Army, besides a large amount supplied to the Military Hospitals in Detroit, nearly six thousand dollars in money was raised, besides nearly two thousand dollars toward a Soldiers' Home, which was established during the year, and furnished forty-two thousand seven hundred and eighty-five meals, and fourteen thousand three hundred and ninety-nine lodgings to five thousand five hundred and ninety-nine soldiers from eight different States. In the organization of this Home, as well as in providing for the families of the soldiers, Miss Campbell was, as usual, the leading spirit. In both the Fairs held at Chicago, September, 1863, and June, 1865, the Michigan Branch of the Sanitary Commission, rendered essential service. Their receipts from the second Fair, were thirteen thousand three hundred and eighty-four dollars and fifty-eight cents less three thousand one hundred and thirty-seven dollars and sixty-five cents expenses, and this balance was expended in the maintenance of the Soldiers' Home, and caring for such of the sick and disabled men as were not provided for in the Hospitals. Of the aggregate amount contributed by this branch to the relief of the soldiers in money and supplies, we cannot as yet obtain a detailed estimate. We only know that it exceeded three hundred thousand dollars.

WOMEN'S PENNSYLVANIA BRANCH OF U. S. SANITARY COMMISSION

PHILADELPHIA was distinguished throughout the war by the intense and earnest loyalty and patriotism of its citizens, and especially of its women. No other city furnished so many faithful workers in the hospitals, the Refreshment Saloons, the Soldiers' Homes and Reading-rooms, and no other was half so well represented in the field, camp, and general hospitals at the "front." Sick and wounded soldiers began to arrive in Philadelphia very early in the war, and hospital after hospital was opened for their reception until in 1863-4, there were in the city and county twenty-six military hospitals, many of them of great extent. To all of these, the women of Philadelphia ministered most generously and devotedly, so arranging their labors that to each hospital there was a committee, some of whose members visited its wards daily, and prepared and distributed the special diet and such delicacies as the surgeons allowed. But as the war progressed, these patriotic women felt that they ought to do more for the soldiers, than simply to minister to those of them who were in the hospitals of the city. They were sending to the active agents in the field, Mrs. Harris, Mrs. Husband, Mrs. Lee, and others large quantities of stores; the "Ladies' Aid Association," organized in April, 1861, enlisted the energies of one class, the Penn Relief Association, quietly established by the Friends, had not long after, furnished an outlet for the overflowing sympathies and kindness of the followers of George Fox and William Penn; and "the Soldiers' Aid Association' whose president, Mrs. Mary A. Brady, represented it so ably in the field, until her incessant labors and hardships brought on disease of the heart, and in May, 1864, ended her active and useful life, had rallied around it a corps of noble and faithful workers. But there were yet hundreds, aye, thousands, who felt that they must do more than they were doing for the soldiers. The organizations we have named, though having a considerable number of auxiliaries in Pennsylvania, New Jersey and

Delaware, did not by any means cover the whole ground, and none of them were acting to any considerable extent through the Sanitary Commission which had been rapidly approving itself as the most efficient and satisfactory agency for the distribution of supplies to the army. In the winter of 1862-3 those friends of the soldier, not as yet actively connected with either of the three associations we have named, assembled at the Academy of Music, and after an address from Rev. Dr. Bellows, organized themselves as the Women's Pennsylvania Branch of the Sanitary Commission, and with great unanimity elected Mrs. Maria C. Grier as their President, and Mrs. Clara J. Moore, Corresponding Secretary. Wiser or more appropriate selections could not have been made. They were unquestionably, "the right women in the right place." Our readers will pardon us for sketching briefly the previous experiences and labors of these two ladies who proved so wonderfully efficient in this new sphere of action.

Mrs. Maria C. Grier is a daughter of the late Rev. Dr. Cornelius C. Cuyler, a clergyman, formerly pastor of the Reformed Dutch Church in Poughkeepsie, and afterward of the Second Presbyterian Church, Philadelphia, and married Rev. M. B. Grier, D. D., now editor of the "Presbyterian," one of the leading papers of the Old School Presbyterian Church. Dr. Grier had been for some years before the commencement of the war pastor of a Presbyterian Church in Wilmington, North Carolina. Wilmington, at the outbreak of the war, shared with Charleston and Mobile the bad reputation of being the most intensely disloyal of all the towns of the South. Dr and Mrs. Grier were openly and decidedly loyal, known everywhere throughout that region as among the very few who had the moral courage to avow their attachment to the Union. They knew very well, that their bold avowals might cost them their lives, but they determined for the sake of those who loved the Union, but had not their courage, to remain and advocate the cause, until it should become impossible to do so longer, bearing in mind that if they escaped, their departure, to be safe, must be sudden.

Early in the morning of the 1st of June word was brought them that there was no time to lose. Dr. Grier's life was threatened. A vessel was ready to sail and they must go. Hurriedly they left a home endeared to them by long years of residence; Dr. Grier's valuable library, a choice collection of paintings and other treasures of art and affection were all abandoned to the ruthless mob, and were stolen or destroyed. Leaving their breakfast untouched upon the table, they hastened to the vessel, and by a circuitous route, at last reached Philadelphia in safety, and were welcomed by kind and sympathizing friends. Mrs. Grier's patriotism was of the active kind, and she was very soon employed among the sick and wounded soldiers who reached Philadelphia after Bull Run and Ball's Bluff, or who were left by the regiments hurrying to the front at the hospitals of the Volunteer and Cooper Shop Refreshment Saloons. With the establishment of the larger hospitals in January, 1862, Airs. Grier commenced her labors in them also, and remained busy in this work till June, 1862, when at the request of the surgeon in charge of one of the Hospital Transports, she went to White House, Virginia, was there when McClellan made his "change of base," and when the wounded were sent on board the transport cared for them and came on to Philadelphia with them, and resumed her work at once in the hospitals. The battles of Pope's campaign and those of South Mountain and Antietam, filled the land with desolate homes, and crowded not only the hospitals, but the churches of Philadelphia with suffering, wounded and dying men, and Mrs. Grier like most of the philanthropic ladies of Philadelphia found abundant employment for heart and hands. Her zeal and faithfulness in this work had so favorably impressed the ladies who met at the Academy of Music to organize the Women's Branch of the Commission that she was unanimously chosen as President.

Mrs. Clara J. Moore, formerly a Miss Jessup, of Boston, is the wife of Mr. Bloomfield H. Moore, a large manufacturer of Philadelphia. She is a woman of high culture, a poetess of rare sweetness, and eminent as a magazine writer. She possessed great energy, and a rare facility of correspondence. In her days of Hospital work, she wrote hundreds of letters for the soldiers, and in the organization of the Women's Branch, of which she was one of the most active promoters, she took upon herself the burden of such a correspondence with the Auxiliaries, and the persons whom she desired to interest in the establishment of local Aid Societies, that when she was compelled by ill health to resign her position, a Committee of nine young ladies was appointed to conduct the correspondence in her place, and all the nine found ample employment. Her daughter married a Swedish Count, and returned with him to Europe, and the mother soon after sought rest and recovery in her daughter's Scandinavian home.

Of the other ladies connected with this Pennsylvania Branch, all were active, but the following, perhaps in part from temperament, and in part from being able to devote their time more fully than others to the work, were peculiarly efficient and faithful. Mrs. W. H. Furness, Mrs. Lathrop, Mrs. C. J. Stills, Mrs. J. Tevis, Mrs. E. D. Gillespie, Mrs. A. D. Jessup, Mrs. Samuel H. Clapp, Mrs. J. Warner Johnson, Mrs. Samuel Field, Mrs. Aubrey H. Smith, Mrs. M. L. Frederick, Mrs. C. Graff, Mrs. Joseph Parrish, Miss M. M. Duane, Miss S. B. Dunlap, Miss. Rachel W. Morris, Miss H. and Miss Anna Blanchard, Miss E. P. Hawley, and Miss M. J. Moss.

Of Mrs. Grier's labors in this position, one of the Associates of the Sanitary Commission, a gentleman who had more opportunity than most others of knowing her faithful and persistent work, writes:

"When the Women's Branch was organized, Mrs. Grier reluctantly consented to take the head of the Supply Department. In this position she continued, working most devotedly, until the work was done. To her labors the success of this undertaking is largely due. To every quality which makes woman admired and loved, this lady added many which peculiarly qualified her for this post; a rare judgment, a wonderful power of organization, and a rare facility for drawing around her the most efficient helpers, and making their labors most useful. During the whole period of the existence of the Association, the greatest good feeling reigned, and if ever differences of opinion threatened to interrupt perfect harmony, a word from Mrs. Grier was sufficient. Her energy in carrying out new plans for the increase of the supplies was most remarkable. When the Women's Pennsylvania Branch disbanded, every person collected with it, regretted most of all the separation from Mrs. Grier. I have never heard but one opinion expressed of her as President of the Association."

A lady, who, from her own labors in the field, and in the promotion of the benevolent plans of the Sanitary Commission, was brought into close and continued intercourse with her, says of her:

"She gave to the work of the Sanitary Commission, all the energies of her mind,—never faltering, or for a moment deterred by the many unforeseen annoyances and trials incident to the position. The great Sanitary Fair added to the cares by which she was surrounded; but that was carried through so successfully and triumphantly, that all else was forgotten in the joy of knowing how largely the means of usefulness was now increased. Her labors ceased not until the war was ended, and the Sanitary Commission was no longer required. Those only who have known her in the work, can form an idea of the vast amount of labor it involved.

"With an extract from the final report of the Women's Pennsylvania Branch, made in the spring of 1866, which shows the character and extent of the work accomplished, we close our account of this very efficient organization.

"On the 26th of March, 1863, the supply department of the Philadelphia agency was transferred to the Executive Committee of the Women's Pennsylvania Branch. A large and commodious building, Number 1307 Chestnut Street, was rented, and the new organization commenced its work. How rapidly the work grew, and how greatly its results exceeded our anticipations are now matters of pleasant memory with us all. The number of contributing Aid Societies was largely increased in a few weeks, and this was accompanied by a corresponding augmentation of the supplies received. The summer came, and with it sanguinary Gettysburg, with its heaps of slain and wounded, giving the most powerful impulse to every loving, patriotic heart. Supplies flowed in largely, and from every quarter; and we found that our work was destined to be no mere holiday pastime, no matter of sudden impulse, but that it would require all the thought, all the time, all the energy we could possibly bring to bear upon it. We had indeed put on the armor, to take it off only when soldiers were no more needed on our country's battle-fields, because the flag of the Union was waving again from every one of her cities and fortresses. Then came the bloody battles and glorious victories, with their depressing and their exhilarating effects. But, through the clouds and through the sunshine alike, our armies marched on, fought on, steadily and persistently advancing towards their final triumph. And so in the cities, in the villages, in the quiet country homes, in the luxurious parlor, in the rustic kitchen, everywhere, always, the women of the country too pursued their patriotic, loving work, content if the toil of their busy fingers might carry comfort to even a few of our bleeding, heroic soldiers. And as they labored in their various spheres, the results of their work poured into the great centres where supplies were collected for the Sanitary Commission. Our Department came to number over three hundred and fifty contributing Societies, besides a large number of individuals contributing with almost the regularity of our auxiliaries. Associate Managers, whose business it was to supervise the work in their own neighborhoods, had been appointed in nearly every county of the entire Department, fifty-six Associate Managers in all. The time came when the work of corresponding with these was too vast to be attended to by only one Corresponding Secretary. The lady who had filled that office with great ability, and to whose energetic zeal our organization owed its first impulse, was compelled by ill health to resign. Her place was filled by a Committee of nine, among whom the duty of correspondence was systematically divided. The work of our Associate Managers deserves more than the passing tribute which this report can give. They were nearly all of them women whose home duties gave them little leisure, and yet the existence of most of our Aid Societies is due to their efforts. In one of the least wealthy and populous counties of Pennsylvania, one faithful, earnest woman succeeded in establishing thirty Aid Societies. When the Great Central Fair was projected their services were found most valuable in the counties under their several superintendence, and they deserve a share of the credit for the magnificent success of that splendid undertaking.

"The total cash value of supplies received is three hundred and six thousand and eighty-eight dollars and one cent. Of this amount, twenty-six thousand three hundred and fifty-nine dollars were contributed to the Philadelphia Agency before the formation of the Women's Branch. The whole number of boxes, barrels, etc., received since the 1st of April, 1863 is fifty-three hundred and twenty-nine. Of these packages, twenty-one bundred and three were received, from April 1st, 1863, until the close of the year; twenty-one hundred and ninety-nine were received in 1864; and one thousand and twenty-seven have been received since January 1st, 1865. During the present year, three hundred and ninety-six boxes have been shipped to various points where they were needed for the Army, and sixteen hundred and ninety-nine were sent to the central office at Washington City. The last item includes the transfer of stock upon closing the depot of this Agency. The total number of boxes shipped from the Women's Pennsylvania Branch, since April 1st, 1863, is two thousand and ninety-five. This means, of course, the articles contributed by Societies, and does not include those purchased by the Commission, excepting the garments made by the Special Belief Committee.

"At length our work is done. Our army is disbanding, and we too must follow their lead. No more need of our daily Committee and their pleasant aids, to unpack and assort supplies for our sick and wounded. God has given us peace at last. Shall we ever sufficiently thank him for this crowning happiness? Bather shall we not thank him, by refusing ever again to be idle spectators when he has work to be done for any form of suffering humanity? And if our country shall, after its baptism of blood and of fire, be found to possess a race of better, nobler American women, with quickened impulses, high thoughts, and capable of heroic deeds, shall not the praise be chiefly due to the better, nobler aims set before them by the United States Sanitary Commission?

"The following is a list of the expenses of the Supply Department, from the time of its organization to January 1st, 1866. These charges were incurred upon goods purchased in this city, as well as upon those contributed to the Women's Pennsylvania Branch. Their total value is five hundred and ninety-six thousand four hundred and sixty-eight dollars and ninety-seven cents."

Rent of Depository $2,87666

Wm, Platt, Jr., Superintendent, for expenses incurred by him on supplies contributed 2, 15973

Salary of Storekeeper and Porter 3,09350

Freight, express charges, cartage 7, 11522

Boxes and material for packing 26178

Labor, extra 35296

Printing and Stationery 92849

Advertising 2,31059

Fuel and Lights 34403

Fitting up Depository, including repairs 61913

Insurance on Stock 24400

Postages 94066

Miscellaneous 66811

Total $21,914.86

RELIEF COMMITTEE.—This Committee was organized in April, 1863, and had for its object, during the first months of its existence, the relief of the wants of soldiers; but finding a Committee of women unequal to the proper performance of this duty, and at the same time having had brought before them the great necessities of the families of our volunteers, they resigned to other hands the care of the soldiers, and determined to devote themselves to the mothers, wives, and children, of those who had gone forth to battle for the welfare of all.

The rooms in which this work has been carried on, are at the South-east corner of Thirteenth and Chestnut streets.

Two Committees have been in attendance daily to receive applications for relief, work, fuel, etc. Persons thus applying for aid are required to furnish proof that their sons or husbands were actually soldiers, and are also obliged to bring from some responsible party a certificate of their own honesty and sobriety. It then becomes the duty of the Committee in charge to visit the applicant, and to afford such aid as may be needed.

The means for supplying this aid have been furnished principally through generous monthly subscriptions from a few citizens, through the hands of Mr. A. D. Jessup. Donations and subscriptions, through the ladies of the Committee, have also been received, and from time to time, acknowledged in the printed reports of the Committee.

It has been the aim of the Committee to provide employment for the women, for which adequate compensation has been given. The Sanitary Commission furnished material, which the Relief Committee had cut and converted into articles required for the use of the soldiers by the Sanitary Commission. Thirty-seven thousand nine hundred and fifteen articles have been made and returned to the Commission, free of charge. Finding the supply of work from this source inadequate to the demands for it, the Committee decided to obtain work from Government contractors, and to pay the women double the price paid by the contractors. Twenty thousand one hundred and seventy-four articles were made in this way, and returned to the contractors who were kind enough to furnish the work. Eleven hundred and twenty-nine articles have been made for the freedmen, and five hundred and five for other charities; making in all, fifty-nine thousand seven hundred and twenty-three articles.

Eight hundred and thirty women have been employed in the two years during which the labors of the Committee have been carried on; and it is due to the women thus employed to state, that of the number of garments made, but two have been missing through dishonesty.

The sources from which work has hitherto been obtained having failed, through the blessed return of peace, and the destitution being great among those near and dear to the men whose lives have been given to purchase that peace, the Committee have determined not to cease their labors during the present winter.

Two hundred women, principally widows, are now employed in making garments from materials furnished by the Committee. These garments are distributed to the most needy among the applicants for relief.

More than four hundred tons of coal have been given out to the needy families of soldiers during the past two years, the coal being the gift of a few coal merchants.

The receipts of the Committee have been as follows:

From Subscriptions and donations $28,300 00

From Entertainment given for the benefit of the Committee 1,444 00

From Contractors in payment for work done 1,681 31

From the Sanitary Commission 2,551 50

Total $33,976 81

This amount has all been expended, with the exception of two hundred and forty-eight dollars and forty-seven cents, which balance remained in the hands of the Treasurer on the 31st of December, 1865.

WISCONSIN SOLDIERS' AID SOCIETY

EARLY in the summer of 1861, Mrs. Margaret A. Jackson, widow of the late Rev. William Jackson, of Louisville, Kentucky, in connection with Mrs. Louisa M. Delafield and others, engaged in awakening an interest among the ladies of Milwaukee, in regard to the sanitary wants of the soldiers, which soon resulted in the formation of a "Milwaukee Ladies' Soldiers' Aid Society," composed of many of the benevolent ladies of this city. The society was very zealous in soliciting aid for the soldiers, and in making garments for their use in the service.

Very soon other Aid Societies in various parts of the State desired to become auxiliaries to this organization, and soon after the battle of Bull Run it became evident that their efficiency could be greatly promoted by the Milwaukee Society becoming a branch of the United States Sanitary Commission, and that relation was effected.

The name of the society was at this time changed to "Wisconsin Soldiers' Aid Society." Mrs. Jackson and Mrs. Delafield continued to be efficient as leaders in all the work of this society, but in its reorganization, Mrs. Henrietta L. Colt was chosen Corresponding Secretary, and commenced her work with great zeal and energy. She visited the Wisconsin soldiers in various localities at the front, and thus brought the wants of the brave men to the particular knowledge of the society, and in this way largely promoted the interest, zeal and efficiency of the ladies connected with it. She described the sufferings, fortitude and heroism of the soldiers with such simple pathos, that thousands of hearts were melted, and contributions poured into the treasury of the society in great abundance.

The number of auxiliaries in the State was two hundred and twenty-nine. The central organization at Milwaukee, beside forwarding supplies, had one bureau to assist soldiers' families in getting payments from the State, one to secure employment for soldiers' wives and mothers through contracts with the Government, under the charge of Mrs. Jackson, one to secure employment for the partially disabled soldiers, and one to provide for widows and orphans. The channels of benevolence through the State were various; the people generally sought the most direct route to the soldiers in the field; but the gifts to the army sent by the Wisconsin Soldiers' Aid Society (their report says without any "Fair"), alone amounted—the packages, to nearly six thousand in number, the value to nearly two hundred thousand dollars.

The Wisconsin Aid Society and its officers also rendered large and valuable aid to the two Sanitary Fairs held in Chicago in September, 1863, and June, 1865.

The Wisconsin Soldiers' Home, at Milwaukee, connected with the Wisconsin Aid Society, was an institution of great importance during the war. Its necessity has not passed away, and will not for many years. The ladies who originated and sustained it were indefatigable in their labors, and the benevolent public gave them their heartiest sanction. It gave thousands of soldiers a place of entertainment as they passed through the city to and from the army, and thus promoted their comfort and good morals. The sick and wounded were there tenderly nursed; the dying stranger there had friends.

During the year ending April 15, 1865, four thousand eight hundred and forty-two soldiers there received free entertainment, and the total number of meals served in the year was seventeen thousand four hundred and fifty-six, an average of forty-eight daily. These soldiers represented twenty different States, two

thousand and ninety belonging in Wisconsin. A fair in 1865 realized upwards of one hundred thousand dollars, which is to be expended on a permanent Soldiers Home, one of the three National Soldiers' Homes having been located at Milwaukee, and the Wisconsin Soldiers' Home being the nucleus of it.

Mrs. Colt was so efficient a worker for the soldiers, that a brief sketch of hex labors, prepared by a personal friend, will be appropriate in this connection.

MRS. HENRIETTA L. COLT, was born March 16th, 1812, in Rensselaerville, Albany County, New York. Her maiden name was Peckham. She was educated in a seminary at Albany, and was married in 1830, to Joseph S. Colt, Esq., a man well known throughout the State, as an accomplished Christian gentleman. Mr. Colt was a member of the Albany bar, and practiced his profession there until 1853, when he removed to Milwaukee. After three years' residence there he returned to New York, where he died, leaving an honored name and a precious memory among men.

The death of Mr. Colt brought to his widow a sad experience. In a letter to the writer, she expresses the deep sense of her loss, and the effect it had in preparing her for that devotion to the cause of her country, which, during the late rebellion, has led her to leave the comforts and refinements of her home to minister to the soldiers of the Union, in hospitals, to labor in the work of the Wisconsin Soldiers' Aid Society, to go on hospital steamers as far as Vicksburg to care for the sick and wounded, as they were brought up the river, where they could be better provided for, to visit the camps and regimental hospitals around the beleagured city, and to return with renewed devotion to the work of sending sanitary supplies to the sick and wounded of the Union army, until the close of the war. After portraying the character of her lamented husband, his chivalric tenderness, his thoughtful affection, his nobility of soul, his high sense of justice, which had made him a representative of the best type of humanity, she goes 77 on to say: "The sun seemed to me to go out in darkness when he went to the skies. Shielding me from every want, from all care, causing me to breathe a continual atmosphere of refinement, and love, and happiness, when he went, life lost its beauty and its charm. In this state of things it was to me as a divine gift—a real godsend—to have a chance for earnest absorbing work. The very first opportunity was seized to throw myself into the work for my country, which had called its stalwart sons to arms to defend its integrity, its liberty, its very existence, from the most gigantic and wicked rebellion known in history."

It is among the grateful memories of the writer of this sketch, that during the winter of 1863, while stationed at Helena, he went on board a steamer passing towards Vicksburg, and met there Mrs. Colt, in company with Mrs. Livermore, and Mrs. Hoge, of Chicago, on their way to carry sanitary stores, and minister to the sick and wounded, then being brought up the river from the first fatal attack on Vicksburg, in which our army was repulsed, and from the battle of Arkansas Post, on the Arkansas river, in which we were successful, and from an expedition up the White river, under General Gorman. He was greatly impressed with her intelligence, her purity of character, the beautiful blending of her religious and patriotic tendencies, the gentleness and tenderness with which she ministered encouragement and sympathy to the sick soldier, and the spirit of humanity and womanly dignity that marked her manners and conversation. The same qualities were characteristic of her companions from Chicago, in varied combination, each having her own individuality, and it was beautiful to see with what judgment and discretion, and union of purpose they went on their mission of love.

On their first visit, she and Mrs. Hoge, improvised a hospital of the steamer on which they went, which came up from Vicksburg loaded with wounded men, under the care of the surgeons. The dressing of their wounds and the amputation of limbs going on during the passage, made the air exceedingly impure, and yet these noble women did not flinch from their duty, nor neglect their gentle ministrations, which were as balm to the wounded heroes who lay stretched on the cabin floors from one end of the boat to the other.

On the renewal of the siege of Vicksburg, by General Grant, and while our army lay encamped for miles around, Mrs. Colt made a second visit to the scene of so much suffering and conflict, and visited the camps and regimental hospitals, where the very air seemed loaded with disease. Men with every variety of complaint were brought to the steamer, where it was known there were ladies on board, from the Sanitary Commissions, in the hope of kinder care and better sustenance. It was amidst dying soldiers, helpless refugees, manacled slaves, and even five hundred worn out and rejected mules, that their path up the Mississippi had to be pursued with patience, and fortitude, and hope.

In a note recently received from Mrs. Colt, she thus speaks of her visits to the hospitals, and of the brave and noble bearing of the wounded soldiers:

"I visited the Southwestern hospitals, in order to see the benefits really conferred by the Sanitary Commission, in order to stimulate supplies at home. Such was my story or the effect of it, that Wisconsin became the most powerful Auxiliary of the Northwestern Branch of the United States Sanitary Commission. I have visited seventy-two hospitals, and would find it difficult to choose the most remarkable among the many heroisms I every day witnessed.

"I was more impressed by the gentleness and refinement that seemed to grow up and in, the men when suffering from horrible wounds than from anything else. It seemed always to me that the sacredness of the cause for which they offered up their lives gave to them a heroism almost super-human—and the sufferings caused an almost womanly refinement among the coarsest men. I have never heard a word nor seen a look that was not respectful and grateful.

"At one time, when in the Adams' Hospital in Memphis, filled with six hundred wounded men with gaping, horrible, head and hip gunshot wounds, I could have imagined myself among men gathered on cots for some joyous occasion, and except one man, utterly disabled for life, not a regret—and even he thanked God devoutly that if his life must be given up then, it should be given for his country.

After a little, as the thought of his wife and babies came to him, I saw a terrible struggle; the great beads of sweat and the furrowed brow were more painful than the bodily suffering. But when he saw the look of pity, and heard the passage, He doeth all things well,' whispered to him, he became calm, and said, ' He knows best, my wife and children will be His care, and I am content.'

"Among the beardless boys, it was all heroism. They gained the victory, they lost a leg there, they lost an arm, and Arkansas Post was taken; they were proud to have helped on the cause. It enabled them apparently with little effort to remember the great, the holy cause, and give leg, arm, or even life cheerfully for its defense.

"I know now that love of country is the strongest love, next to the love of God, given to man."

Besides the good done to the sick and wounded of our army by these visits, an equal benefit resulted in their effect upon the people at home, in inspiring them to new zeal and energy, and increasing generosity on behalf of the country and its brave defenders.

Another service of great value to the soldiers, was rendered by Mrs. Colt, under an appointment from the Governor of Wisconsin, to visit the Army of the Cumberland, and see personally all sick Wisconsin men. She went under the escort of Rev. J. P. T. Ingraham, and saw every sick soldier of the Wisconsin troops in hospital. Their heroic endurance and its recital after her return, stimulated immensely the generosity of the people.

In such services as these Mrs. Colt passed the four years of the war, and by her self-sacrifice and devotion to the cause, in which her heart and mind were warmly enlisted, by the courage and fortitude with which she braved danger and death, in visiting distant battle-fields, and camps and hospitals, and ministering at the couch of sickness, and pain, and death, that she might revive the spirit, and save the lives of those who were battling for Union and Liberty, she has won the gratitude of her country, and deserves the place accorded to her among the heroines of the age.

MRS. ELIZA SALOMON, the accomplished and philanthropic wife of Governor Salomon, of Wisconsin, was at the outbreak of the war living quietly at Milwaukee, and amid the patriotic fervor which then reigned in Wisconsin, she sought no prominence or official position, but like the other ladies of the circle in which she moved, contented herself with working diligently for the soldiers, and contributing for the supply of their needs. In the autumn of 1861, her husband was elected Lieutenant Governor of the State, on the same ticket which bore the name of the lamented Louis Harvey, for Governor. On the death of Governor Harvey, in April, 1862, at Pittsburg Landing, Lieutenant Governor Salomon was at once advanced by the Constitution of Wisconsin, to his place for the remainder of his term, about twenty-one months. Both Governor and Mrs. Salomon, were of German extraction, and it was natural that the German soldiers, sick, wounded or suffering from privation, should look to the Governor's wife as their State-mother, and should expect sympathy and aid from her. She resolved not to disappoint their expectation, but to prove as far as lay in her power a mother not only to them, but to all the brave Wisconsin boys of whatever nationality, who needed aid and assistance.

At home and abroad, her time was almost entirely occupied with this noble and charitable work. She accompanied her husband wherever his duty and his heart called him to look after the soldiers. She visited the hospitals East and West, in Indiana, Illinois, St. Louis, and the interior of Missouri, and all along the Mississippi, as far South as Vicksburg, stopping at every place where Wisconsin troops were stationed.

Her voyage to Vicksburg in May, 1863, was one of considerable peril, from the swarms of guerrillas all along the river, who on several occasions fired at the boat, but fortunately did no harm.

She found at Vicksburg, a vast amount of suffering to be relieved, and abundant work to do, and possessing firm health and a vigorous constitution, she was able to accomplish much without impairing her health. At the first Sanitary Fair at Chicago, Mrs. Salomon organized a German Department, in which she sold needle and handiwork contributed by German ladies of Wisconsin and Chicago, to the amount of six thousand dollars. When, in January 1864, Governor Salomon returned to private life, Mrs. Salomon did not intermit her efforts for the good of the soldiers; her duty had become a privilege, and she continued her efforts for their relief and assistance, according to her opportunity till the end of the war.

PITTSBURG BRANCH, U. S. SANITARY COMMISSION

PITTSBURG, as the Capital of Western Pennsylvania, and the center of a large district of thoroughly loyal citizens, early took an active part in furnishing supplies for the sick and wounded of our armies. As its commercial relations and its readiest communications were with the West, most of its supplies were sent to the Western Armies, and after the battle of Belmont, the capture of Fort Donelson, and the terrible slaughter at Shiloh, the Pittsburg Subsistence Committee, and the Pittsburg Sanitary Committee, sent ample supplies and stores to the sufferers. The same noble generosity was displayed after the battles of Perryville, Chickasaw Bluffs, Murfreesboro' and Arkansas Post. In the winter of 1863, it was deemed best to make the Pittsburg Sanitary Committee, which had been reorganized for the purpose, an auxiliary of the United States Sanitary Commission, and measures were taken for that purpose by Mr. Thomas Bakewell, the President, and the other officers of the Committee. The Committee still retained its name, but in the summer of 1863, a consolidation was effected of the Sanitary and Subsistence Committees, and the Pittsburg Branch of the Commission was organized. Auxiliaries had previously been formed in the circumjacent country, acknowledging one or the other of these Committees as their head, and sending their contributions and supplies to it. The number of these was now greatly increased, and though latest in the order of time of all the daughters of the Commission, it was surpassed by few of the others in efficiency. The Corresponding Secretary and active manager of this new organization was Miss Rachael W. Me Fadden, a lady of rare executive ability, ardent patriotism, untiring industry, and great tact and discernment. Miss McFadden was ably seconded in her labors by Miss Mary Bissell, Miss Bakewell, and Miss Annie Bell, and Miss Ellen E. Murdoch, the daughter of the patriotic actor and elocutionist, gave her services with great earnestness to the work. In the spring of 1864, the people of Pittsburg, infected by the example of other cities, determined to hold a Sanitary Fair in their enterprising though smoke-crowned city. In its inception, development and completion, Miss McFadden was the prime mover in this Fair. She was at the head of the Executive Committee, and Miss Bakewell, Miss Ella Steward, and Mrs. McMillan, were its active and indefatigable Secretaries. The appeals made to all classes in city and country for contributions in money and goods were promptly responded to, and on the first of June, 1864, the Fair opened in buildings expressly erected for it in Alleghany, Diamond Square. The display in all particulars, was admirable, but that of the Mechanical and Floral Halls was extraordinary in its beauty, its tasteful arrangement and its great extent. The net results of the Fair, were three hundred and thirty thousand four hundred and ninety dollars, and eighty cents, and while it was in progress, fifty thousand dollars were also raised in Pittsburg, for the Christian Commission. The great Central Fair in Philadelphia, was at the same time in progress, so that the bulk of the contributions were drawn from the immediate vicinage of Pittsburg.

The Pittsburg Branch continued its labors to the close of the war.

After the fair, a special diet kitchen on a grand scale was established and supplied with all necessary appliances by the Pittsburg Branch. Miss Murdoch gave it her personal supervision for three months, and in August, 1864, prepared sixty-two thousand dishes.

MRS. ELIZABETH S. MENDENHALL

THIS lady and Mrs. George Hoadly, were the active and efficient managers of the Soldiers Aid Society, of Cincinnati, which bore the same relations to the branch of the United States Sanitary

Commission, at Cincinnati, which the Woman's Central Association of Relief did to the Sanitary Commission itself. Mrs. Mendenhall is the wife of Dr. George Mendenhall, an eminent and public-spirited citizen of Cincinnati. Mrs. Mendenhall was born in Philadelphia, in 1819, but her childhood and youth were passed in Richmond, Virginia, where a sister, her only near relative, still resides. Her relatives belonged to the society of Friends, and though living in a slaveholding community, she grew up with an abhorrence of slavery. On her marriage, in 1838, she removed with her husband to Cleveland, Ohio, and subsequently to Cincinnati, where she has since resided, and where her hatred of oppression increased in intensity.

When the first call for troops was made in April, 1861, and thenceforward throughout the summer and autumn of that year, and the winter of 1861–2, she was active in organizing sewing circles and aid societies to make the necessary clothing and comforts which the soldiers so much needed when suddenly called to the field. She set the example of untiring industry in these pursuits, and by her skill in organizing and systematizing their labor, rendered them highly efficient. In February, 1862, the sick and wounded began to pour into the government hospitals of Cincinnati, from the siege of Fort Donelson, and ere these were fairly convalescent, still greater numbers came from Shiloh; and from that time forward, till the close of the war, the hospitals were almost constantly filled with sick or wounded soldiers. To these suffering heroes Mrs. Mendenhall devoted herself with the utmost assiduity. For two and a half years from the reception of the first wounded from Fort Donelson, she spent half of every day, and frequently the whole day, in personal ministrations to the sick and wounded in any capacity that could add to their comfort. She procured necessaries and luxuries for the sick, waited upon them, wrote letters for them, consoled the dying, gave information to their friends of their condition, and attended to the necessary preparations for the burial of the dead. During the four years of the war she was not absent from the city for pleasure but six days, and during the whole period there were not more than ten days in which she did not perform some labor for the soldiers' comfort.

Her field of labor was in the four general hospitals in the city, but principally in the Washington Park Hospital, over which Dr. J. B. Smith, who subsequently fell a martyr to his devotion to the soldiers, presided, who gave her ample opportunities for doing all for the patients which her philanthropic spirit prompted. During all this time she was actively engaged in the promotion of the objects of the Women's Soldiers' Aid Society, of which, she was at this time, president, having been from the first an officer. The enthusiasm manifested in the northwest in behalf of the Sanitary Fair at Chicago, led Mrs. Mendenhall to believe that a similar enterprise would be feasible in Cincinnati, which should draw its supplies and patrons from all portions of the Ohio valley. With her a generous and noble thought was sure to be followed by action equally generous and praiseworthy. She commenced at once the agitation of the subject in the daily papers of the city, her first article appearing in the Times, of October 31, 1863, and being followed by others from her pen in the other loyal papers of the city. The idea was received with favor, and on the 7 th of November an editorial appeared in the Cincinnati Gazette, entitled "Who speaks for Cincinnati?" This resulted in a call the next day for a meeting of gentlemen to consider the subject. Committees were appointed, an organization effected and circulars issued on the 13th of November. On the 19th, the ladies met, and Mrs. Mendenhall was unanimously chosen President of the ladies' committee, and subsequently second Vice-President of the General Fair organization, General Rosecrans being President, and the Mayor of the city, first Vice-President. To the furtherance of this work, Mrs. Mendenhall devoted all her energies. Eloquent appeals from her facile pen were addressed to loyal and patriotic men and women all over the country, and a special circular and appeal to the patriotic young ladies of Cincinnati and the Ohio valley for their hearty co-operation in the good work. The correspondence and supervision of that portion of the fair which necessarily came under the direction of the ladies, required all her time and strength, but the results were highly satisfactory. Of the two hundred and thirty-five thousand dollars which was the net product of this Sanitary Fair, a very liberal proportion was called forth by her indefatigable exertions and her extraordinary executive ability.

The aggregate results of the labors of the Women's Aid Society, before and after the fair, are known to have realized about four hundred thousand dollars in money, and nearly one million five hundred thousand in hospital stores and supplies.

The Soldiers' Home of Cincinnati, one of the best managed of these institutions, was also established by the energy of Mrs. Mendenhall, and her associates. Up to the close of 1864, eighty thousand soldiers had been entertained in this "Home," and three hundred and seventy-two thousand meals dispensed. They also obtained by their exertions, a burial place for Ohio soldiers, dying in Cincinnati, at the Spring Grove Cemetery, the Trustees of the Cemetery giving one lot, and the Legislature purchasing two more at a small price.

The fair closed, she resumed her hospital work and her duties as President of the Women's Soldiers' Aid Society, and continued to perform them to the close of the war. Near the close of 1864, she exerted her energies in behalf of a Fair for soldiers' families, in which fifty thousand dollars were raised for this deserving object. The testimonies of her associates to the admirable manner in which her hospital work was performed are emphatic, and the thousands of soldiers who were the recipients of her gentle ministries, give equally earnest testimonies to her kindness and tenderness of heart.

The freedmen and refugees have also shared her kindly ministrations and her open-handed liberality, and since the close of the war her self-sacrificing spirit has found ample employment in endeavoring to lift the fallen of her own sex out of the depths of degradation, to the sure and safe paths of virtue and rectitude.

With the modesty characteristic of a patriotic spirit, Mrs. Mendenhall depreciates her own labors and sacrifices. "What," she says in a letter to a friend, "are my humble efforts for the soldiers, compared with the sacrifice made by the wife or mother of the humblest private who ever shouldered a musket?"

DEPARTMENT OF THE SOUTH

R. M. M. MARSH was Medical Inspector of the Department of the Gulf and South, his charge comprising the States of Georgia, South Carolina, and Florida. He held his appointment in the capacity mentioned from the Sanitary Commission, and from Government, the latter conferring upon him great authority over hospitals and health matters in general throughout his district.

It was in the early part of the year 1863 that Mrs. Marsh left her home in Vermont and joined her husband at Beaufort.

The object of Mrs. Marsh in going thither, was to establish a home with its comforts amidst the unfamiliar scenes and habitudes of the South.

Everything was strange, unnatural, unreal. Beaufort was in conquered territory occupied by its conquerors The former inhabitants had fled, leaving lands, houses and negroes—all that refused to go with them, or could not be removed. Military rule prevailed, and the new population were Northern soldiers, and a few adventurous women. Besides these were blades, men, women and children, many of them far from the homes they had known, and strange alike to freedom and a life made independent by their own efforts. From order to chaos, that was the transition a Northern woman underwent in coming to this place and state of society.

Mrs. Marsh had no sooner arrived than she found there was work to do and duties to perform in her new home on which she had not calculated. Her husband was frequently absent, sometimes for long periods. To his charge came the immense stores of supplies constantly forwarded by the Sanitary Commission, which were to be received, accounted for, unpacked, dealt out to the parties for whom they were intended. All this must be done bv an intelligent person or persons, and by the same, reports of the condition of the hospitals must be made, together with the needful requisitions.

Here was business enough to employ the time, exhaust the strength, and occupy the thoughts of any single individual. It was a "man's work," as Mrs. Marsh often declares. Be that as it may, it v as accomplished by a woman, and in the most admirable manner. The

Sanitary Commission feels both proud and grateful, whenever the name of Mrs. Marsh is mentioned.

Her services were not of a nature to elicit great applause, or to attract much attention. They were quietly performed, and at a point quite aside from battle-fields, or any great center where thousands of spectators had the opportunity to become cognizant of them. But they were not, on account of these facts, less beneficent or useful.

Mrs. Marsh often visited the hospitals and made the acquaintance of the sick and wounded, becoming frequently, deeply interested in individuals. This was a feeling entirely different from that general interest in the welfare of every Union soldier which arose as much from the instincts of a patriotic heart, as from philanthropy.

She never became a hospital nurse, however, for she was fully occupied in other ways, and her husband, Dr. Marsh did not cordially approve, save in a few particular instances, of the introduction of women to the hospitals in that capacity. But living in the immediate vicinity of the hospitals, her benevolent face was often seen there, and welcomed with grateful smiles from many a bed of suffering.

A young officer from one of the Northern States and regiments, wounded at the battle of Olustee, was brought to Beaufort Hospital for treatment and care. Long previously there had been a compact between him and a comrade that the one first wounded should be cared for by the other if possible. The exigencies of the service were at that time such that this comrade could not without much difficulty obtain leave of absence. He finally, however, triumphed over all obstacles, and took his place beside his friend. Mrs. Marsh often- saw them together, and listened, at one time, to a discussion or comparison of views which revealed the character and motives of both.

The unwounded one was rejoicing that his term of service was nearly expired. It was at a time when many were re-enlisting, but he emphatically declared he would not. "I would, then," replied the wounded man, "if I had the strength to enter upon another term of service, I would do so. When I did enlist it was because of my country's need, and that need is not less imminent now. Yes," he added, with a sigh, "if God would restore me to health, I would remain in the service till the end of the war. The surgeon tells me I shall not recover, that the next hemorrhage will probably be the last. But I am not sorry, I am glad, that I have done what I have done, and would do it again, if possible."

That this was the spirit of many of the wounded men, Mrs. Marsh delights to testify. This man was God's soldier, as well as the Union's. He had learned to think amid the awful scenes of Fort Wagner, and when wounded at Olustee was prepared to live or die, whichever was God's will. Mrs. Marsh was sitting beside his bed, in quiet conversation with him, when without warning, the hemorrhage commenced. The plash of blood was heard, as the life-current burst from his wound, and, "Go now," he said in his low calm voice. "This is the end, and I would not have you witness it."

The hemorrhage was, however, checked, but he died soon after. Meantime the Sanitary Commission stores were constantly arriving, and Mrs. Marsh continued to take the entire charge of them. A portion of her house was used for store-rooms, and there were received thousands of dollars' worth of comforts of all kinds from the North—a constant, never-failing flood of beneficence.

The first prisoners seen by Mrs. Marsh had come from Charleston. There were nine privates and three or four officers. Their rags scarcely covered them decently. They were filthy, squalid, emaciated. They halted at a point several miles from Beaufort, and a requisition was sent by the officers at this outpost, for clothing and other necessaries for the officers of the party. These were sent, but Mrs. Marsh thought there must be others—private soldiers, perhaps, for whom no provision had been made. She accordingly dispatched her nephew, who was a member of her family, to make inquiries and see that the wants of such were provided for.

In a short time she saw him returning at the head of his ragged brigade. The poor fellows were indeed a loathsome sight, worn, feeble, clad only in the unsightly rags which had been their prison wear. They were not shown into the office, but to a vestibule without, and their first desire was for water, soap—the materials for cleanliness. Mrs. Marsh examined her stores for clothing. That which was on hand was mainly designed for hospital use. She would have given each an entire suit, but could find only two or three pairs of coarse blue overalls, such as are worn by laborers at the North. As she stepped to the door to give them this clothing, she remarked upon the scarcity, and said the overalls must be given to the men that most needed them, but at once saw that where all were in filthy rags, there seemed no choice. The one who stood nearest her had taken a pair of the overalls, and was surveying them with delight, but he at once turned to another, "I guess he needs 'em most, I can get along with the old ones, a while," he said, in a cheerful tone, and smothering a little sigh he turned away.

This spirit of self-sacrifice was almost universal among the men of our army, and was shown to all who had any care over them. How much every man needed an entire change of clean, comfortable garments, was shown the instant they left, when the nephew of Mrs. Marsh commenced sweeping the vestibule where they had stood, with great vigor, replying to the remonstrances of his aunt, only "I must," and adding, in a lower tone, "They can't help it, poor fellows," as he made the place too hot to hold anything with life.

It was in the summer of 1864, that communication was first obtained with the prisoners in Charleston, a communication afterwards extended to all the loathsome prison-pens of the South, where our men languished in filth, disease, and starvation.

At this time Dr. Marsh's duties kept him almost entirely at Folly Island, and there he received a letter from General Seymour who was confined, with other Union officers, in Charleston, a part of the time under fire, asking that if possible certain needful articles might be sent to him. This letter was immediately sent to Mrs. Marsh, who at once prepared a box containing more than twice the amount of articles asked for, and forwarded them to the confederate authorities at Charleston, for General Seymour. Almost contrary to all expectations, this box reached the General, and but a short time elapsed before its receipt was acknowledged. The General wrote touchingly of their privations, and while thanking Mrs. Marsh warmly for the articles already sent, represented the wants of some of the other gentlemen, his companions. Supplies were sent them, received and acknowledged, and thus a regular channel of communication was opened.

One noticeable fact attended this correspondence—namely, the extreme modesty of the demands made; no one ever asking for more than he needed at the time, as a pair of stockings, or a single shirt, and always expressing a fear lest others might need these favors more than himself.

When, soon after, by means of this entering wedge, the way to the prisons of Andersonville, Florence, and Salisbury, was 79 opened, the same fact was observed. In the midst of all their dreadful suffering and misery, the prisoners there made no large demands. They asked for but little—the smallest possible amount, and were always fearful lest they might absorb the bounty to which others had a better claim.

After this communication was opened, Mrs. Marsh found a delightful task in preparing the boxes which in great numbers were constantly being sent forward to the prisons. It was a part of her duty, also, to inspect the letters which went and came between the prisons and the outside world.

The pathos of many of these was far beyond description. Touching appeals constantly came to her from distant Northern homes for some tidings of the sons, brothers, fathers of whose captivity they had heard, but whose further existence had been a blank. Where are they? and how are they? were constantly recurring questions, which alas! it was far too often her sad duty to answer in a way to destroy all hope.

And the letters of the prisoners, filled to the uttermost, not with complaints, but with the pervading sadness that could not for one moment be banished from their horrible lives! No words can describe them, they were simply heart-breaking! Just as the horror of the prison-pens is beyond the power of words to fitly tell, so are the griefs which grew out of them.

Mrs. Marsh continued busily employed in this work of mercy until it was suddenly suspended. Some formality had not been complied with, and the privilege of communication was discontinued; and all their friends disappointed and disheartened. This we can easily imagine, but not what the suspension was to the suffering prisoners who had for a short season enjoyed this one gleam of light from the outer world, and were now plunged into a rayless hopeless night. When the time of deliverance came, as we all know, many of them were past the power of rejoicing in it.

Dr. Marsh was for a long time detained at Folly and Morris Islands. The force at Beaufort was quite inadequate, and exceedingly onerous and absorbing duties fell to the share of Mrs. Marsh. Communication was difficult. Dr. Marsh at times could not reach his home. Vessels which had been running between New York and Port Royal and Hilton Head were detained at the North. The receipt and transmission of sanitary stores, and the immense correspondence growing out of it; the general oversight of the needs of the hospitals, and the monthly reports of the same all fell heavily upon one brain and one pair of hands.

It was at just such an emergency that the army of Sherman, the "Great March" to the sea nearly completed, arrived upon the scene. The sick and disabled arrived by hundreds, the hospitals were filled up directly, and even thronged; while so numerous were the cases of small-pox, which had appeared in the army, that a large separate hospital had to be provided for them.

We may perhaps imagine how busy was the brave woman, left with such an immense responsibility on her hands.

Early in 1865, Dr. Marsh received notice that it had been determined to send him to Newbern, North Carolina, but he never went, being attacked soon after by a long and dangerous illness which for a time rendered it improbable that he would ever see his Northern home again.

It was at this time that a cargo of sanitary supplies arrived from New York. A part of these were a contribution from Montreal. Montreal had before sent goods to the Commission, but these were forwarded to Mrs. Marsh herself. A letter of hers written not long previous to a friend in New York, had been 'forwarded to Montreal, and had aroused a strong desire there to help her in her peculiar work. A large portion of this gift was from an M. P., who, though he might, like others, lift his voice against the American war, had yet enough of the milk of human kindness in his heart to lead him to desire to do something for her suffering soldiers and prisoners.

This gift Mrs. Marsh never saw, it being sent with the rest of the unbroken cargo back to Newbern in view of the expected arrival of her family there.

The surrender of Lee virtually closed the war, and the necessity of Dr. Marsh's stay in the South was no longer an important one. Besides this, his health would not permit it, and he returned to New York where he had long been wanted to take charge of the "Lincoln Home" in Grove Street, a hospital opened by the Sanitary Commission for lingering cases of wounds and sickness among homeless and destitute soldiers.

Of this hospital and home Dr. Marsh was surgeon, and Mrs. Marsh matron. Dr. Hoadly who had been with Dr. Marsh at the South, still retained the position of assistant. The health of Dr. Marsh improved, but he has never entirely recovered.

They entered the Lincoln Home on the 1st of May, 1865, and the house was immediately filled with patients. They remained there until June of the following year, 1866. During their stay between three and four hundred patients were admitted, and of those who were regular patients none died. One soldier, a Swede, was found in the street in the last stages of exhaustion and suffering, and died before the morning following his admission. He bore about him evidences of education and gentle birth, but he could not speak English, and carried with him into another world the secret of his name and identity. He had no disease, but the foundations of his life had been sapped by the irritation caused by filth and vermin.

As at the South, in the services of Mrs. Marsh here, there was a great disproportion between their showiness and their usefulness. She pursued her quiet round of labors, the results of which will be seen and felt for years, as much as in the present. Her kind voice, and pleasant smile will be an ever living and delightful memory in the hearts of all to whom she ministered during those long hours of the nation's peril, in which the best blood of her sons was poured out a red libation to Liberty.

After the close of the Lincoln Home, Mrs. Marsh continued to devote herself to suffering soldiers and their families, making herself notably useful in this important department of the nation's work.

SAINT LOUIS LADIES' UNION AID SOCIETY

THIS Society, the principal Auxiliary of the "Western Sanitary Commission, and holding the same relation to it that the Women's Central Association of Relief in New York, did to the United States Sanitary Commission had its origin in the summer of 1861. On the 26th of July, of that year, a few ladies met at the house of Mrs. F. Holy, in St. Louis, to consider the propriety of combining the efforts of the loyal ladies of that city into a single organization in anticipation of the conflict then impending within the State. At an adjourned meeting held a week later, twenty-five ladies registered themselves, as members of the "Ladies' Union Aid Society," and elected a full board of officers. Most of these resigned in the following autumn, and in November, 1861, the following list was chosen, most of whom served through the war.

President: Mrs. Alfred Clapp; Vice Presidents, Mrs. Samuel C. Davis, Mrs. T. M. Post, Mrs. Robert Anderson; Recording Secretary, Miss H. A. Adams; Treasurer, Mrs. S. B. Kellogg; Corresponding Secretary, Miss Belle Holmes; afterwards, Miss Anna M. Debenham. An Executive Committee was also appointed, several of the members of which, and among the number, Mrs. C. R. Springer, Mrs. S. Palmer, Mrs. Joseph Crawshaw, Mrs. Washington King, Mrs. Charles L. Ely, Mrs. F. F. Maltby, Mrs. C. N. Barker, Miss Susan J. Bell, Miss Eliza S. Glover, and Miss Eliza Page, were indefatigable in their labors for the soldiers.

This Society was from the beginning, active and efficient. It conducted its business with great ability and system, and in every direction made itself felt as a power for good throughout the Mississippi Valley. Its officers visited for a considerable period, fourteen hospitals in the city and vicinity, and were known in the streets by the baskets they earned. Of one of these baskets the recording Secretary, Miss Adams, gives us an interesting inventory in one of her reports: "Within was a bottle of cream, a home-made loaf, fresh eggs, fruit and oysters; stowed away in a corner was a flannel shirt, a sling, a pair of spectacles, a flask of cologne; a convalescent had asked for a lively book, and the lively book was in the basket; there was a dressing-gown for one, and a white muslin handkerchief for another; and paper, envelopes and stamps for all."

The Christian Commission made the ladies of the Society their agents for the distribution of religious reading, and they scattered among the men one hundred and twenty-five thousand pages of tracts, and twenty thousand books and papers.

The Ladies' Union Aid Society, sent delegates to all the earlier battle-fields, as well as to the camps and trenches about Vicksburg, and these ladies returned upon the hospital steamers, pursuing their heroic work, toiling early and late, imperilling in many cases their health, and even their lives, in the midst of the trying and terrible scenes which surrounded them. During the fall and winter of 1862-3, the Society's rooms were open day and evening, for the purpose of bandage-rolling, so great was the demand for supplies of this kind.

Amid their other labors, they were not unmindful of the distress which the families of the soldiers were suffering. So great was the demand for hospital clothing, that they could not supply it alone, and they expended five thousand five hundred dollars received for the purpose from the Western Sanitary Commission, in paying for the labor on seventy-five thousand garments for the hospitals. The Medical Purveyor, learning of their success, offered the Aid Society a large contract for army work. They accepted it, and prepared the work at their rooms, and gave out one hundred and twenty-eight thousand articles to be made, paying out over six thousand dollars for labor. Several other contracts followed, particularly one for two hundred and sixty-one thousand yards of bandages, for the rolling of which six hundred and fifty-two dollars were paid. By these means and a judicious liberality, the Society prevented a great amount of suffering in the families of soldiers. The Benton Barracks Hospital, one of the largest in the West, to which reference has been frequently made in this volume, had for its surgeon-in-charge, that able surgeon and earnest philanthropist, Dr. Ira Russell. Ever anxious to do all in his power for his patients, and satisfied that more skilfully prepared special diet, and in greater variety than the government supplies permitted would be beneficial to them, he requested the ladies of the UnionAid Society, to occupy a reception-room, storeroom, and kitchen at the hospital, in supplying this necessity. Donations intended for the soldiers could be left at these rooms for distribution; fruit, vegetables, and other offerings could here be prepared and issued as required. Thus all outside bounty could be systematized, and the surgeon could regulate the diet of the entire hospital. Miss Bettie Broadhead, was the first superintendent of these rooms which were subsequently enlarged and multiplied. Bills of fare were distributed in each ward every morning; the soldiers wrote their names and numbers opposite the special dishes they desired; the surgeon examined the bills of fare, and if he approved, endorsed them. At the appointed time the dishes distinctly labelled, arrived at their destination in charge of an orderly. Nearly forty-eight thousand dishes were issued in one year.

In the fall of 1863, the Society established a branch at Nashville, Tennessee, Mrs. Barker and Miss H. A. Adams, going thither with five hundred dollars and seventy-two boxes of stores. Miss Adams, though surrounded with difficulties, and finding the surgeons indifferent if not hostile, succeeded in establishing a special diet kitchen, like that at Benton Barracks' Hospital. This subsequently became a very important institution, sixty-two thousand dishes being issued in the single month of August, 1864. The supplies for this kitchen, were mostly furnished by the Pittsburg Subsistence Committee, and Miss Ellen Murdoch, the daughter of the elocutionist to whom we have already referred, in the account of the Pittsburg Branch, prepared the supplies with her own hands, for three months. During this period, no reasonable wish of an invalid ever went ungratified.

This Society also did a considerable work for the freedmen— and the white refugees, in connection with the Western Sanitary

Commission. On the formation of the Freedmen's Relief Society, this part of their work was transferred to them.

We have no means of giving definitely the aggregate receipts and disbursements of this efficient Association. They were so involved with those of the Western Sanitary Commission, that it would be a difficult task to separate them. The receipts of the Commission were seven hundred and seventy-one thousand dollars in money, and about three millions five hundred thousand dollars in supplies. Of this sum we believe we are not in the wrong in attributing nearly two hundred thousand dollars in cash, and one million dollars in supplies to the Ladies' Union Aid Society, either directly or indirectly.

Believing that the exertions of the efficient officers of the Society deserve commemoration, we have obtained the following brief sketches of Mrs. Clapp, Miss Adams, (now Mrs. Collins), Mrs. Springer, and Mrs. Palmer.

Among the earnest and noble women of St. Louis, who devoted themselves to the cause of their country and its heroic defenders at the beginning of the great Rebellion, and whose labors and sacrifices were maintained throughout the struggle for naso tional unity and liberty, none are more worthy of honorable mention, in a work of this character, than MRS. ANNA L. CLAPP.

She was distinguished among those ladies whose labors for the Charities of the war, and whose presence in the Hospitals, cheered and comforted the soldiers of the Union, and either prepared them for a tranquil and happy deliverance from their sufferings, or sent them back to the field of battle to continue the heroic contest until success should crown the victorious arms of the nation, and give peace and liberty to their beloved country.

The maiden name of Mrs. Clapp was Wendell, and her paternal ancestors originally emigrated from Holland. She was born in Cambridge, Washington county, New York, and was educated at Albany.

For three years she was a teacher in the celebrated school of Rev. Nathaniel Prime, at Newburgh, New York. In the year 1838, she was married to Alfred Clapp, Esq., an enterprising merchant, and lived for several years in New York City, and Brooklyn, where she became an active member of various benevolent associations, and performed the duties of Treasurer of the Industrial School Association.

Just previous to the Rebellion, she emigrated with her husband and family to St. Louis, and after the war had commenced, and the early battles in the West had begun to fill every vacant public building in that city with sick and wounded men, she, with many other noble women of like heroic temperament, found a new sphere for their activity and usefulness. In the month of August, 1861, the Ladies' Union Aid Society, of St. Louis, was organized for the purpose of ministering to the wants of the sick and wounded soldiers, providing Hospital garments and Sanitary stores, in connection with similar labors by the Western Sanitary Commission, assisting soldiers' families, and visiting the Hospitals, to give religious counsel, and minister consolation to the sick and dying, in a city where only a few of the clergy of the various denominations who were distinguished for their patriotism and loyalty, attended to this duty; the majority, both Protestant and Catholic, being either indifferent to the consequences of the rebellion, or in sympathy with the treason which was at that time threatening the Union and liberties of the country with disruption and overthrow.

Of this Association of noble and philanthropic women, which continued its useful labors during the war, Mrs. Clapp was made President in the fall of 1861, holding that office during the existence of the organization, giving nearly all her time and energies to this great work of helping and comforting her country's defenders.

After the great battles of Shiloh and Vicksburg, and Arkansas Post, she, with other ladies of the Association, repaired on Hospital Steamers to the scene of conflict, taking boxes of Sanitary stores, Hospital garments and lint for the wounded, and ministered to them with her own hands on the return trips to the Hospitals of St. Louis.

As President of the Ladies' Union Aid Society, her labors were arduous and unremitting. The work of this association was always very great, consisting in part of the manufacture of hospital garments, by contract with the medical purveyor, which work was given out to the wives of soldiers, to enable them the better to support themselves and children, during the absence of their husbands in the army. The work of cutting out these garments, giving them out, keeping an account with each soldier's wife, paying the price of the labor, etc., was no small undertaking, requiring much labor from the members of the society. It was an interesting sight, on Thursday of each week, to see hundreds of poor women filling the large rooms of the association on Chestnut Street, from morning to night, receiving work and pay, and to witness the untiring industry of the President, Secretary, Treasurer, and Committees, waiting upon them.

The visitation of these families by committees, and their reports, to say nothing of the general sanitary and hospital work performed by the society, required a large amount of labor; and in addition to this the aid rendered to destitute families of Union refugees, and the part taken by Mrs. Clapp in organizing a Refugee Home, and House of Industry, would each of itself make quite a chapter of the history of the association.

In all these labors Mrs. Clapp showed great executive and administrative ability, and must be reckoned by all who know her, among the truly patriotic women of the land. And in all the relations of life her character stands equally high, adorning, as she does, her Christian profession by works of piety, and patriotism, and love, and commanding the highest confidence and admiration of the community in which she lives.

The devoted labors of Miss H. A. ADAMS, in the service of the soldiers of the Union and their families, from the beginning of the war, till near its close, entitle her to a place in the records of this volume. She was born in Fitz William, New Hampshire, at the foot of Mount Monadnock, and grew to maturity amid the beautiful scenery, and the pure influences of her New England home. Her father, Mr. J. S. Adams, was a surveyor, a man of character and influence, and gave to his daughter an excellent education. At fifteen years of age she became a teacher, and in 1856 came West for the benefit of her health, having a predisposition to pulmonary consumption, and fearing the effect of the east winds and the trying climate of the Eastern States.

Having connections in St. Louis she came to that city, and, for a year and a half, was employed as a teacher in the public schools. In this, her chosen profession, she soon acquired an honorable position, which she retained till the commencement of the war. At this time, however, the management of the schools was directed by a Board of Education, the members of which were mostly secessionists, the school fund was diverted from its proper uses by the disloyal State government, under Claib. Jackson, and all the teachers, who were from New England, were dismissed from their situations, at the close of the term in 1861. Miss

Adams, of course, was included in this number, and the unjust proscription only excited more intensely the love of her country and its noble defenders, who were already rallying to the standard of the Union, and laying down their lives on the altars of justice and liberty.

In August, 1861, the Ladies' Union Aid Society, of St. Louis, was organized. Miss Adams was present at its first meeting and assisted in its formation. She was chosen as its first secretary, which office she filled with untiring industry, and to the satisfaction of all its members, for more than three years.

In the autumn of 1863, her only brother died in the military service of the United States. With true womanly heroism, she went to the hospital at Mound City, Illinois, where he had been under surgical treatment, hoping to nurse and care for him, and see him restored to health, but before she reached the place he had died and was buried. From this time her interest in the welfare of our brave troops was increased and intensified, and there was no sacrifice she was not willing to undertake for their benefit. Moved by the grief of her own personal bereavement, her sympathy for the sick and wounded of the army of the Union, was manifested by renewed diligence in the work of sending them all possible aid and comfort from the ample stores of the Ladies' Union Aid Society, and the

Western Sanitary Commission, and by labors for the hospitals far and near.

The duties of Miss Adams, as Secretary of the Ladies' Union Aid Society, were very arduous.

The Society comprised several hundred of the most noble, efficient and patriotic women of St. Louis. The rooms were open every day, from morning to night. Sanitary stores and Hospital garments were prepared and manufactured by the members, and received by donation from citizens and from abroad, and had to be stored and arranged, and given out again to the Hospitals, and to the sick in regimental camps, in and around St. Louis, and also other points in Missouri, as they were needed. Letters of acknowledgement had to be written, applications answered, accounts kept, proceedings recorded, information and advice given, reports written and published, all of which devolved upon the faithful and devoted Secretary, who was ever at her post, and constant and unremitting in her labors. Soldiers' families had also to be assisted; widows and orphans to be visited and cared for; rents, fuel, clothing, and employment to be provided, and the destitute relieved, of whom there were thousands whose husbands, and sons, and brothers, were absent fighting the battles of the Union.

Missouri was, during the first year of the war, a battle-ground. St. Louis and its environs were crowded with troops; the Hospitals were large and numerous; during the winter of 1861-2, there were twenty thousand sick and wounded soldiers in them; and the concurrent labors of the Ladies' Union Aid Society, and the Western Sanitary Commission, were in constant requisition. The visiting of the sick, ministering to them at their couches of pain, reading to them, cheerful conversation with them, were duties which engaged many of the ladies of the Society; and numerous interesting and affecting incidents were preserved by Miss Adams, and embodied in the Reports of the Association. She also did her share in this work of visiting; and during the winter of 1863-4, she went to Nashville, Tennessee, and established there a special diet kitchen, upon which the surgeons in charge of the hospitals, could make requisitions for the nicer and more delicate preparations of food for the very sick.

She remained all winter in Nashville, in charge of a branch of the St. Louis Aid Society, and, by her influence, secured the opening of the hospitals to female nurses, who had hitherto not been employed in Nashville. Knowing, as she did, the superior gentleness of women as nurses, their more abundant kindness and sympathy, and their greater skill in the preparation of food for the sick; knowing also the success that had attended the experiment of introducing women nurses in the Military Hospitals in other cities, she determined to overcome the prejudices of such of the army surgeons as stood in the way, and secure to her sick and wounded brothers in the hospitals at Nashville, the benefit of womanly kindness, and nursing, and care. In this endeavor she was entirely successful, and by her persuasive manners, her womanly grace and refinement, and her good sense, she recommended her views to the medical authorities, and accomplished her wishes.

Returning to St. Louis in the spring of 1864, she continued to perform the duties of Secretary of the Ladies' Union Aid Society, till the end of the year, when, in consequence of a contemplated change in her life, she resigned her position, and retired from it with the friendship and warm appreciation of her coworkers in the useful labors of the society. In the month of June, 1865, she was married to Morris Collins, Esq., a citizen of St. Louis.

MRS. C. R. SPRINGER, who has labored so indefatigably at St. Louis, for the soldiers of the Union and their families during the war, was born in Parsonsfield, Maine. Her maiden name was Lord. Previous to her marriage to Mr. Springer, a respectable merchant of St. Louis, she was a teacher in New Hampshire. On the event of her marriage, she came to reside at St. Louis, about ten years ago, and on the breaking out of the war, espoused with patriotic ardor the cause of her country in its struggle with the great slaveholding rebellion. To do this in St. Louis, at that period, when wealth and fashion, and church influence were so largely on the side of the rebellion, and every social circle was more or less infected with treason, required a high degree of moral courage and heroism.

From the first opening of the hospitals in St. Louis, in the autumn of 1861, Mrs. Springer became a most untiring, devoted and judicious visiter, and by her kind and gracious manners, her words of sympathy and encouragement, and her religious consolation, she imparted hope and comfort to many a poor, sick, and wounded soldier, stretched upon the bed of languishing.

Besides her useful labors in the hospitals, Mrs. Springer was an active member of the Ladies' Union Aid Society in St. Louis, from the date of its organization in August, 1861, to its final disbanding—October, 1865—in the deliberations of which her counsel always had great weight and influence. During the four years of its varied and useful labors for the soldiers and their families, she has been among its most diligent workers. In the winter of 1862, the Society took charge of the labor of making up hospital garments, given out by the Medical Purveyor of the department, and she superintended the whole of this important work during that winter, in which one hundred and twenty-seven thousand five hundred garments were made.

Mrs. Springer is a highly educated woman, of great moral worth, devoted to the welfare of the soldier, inspired by sincere love of country, and a high sense of Christian duty. No one will be more gratefully remembered by thousands of soldiers and their families, to whom she has manifested kindness, and a warm interest in their welfare. These services have been gratuitously rendered, and she has given up customary recreations, and sacrificed ease and social pleasure to attend to these duties of humanity. Her reward will be found in the consciousness of having done good to the defenders of her native land, and in the blessing of those who were ready to perish, to whom her kind services, and words of good cheer came as a healing balm in the hour of despondency, and strengthened them for a renewal of their efforts in the cause of country and liberty.

Among the devoted women who have made themselves martyrs to the work of helping our patriotic soldiers and their families in St. Louis, was the late MRS. MARY E. PALMER. She was born in Elizabethtown, New Jersey, June 28th, 1827, and her maiden name was Locker. She was married in February, 1847, to Mr. Samuel Palmer. In 1855 she removed to Kansas, and in 1857 returned as far eastward as St. Louis, where she resided until her death.

In the beginning of the war, when battles began to be fought, and the sick and wounded were brought to our hospitals to be treated and cared for, Mrs. Palmer with true patriotic devotion and womanly sympathy offered her services to this good cause, and after a variety of hospital work in the fall of 1863, she entered into the service of the Ladies Union Aid Society of St. Louis as a regular visiter among the soldiers' families, many of whom needed aid and work, during the absence of their natural protectors in the army. It was a field of great labor and usefulness; for in so large a city there were thousands of poor women, whose husbands often went months without pay, or the means of sending it home to their families, who were obliged to appeal for assistance in taking care of themselves and children. To prevent imposition it was necessary that they should be visited, the requisite aid rendered, and sewing or other work provided by which they could earn a part of their own support, a proper discrimination being made between the worthy and unworthy, the really suffering, and those who would impose on the charity of the society under the plea of necessity.

In this work Mrs. Palmer was most faithful and constant, going from day to day through a period of nearly two years, in summer and winter, in sunshine and storm, to the abodes of these people, to find out their real necessities, to report to the society and to secure for them the needed relief.

Her labors also extended to many destitute families of refugees, who had found their way to St. Louis from the impoverished regions of Southern Missouri, Arkansas, Tennessee, Mississippi, Louisiana, and Texas, and who would have died of actual want, but for the charity of the Government and the ministering aid of the Western Sanitary Commission and the Ladies Union Aid Society. In her visits and her dispensations of charity Mrs. Palmer was always wise, judicious, and humane, and enjoyed the fullest confidence of the society in whose service she was engaged. In the performance of her duties she was always thoroughly cousi seientious, and actuated by a high sense of religious duty. From an early period of her life she had been a consistent member of the Baptist Church, and her Christian character was adorned by a thorough consecration to works of kindness and humanity which were performed in the spirit of Him, who, during his earthly ministry, "went about doing good."

By her arduous labors, which were greater than her physical constitution could permanently endure, Mrs. Palmer's health became undermined, and in the summer of 1865 she passed into a fatal decline, and on the 2d of August ended a life of usefulness on earth to enter upon the enjoyments of a beatified spirit in heaven.

LADIES' AID SOCIETY OF PHILADELPHIA

ONE of the first societies formed by ladies to aid and care for the sick and wounded soldiers, was the one whose name we have placed at the head of this sketch. The Aid Society of Cleveland, and we believe one in Boston claim a date five or six days earlier, but no others. The ladies who composed it met on the 26th of April, 1861, and organized themselves as a society to labor for the welfare of the soldiers whether in sickness or health. They continued their labors with unabated zeal until the close of the war rendered them unnecessary. The officers of the society were Mrs. Joel Jones, President; Mrs. John Harris, Secretary; and Mrs. Stephen Colwell, Treasurer. Mrs. Jones is the widow of the late Hon. Joel Jones, a distinguished jurist of Philadelphia, and subsequently for several years President of Girard College. A quiet, self-possessed and dignified lady, she yet possessed an earnestly patriotic spirit, and decided business abilities. Of Mrs. Harris, one of the most faithful and persevering laborers for the soldiers in the field, throughout the war, we have spoken at length elsewhere in this volume. Airs. Colwell, the wife of Hon. Stephen Colwell, a mail of rare philosophic mind and comprehensive views, who had acquired a reputation alike by his writings, and his earnest practical benevolence, was a woman every way worthy of her husband.

It was early determined to allow Mrs. Harris to follow the promptings of her benevolent heart and go to the field, while her colleagues should attend to the work of raising supplies and money at home, and furnishing her with the stores she required for her own distribution and that of the zealous workers who were associated with her. The members of the society were connected with twenty different churches of several denominations, and while all had reference to the spiritual as well as physical welfare of the soldier, yet there was nothing sectarian or denominational in its work. From the fact that its meetings were held and its goods packed in the basement and vestry of Dr. Boardman's Church, it was sometimes called the Presbyterian Ladies' Aid Society, but the name, if intended to imply that its character was denominational, was unjust. As early as October, 1861, the pastors of twelve churches in Philadelphia united in an appeal to all into whose hands the circular might fall, to contribute to this society and to form auxiliaries to it, on the ground of its efficiency, its economical management, and its unsectarian character.

The society, with but moderate receipts as compared with those of the great organizations, accomplished a great amount of good. Not a few of the most earnest and noble workers in the field were at one time or another the distributors of its supplies, and thus in some sense, its agents. Among these we may name besides Mrs. Harris, Mrs. M. M. Husband, Mrs. Mary W. Lee, Miss M. M. C. Hall, Miss Cornelia Hancock, Miss Anna M. Ross, Miss Nellie Chase, of Nashville, Miss Hetty K. Painter, Mrs. Z. Denham, Miss Pinkham, Miss Biddle, Mrs. Sampson, Mrs. Waterman, and others. The work intended by the society, and which its agents attempted to perform was a religious as well as a physical one; hospital supplies were to be dispensed, and the sick and dying soldier carefully nursed; but it was also a part of its duty to point the sinner to Christ, to warn and reprove the erring, and to bring religious consolation and support to the sick and dying; the Bible, the Testament, and the tract were as truly a part of its supplies as the clothing it distributed so liberally, or the delicacies it provided to tempt the appetite of the sick. Mrs. Harris established prayer-meetings wherever it was possible in the camps or at the field hospitals, and several of the other ladies followed her example.

In her first report, Mrs. Harris said:—"In addition to the dispensing of hospital supplies, the sick of two hundred and three regiments have been personally visited. Hundreds of letters, bearing last messages of love to dear ones at home, have been written for sick and dying soldiers. We have thrown something of home light and love around the rude couches of at least five hundred of our noble citizen soldiers, who sleep their last sleep along the Potomac.

"We have been permitted to take the place of mothers and sisters, wiping the chill dew of death from the noble brow, and breathing words of Jesus into the ear upon which all other sounds fell unheeded. The gentle pressure of the hand has carried the dying one to the old homestead, and, as it often happened, by a merciful illusion, the dying soldier has thought the face upon which his last look rested, was that of a precious mother, sister, or other cherished one. One, a German, in broken accents, whispered: 'How good you have come, Eliza; Jesus is always near me;' then, wrestling with that mysterious power, death, slept in Jesus. Again, a gentle lad of seventeen summers, wistfully then joyfully exclaimed: 'I knew she would come to her boy,' went down comforted into the dark valley. Others, many others still, have thrown a lifetime of trustful love into the last look, sighing out life with 'Mother, dear mother!'

"It has been our highest aim, whilst ministering to the temporal well-being of our loved and valued soldiers, to turn their thoughts and affections heavenward. We are permitted to hope that not a few have, through the blessed influence of religious tracts, soldiers' pocket books, soldiers' Bibles, and, above all, the Holy Scriptures distributed by us, been led to cast anchor upon that which is within the veil, whither the forerunner is for us entered, even Jesus.'"

The society did not attempt, and wisely, to compete with the great commissions in their work. It could not supply an entire army or throw upon the shoulders of its hard-working voluntary agents the care of the sick and wounded of a great battle. Its field of operations was rather here and there a field hospital, the care of the sick and wounded of a single division, or at most of a small army corps, when not engaged in any great battles; the providing for some hundreds of refugees, the care of some of the freedmen, and the assistance of the families of the soldiers. Whatever it undertook to do it did well. Its semi-annual reports consisted largely of letters from its absent secretary, letters full of pathos and simple eloquence, and these widely circulated, produced a deep impression, and stirred the sympathies of those who read, to more abundant contributions.

As an instance of the spirit which actuated the members of this society we state the following incident of which we were personally cognizant; one of the officers of the society soon after the commencement of the war had contributed so largely to its funds that she felt that only by some self-denial could she give more. Considering for a time where the retrenchment should begin, she said to the members of her family; "these soldiers who have gone to fight our battles have been willing to hazard their lives for us, and we certainly cannot do too much for them. Now, I propose, if you all consent, to devote a daily sum to the relief of the army while the war lasts, and that we all go without some accustomed luxury to procure that sum. Suppose we dispense with our dessert during the war?" Her family consented, and the cost of the dessert was duly paid over to the society as an additional donation throughout the war.

The society received and expended during the four years ending April 30, 1865, twenty-four thousand dollars in money, beside five hundred and fifty dollars for soldiers' families, and seven hundred dollars with accumulated interest for aiding disabled soldiers to reach their homes. The supplies distributed were worth not far from one hundred and twenty-five thousand dollars, aside from those sent directly to Mrs. Harris from individuals and societies, which were estimated at fully two hundred thousand dollars.

In this connection it may be well to say something of two other associations of ladies in Philadelphia for aiding the soldiers, which remained independent of the Sanitary or Christian Commissions through the war, and which accomplished much good.

THE PENN RELIEF ASSOCIATION was organized early in 1862, first by the Hicksite Friends, to demonstrate the falsity of the commonly received report that the "Friends," being opposed to war, would not do anything for the sick and wounded. Many of the "Orthodox Friends" afterwards joined it, as well as considerable numbers from other denominations, and it proved itself a very efficient body. Mrs. Rachel S. Evans was its President, and Miss Anna P. Little and Miss Elizabeth Newport its active and hard-working Secretaries, and Miss Little doubtless expressed the feeling which actuated all its members in a letter in which she said that "while loyal men were suffering, loyal women must work to alleviate their sufferings." The "Penn Relief" collected supplies to an amount exceeding fifty thousand dollars, which were almost wholly sent to the "front," and distributed by such judicious and skilful hands as Mrs. Husband, Mrs. Hetty K. Painter, Mrs. Mary W. Lee, and Miss Anna Carver.

"THE SOLDIERS' AID ASSOCIATION," was organized on the 28th of July, 1862, mainly through the efforts of Mrs. Mary A. Brady, a lady of West Philadelphia, herself a native of Ireland, but the wife of an English lawyer, who had made his home in Philadelphia, in 1849. Mrs. Brady was elected President of the Association, and the first labors of herself and her associates were expended on the Sattcrlcc Hospital, one of those vast institutions created by the Medical Department of the Government, which had over three thousand beds, each during those dark and dreary days occupied by some poor sufferer. In this great hospital these ladies found, for a time, full employment for the hearts and hands of the Committees who, on their designated days of the week, ministered to these thousands of sick and wounded men, and from the depot of supplies which the Association had established at the hospital, prepared and distributed fruits, food skilfully prepared, and articles of hospital clothing, of which the men were greatly in need. Those cheering ministrations, reading and singing to the men, writing letters for them, and the dressing and applying of cooling lotions to the hot and inflamed wounds were not forgotten by these tender and kind-hearted women.

But Mrs. Brady looked forward to work in other fields, and the exertion of a wider influence, and though for months, she and her associates felt that the present duty must first be done, she desired to go to the front, and there minister to the wounded before they had endured all the agony of the long journey to the hospital in the city. The patients of the Satterlee Hospital were provided with an ample dinner on the day of the National Thanksgiving, by the Association, and as they were now diminishing in numbers, and the

Auxiliary Societies, which had sprung up throughout the State, had poured in abundant supplies, Mrs. Brady felt that the time had come when she could consistently enter upon the work nearest her heart. In the winter of 1863" she visited Washington, and the hospitals and camps which were scattered around the city, at distances of from five to twenty miles. Here she found multitudes of sick and wounded, all suffering from cold, from hunger, or from inattention. "Camp Misery," with its twelve thousand convalescents, in a condition of intense wretchedness moved her sympathies, and led her to do what she could for them. She returned home at the beginning of April, and her preparations for another journey were hardly made, before the battles of Chancellorsville and its vicinity occurred. Here at the great field hospital of Sedgwick's (Sixth) Corps, she commenced in earnest her labors in the care of the wounded directly from the field. For five weeks she worked with an energy and zeal which were the admiration of all who saw her, and then as Lee advanced toward Pennsylvania, she returned home for a few days of rest.

Then came Gettysburg, with its three days of terrible slaughter, and Mrs. Brady was again at her work day and night, furnishing soft food to the severely wounded, cooling drinks to the thirsty and fever-stricken, soothing pain, encouraging the men to heroic endurance of their sufferings, everywhere an angel of comfort, a blessed and healing presence. More than a month was spent in these labors, and at their close Mrs. Brady returned to her work in the Hospitals at Philadelphia, and to preparation for the autumn and winter campaigns. When early in January, General Meade made his Mine Run Campaign, Mrs. Brady had again gone to the front, and was exposed to great vicissitudes of weather, and was for a considerable time in peril from the enemy's fire. Her exertions and exposures at this time brought on disease of the heart, and her physician forbade her going to the front again. She however made all the preparations she could for the coming campaign, and hoped, though vainly, that she might be permitted again to enter upon the work she loved. When the great battles of May, 1864, were fought, the dreadful slaughter which accompanied them, so disquieted her, that it aggravated her disease, and on the 27th of May, she died, greatly mourned by all who knew her worth, and her devotion to the national cause.

The Association continued its work till the close of the war. The amount of its disbursements, we have not been able to ascertain.

WOMEN'S RELIEF ASSOCIATION OF BROOKLYN AND LONG ISLAND

THE city of Brooklyn, Long Island, and the Island of which it forms the Western extremity, were from the commencement of the war intensely patriotic. Regiment after regiment was raised in the city, and its quota filled from the young men of the city, and the towns of the island, till it seemed as every man of military age, and most of the youth between fifteen and eighteen had been drawn into the army. An enthusiastic zeal for the national cause had taken as complete possession of the women as of the men. Everywhere were seen the badges of loyalty, and there was no lack of patient labor or of liberal giving for the soldiers on the part of those who had either money or labor to bestow. The news of the first battle was the signal for an outpouring of clothing, hospital stores, cordials, and supplies of all sorts, which were promptly forwarded to the field. After each successive engagement, this was repeated, and at first, the Young Men's Christian Association of the city, a most efficient organization, undertook to be the almoners of a part of the bounty of the citizens. Distant as was the field of Shiloh, a delegation from the Association went thither, bearing a large amount of hospital stores, and rendered valuable assistance to the great numbers of wounded. Other organizations sprang up, having in view the care of the wounded and sick of the army, and many contributors entrusted to the earnest workers at Washington, the stores they were anxious to bestow upon the suffering.

After the great battles of the summer and autumn of 1862, large numbers of the sick and wounded were brought to Brooklyn, for care and treatment filling at one time three hospitals. They came often in need of all things, and the benevolent women of the city formed themselves into Committees, to visit these hospitals in turn, and prepare and provide suitable dishes, delicacies, and special diet for the invalid soldiers, to furnish such clothing as was needed, to read to them, write letters for them, and bestow upon them such acts of kindness as should cause them to feel that their services in defense of the nation were fully appreciated and honored.

There was, however, in these varied efforts for the soldiers a lack of concentration and efficiency which rendered them less serviceable than they otherwise might have been. The different organizations and committees working independently of each other, not unfrequently furnished over-abundant supplies to some regiments or hospitals, while others were left to lack, and many who had the disposition to give, hesitated from want of knowledge or confidence in the organizations which would disburse the funds. The churches of the city though giving freely when called upon, were not contributing systematically, or putting forth their full strength in the service. It was this conviction of the need of a more methodical and comprehensive organization to which the churches, committees, and smaller associations should become tributary, which led to the formation of the Women's Belief Association, as a branch of the United States Sanitary Commission. This Association was organized November 23d, 1862, at a meeting held by the Ladies of Brooklyn, in the Lecture Boom of the Church of the Pilgrims, and MRS. MARIAMNE FITCH STRANAHAN, was chosen President, and Miss Kate E. Waterbury, Secretary, with an Executive Committee of twelve ladies of high standing and patriotic impulses. The selection of President and Secretary was eminently a judicious one. MRS. STRANAHAN was a native of Westmoreland, Oneida County, New York, and had received for the time, and the region in which her childhood and youth was passed, superior advantages of education. She was married in 1837, to Mr. James S. T. Stranahan, then a merchant of Florence, Oneida County, New York, but who removed with his family in 1840, to Newark, New Jersey, and in 1845, took up his residence in Brooklyn. Here they occupied a high social position, Mr. Stranahan having been elected a Representative to the Thirty-fourth Congress, and subsequently appointed to other positions of responsibility in the city and State. Mrs. Stranahan was active in every good work in the city of her adoption, and those who knew her felt that they could confide in her judgment, her discernment, her tact, and her unflinching integrity and principle. For eight years she was the first Directress of the "Graham Institute, for the relief of Aged and Indigent Females," a position requiring the exercise of rare abilities, and the most skilful management, to harmonize the discords, and quiet the misunderstandings, inevitable in such an institution. Her discretion, equanimity, and tact, were equal to the duties of the place, and under her administration peace and quiet reigned. It was probably from the knowledge of her executive abilities, that she was unanimously chosen to preside over the Women's Relief Association. This position was also one requiring great tact and skill in the presiding officer. About eighty churches of different denominations in Brooklyn, cooperated in the work of the Association, and it had also numerous auxiliaries scattered over the Island. These diverse elements were held together in perfect harmony, by Mrs. Stranahan's skilful management, till the occasion ceased for their labors. The Association was from first to last a perfect success, surpassing in its results most of the branches of the Commission, and surpassed in the harmony and efficiency of its action by none.

In her final report Mrs. Stranahan said: "The aggregate of our efforts including the results of our Great Fair, represents a money value of not less than half a million of dollars." Three hundred thousand dollars of this sum were paid into the treasury of the United States Sanitary Commission in cash; and hospital supplies were furnished to the amount of over two hundred thousand more. The Great Fair of Brooklyn had its origin in the Women's Relief Association. At first it was proposed that Brooklyn should unite with New York in the Metropolitan Fair; but on further deliberation it was thought that a much larger result would be attained by an independent effort on the part of Brooklyn and Long Island, and the event fully justified the opinion. The conducting of such a fair involved, however, an excessive amount of labor on the part of the managers; and notwithstanding the perfect equanimity and self-possession of Mrs. Stranahan, her health was sensibly affected by the exertions she was compelled to make to maintain the harmony and efficiency of so many and such varied interests. It is much to say, but the proof of the statement is ample, that no one of the Sanitary Fairs held from 1863 to 1865 equalled that of Brooklyn in its freedom from all friction and disturbing influences, in the earnestness of its patriotic feeling, and the complete and perfect harmony which reigned from its commencement to its close. This gratifying condition of affairs was universally attributed to the extraordinary tact and executive talent of Mrs. Stranahan.

Rev. Dr. Spear, her pastor, in a touching and eloquent memorial of her, uses the following language in regard to the success of her administration as President of the Women's Relief Association; "It is due to truth to say that this success depended very largely upon her wisdom and her efforts. She was the right woman in the right place. She gave her time to the work with a zeal and perseverance that never faltered, and with a hopefulness for her country that yielded to no discouragement or despondency. As a presiding officer she discharged her duties with a self-possession, courtesy, skill, and method, that commanded universal admiration. She had a quick and judicious insight into the various ways and means by which the meetings of the Association would be rendered interesting and attractive. The business part of the work was constantly under her eye. No woman ever labored in a sphere more honorable; and but few women could have filled her place. Her general temper of mind, her large and catholic views as a Christian, and then her excellent discretion, eminently fitted her to combine all the churches in one harmonious and patriotic effort. This was her constant study; and well did she succeed. As an evidence of the sentiments with which she had inspired her associates, the following resolution offered at the last meeting of the Association, and unanimously adopted, will speak for itself:—

"Resolved, That the thanks of the Women's Relief Association are pre-eminently due to our President, Mrs. J. S. T. Stranahan, for the singular ability, wisdom, and patience with which she has discharged the duties of her office, at all times arduous, and not unfrequently requiring sacrifices to which nothing short of the deepest love of country could have been equal. It is due to justice, and to the feelings of our hearts, to say that the usefulness, the harmony, and the continued existence of the Women's Relief Association, through the long and painful struggle, now happily ended, have been in a large measure owing to the combination of rare gifts, which have been so conspicuous to us all in the guidance of our public meetings, and which have marked not less the more unnoticed, but equally essential, superintendence of the work in private.'"

The Rev. Dr. Bellows, President of the United States Sanitary Commission, thus speaks of Mrs. Stranahan and of the Brooklyn Woman's Relief Association, of which she was the head:

"Knowing Mrs. Stranahan only in her official character, as head of the noble band of women who through the war, by their admirable organization and efficient, patient working, made Brooklyn a shining example for all other cities—I wonder that she should have left so deep a personal impression upon my heart; and that from a dozen interviews confined wholly to one subject, I should have conceived a friendship for her which it commonly takes a life of various intercourse and intimate or familiar relations to establish. And this is the more remarkable, because her directness, clearness of intention, and precision of purpose always kept her confined, in the conversations I held with her, to the special subject on which we met to take counsel. She had so admirably ordered an understanding, was so businesslike and clear in her habits of mind, that not a minute was lost with her in beating the bush. With mild determination, and in a gentle distinctness of tone, she laid her views or wishes before me, in a way that never needed any other explanation or enforcement than her simple statement carried with it. In few, precise, and transparent words, she made known her business, or gave her opinion, and wasted not a precious minute in generalities, or on matters aside from our common object. This rendered my official intercourse with her peculiarly satisfactory. She always knew just what she wanted to say, and left no uncertainty as to what she had said; and what she said, had always been so carefully considered, that her wishes were full of reason, and her advice full of persuasion. She seemed to me to unite the greatest discretion with the finest enthusiasm. As earnest, large, and noble in her views of what was due to the National cause, as the most zealous could be, she was yet so practical, judicious, and sober in her judgment, that what she planned, I learned to regard as certain of success. No one could see her presiding with mingled modesty and dignity over one of the meetings of the Women's Relief Association, without admiration for her self-possession, propriety of utterance, and skill in furthering the objects in view. I have always supposed that her wisdom, resolution, and perseverance, had a controlling influence in the glorious success of the Brooklyn Relief Association— the most marked and memorable fellowship of women, united from all sects and orders of Christians, in one practical enterprise, that the world ever saw." after the disbanding of the Women's Relief Association, Mrs. Stranahau, though retaining her profound interest in the welfare of her country, and her desire for its permanent pacification by such measures as should remove all further causes of discord and strife, returned to the quiet of her home, and except her connection with the Graham Institute, gladly withdrew from any conspicuous or public position. Her health was as we have said impaired somewhat by her assiduous devotion to her duties in connection with the Association, but she made no complaint, and her family did not take the alarm. The spring of 1866 found her so feeble, that it was thought the pure and bracing air of the Green Mountains might prove beneficial in restoring her strength, but her days were numbered. On the 30th of August she died at Manchester, Vermont.

In closing our sketch of this excellent woman, we deem it due to her memory to give the testimony of two clergymen who were well acquainted with her work and character, to her eminent abilities, and her extraordinary worth. Kev. Dr. Farley, says of her:

"When I think of the amount of time, thought, anxious and painstaking reflection, and active personal attention and effort she gave to this great work; when I recall how for nearly three years, with other weighty cares upon her, and amid failing health, she contrived to give herself so faithfully and devotedly to carrying it on, I am lost in admiration. True, she had for coadjutors a company of noble women, worthy representatives of our great and beautiful city. They represented every phase of our social and religious life; they were distinguished by all the various traits which are the growth of education and habit; they had on many subjects few views or associations in common. In one thing, indeed, they were united—the desire to serve their country in her hour of peril, by ministering to the sufferings of her heroic defenders in the field. Acting on this thought—knowing no personal distinctions where this was the prevailing sentiment— and treating all with the like courtesy—she had yet the nice tact to call into requisition for special emergencies the precise talent which was wanted, and give it its right direction. Now and then—strange if it had not been so—there would be some questioning of her proposed measures, some demur to, or reluctance to accept her suggestions; but among men, the case would be found a rare one, where a presiding officer carried so largely and uniformly, from first to last, the concurrent judgment and approval of his compeers.

"I shall always call her to mind as among the remarkable women whom I have had the good fortune to know. With no especial coveting of notoriety, she was—as one might say—in the course of nature, or rather—as I prefer to say—in the order of the Divine Providence, called to occupy very responsible positions bearing largely on the public weal; and she was not found wanting. Nay, she was found eminently fit. All admitted it. And all find, now that she has been taken to her rest, that they owe her every grateful and honored remembrance."

The Rev. W. J. Budington, D.D., who had known her activity and zeal in the various positions she had been called to fill, pays the following eloquent tribute to her memory:

"Iliad known Mrs. Stranahan chiefly, in common with the citizens of Brooklyn, as the head of the 'Women's Relief Association,' and thus, as the representative of the patriotism and Christian benevolence of the Ladies of Brooklyn, in that great crisis of our national history which drew forth all that was best in our countrymen and countrywomen, and nowhere more than i n our own city. Most naturally—inevitably, I may say—she became the presiding officer of this most useful and efficient Association.

Possessed naturally of a strong mind, clear in her perceptions, and logical in her courses of thought, she had, at the outset of the struggle, the most decided convictions of duty, and entered into the work of national conservation with a heartiness and selfdevotion, which, in a younger person, would have been called enthusiasm, but which in her case was only the measure of an enlightened Christianity and patriotism. She toiled untiringly, in season and out of season; when others flagged, she supplied the lack by giving more time, and redoubling her exertions; as 83 the war wore wearily on, and disasters came, enfeebling some, and confounding others, she rose to sublimer efforts, and supplied the ranks of the true and faithful who gathered round her, with the proper watchwords and fresh resources. I both admired and wondered at her in this regard; and when success came, crowning the labors and sacrifices of our people, her soul was less filled with mere exultation than with sober thoughtfulness as to what still remained to be done.

"I regard Mrs. Stranahan as one of the most extraordinary of that galaxy of women, whom the night of our country's sorrow disclosed, and whose light will shine forever in the land they have done their part—I dare not say, how great a part—to save." We should do gross injustice to this efficient Association, if we neglected to give credit to its other officers, for their faithfulness and persevering energy during the whole period of its existence. Especially should the services of its patient and hard-working Corresponding Secretary, Miss Kate E. Waterbury, be acknowledged. Next to the president, she was its most efficient officer, ever at her post, and performing her duties with a thoroughness and heartiness which called forth the admiration of all who witnessed her zeal and devotion. Miss Perkins, the faithful agent in charge of the depot of supplies and rooms of the Association, was also a quiet and persevering toiler for the promotion of its great objects.

LADIES' UNION RELIEF ASSOCIATIONS OF BALTIMORE

AMIDST the malign influences of secession and treason, entire and unqualified devotion to the Union, shone with additional brightness from its contrast with surrounding darkness. In all portions of the South were found examples of this patriotic devotion, and nowhere did it display itself more nobly than in the distracted city of Baltimore. The Union people were near enough to the North with its patriotic sentiment, and sufficiently protected by the presence of Union soldiery, to be able to act with the freedom and spontaneity denied to their compatriots of the extreme South, and they did act nobly for the cause of their country and its defenders.

Among the ladies of Baltimore, few were more constantly or conspicuously employed, for the benefit of sufferers from the war, than MRS. ELIZABETH M. STREETER. With the modesty that almost invariably accompanies great devotion and singleness of purpose she sought no public notice; but in the case of one so actively employed in good works, it was impossible to avoid it.

More than one of the Associations of Ladies formed in Baltimore for the relief of soldiers, of their families, and of refugees from secession, owes its inception, organization, and successful career to the mind and energies of Mrs. Streeter. It may truly be said of her that she has refused no work which her hands could find to accomplish.

Mrs. Streeter was the wife of the late Hon. S. F. Streeter, Esq., a well-known citizen of Baltimore, a member of the city Government during the war, an active Union man, devoted to the cause of his country and her defenders as indefatigably as his admirable wife. Working in various organizations, he was made an almoner of the city funds bestowed upon the families of soldiers, and upon hospitals, and afterwards appointed in conjunction with George R. Dodge, Esq., to distribute the appropriation of the State, for the families of Maryland soldiers. Thus the two were continually working side by side, or in separate spheres of labor, for the same cause, all through the dark days of the rebellion.

Mrs. Streeter was born in Plymouth, Massachusetts, her ancestors, the Jacksons, having been among the original settlers of the old Colony, and she has doubtless inherited the ancestral love of freedom. For thirty years she has been a resident of Baltimore.

On the 16th of October, 1861, she originated the Ladies' Union Relief Association, of Baltimore, and in connection with other zealous loyal ladies, carried on its operations for more than a year with great success. From this as a center, sprang other similar associations in different parts of the city, and connected with the various hospitals.

After the battle of Antietam, Mrs. Streeter, with Mrs. Pancoast, a most energetic member of the Association, spent some time on the field dispensing supplies, and attending to the wants of the wounded, suffering and dying.

Exhausted by her labors and responsibilities, at the end of a year, Mrs. Streeter resigned her official connection with the Ladies' Relief Association, and after a brief period of repose, she devoted herself to personal visitation of the hospitals, dispensing needed comforts and delicacies, and endeavoring by conversation with the inmates to cheer them, stimulate their patriotism, and to make their situation in all respects, more comfortable.

Subsequently, she connected herself with the hospital attached to the Union Relief Association, located at 120 South Eutaw Street, Baltimore. Up to the time of the discontinuance of the work of the Association, she gave it her daily attendance, and added largely to its resources by way of supplies.

At this time, Baltimore was thronged by the families of refugees, who were rendered insecure in their homes by the fact of their entertaining Union sentiments, or homeless, by some of the bands of marauders which followed the advance of the Confederate troops when they invaded Maryland, or, who perhaps, living unfortunately in the very track of the conflicting armies, found themselves driven from their burning homesteads, and devastated fields, victims of a wanton soldiery. Destitute, ragged and shelterless, their condition appealed with peculiar force to the friends of the Union. State aid was by no means sufficient, and unorganized charity unavailable to any great extent.

Mrs. Streeter was one of the first to see the need of systematic assistance for this class. On the 16th of November, 1863, the result of her interest was seen in the organization of the "Ladies' Aid Society, for the Relief of Soldiers' Families," which included in its efforts the relief of all destitute female refugees. A house was taken more particularly to accommodate these last, and the Association, which consisted of twenty-five ladies, proceeded to visit the families of soldiers and refugees in person, inquiring into their needs, and dispensing money, food, clothing, shoes, fuel, etc., as required. Over twelve hundred families were thus visited and relieved, in addition to the inmates of the Home. For this purpose they received from the city and various associations about seven thousand dollars, and a large amount from private contributions. In this and kindred work, Mrs. Streeter was engaged till the close of the war.

The second report of the Maryland Committee of the Christian Commission thus speaks of the services of the devoted women who proceeded to the field after the battle of Antietam, and there ministered to the wants of the suffering and wounded soldiers.

"Attendance in the hospitals upon the wounded at Antietam, was required for several months after the battle. Services and supplies were furnished by the Committee, principally through the agency of the ladies of the Relief Associations, to whom the Committee acknowledge its indebtedness for important and necessary labors, which none but themselves could so well perform. The hospitals were located near the battle-field, and the adjacent towns, and in Baltimore and Frederick cities. Connected with each of them there was a band of faithful and devoted women, who waited about the beds of the suffering objects of their concern, and ministered to their relief and comfort during the hours of their affliction. Through the months of September, October, and November, these messengers of mercy labored among the wounded of Antietam, and were successful in saving the lives of hundreds of the badly wounded. They had not yet cleared the hospitals, when other battles added to their number, and made new drafts for services, which were promptly and cheerfully rendered."

Many times the Committee take occasion to mention the valuable services of the loyal ladies of Baltimore, and the services of Mrs. Streeter are specially noticed in the third report in connection with the Invalid Camp Hospital located at the boundary of the city and county of Baltimore in the vicinity of Northern avenue.

"The services to this camp, usually performed by ladies, were under the supervision of Mrs. S. F. Streeter, who visited the grounds daily, on several occasions several times a day. The Secretary of the Committee has frequently met Mrs. Streeter on her errand of benevolence, conveying to the sufferers the delicacies she had prepared. Her active and faithful services were continued until the breaking up of the camp."

The ladies of Baltimore worked in connection with the Sanitary and Christian Commissions, both of which organizations take occasion frequently to acknowledge their services.

Late in 1864, Mrs. Streeter was called to deep affliction. Her noble-hearted and patriotic husband, who had been as active as herself in all enterprises for the welfare of the soldiers, and the promotion of the cause for which the war was undertaken, was suddenly taken from her, falling a victim to fever contracted in his ministrations to the sick and wounded of the Army of the Potomac, and the home and city where his presence had been to her a joy and delight, became, since he was gone too full of gloom and sorrow to be borne. Mrs. Streeter returned to her New England home in the hope of finding there some relief from the grief which overwhelmed her spirit.

Two other ladies of Baltimore, and doubtless many more, deserve especial mention in this connection, Miss TYSON, and Mrs. BECK. Active and efficient members of the Ladies' Relief Association of that city, they were also active and eminently useful in the field and general hospitals. To the hospital work they seem both to have been called by Mrs. John Harris, who to her other good qualities added that of recognizing instinctively, the women who could be made useful in the work in which she was engaged.

Miss Tyson was with Mrs. Harris at French's Division Hospital, after Antietam, and subsequently at Smoketown General Hospital, and after six or eight weeks of labor there, was attacked with typhoid fever. Her illness was protracted, but she finally recovered and resumed her work, going with Mrs. Harris to the West, and during most of the year 1864, was in charge of the Low Diet Department of the large hospital on Lookout Mountain. Few ladies equalled her in skill in the preparation of suit able food and delicacies for those who needed special diet. Miss Tyson was a faithful, indefatigable worker, and not only gave her services to the hospitals, but expended largely of her own means for the soldiers. She was always, however, disposed to shrink from any mention of her work, and we are compelled to content ourselves with this brief mention of her great usefulness.

Mrs. Beck was also a faithful and laborious aide to Mrs. Harris, at Falmouth, and afterwards at the West. She was, we believe, a native of Philadelphia, though residing in Baltimore. Her earnestness and patience in many very trying circumstances, elicited the admiration of all who knew her. She was an excellent singer, and when she sang in the hospitals some of the popular hymns, the words and melody would often awaken an interest in the heart of the soldier for a better life.

MRS. C. T. FENN

BERKSHIRE County, Massachusetts, has long been noted as the birth-place of many men and women distinguished in the higher ranks of the best phases of American life, literature, law, science, art, philosophy, as well as religion, philanthropy, and the industrial and commercial progress of our country have all been brilliantly illustrated and powerfully aided by those who drew their first breath, and had their earliest home among the green hills and lovely valleys of Berkshire. Bryant gained the inspiration of his poems—sweet, tender, refined, elevating—from its charming scenery; and from amidst the same scenes Miss Sedgwick gathered up the quiet romance of country life, often as deep as silent, and wove it into those delightful tales which were the joy of our youthful hearts.

The men of Berkshire are brave and strong, its women fair and noble. Its mountains are the green altars upon which they kindled the fires of their patriotism. And these fires brightened a continent, and made glad the heart of a nation.

Berkshire had gained the prestige of its patriotism in two wars, and at the sound of the signal gun of the rebellion its sons— "brave sons of noble sires"—young men, and middle-aged, and boys, sprang to arms. Its regiments were among the first to answer the call of the country and to offer themselves for its defense. Let Ball's Bluff and the Wilderness, the Chickahoininy, and the deadly swamps and bayous of the Southwest, tell to the

S4065 listening world the story of their bravery, their endurance and their sacrifices.

But these men who went forth to fight left behind them, in their homes, hearts as brave and strong as their own. If Berkshire has a proud record of the battle-field, not less proud is that which might be written of her home work. Its women first gave their best beloved to the defense of the country, and then, in their desolate homes, all through the slow length of those horrible, sometimes hopeless years, by labor and sacrifice, by thought and care, they gave themselves to the more silent but not less noble work of supplying the needs and ministering to the comforts of the sick and wounded soldiery.

Foremost among these noble women, as the almoner of their bounty, and the organizer of their efforts, stands the subject of this sketch, Mrs. C. T. Fenn, of Pittsfield, whose devotion to the work during the entire war was unintermitted and untiring.

Mrs. Fenn, whose maiden name was Dickinson, was born in Pittsfield just before the close of the last century, and with the exception of a brief residence in Boston, has passed her entire life there. Her husband, Deacon Curtis T. Fenn, an excellent citizen, and enterprising man of business, in his "haste to be rich," was at one time tempted to venture largely, and became bound for others. The result was a failure, and a removal to Boston with the idea of retrieving his fortunes in new scenes. Here his only son, a promising young man of twenty-two years, fell ill, and with the hope of arresting his disease, and if possible saving his precious life, his parents returned to his native place, giving up their flattering prospects in the metropolis. It was in vain, however—in a few months the insidious disease, always so fatal in New England, claimed its victim, and they were bereaved in their dearest hopes.

This affliction did not change, but perhaps intensified, the character of Mrs. Fenn. She was now called to endure labor, and to make many sacrifices, while her husband was slowly winning his way back to competence. But ever full of kindness and sympathy, she devoted her time more unsparingly to doing good. Her name became a synonym for spontaneous benevolence in her native town. By the bed-sides of the sick and dying, in the home of poverty, and the haunts of disease, where sin, and sorrow and suffering, that trinity of human woe are ever to be found, she became a welcome and revered visitant. All sought her in trouble, and she withheld not counsel nor aid in any hour of need, nor from any who claimed them.'

This was the prestige with which she was surrounded at the opening of the war, and her warm heart, as well as her patriotic instincts were at once ready for any work of kindness or aid it should develop. The following extract from the Berkshire County Eagle, of May, 1862, tells better than we can of the estimation in which she was held in her native town.

"Mrs. Eenn, as most of our Pittsfield readers know, has been for many years the kind and familiar friend of the sick and suffering. Familiar with its shades, her step in the sick chamber has been as welcome and as beneficial as that of the physician. When the ladies were appealed to for aid for our soldiers suffering from wounds or disease, she entered into the work with her whole soul and devoted all her time and the skill learned in years of attendance on the sick to the new necessities. Possessing the entire confidence of our citizens, and appealing to them personally and assiduously, she was met by generous and well selected contributions which we have, from time to time, chronicled. In her duties at the work room, in preparing the material contributed, she has had constant and reliable assistance, but very much less than was needed, a defect which we hope will be remedied. Surely many of our ladies have leisure to relieve her of a portion of her work, and we trust that some of our patriotic boys will give their aid, for we learn that even such duties as the sweeping of the rooms devolve upon her.

"Knowing that Mrs. Fenn's entire time had been occupied for months in this great and good cause, and that all her time was not adequate to the manifold duties imposed upon her, we were somewhat surprised to see a letter addressed to her in print a few weeks since, complimenting her upon her efforts for the soldiers and asking her to give her aid in collecting hospital stores for the clinic at the Medical College. Surely thought we, there ought to be more than one Dorcas in Pittsfield. Indeed, it occurred to us that there were ladies here who, however repugnant to aid the soldiers of the North, could, without violence to their feelings so far as the object is concerned, gracefully employ a share of their elegant leisure in the service of the Medical College. But Mrs. Fenn did not refuse the new call, and having let her charity begin at home with those who are dearest and nearest to our hearts, our country's soldiers, expanded it to embrace those whose claim is also imperative, the poor whom we have always with us, and made large collections for the patients of the clinic.

"We have thus briefly sketched the services of this noble woman, partly in justice to her, but principally as an incentive to others."

Very early in the war, a meeting of the ladies of Pittsfield was called with the intention of organizing the services, so enthusiastically proffered on all hands, for the benefit of the soldiers. It was quite numerously attended, and the interest and feeling was evidently intense. But they failed to organize anything beyond a temporary association. All wanted to work, but none to lead. All looked to Mrs. Fenn as head and leader, while she was more desirous of being hand and follower. No constitution was adopted, nor officers elected. But as the general expression of feeling seemed to be that all should be left in the hands of Mrs. Fenn, the meeting adjourned with a tacit understanding to that effect.

And so it remained until the close of the work. Mrs. Fenn continued to be the life and soul of the movement, and there was never any organization. In answer to her appeals, the people of

Pittsfield, of many towns in Berkshire, as well as numbers of the adjoining towns in the State of New York, forwarded to her their various and liberal contributions. She hired rooms in one of the business blocks, where the ladies were invited to meet daily for the purpose of preparing clothing, lint, and bandages, and where all articles and money were to be sent.

Such was the confidence and respect of the people, that they freely placed in her hands all these gifts, without stint or fear. She received and disbursed large sums of money and valuable stores of all kinds, and to the last occupied this responsible position without murmur or distrust on the part of any, only from time to time acknowledging her receipts through the public prints.

Pittsfield is a wealthy town, with large manufacturing interests, and Mrs. Fenn was well sustained and aided in all her efforts, by valuable contributions. She received also the most devoted and efficient assistance from numerous ladies. Among these may be named, Mrs. Barnard, Mrs. Oliver, during the whole time, Mrs. Brewster, Mrs. Dodge, Mrs. Pomeroy, and many others, either constantly or at all practicable periods. Young ladies, reared in luxury, and unaccustomed to perform any laborious services in their own homes, would at the Sanitary Rooms sew swiftly upon the coarsest work, and shrink from no toil. A few of this class, during the second winter of the war manufactured thirty-one pairs of soldiers trowsers, and about fifty warm circular capes from remnants of heavy cloth contributed for this use by Robert Pomeroy, Esq., a wealthy manufacturer of Pittsfield. The stockings, mittens of yarn and cloth, and hospital clothing of every variety, are too numerous to be mentioned.

Meanwhile supplies of every kind and description poured in. All of these Mrs. Fenn received, acknowledged, collected many of them by her own personal efforts, and then with her own hands arranged, packed, and forwarded them. During the war more than nine thousand five hundred dollars' worth of supplies thus passed directly through her hands, and of these nothing save one barrel of apples at David's Island, was ever lost.

During the entire four years of the war, she devoted three days of the week to this work, often all the days. But these three she called the "soldiers' days," and caused it to be known among her friends that this was not her time, and could not be devoted to personal work or pleasure.

The Sanitary Booms were more than half a mile distant from her own home. But on all these mornings, immediately after breakfast, she proceeded to them, on foot, (for she kept no carriage), carrying with her, her lunch, and at mid-day, making herself that old lady's solace, a cup of tea, and remaining as long as she could see; busily at work, receiving letters, supplies, acknowledging the same, packing and unpacking, buying needed articles, cutting out and preparing work, and answering the numerous and varied calls upon her time. After the fatiguing labors of such a day, she would again return to her home on foot, unless, as was very frequently the case, some friend took her up in the street, or was thoughtful enough to come and fetch her in carriage or sleigh. When we reflect that these tasks were undertaken in all weathers, and at all seasons, by a lady past her sixtieth year, during so long a period, we are astonished at learning that her health was never seriously injured, and that she was able to perform all her duties with comfort, and without yielding to fatigue.

In addition to these labors, she devoted much time and persona attention to such sick and wounded soldiers as fell in her way cheered and aided many a raw recruit, faltering on the threshhold of his new and dangerous career. Twice, at least, in each year, she herself proceeded to the hospitals at New York, or some other point, herself the bearer of the bounties she had arranged, and in some years she made more frequent visits.

Early in her efforts, she joined hands with Mrs. Col. G. T. M. Davis, of New York, (herself a native of Pittsfield, and a sister of Robert Pomeroy, Esq., of that place), in the large and abundant efforts of that lady, for the welfare of the sick and wounded soldiers. Mrs. Davis was a member of the Park Barracks' Ladies' Aid Society, and through her a large part of the bounty of Berkshire was directed in that channel. The sick and weary, and fainting men at the

Barracks, at the New England Rooms, and Bedloe's Island, were principally aided by this Association, which were not long in discovering the great value of the nicely selected, arranged and packed articles contained in the boxes which had passed through the hands of Mrs. Fenn, and came from Pittsfield.

But the ladies of this Association, were desirous of concentrating all their efforts upon the sufferers who had reached New York, while Mrs. Fenn, and her associates in Berkshire, desired to place no bound or limit to their divine charity. The soldiers of the whole army were their soldiers, and all had equal wants, and equal rights. Thus they often answered individual appeals from a variety of sources, and their supplies often helped to fit out expeditions, and were sent to Sherman's and Grant's, and Burnside's forces—to Annapolis, to Alexandria, to the Andersonville and Libby prisoners, and wherever the cry for help seemed most importunate.

Among other things, Mrs. Fenn organized a plan for giving refreshments to the weary soldiers, who from time to time passed through Pittsfield. A signal gun would be fired when a transport-train reached the station at Richmond, ten miles distant, and the ladies would hasten to prepare the palatable lunch and cooling drink, against the arrival of the wearied men, and to distribute them with their own hands.

In the fall of 1862, Mrs. Fenn, herself, conveyed to New York the contribution of Berkshire, to the Soldiers' Thanksgiving Dinner at Bedloe's Island. Among the abundance of good things thus liberally collected for this dinner, were more than a half ton of poultry, and four bushels of real Yankee doughnuts, besides cakes, fruit and vegetables, in enormous quantities. These she greatly enjoyed helping to distribute.

In the fall of 1864, she had a similar pleasure in contributing to the dinner at David's Island, where several thousand sick and wounded soldiers, (both white and colored) returned prisoners, and freed men were gathered, fourteen boxes and parcels of similar luxuries. Various accidents combined to prevent her arrival in time, and her good things were consequently in part too late for the dinner. There was fortunately a plenty beside, and the Berkshire's contribution was reserved for the feast of welcome to the poor starved wrecks so soon to come home from the privations and cruelties of Andersonville.

Mrs. Fenn however enjoyed the occasion to the fullest, and was welcomed with such joy and gratitude, by the men who had so often shared the good things she had sent to the hospitals, as more than repaid her for all her labors and sacrifices. Many thousands of all classes, sick and wounded convalescents, and returned prisoners, white and colored troops, were then gathered there, and on the last day of her stay, Mrs. Fenn enjoyed the pleasure of personally distributing to each individual in that vast collection of suffering men, some little gift from the stores she had brought. Fruit, (apples, or some foreign fruit), cakes, a delicacy for the failing appetite, stores of stationery, contributed by the liberal Berkshire manufacturers, papers, books—to each one some token of individual remembrance. And, with great gusto, she still tells how she came at last to the vast pavilion where the colored troops were stationed, and how the dusky faces brightened, and the dark eyes swam in tears, and the white teeth gleamed in smiles, half joyful, half sad; and how, after bestowing upon each some token of her visit, and receiving their enthusiastic thanks, she paused at the door, before bidding them farewell, and asked if any were there who were sorry for their freedom, regretted the price they had paid for it, or wished to return to their old masters, they should say—Aye. "The gentleman from Africa," perhaps for the first time in his life had a vote. He realized the solemnity of the moment. A dead silence fell upon the crowd, and no voice was lifted in that important affirmative. "Very well, boys," again spoke the clear, kind voice of Mrs. Fenn. "Each of you who is glad to be free, proud to be a free soldier of his country, and ready for the struggles which freedom entails, will please to say Aye." Instantly, such a shout arose, as startled the sick in their beds in the farthest pavilion. No voice was silent. An irrepressible, exultant, enthusiastic cry answered her appeal, and told how the black man appreciated the treasure won by such blood and suffering.

As has been said before, the personal labors of Mrs. Fenn were unintermitted as long as a sick or wounded soldier remained in any hospital. After all the hospitals in the neighborhood of New York were closed, except that of David's Island, months after the suspension of hostilities, she continued to be the medium of sending to the men there the contributions of Berkshire, and the supplies her appeals drew from various sources.

The United Societies of Shakers, at Lebanon and Hauck, furnished her with many supplies—excellent fruit, cheese, eatables of various kinds, all of the best, cloth, linen new and old, towels, napkins, etc., etc., all of their own manufacture and freely offered. The Shakers are no less decided than the Quakers in their testimony against war, but they are also, as a body, patriotic to a degree, and full of kindly feelings which thus found expression.

At one time Mrs. Fenn with a desire of saving for its legitimate purpose even the small sum paid for rent, gave up the rooms she had hired, and for more than a year devoted the best parlor of her own handsome residence to the reception of goods contributed for the soldiers. Thousands of dollars' worth of supplies were there received and packed by her own hands.

Among other things accomplished by this indefatigable woman was the making of nearly one hundred gallons of blackberry cordial. Most of the bandages sent from Pittsfield were made by her, and so nicely, that Mrs. Fenn's bandages became famed throughout the army and hospitals. In all, they amounted to many thousand yards. One box which accompanied Burnside's expedition, alone contained over four thousand yards of bandages, which she had prepared.

Though the bounties she so lavishly sent forth were in a very large measure devoted to the hospitals in the neighborhood of New York, to the Soldiers' Rest in Howard Street; New England Rooms, Central Park, Ladies' Home and Park Barracks, they were still diffused to all parts of the land. The Army of the Potomac, and of the Southwest, and scores of scattered companies and regiments shared them. The Massachusetts Regiments, whether at home or abroad, were always remembered with the tenderest care, and especially was the gallant

Forty-ninth, raised almost entirely in Berkshire, the object of that helpful solicitude which never wearied of well-doing.

Almost decimated by disease in the deadly bayous of the Southwest, and in the fearful conflicts at Port Hudson and its neighborhood in the summer of 1863, the remnant at length returned to Berkshire to receive such a welcome and ovation at Pittsfield, on the 22d of August of that year, as has seldom been extended to our honored soldiery. About fifty of these men were at once taken to the hospital, and long lay ill, the constant recipients of unwearied kind attentions from Mrs. Fenn and her coadjutors.

Much as we have said of the excellent and extensive work performed by this most admirable woman, space fails us for the detail of the half. Her work was so various, and so thoroughly good in every department, both head and hands were so entirely at the service of these her suffering countrymen, that it would be impossible to tell the half. The close of the war has brought her a measure of repose, but for such as she there is no rest while human beings suffer and their cry ascends for help. Her charities are large to the freedmen, and the refugees who at the present time so greatly need aid. She is also lending her efforts to the collection of the funds needful for the erection of a monument to her fallen soldiers which Pittsfield proposes to raise at an expense of several thousands of dollars contributed by the people.

At sixty-eight, Mrs. Fenn is still erect, active, and with a countenance beaming with animation and benevolence, bids fair to realize the wish which at sight of her involuntarily springs to all lips that her life may long be spared to the good words and works to which it is devoted. She has been the recipient of several handsome testimonials from her towns-people and from abroad, and many a token of the soldier's gratitude, inexpensive, but most valuable, in view of the laborious and painstaking care which formed them, has reached her hands and is placed with worthy pride among her treasures.

MRS. JAMES HARLAN

THERE have been numerous instances of ladies of high social position, the wives and daughters of generals of high rank, and commanding large bodies of troops, of Governors of States, of Senators and Representatives in Congress, of Members of the Cabinet, or of other Government officials, who have felt it an honor to minister to the defenders of their country, or to aid in such ways as were possible the blessed work of relieving pain and suffering, of raising up the downtrodden, or of bringing the light of hope and intelligence back to the dull and glazed eyes of the loyal whites who escaped from cruel oppression and outrages worse than death to the Union lines. Among these will be readily recalled, Mrs. John C. Fremont, Mrs. General W. H. L. Wallace, Mrs. Harvey, Mrs. Governor Salomon, Mrs. William H. Seward, Mrs. Ira Harris. Mrs. Samuel C. Pomeroy, Mrs. L. E. Chittenden, Mrs. John S. Phelps, and, though last named, by no means the least efficient, Mrs. James Harlan.

Mrs. Harlan is a native of Kentucky, but removed to Indiana in her childhood. Hero she became acquainted with Mr. Harlan to whom she was married in 1845 or 1846. In the rapid succession of positions of honor and trust to which her husband was elevated by the people, as Superintendent of Public Instruction, President of Mount Pleasant University, United States Senator, Secretary of the Interior, and again United States Senator, Mrs. Harlan proved herself worthy of a position by his side. Possessing great energy and resolution and a highly cultivated intellect, she acquitted herself at all times with dignity and honor. When the nominal became the actual war, and great battles were fought, she was among the first to go to the bloody battle-fields and minister to the wounded and dying. After the battle of Shiloh she was one of the first ladies on the field, and her labors were incessant and accomplished great good. Her position as the wife of a distinguished senator, and her energy and decision of character were used with effect, and she was enabled to wring from General Halleck the permission previously refused to all applicants to remove the wounded to hospitals at Mound City, St. Louis, Keokuk, and elsewhere, where their chances of recovery were greatly improved. At Washington where she subsequently spent much of her time, she devoted her energies first to caring for the

Iowa soldiers, but she soon came to feel that all Union soldiers were her brothers, and she ministered to all without distinction of State lines. She lost during the war a lovely and beautiful daughter, Jessie Fremont Harlan, and the love which had been bestowed upon her overflowed after her death upon the soldiers of the Union. Her faithfulness, energy, and continuous labors in behalf of the soldiers, her earnestness in protecting them from wrongs or oppression, her quick sympathy with their sorrows, and her zealous efforts for their spiritual good, will be remembered by many thousands of them all over the country. Mrs. Harlan early advocated the mingling of religious effort with the distribution of physical comforts among the soldiers, and though she herself would probably shrink from claiming, as some of her enthusiastic friends have done for her, the honor of inaugurating the movement which culminated in the organization of the Christian Commission, its plan of operations was certainly fully in accordance with her own, and she was from the beginning one of its most active and efficient supporters.

Mrs. Harlan was accompanied in many of her visits to the army by Mrs. Almira Fales, of whom we have elsewhere given an account, and whose husband having been the first State Auditor of Iowa, was drawn to her not only by the bond of a common benevolence, but by State ties, which led them both to seek the good of the soldiers in whom both felt so deep an interest. Mrs. Harlan continued her labors for the soldiers till after the close of the war, and has been active since that time in securing for them their rights. Her health was much impaired by her protracted efforts in their behalf, and during the year 1866 she was much of the time an invalid.

NEW ENGLAND SOLDIERS' RELIEF ASSOCIATION

THE "New England Society," of New York City, is an Association of long standing, for charitable and social purposes, and is composed of natives of New England, residing in New York, and its vicinity. Soon after the outbreak of the war, this society became the nucleus of a wider and less formal organization—the Sons of New England. In April, 1862, these gentlemen formed the New England Soldiers' Relief Association, whose object was declared to be "to aid and care for all sick and wounded soldiers passing through the city of New York, on their way to or from the war." On the 8th of April, its "Home," a building well adapted to its purposes, was opened at No. 198 Broadway, and Hr. Everett Herrick, was appointed its resident Surgeon, and Mrs. E. A. Russell, its Matron. The Home was a hospital as well as a home, and in its second floor accommodated a very considerable number of patients. Its Matron was faithful and indefatigable in her performance of her duties, and in the three years of her service had under her care more than sixty thousand soldiers, many of them wounded or disabled.

A Women's Auxiliary Committee was formed soon after the establishment of the Association, consisting of thirty ladies who took their turn of service as nurses for the sick and wounded through the year, and provided for them additional luxuries and delicacies to those furnished by the Association and the Government rations. These ladies, the wives and daughters of eminent merchants, clergymen, physicians, and lawyers of the city, performed their work with great faithfulness and assiduity. The care of the sick and wounded men during the night, devolved upon the Night Watchers' Association, a voluntary committee of young men of the highest character, who during a period of three years never failed to supply the needful watchers for the invalid soldiers.

The ladies in addition to their services as nurses, took part in a choir for the Sabbath services, in which all the exercises were by volunteers.

The Soldiers' Depot in Howard Street, New York, organized in 1863, was an institution of somewhat similar character to the New England Soldiers' Relief, though it recognized a primary responsibility to New York soldiers. It was founded and sustained mainly by State appropriations, and a very earnest and faithful association of ladies, here also bestowed their care and services upon the soldiers. Mrs. G. T. M. Davis, was active and prominent in this organization.

AMONG THE FREEDMEN AND REFUGEES

MRS. FRANCES D. GAGE.

ON the 12th of October, 1808, was born in the township of Union, Washington County, Ohio, Frances Dana Barker. Her father had, twenty years before that time, gone a pioneer to the Western wilds. His name was Joseph Barker, a native of New Hampshire. Her mother was Elizabeth Dana, of Massachusetts, and her maternal grandmother was Mary Bancroft. She was thus allied on the maternal side to the well-known Massachusetts families of Dana and Bancroft.

During her childhood, schools were scarce in Ohio, and in the small country places inferior. A log-cabin in the woods was the Seminary where Frances Barker acquired the rudiments of education. The wolf's howl, the panther's cry, the hiss of the copperhead, often filled her young heart with terror.

Her father was a farmer, and the stirring life of a farmer's daughter in a new country, fell to her lot. To spin the garments she wore, to make cheese and butter, were parts of her education, while to lend a hand at out-door labor, perhaps helped her to acquire that vigor of body and brain for which she has since been distinguished.

She made frequent visits to her grandmother, Mrs. Mary Bancroft Dana, whose home was at Belpre, Ohio, upon the Ohio river, only one mile from Parkersburg, Virginia, and opposite Blennerhasset's Island. Mrs. Dana, was even then a radical on the subject of slavery, and Frances learned from her to hate the word, and all it represented. She never was on the side of the oppressor, and was frequently laughed at in childhood, for her sympathy with the poor fugitives from slavery, who often found their way to the neighborhood in which she lived, seeking kindness and charity of the people.

It had not then become a crime to give a crust of bread, or a cup of milk to the "fugitive from labor," and Mrs. Barker, a noble, true-thinking woman, often sent her daughter on errands of mercy to the neighboring cabins, where the poor creatures sought shelter, and would tarry a few days, often to be caught and sent back to their masters. Thus she early became familiarized with their sufferings, and their wants.

At the age of twenty, on the 1st of January, 1829, Frances Barker became the wife of James L. Gage, a lawyer of McConnellsville, Ohio, a good and noble man, whose hatred of the system of slavery in the South, was surpassed only by that of the great apostle of anti-slavery, Garrison, himself. Moral integrity, and unflinching fidelity to the cause of humanity, were leading traits of his character.

A family of eight children engrossed much of their attention for many years, but still they found time to wage moral warfare with the stupendous wrong that surrounded them, and bore down their friends and neighbors beneath the leaden weight of its prejudice and injustice.

Mrs. Gage records that "it never seemed to her to require any sacrifice to resist the popular will upon the subjects of freedom for the slave, temperance, or even the rights of woman." They were all so manifestly right, in her opinion, that she could not but take her stand as their advocates, and it was far easier for her to maintain them than to yield one iota of her conscientious views.

Thus she always found herself in a minority, through all the struggling years between 1832 and 1865. She had once an engagement with the editor of a "State Journal" to write weekly for his columns during a year. This, at that time seemed to her a great achievement. But a few plain words from her upon the Fugitive Slave Law, brought a note saying her services were no longer wanted; "He would not," the editor wrote, "publish sentiments in his Journal, which, if carried out, would strike at the foundations of all law, order, and government," and added much good advice. Her reply was prompt:

"Yours of— is at hand. Thanking you for your unasked counsel, I cheerfully retire from your columns." Respectfully yours,

"F. D. GAGE."

She has lived to see that editor change many of his views, and approach her standard.

The great moral struggle of the thirty years preceding the war, in her opinion, required for its continuance far more heroism than that which marshalled our hosts along the Potomac, prompted Sheridan's raids, or Sherman's triumphant "march to the sea."

In all her warfare against existing -wrong, that which she waged for the liberties of her own sex subjected her to the most trying persecution, insult and neglect. In the region of Ohio where she then resided, she stood almost alone, but she was never inclined to yield. Probably, unknown to herself, this very discipline was preparing her for the events of the future, and its supreme tests of her principles.

A member of Congress once called to urge her to persuade her husband to yield a point of principle (which he said if adhered to would prove the political ruin of Mr. Gage) holding out the bribe of a seat in Congress, if he would stand by the old Whig party in some of its tergiversations, and insisting that if he persisted in doing as he had threatened, he would soon find himself standing alone. She promised the gentleman that she would repeat to her husband what he had said, and as soon as he had gone seized her pencil and wrote the following impromptu, which serves well to illustrate her firm persistence in any course she believes right, as well as the principle that animates her.

She handed this poem to the gentleman with whom she had been conversing, and he afterwards told her that it decided him to give up all for principle. He led off in his district in what was soon known as the Free Soil party, the root of the present triumphant Republican party.

In 1853 the family of Mrs. Gage removed to St. Louis. Those who fought the anti-slavery battle in Massachusetts have little realization of the difficulty and danger of maintaining similar sentiments in a slaveholding community, and a slave State. Mrs. Gage spoke boldly whenever her thought seemed to be required, and soon found herself branded as an "abolitionist" with every adjective appended that could tend to destroy public confidence.

While Colonel Chambers, the former accomplished editor of the Missouri Republican lived, she wrote for his columns, and at one time summing up the resources of that great State, she advanced this opinion: "Strike from your statute books the laws that give man the right to hold property in man, and ten years from this time Missouri will lead its sister State on the eastern shore of the Mississippi."

After the publication of this article, Colonel Chambers was waited upon and remonstrated with by some old slaveholders, for allowing an abolitionist to write for his journal. "Such sentiments," they said, "would destroy the Union." "If your Union," replied he, "is based upon a foundation so unstable that one woman's breath can blow it down, in God's name let her do it. She shall say her say while I live and edit this paper."

He died soon after, and Mrs. Gage was at once excluded from its columns, by the succeeding editors, refused payment for past labors, or a return of her manuscripts.

The Missouri Democrat soon after hoisted the flag of Emancipation, under the leadership of Frank Blair. She became one of its correspondents, and for several years continued to supply its columns with an article once or twice a week. Appearing in 1858 upon the platform of the Boston Anti-Slavery Society, she was at once excluded as dangerous to the interests of the party which the paper represented.

During all the years of her life in Missouri Mrs. Gage frequently received letters threatening her with personal violence, or the destruction of her husband's property. Slaves came to her for aid, and were sent to entrap her, but she succeeded in evading all positive difficulty and trial.

During the Kansas war she labored diligently with pen, tongue, and hands, for those who so valiantly fought the oppressor in that hour of trial. She expected to be waylaid and to be made to suffer for her temerity, and perhaps she did; for about the close of that perilous year three disastrous fires, supposed to be the work of incendiaries, greatly reduced the family resources.

This portion of the life of Mrs. Gage has been dwelt upon at considerable length, because she regards the struggle then made against the wickedness, prejudice, and bigotry of mankind, as the main bravery of her life, and that if there has been heroism in any part of it, it was then displayed. "If as a woman," she says, "to take the platform amidst hissing, and scorn, and newspaper vituperations, to maintain the right of woman to the legitimate use of all the talents God invests her with; to maintain the rights of the slave in the very ears of the masters; to hurl anathemas at intemperance in the very camps of the dram-sellers; if to continue for forty years, in spite of all opposing forces, to press the triune cause persistently, consistently, and unflinchingly, entitles me to a humble place among those noble ones who have gone about doing good, you can put me in that place as it suits you."

At the breaking out of the war, by reason of her husband's failure in business at St. Louis, and his ill-health, Mrs. Gage found herself filling the post of Editor of the Home Department of an Agricultural paper in Columbus, Ohio. The call for help for the soldiers, was responded to by all loyal women. Airs. Gage did what she could with her hands, but found them tied by unavoidable labors. She offered tongue and pen, and found them much more efficient agents. The war destroyed the circulation of the paper, and she was set free.

The cry of suffering from the Freedmen reached her, and God seemed to speak to her heart, telling her that there was her mission.

In the autumn of 1862, without appointment, or salary, with only faith in God that she should be sustained, and with a firm reliance on the invincible principles of Truth and Justice, in the hope of doing good, she left Ohio, and proceeded directly to Port Royal.

She remained among the freedmen of Beaufort, Paris, Fernandina, and other points, thirteen months; administering also to the soldiers, as often as circumstances gave opportunity. Her own four boys were in the Union army, and this, if no more, would have given every "boy in blue," a claim upon her sympathy and kindness.

In the fall of 1863, Mrs. Gage returned North, and with head and heart filled to overflowing with the claims of the great mission upon which she had entered, she commenced a lecturing tour, speaking to the people of her "experiences among the Freedmen." To show them as they were, to give a truthful portrayal of Slavery, its barbarity and heinousness, its demoralization of master and man, its incompatibility with all things beautiful or good, its defiance of God and his truth; and to show the intensely human character of the slave, who, through this fearful ordeal of two hundred years, had preserved so much goodness, patient hope, unwavering trust in Jesus, faith in God, such desire for knowledge and capability of self-support—such she felt to be her mission, and as such she performed it! She believed that by removing prejudice, and inspiring confidence in the Emancipation Proclamation, and by striving to unite the people on this great issue, she could do more than in any other way toward ending the war, and relieving the soldier—such was the aim of her lectures, while she never omitted to move the hearts of the audience toward those so nobly defending the Union and the Government.

Thus, in all the inclement winter weather, through Pennsylvania, New York, Ohio, Illinois, and Missouri, she pursued her labors of love, never omitting an evening when she could get an audience to address, speaking for Soldiers' Aid Societies, and giving the proceeds to those who worked only for the soldier, —then for Freed men's Associations. She worked without fee or reward, asking only of those who were willing, to give enough to 87 defray her expenses—for herself—thankful if she received, cheerful if she did not.

Following up this course till the summer days made lecturing seem impossible, she started from St. Louis down the Mississippi, to Memphis, Vicksburg, and Natchez. On this trip she went as an unsalaried agent of the Western Sanitary Commission—receiving only her expenses, and the goods and provisions wherewith to relieve the want and misery she met among our suffering men.

A few months' experience among the Union Refugees, and unprotected fugitives, or unprotected Freedmen, convinced her that her best work for all was in the lecturing field, in rousing the hearts of the multitude to good deeds.

She had but one weak pair of hands, while her voice might set a hundred, nay, a thousand pairs in motion, and believing that we err if we fail to use our best powers for life's best uses, she again, after a few months with the soldiers and other sufferers, entered the lecturing field in the West, speaking almost nightly.

In the month of September, she was overturned in a carriage at Galesburg, Illinois. Some bones were broken, and she was otherwise so injured as to be entirely crippled for that year. She has since been able to labor only occasionally, and in great weakness for the cause. This expression she uses for all struggle against wrong. "Temperance, Freedom, Justice to the negro, Justice to woman," she says, "are but parts of one great whole, one mighty temple whose maker and builder is God."

Through all the vicissitudes of the past; through all its years of waiting, her faith in Him who led, and held, and comforted, has never wavered, and to Him alone does she ascribe the Glory of our National Redemption.

MRS. LUCY GAYLORD POMEROY.

IN 1803, some families from Bristol and Meriden, Connecticut, removed to the wilderness of New York, and settled in what is now Otisco, Onondaga County. Among these were Chauncey Gaylord, a sturdy, athletic young man, just arrived at the age of twenty-one, and "a little, quiet, black-eyed girl, with a sunny, thoughtful face, only eleven years old." Her name was Dema Cowles. So the young man and the little girl became acquaintances, and friends, and in after years lovers. In 1817 they were married. Their first home was of logs, containing one room, with a rude loft above, and an excavation beneath for a cellar.

In this humble abode was born Lucy Ann Gaylord, the subject of this sketch, who afterwards became the wife of Samuel C. Pomeroy, United States Senator from Kansas.

Plain and humble as was this home, it was a consecrated one, where God was worshipped, and the purest religious lessons taught. Mrs. Gaylord was a woman of remarkable strength of character and principles, one who carried her religion into all the acts of daily life, and taught by a consistent example, no less than by a wise precept. Her mother had early been widowed, and had afterwards married Mr. Eliakim Clark, from Massachusetts, and had become the mother of the well-known twin-brothers, Lewis Gaylord, and Willis Gaylord Clark, destined to dcvelope into scholars and poets, and to leave their mark upon the literature of America. She had been entrusted with the care of these beautiful and noble boys for some years, and was already experienced in duties of that kind, before children of her own were given her. Doubtless to her high order of intellect, refined taste, amiable disposition, and sterling good sense, all the children who shared her care are indebted to a great extent for the noble qualities they possess.

Other children succeeded Lucy, and as the elder sister, she shared, in their primitive mode of life, her mother's cares and duties. Her character developed and expanded, and she grew in mental grace as in stature, loving all beautiful things and noble thoughts, and early making a profession of religion.

By this time the family occupied a handsome rural homestead, where neatness, order, regularity, industry and kindness reigned, and where a liberal hospitality was always practiced. Here gathered all the large group of family relatives, here the aged grandmother Clark lived, and hither came her gifted twin sons, from time to time, as to their home. The most beautiful scenery surrounded this homestead; peace, order, intelligence, truth and godliness abounded there, and amidst such influences Lucy Gaylord had the training which led to the future usefulness of her life. Even in her youth she was the friend and safe counsellor of her brothers, as in her maturer years she was of her gifted husband.

At eighteen she made a public profession of religion, and soon after the thought of consecrating herself to the missionary work took possession of her mind. To this end she labored and studied for several years, steadfastly educating herself for a vocation to which she believed herself called, though often afflicted with serious doubts as to whether she, being an only daughter, could leave her parents.

In early life she became an earnest and efficient teacher in Sunday-schools, her intellectual pursuits furnishing her with ever fresh means of rendering her instruction interesting and useful to her classes. She undoubtedly at the first considered this as a training for the work to which, in time, she hoped to devote herself.

But this hope was destined to disappointment. One violent illness after another finally destroyed her health, and she never quite recovered the early tone of her system. Yet she worked on, doing good wherever the means presented.

Soon afterwards she met with the great sorrow of her life. The young man to whom she was soon to be married, between whom and herself the strongest attachment existed, cemented by a mutual knowledge of noble qualities,'was suddenly snatched from her, and she became a widow in all but the name.

This sorrow still more refined and beautified her character. By degrees the sharpness of the grief wore away, and it became a sweet, though saddened memory. Eight years after her loss, she became the wife of Samuel C. Pomeroy, of Southampton, Massachusetts. "They were of kindred feelings in life's great work, had suffered alike by early bereavement, and were drawn together by that natural affinity which unites two lives in one."

He had given up mercantile business in Western New York not long before, and had returned to his early home to care for the declining years of his aged parents. And this was the missionary work to which Mrs. Pomeroy found herself appointed. She was welcomed heartily, and found her duties rendered light by appreciation and affection.

Here, as elsewhere, Mrs. Pomeroy made herself actively useful beyond, as well as within, her home. She performed duties of Sabbath School and general religious instruction, that might be called arduous, especially when added to her domestic cares and occupations. These, with other labors, exhausted her strength and a protracted season of illness followed.

From that time, 1850, for five or six years, she continued to suffer, being most of the time very ill, her life often despaired of. During all this season of peculiar trial she never lost her faith and courage, even when her physicians gave no hope of her recovery, being contented to abide by the will of Providence, convinced that if God had any work for her to do He would spare her life. During this time her husband was often absent, being first in the Massachusetts Legislature, and afterwards sent out as Agent by the Northeastern Aid Society to Kansas, which they were desirous to settle as a free State. Into this last duty she insisted with energy that he should enter. During his absence she experienced other afflictions, but her health notwithstanding rallied, and as soon as possible she made preparations to remove to Kansas where Mr. Pomeroy wished to make a home. In the spring of 1857 she finally arrived there, and there she remained until the spring of 1861, when she accompanied her husband to Washington, when he went thither to take his seat in the Senate.

The hardships and the usefulness of her life in Kansas are matters of history, and it is truly surprising to read how one so long an invalid was enabled to perform such protracted and exhausted labors. All who knew her there bear ample and enthusiastic testimony to the usefulness of her life. To the whites she was friend, hostess, counsellor, assistant, in sickness and in health. To the poor and despised blacks, striving to find freedom, she AA as friend and teacher, even at the time when her near neighborhood to the slave State of Missouri, made the service most dangerous. Then followed the terrible famine year of 1860. During all that time she freely gave her services in the work of providing for the sufferers. Mr. Pomeroy, aided by the knowledge he had acquired in his experience as Agent of Emigration, was able at once to put the machinery in motion for obtaining supplies from the East, and Mrs. Pomeroy transformed her home into an office of distribution, of which she was superintendent and chief clerk. It AATIS a year that taxed far too heavily her already much exhausted strength.

When she accompanied her husband to Washington in the spring, her health failed, cough and hoarseness troubled her, and she was obliged to leave for visits in her native air, and for a stay of some months at Geneva Water Cure.

From the breaking out of the war Mrs. Pomeroy, on all occasions, proved herself desirous of the welfare of our soldiers. The record of her deeds of kindness in their behalf is not as ample as that of some others, for her health forbade the active nursing, and visiting of the sick in hospitals, which is the most showy part of the work. But her contributions of supplies were always large; and she had always a peculiar care and interest in the religious and moral welfare of the volunteers, who, far from the influences of home, and exposed to new and numerous temptations, were, she felt, in more than one sense encircled by peculiar dangers.

Only once did she revisit her Kansas home, and in the autumn of 1862 spent some months there. There was at that time a regiment in camp at Atchison, and she was enabled to do great good to the sick in hospital, not only with supplies, but by her own personal efforts for their physical and spiritual welfare.

On her return to Washington she there entered as actively as possible into this work. Her form became known in the hospitals, and many a suffering man hailed her coming with a new light kindling his dimmed eyes. She brought them comforts and delicacies, and she added her prayers and her precious instructions. She cared both for souls and bodies, and earned the immortal gratitude of those to whom she ministered.

In January, 1863, her last active benevolent work was commenced, namely the foundation of an asylum at the National Capital for the freed orphans and destitute aged colored women whom the war, and the Proclamation of Emancipation, had thrown upon the care of the benevolent. For several months she was actively engaged in this enterprise. A charter was immediately obtained, and when the Association was organized, Mrs. Pomeroy was chosen President.

Almost entirely by her exertions, a building for the Asylum was obtained, as well as some condemned hospital furniture, which was to be sold at auction by the Government, but was instead transferred—a most useful gift—to the Asylum.

But when the time came, about the 1st of June, 1863, for the Association to be put in possession of the buildings and grounds assigned them, Mrs. Pomeroy was too ill to receive the keys, and the Secretary took her place. She was never able to look upon the fruit of her labors. Again, she had exhausted her feeble powers, and she was never more to rally.

A slow fever followed, which at last assumed the form of typhoid. She lingered on, slightly better at times, until the 17th of July, when preparations were completed for removing her to the Geneva Water Cure, and she started upon her last journey. She went by water, and arrived at New York very comfortably, leaving there again on the boat for Albany, on the morning of the 20th. But death overtook her before even this portion of the journey was finished. She died upon the passage, on the afternoon of July 20th, 1863. After her life of usefulness and devotion, her name at last stands high upon the roll of martyr-women, whom this war has made.

MARIA R. MANN.

AMONG the heroic women who labored most efficiently and courageously during the late civil war for the good of our soldiers, and the poor "contrabands," as the freed people were called, was Miss Maria R. Mann, an educated and refined woman from Massachusetts, a near relative of the first Secretary of the Board of Education of that renowned Commonwealth, who gave his life and all his great powers to the cause of education, and finished his noble career as the President of Antioch College, in Ohio.

Miss Mann, is a native of Massachusetts, and spent the greater portion of her mature life previous to the war, as a teacher. In this, her chosen profession, she attained a high position, and for a number of years taught in the High Schools. As a teacher she was highly esteemed for her varied and accurate knowledge, the care and minuteness with which she imparted instruction to her pupils, the high moral and religious principle which controlled her actions, and made her life an example of truth and goodness to her pupils, and for her enthusiastic interest in the cause of education, of freedom and justice for the slave, and of philanthropy and humanity towards the orphan, the prisoner, the outcast, the oppressed and the poor, to whom her heart went out in kindly sympathies, and in prayer and effort for the improvement of their condition.

During the first year of the rebellion, she left all her pleasant associations in New England, and came out to St. Louis, that she might be nearer to the scene of conflict, and aid in the work of the "Western Sanitary Commission, and in nursing the sick and wounded soldiers, with whom the hospitals at St. Louis were crowded that year. On her arrival, she was duly commissioned by Mr. Yeatman, (the agent of Miss Dix for the employment of women nurses), and entered upon her duties in the Fifth Street Hospital.

For several months, she devoted herself to this work with great fidelity and patience, and won the gratitude of many a poor sufferer by her kindness, and the respect of the surgeons, by her good judgment and her blended gentleness and womanly dignity.

Late in the fall of 1862, the Western Sanitary Commission was moved to establish an agency at Helena, Ark., for the special relief of several hundred colored families at that military post who had gathered there from the neighboring country, and from the opposite shore in Mississippi, as a place of refuge from their rebel owners. It was at that time a miserable refuge, for the post was commanded by pro-slavery Generals, who succeeded the humane and excellent Major-General Curtis, who was unfortunately re-' lieved of his command, and transferred to St. Louis, in consequence of slanders against him at Washington, which some of his pro-slavery subordinates had been busy in fabricating; and the free papers which he gave to the colored people were violated; they were subjected to all manner of cruelties and hardships; they were put under a forced system of labor; driven by mounted orderlies to work on the fortifications, and to unload steamboats and coal barges; and discharged at night without compensation, or a comfortable shelter. No proper record was kept of their services, and most of them never received any pay for months of incessant toil. They were compelled to camp together in the outskirts of the town, in huts and condemned tents, and the rations issued to them were cut down to a half ration for the women and children; so that they were neither well fed nor sheltered properly from the weather, while they were entirely destitute of comfortable clothing, and were without the means of purchasing new. Subjected to this treatment, very great sickness and mortality prevailed among them. In the miserable building assigned them for a hospital, which was wholly unprovided with hospital furniture and bedding, and without regular nurses or attendants, they were visited once a day by a contract surgeon, who merely looked in upon them, administered a little medicine, and left them to utter neglect and miseiy. Here they died at a fearful rate, and their dead bodies were removed from the miserable pallet of straw, or the bare floor where they had breathed their last, and buried in rude coffins, and sometimes coffinless, in a low piece of ground near by. The proportion of deaths, was about seventy-five percent of all who were carried sick to this miserable place, so that the colored people became greatly afraid of being sent to the hospital, considering it the same as going to a certain death; and many of them refused to go, even in the last stages of sickness, and died in their huts, and in and out of the very places into which they had crawled for concealment, neglected and alone.

This state of things was fully known to the Generals commanding, and to the medical director, and the army surgeons at Helena, without the least effort being made on their part towards their improvement or alleviation. From August, 1862, to January, 1863, they continued to suffer in this manner, until the printed report and appeal of the chaplains at Helena for aid, brought some voluntary contributions of clothing, and secured the attention of the Western Sanitary Commission, at St. Louis, to the great need of help at Helena, for the "contrabands."

It was at this juncture that the Commission proposed to Miss Mann to go to Helena, and act the part of the Good Samaritan to the colored people who had congregated there; to establish a hospital for the sick among them; to supply them with clothing and other necessaries, and in all possible ways to improve their condition the offer was readily accepted by her, and in the month of January she arrived at Helena, with an ample supply of sanitary goods and clothing, and with letters commending her to the protection and aid of the commanding general, and to the chaplain of the post, (who now furnishes this sketch from his memory), and to the superintendent of freedmen, who welcomed her as a providential messenger whom God had sent to his neglected and suffering poor.

The passage from St. Louis to Helena, a distance of sis hundred miles, in mid-winter, at a time when the steamers were fired on by guerrillas from the shore, and sometimes captured, was made by Miss Mann, unattended, and without knowing where she would find a shelter when she arrived. The undertaking was attended with difficulty and danger, and many obstacles were to be overcome, but the brave spirit of this noble woman knew no such word as fail. Fortunately, the post chaplain, who had been detailed to a service requiring clerks, was able to receive Miss Mann, provide rooms for her, give her a place at the mess board, and render useful aid in her work. He remembers with a grateful interest how bravely she encountered every difficulty, and persevered in her humane undertaking, until almost every evil the colored people suffered was removed. A new hospital building was secured, furnished, and provided with good surgeons and nurses, and the terrible sickness and mortality reduced to the minimum per-centage of the best regulated hospitals; a new and better camping ground was obtained, and buildings erected for shelter; a school for the children was established, and the women taught how to cut and make garments, and advised and instructed how to live and be useful to themselves and their families. Material for clothing was furnished them, which they made up for themselves. As the season of spring came, the able-bodied men were enlisted as soldiers, by a new order of the Government; those who were not fit for the military service were hired by the new lessees of the plantations, and the condition of the colored people was changed from one of utter misery and despair, to one of thrift, improvement and comparative happiness.

In all these changes Miss Mann was a moving spirit, and with the co-operation of the chaplains, and the friendly sanction and aid of Major-General Prentiss—who on his arrival in February, 1863, introduced a more humane treatment of the freed people— she was able to fulfil her benevolent mission, and remained till the month of August of that year.

The heroism of Miss Mann during the winter season at Helena, was a marvel to us all. It was an exceedingly rainy winter, and the streets were often knee deep with mud. The town is built on a level, marshy region of bottom land, and for weeks the roads became almost impassable, and had to be waded on horseback, or the levee followed, and causeways had to be built by the military. But Miss Mann was not to be prevented by these difficulties from visiting the "Contraband Hospital," as it was called, and from going her rounds to the families of the poor colored people who needed her advice and assistance. I have often taken her myself in an open wagon with which we carried the mail bags to and from the steamers—having charge of the military post-office— and conveyed her from place to place, when the wheels would sink almost to the hubs, and returned with her to her quarters; and on several occasions when she had gone on foot when the side-walks were dry, and she came to a crossing that required deep wading, I have known her to call some stout black man to her aid, to carry her across, and set her down on the opposite sidewalk. In these cases the service was rendered with true politeness and gallantry, and with the remark, "Bress the Lord, missus, it's no trouble to carry you troo de mud, and keep your feet drv, you who does so much for us black folks. You's light as a fedder, anyhow, and de good Lord gibs you a wonderful sight of strength to go'bout dis yere muddy town, to see de poor culled folks, and gib medicines to the sick, and feed the hungry, and clothe de naked, and I bress de good Lord dat he put it into your heart to come to Helena."

In the autumn of 1863 Miss Mann felt that her work in Helena was accomplished, and she returned to St. Louis, the colored people greatly lamenting her departure. In her work there she not only had the co-operation and assistance of the Western Sanitary Commission, but of many benevolent ladies in New England, personal friends of Miss Mann and others, who, through Rev. Dr. Eliot of St. Louis, supplied a large portion of the funds that were necessary to defray the expenses of our mission.

A new call to a theatre of usefulness in Washington City, in the District of Columbia, now came to Miss Mann, to become the teacher of a colored orphan asylum, which she accepted, where she devoted her energies to the welfare of the children of those who in the army, or in some other service to their country and race have laid down their lives, and left their helpless offspring to be cared for by Him, who hears even the young ravens when they cry, and moves human hearts to fulfil the ministry of his love; and who by his Spirit is moving the American people to do justly to the freed people of this land, and to make reparation for the oppression and wrong they have endured for so many generations.

After rendering a useful and excellent service as a teacher in the Colored Orphan Asylum at Washington, she was induced by the colored people, who greatly appreciated her work for their children, to establish an independent school in Georgetown. Friends at the North purchased a portable building for a schoolhouse; the Freed men's Bureau offered her a lot of ground to put it on, but not being in the right locality she rented one, and the building was sent to her, and has been beautifully fitted up for the purpose. The school has been successfully established, and under her excellent management, teaching, and discipline, it has become a model school. Intelligent persons visiting it are impressed by the perfect order maintained, and the advancement of the scholars in knowledge and good behaviour.

Miss Mann has made many personal sacrifices in establishing and carrying forward this school without government patronage or support, and the only fear concerning it is that the colored people will not be able from their limited resources to sustain it. It is her wish to prepare her scholars to become teachers of other colored schools, a work she is amply and remarkably qualified to do, and one in which she would be sustained by philanthropic aid, if the facts were known to those who feel the importance of all such efforts for the education and improvement of the colored people of this country, in the new position upon which they have entered as free citizens of the republic.

Among the gratifying results which Miss Mann has found in this work of instruction among the colored people are the rapid improvement she has witnessed among them, the capacity and eagerness with which they pursue the acquisition of knowledge, the gratitude they have evinced to her, and the consciousness that she has contributed to their welfare and happiness.

As a noble, self-sacrificing woman, devoted to the service of her fellow-beings, and endowed with the best attributes of human nature, Miss Mann deserves the title of a Christian philanthropist, and her life and labors will be remembered with gratitude, and the blessing of him that was ready to perish, and of those who had no helper, will follow her all the remainder of her days.

SARAH J. HAGAR.

IT is due to the memory of this noble young woman that she should be included in the record of those sainted heroines who fearlessly went into the midst of danger and death that they might minister to the poor and suffering freedmen, whom our victorious arms had emancipated from their rebel masters, and yet had left for a time without means or opportunity to fit themselves for the new life that opened before them. To this humane service she freely devoted herself and became a victim to the climate of the lower Mississippi, while engaged in the arduous work of ministering to the physical wants and the education of the freed people, who in the winter and spring of 1864, had gathered in camps around Vicksburg, and along the Louisiana shore.

Miss Hagar was the eldest daughter of Mrs. C. C. Hagar, who also was one of the army of heroic nurses who served in the hospitals of St. Louis during the greater part of the war. For many months they had served together in the same hospital, and by their faithfulness and careful ministrations to the sick and wounded soldier had won the highest confidence of the Western Sanitary Commission, by whose President they were appointed.

During the fall of 1863 the National Freed men's Aid Commission of New York, under the presidency of Hon. Francis G. Shaw, sent two agents, Messrs. William L. Marsh and H. R. Foster, to Vicksburg, to establish an agency there, and at Natchez, for the aid of the freed people, in furnishing supplies of food and clothing to the destitute, and establishing schools for the children of the freedmen, and for such adults as could attend, and to help them in all possible ways to enter upon the new and better civilization that awaited them. In this work the Western Sanitary Commission co-operated, and Messrs. Marsh and Foster wrote to the writer of this sketch, then acting as Secretary of the above Commission, to send them several teachers and assistants in their work. Among those who volunteered for the service was Miss Hagar, who was wanted in another situation in St. Louis, but preferred this more arduous work for the freedmen.

The reasons she gave for her choice were, that she was well and strong, and felt a real interest in the welfare of the freed people; that she had no prejudices against them, and that while there were enough who were willing to fill the office of nurse to the white soldiers, it was more difficult to get those who would render equal kindness and justice to the black troops, and to the freed people, and therefore she felt it her duty and pleasure to go. She was accordingly commissioned, and with Miss A. M. Knight, of Sun Prairie, Wisconsin, (another worthy laborer in the same cause) went down the river to Vicksburg, in the winter of 1864.

For several months she labored there with untiring devotion to the interests and welfare of the colored people, under the direction of Messrs. Marsh and Foster. No task was too difficult for her to undertake that promised good results, and in danger of all kinds, whether from disease, or from the assaults of the enemy, she never lost her presence of mind, nor was wanting in the requisite courage for that emergency. In person she was above the medium height, and had a face beaming with kindness, and pleasant to look upon. Her mind had received a good degree of culture, and her natural intelligence was of a high order. And better than all within her earthly form dwelt a noble and heroic soul.

Late in April of that year, she had au attack of malarial fever, which prostrated her very suddenly, and just in the proportion 89 that she had been strong and apparently well fortified against disease, it took a deep hold of her vital powers, and on the 3d of May, she yielded to the fell destroyer, and breathed no more.

The following tribute to her character, is taken from the letter of Mr. Marsh, in which he communicated the sad tidings of her death.

"In her death the National Freedmen's Aid Association, has lost a most earnest, devoted, Christian laborer. She entered upon her duties at a time of great suffering and destitution among the Freedmen at Vicksburg, and when we were much in need of aid. The fidelity with which she performed her labors, and the deep interest she manifested in them soon endeared her to us all. We shall miss her sorely; but the noble example she has left us will encourage us to greater efforts, and more patient toil. She seemed also to realize the magnitude and importance of this work upon which she had entered, and the need of Divine assistance in its performance. She seemed also to realize what sacrifice might be demanded of one engaged in a work like this, and the summons, although sudden, did not find her unprepared to meet it. She has done a noble work, and done it well.

"The sacrifice she made is the greatest one that can be made for any cause, the sacrifice of life. 'Greater love than this hath no man, that a man lay down his life for his friends.' She has gone to receive her reward."

Her remains were brought to her native town in Illinois, and deposited there, where the blessed memory she has left among her friends and kindred, is cherished with heartfelt reverence and affection.

MRS. JOSEPHINE R. GRIFFIN.

IF the most thoroughly unselfish devotion of an earnest and gifted woman to the interests and welfare of a despised and down-trodden race, to the manifest injury and detriment of her own comfort, ease, or pecuniary prospects, and without any hope or desire of reward other than the consciousness of having been their benefactor, constitutes a woman a heroine, then is Mrs. Griffin one of the most remarkable heroines of our times.

Of her early history we know little. She was a woman of refinement and culture, has always been remarkable for her energy and resolution, as well as for her philanthropic zeal for the poor and oppressed. The beginning of the war found her a widow, with, we believe, three children, all daughters, in Washington, D. C. Of these daughters, the eldest has a position in the Treasury Department, a second has for some time assisted her mother in her labors, and the youngest is in school. Mrs. Griffin was too benevolent ever to be rich, and when the freedmen and their families began to concentrate in the District of Columbia, and on Arlington Heights, across the Potomac, she sought them out, and made the effort to ameliorate their condition. At that time they hardly knew whether they were to be permanently free or not, and massed together as they were, their old slave habits of recklessness, disorder, and over-crowding soon gained the predominance, and showed their evil effect in producing a fearful amount of sickness and death. They were not, with comparatively few exceptions, indolent; but they had naturally lapsed into the easy, slovenly methods, or rather want of method of the old slave life, and a few were doing the greater part of what was done. They were mere children in capacity, will and perseverance. Mrs. Griffin, with her intensely energetic nature, soon effected a change. Order took the place of disorder, under her direction; new cabins were built, neatness and system maintained, till their good effects were so apparent, that the freedmen voluntarily pursued the course advised by their teacher and friend; all who were able to do any work were provided as far as possible with employment, and schools for the children in the day time, and for adults in the evening, were established. In this good work she received material assistance from that devoted young Christian now gone to his rest, the late Cornelius M. Welles. After awhile, the able-bodied men were enlisted in the army, and the stronger and healthier women provided with situations in many instances at the North, and the children, and feeble, decrepit men and women, could not perform work enough for their maintenance. Mrs. Griffin began to solicit aid for them, and carried them through one winter by the assistance she was able to collect, and by what she gave from her own not over-full purse. Some land was now allotted to them, and by the utmost diligence they were enabled to provide almost entirely for themselves, till autumn; but meantime the Act of Emancipation in the District of Columbia had drawn thither some thousands of people of color from the adjacent states of Maryland and Virginia. All looked up to Mrs. Griffin as their special Providence. She was satisfied that it was better for them, as far as possible, to find places and work in the Northern States, than to remain there, where employment was precarious, and where the excessive number of workers had reduced the wages of such as could find employment. She accordingly commenced an extensive correspondence, to obtain from persons at the North in want of servants, orders for such as could be supplied from the colored people residing in the District of Columbia. Having completely systematized the matter, she has been in the habit, for nearly two years past, of leaving Washington once or twice a week, with a company of colored persons, for whom she had obtained situations in Philadelphia, New York, Boston, Pittsburg, Cincinnati, or smaller cities, paying their fare, providing them with food on the journey, and at its termination until she could put them into the families who had engaged them, and then returning to make up another company. The cost of these expeditions she has provided almost entirely from her own means, her daughters who have imbibed their mother's spirit, helping as far as possible in this noble work. In the autumn of 1865 she found that notwithstanding all for whom she could provide situations, there were likely to be not less than twenty thousand colored persons, freedmeu and their families, in a state of complete destitution before the 1st of December, and she published in the Washington and other papers, an appeal to the benevolent to help. The Freedmen's Bureau at first denied the truth of her statements, but further investigation convinced them that she was right, and they were wrong, and Congress was importuned for an appropriation for their necessities. Twenty-five thousand dollars were appropriated, and its distribution left to the Freedmen's Bureau. It would have been more wisely distributed had it been entrusted to Mrs. Griffin, as she was more thoroughly cognizant of the condition and real wants of the people than the Bureau could be. Mrs. Griffin has pursued her work of providing situations for the freedmen, and watching over their interests to the present time; and so long as life and health lasts, she is not likely to give it up.

MRS. M. M. HALLOWELL

THE condition of the loyal whites of East Tennessee and Northern Alabama and Georgia, deservedly excited the sympathy and liberality of the loyal North. No portion of the people of the United States had proved their devotion to the Union by more signal sacrifices, more patient endurance, or more terrible sufferings. The men for the mere avowal of their attachment to the Union flag and the Constitution were hunted like deer, and if caught, murdered in cold blood. Most of them managed, though with great peril, to escape to the Union army, where they became valuable soldiers, and by their thorough knowledge of the country and their skill in woodcraft rendered important service as scouts and pioneers. Whenever they escaped the Rebels visited them, their houses were plundered, their cattle and other live stock seized, and if the house was in a Rebel neighborhood or in a secluded situation, it was burned and the wife and children driven out penniless, and often maltreated, outraged or murdered. If they escaped with their lives they were obliged to hide in the caves or woods by day, and travel often hundreds of miles by night, to reach the Union lines. They came in, wearied, footsore, in rags, and often sick and nearly dead from starvation. When they reached Nashville, or Knoxville after it came into our possession, they were in need of all things; shelter, food, clothing, medicine and care. A few of them were well educated; the majority were illiterate so fai as book knowledge was concerned, but intelligent and thoughtful on the subject of loyalty and the war; not a few were almost reduced to a state of fatuity by their sufferings, and seemed to have lost all distinct consciousness of what was occurring around them. Nashville and Knoxville a little later, Memphis, Cairo, St. Louis, and Louisville swarmed with these poor loyal people, and efforts were made in each city to aid them. In the Northern cities large contributions of money and clothing were made for their relief. In Boston, Edward Everett, ever ready to aid the suffering, gave the great influence of his name, as well as his personal efforts, (almost the last act of his well-spent life) in raising a liberal fund for their help. In New York, Brooklyn and other cities, efforts were made which resulted in large contributions. In Philadelphia, Mrs. M. M. Hallowell, a lady of high position and great energy, appealed to the public for aid for these unfortunate people, and Governor Curtin and many other State and National official personages, gave their influence and contributions to the work. A large amount of money and stores having been collected, Mrs. Hallowell and a committee of ladies from Philadelphia visited Nashville, Knoxville, Chattanooga and Huntsville to distribute their stores in person. The journey undertaken early in May, 1864, was not unattended with danger; for, though General Sherman had commenced his great march toward Atlanta, Forrest, Morgan and Wheeler were exerting themselves to cut his communications and break up his connection with his base. Along some portions of the route the guerrillas swarmed, and more than once the cars were delayed by reports of trouble ahead. The courageous ladies, however, pushed forward and received from the generals in command the most hearty welcome, and all the facilities they required for their mission. They found that the suffering of the loyal refugees had not been exaggerated; that in many cases their misery was beyond description, and that from hunger, cold, nakedness, the want of suitable shelter, and the prevalence of malignant typhoid fever, measles, scarlet fever and the other diseases which usually prevail among the wretched and starving poor, very many had died, and others could not long survive. They distributed their stores freely yet judiciously, arranged to aid a home and farm for Refugees and Orphans which had been established near Nashville, and to render future assistance to those in need at Knoxville, Chattanooga, &c., and returned to Philadelphia. Mrs. Hallowell visited them again in the autumn, and continued her labors for them till after the close of the war. The Home for Refugees and Orphans near Nashville, formed a part of the battle ground in the siege and battles of Nashville in December, 1864, and was completely ruined for the time. Some new buildings of a temporary character were subsequently erected, but the close of the war soon rendered its further occupation unnecessary.

Mrs. Hallowell's earnest and continued labors for the refugees drew forth from the loyal men and women of East Tennessee letters full of gratitude and expressive of the great benefits she had conferred on them. Colonel N. G. Taylor, representative in Congress from East Tennessee, and one of the most eloquent speakers and writers in the West, among others, addressed her an interesting and touching letter of thanks for what she had done for his persecuted and tried constituents, from which we quote a single paragraph.

"Accept, my dear madam, for yourself and those associated with you, the warmest thanks of their representative, for the noble efforts you have been and are making for the relief of my poor, afflicted, starving people. Most of the men of East Tennessee are bleeding at the front for our country (this letter was written before the close of the war) whilst their wives and little ones are dying of starvation at home. They are worthy of your sympathy and your labor, for they have laid all their substance upon the altar of our country and have sacrificed everything they had for their patriotism."

OTHER FRIENDS OF THE FREEDMEN AND REFUGEES.

IN many of the preceding sketches we have had occasion to notice the labors of ladies who had been most distinguished in other departments of the great Army work, in behalf of the Freedmen, or the Refugees. Mrs. Harris devoted in all five or six months to their care at Nashville and its vicinity. Miss Tyson and Mrs. Beck gave their valuable services to their relief. Miss Jane Stuart Woolsey was, and we believe still is laboring in behalf of the Freedmen in Richmond or its vicinity. Mrs. Governor Hawley of Connecticut was among the first to instruct them at Fernandina and Hilton Head. Miss Gilson devoted nearly the whole of the last year of her service in the army to the freedmen and the hospital for colored soldiers. In the West, Mrs. Lucy E. Starr, while Matron of the Soldiers' Home at Memphis, bestowed a large amount of labor on the Refugees who were congregated in great numbers in that city. Mrs. Clinton B. Fisk, the wife of the gallant Christian, General Fisk, exerted herself to collect clothing, money and supplies for the Refugees, black and white, at Pilot Knob, Missouri, and distributed it to them in person. Mrs. H. F. Hoes and Miss Alice F. Royce of Wisconsin, were very active in instructing and aiding the children of Refugees at Rolla, Missouri, in 1864 and 1865. Mrs. John S. Phelps established with the aid of a few other ladies a school for the children of Refugees 90713 at Springfield, Missouri, and Mrs. Mary A. Whitaker, an excellent and efficient teacher, had charge of it for two years.

At Leavenworth and Fort Scott, large and well conducted schools for the children of Refugees and Freedmen were established, and several teachers employed, one of them, Mrs. Nettie C. Constant, at Leavenworth, winning a very high reputation for her faithfulness and skill as a teacher.

The Western Sanitary Commission, the National Freedmen's Relief Association, Relief Societies in Cincinnati, Chicago, St. Louis and elsewhere, and later the American Union Commission, were all engaged in labor for either the Freedmen or the Refugees or both.

All these organizations employed or supported teachers, and all worked in remarkable harmony. At Vicksburg the Western Sanitary Commission sent, in the spring of 1864, Miss G. D. Chapman of Exeter, Maine, to take charge of a school for the children of Refugees, of whom there were large numbers there. Miss Chapman served very faithfully for some months, and then was compelled by her failing health, to return home. The Commission then appointed Miss Sarah E. M. Lovejoy, daughter of Hon. Owen Lovejoy, to take charge of the school. It soon became one of the largest in the South, and was conducted with great ability by Miss Lovejoy till the close of the War.

The National Freedmen's Relief Association had, at the same time, a school for Freedmen and the children of Freedmen there, and Miss Mary E. Sheffield, a most faithful and accomplished teacher from Norwich, Connecticut, was in charge of it. The climate, the Rebel prejudices and the indifference or covert opposition to the school of those from whom better things might have been expected, made the position one of great difficulty and responsibility; but Miss Sheffield was fully equal to the work, and continued in it with great usefulness until late in May, 1865, when finding herself seriously ill she attempted to return North, but on reaching Memphis was too ill to proceed farther, and died there on the 5th of June, 1865, a martyr to her faithfulness and zeal.

In Helena, a Refugee Home was established by the Western Sanitary Commission, and Mrs. Sarah Coombs, a benevolent and excellent lady of that town, placed in charge of it. At Nashville, Tennessee, the Nashville Refugee Relief Society, under the management of Mrs. Mary R. Fogg, established a Refugees' Home which was aided by the Western Sanitary Commission, the Philadelphia ladies, and other associations. At Little Rock, Arkansas, was another Home which did good service. But the most extensive institution of this description, was the Refugee and Freedmen's Home at St. Louis, occupying the Lawson Hospital in that city, and established by the Western Sanitary Commission with the co-operation of the Ladies' Union Aid Society, and the Ladies' Freedmen's Relief Association. Mrs. H. M. Weed was its efficient matron, and was supported by a staff of six or seven assistants and teachers. Over three thousand Refugees were received and aided here in the six months from February to July, 1865, and both children and adults were taught not only elementary studies but housework, cooking and laundry work; the women were paid moderate wages with which to clothe themselves and their children, and were taught some of the first lessons of a better civilization. In. the superintendence of this good work, Mrs. Alfred Clapp, the President of the Ladies' Union Aid Society, Mrs. Joseph Crawshaw, an active member of that Society, Mrs. Lucien Eaton, the President of the Ladies' Freedmen's Association, and Mrs. N. Stevens, one of the managers of that Society, were assiduous and faithful.

There were great numbers of other ladies equally efficient in the Freedmen's Schools and Homes in the Atlantic States, but their work was mainly under the direction of the Freedmen's Relief, and subsequently of the American Union Commission, and it is not easy to obtain from them accounts of the labors of particular individuals. The record of the women who have labored faithfully, and not a few of them to the loss of their health or lives in work which was in some respects even more repulsive to the natural sensibilities than that in the hospitals, if smaller in numbers, is not less honorable than that of their sisters in the hospitals.

SOLDIERS' HOMES, REFRESHMENT SALOONS, HOSPITAL TRANSPORTS

MRS. O. E. HOSMER.

AT the opening of the late war, the subject of this sketch, Mrs. O. E. Hosmer, was residing with her family in Chicago, Illinois. Hers was by no means a vague patriotism that contented itself with verbal expressions of sympathy for her country's cause and defenders. She believed that she had sacrifices to make, and work to do, and could hope for no enjoyment, or even comfort, amidst the luxuries of home, while thousands to whom these things were as dear as to herself, had resolutely turned away from them, willing to perish themselves, if the national life might be preserved.

Her first sacrifice was that of two of her sons, whom she gave to the service of the country in the army. Then, to use her own words, "feeling a burning desire to aid personally in the work, I did not wait to hear of sufferings I have since so often witnessed, but determined, as God had given me health and a good husband to provide for me, to go forth as a volunteer and do whatever my hands found to do." Few perhaps will ever know to the full extent, how much the soldier benefited by this resolve.

To such a spirit, waiting and ardent, opportunities were not long in presenting themselves. Mrs. Hosmer's first experiences, away from home, were at Tipton, and Smithtown, Missouri. This was early in the winter of 1862, only a few months after the commencement of the War; but as all will remember there had already been desperate campaigns, and hard fighting in Missouri,

719 and there were the usual consequences, devastation, want and suffering to be met on all sides.

At this time the effects of that beneficent and excellent institution, the Northwestern Sanitary Commission, had not been felt at all points where need existed; for the field was vast, and even with the wonderful charities of the great Northwest, pouring into its treasury and store-houses, with a powerful organization, and scores of willing hands and brains at command, time was necessary to enable it to assume that sort of omnipresence which afterward caused it to be found in all places where battles were fought, or hospitals erected, or men suffered from the casualties of war, throughout that great territory.

Mrs. Hosmer found the hospitals at Tipton and Smithtown in the worst possible condition, and the men suffering for almost everything required for their comfort. This, under the circumstances, caused no surprise, for medical stores were not readily available at points so remote. But Mrs. Hosmer had the pleasure of causing a large box of Sanitary stores and comforts to be sent them by the kind and efficient agent at St. Louis, which she helped to distribute. She was thus enabled to leave them in a much more comfortable condition.

On her return to Chicago, a number of influential ladies residing there, formed an association to which the name of the "Ladies' "War Committee" was given. Mrs. Hosmer was appointed secretary of this organization.

This association was very useful and efficient, and met daily to work for the soldiers, particularly in making up garments for the Regiments sent out by the Board of Trade of Chicago.

When these, the Eighty-eighth and Seventy-second Illinois Regiments, and the Board of Trade Battery, participated in any battle, they volunteered to go and look after the wounded. The first volunteers were sent out upon this charitable mission after the battle of Stone River, about the 1st of January, 1863, when two ladies, Mrs. Hosmer and Mrs. Smith Tinkham proceeded to Murfreesboro, Tennessee, with a large quantity of supplies. They remained there, in constant and unwearied attendance upon the large number of wounded from this important battle, for nine or ten weeks.

The writer of this sketch was at that time in Chicago, and well remembers the return of these ladies from this errand of mercy, and the simple pathos of the report they then made, to the Board of Trade, of their work and their stewardship of the funds entrusted to them by that body for the expenses of the expedition, and the use of the wounded.

As these ladies were the first volunteers upon the ground, they were warmly welcomed by the medical director and surgeons, and their services at once rendered available both in the preparation of delicacies for the sufferers, and in personal attendance upon them. Here Mrs. Hosmer met with a most singular and touching incident. A soldier who had been wounded in the leg, and taken prisoner, had his leg amputated by a Rebel surgeon. He was afterwards recaptured, and being found in a dreadful and dangerous condition, had to suffer a second amputation. It was only by the closest and best of care that there remained a possibility that his life might be saved; and this the surgeon in charge requested of Mrs. Hosmer.

On approaching his bed, Mrs. Hosmer was almost painfully struck by his strong resemblance to one of her sons, while he was at the same instant, bewildered and excited by discovering in her an equally strong likeness to the mother he was never to see again.

It need hardly be said that this accidental likeness caused a strong bond of feeling between those till that moment utter strangers. The soldier begged to be allowed to call the lady mother, and she was only too glad to minister to him as she hoped some kind soul might do to the son he resembled, should an hour of need occur. She found him to be an educated and intelligent young man. She did for him all she could, and 91 watched and tended him with real devotion, but in vain. It was found impossible to save him; and when he was gone, she performed the last of her sad offices, by cutting from above his brow a mass of clustering, raven curls, which she enclosed in a letter to his mother, telling her all she knew of her boy's bravery, and his fate.

These days at Murfreesboro were days of hard labor, but of great satisfaction. There had been more than five thousand men in hospital, but these were thinned out by deaths, convalescence, etc., until but few remained. Then Mrs. Hosmer and her friend returned to their home.

The following summer that admirable and most useful institution, the "Soldiers' Home," was established in Chicago, and Mrs. Hosmer was appointed first vice-president.

This "Home" occupied much of her time for the following year. In connection with this was the Soldiers' Rest, where hundreds, and sometimes thousands of men, in transitu, were furnished with good warm meals, and with lodging for the sick, to the extent of its accommodations. This was entirely sustained and carried on by the ladies of Chicago, and Mrs. Hosmer often passed entire days and nights there, in these labors of love.

After the battle of Chickamauga she again felt it a duty and privilege to proceed to the field, on a mission of mercy. Her friend, Mrs. Tinkham, again accompanied her. As they neared Chattanooga, they were unfortunately taken prisoners. They suffered much fatigue, and many privations, but no other illtreatment, though they were, a part of the time, in great danger from the shells which were exploding all about them. They were however soon recaptured, and proceeded on their way.

Having lost their supplies, however, they found they could be of little service. Provisions were very scarce, as in fact were all necessaries, both for the wounded and well. Therefore, being provided with an escort, they slowly retraced their way, and, after a disastrous and fatiguing journey, arrived in Chicago, completely worn and exhausted, and without the cheering influence of the consciousness of having accomplished much good by their efforts.

From this time, with the exception of occasional trips to Cairo, to look after the sick and wounded there, Mrs. Hosmer remained in Chicago, laboring for the soldiers at the "Home" and "Rest," until the close of the year, 1864. The "Northwestern Sanitary and Soldiers' Home Fair," was then in contemplation, and was to take place in June, 1865. Mrs. Hosmer had been appointed one of the Executive Committee, and Corresponding Secretary of the organization, which had the mammoth fair in charge.

In pursuance of the objects in view, she then went down the Mississippi River, to solicit donations of money and articles for the fair. Thinking she eonld materially aid the object, by visiting hospitals, and giving her testimony that supplies -were still needed, she paid particular attention to this part of her duty, and visited nearly every hospital from Cairo to New Orleans. She had the satisfaction of raising about five thousand dollars in money for the fair, besides obtaining a variety and large amount of valuable articles for sale. She also had the pleasure of causing supplies to be sent, at that time, to points where they were much needed.

She was at Vicksburg when five thousand emaciated wrecks of manhood from the prisons of Andersonvilie and Catawba, were brought thither to be exchanged, and often visited their camp and aided in distributing the supplies so greatly needed.

Many a time her kind heart was bursting with pain and sympathy for these suffering men, many of whom had been tortured and starved till already beyond the reach of help. But she was to see still greater horrors, when, as the culmination of their fate, the steamer Sultana, on which their homeward passage was taken, exploded, and, she, being near, beheld hundreds who had escaped the sufferings of the prison pens, drawn from the water, dying or dead, drowned or scalded, in that awful accident. As she says, herself, her heart was nearly broken by this dreadful sight.

Mrs. Hosmer returned to Chicago, and did not cease her labors until the Soldiers' Rest was closed, and the war ended. For about four years she gave untiring devotion to the cause, and few have accomplished more real, earnest and persistent service. Since the close of the war, Mrs. Hosmer has become a resident of Hew York, though she is, at this present writing, established at St. Paul, Minnesota, in charge of a sick son, who seeks the recovery of his health in that bracing climate.

MISS HATTIE WISWALL.

MISS HATTIE WISWALL entered the service as Hospital Nurse, May 1, 1863. For the first five or six months she was employed in the Benton Barracks Hospital at St. Louis. At that time the suffering of our boys in Missouri was very great, and all through that summer the hospitals of St. Louis were crowded to overflowing. From one thousand to fifteen hundred were lying in Benton Barracks alone. Men, wounded in every conceivable manner, were frequently arriving from the battle-fields, and our friend went through the same experience to which so many brave women, fresh from the quiet and happy scenes of their peaceful homes, have been willing to subject themselves for the sake of humanity. Sensitive and delicate though she was, she acquired here, by constant attention to her duties, a coolness in the presence of appalling sights that we have rarely seen equaled even in the stronger sex, and which, when united with a tender sympathy, as in her case, makes the model nurse. The feeling of horror which shrinks from the sight of agony and vents itself in vapid exclamations, she rightly deemed had no place in the character of one who proposes to do anything. So putting this aside she learned to be happy in the hospital, and consequently made others happy. Never in our observation has this first condition of success in nursing been so completely met. It became so intense a satisfaction to her to lessen, in ever so slight a degree, the misery of a sick or wounded soldier that the horror of the case seemed never to occur to her. It was often remarked that "Miss Hattie was never quite so happy as when administering medicine or dressing a wound."

From Benton Barracks she was ordered in the autumn of 1863 to Nashville, Tennessee, where she remained a short time and was then ordered to Vicksburg, Mississippi, to assist in conducting a Soldiers' Home. Here she remained until the close of the war. How faithfully she discharged her duties, first as assistant and then as principal Matron, the one hundred and fifteen thousand guests who were entertained there during her stay know, and the living can testify. Her position for much of the time was an extremely responsible and laborious one, the capacities of the Home being sometimes extended to the accommodation of six hundred men, and averaging, for nearly the whole period of her stay, two hundred daily. The multiplicity of duties in the charge of the household affairs of such an institution, with the uncertain assistance to be found in such a place, may be better imagined than told. Under her satisfactory management the Vicksburg Home acquired an enviable reputation, and was the favorite stopping-place on the river. The great difficulty in conducting a Soldiers' Horae in time of war, as every one knows who has been connected with one, is to keep it neat and clean, to have the floors, the tables, the beds sufficiently respectable to remind the soldier of the home he has left. Nothing but ceaseless vigilance could do this at Vicksburg, as men were constantly arriving from filthy camps, and still filthier prisons, covered not with greenbacks but with what was known there as the rebel "currency." But on any one of the hundreds of beds that filled the dormitories of this Home our most fastidious reader could have slept in peace and safety; and, but for the fact that the bill of fare was mostly limited to the army ration, could have set down at any of the tables and enjoyed a meal.

The good work of Miss Wiswall in Vicksburg was not confined to the Soldiers' Home. She did not forget the freedmen, but was true to the teachings of her uncles, the great and good Lovejoys. Of the sufferings of these poor people she had opportunity to see much, and often did her sympathies lead her beyond the sphere of her ordinary duties, to carry food and clothing and medicine to such as were ready to perish.

In these charities, which were extended also to the white refugees, Miss Wiswall did not lose sight of the direct line of her duty, the work she had set out to do. The needs of the loyal soldier took precedence in her mind of all others. No service so delighted her as this, and to none was she so well fitted.

We remember after the calamitous Red River expedition, boatload after boat-load of the wounded were sent up to Vicksburg. As soon as they touched the shore, our friend and her companions met the poor fellows stretched upon the decks and scattered through the cabins and around the engines, with words of womanly cheer, and brought the delicacies and refreshments prepared by thoughtful hands at home. Many a brave man will remember to his dying day how he shed tears of joy at sight of the first true Northern woman's face that met him after that toilsome, disastrous march.

At length a boat-load of the severely wounded were about to be sent up the river to Northern hospitals, or on furlough to go to their homes. The surgeon in charge desired the aid of a competent lady assistant; and Miss Wiswall obtained temporary leave of absence to accompany him and help take care of the sufferers. Her influence, we were told, was inspiriting to all on board. She was once more in hospital and entirely at home. At Cairo, where a portion of the wounded were discharged, she took charge of an officer, whose limb had been amputated, and saw him safely to his home in Elgin, Illinois. Making her friends in Chicago a brief visit, she returned to her duties at Vicksburg, where she remained until, with the close of the war, the Soldiers' Home was discontinued about the 1st of June, 1865.

MRS. LUCY E. STARR.

R an early period of the civil war this heroic woman left her home at Griggsville, Illinois, came to St. Louis and offered her services to the Western Sanitary Commission as a nurse in the hospitals. She was already known as a person of excellent Christian character, of education and refinement of real practical ability, the widow of a deceased clergyman, and full of the spirit of kindness and patriotic sympathy towards our brave soldiers in the field. Her services were gladly accepted, and she entered at once upon her duties as a nurse in the Fifth Street Hospital at St. Louis, which was in charge of the excellent Dr. John T. Hodgen, an eminent surgeon of that city.

For nearly two years Mi's. Starr served as nurse in this hospital, having charge of one of the special diet kitchens, and ministering with her OAVII hands to the sick and wounded inmates. In these services the great kindness of her manners, the cheerful and hopeful spirit that animated her, the words of sympathy and encouragement she gave her patients, and the efficiency and excellence of everything she did won for her a large measure of esteem and confidence, and made her a favorite nurse with the authorities of the hospital, and with the sick and wounded, who received her ministrations and care. Small in stature, it was wonderful how much labor she was able to accomplish, and she was sustained by a soul full of noble purposes and undoubting faith.

In the autumn of 1863 Mrs. Starr was needed by the Western Sanitary Commission to take the position of Matron of the Soldiers' Home at Memphis, to have charge of the domestic arrangements of the institution, and to extend a true hospitality to the many invalid soldiers going on furlough to their homes or returning to the hospitals, or to their regiments, passing through Memphis on their way. The number thus entertained sometimes reached as high as three hundred and fifty in one day. The average daily number for two years and a half was one hundred and six. When the Home was first opened, and before it was much known, the first guests were brought in by Mrs. Governor Harvey, of Wisconsin, who found them wandering in the streets, sadly in need of a kind friend to give them assistance and care. Sometimes the Superintendent, Mr. O. E. Waters, would have from twenty to thirty discharged, furloughed and invalid soldiers to aid, in collecting their pay, procuring transportation, many of whom he found lying on the hard pavements in the streets and on the bluff near the steamboat landing, in a helpless condition, with no friend to assist them. The object of the Soldiers' Home was to take care of such, give them food and lodging without charge, make them welcome while they stayed, and send them rejoicing on their way.

In the internal management of this institution, and in the kind hospitality extended to the soldiers Mrs. Starr was doing a congenial work. For two years she filled this position with great fidelity and success, and to the highest satisfaction of those who placed her here, and of all who were the guests of the Home. At the end of this service, on the closing of the Home, the Superintendent in his final report to the Western Sanitary Commission, makes this acknowledgment of her services:

"It would not only be improper but unjust, not to speak of the faithfulness and hearty co-operation of the excellent and much esteemed Matron, Mrs. Lucy E. Starr. Her mission has been full of trials and discouragements, yet she has patiently and uncomplainingly struggled through them all; and during my frequent absences she has cheerfully assumed the entire responsibility of the Home. Her Christian forbearance and deep devotion to the cause of humanity have won the admiration of all who have come within the sphere of her labors."

On the closing of the Soldiers' Home, Mrs. Starr became connected with an institution for the care of suffering refugees and freedmen at Memphis, under the patronage of the Freedmen's Aid Commission of Cincinnati, Ohio. She took a great interest in the thousands of this class of destitute people who had congregated in the vicinity of Memphis; visited them for weeks almost daily; and in the language of Mr. Waters' report, "administered to the sick with her own hands, going from pallet to pallet, giving nourishing food and medicines to many helpless and friendless beings."

Thus she continued to be a worker for the suffering soldiers of the Union army from the beginning to the end of the war, and when peace had come, devoted herself to the poor and suffering refugees and freedmen, whom the war had driven from their homes and reduced to misery and want. With a wonderful fortitude, endurance and heroism she persevered in her faithfulness to the end, and through the future of her life on earth and in heaven, those whom she has comforted and relieved of their sorrows and distresses will constitute for her a crown of rejoicing, and their tears of gratitude will be the brightest jewels in her diadem.

CHARLOTTE BRADFORD.

THIS lady, like her friend, Miss Abby W. May, of Boston, though a woman of extraordinary attainments and culture, and an earnest outspoken advocate of the immediate abolition of slavery before the "War, is extremely averse to any mention of her labors in behalf of the soldiers, alleging that they were not worthy to be compared with the sacrifices of those humbler and unnamed heroines, who in their country homes, toiled so incessantly for the boys in blue. We have no desire to detract one iota of the honors justly due to these noble and self-sacrificing women; but when one is called to a position of more prominent usefulness than others, and performs her duties with great ability, system and perseverance, though her merits may be no greater than those of humbler and more obscure persons, yet the public position which she assumes, renders her service so far public property, that she cannot with justice, refuse to accept the consequences of such public action or the sacrifices it entails. Holding this opinion we deem it a part of our duty to speak of Miss

Bradford's public and official life. With her motives and private feelings we have no right to meddle.

So far as we can learn, Miss Bradford's first public service in connection with the Sanitary Commission, was in the Hospital Transport Corps in the waters of the Peninsula, in 1862. Here she was one of the ladies in charge of the Elm City, and afterward of the Knickerbocker, having as associates Mrs. Bailey, Miss Helen L. Gilson, Miss Amy M. Bradley, Mrs. Balestier, Miss Gardner and others.

Miss Bradley was presently called to Washington by the officers of the Sanitary Commission, to take charge of the Soldiers' Horae then being established there, and Miss Bradford busied herself in other Relief work. In February following, Miss Bradley relinquished her position as Matron of the Home, to enter upon her great work of reforming and improving the Rendezvous of Distribution, which under the name of "Camp Misery," had long been the opprobrium of the War Department, and Miss Bradford was called to succeed her in charge of the Soldiers' Home at Washington. Of the efficiency and beneficence of her administration here for two and a half years there is ample testimony. Thoroughly refined and ladylike in her manners, there was a quiet dignity about her which controlled the wayward and won the respect of all. Her executive ability and administrative skill were such, that throughout the realm where she presided, everything moved with the precision and quietness of the most perfect machinery. There was no hurry, no bustle, no display, but everything was done in time and well done. To thousands of the soldiers just recovering from sickness or wounds, feeble and sometimes almost disheartened, she spoke words of cheer, and by her tender and kind sympathy, encouraged and strengthened them for the battle of life; and in all her intercourse with them she proved herself their true and sympathizing friend.

After the close of the war, Miss Bradford returned to private life at her home in Duxbury, Massachusetts.

UNION VOLUNTEER REFRESHMENT SALOON OF PHILADELPHIA

WE have already in our sketch of the labors of Mrs. Mary W. Lee, one of the most efficient workers for the soldiers in every position in which she was placed, given some account of this institution, one of the most remarkable philanthropic organizations called into being by the War, as in the sketch of Miss Anna M. Ross we have made some allusions to the Cooper Shop Refreshment Saloon, its rival in deeds of charity and love for the soldier. The vast extent, the wonderful spirit of self-sacrifice and persevering patience and fidelity in which these labors were performed, demand, however, a more than incidental notice in a record like this.

No philanthropic work during the war was more thoroughly free from self-seeking, or prompted by a higher or nobler impulse than that of these Refreshment Saloons. Beginning in the very first movements of troops in the patriotic feeling which led a poor man to establish his coffee boilers on the sidewalk to give a cup of hot coffee to the soldiers as they waited for the train to take them on to Washington, and in the generous impulses of women in humble life to furnish such food as they could provide for the soldier boys, it grew to be a gigantic enterprise in its results, and the humble commencement ere long developed into two rival but not hostile organizations, each zealous to do the most for the defenders of their country. Very early in the movement some men of larger means and equally earnest sympathies were attracted to it, and one of them, a thorough patriot, Samuel B. Fales, Esq., gave himself wholly to it for four and a half years. The interest of the community was excited also in the labors of these humble men and women, and the enterprise seldom lacked for funds; the zealous and earnest Chairman, Mr. Arad Barrows, and Corresponding Secretary, Mr. Fales, of the Union Volunteer Refreshment Saloon, took good care of that part of the work, and Mr. W. M. Cooper and his associates did the same for the Cooper Shop Saloon.

Ample provision was made to give the regiments the benefit of a bath and an ample repast at whatever hour of day or night they might come into the city. In the four and a half years of their labors, the Volunteer Refreshment Saloon fed between eight hundred thousand and nine hundred thousand soldiers and expended about one hundred thousand dollars in money, aside from supplies. The Cooper Shop Saloon, closing a little earlier, fed about four hundred thousand men and expended nearly seventy thousand dollars. Both Saloons had hospitals attached to them for sick and wounded soldiers. The Union Volunteer Refreshment Saloon had, during the war, nearly fifteen thousand patients, the Cooper Shop, perhaps half that number.

But noble and patriotic as were the labors of the men connected with these Saloons, they were less deserving of the highest meed of praise than those of the women who, with a patience and fidelity which has never been surpassed, winter and summer, in cold and heat, at all hours of night as well as in the day, at the boom of the signal gun, hastened to the Refreshment Saloons and prepared those ample repasts which made Philadelphia the Mecca to which every soldier turned longingly during his years of Army life. These women were for the most part in the middle and humbler walks of life; they were accustomed to care for their own households, and do their own work; and it required no small degree of self-denial and patriotic zeal MU their part, after a day of the housekeeper's never ending toil, to rise from their beds at midnight (for the trains bringing soldiers came oftener at night than in the day time), and go through the darkness or storm, a considerable distance, and toil until after sunrise at the prosaic work of cooking and dish-washing.

Of some of these noble women we haye the material for brief sketches, and we know of none more deserving a place in our record.

MRS. ELIZA G. PLUMMER was a native of Philadelphia, of revolutionary stock, born in 1812, and had been a widow for nearly twenty-five years. Though possessed of but little property, she had for many years been the friend and helper of the poor, attending them in sickness, and from her scanty purse and by her exertions, securing to them a decent and respectable Christian burial when they were called to die. At the very commencement of the War, she entered into the Refreshment Saloon enterprise with a zeal and perseverance that never flagged. She was particularly devoted to the hospital, and when the accommodations of the Union Volunteer Refreshment Saloon Hospital were too limited for the number who needed relief, as was the case in 1862, she received a considerable number of the worst eases of sick or wounded soldiers into her own house, and nursed them without any compensation till they recovered. At the second fair held by the Saloon in June, 1863, she was instant in season and out of season, feeding the soldiers as well as attending the fair; and often remaining at her post till long after midnight. In July and August, 1863, she was constantly engaged in nursing the wounded from Gettysburg, who crowded the Saloon Hospitals for some time, and in supplying the needs of the poor fellows who passed through in the Hospital Cars on their way to Northern hospitals. For these she provided tea and toast always, having everything ready immediately on their arrival. These excessive labors impaired her health, and being called to nurse her aged blind mother during a severe fit of sickness, her strength failed and she sank rapidly, and died on the 21st of October, 1863. The soldier has lost no more earnest or faithful friend than she.

MRS. MARY B. WADE, a widow and now nearly eighty years of age, but a woman of remarkable energy and perseverance, was throughout the whole four and a half years, as constantly at her post, as faithful and as efficient as any of the Executive Committee of the Saloon. Suffering from slight lameness, she literally hobbled down to the Saloon with a cane, by night or day; but she was never absent. Her kind, winning and motherly ways made her always a great favorite with the soldiers, who always called her Mother Wade. She is a woman of rare conscientiousness, truthfulness and amiability of character. She is a native of Southwark, Philadelphia, and the widow of a sea-captain.

MRS. ELLEN J. LOWRY, a widow upwards of fifty years of age, a native of Baltimore, was in the beginning of the War a woman of large and powerful frame, and was surpassed by none in faithfulness and efficiency, but her labors among the wounded from Gettysburg seriously injured her health, and have rendered her, probably a permanent invalid; she suffered severely from typhoid fever, and her life was in peril in the summer of 1864.

MRS. MARGARET BOYER, a native of Philadelphia, the wife of a sea-captain, but in very humble circumstances, and advanced in years, was also one of the faithful untiring workers of the Union Saloon, but like Mrs. Lowry, lost her health by her care of the Gettysburg wounded, and those from the great battles of Grant's Campaign.

MRS. PRISCILLA GROVER and MRS. GREEN, both women about sixty years of age, were constant in their attendance and remarkably faithful in their services at the Saloon. Our record of these remarkable women of advanced age would be incomplete did we omit MRS. MARY GROVER, MRS. HANNAH SMITH, MRS. SARAH FEMINGTON and Miss SARAH HOLLAND, all noble, persevering and efficient nurses, and strongly attached to their work. Nor were the younger women lacking in skill, patience or activ-

ity. Mrs. Ellen B. Barrows, wife of the Chairman of the Saloon, though blessed with more ample means of usefulness than some of the others, was second to none in her untiring energy and persistency in the discharge of her duties both in the hospitals and the Saloon. Mrs. Eliza J. Smith, whose excessive labors have nearly cost her her life, Mrs. Mary A. Cassedy, Mrs. Kate B. Anderson, Mrs. Mary E. Field, Mrs. Emily Mason, Mrs. Anna A. Elkinton and Mrs. Hannah F. Bailey were all notable women for their steady and efficient work in the hospitals and Saloon. Of Mrs. Mary "NY. Lee and her daughter, Miss Amanda Lee, we have spoken elsewhere.

Miss Catharine Bailey, Mrs. Eliza Helmbold, Mrs. Mary Courteney, Mrs. Elizabeth Horton and Misses Grover, Krider and Field were all useful and active, though their duties were less severe than those we have previously named.

The Cooper Shop Saloon was smaller and its work consequently less severe, yet, as we have seen, the labors of Miss Ross in its hospital proved too severe for even her vigorous constitution, and she added another to the long list of blessed martyrs in the cause of liberty. Others there were in that Saloon and hospital, who, by faithful labor, patient and self-denying toil, and great sacrifices, won for themselves an honorable place in that record which the great day of assize shall reveal. We may not know their names, but God knows them, and will reward them for their deeds of mercy and love.

MRS. R. M. BIGELOW.

IN the ordinary acceptation of the term, Mrs. Bigelow has not been connected with Soldiers Homes either in Washington or elsewhere; yet there are few if any ladies in the country who have taken so many sick or wounded soldiers to their own houses, and have made them at home there, as she. To hundreds, if not thousands, of the soldiers of the Army of the Potomac, the name of "Aunty Bigelow the title by which she was universally known among the sick and wounded soldiers, is as carefully, and quite as gratefully cherished as the name of their commanders. Mrs. Bigelow is a native of Washington, in which city she has always resided. She-was never able, in consequence of her family duties, to devote herself exclusively to hospital work, but was among the first to respond to the call for friendly aid to the sick soldier. She was, in 1861, a daily visitor to the Indiana Hospital in the Patent Office Building, coming at such hours as she could spare from her home duties; and she was always welcome, for no one was more skillful as a nurse than she, or could cheer and comfort the sick better. When she could not come, she sent such delicacies as would tempt the appetite of the invalid to the hospital. Many a soldier remembers to this day the hot cakes, or the mush and milk, or the custard which came from Aunty Bigelow s, on purpose for him, and always exactly at the right time. Mrs. R. K. Billing, a near relative of Mrs. Bigelow, and the mother of that Miss Rose M. Billing whose patriotic labors ended only with her life—a life freely sacrificed for the relief of our poor returned prisoners from Andersonville, as related in our sketch of the Annapolis Hospital Corps,—was the co-laborer of her kinswoman in these labors of love. Both were indefatigable in their labors for the sick soldiers; both knew how to make "that bread which tasted exactly like mother's" to the convalescent soldier, whose feeble appetite was not easily tempted; and both opened their houses, as well as their hearts to these poor suffering invalids, and many is the soldier who could and did say: "I don't know what would have become of me if I had not met -with such good friends."

Mrs. Bigelow became, ere long, the almoner of the bounty of many Aid Societies at the North, and vast quantities of supplies passed through her hands, to the patients of the hospitals; and they were always judiciously distributed. She not only kept up a constant correspondence with these societies, but wrote regularly to the soldier-boys who had been under her care, after they returned to their regiments, and thus retained her influence over them, and made them feel that somebody cared for them, even when they were away from all other home influences.

Besides these labors, which were seemingly sufficient to occupy her entire time, she visited continually the hospitals about the city, and always found room in her house for any sick one, who came to her begging that he might "come home," rather than go to a boarding-house or to a hospital. Three young officers, who came to her with this plea, were received and watched over till death relieved them of their sufferings, and cared for as tenderly as they could have been in their own homes; and those who came thither were nursed and tended till their recovery were numbered by scores.

To all the hospital workers from abroad, and the number was not few, her house was always a home. There was some unappropriated room or some spare bed in which they could be accommodated, and they were welcome for the sake of the cause for which they were laboring. Had she possessed an ample fortune, this kindness, though honorable, might not have been so noteworthy, but her house was small and her means far from ample. In the midst of these abundant labors for the soldiers, she was called to pass through deep affliction, in the illness and death of her husband; but she suffered no personal sorrow to so absorb her interest as to make her unmindful of her dear hospital and home-work for the soldiers. This was continued unfalteringly as long as there was occasion for it.

Few, if any, of the "Women of the War," have been or have deserved to be, more generally beloved by the soldiers and by all true hospital-workers than Mrs. Bigelow.

MISS SHARPLESS AND ASSOCIATES.

THAT the Hospital Transport service was under the management of the Sanitary Commission, we have elsewhere detailed, and have also given some glimpses of its chaotic confusion, its disorder and wretchedness under the management of government officials, early in the war. Under the efficient direction of Surgeon General Hammond, and his successor, Surgeon-General Barnes, there was a material improvement; and in the later years of the war the Government Hospital Transports bore some resemblance to a well ordered General Hospital. There was not, indeed, the complete order and system, the thorough ventilation, the well regulated diet, and the careful and systematic treatment which marked the management of the great hospitals, for these were to a considerable extent impossible on shipboard, and especially where the changes of patients were so frequent.

For a period of nearly seventeen months, during the last two years of the war, the United States Steamship Connecticut was employed as a hospital transport, bringing the sick and wounded from City Point to Washington and Baltimore, and later, closing up one after another, the hospitals in Virginia and on the shores of Maryland and Delaware, and transferring their patients to convalescent camps or other hospitals, or some point where they could be put en route for home. On this steamship Miss HATTIE B. SHARPLESS commenced her labors as matron, on the 10th of May, 1864, and continued with only a brief intermission till September 1st, 1865. She was no novice in hospital work when she assumed this position. A native and resident of Bloomsburg, Colombia County, Pa., she had first entered upon her duties as nurse in the Army in July, 1862, when in connection with Miss Rose M. Billing and Miss Belle Robinson, the latter being also a Pennsylvanian, she commenced hospital work at Fredericksburg. Subsequently, with her associate, she was at the Falls Church Hospital and at Antietam, and we believe also at Chancellorsville and Gettysburg. She is a lady admirably adapted to the hospital-work; tender, faithful, conscientious, unselfish, never resting while she could minister to the suffering, and happiest when she could do most for those in her care. During her service on the Connecticut, thirty-three thousand sick and wounded men were conveyed on that steamer to hospitals in Washington, Alexandria, Baltimore and other points. Constant and gentle in the discharge of her duties, with a kind and if possible a cheering word for each poor sufferer, and skillful and assiduous in providing for them every needed comfort so far as lay in her power, she proved herself a true Christian heroine in the extent and spirit of her labors, and sent joy to the heart of many who were on the verge of despair.

Her religious influence upon the men was remarkable. Never obtrusive or professional in her treatment of religious subjects, she exhibited rare tact and ability in bringing those who were in the possession of their reason and consciousness to converse on their spiritual condition, and in pointing them affectionately to the atoning Sacrifice for sin.

In these works of mercy and piety she was ably seconded by her cousin, Miss Hattie S. Reifsnyder, of Catawissa, Columbia County, Pa., a lady of very similar spirit and tact, who was with her for about eight months; and subsequently by Mrs. Cynthia Case, of Newark, Ohio, who succeeded Miss Reifsnyder, and entered into her work in the same thorough Christian spirit.

Miss W. F. HARRIS is a native, and was previous to the war, a resident of Providence, Rhode Island. She was a faithful worker through the whole war, literally wearing herself out in the service. She commenced her work at the Indiana Hospital, in the Patent Office, Washington, in the spring of 1862. After the closing of that hospital, she transferred her service to Ascension Church Hospital, and subsequently early in 1863, to the Carver Hospital, both in Washington, where she labored with great assiduity and faithfulness. Early in May, 1864, she was appointed to service on the Transport Connecticut, where she was indefatigable in her service, and manifested the same tender spirit, and the same skill and tact, as Miss Sharpless. Of less vigorous constitution than her associates, she was frequently a severe sufferer from her over exertions. In the summer of 1864, she was transferred to the Hospital at Harper's Ferry, and at that hospital and at Winchester continued her service faithfully, though amid much pain and weariness, to the close of the war. Though her health was much shattered by her labors she could not rest, and has devoted herself to the instruction and training of the Freedmen from that time to the present. A gentleman who was associated with her in her service in the Carver Hospital and afterward on the Transport Connecticut, says of her: "I know of no more pure-minded, unselfish and earnest laborer among all the women of the war that came under my notice."

LADIES DISTINGUISHED FOR OTHER SERVICES

MRS. ANNIE ETHERIDGE.

NO woman attached to a regiment, as vivandiére, cantiniére, or file du regiment (we use the French terms because we have no English ones which fully correspond to them), during the recent war, has won so high and pure a renown as Annie Etheridge. Placed in circumstances of peculiar moral peril, her goodness and purity of character were so strongly marked that she was respected and beloved not only by all her own regiment, but by the brigade division and corps to which that regiment belonged, and so fully convinced were the officers from the corps commander down, of her usefulness and faithfulness in the care of the wounded, that at a time when a peremptory order was issued from the headquarters of the array that all women, whatever their position or services should leave the camp, all the principal field officers of the corps to which her regiment was attached united in a petition to the general-inchief, that an exception might be made in her favor.

The greater part of Annie Etheridge's childhood was passed in Wisconsin. Her father was a man of considerable property, and her girlhood was passed in ease and luxury; but as she drew near the age of womanhood, he met with misfortunes by which he lost nearly all he had possessed, and returned to her former home in Michigan. Annie remained in Wisconsin, where she had married, but was on a visit to her father in Detroit at the outbreak of the war, and joined the Second Michigan Regiment when they departed for the seat of war, to fulfil the office of a daughter of the regiment, in attending to its sick and wounded. When that regiment was sent to Tennessee she went to the Third Regiment in which she had many friends, and was with them in every battle in which they were engaged. When their three years' service was completed, she with the re-enlisted veterans joined the Fifth Michigan. Through this whole period of more than four years' service she conducted herself with such modesty and propriety, and was at the same time so full of patriotism and courage, that she was a universal favorite with the soldiers as well as officers.

She was in the skirmish of Blackburn's Ford, and subsequently in the first battle of Bull Run, where she manifested the same courage and presence of mind which characterized her in all her subsequent career in the army. She never carried a musket, though she had a pair of pistols in her holsters, but seldom or never used them. She was for a time during the winter following engaged in hospital service, and when the Army of the Potomac went to the Peninsula, during the Chickahominy campaign she was on a hospital transport with Miss Amy M. Bradley, and rendered excellent service there. She was a very tender and careful nurse, and seemed to know instinctively what to do for the sick and wounded. She returned to Alexandria with her regiment, and was with them at the second battle of Bull Run, on the 29th of August, 1862. Early in this battle she was on a portion of the battle-field which had been warmly contested, where there was a rocky ledge, under shelter of which, some of the wounded had crawled. Annie lingered behind the troops, as they changed position, assisted several poor helpless fellows to this cover and dressed their wounds. One of these was Williamof the Seventh New York Infantry, a noble looking boy, to whose parched lips she had held the cooling draught, and had bound up his wounds, receiving in return a look of unutterable gratitude from his bright blue eyes, and his faintly murmured "God's blessing on you," when a shot from the rebel battery tore him to pieces under her very hands. She discovered at the same moment that the rebels were near, and almost upon her, and she was forced to follow in the direction taken by her regiment. On another portion of that bloody field, Annie was kneeling by the side of a soldier binding up his wounds, when hearing a gruff voice above her, she looked up and to her astonishment saw General Kearny checking his horse beside her. He said, "That is right; I am glad to see you here helping these poor fellows, and when this is over, I will have you made a regimental sergeant" meaning of course that she should receive a sergeant's pay and rations. But two days later the gallant Kearny was killed at Chantilly, and Annie never received the appointment, as has been erroneously asserted.

At Chancellorsville on the 2d of May, 1863, when the Third Corps were in such extreme peril, in consequence of the panic by which the

Eleventh Corps were broken up, one company of the Third Michigan, and one of the sharp-shooters were detailed as skirmishers. Annie, although advised to remain in the rear accompanied them, taking the lead; meeting her colonel however, he told her to goback, as the enemy was near, and he was every moment expecting an attack. Very loth to fall back, she turned and rode along the front of a line of shallow trenches filled with our men; she called to them, "Boys, do your duty and whip the rebels." The men partially rose and cheered her, shouting "Hurrah for Annie," "Bully for you." This revealed their position to the rebels, who immediately fired a volley in the direction of the cheering; Annie rode to the rear of the line, then turned to see the result; as she did so, an officer pushed his horse between her and a large tree by which she was waiting, thus sheltering himself behind her. She looked round at him with surprise, when a second volley was fired, and a Minié ball whizzing by her, entered the officer's body, and he fell a corpse, against her and then to the ground. At the same moment another ball grazed her hand, (the only wound she received during the war), pierced her dress, the skirt of which she was holding, and slightly wounded her horse. Frightened by the pain, he set off on a run through a dense wood, winding in and out among the trees so rapidly that Annie feared being torn from her saddle by the branches, or having her brains dashed out by violent contact with the trunks. She raised herself upon the saddle, and crouching on her knees clung to the pommel. The frightened animal as he emerged from the woods plunged into the midst of the Eleventh Corps, when his course was soon checked. Many of the men, recognizing Annie, received her with cheers. As she was IIOAV at a distance from her regiment, she felt a strong impulse to see and speak with General Berry, the commander of her division, with whom she was well acquainted. Meeting an aid, she asked where the General was. "He is not here," replied the aid. "He is here," replied Annie; "He is my Division General, and has command on the right to-day. I must see him." The aid turned his horse and rode up to the General, who was near at hand, and told him that a woman was coming up who insisted on seeing him. "It is Annie," said General Berry, "let her come; let her come, I would risk my life for Annie, any time." As she approached from one side, a prisoner was brought up on the other, said to be an aid of General Hill's. After some words with him, and receiving his Sword, the General sent him to the rear; and after giving Annie a cordial greeting and some kind words, he put the prisoner under her charge, directing him to AA alk by her horse. It was her last interview with the brave General. Early the next morning he was slain, in the desperate fight for the possession of the plank road past the Chancellor House. In the neighborhood of the hospital, Annie, working as usual among the wounded, discovered an artillery man badly injured and very much in need of her assistance. She bound up his wounds and succeeded in having him brought to the hospital. The batteries were not usually accompanied by surgeons, and their men were often very much neglected, when wounded, as the Infantry Surgeons with their hands full with their own wounded would not, and perhaps could not, always render them speedy assistance. A year later Annie received the following letter, which was found on the body of a Lieutenant Straehan, of her division, who was killed in one of the early battles of Grant's campaign.

WASHINGTON, D. C., January 14th, 1864.

ANNIE—Dearest Friend: I am not long for this world, and I wish to thank you for your kindness ere I go.

You were the only one who was ever kind to me, since I entered the Army. At Chancellorsville, I was shot through the body, the ball entering my side, and coming out through the shoulder. I was also hit in the arm, and was carried to the hospital in the woods, where I lay for hours, and not a surgeon would touch me; when you came along and gave me water, and bound up my wounds. I do not know what regiment you belong to, and I don't know if this will ever reach you. There is only one man in your division that I know. I will try and send this to him; his name is Straehan, orderly sergeant in Sixtythird Pennsylvania volunteers.

But should you get this, please accept my heartfelt gratitude; and may God bless you, and protect you from all dangers; may you be eminently successful in your present pursuit. I enclose a flower, a present from a sainted mother; it is the only gift I have to send you.

Had I a picture, I would send you one; but I never had but two, one my sister has; the other, the sergeant I told you of; he would give it you, if you should tell him it is my desire. I know nothing of your history, but I hope you always have, and always may be happy; and, since I will be unable to see you in this world, I hope I may meet you in that better world, where there is no war. May God bless you, both now and forever, is the wish of your grateful friend,

GEORGE H. HILL,

CLEVELAND, OHIO.

Daring the battle of Spottsylvania, Annie met a number of soldiers retreating. She expostulated with them, and at last shamed them into doing their duty, by offering to lead them back into the fight, which she did under a heavy fire from the enemy. She had done the same thing more than once on other battlefields, not by flourishing a sword or rifle, for she carried neither; nor by waving a flag, for-she was never color-bearer; but by inspiring the men to deeds of valor by her own example, her courage, and her presence of mind. On the 1st or 2nd of June, when the Second Corps attacked the enemy at Deep Bottom, Annie became separated from her regiment, and with her usual attendant, the surgeon's orderly, who carried the "pill box" (the medicine chest), she started in search of it, and before long, without being aware of the fact, she had passed beyond the line of Union pickets. Here she met an officer, apparently reconnoitcring, who told her she must turn back, as the enemy was near; and hardly were the words spoken, when their skirmishers suddenly appeared. The officer struck his spurs into his horse and fled, Annie and the orderly following with all speed, and arrived safe within our lines. As the Rebels hoped to surprise our troops, they did not fire lest they should give the alarm; and to this fact Annie probably owed her escape unscathed.

On the 27th of October, 1864, in one of the battles for the possession of Hatcher's Run and the Boydtown Plank Road, a portion of the Third Division of the Second Corps, was nearly surrounded by the enemy, in what the soldiers called the "Bull Ring." The regiment to which Annie was attached was sorely pressed, the balls flying thick and fast, so that the surgeon advised her to accompany him to safer quarters • but she lingered, watching for an opportunity to render assistance. A little drummer boy stopped to speak to her, when a ball struck him, and he fell against her, and then to the ground, dead. This so startled her, that she ran towards the line of battle. But to her surprise, she found that the enemy occupied every part of the ground held a few moments before by Union troops. She did not pause, however, but dashed through their line unhurt, though several of the chivalry fired at her.

So strong was the confidence of the soldiers in her courage and fidelity to her voluntarily assumed duties, that whenever a battle was to be fought it was regarded as absolutely certain that "Gentle Annie" (so the soldiers named her) would be at hand to render assistance to any in need. General Birney never performed an act more heartily approved by his entire command, than when in the presence of his troops, he presented her with the Kearny cross.

At the close of the war, though her health had been somewhat shaken by her varied and trying experiences, she felt the necessity of engaging in some employment, by which she could maintain herself, and aid her aged father, and accepted an appointment in one of the Government departments, where she labors assiduously for twelve hours daily. Her army experiences have not robbed her of that charming modesty and diffidence of demeanor, which are so attractive in a woman, or made her boastful of her adventures. To these she seldom alludes, and never in such a way as to indicate that she thinks herself in the least a heroine.

DELPHINE P. BAKER.

THOUGH her attentions and efforts have had a specific direction widely different, for the most part, from those of the majority of the American women, who have devoted themselves to the cause of the country and its defenders, few have been more actively and energetically employed, or perhaps more usefully, than the subject of the following sketch. To her efforts, persistent, untiring, self-sacrificing, almost entirely does the Nation owe the organization of the National Military Asylum—a home for the maimed and permanently disabled veterans who gave themselves to the cause which has so signally triumphed.

Delphine P. Baker was born in Bethlehem, Grafton County, New Hampshire, in the year 1828, and she resided in New England during her early youth. Her father was a respectable mechanic of good family, an honest, intellectual, industrious man, of sterling principle and a good member of society. Her mother possessed a large self-acquired culture, a mind of uncommon scope, and a vivid and powerful imagination. She was in a large degree capable of influencing the minds of others, and was endowed with a natural power of leadership.

These qualities and traits of both parents we find remarkably developed in the daughter, and to them is doubtless largely due the successful achievement of the great object of her later labors. A feeling, from some cause always cherished by her mother, until it became an actual belief, that her child was destined to an ex754 traordinary career, was so impressed upon her daughter's mind, and inwrought with her higher being as to become a controlling impulse. It is easy, in tracing the history of Miss Baker, to mark the influence of this fixed idea in every act of her life.

For some years previous to the breaking out of the war, Miss Baker had devoted herself to the inculcation of proper ideas of the sphere and culture of woman. She belonged to no party, or clique, had no connection with the Women's Rights Movement, but desired to see her sex better educated, and in the enjoyment of the fullest mental development. To that end she had travelled in many of the Western States, giving lectures upon her favorite subject, and largely influencing the public mind. In this employment her acquaintance had become very extensive.

At the time of the first breaking out of hostilities, Miss Baker was residing in Chicago, Illinois, enjoying a respite from public labors, and devoting herself to her family. But she soon saw that there was much need of the efforts of woman—a great deal to be done by her in preparing for the sudden emergency into which the nation had been plunged. Government had not at hand all the appliances for sending its newly raised forces into the field properly equipped, and women, who could not wield the bayonet, were skillful in the use of another implement as sharp and bright, and which just at that period could be as usefully brought into action.

The devoted labors of the women of Chicago for the soldiers, have long since become a part of the history of the war. In these Miss Baker had her own, and a large share. She collected materials for garments, exerted her influence among her extensive circle of acquaintances in gathering up supplies, and providing for the yet small, but rapidly increasing, demand for hospital comforts. She took several journeys to St. Louis and Chicago, ministered in the hospitals, and induced others to enter upon the same work. Perceiving, with a quick eye, what was most needed in the hastily-arranged and half-furnished places to which the sick and wounded were consigned, she journeyed backward and forward, gathering up from the rich and well-disposed the Deeded articles, and then conveying them herself to those points where they were most wanted.

Not in strong health, a few months of such indefatigable labors exhausted her strength. She returned to Chicago, but her ardent spirit chafed in inaction. After a time she resolved to commence a literary enterprise in aid of the object she had so much at heart, and in the spring of 1862 she announced the forthcoming publication of the "National Banner," a monthly paper of sixteen pages, the profits of which were to be devoted to the needs of the volunteer soldiery of the United States.

After publishing in Chicago a few numbers of this very readable paper, she removed it to Washington, D. C., where its publication was for some time continued. It was then transferred to New York.

The National Banner did not meet with all the success, its patriotic object and its real literary excellence, demanded. During the last year of the war it was not published with complete regularity, owing to this cause, and to the lack of pecuniary means. But it was undoubtedly the means of doing a great deal of good. Among other things it kept constantly before the people the great object into which Miss Baker had now entered with all the ardor and the persistence of her nature.

This object was the founding of a National Home for totally disabled volunteers of the Union service, and included all who had in their devotion to the cause of the nation become incompetent to provide for their own wants or those of their families.

For years, with a devotion seldom equalled, and a self-sacrifice almost unparalleled, Miss Baker gave herself to this work. She wrote, she travelled, she enlisted the aid of her numerous friends, she importuned the Executive, Heads of Departments, and members of Congress. She gave herself no rest, she flinched at no privations. She apparently existed by the sheer necessity of living for her object, and in almost total self-abnegation she encountered opposition, paralyzing delays, false promises, made only to be broken, and hypocritical advice, intended only to mislead.

Hopeful, unsubdued, unchanged, she at last saw herself nearing success. The session of 1865 was drawing to a close, and repeated promises of reporting the bill for the establishment of the Asylum had been broken. But at length her almost agonized pleadings had their effect. Three days before the adjournment of Congress Hon. Henry Wilson, chairman of the Committee on Military Affairs, in the Senate introduced the bill. It provided for the establishment of a National Military and Naval Asylum for the totally disabled of both branches of the service.

In the confusion and hurry of the closing scenes of the session the bill did not probably meet the attention it would have done under other circumstances. But it was well received, passed by a large vote of both houses, was sanctioned by the signature of President Lincoln, and became a law before the adjournment of Congress.

The bill appointed one hundred corporators who were to organize and assume the powers granted them under its provisions, for the immediate foundation of the proper establishment or establishments, for the reception of the contemplated recipients of its benefits. The fund accrued from military fines and unclaimed pay of members of the service, was to be handed over to the use of the Asylum as soon as a corresponding sum was raised by public gift.

Unfortunately for the success of the organization, the meeting of the corporators for that purpose was appointed for the day afterward so mournfully conspicuous as that of the funeral obsequies of our assassinated President. Amidst the sad and angry excitement of the closing scenes of that terrible tragedy, it was found impossible to eonvene a sufficient number of the corporators (although present in the city) to form a quorum for the transaction of business. The opportunity thus lost did not recur, and though an effort was made to substitute proxies for actual members of the body, it was unsuccessful, and an organization was not effected.

Thus a year dragged its length along. Miss Baker was busy enlarging her sphere of influence—encountering and overcoming opposition and obstacles, endeavoring to secure co-operation, and in securing also personal possession of the property at Point Lookout, Maryland, which she believed to be a desirable site for the Asylum. Her object in this was that she might hold this property until the organization was effected, and it might be legally transferred to the corporators.

Point Lookout was a watering-place previous to the war. The hospital property there consists of three hundred acres of land, occupying the point which divides the mouth of the Potomac River from Chesapeake Bay, at the confluence of the former with the Bay. One or more large hotels, numerous cottages and other buildings remained from the days of peace. The Government also established there, during' the war, Hammond General Hospital with its extensive buildings, and a stockade and encampment for prisoners. The air is salubrious, the land fertile, a supply of excellent water brought from neighboring heights, and an extensive oyster-bed and a fine beach for bathing, add to its attractions. BelieAnng the place well calculated to meet the AA ants of the Asylum, Miss Baker desired to secure the private property together with a grant from the Go ernment of that portion which belongs to it. She succeeded in securing the latter, and in delaying the contemplated sale of the former.

A change being imperatively demanded in the Act of Incorporation, efforts were immediately commenced at the next session of Congress to effect this purpose. Again the painful, anxious delays, again the wearisome opposition were encountered. But Miss Baker and the movement had friends—and in the highest quarters. Her efforts were countenanced and aided by these, but it was not till the session of 1866 approached its close that the amended bill was reached, and the votes of both Houses at last placed the whole matter on a proper footing, and in competent hands.

With Major-General Butler at the head of the Managing Board of Trustees, the successful commencement of the Institution is a foregone conclusion. The Board is composed of some of the best men of the Nation—men, some of them unequalled in their various spheres. The United States will soon boast for its disabled defenders Institutions (for the present management contemplate the establishment of Homes at several points), fully equal to those which the great Powers of Europe have erected for similar purposes. In the autumn and winter of 1866-7 Miss Baker succeeded in consummating the purchase, and tender to the Trustees of the - Asylum of the Point Lookout property.

The labors of Miss Baker for this purpose are now ended. She retires, not to rest or idleness, but still to lend her efforts to this or any other great and worthy cause. She has no official connection with the organization which controls the destiny of the Asylum. But it will not cease to be remembered in this country that to her efforts the United States owes in great part all that, as a nation, it has done for the men who have thus given all but life itself to its cause.

MRS. S. BURGER STEARNS.

THIS lady is a native of New York city, where she resided for the first seven years of her life. In 1844 her parents removed to Michigan, where she has lived ever since, receiving her education at the best schools, and spending much time in preparation for a classical course at the State University. She was, however, with other young ladies, denied admission there, on the ground of expediency; and finally entered the State Normal School where she graduated with high honors.

She soon after became Mrs. Stearns, her husband being a graduate of the Literary and Law Departments of the Michigan University. But choosing to devote himself to the service of his country, he entered the army as First Lieutenant, afterwards rising to the rank of Colonel.

Mrs. Stearns determined to devote herself to the work of lecturing in behalf of the Aid movement, and did extensive, and much appreciated services in this direction. From time to time she visited the hospitals, and learned the details of the work, as well as the necessities required there; in that way rendering herself peculiarly competent for her chosen field of labor. She continued in this service until the close of the war, accomplishing much good, and laboring with much acceptance.

BARBARA FRIETCHIE.

BARBARA FRIETCHIE was an aged lady of Frederick, Maryland, of German birth, but intensely patriotic. In September, 1862, when Lee's army were on their way to Antietam, "Stonewall" Jackson's corps passed through Frederick, and the inhabitants, though a majority of them were loyal, resolved not to provoke the rebels unnecessarily, knowing that they could make no effectual resistance to such a large force, and accordingly took down their flags; but Dame Barbara though nearly eighty years of age could not brook that the flag of the Union should be humbled before the rebel ensign, and from her upper window waved her flag, the only one visible that day in Frederick. Whittier has told the whole story so admirably that we cannot do better than to transfer his exquisite poem to our pages. Dame Barbara died in 1865.

MRS. HETTY M. McEWEN.

MRS. McEWEN is an aged woman of Nashville, Tennessee, of revolutionary stock, having had six uncles in the revolutionary war, four of whom fell at the battle of King's Mountain. Her husband, Colonel Robert H. McEwen, was a soldier in the war of 1812, as his father had been in the revolution. Her devotion to the Union, like that of most of those who had the blood of our revolutionary fathers in their veins is intense, and its preservation and defense were the objects of her greatest concern. Making a flag with her own hands, she raised it in the first movements of secession, in Nashville, and when through the treachery of Isham Harris and his co-conspirators, Tennessee was dragged out of the Union, and the secessionists demanded that the flag should be taken down, the brave old couple nailed it to the flag-staff, and that to the chimney of their house. The secessionists threatened to fire the house if it was not lowered, and the old lady armed with a shot-gun, undertook to defend it, and drove them away. She subsequently refused to give up her fire-arms on the requisition of the traitor Harris. Mrs. Lucy H. Hooper has told the story of the rebel efforts to procure the lowering of her flag very forcibly and truthfully:

OTHER DEFENDERS OF THE FLAG

BARBARA FRIETCHIE and Hettie McEwen were not the only women of our country who were ready to risk their lives in the defense of the National Flag. Mrs. Effie Titlow, as we have already stated elsewhere, displayed the flag, wrapped about her, at Middletown, Maryland, when the Rebels passed through that town in 1863. Early in 1861, while St. Louis yet trembled in the balance, and it seemed doubtful whether the Secessionists were not in the majority, Alfred Clapp, Esq., a merchant of that city, raised the flag on his own house, then the only loyal house for nearly half a mile, on that street, and nailed it there. His secession neighbors came to the house and demanded that it should be taken down. Never! said his heroic wife, afterwards president of the Union Ladies Aid Society. The demand was repeated, and one of the secessionists at last said, "Well, if you will not take it down, I will, and moved for the stairs leading to the roof. Quick as thought, Mrs. Clapp intercepted him. "You can only reach that flag over my dead body, said she. Finding her thus determined, the secessionist left, and though frequent threats were muttered against the flag, it was not disturbed.

Mrs. Moore (Parson Brownlow s daughter) was another of these fearless defenders of the flag. In June, 1861, the Rebels were greatly annoyed at the sturdy determination of the Parson to keep the Stars and Stripes floating over his house; and delegation after delegation came to his dwelling to demand that they should be lowered. They were refused, and generally went off in a rage. Oil one of these occasions, nine men from a Louisiana regiment stationed' at Knoxville, determined to see the flag humbled. Two men were chosen as a committee to proceed to the parson's house to order the Union ensign down. Mrs. Moore (the parson's daughter) answered the summons. In answer toher inquiry as to what was their errand, one said, rudely: "We have come to take down that d—d rag you flaunt from your roof—the Stripes and Stars."

Mrs. Moore stepped back a pace or two within the door, drew a revolver from her dress pocket, and leveling it, answered: "Come on, sirs, and take it down!"

The chivalrous Confederates were startled!

"Yes, come on!" she said, as she advanced toward them.

They cleared the piazza, and stood at bay on the wall.

"We'll go and get more men, and then d—d if it don't come down!"

"Yes, go and get more men—you are not men!" said the heroic woman, contemptuously, as the two backed from the place and disappeared.

Miss Alice Taylor, daughter of Mrs. Nellie Maria Taylor, of New Orleans, a young lady of great beauty and intelligence, possessed much of her mother's patriotic spirit. The flag was always suspended in one or another of the rooms of Mrs. Taylor's dwelling, and notwithstanding the repeated searches made by the Rebels it remained there till the city was occupied by Union troops. The beauty and talent of the daughter, then a young lady of seventeen, had made her very popular in the city. In she had made a presentation speech when a flag was presented to one of the New Orleans Fire Companies. In May, a committee of thirteen gentlemen called on Mrs. Taylor, and informed her that the ladies of the district had wrought a flag for the Crescent City (Rebel) regiment to carry on their march to Washington, and that the services of her daughter Alice were required to make the presentation speech. Of course

Mrs. Taylor's consent was not given, and the committee insisted that they must see the young lady, and that she must make the presentation address. She was accordingly called, and after hearing their request, replied that she would readily consent on two conditions. First, that her mother's permission should be obtained; and second, that the Stars and Stripes should wave around her, and decorate the arch over her head, as on the former occasion. The committee, finding that they could get no other terms, withdrew, vexed and mortified at their failure.

Mrs. Booth, the widow of Major Booth, who fell contending against fearful odds at Fort Pillow, at the time of the bloody massacre, a few weeks after presented the blood-stained flag of the fort which had been saved by one of the few survivors, to the remnant of the First Battalion of Major Booth's regiment, then incorporated with the Sixth United States Heavy Artillery, with these thrilling words, "Boys, I have just come from a visit to the hospital at Mound City. There I saw your comrades, wounded at the bloody struggle in Fort Pillow. There I found the flag—you recognize it! One of your comrades saved it from the insulting touch of traitors. I have given to my country all I had to give—my husband—such a gift! Yet I have freely given him for freedom and my country. Next to my husband's cold remains, the dearest object left to me in the world, is that flag—the flag that waved in proud defiance over the works of Fort Pillow! Soldiers! this flag I give to you, knowing that you will ever remember the last words of my noble husband, 'never surrender the flag to traitors'"

Colonel Jackson received from her hand—on behalf of his command—the blood-stained flag, and called upon his regiment to receive it as such a gift ought to be received. At that call, he and every man of the regiment fell upon their knees, and solemnly appealing to the God of battles, each one swore to avenge their brave and fallen comrades, and never, never surrender the flag to traitors.

MILITARY HEROINES

THE number of women who actually bore arms in the war, or who, though generally attending a regiment as nurses and vivandires, at times engaged in the actual conflict was much larger than is generally supposed, and embraces persons of all ranks of society. Those who from whatever cause, whether romance, love or patriotism, and all these had their influence, donned the male attire and concealed their sex, are hardly entitled to a place in our record, since they did not seek to be known as women, but preferred to pass for men; but aside from these there were not a few who, without abandoning the dress or prerogatives of their sex, yet performed skillfully and well the duties of the other.

Among these we may name Madame Turchin, wife of General Turchin, who rendered essential service by her coolness, her thorough knowledge of military science, her undaunted courage, and her skill in command. She is the daughter of a Russian officer, and had been brought up in the camps, where she was the pet and favorite of the regiment up to nearly the time of her marriage to General Turchin, then a subordinate officer in that army. When the war commenced she and her husband had been for a few years residents of Illinois, and when her husband was commissioned colonel of a regiment of volunteers she prepared at once to follow him to the field. During the march into Tennessee in the spring of 1862, Colonel Turchin was taken seriously ill, and for some days was carried in an ambulance on the route.

Madame Turchin took command of the regiment during his illness, and while ministering kindly and tenderly to her husband, filled his place admirably as commander of the regiment. Her administration was so judicious that no complaint or mutiny was manifested, and her commands were obeyed with the utmost promptness. In the battles that followed, she was constantly under fire, now encouraging the men, and anon rescuing some wounded man from the place where he had fallen, administering restoratives and bringing him off to the field-hospital. When, in consequence of the "Athens affair," Colonel Turchin was court-martialed and an attempt made by the conservatives to have him driven from the army, she hastened to Washington, and by her skill and tact succeeded in having the court-martial set aside and her husband promoted to the rank of Brigadier-General, and confounded his accusers by bringing his commission and the order to abandon the trial into court, just as the officers comprising it were about to find him guilty. In all the subsequent campaigns at the West, Madame Turchin was in the field, confining herself usually to ministrations of mercy to the wounded, but ready if occasion required, to lead the troops into action and always manifesting the most perfect indifference to the shot and shell or the whizzing minie balls that fell around her. She seemed entirely devoid of fear, and though so constantly exposed to the enemy's fire never received even a scratch.

Another remarkable heroine who, while from the lower walks of life, was yet faithful and unwearied in her labors for the relief of the soldiers who were wounded and who not unfrequently took her place in the ranks, or cheered and encouraged the men when they were faltering and ready to retreat, was Bridget Divers, better known as "Michigan Bridget," or among Sheridan's men as "Irish Biddy." A stout robust Irish woman, she accompanied the First Michigan Cavalry regiment in which her husband was a private soldier, to the field, and remained with that regiment and the brigade to which it belonged until the close of the war. She became well known throughout the brigade for her fearlessness and daring, and her skill in bringing oft' the wounded. Occasionally when a soldier whom she knew fell in action, after rescuing him if he was only wounded, she would take his place and fight as bravely as the best. In two instances and perhaps more, she rallied and encouraged retreating troops and brought them to return to their position, thus aiding in preventing a defeat. Other instances of her energy and courage are thus related by Mrs. M. M. Husband, who knew her well.

"In one of Sheridan's grand raids, during the latter days of the rebellion, she, as usual, rode with the troops night and day wearing out several horses, until they dropped from exhaustion. In a severe cavalry engagement, in which her regiment took a prominent part, her colonel was wounded, and her captain killed. She accompanied the former to the rear, where she ministered to his needs, and when placed in the cars, bound to City Point Hospitals, she remained with him, giving all the relief in her power, on that fatiguing journey, although herself almost exhausted, having been without sleep four days and nights. After seeing her colonel safely and comfortably lodged in the hospital, she took one night's rest, and returned to the front. Finding that her captain's body had not been recovered, it being hazardous to make the attempt, she resolved to rescue it, as "it never should be left on rebel soil." So, with her orderly for sole companion, she rode fifteen miles to the scene of the late conflict, found the body she sought, strapped it upon her horse, rode back seven miles to an embalmer's, where she waited whilst the body was embalmed, then again strapping it on her horse, she rode several miles further to the cars in which, with her precious burden she proceeded to City Point, there obtained a rough coffin, and forwarded the whole to Michigan. Without any delay Biddy returned to her Regiment, told some officials, that wounded men had been left on the field from which she had rescued her Captain's body. They did not credit her tale, so she said, "Furnish me some ambulances and I will bring them in." The conveyances were given her, she retraced her steps to the deserted battlefield, and soon had some eight or ten poor sufferers in the wagons, and on their way to camp. The roads were rough, and their moans and cries gave evidence of intense agony. While still some miles from their destination, Bridget saw several rebels approaching, she ordered the drivers to quicken their pace, and endeavoured to urge her horse forward, but he baulked and refused to move. The drivers becoming alarmed, deserted their charge and fled to the woods, while the wounded men begged that they might not be left to the mercy of the enemy, and to suffer in Southern prisons. The rebels soon came up, Bridget plead with them to leave the sufferers unmolested, but they laughed at her, took the horses from the ambulances, and such articles of value as the men possessed, and then dashed off the way they came. Poor Biddy was almost desperate, darkness coming on, and with none to help her, the wounded men beseeching her not to leave them. Fortunately, an officer of our army rode up to see what the matter was, and soon sent horses and assistance to the party."

When the war ended, Bridget accompanied her regiment to Texas, from whence she returned with them to Michigan, but the attractions of army life were too strong to be overcome, and she has since joined one of the regiments of the regular army stationed on the plains in the neighborhood of the Pocky Mountains.

Mrs. Kady Brownell, the wife of an Orderly Sergeant of the First and afterwards of the Fifth Rhode Island Infantry, who, like Madame Turchin was born in the camp, and was the daughter of a Scottish soldier of the British army, was another of these half soldier heroines; adopting a semi-military dress, and practicing daily with the sword and rifle, she became as skillful a shot and as expert a swordsman as any of the company of sharp-shooters to which she was attached. Of this company she was the chosen color-bearer, and asking no indulgence, she marched with the men, carrying the flag and participating in the battle as bravely as any of her comrades. Inthe first battle of Bull Bun, she stood by her colors and maintained her position till all her regiment and several others had retreated, and came very near falling into the hands of the enemy. She was in the expedition of General Burnside to Roanoke Island and Newbern and by her coolness and intrepidity saved the Fifth Rhode Island from being fired upon by our own troops by mistake. Her husband was severely wounded in the engagement at Newbern, and she rescued him from his position of danger and having made him as comfortable as possible attempted to rescue others of the wounded, both rebel and Union troops. By some of the rebels, both men and women, she was grossly insulted, but she persevered in her efforts to help the wounded, though not without some heart-burnings for their taunts. Her husband recovering very slowly, and being finally pronounced unfit for service, she returned to Rhode Island with him after nursing him carefully for eighteen months or more, and received her discharge from the army.

There were very, probably, many others of this class of heroines who deserve a place in our record; but there is great difficulty in ascertaining the particulars of their history, and in some cases they failed to maintain that unsullied reputation without which courage and daring are of little worth.

THOSE who have read Miss Georgiana Woolsey's charming narrative "Three Weeks at Gettysburg" in this volume, will have formed a higher estimate of the women of Gettysburg than of the men. There were some exceptions among the latter, some brave earnest-hearted men, though the farmers of the vicinity were in general both cowardly and covetous; but the women of the village have won for themselves a high and honorable record, for their faithfulness to the flag, their generosity and their devotion to the wounded.

Chief among these, since she gave her life for the cause, we must reckon MRS. JENNIE WADE. Her house was situated in the valley between Oak Ridge and Seminary Hill, and was directly in range of the guns of both armies. But Mrs. Wade was intensely patriotic and loyal, and on the morning of the third day of the battle, that terrible Friday, July 3, she volunteered to bake bread for the Union troops. The morning passed without more than an occasional shot, and though in the midst of danger, she toiled over her bread, and had succeeded in baking a large quantity. About two o'clock, P. M., began that fearful artillery battle which seemed to the dwellers in that hitherto peaceful valley to shake both earth and heaven. Louder and more deafening crashed the thunder from two hundred and fifty cannon, but as each discharge shook her humble dwelling, she still toiled on unterrified and only intent on her patriotic task. The rebels, who were nearest her had repeatedly ordered her to quit the premises, but she steadily refused. At length a shot from the rebel batteries struck her in the breast killing her instantly. A rebel officer of high rank was killed almost at the same moment near her door, and the rebel troops hastily constructing a rude coffin, were about to place the body of their commander in it for burial, when, in the swaying to and fro of the armies, a Union column drove them from the ground, and finding Mrs. Wade dead, placed her in the coffin intended for the rebel officer. In that coffin she was buried the next day amidst the tears of hundreds who knew her courage and kindness of heart.

Miss CARRIE SHEADS, the principal of Oak Ridge Female Seminary, is also deserving of a place in our record for her courage, humanity and true womanly tact. The Seminary buildings were within a few hundred yards of the original battle-field of the first day's fight, and in the course of the day's conflict, after the death of General Reynolds, the Union troops were driven by the greatly superior force of the enemy into the grounds of the Seminary itself, and most of them swept past it. The Ninety-seventh New York volunteer infantry commanded on that day by Lieutenant-Colonel, afterwards General Charles Wheelock, were surrounded by the enemy in the Seminary grounds, and after repeated attempts to break through the ranks of the enemy, were finally compelled to surrender. Miss Sheads who had given her pupils a holiday on the previous day, and had suddenly found herself transformed into the lady superintendent of a hospital, for the wounded were brought to the Seminary, at once received Colonel Wheelock and furnished him with the signal for surrender. The rebel commander demanded his sword, but the colonel refused to give it up, as it was a gift of friends. An altercation ensued and the rebel officer threatened to kill Colonel Wheelock. Mr. Sheads, Miss Carrie's father, interposed and endeavored to prevent the collision., but was soon pushed out of the way, and the rebel officer again presented his pistol to shoot his prisoner. Miss Sheads now rushed between them and remonstrated with the rebel on his inhumanity, while she urged the colonel to give up his sword. He still refused, and at this moment the entrance of other prisoners attracted the attention of the rebel officer for a few moments, when Miss Sheads unbuckled his sword and concealed it in the folds of her dress unnoticed by the rebel officer. Colonel Wheelock, when the attention of his foe was again turned to him, said that one of his men who had passed out had his sword, and the rebel officer ordered him with the other prisoners to march to the rear. Five days after the battle the colonel, who had made his escape from the rebels, returned to the Seminary, when Miss Sheads returned his sword, with which he did gallant service subsequently the Seminary buildings were crowded with wounded, mostly rebels, who remained there for many weeks and were kindly cared for by Miss Sheads and her pupils. The rebel chief undertook to use the building and its observatory as a signal station for his army, contrary to Miss Sheads' remonstrances, and drew the fire of the

Union army upon it by so doing. The buildings were hit many times and perforated by two shells. But amid the danger, Miss Sheads was as calm and self-possessed as in her ordinary duties, and soothed some of her pupils who were terrified by the hurtling shells. From the grounds of the Seminary she and several of her pupils witnessed the terrible conflict of Friday. The severe exertion necessary for the care of so large a number of wounded, for so long a period, resulted in the permanent injury of Miss Sheads' health, and she has been since that time an invalid. Two of her brothers were slain in the war, and two others disabled for life. Few families have made greater sacrifices in the national cause.

Another young lady of Gettysburg, Miss Amelia Harmon, a pupil of Miss Sheads, displayed a rare heroism under circumstances of trial. The house where she resided with her aunt was the best dwelling-house in the vicinity of Gettysburg, and about a mile west of the village, on Oak or Seminary Ridge. During the fighting on Wednesday (the first day of the battle) it was for a time forcibly occupied by the Union sharp-shooters who fired upon the rebels from it. Towards evening the Union troops having retreated to Cemetery Hill, the house came into possession of the rebels, who bade the family leave it as they were about to burn it, in consequence of its having been used as a fort. Miss Harmon and her aunt both protested against this, explaining that the occupation was forcible and not with their consent. The young lady added that her mother, not now living, was a Southern woman, and that she should blush for her parentage if Southern men would thus fire the house of defenseless females, and deprive them of a home in the midst of battle. One of the rebels, upon this, approached her and proposed in a confidential way, that if she would prove that she was not a renegade Southerner by hurrahing for the Southern Confederacy, he would see what could be done. "Never!" was the indignant reply of the truly loyal girl, "burn the house if you will! I will never do that, while the Union which has protected me and my friends, exists." The rebels at once fired the house, and the brave girl and her aunt made their way to the home of friends, running the gauntlet of the fire of both armies, and both were subsequently unwearied in their labors for the wounded.

WE have already had occasion to mention some of those whose labors had been conspicuous, and especially Mrs. Sarah R. Johnson, Mrs. Nellie M. Taylor, Mrs. Grier, Mrs. Clapp, Miss Breckinridge, Mrs. Phelps, Mrs. Shepard Wells, and others. There was however, beside these, a large class, even in the chief cities of the rebellion, who not only never bowed their knee to the idol of secession, but who for their fidelity to principle, their patient endurance of proscription and their humanity and helpfulness to Union men, and especially Union prisoners, are deserving of all honor.

The loyal women of Richmond were a noble band. Amid obloquy, persecution and in some cases imprisonment (one of them was imprisoned for nine months for aiding Union prisoners) they never faltered in their allegiance to the old flag, nor in their sympathy and services to the Union prisoners at Libby and Belle Isle, and Castle Thunder. With the aid of twenty-one loyal white men in Richmond they raised a fund of thirteen thousand dollars in gold, to aid Union prisoners, while their gifts of clothing, food and luxuries, were of much greater value. Some of these ladies were treated with great cruelty by the rebels, and finally driven from the city, but no one of them ever proved false to loyalty. In Charleston, too, hot-bed of the rebellion as it was, there was a Union league, of which the larger proportion were women, some of them wives or daughters of prominent rebels, who dared everything, even their life, their liberty and their social position, to render aid and comfort to the Union soldiers, and to facilitate the return of a government of liberty and law. Had we space we might fill many pages with the heroic deeds of these noble women. Through their assistance, scores of Union men were enabled to make their escape from the prisons, some of them under fire, in which they were confined, and often after almost incredible sufferings, to find their way to the Union lines. Others suffering from the frightful jail fever or wasted by privation and wearisome marches with little or no food, received from them food and clothing, and were thus enabled to maintain existence till the time for their liberation came. The negro women were far more generally loyal than their mistresses, and their ready wit enabled them to render essential service to the loyal whites, service for which, when detected, they often suffered cruel tortures, whipping and sometimes death.

In New Orleans, before the occupation of the city by the Union troops under General Butler, no woman could declare herself a Unionist without great personal peril; but as we have seen there were those who risked all for their attachment to the Union even then. Mrs. Taylor was by no means the only outspoken Union woman of the city, though she may have been the most fearless. Mrs. Minnie Don Carlos, the wife of a Spanish gentleman of the city, was from the beginning of the war a decided Union woman, and after its occupation by Union troops was a constant and faithful visitor at the hospitals and rendered great service to Union soldiers. Mrs. Flanders, wife of Hon. Benjamin Flanders, and her two daughters, Miss Florence and Miss Fanny Flanders were also well known for their persistent Unionism and their abundant labors for the sick and wounded. Mrs and Miss Carrie Wolfley, Mrs. Dr. Kirchner, Mrs. Mills, Mrs. Bryden, Mrs. Barnett and Miss Bennett, Mrs. Wibrey, Mrs. Richardson, Mrs. Hodge, Mrs. Thomas, Mrs. Howell, Mrs. Charles Howe of Key West, and Miss Edwards from Massachusetts, were all faithful and earnest workers in the hospitals, throughout the war, and Union women when their Unionism involved peril. Miss Sarah Chappell, Miss Cordelia Baggett and Miss Ella Gallagher, also merit the same commendation.

Nor should we fail to do honor to those loyal women in the mountainous districts and towns of the interior of the South. Our prisoners as they were marched through the towns of the South always found some tender pitying hearts, ready to do something for their comfort, if it were only a cup of cold water for their parched lips, or a corn dodger slyly slipped into their hand. Oftentimes these humble but patriotic women received cruel abuse, not only from the rebel soldiers, but from rebel Southern women, who, though perhaps wealthier and in more exalted social position than those whom they scorned, had not their tenderness of heart or their real refinement. Indeed it would be difficult to find in history, even among the fierce brutal women of the French revolution, any record of conduct more absolutely fiendish than that of some of the women of the South during the war. They insisted on the murder of helpless prisoners; in some instances shot them in cold blood themselves, besought their lovers and husbands to bring them Yankee skulls, scalps and bones, for ornaments, betrayed innocent men to death, engaged in intrigues and schemes of all kinds to obtain information of the movements of Union troops, to convey it to the enemy, and in every manifestation of malice, petty spite and diabolical hatred against the flag under which they had been reared, and its defenders, they attained a bad pre-eminence over the evil spirits of their sex since the world began. It is true that these were not the characteristics of all Southern, disloyal women, but they were sufficiently common to make the rebel women of the south the objects of scorn among the people of enlightened nations. Many of these patriotic loyal -women, of the mountainous districts, rendered valuable aid to our escaping soldiers, as well as to the Union scouts who were in many cases their own kinsmen. Messrs. Richardson and Browne, the Tribune correspondents so long imprisoned, have given due honor to one of this class, "the nameless heroine" as they call her, Miss Melvina Stevens, a young and beautiful girl who from the age of fourteen had guided escaping Union prisoners past the most dangerous of the rebel garrisons and outposts, on the borders of North Carolina and East Tennessee, at the risk of her liberty and life, solely from her devotion to the national cause. The mountainous regions of East Tennessee, Northern Alabama and Northern Georgia were the home of many of these loyal and energetic Union women—women, who in the face of privation, persecution, death and sometimes outrages worse than death, kept up the courage and patriotic ardor of their husbands, brothers and lovers, and whose lofty self-sacrificing courage no rebel cruelties or indignities could weaken or abate.

MISS HETTY A. JONES

AMONG the thousands of noble women who devoted their time and services to the cause of our suffering soldiers during the rebellion there were few who sacrificed more of comfort, money or health, than Miss Hetty A. Jones of Roxborough, in the city of Philadelphia. She was a daughter of the late Rev. Horatio Gates

Jones, D D., for many years pastor of the Lower Merion Baptist Church, and a sister of the Hon. J. Richter Jones, who was Colonel of the Fifty-eighth Regiment Pennsylvania Volunteers, and who was killed at the head of his regiment, near Newbern, N. C., in May, 1863, and grand-daughter of Rev. Dr. David Jones, a revolutionary chaplain, eminently patriotic.

At the commencement of the war Miss Jones freely gave of her means to equip the companies which were organized in her own neighborhood, and when the news came of the death of her brave oldest brother, although for a time shocked by the occurrence, she at once devoted her time and means to relieve the wants of the suffering. She attached herself to the Filbert Street Hospital in Philadelphia, and thither she went for weeks and months, regardless of her own comfort or health. Naturally of a bright and cheerful disposition, she carried these qualities into her work, and wherever she went she dispensed joy and gladness, and the sick men seemed to welcome her presence. One who had abundant means of observing, bears testimony to the power of her brave heart and her pleasant winning smile. He says, "I have often seen her sit and talk away the pain, and make glad the heart of the wounded." Nor did she weary in AA ell-doing. Her services at the hospital were constant and efficient, and when she heard of any sick soldier in her Aullage she would visit him there and procure medicine and comforts for him.

In the fall of 1864 she accompanied a friend to Fortress Monroe to meet his sick and wounded son, and thus was led to see more of the sufferings of our brave patriots. On returning home she expressed a wish to go to the front, and although dissuaded on account of her delicate health, she felt it to be her duty to go, and accordingly on the 2d of November, 1864, she started on her errand of mercy, to City Point, Va., the Headquarters of General Grant. The same untiring energy, the same forgetfulness of self, the same devotion to the sick and wounded, were exhibited by her in this new and arduous field of labor. She became attached to the Third Division Second Corps Hospital of the Army of the Potomac, and at once secured the warm affections of the soldiers.

She continued her work with unremitting devotion until the latter part of November, when she had an attack of pleurisy, caused no doubt, by her over exertions in preparing for the soldiers a Thanksgiving Dinner. On her partial recovery she wrote to a friend, describing her tent and its accommodations. She said: "When I was sick, I did want some home comforts; my straw bed was very hard. But even that difficulty was met. A kind lady procured some pillows from the Christian Commission, and sewed them together, and made me a soft bed. But I did not complain, for I was so much better off than the *sich* boys." The italics are ours, not hers. She never put her ease before her care for "the sick boys."

She not only attended to the temporal comforts of the soldiers, but she was equally interested in their spiritual welfare, and was wont to go to the meetings of the Christian Commission. Her letters home and to her friends, were full of details of these meetings, and her heart overflowed with Christian love as she spoke of the brave soldiers rising in scores to ask for the prayers of God's people.

She continued her labors, as far as possible, on her recovery, but was unable to do all that her heart prompted her to attempt. She was urged by her friends at home to return and recruit her strength. In her brief journal she alludes to this, but says, "Another battle is expected; and then our poor crippled boys will need all the care that we can give. God grant that we may do something for them!"

Two days after writing this, in her chilly, leaking tent, she was prostrated again. She was unwilling at first that her family should be made uneasy by sending for them. But her disease soon began to make rapid and alarming progress. She consented that they should be summoned. But on the 21st of December, 1864, the day after this consent was obtained, she passed away to her rest. Like a faithful soldier, she died at her post.

She was in early life led to put her trust in Christ, and was baptized about thirty years ago, by her father, on confession of her faith. She continued from that time a loved member of the Lower Merion Baptist church. In her last hours she still rested with a calm, child-like composure on the finished work of Christ. Though called to die, with none of her own kindred about her, she was blessed with the presence of her Lord, who, having loved his own, loves them unto the end.

Her remains were laid beside those of her father, in the cemetery of the Baptist church at Boxborough, Pa., on Friday, the 30th of December, 1864. A number of the convalescent soldiers from the Filbert Street Hospital in the city, with which she was connected, attended her funeral; and her bier was borne by four 99 of those who had so far recovered as to be able to perform this last office for their departed friend.

Her memory will long be cherished by those who knew her best, and tears often shed over her grave by the brave soldiers whom she nursed in their sickness the soldiers of the Filbert Street Hospital, on receiving the intelligence of her death, met and passed resolutions expressive of their high esteem and reverence for her who had been their faithful and untiring friend, and deep sympathy with her friends in their loss.

THE FAITHFUL BUT LESS CONSPICUOUS LABORERS

SO abundant and universal was the patriotism and self-sacrifice of the loyal women of the nation that the long list of heroic names whose deeds of mercy we have recorded in the preceding pages gives only a very inadequate idea of woman's work in the war. These were but the generals or at most the commanders of regiments, and staff officers, while the great army of patient workers followed in their train. In every department of philanthropic labor there were hundreds and in some, thousands, less conspicuous indeed than these, but not less deserving. We regret that the necessities of the case compel us to pass by so many of these without notice, and to give to others of whom we know but little beyond their names, only a mere mention.

Among those who were distinguished for services in field, camp or army hospitals, not already named, were the following, most of whom rendered efficient service at Antietam or at the Naval Academy Hospital at Annapolis. Some of them were also at City Point; Miss Mary Cary, of Albany, N. Y., and her sister, most faithful and efficient nurses of the sick and wounded, as worthy doubtless, of a more prominent position in this work as many others found in the preceding pages, Miss Agnes Gillis, of Lowell, Mass., Mrs. Guest, of Buffalo, N. Y., Miss Maria Josslvn, of Roxbury, Mass., Miss Ruth L. Ellis, of Bridgewater, Mass., Miss Kate P. Thompson, of Koxbury, Mass., whose labors at Annapolis, have probably made her permanently an invalid, Miss Eudora Clark, of Boston, Mass., Miss Sarah Allen, of Wilbraham, Mass., Miss Emily Gove, of Peru, N. Y., Miss Caroline Cox, of Mott Haven, N. Y., first at David's Island and afterward at Beverly Hospital, N. J., with Mrs. Gibbons, Miss Charlotte Ford, of Morristown, N.Y.., Miss Ella Wolcott, of Elmira, N. Y., who was at the hospitals near Fortress Monroe, for some time, and subsequently at Point Lookout.

Another corps of faithful hospital workers were those in the Benton Barracks and other hospitals, in and near St. Louis. Of some of these, subsequently engaged in other fields of labor we have already spoken; a few others merit special mention for their extraordinary faithfulness and assiduity in the service; Miss Emily E. Parsons, the able lady superintendent of the Benton Barracks Hospital, gives her testimony to the efficiency and excellent spirit of the following ladies; Miss S. K. Lovell, of Galesburg, Michigan, whose labors began in the hospitals near Nashville, Tennessee, and in 1864 was transferred to Benton Barracks, but was almost immediately prostrated by illness, and after her recovery returned to the Tennessee hospitals. Her gentle sympathizing manners, and her kindness to the soldiers won for her their regard and gratitude.

Miss Lucy J. Bissell, of Meremec, St. Louis County, Mo., offered her services as volunteer nurse as soon as the call for nurses in 1861, was issued; and was first sent to one of the regimental hospitals at Cairo, in July, 1861, afterward to Bird's Point, where she lived in a tent and subsisted on the soldiers' rations, for more than a year. After a short visit home she was sent in January, 1863, by the Sanitary Commission to Paducah, Ky., where she remained till the following October. In February, 1864, she was assigned to Benton Barracks Hospital where she continued till June 1st, 1864, except a short sickness contracted by hospital service. In July, 1864, she was transferred to Jefferson Barracks Hospital and continued there till June, 1865, and that hospital being closed, served a month or two longer, in one of the others, in which some sick and wounded soldiers were still left. Many hundreds of the soldiers will testify to her untiring assiduity in caring for them.

Mrs. Arabella Tannehill, of Iowa, after many months of assiduous work at the Benton Barracks Hospital, went to the Nashville hospitals, where she performed excellent service, being a most conscientious and faithful nurse, and winning the regard and esteem of all those under her charge.

Mrs. Rebecca S. Smith, of Chelsea, Ill., the wife of a soldier in the army, had acquitted herself so admirably at the Post Hospital of Bentou Barracks, that one of the surgeons of the General Hospital, who had formerly been surgeon of the Post, requested Miss Parsons to procure her services for his ward. She did so, and found her a most excellent and skillful nurse.

Mrs. Caroline E. Gray, of Illinois, had also a husband in the army; she was a long time at Benton Barracks and was one of the best nurses there, an estimable woman in every respect.

Miss Adeline A. Lane, of Quincy, 111., a teacher before the war, came to Benton Barracks Hospital in the Spring of 1863, and after a service of many months there, returned to her home at Quincy, where she devoted her attention to the care of the sick and wounded soldiers sent there, and accomplished great good.

Miss Martha Adams, of New York city, was long employed in the Fort Schuyler Hospital and subsequently at Benton Barracks, and was a woman of rare devotion to her work.

Miss Jennie Tileston Spaulding, of Roxbury, Mass., was for a long period at Fort Schuyler Hospital, where she was much esteemed, and after her return home busied herself in caring for the families of soldiers around her.

Miss E. M. King, of Omaha, Nebraska, was a very faithfiL and excellent nurse at the Benton Barracks Hospital.

Mrs. Juliana Day, the wife of a surgeon in one of the Nashville hospitals, acted as a volunteer nurse for them, and by her protracted services there impaired her health and died before the close of the war.

Other efficient nurses appointed by the Western Sanitary Commission (and there were none more efficient anywhere) were, Miss Carrie C. McNair, Miss N. A. Shepard, Miss C. A. Harwood, Miss Rebecca M. Craighead, Miss Ida Johnson, Mrs. Dorothea Ogden, Miss Harriet N. Phillips, Mrs. A. Reese, Mrs. Maria Brooks, Mrs. Mary Otis, Miss Harriet Peabody, Mrs. M. A. Wells, Mrs. Florence P. Sterling, Miss N. L. Ostram, Mrs. Anne Ward, Miss Isabella M. Hartshorn, Mrs. Mary Ellis, Mrs. L. E. Lathrop, Miss Louisa Otis, Mrs. Lydia Leach, Mrs. Mary Andrews, Mrs. Mary Ludlow, Mrs. Hannah A. Haines and Mrs. Mary Allen. Most of these were from St. Louis or its vicinity.

The following, also for the most part from St. Louis, were appointed somewhat later by the Western Sanitary Commission, but rendered excellent service. Mrs. M. I. Ballard, Mrs. E. O. Gibson, Mrs. L. D. Aldrich, Mrs. Ploughton, Mrs. Sarah A. Barton, Mrs. Olive Freeman, Mrs. Anne M. Shattuck, Mrs. E. C. Brendell, Mrs. E. J. Morris, Miss Fanny Marshall, Mrs. Elizabeth A. Nichols, Mrs. H. A. Reid, Mrs. Reese, Mrs. M. A. Stetler, Mrs. M. J. Dykemau, Misses Marian and Clara McClintock, Mrs. Sager, Mrs. Peabody, Mrs. C. C. Hagar, Mrs. J. E. Hickox, Mrs. L. L. Campbell, Miss Deborah Dougherty and Mrs. Ferris.

As in other cities, many ladies of high social position, devoted themselves with great assiduity to voluntary visiting and nursing at the hospitals. Among these were Mrs. Chauncey I. Filley, wife of Mayor Filley, Mrs. Robert Anderson, wife of General Anderson, Mrs. Jessie B. Fremont, wife of General Fremont, Mrs. Clinton B. Fisk, wife of General Fisk, Mrs. E. M. Webber, Mrs. A. M. Clark, Mrs. John Campbell, Mrs. W. F. Cozzens, Mrs. E. W. Davis, Miss S. F. McCracken, Miss Anna M. Debenham, since deceased, Miss Susan Bell, Miss Charlotte Ledergerber, Mrs. S. C. Davis, Mrs. Hazard, Mrs. T. D. Edgar, Mrs. George Partridge, Miss E. A. Hart, since deceased, Mrs. H. A. Nelson, Mrs. E. A. Holden, Mrs. Hicks, Mrs. Baily, Mrs. Elizabeth Jones, Mrs. C. V. Barker, Miss Bettie Brodhead, Mrs. T. M. Post, Mrs. E. J. Page, Miss Jane Patrick, since deceased, Mrs. R. H. Stone, Mrs. C. P. Coolidge, Mrs. S. R. "Ward, Mrs. Washington King, Mrs. Wyllys King, Miss Fales, since deceased.

The following were among the noble women at Springfield, 111., who were most devoted in their labors for the soldier in forwarding sanitary supplies, in visiting the hospitals in and near Springfield, in sustaining the Soldiers' Home in that city, and in aiding the families of soldiers. Mrs. Lucretia Jane Tilton, Miss Catharine Tilton, Mrs. Lucretia P. Wood, Mrs. P. C. Latham, Mrs. M. E. Halbert, Mrs. Zimmerman, Mrs. J. D. B. Salter, Mrs. John Ives, Mrs. Mary Engleman, Mrs. Paul Selby, Mrs. S. H. Melvin, Mrs. Stoneberger, Mrs. Schaums, Mrs. E. Curtiss, Mrs. L. Snell, Mrs. J. Nutt and Mrs. J. P. Reynolds. Mrs. R. H. Bennison, of Quincy, 111., was also a faithful hospital visitor and friend of the soldier. Mrs. Dr. Ely, of Cedar Rapids, Iowa, efficient in every good work throughout the war, and at its close the active promoter and superintendent of a Home for Soldiers' Orphans, near Davenport, Iowa, is deserving of all honor.

Miss Georgiana Willets, of Jersey City, N. J., a faithful and earnest helper at the front from 1864 to the end of the war, deserves especial mention, as do also Miss Molineux, sister of General Molineux and Miss McCabe, of Brooklyn, N. Y., who were, throughout the war, active in aiding the soldiers by all the means in their power. Miss Sophronia Bucklin, of Auburn, N. Y., an untiring and patient worker among the soldiers of the Army of the Potomac, also deserves a place in our record.

Cincinnati had a large band of noble hospital workers, women who gave freely of their own property as well as their personal services for the care and comfort of the soldier. Among these were, Mrs. Crafts J. Wright, wife of Colonel Crafts J. Wright, was among the first hospital visiters of the city, and was unwearied in her efforts to provide comforts for the soldiers in the general hospitals of the city as well as for the sick or wounded soldiers of her husband's regiment in the field. Mrs. C. W. Starbuck, Mrs. Peter Gibson, Mrs. William Woods and Mrs. Caldwell, were also active in visiting the hospitals and gave largely to the soldiers who were sick there. Miss Penfield and Mrs. Elizabeth S. Comstock, of Michigan, Mrs. C. E. Russell, of Detroit, Mrs. Harriet B. Dame, of Wisconsin and the Misses Rexford, of Illinois, were remarkably efficient, not only in the hospitals at home, but at the front, where they were long engaged in caring for the soldiers.

From Niagara Falls, N. Y., Miss Elizabeth L. Porter, sister of the late gallant Colonel Peter A. Porter, went to the Baltimore Hospitals and for nineteen months devoted her time and her ample fortune to the service of the soldiers, with an assiduity which has rendered her an invalid ever since in Louisville, Ky., Mrs. Menefee and Mrs. Smith, wife of the Bishop of the Protestant Episcopal Church for the diocese of Kentucky, were the leaders of a faithful band of hospital visitors in that city.

Boston was filled with patriotic women; to name them all would be almost like publishing a directory of the city. Mrs. Lowell, who gave two sons to the war, both of whom were slain at the head of their commands, was herself one of the most zealous laborers in behalf of the soldier in Boston or its vicinity. Like Miss Wormeley and Miss Gilson, she took a contract for clothing from the government, to provide work for the soldiers' families, preparing the work for them and giving them more than she received. Her daughter, Miss Anna Lowell, was on one of the Hospital Transports in the Peninsula, and arrived at Harrison's Landing, where she met the news of her brother's death in the battles of the Seven Days, but burying her sorrows in her heart, she took chai'ge of a ward on the Transport when it returned, and from the summer of 1862 till the close of the war was in charge as lady superintendent, of the Armory Square Hospital, Washington. Other ladies hardly less active were Mrs. Amelia L. Holmes, wife of the poet and essayist, Miss Hannah E. Stevenson, Miss Ira E. Loring, Mrs. George H. Shaw, Mrs. Martin Brimmer and Mrs. William B. Rogers. Miss Mary Felton, of Cambridge, Mass., served for a long time with her friend, Miss Anna Lowell, at Armory Square Hospital, Washington. Miss Louise M. Alcott, daughter of A. B. Alcott, of Concord, Mass., and herself the author of a little book on "Hospital Scenes," as well as other works, was for some time an efficient nurse in one of the Washington hospitals.

Among the leaders in the organization of Soldiers' Aid Societies in the smaller cities and towns, those ladies who gave the impulse which during the whole war vibrated through the souls of those who came within the sphere of their influence, there are very many eminently deserving of a place in our record. A few we must name. Mrs. Heyle, Mrs. Ide and Miss Swayne, daughter of Judge Swayne of the United States Supreme Court, all of Columbus, Ohio, did an excellent work there. The Soldiers' Home of that city, founded and sustained by their efforts, was one of the best in the country. Mrs. T. W. Seward, of Utica, was indefatigable in her efforts for maintaining in its highest condition of activity the Aid Society of that city. Mrs. Sarah J. Cowen was similarly efficient in Hartford, Conn. Miss Long, at Rochester, N. Y., was the soul of the efforts for the soldier there, and her labors were warmly seconded by many ladies of high standing and earnest patriotism. In Norwalk, Ohio, Mrs. Lizzie H.

Farr was one of the most zealous coadjutors of those ladies who managed with such wonderful ability the affairs of the Soldiers' Aid Society of Northern Ohio, at Cleveland. To her is due the origination of the Alert Clubs, associations of young girls for the purpose of working for the soldiers and their families, which rapidly spread thence over the country. Never flagging in her efforts for the soldiers, Mrs. Farr exerted a powerful and almost electric influence over the region of which Norwalk is the centre.

Equally efficient, and perhaps exerting a wider influence, was the Secretary of the Soldiers' Aid Society at Peoria, Ill., Miss Mary E. Bartlett, a lady of superior culture and refinement, and indefatigable in her exertions for raising supplies for the soldiers, from the beginning to the close of the war. The Western Sanitary Commission had no more active auxiliary out of St. Louis, than the Soldiers' Aid Society of Peoria.

Among the ladies who labored for the relief of the Freedmen, Miss Sophia Knight of South Reading, Mass., deserves a place. After spending five or six months in Benton Barracks Hospital (May to October, 1864) she went to Natchez, Miss., and engaged as teacher of the Freedmen, under the direction of the Western Sanitary Commission. Not satisfied with teaching the colored children, she instructed also the colored soldiers in the fort, and visited the people in their homes and the hospitals for sick and wounded colored soldiers. She remained in Natchez until May, 1865. In the following autumn she accepted an appointment from the New England Freedman's Aid Society as teacher of the Freedmen in South Carolina, on Edisto Island, where she remained until July, 1866; she then returned to Boston, where she is still engaged in teaching freedmen.

But time and space would both fail us were we to attempt to put on record the tithe of names which memory recalls of those whose labors and sacrifices of health and life for the cause of the nation, have been not less heroic or noble than those of the soldiers whom they have sought to serve. In the book of God's remembrance their names and their deeds of love and mercy are all inscribed, and in the great day of reckoning, when that record shall be proclaimed in the sight and hearing of an assembled universe, it will be their joyful privilege to hear from the lips of the Supreme Judge, the welcome words, "Inasmuch as ye did it unto one of the least of these, my brethren, ye did it unto me."

THE END.

BIG BYTE BOOKS is your source for great lost history!

Made in the USA
San Bernardino, CA
27 June 2018